THE *AMICUS CURIAE* IN INTERNATIONAL CRIMINAL JUSTICE

The *amicus curiae* – or friend of the court – is the main mechanism for actors other than the parties, including civil society actors and states, to participate directly in proceedings in international criminal tribunals. Yet reliance on this mechanism raises a number of significant questions concerning: the functions performed by *amici*, which actors seek to intervene and why, and the influence of *amicus* interventions on judicial outcomes. Ultimately, the *amicus curiae* may have a significant impact on the fairness, representativeness and legitimacy of the tribunals' proceedings and decisions.

This book provides a comprehensive examination of the *amicus curiae* practice of the International Criminal Court and other major international criminal tribunals and offers suggestions for the role of the *amicus curiae*. In doing so, the authors develop a framework to augment the potential contributions of *amicus* participation in respect of the legitimacy of international criminal tribunals and their decisions, while minimising interference with the core judicial competence of the tribunal and the right of the accused to a fair and expeditious trial.

Volume 18 in the series Studies in International and Comparative Criminal Law

Studies in International and Comparative Criminal Law
General Editor: Michael Bohlander

Criminal law had long been regarded as the preserve of national legal systems, and comparative research in criminal law for a long time had something of an academic ivory tower quality. However, in the past 15 years it has been transformed into an increasingly, and moreover practically, relevant subject of study for international and comparative lawyers. This can be attributed to numerous factors, such as the establishment of ad hoc international criminal tribunals and the International Criminal Court, as well as to developments within the EU, the UN and other international organisations. There is a myriad of initiatives related to tackling terrorism, money laundering, organised crime, people trafficking and the drugs trade, and the international 'war' on terror. Criminal law is being used to address global or regional problems, often across the borders of fundamentally different legal systems, only one of which is the traditional divide between common and civil law approaches. It is therefore no longer solely a matter for domestic lawyers. The need exists for a global approach which encompasses comparative and international law.

Responding to this development this new series will include books on a wide range of topics, including studies of international law, EU law, the work of specific international tribunals, and comparative studies of national systems of criminal law. Given that the different systems to a large extent operate based on the idiosyncracies of the peoples and states that have created them, the series will also welcome pertinent historical, criminological and socio-legal research into these issues.

Recent titles in this series:

Genocide and Crimes against Humanity: Misconceptions and Confusion in French Law and Practice
Caroline Fournet

The Emergence of EU Criminal Law: Cyber Crime and the Regulation of the Information Society
Sarah Summers, Christian Schwarzenegger, Gian Ege and Finlay Young

Transitional Justice and the Prosecution of Political Leaders in the Arab Region: A Comparative Study of Egypt, Libya, Tunisia and Yemen
Noha Aboueldahab

Caribbean Anti-Trafficking Law and Practice
Jason Haynes

The Construction of Guilt in China: An Empirical Account of Routine Chinese Injustice
Yu Mou

The *Amicus Curiae* in International Criminal Justice
Sarah Williams, Hannah Woolaver and Emma Palmer

The *Amicus Curiae* in International Criminal Justice

Sarah Williams
Hannah Woolaver
and
Emma Palmer

•HART•
OXFORD • LONDON • NEW YORK • NEW DELHI • SYDNEY

HART PUBLISHING
Bloomsbury Publishing Plc
Kemp House, Chawley Park, Cumnor Hill, Oxford, OX2 9PH, UK
1385 Broadway, New York, NY 10018, USA

HART PUBLISHING, the Hart/Stag logo, BLOOMSBURY and the Diana logo are trademarks of Bloomsbury Publishing Plc

First published in Great Britain 2020

A catalogue record for this book is available from the British Library.

Library of Congress Cataloging-in-Publication data

Names: Williams, Sarah (Writer on law), author. | Woolaver, Hannah, author. | Palmer, Emma (Writer on law), author.

Title: The *amicus curiae* in international criminal justice / Sarah Williams, Hannah Woolaver, Emma Palmer.

Description: Chicago : Hart Publishing, an imprint of Bloomsbury Publishing, 2020. | Series: Studies in international and comparative criminal law; volume 18 | Includes bibliographical references and index.

Identifiers: LCCN 2019044119 (print) | LCCN 2019044120 (ebook) | ISBN 9781509913329 (hardback) | ISBN 9781509913336 (Epub)

Subjects: LCSH: *Amicus curiae* | Criminal justice, Administration of—International cooperation. | International criminal courts. | Criminal procedure (International law)

Classification: LCC KZ7235 .W55 2020 (print) | LCC KZ7235 (ebook) | DDC 345/.05—dc23

LC record available at https://lccn.loc.gov/2019044119

LC ebook record available at https://lccn.loc.gov/2019044120

ISBN: HB: 978-1-50991-332-9
ePDF: 978-1-50991-334-3
ePub: 978-1-50991-333-6

Typeset by Compuscript Ltd, Shannon

Foreword

THIS ERUDITE WORK is an important and timely contribution to the system of utilising *amicus curiae* in the dynamic but rather arcane world of international criminal and humanitarian law. In respect of the International Criminal Court the only avenue for civil society to contribute to the formal proceedings, other than as a factual or expert witness, is to appear as *amici*. The same is true in respect of State participation where the legal avenues within the Rome Statute do not otherwise provide formal rights of participation.

The use of *amicus curiae* in both domestic and, latterly, international legal forums has a long and distinguished history. It found its origins in Roman law and by the 9th century was a recognised feature of English law. It has spread into most mature legal systems, common law and civil alike. The United States Supreme Court has specific and special rules covering the admission of *amicus curiae* briefs, not least that such briefs should cover 'relevant matter' that has not been dealt with by the parties to the case.

As both counsel and judge in domestic and international cases I have found the submissions of *amici* of great assistance, in particular as an appeal judge at the ICC. They provide a conduit for academic assistance and a source of pragmatic submissions. Such a broadening of the scope of material before a court or tribunal not only assists in the determination of a particular case or issue but also impacts upon the broader legitimacy of the tribunals themselves. This is the thrust of this important work relating to both normative and socio-political legitimacy, and overall functioning transparency. Those aspects are very important given the criticisms that emanate from affected parties or observers who sometimes perceive international courts and tribunals of being (at least sub-consciously) politically and/or culturally biased against individuals or their mother states for extra-judicial reasons. This is so even where the object is to determine individual criminal responsibility within the structure of accepted due process.

I recommend this comparative analysis to all those engaged in or with international litigation of whatever nature. It provides a valuable platform for the better understanding of the function and vital importance of the proper utilisation of *amici* and, from the judicial perspective at least, an encouragement to engage even further with this ancient aid to better judgements based upon a broader understanding of both the discreet and wider implications of the issues to be resolved and adjudicated upon.

Judge Sir Howard Morrison KCMG CBE QC
International Criminal Court

Acknowledgements

This book is the major output from a four-year project that was supported by the Australian Government through the Australian Research Council's *Discovery Projects* funding scheme project DP140101347. Those parts of the book addressing representation in reparations proceedings were partially supported by project DP14010227. We are grateful for the support of the Australian Research Council, which facilitated the collaboration between our institutions and workshops in Cape Town, the Hague and London. Of course, the views expressed herein are our views and are not necessarily those of the Australian Government or Australian Research Council.

We also acknowledge the financial and in-kind contributions made by UNSW Law and the Department of Public Law at the University of Cape Town to project workshops and events as well as funding research sabbaticals for us during the lifetime of the project. The former Australian Human Rights Centre and the irreplaceable Di McDonald provided an institutional home for our research and facilitated many events. Sarah also benefited from a sabbatical at the Lauterpacht Centre for International Law at Cambridge University from September 2018 to July 2019, which enabled completion of the manuscript. Thank you to the staff and fellow visitors at the Centre for their encouragement and interest in the project and for the opportunity to present preliminary findings as part of the lunchtime seminar series in November 2018.

Our project would not have been possible without the excellent research assistance provided by several former undergraduate students over its lifetime: Sam Hartridge for his assistance with data collection for the ICTY and ICTR; Caitlin Eaton, Isobel O'Brien and Mark Knepsal for assisting with collating the national and international comparative practice; Josh Gibson for his assistance with the bibliography; and, in particular, Natalie Hodgson for her meticulous proof reading and assistance with referencing and finalising the bibliography, table of legislation and other supporting material for the book.

Intellectually, our research was informed by those individuals – judges, personnel at the ICTs, practitioners, civil society organisations and fellow academics – who generously agreed to be interviewed for our project and/or participated in project workshops. These include the workshop held in Cape Town in February 2015, a workshop co-hosted by Carsten Stahn at the Grotius Centre for International Law held in January 2016 and the workshop jointly hosted by Chatham House and Doughty Street Chambers in January 2016. This book was much improved by their input and practical perspective.

At Bloomsbury, Bill Asquith and Judge Michael Bohlander (series editor) enthusiastically supported our project. Sasha Jawed, Claire Banyard and Linda Staniford steered us masterfully through the review and production process and tolerated our queries and requests for extensions.

Our families, friends and colleagues have supported and listened to us discuss this topic for several years, tolerating absences and distraction. In particular, thank you to our families: Isobel, Lucy, Jamie, Alistair, Hudson, Jesse and our parents.

Table of Contents

Table of Abbreviations

Abbreviation	Phrase
ADAD	Association of Defence Counsel for the International Criminal Tribunal for Rwanda
ADC-ICTY	Association of Defence Counsel for the International Criminal Tribunal for Yugoslavia
ASF	Avocats Sans Frontières
ASP	Assembly of State Parties
DRC	Democratic Republic of Congo
DSB	Dispute Settlement Body
DSS	Defence Support Service
EAC	Extraordinary African Chambers
ECCC	Extraordinary Chambers in the Courts of Cambodia
ECtHR	European Court of Human Rights
FARC	Colombian Revolutionary Armed Forces – People's Army
FOCDP	Fondation Congolaise pour la Promotion des Droits humains et la Paix
FTC	NAFTA Free Trade Commission
IACHR	Inter-American Court of Human Rights
ICC	International Criminal Court
ICD	International Crimes Division
ICDAA	International Criminal Defence Attorneys Association
ICJ	International Court of Justice
ICRC	International Committee of the Red Cross
ICTR	International Criminal Tribunal for Rwanda
ICTY	International Criminal Tribunal for the former Yugoslavia

IMT	International Military Tribunal
IMTFE	International Military Tribunal for the Far East
ISA	International Seabed Authority
ITLOS	International Tribunal on the Law of the Sea
JCE	Joint Criminal Enterprise
LRV	Legal Representative of Victims
JEP	Special Jurisdiction for Peace
MICT	United Nations International Residual Mechanism for Criminal Tribunals
MONUSCO	UN Mission in the DRC
NAFTA	North American Free Trade Agreement
NGO	Non-Governmental Organisation
OPCD	Office of Public Counsel for the Defence
OPCV	Office of Public Counsel for Victims
OSC	Ombudsperson of the Specialist Chambers
OTP	Office of the Prosecutor
RPE	Rules of Procedure and Evidence
SCC	Supreme Court Chamber
SCSL	Special Court for Sierra Leone
SCSL Residual Mechanism	Residual Special Court for Sierra Leone
STL	Special Tribunal for Lebanon
Tokyo Tribunal or IMTFE	International Military Tribunal for the Far East
TFV	Trust Fund for Victims
UN	United Nations
UNCITRAL	United Nations Commission on International Trade Law
UNCLOS	UN Convention on the Law of the Sea

UNESCO	United Nations Educational, Scientific and Cultural Organisation
UNICEF	United Nations International Children's Emergency Fund
WIGJ	Women's Initiatives for Gender Justice
WTO	World Trade Organization

Table of Cases and Decisions

Decisions of international tribunals

International Court of Justice

World Trade Organisation

Judgments, decisions and other practice of ICTs

Extraordinary Chambers in the Courts of Cambodia

Case 001 (KAING Guek Eav, alias DUCH)

CASE 002 (NUON Chea, KHIEU Samphan, IENG Sary and IENG Thirith)

CASE 003 (MEAS Muth)

International Criminal Court

AL-BASHIR, Omar Hassan Ahmad

BEMBA GOMBO, Jean-Pierre

BLÉ GOUDÉ, Charles

CHUI, Mathieu Ngudjolo

GADDAFI, Saif Al-Islam and AL-SENUSSI, Abdullah

GBAGBO, Laurent

GBAGBO, Simone

Situation in the Islamic Republic of Afghanistan

Situation in the Republic of Burundi

Situation in the Republic of Kenya

Situation on Registered Vessels of the Union of the Comoros, the Hellenic Republic and the Kingdom of Cambodia

HARTMANN, Florence

JANKOVIĆ, Gojko

KARADŽIĆ, Radovan

KRAJIŠNIK, Momčilo

International Residual Mechanism for Criminal Tribunals

KAMUHANDA, Jean de Dieu

Special Court for Sierra Leone

KALLON, Morris

NORMAN, Sam Hinga

NORMAN, Sam Hinga, FOFANA, Moinina and KONDEWA, Allieu

Special Tribunal for Lebanon

National Cases

Australia

Canada

Indonesia

South Africa

Table of Treaties, Legislation and Selected Primary Materials

Treaties and Resolutions

UN Documents and Security Council Resolutions

Rules, Procedure and Other Documents of ICTs

Extraordinary Chambers in the Courts of Cambodia

International Criminal Court

International Criminal Tribunal for Rwanda

International Criminal Tribunal for the Former Yugoslavia

International Residual Mechanism for Criminal Tribunals

Iraqi High Tribunal

Special Court for Sierra Leone

Special Tribunal for Lebanon

Others

National Laws and Instruments

Australia

Canada

Colombia

Indonesia

Kosovo

South Africa

1

International Criminal Tribunals, Legitimacy and the Amicus Curiae

I. INTRODUCTION

THE INTERNATIONAL CRIMINAL Court (ICC; the Court) faces a crisis of legitimacy. As we write in May 2019, the Court faces challenges on several fronts. The rate of ratification of and accession to the Rome Statute has slowed. The Court's focus on African situations has led to continued accusations of bias and selectivity, leading to calls for states to withdraw from the Rome Statute and not to cooperate with the institution.[1] Several states[2] have announced their intention to withdraw from the Rome Statute, although only Burundi and the Philippines have followed through on this threat.[3] The decision not to authorise an investigation into the situation in Afghanistan,[4] in the face of US pressure,[5] has been criticised by many.[6] Critics point to the low rate of 'successful' trials, judging the ICC on its convictions as the primary measure of success: as at May 2019, only six trials have been completed, leading to three

[1] African Union Assembly, 'Decision on the Meeting of African States Parties to the Rome Statute of the International Criminal Court (ICC)' (1–3 July 2009) 13th Ordinary Session, African Union Assembly Document Dec.245(XIII) Rev.1, available at https://au.int/sites/default/files/decisions/9560-assembly_en_1_3_july_2009_auc_thirteenth_ordinary_session_decisions_declarations_message_congratulations_motion_0.pdf.

[2] eg, South Africa, The Gambia, Burundi, Kenya, The Philippines and Malaysia.

[3] 'Burundi: Withdrawal', UN Depositary Notification C.N.805.2016.TREATIES-XVIII.10, available at https://treaties.un.org/doc/publication/cn/2016/cn.805.2016-eng.pdf; 'Philippines: Withdrawal', UN Depositary Notification C.N. 138.2018.TREATIES-XVIII.10, available at https://treaties.un.org/doc/Publication/CN/2018/CN.138.2018-Eng.pdf. Malaysia withdrew its instrument of accession in April 2019, the month after it was deposited.

[4] *Situation in the Islamic Republic of Afghanistan*, ICC PTC II, 12 April 2019, ICC-02/17-33. At the time of writing, this decision was subject to a possible appeal.

[5] Senior US officials have threatened the Court: 'Full Text of John Bolton's Speech to the Federalist Society', *Al Jazeera* (11 September 2018), available at www.aljazeera.com/news/2018/09/full-text-john-bolton-speech-federalist-society-180910172828633.html. This extended to the decision to withdraw the US visa from the ICC Prosecutor in April 2019: P Wintour, O Bowcott and J Borger, 'US Revokes ICC Prosecutor's Visa Over Afghanistan Inquiry', *The Guardian* (5 April 2019), available at www.theguardian.com/law/2019/apr/05/us-revokes-visa-of-international-criminal-courts-top-prosecutor.

[6] See, eg M Kersten, 'The ICC was Wrong to Deny Prosecution Request for Afghan Probe', *Al Jazeera* (12 April 2019), available at www.aljazeera.com/indepth/opinion/icc-wrong-deny-prosecution-request-afghan-probe-190412101757533.html.

convictions.[7] The Court is struggling to give effect to its victim participation regime, the challenges of which were brought into stark relief when the Appeals Chamber overturned the conviction of Jean-Pierre Bemba in 2018,[8] thus signalling the end of participation and any prospect of reparations.[9] The enthusiasm and support the Court has enjoyed from its creation and establishment has been replaced by growing criticism, frustration and alarm. This has led to calls, including by former Presidents of the Assembly of States Parties, for an independent assessment of the Court and its functioning.[10]

The ICC is not the first international criminal tribunal to face criticism from a diverse range of actors and across a number of issues. Its predecessors, the International Criminal Tribunal for the former Yugoslavia (ICTY) and the International Criminal Tribunal for Rwanda (ICTR), were certainly not immune. Earlier institutions, such as the International Military Tribunal (IMT) and the International Military Tribunal for the Far East (IMTFE), were also criticised, often with justification. Other tribunals, including the Special Court for Sierra Leone (SCSL), the Extraordinary Chambers in the Courts of Cambodia (ECCC) and the Special Tribunal for Lebanon (STL), have their detractors. However, as the first permanent international criminal tribunal, the criticism directed at the ICC is concerning, potentially threatening the belief that the institution can achieve its aspiration of ending impunity for international crimes. What is also significant is that much of the criticism directed against the ICC (and other international criminal tribunals) is expressed in terms of the impact of certain actions or actors on the legitimacy of the Court's decisions and on the legitimacy of the institution itself.

As we will explore in section III below, legitimacy is one framework for assessing the performance of an international institution.[11] Scholars have considered the ICC and other international criminal tribunals within this broader critical approach. This book furthers this trend by exploring how the *amicus curiae* mechanism may enhance – or undermine – the legitimacy of international criminal tribunals, and the ICC in particular. Historically, as detailed in chapter two, the *amicus curiae* or 'friend of the court' acted within the common law as an impartial adviser to the court whose role was simply to inform and not to advocate.[12] This filled a *lacuna* by permitting

[7] Appeals are pending from the acquittal of Laurent Gbagbo and Charles Blé Goudé.

[8] *Prosecutor v Bemba,* ICC AC, 8 June 2018, ICC-01/05-01/08-3636-Red.

[9] Although note that the Trust Fund for Victims has set up a trust fund for victims: Trust Fund for Victims, 'Following Mr Bemba's acquittal, Trust Fund for Victims at the ICC decides to accelerate launch of assistance programme in Central African Republic', *International Criminal Court* (13 June 2018), available at www.icc-cpi.int/Pages/item.aspx?name=180613-TFVPR.

[10] Zeid Raad Al Hussein et al, 'The International Criminal Court Needs Fixing' *Atlantic Council* (24 April 2019), available at www.atlanticcouncil.org/blogs/new-atlanticist/the-international-criminal-court-needs-fixing.

[11] C Stahn, 'Between "Faith" and "Facts": By What Standards Should We Assess International Criminal Justice?' (2012) 25 *LJIL* 251.

[12] S Krislov, 'The *Amicus Curiae* Brief: From Friendship to Advocacy' [1963] 72 *Yale LJ* 694.

the representation of interests beyond those of the primary parties to the case. This is, on first glance, a narrow procedural issue with little apparent relevance to the legitimacy of the ICC or any other international institution. However, we argue that this is too simplistic a view of the *amicus curiae* function. Instead, we suggest that the *amicus curiae* mechanism offers a significant avenue for participation in formal proceedings. As such, the *amicus curiae* mechanism is important for building and maintaining the legitimacy of any international criminal tribunal, but especially for a permanent tribunal such as the ICC. Yet, despite its potential contribution to legitimacy, there has not been a comprehensive study of the *amicus curiae* practice of international criminal tribunals. Our primary aim in this study is to explore the legal framework and practice of various international criminal tribunals concerning the *amicus curiae* mechanism. We use the terms *amicus curiae*, *amici curiae* and *amici* to refer to submissions formally identified as *amicus* submissions as well as to refer to submissions by non-parties (ie, not prosecution or defence) where the participant does not have a separate formal right to participate. In particular, we focus on the ways in which and under what circumstances the *amicus curiae* mechanism may contribute to – or undermine – the legitimacy of an institution and its decisions. Our study thus goes beyond existing scholarship both in the comprehensiveness of its analysis and in its normative focus.

II. WHY INTERNATIONAL CRIMINAL TRIBUNALS? AND WHICH ONES?

This project emerged from an article co-authored by two of us in 2006,[13] at a time when the ICC had yet substantially to commence operations and other tribunals studied were at an early stage of their practice. Our preliminary study revealed some interesting trends. We concluded that further research would be warranted once the *amicus curiae* practice had developed. During the following decade or so, we have monitored this practice in various tribunals. Securing funding from the Australian Research Council in 2014 allowed us to embark on an updated and more comprehensive study. By that point, there was a considerable body of practice to examine across a number of institutions. Moreover, despite the significant literature concerning civil society engagement with international criminal tribunals,[14] which occasionally examines notable uses of *amicus curiae* briefs, there has not yet been a systematic empirical examination of the use of *amicus curiae* briefs in international criminal tribunals.

Our focus on international criminal tribunals – rather than a broader range of international institutions – is both principled and pragmatic. The decision to

[13] H Woolaver and S Williams, 'The Role of the *Amicus Curiae* Before International Criminal Tribunals' (2006) 6 *ICLR* 15.

[14] eg, see H Nichols Haddad, *The Hidden Hands of Justice: NGOs, Human Rights and International Courts* (Cambridge, CUP, 2018).

limit our focus was principled in the sense that we view international criminal tribunals as distinct in important ways from their international counterparts, creating key legal, structural and institutional differences that are relevant to their *amicus curiae* practice. While these differences are addressed in more detail in this study, particularly in chapter two, it is evident almost immediately that international criminal tribunals do not conform to the traditional model of international adjudication of a single issue between states. International criminal trials are different to other international proceedings in that they are concerned with individual criminal responsibility rather than with determining a particular dispute between or involving states. Instead, the primary actors – the parties to the proceedings – are the prosecution and the defence. States, normally the primary actors in international adjudication are, to an extent, excluded as participants. Given these differences, a separate and focused study of the *amicus curiae* in international criminal tribunals is required. The decision was also pragmatic as there is an increasing number of international criminal tribunals, including the establishment of a permanent institution, with the extent and variation in the *amicus curiae* practice of those tribunals significant. We recognised that locating, collating and analysing that practice would be a significant undertaking and extending our data collection to other international institutions would have made the project too large and impractical with the time and resources available to us. That is not to say that we do not consider comparative analysis of other international institutions relevant. International criminal tribunals remain creatures of international law, albeit to varying extents. However, we have relied largely on existing studies and literature for the comparative dimension instead of creating our own data set of *amicus curiae* practice.

In addition to other international institutions, we also considered whether and how the *amicus curiae* features in national legal systems. The *amicus curiae* is found in several legal systems, mainly common law systems such as the US and the United Kingdom (UK). However, the mechanism has a different scope even within traditional common law systems, with the functions we identified that are performed by the *amicus curiae* in international criminal tribunals (see section IV) performed by other mechanisms in some systems. Despite the key differences between national courts and international criminal tribunals, we decided to include some comparative material from national systems, focusing in particular on two aspects of the *amicus curiae* (or similar mechanisms): (1) its use in domestic proceedings concerning the commission of international crimes (not necessarily criminal trials), and (2) its use in criminal proceedings. The methodological approach we adopt, and its limits, are explored in section V and in Annex A.

Thus our study primarily considers six international criminal tribunals: the ICC; the ICTY; the ICTR; the SCSL; the STL; and the ECCC. For ease, we have referred to them collectively and individually as international criminal tribunals (the Tribunals), although we appreciate that there are different ways of classifying such tribunals (international, hybrid, internationalised).[15] We have also captured the legal framework and practice of the United Nations International Residual Mechanism for Criminal Tribunals (the MICT) and the Residual Special Court for Sierra Leone (SCSL Residual Mechanism), as the successor institutions to the ICTY, the ICTR and the SCSL.[16] Having selected the focus of the study, we then gathered relevant documents and analysed them (see Annex A). We also identified a normative framework for our study: legitimacy.

III. LEGITIMACY IN INTERNATIONAL CRIMINAL JUSTICE

Over the past two decades or so, scholars have established a body of literature addressing the legitimacy of international law and international institutions.[17] Studies have focused on particular areas of law, for example, environmental law,[18] or specific institutions, such as the World Trade Organisation[19] or the Security Council.[20] There are many definitions of legitimacy, but we use the term legitimacy to refer to 'the justification of authority – the authority, for example, of legislatures to prescribe legal rules or of courts to decide cases'.[21] For international institutions, legitimacy offers an assessment of whether the institution deserves our support[22] as well as 'a potentially important basis of effectiveness, in addition to power and self-interest': 'the more an institution is perceived as legitimate, the more stable and effective it is likely to be'.[23] Actors are more likely to defer to an institution's decisions where that institution is believed to be legitimate, even when it is not in the actor's self-interest to do so, thus legitimacy is linked to compliance.[24] Bodansky argues for a differentiated, contextual approach to questions of legitimacy, as not all international institutions are the

[15] S Williams, *Hybrid & Internationalised Criminal Tribunals: Selected Jurisdictional Issues* (Oxford, Hart Publishing, 2012).

[16] This practice was included with the figures for the ICTY, ICTR and SCSL and not separately analysed.

[17] See D Bodansky, 'Legitimacy in International Law and International Relations' in JL Dunoff and MA Pollack (eds), *Interdisciplinary Perspectives on International Law and International Relations: The State of the Art* (New York, CUP, 2013).

[18] D Bodansky, 'The Legitimacy of International Governance: A Coming Challenge for International Environmental Law?' (1999) 93 *AJIL* 596.

[19] eg, R Howse 'The World Trade Organization 20 Years On: Global Governance by Judiciary' (2016) 27 *EJIL* 9.

[20] eg, I Hurd, *After Anarchy: Legitimacy and Power in the United Nations Security Council* (Princeton, Princeton University Press, 2007).

[21] Bodansky (n 18), 601.

[22] Bodansky (n 17), 326.

[23] Bodansky (n 18), 603, citing M Weber in G Roth and C Wittich (eds), *Economy and Society* (1968) 31.

[24] See, eg TM Franck, *The Power of Legitimacy Among Nations* (Oxford, OUP, 1990); D Bodansky, 'The Concept of Legitimacy in International Law' in R Wolfrum and V Röben (eds), *Legitimacy in International Law* (Berlin, Springer, 2008); A Cassese, 'The Legitimacy of International Criminal Tribunals and the Current Prospects of International Criminal Justice' (2012) 25 *LJIL* 491.

same and different areas of law may present different challenges for legitimacy.[25] Accordingly, while we draw on the broader legitimacy literature, this section explores conceptualisations of legitimacy regarding international criminal law and its institutions.

Legitimacy is an important concern for international criminal tribunals. Mégret writes that 'In a context where a radical new form of power is being exercised, questions are bound to arise about the nature of international tribunals' authority … Failure to establish the legitimacy of international criminal tribunals on solid ground will expose the tenuous bases for their exercise of power'.[26] The absence of a proper understanding of legitimacy in international criminal justice allows critics to advance legitimacy challenges on a number of issues without proper response. Vasiliev suggests that legitimacy has been under-theorised in international criminal law due to the dormancy of the field during the Cold War and a reluctance to undermine or critique the fragile international criminal justice project.[27] However, scholars have started to explore the notion of legitimacy in international criminal law and tribunals. We focus on this literature and aim partly to address this under-theorisation by exploring a particular mechanism that we argue can contribute to building legitimacy. Much of that literature is directed at the ICC as the permanent international criminal court; hence, our discussion in this section also concentrates on the ICC.

For the purposes of our study, we understand legitimacy in two senses.[28] First, **normative** legitimacy is considered to be the right to rule, which is derived from the rules, process and outputs of a particular institution.[29] Secondly, **sociological** (or descriptive or social) legitimacy is the subjectively held belief on the part of key constituents and actors that an institution has the right to rule. There is a degree of inter-connectedness between normative legitimacy and sociological legitimacy, but the two concepts are distinct: normative legitimacy evaluates the institution itself while sociological legitimacy is an evaluation of attitudes towards that institution.[30] International criminal tribunals should have both sociological legitimacy and normative legitimacy.

An important starting point is that the literature on legitimacy does not reveal a singular conception of legitimacy. Instead, legitimacy is a socially constructed and contested notion that may mean different things to different people in different contexts. Both normative and sociological legitimacy are linked to the perceptions of stakeholders. International criminal tribunals have a number and range of stakeholders. Schiff lists the constituencies of the

[25] Bodansky (n 24).

[26] F Mégret, 'The Anxieties of International Criminal Justice' (2016) 29 *LJIL* 197, 205–6.

[27] S Vasiliev, 'Between International Criminal Justice and Injustice: Theorising Legitimacy' in N Hayashi and CM Bailliet (eds), *The Legitimacy of International Criminal Tribunals* (Cambridge, CUP, 2017).

[28] Drawn from the literature: see A Buchanan and RO Keohane, 'The Legitimacy of Global Governance Institutions' (2006) 20 *Ethics & International Affairs* 405; Bodansky (n 17), 326.

[29] Buchanan and Keohane (n 28).

[30] See Bodansky (n 18), 602; Bodansky (n 17).

ICC (roughly in order of their significance) as 'states (members and non-members), international organizations, non-governmental organizations (humanitarian, human rights), victims, expert observers and perpetrators'.[31] We could also add to this list other non-state actors, such as non-state armed groups, unrecognised entities and transitional authorities, and corporations and other private entities. Stakeholder 'groups' are not homogenous; states may have different interests, victims have different priorities and civil society actors pursue distinct and often competing agendas. Thus a disaggregated approach to legitimacy is required. Another dimension of international criminal tribunals is that they have dual constituencies with stakeholders at both the international and the local levels.[32] Stahn tells us that 'There is no unified local';[33] instead, a range of different actors may be considered local – individuals, communities, local groups. Moreover, local does not equate to national and it cannot be assumed that national interests, as represented by the state, are the same as all – or any – local actors within that state.[34] Although '"the local" may serve as a parameter to consider the legitimacy of an institution', the perspectives of local actors have been under-studied in international criminal law.[35]

Traditionally, the **normative legitimacy** of international law and of international institutions has been based on state consent. International institutions were legitimate because states had consented to their mandate, jurisdiction and authority. However, while states remain an essential aspect of the international legal system, international institutions increasingly make law and are tasked with developing and maintaining normative frameworks in areas such as trade, environment and human rights.[36] Their decisions may shape the law and behaviour of actors beyond the outcome of a particular dispute.[37] Therefore state consent alone is no longer considered a sufficient (or arguably a necessary) basis for normative legitimacy.[38] Instead, 'a theory of legitimacy of international courts, must, at a minimum recognize the role and rights of actors beyond the state and the changed purposes of international adjudication'.[39]

[31] B Schiff, 'Evolution of ICC Legitimacy' (International Studies Association Annual Meeting, New Orleans, February 2010) 6.

[32] F Mégret, 'In Whose Name? The ICC and the Search for Constituency' in C De Vos, S Kendall and C Stahn (eds), *Contested Justice: The Politics and Practice of International Criminal Court Interventions* (Cambridge, CUP, 2015); Mégret (n 26), 208.

[33] C Stahn, 'Justice Civilisatrice? The ICC, Post-colonial Theory, and Faces of "the Local"' in C De Vos, S Kendall and C Stahn (eds), *Contested Justice: The Politics and Practice of International Criminal Court Interventions* (Cambridge, CUP, 2015) 46.

[34] ibid, 62.

[35] ibid.

[36] Bodansky (n 18), 606.

[37] N Grossman, 'The Normative Legitimacy of International Courts' (2013) 86 *Temple Law Review* 61.

[38] See, eg, Bodansky (n 18); Buchanan and Keohane (n 28), 412–14; A Buchanan, 'The Legitimacy of International Law' in S Besson and J Tasioulas (eds), *The Philosophy of International Law* (Oxford, OUP, 2010); Bodansky (n 17) 330.

[39] Grossman (n 37), 65.

This is true of international criminal tribunals. State consent plays an important legitimating role, particularly for those tribunals based on treaties, namely the SCSL, ECCC, EAC and the ICC, and arguably also for those tribunals established by or drawing on the authority of the Security Council (the ICTY, ICTR, STL and – in some circumstances – the ICC).[40] However, international criminal tribunals are dependent on state cooperation for their effective operation so tribunals must maintain state support after initial consent to the treaty is given. The challenge of maintaining state support clearly demonstrates the connection between normative and sociological legitimacy and the challenges tribunals face when seeking to build legitimacy. Ongoing cooperation with an international criminal tribunal, including meeting statutory obligations, is more likely where that state considers the tribunal to be legitimate.[41] States may also instrumentalise their engagement with international criminal tribunals for their own purposes, using their interactions to signal various views or commitments both to the tribunal and to internal and external constituencies.[42] Thus the need to remain legitimate in the eyes of states, arguably the key stakeholders, operates as a significant constraint on international criminal tribunals.[43] Moreover, states are not homogenous nor are they uniform in their support of particular institutions or international criminal justice more broadly and their support may vary over time (particularly where a state becomes the focus of an investigation).[44] Maintaining the support of states (or an individual state or group of states) may often be inconsistent with building or maintaining legitimacy with other key stakeholders. Mégret observes that 'The impossibility of both relying on the powers that be and remaining at a safe distance from them underscores one of the crucial dimensions of international criminal tribunals' anxiety vis-à-vis the question of power: the difficulty of claiming to constrain the very actors one relies upon'.[45] Engagement with states is therefore an issue we return to throughout this study, particularly in chapter seven, with a focus on the potential role of the *amicus curiae* mechanism in assisting tribunals to perform this tenuous balancing act.

Given the limits of state consent as a sufficient source of normative legitimacy for international criminal tribunals, scholars have explored various additional sources, suggesting that these other sources could be used to compensate for

[40] See Cassese (n 24) for discussion of the legitimacy of their establishment.

[41] Schiff (n 31), 3.

[42] ibid, 4–5. See also S MH Nouwen and WG Werner, 'Doing Justice to the Political: The International Criminal Court in Uganda and Sudan' (2010) 21 *EJIL* 941.

[43] M Damaška, 'Reflections on Fairness in International Criminal Justice' (2012) 10 *JICJ* 611, 613; JN Clark, 'International Criminal Tribunals and Normative Legitimacy: An Achievable Goal?' (2015) 15 *ICLR* 763.

[44] Struett, for example, highlights the need to engage with weak as well as strong states: MJ Struett, 'The Politics of Discursive Legitimacy: Understanding the Dynamics and Implications of Prosecutorial Discretion at the International Criminal Court' in SC Roach (ed), *Governance, Order, and the International Criminal Court* (Oxford, OUP, 2009).

[45] Mégret (n 26), 202.

the absence or inadequacies of state consent by 'boot-strapping' a tribunal's legitimacy.[46] We now explore some potential sources of normative legitimacy in international criminal tribunals. This provides the basis for our discussion in the next section of the potential ways in which the *amicus curiae* mechanism might contribute to normative legitimacy.

First, scholars have pointed to legality as an important source of legitimacy, often alongside state consent.[47] This involves an assessment of the content of the institution's founding document: does this represent accepted normative commitments, such as clearly accepted definitions of crimes, jurisdictional bases and rules of procedure and evidence that conform to accepted judicial and legal principles? Legitimacy can also be built from the extent to which the institution acts consistently with its normative framework (including the commitment to fairness) and does not exceed its legal mandate. Schiff labels this 'operational legitimacy',[48] while Cassese refers to 'performance legitimacy'.[49] Other scholars have considered legality as requiring the adoption of clear legal criteria for the exercise of discretion.[50]

While legality is certainly a basis for legitimacy, we do not consider it to be, of itself, a sufficient basis. Although the Rome Statute restricts the scope for 'judicial activism' in comparison to the ICTY and the ICTR, there remain many areas of uncertainty that are ripe for judicial interpretation in the ICC and give rise to a range of possible interpretations. This means that there will be reasonable disagreement between stakeholders as to whether the standard of legality is met in a particular instance. Such genuine contestation of legality is evident in the varied, strongly held and competing views of states and other stakeholders regarding the immunities of heads of state of states that are not party to the Rome Statute, which is one of the most pressing challenges to the ICC.[51] Moreover, an exclusive focus on legality ignores that 'the ICC is often "trapped" in-between the demands of legalism and the demands arising

[46] See L May and S Fyfe, 'The Legitimacy of International Criminal Tribunals' in N Hayashi and CM Bailliet (eds), *The Legitimacy of International Criminal Tribunals* (Cambridge, CUP, 2017).

[47] eg Franck (n 24); Bodansky (n 18), 605; J Brunee and S Toope, *Legitimacy and Legality in International Law: An Interactional Account* (Cambridge, CUP, 2010).

[48] Schiff (n 31), 11.

[49] Cassese's notion of performance legitimacy is broader than legality and captures several of the bases we discuss here: Cassese (n 24).

[50] eg AM Danner, 'Enhancing the Legitimacy and Accountability of Prosecutorial Discretion at the International Criminal Court' (2003) 97 *AJIL* 510; A KA Greenawalt, 'Justice Without Politics? Prosecutorial Discretion and the International Criminal Court' (2007) 39 *New York University Journal of International Law and Politics* 583; MM DeGuzman, 'Gravity and the Legitimacy of the International Criminal Court' (2009) 32 *Fordham International Law Journal* 1400. Although DeGuzman also highlights the need to take into account different perspectives, while Danner notes that the Prosecutor should reach decisions in a fair and non-discriminatory way.

[51] For further discussion, see A Kiyani, 'Legitimacy, Legality and the Possibility of a Pluralist International Criminal Law' in N Hayashi and CM Bailliet (eds), *The Legitimacy of International Criminal Tribunals* (Cambridge, CUP, 2017). The five days of debate on this question before the Appeals Chamber in September 2018 highlighted the different possible interpretations of the Rome Statute and customary international law.

out of the broader political and social contexts in which it operates' and the importance of the Court being 'able to strike the *right* balance between these competing demands'.[52]

Secondly, given the criminal focus of international criminal tribunals, scholars suggest a separate but related source for legitimacy, namely that a tribunal that conducts fair trials is legitimate and will be perceived as legitimate. For Luban, fair trials are the only necessary basis of legitimacy: 'the legitimacy of international tribunals comes not from the shaky political authority that creates them, but from the manifested fairness of their procedures and punishment. Tribunals bootstrap themselves into legitimacy by the quality of justice they deliver; their rightness depends on their fairness'.[53] Fitchelberg goes further: for him, fairness and the protection of individual rights should be the *only* measures against which the legitimacy of an international criminal tribunal is assessed.[54] For both Fitchelberg and Luban the legitimacy of the ICC is assessed by the extent to which the ICC satisfies the fair trial rights as set out in the Rome Statute and RPE.[55]

However, this emphasis on fair trial rights is too limited. It looks almost exclusively at the trial phase and neglects both questions of jurisdiction[56] and the broader roles accorded to international criminal tribunals, including the emphasis placed on the rights of victims and the political dimensions of international criminal justice.[57] As Grossman observes, albeit in the context of non-criminal proceedings, a focus on the fairness of procedures looks only to the parties in proceedings and neglects interested or potentially affected actors beyond the courtroom,[58] which 'leaves an enormous blind spot in assessments of normative legitimacy'.[59] The ICC in particular has a much closer link to national systems and its processes incorporate a range of phases that are linked to but not focused on the criminal trial, for example challenges to jurisdiction and admissibility, as

[52] TO Hansen, 'The International Criminal Court and the Legitimacy of Exercise' in P Andersen, Cecilie Eriksen and B Viskum (eds), *Law and Legitimacy* (Denmark, DJØF Publishing, 2015) 75.

[53] D Luban, 'Fairness to Rightness: Jurisdiction, Legality and the Legitimacy of International Criminal Law' in S Besson and J Tasioulas (eds), *The Philosophy of International Law* (Oxford, OUP, 2010) 590.

[54] A Fitchelberg, 'Democratic Legitimacy and the International Criminal Court: A Liberal Defence' (2006) 4 *JICJ* 765, 767.

[55] ibid, 779. See further Rome Statute of the International Criminal Court (opened for signature 17 July 1998, entered into force 1 July 2002) 2187 UNTS 38544, Arts 66, 67.

[56] M Morris, 'The Democratic Dilemma of the International Criminal Court' (2002) 5 *Buffalo Criminal Law Review* 591; A Duff, 'Authority and Responsibility in International Criminal Law' in S Besson and J Tasioulas (eds), *The Philosophy of International Law* (Oxford, OUP, 2010).

[57] For discussion as to what standards of fair trial should apply to international criminal tribunals see C Warbrick, 'International Criminal Courts and Fair Trial' (1998) 3 *Journal of Armed Conflict Law* 45; F Mégret, 'Beyond Fairness: Understanding the Determinants of International Criminal Procedure' (2009) 14 *UCLA Journal of International Law and Foreign Affairs* 37; Damaška (n 43).

[58] Grossman (n 37), 68. Damaška makes this point in relation to other interests excluded from the trial, something we will explore in more detail in subsequent chapters: M Damaška, 'Unacknowledged Presences in International Criminal Justice' (2012) 10 *JICJ* 1239.

[59] Grossman (n 37), 78.

well as non-cooperation and reparations proceedings. The insufficiency of fair trials as the sole sufficient source of legitimacy is demonstrated by considering the range of legitimacy challenges currently facing the ICC. While criticism has certainly been directed at the fairness of its trials, many of the current challenges to its legitimacy arise not from the trial itself, but from related phases, in particular jurisdiction, admissibility and non-cooperation, as well as the effectiveness of the victim participation and reparations regime.

Thus, we conceive of the fairness of criminal trials as a necessary, but not sufficient, source of legitimacy for international criminal tribunals. For our study, it operates as an important constraint. Moreover, in other phases of proceedings the requirement for fairness moves away from the rights of the accused and may incorporate other notions of fairness, including transparency, equal treatment, and participation. We will consider fair trial rights and broader notions of fairness throughout the study.

Discussions of both legality and fairness as sources of legitimacy generally refer to the need for international criminal tribunals to be independent of states (and other actors) and for decision makers to be impartial.[60] However, this gives rise to the tension, as noted above, between the need to rely on and engage states while also seeking to restrain their actions. It also ignores the formal role given to states, especially through the Assembly of States Parties under the Rome Statute framework. Moreover, independence, and impartiality and 'fairness' are often linked to perceptions of different stakeholders, that is, affected communities rather than formal, objective standards of fairness.[61] As Nouwen and Werner conclude, we cannot ignore the political dimensions of international criminal tribunals, in particular the ICC, which through their processes and outcomes delimit friends and enemies of the international community. Therefore: 'a sound normative assessment of the Court should be based on an acknowledgement and understanding of the political aspects of the ICC'.[62] This means that relying on independence or impartiality may require a more nuanced approach than found in national systems, as international criminal tribunals have greater need to engage with stakeholders, particularly states. We explore independence and impartiality in the context of the *amicus curiae*.

Commentators highlight democracy as an alternative basis for legitimacy, pointing to the democratic deficit in international institutions as a reason why such institutions can never be considered normatively legitimate. This approach equates international institutions with the notions of participatory democracy found in national systems.[63] A form of democracy is found in the agreement of

[60] This is a possible base of legitimacy for other institutions: see Bodansky (n 18), 599. In the context of international criminal tribunals see, eg Cassese (n 24).

[61] Stahn (n 11), 269–70.

[62] Nouwen and Werner (n 42), 946. For the contrary view, see MJ Struett, 'Why the International Criminal Court Must Pretend to Ignore Politics' (2012) 26 *Ethics & International Affairs* 83.

[63] This is a simplified discussion of what democracy may entail given the limited space available. For further discussion, see Bodansky (n 18), 612–17.

states to be bound by a treaty or to cooperate with an international criminal tribunal. However, states are not necessarily democratic, nor are the institutions they establish.[64] Nor are states necessarily the same as or representative of the victims or the perpetrators, and their interests may diverge significantly. Similarly, civil society actors are not themselves democratic or representative, nor do they necessarily have a close connection to affected communities. We agree that it is unlikely that international criminal tribunals will ever meet – or should even aspire to meet – the notions of democratic governance.[65] Therefore, as Glasius concludes, democratic participation in a direct representative sense should not be considered an essential source of legitimacy in international criminal tribunals.[66] Given the focus of international criminal justice on a criminal trial and fair trial rights, as well as the need to maintain state support, it may not be appropriate or desirable for them to do so.[67] However, Glasius also finds that international criminal tribunals should strive for some form of social legitimation through adopting a 'communicative' strategy that would enhance transparency, explain decisions and encourage debate.[68] Moreover, a communicative court should 'be open to considering institutional (re-)designs that systematically offer carefully circumscribed citizen deliberation in certain stages of adjudication'.[69]

Buchanan too suggests a complex standard of legitimacy, suggesting that 'the key values that underlie the demand for global democracy can be reasonably approximated if those institutions satisfy other more feasible conditions'.[70] Such values would include broad accountability, meaning that 'these institutions must cooperate with external epistemic actors – individuals and groups outside the institution, in particular transnational civil society organisations – to create conditions under which the goals and processes of the institution as well as the current terms of institutional accountability, can be contested and critically revised over time, and in a manner that helps to ensure an increasingly inclusive consideration of legitimate interests, through largely transparent deliberative processes'.[71] This approach highlights the significance of participation and representation of interests in an institution's processes, as well as the fairness of the processes, transparency, accountability and the expertise in or otherwise available to the decision-making body. Clark, for example, highlights the need for transparency in the way the Tribunals engage with constituencies, including

[64] Bodansky (n 17), 330.

[65] For detailed discussion of the extent to which the tribunals studied here meet the ideal of democratic consent of local populations in their establishment, see M Glasius, 'Do International Criminal Courts Require Democratic Legitimacy?' (2012) 23 *EJIL* 43.

[66] ibid, 63.

[67] See Fitchelberg (n 54), 778: the legitimacy of a criminal trial 'is logically distinct from its relationship to a democratic institution because of its unique tasks (punishing the guilty and exonerating the innocent)'.

[68] Glasius (n 65), 64.

[69] ibid, 65.

[70] Buchanan (n 38), 97.

[71] ibid.

the need to be 'explicit in their judgements and public announcements about the broader moral significance of their work'.[72] Arguments for including democratic values parallel the suggestions above that fair trials should be interpreted broadly to include principles of natural justice and the notion of equal – or at least fair – treatment of different actors within a system. We therefore return to these key values in our study of the *amicus curiae* in the Tribunals.

Mégret suggests that as a result of the weaknesses in other sources of legitimacy, 'international criminal tribunals have gradually reoriented themselves towards a politics of representation, of standing in for certain constituencies'.[73] He suggests that this is done by highlighting consent – particularly state consent – for their mandate or, alternatively, through claiming to 'more deeply incarnate the 'true' aspirations of local or global public opinion, the masses, or the victims … as actors endowed with a certain democratic legitimacy'.[74] There are certainly elements of this attempt to build representative legitimacy in the practice of the ICC and other tribunals: the Tribunals and their organs are at various times claimed to act on behalf of the international community, the victims and humanity. Kendall and Nouwen explore the discursive reliance on the abstract notion of 'the Victims' (as distinct from the formal representation of victims in proceedings), whereby 'the moral currency of victimhood is thus appropriated to shore up the legitimacy of the ICC's actions'.[75]

However, we agree with Mégret that this approach is problematic: there is no mechanism for determining whether 'international criminal tribunals "represent" the constituencies they claim to represent'.[76] Moreover, tribunals struggle when forced to translate these broad claims of representation of 'abstract' stakeholders to direct representation of actual stakeholder interests in proceedings.[77] This tension has been particularly acute in relation to victim participation in criminal proceedings.[78] Thus these broader discursive claims that international criminal tribunals represent victims and other stakeholders do not constitute direct representation in any meaningful sense – certainly not democratic representation – and cannot of themselves legitimise the ICC. We explore this role of representation and its potential contribution to legitimacy in the context of the *amicus curiae* mechanism, looking particularly at the interests that are or should be represented in proceedings and how. Further, to the extent the ICC considers that it represents particular groups or 'public opinion', we explore whether this is an appropriate function for a criminal tribunal and how that function may be facilitated through the *amicus curiae* mechanism.

[72] Clark (n 43), 780.
[73] Mégret (n 26), 207.
[74] ibid.
[75] S Kendall and S Nouwen, 'Representational Practices at the International Criminal Court: The Gap Between Juridified and Abstract Victimhood' (2013) 76 *Law and Contemporary Problems* 235, 255.
[76] Mégret (n 26), 207.
[77] ibid.
[78] Kendall and Nouwen (n 75).

So far, we have been focusing on normative legitimacy, although many of the sources identified as potentially 'boot-strapping' legitimacy also overlap to an extent with potential indicators of sociological legitimacy. Although some of these sources of normative legitimacy are objective measures, most also rely on some aspect of the tribunal's performance or operations to build legitimacy claims. Our discussion demonstrates that there is no singular conception of legitimacy for the Tribunals, including the ICC. None of the suggested sources for normative legitimacy on their own sufficiently establish legitimacy. This is consistent with other studies of legitimacy.[79] Rather, legitimacy requires a complex and contextualised approach, drawing on different potential sources and indicators. This also shows the interconnectedness between normative and sociological legitimacy, as different stakeholders will prioritise different sources and the relative importance of sources may vary over time and in different contexts. As highlighted above, the ICC and other international criminal tribunals have a range of stakeholders. Many were involved in establishing the ICC and are deeply committed to it, which provides a strong foundation for building sociological legitimacy. Sociological legitimacy is more difficult to explore than normative legitimacy, as it tends to require empirical research being based on subjectively held views. This also makes it challenging to determine whether particular factors lead to sociological legitimacy. The bases identified above for normative legitimacy are likely to be relevant but we should not assume that the same bases apply for both normative and sociological legitimacy.[80] While we have focused on normative legitimacy, our study makes some contribution to an empirical study of sociological legitimacy, by focusing on a particular mechanism and its potential influence on legitimacy through a detailed study of practice, supplemented by interviews with various stakeholders.

According to Stahn, international criminal tribunals should harness their expressivist function: 'International courts have a more "attentive public" than most other judicial entities. They have a "global reach" and "audience". Like supreme courts or other highest judiciaries in a domestic system, their strength and virtue may lie in their ability to "send messages", shape debates and discourse, and influence the generation and perception of norms'.[81] Schiff describes international criminal justice as a dynamic and discursive model of building legitimacy,[82] which by providing mechanisms for contestation and responding to calls from stakeholders by revising practices helps to build legitimacy. Clark agrees that tribunals are 'necessarily dialectical',[83] while Vasiliev

[79] See, eg Bodansky (n 17). See also S Aambø Langvatn and T Squatrito, 'Conceptualising and Measuring the Legitimacy of International Criminal Tribunals' in N Hayashi and CM Bailliet (eds), *The Legitimacy of International Criminal Tribunals* (Cambridge, CUP, 2017) 41.

[80] See critique by Bodansky of studies that assume sociological legitimacy follows normative: Bodansky (n 17), 329.

[81] Stahn (n 11), 279–80.

[82] Schiff (n 31). See also L Chappell, *The Politics of Gender Justice at the International Criminal Court: Legacies and Legitimacy* (Oxford, OUP, 2016) 22–23.

[83] Clark (n 43), 781.

writes of the legitimacy debate as 'a multilateral communication about the expectations towards international criminal justice between the actors in charge and those subject to their powers or affected by their operations'.[84]

Kiyani highlights how the flexibility and indeterminacy of the concept of legitimacy makes it a useful analytical tool:[85] 'legitimacy discourse acts as a vehicle for introducing and/or excluding alternative or marginalised voices and interests in the analysis of international criminal law and its institutions'.[86] An interactional approach 'implies that certain acts of the institution will help to legitimate it, others will have no effect, and still others will delegitimise it. Again, this evidences a shift from legitimacy as an all-or-nothing concept to one more concerned with specific decisions, acts and individuals as part of a dynamic sense of legitimacy for the institution'.[87] For Kiyani, a critical approach based on legitimacy may force the discourse around international criminal law 'to become more inclusive of non-Western views'.[88] For Varaki, too, it is important that the Court engage with affected communities, 'otherwise the Court becomes the subject of discourse among a small elite, who share thorough knowledge and access to its functions, while excluding those who are immediately affected by its decision'.[89] Stahn similarly argues for a 'pluralist vision' of the ICC's constituency, one that 'work[s] towards a better communication between global, national, and local audiences … and to improve the conditions of this dialogue'.[90]

This conception of international criminal justice as a communicative, discursive process that builds legitimacy by recognising and responding to the concerns of different stakeholders offers us a useful analytical framework to understand the potential role and limits of the *amicus curiae* mechanism. This framework allows us to look at the different constituencies and their often incompatible, competing and sometimes changing interests and demands on the institution.[91] Chappell argued for a more nuanced study of various stakeholders and their impact on legitimacy of the ICC; her study concentrated on the influence of 'gender justice' stakeholders.[92] Rather than consider a

[84] Vasiliev (n 27), 91.

[85] A Kiyani, 'The Antinomies of Legitimacy: On the (Im)possibility of a Legitimate International Criminal Court' (2015) 8 *African Journal of Legal Studies* 1.

[86] Kiyani (n 51), 93.

[87] ibid, 109.

[88] Kiyani (n 85), 3. See also Stahn emphasising the need to look 'at very different spectrums of its interventions, that is, regional implications; impact on states; effects on communities': Stahn (n 33), 83.

[89] M Varaki, 'Introducing a Fairness-Based Theory of Prosecutorial Legitimacy before the International Criminal Court' (2016) 27 *EJIL* 769, 785.

[90] Stahn (n 11), 282.

[91] See, eg Sheffield, demonstrating the very different perceptions among different groups in Sudan: K Sheffield, 'Speak Softly and Carry a Sealed Warrant: Building the International Criminal Court's Legitimacy in the Wake of Sudan' (2013) 18 *Appeal* 163; J Subotić, 'Legitimacy, Scope, and Conflicting Claims on the ICTY: In the Aftermath of *Gotovina*, *Haradinaj* and *Perišić*' (2014) 13 *Journal of Human Rights* 170.

[92] Chappell (n 82), 23.

category of stakeholder we examine a range of key stakeholders (considered separately in our study) focusing on their intersection with a particular mechanism that we argue can promote both normative and sociological legitimacy, the *amicus curiae*.

This means that our focus is predominantly on the Chambers, as we assume that most *amici* are primarily motivated by a desire to influence the judges and the substantive outcomes of legal proceedings. Our impression of the legitimacy literature is that it often conceives of stakeholders as largely passive, waiting to receive and assess key outcomes and actions. However, many stakeholders are not passive and try to shape the Court and to instrumentalise its proceedings for their own interests, including through submission of *amicus curiae* submissions. Tribunals too can deliberately become 'agents of their own legitimacy' 'through a range of choices and strategies'.[93] Drawing on Haddad's study of NGOs, tribunals will increase opportunities for communication with stakeholders – and their responsiveness to their concerns – where the tribunal needs to build legitimacy or faces legitimacy challenges.[94]

We argue that judges actively seek to build legitimacy. Aloisi and Meernik explore how 'international judicial decisions have been the instruments through which judges have answered the many challenges of legitimacy and authority raised by defendants and critics'.[95] Aliosi and Meernik suggest that judges at international criminal tribunals, applying a model of 'entrepreneurial judicial making', are concerned with entering into a dialogue with those affected by the crimes before them and with various constituencies so as to maximise the expressive potential of their judgments and to create a legacy, while accepting that their ability to do so is to an extent circumscribed by the interests of those constituencies.[96] Helfer and Slaughter, in a study of the European Court of Justice and the European Court of Human Rights, identified several judicial behaviours that can contribute to establishing and maintaining legitimacy.[97] Of particular relevance for this study are the following behaviours: (1) awareness of the audience(s) for a tribunal; (2) demonstrating autonomy from political interests; (3) the quality of legal reasoning; (4) incremental decision-making; and (5) allowing interested participants to air their views and to have those views acknowledged and treated with respect.[98]

[93] Mégret (n 32), 23. See also Roach, arguing that the ICC should and has used its judicial power towards 'negotiated justice' so as to boost legitimacy: SC Roach, 'Legitimising Negotiated Justice: The International Criminal Court and Flexible Governance' (2013) 17 *International Journal of Human Rights* 619.

[94] See, eg, Haddad (n 14), 163.

[95] R Aloisi and J Meernik, *Judgment Day: Judicial Decision Making at the International Criminal Tribunals* (Cambridge, CUP, 2017) 14–15.

[96] ibid, 20–22, ch 2.

[97] LR Helfer and A Slaughter, 'Toward a Theory of Effective Supranational Adjudication' [1997] *Yale LJ* 273.

[98] ibid, 308–28.

Schlensinger notes that specific legitimacy building behaviours for 'increasing opportunities for participation may take the form of the promulgation of rules, policies or practices enabling the participation of parties other than those directly involved by a process or decision, an expansive approach to interpretation of such rules, and comprehensively reasoned judicial decisions, acknowledging and dignifying opposing viewpoints'. This process, she argues, creates a 'voice effect', whereby participation in the process generates greater support for an outcome, even when that outcome is not favourable to the participant (ie, boosting sociological legitimacy).[99] The *amicus curiae* is one mechanism that potentially enables judges to increase participation and dialogue and hence boost any voice effect. Having outlined our analytical framework, we now turn to a more detailed consideration of the *amicus curiae* mechanism.

IV. LEGITIMACY AND THE *AMICUS CURIAE*

As we explore further in chapter two, the *amicus curiae* mechanism is included – either formally or informally – in the rules and practice of most international and regional tribunals. The mechanism or some variation of it is found in many common law jurisdictions and is increasingly evident in civil law jurisdictions. Reliance on the mechanism appears to be increasing. The mechanism, being discretionary, is flexible: in fact, we argue that this is one of its strengths. There are differences in how the mechanism is labelled or used in different jurisdictions. However, the study of the *amicus curiae* in international criminal tribunals in chapters three and four demonstrates a shared sense of what is at the core of the mechanism and, in particular, the functions it is intended to perform.

We present a typology of functions performed by the *amicus curiae* role based on our review of the legal provisions and practice in the Tribunals. The typology incorporates three functions for the *amicus curiae* in the Tribunals, as set out in Table 1.1. We consider that each of these three functions of the *amicus curiae* has implications for legitimacy. We argue that these functions contribute to both *normative* and *sociological* legitimacy by providing a mechanism that at least partly realises the key values we have identified in the legitimacy literature, in particular representation, participation, transparency, accountability and expertise, as well as broader notions of natural justice. The *amicus curiae* mechanism may also aid in facilitating a broader communicative strategy.

[99] N Schlesinger, 'Making International Criminal Law: Factors Influencing Judicial Behaviour at the ICTY and ICTR' (PhD thesis, the University of Melbourne) 172.

Table 1.1 Typology of *amicus curiae* functions in international criminal tribunals

	Expertise	Representative	Communicative
Purpose	Provision of specific expertise – predominantly legal expertise – to the Chamber. Provision of information that would not otherwise be available to the Chamber.	To allow those actors with an interest that is directly affected by the proceedings or the outcome to participate – in a limited manner – in proceedings.	Enables those stakeholders, not 'directly affected' or providing particular expertise or information, to participate. This includes *amici* seeking to represent the public interest, community interests or to make more indirect representative claims.
Link to legitimacy	Enhances the quality and accuracy of judicial decision-making, thus promoting normative legitimacy through principles of legality and fair trials. Promotes sociological legitimacy as actors are more likely to accept a decision that is more accurate and adheres to legal rules and arguments.	Recognises the key values of participation, transparency and natural justice. Decisions are more accurate and fair, in that they have heard from the actors affected by their decision. Promotes sociological legitimacy as actors are more likely to accept a decision where the Chamber has recognised and heard their interest in proceedings.	Facilitates the key values of participation, representativeness and transparency, as well as accountability, through broader discursive interactions between the Chambers and key stakeholders.
Key challenges	Identifying the required expertise or information and who is best to provide it. Ensuring that expertise is provided in an independent and impartial manner. Determining the most appropriate mechanism for obtaining required expertise, including as expert witnesses, institutionalise actors, or experts assisting the parties.	Identifying where an actor has a directly affected interest that warrants participation and managing the impact of that participation on the parties, particularly the accused.	Identifying what the public interest(s) in an issue is and who is best able to represent that interest. Managing multiple and often competing and inconsistent views of what the public interest requires. Managing the impact of participation by a number of actors in a criminal trial on the parties, in particular the fair trial rights of the accused.

The first function of the *amicus curiae* we label as the **'expertise'** function. This function enables *amici* to place before the Chamber information or expertise – predominantly legal expertise – that would otherwise be unavailable to it. This information or expertise improves the quality of judicial outcomes, by ensuring the judges are better informed and produce more 'accurate' decisions. Such material or expertise may also contribute to the coherence of international law, for example, if *amici* provide information concerning cases from other tribunals or arguments as to the state of customary international law. Here, we assume that actors are attempting to influence the development of the relevant legal and institutional framework and its interpretation and application. The 'expertise' function equates with the value of 'expertise' identified by Buchanan and Keohane.[100] Expertise contributes to both normative and sociological legitimacy as better, more accurate decisions speak to legality and outcomes as sources of legitimacy. A fully informed decision-maker is also consistent with notions of fairness and natural justice. Moreover, by allowing experts or those with relevant information to participate in proceedings, key stakeholders are more likely to accept the outcome of the decision. We explore the extent to which the *amicus curiae* mechanism enables the provision of expertise to Chambers and its impact on legitimacy.

The second function – which we label the **'representative' function** – facilitates the realisation of three key values: participation, transparency and fairness. The *amicus curiae* mechanism is often the only mechanism for key stakeholders to participate in international criminal proceedings. When performing the representative function, the *amicus curiae* represents otherwise unrepresented interests in proceedings, for example victims of international crimes or the perspective of the state in which the crimes occurred. This function therefore aligns with one of the traditional roles of the *amicus curiae*, explored in chapter two. The representative function enhances the transparency of decision-making as those with directly affected interests participate formally in the proceedings and not through other non-legal, secret or political processes. Applying principles of natural justice, allowing those directly affected to present their views enables a better-informed, more accurate and a fairer outcome, at least in the procedural sense. Actors are also more likely to accept the outcome, even if it affects their interest, when they have been heard. Thus, the representative function of the *amicus curiae* promotes both normative and sociological legitimacy. However, under our typology, *amici* should fulfil the representative function only where the interests of the stakeholder are directly affected by the proceedings. We explore in the study what 'directly affected' might mean for certain actors in chapters five–seven, namely victims, civil society actors, accused in related proceedings, and states and international organisations.

The third and final function we have labelled the **'communicative' function.** This function enables other stakeholders, those not 'directly affected' or providing

[100] Buchanan and Keohane (n 28).

particular expertise or information, to participate in proceedings. In this category we include *amici* seeking to represent the public interest, community interests or to make more indirect representative claims. The communicative function facilitates participation by a broader range of actors in the decision-making processes of international criminal tribunals and recognises the discursive dimensions of international criminal justice outlined above. The potential contribution of the communicative function to building sociological legitimacy in the Tribunals is evident: if key stakeholders, even those not directly affected by the proceedings, have participated and been heard they are more likely to accept the decision, even if the outcome is not as they would have liked. However, the communicative function is the most controversial role for the *amicus curiae* as it has the greatest potential to undermine other sources of legitimacy, including fair trials, legality, independence and impartiality. Moreover, when an actor seeks to participate on behalf of 'the public interest', additional challenges are raised. Public interest participation would require judges to determine what the 'public interest' (or interests) in an issue is, why that public interest should be communicated and whether a particular actor can rightly claim to speak for the public interest.

We consider that a communicative function is problematic in the context of criminal proceedings. One method of determining the public interest is to link the notion to the goals of international criminal justice. The goals of international criminal justice are many and wide, and often inconsistent or competing with one another. The goals and potential public interests include: ending impunity through accountability for international crimes; deterrence of future crimes; reconciliation; recognising and restoring harm suffered by victims; truth-telling; producing an authoritative historical record; contributing to building peace; fair trials; developing international criminal law; and building domestic capacity. These are broad and aspirational aims and we suggest are not sufficiently determinate to form the 'test' for participation. Stakeholders will hold a range of views as to what the public interest requires, and it will be challenging for a Chamber to accommodate these divergent and often inconsistent claims within the context of specific criminal trials. Moreover, given the focus of international criminal justice on individual criminal responsibility, we suggest that in most circumstances, it is inappropriate for a Chamber to permit *amici* to perform a communicative role, particularly during the trial. Instead, the discursive dimensions of international criminal justice require different mechanisms. However, we explore whether there may be some scope for a communicative function for an *amicus curiae* in certain circumstances, for example in non-cooperation proceedings.

We are not suggesting that simply increasing the number of *amicus curiae* submissions fulfilling these three functions will enhance legitimacy. The *amicus curiae* is one narrow facet of how various actors engage with international criminal tribunals. Perhaps more importantly for our study, there are significant constraints on the extent to which an international criminal tribunal can and should be allowing *amicus curiae* participation, including the legitimacy sources explored in the previous section. These constraints are explored throughout this study, but we outline them briefly here.

First, as Fitchelberg notes, the ICC 'is a criminal court – not a world government or a global constitutional court – and is thus charged with adjudicating a narrow sliver of issues regarding the guilt or innocence of an accused'.[101] Two key limits emerge from this: the right of the accused to a fair and expeditious trial and the primary responsibility of the judges to determine the guilt or innocence of the accused based on evidence and the law. *Amicus curiae* participation that is inconsistent with these limits may actually undermine legitimacy. That said, we explore *amicus curiae* participation in other phases of proceedings, where these limits may not be as significant and more flexible approaches to *amicus curiae* participation may be possible.

Secondly, increasing the number of *amicus curiae* submissions would generate a considerable burden, for the parties to proceedings and other participants (states, victims) and also for the judges. An unregulated policy towards *amicus curiae* submissions risks overwhelming the institution, in addition to having consequences for the expeditiousness and efficiency of proceedings. Thirdly, as is explored further in chapter four, the *amicus curiae* mechanism is discretionary and only arises where there are legal proceedings (it is not generally an option at the investigative phase). Submissions by *amici* are also voluntary, in the sense that even where a chamber may invite specific *amici* or class of *amici* to participate, it has no means to compel them to do so. Thus, the mechanism is not well-suited to responding to issues that affect the system as a whole or that may require a strategic response. Fourthly, there is no guarantee that *amici* are themselves representative or democratic or even transparent in their identity, funding or goals.

We argue that the ICC and other tribunals should 'manage' their *amicus curiae* practice in accordance with the legitimacy framework identified in the previous section. The key values of participation, transparency, accountability and expertise, as well as broader notions of fairness, including independence, impartiality, equal treatment and fair processes should guide the ICC in its *amicus curiae* practice. This reduces the risk that *amicus curiae* interventions will negatively affect legitimacy. As we explore in chapter four, this is where there could be improvement in the practice. In particular, blurring the distinctions between the three functions of the *amicus curiae* explains some of the confusion concerning the role of the *amicus* and its inconsistent labelling and use. We suggest that different functions and stakeholders may require different criteria and approaches to the *amicus curiae*.

It is perhaps easy to conclude that with a few notable exceptions *amicus curiae* submissions have limited influence on substantive outcomes, as we explore in chapter four. For us, this understates the potential contribution of

[101] Fitchelberg (n 54), 781.

the *amicus curiae* mechanism for a number of reasons. A focus on legitimacy, and the ways in which the *amicus curiae* and our typology of functions can promote legitimacy, shifts the conversation from assessing influence on the formal outcomes in proceedings to recognising the potential discursive role of the *amicus curiae* mechanism. Thus, while we explore instances of impact on particular substantive outcomes, that is not our primary focus or means of assessing the utility of the *amicus curiae*. Instead, our priority is the broader contribution of the *amicus curiae* mechanism to building legitimacy over time.

V. METHOD AND CHAPTER OVERVIEW

This study adopts both an analytical and a normative approach to the role of the *amicus curiae* in international criminal tribunals. This chapter has detailed our main normative claim: that the *amicus curiae* should and could contribute to enhancing the legitimacy of an international criminal tribunal, in particular the ICC. We then identified three functions of the *amicus curiae* and their potential contribution to legitimacy, before detailing the limits that should guide a tribunal in managing its *amicus curiae* practice so as to maximise – or not undermine – the potential contribution to legitimacy.

In chapter two, we undertake a comparative study of practice concerning the *amicus curiae* in certain international and regional institutions and selected national jurisdictions, using a functional approach. This means that we have included in our study mechanisms that may not be labelled '*amicus curiae*' but which are intended to fulfil the three functions we have identified (expertise, representative and communicative), resulting in a more inclusive study. This analysis highlights differences in the approaches in various tribunals, dictated by their subject matter, mandate and legal framework, and how this influences the functions performed by *amici curiae* and its influence on legitimacy. These differences justify the variations we see in the *amicus curiae* practice of international criminal tribunals.

The detailed analytical and empirical study of the *amicus curiae* practice in the Tribunals is set out in chapters three and four. As explained above, the analysis explores the practice of six international criminal tribunals: the ICC; the ICTY; the ICTR; the SCSL; the STL; and the ECCC. Chapter three first outlines the history of the inclusion of the *amicus curiae* mechanism in the legal framework of each tribunal, before providing an overview of the relevant provisions and associated instruments. Next, it details other aspects of the Tribunals' institutional and legal framework that may impact the *amicus curiae* practice, namely the core judicial competence of judges, the requirement to respect fair trial rights and other potential mechanisms for fulfilling the functions we have identified for the *amicus curiae* (such as alternative sources of expertise, or victim participation).

Chapter four then presents the detailed analysis of the *amicus curiae* practice. The method for the research in this chapter is detailed in Annex A. For each tribunal, we collated the following data: (1) relevant legal provisions, including rules of procedure and practice directions; (2) requests to participate as *amicus curiae*, all open calls for *amicus* submissions and invitations to participate as an *amicus* addressed to specific individuals or organisations; (3) the judicial decision on the participation of the *amicus curiae*, if available; (4) associated filings, in particular the *amicus* submission(s) and responses, if any, by parties to proceedings; and (5) the judicial or other 'outcome' of the proceedings, especially concerning the issues addressed by any *amicus curiae*. Data was collected, as relevant, across all stages of proceedings: investigation; pre-trial; trial; appellate; sentencing; (non)cooperation proceedings; and reparations. As detailed in chapter four, while we considered representations in reparations proceedings under Article 75 of the Rome Statute in our study, we have separated this practice to identify different patterns and functions at this unique stage of proceedings. We also excluded the *amicus curiae* as substitute defence from our data (although this role is discussed in chapter six), and excluded the *amicus* prosecutor (discussed briefly in chapter three, section IV(A)).

The resulting database included 408 applications and responses to invitations or calls from the Tribunals, including 157 from the ICC. The inclusion of all, or at least nearly all, requests and related filings enables a comprehensive overview of the practice, rather than focusing on a descriptive analysis of selected cases. However, as described below, the study also examines certain *amicus curiae* submissions in more detail to demonstrate particular points. The data was current up to April 2019. The data was analysed both quantitatively and qualitatively, applying the analytical framework provided by legitimacy and our typology. Further details concerning the method for this study are set out in Annex A. We make suggestions as to how this practice could be improved to enhance both the legitimacy of the *amicus curiae* process and the contribution to the legitimacy of the institution itself.

This mainly desk-based research was complemented by a series of semi-structured interviews with a range of actors involved in international criminal justice: judges; prosecutors; defence lawyers; civil society actors; academics; and victims' representatives. Interviews were conducted in accordance with UNSW ethics approval.[102] Findings were presented and debated at three workshops: a two-day meeting held at the University of Cape Town in February 2015 on the broader issue of Civil Society and International Criminal Justice in Africa;[103] a one-day expert workshop hosted in The Hague with the Grotius Centre

[102] UNSW HREAP B: Arts, Humanities & Law, HREAP 14122.

[103] For the report from this workshop, see 'Civil Society and International Criminal Justice in Africa' (4–5 February 2015), available at http://archive.ahrcentre.org/sites/ahrcentre.org/files/Civil%20Society%20and%20ICJ%20in%20Africa%20Exec%20Summary.pdf. Papers from the workshop were published as H Woolaver and S Williams (eds), *Civil Society and International Criminal Justice in Africa Challenges and Opportunities* (Cape Town, Juta Law, 2016).

for International Legal Studies in January 2016;[104] and an evening seminar co-hosted by Doughty Street Chambers and Chatham House (the Royal Institute of International Affairs) in London in January 2016.[105] We encountered a high level of interest in the topic of the *amicus curiae* and remain grateful to those individuals who took time from their busy schedules to discuss their own views and experiences.

Chapters five, six and seven analyse the *amicus curiae* from the perspectives of three key stakeholder groups: civil society (including NGOs, academics and victims) in chapter five; defence and defence associations in chapter six; and states and international organisations in chapter seven. For the purpose of our study, civil society is defined broadly to include: local and international NGOs, academics, individuals, and representatives of intergovernmental organisations (eg, UN special rapporteurs).[106] Applying our typology of functions, these chapters explore how different stakeholder groups use the *amicus curiae* mechanism. We also consider how the judges and stakeholders have managed this process and the extent to which the *amicus curiae* practice has contributed to enhancing or undermining legitimacy. The study is not simply analytical; rather, in these chapters we seek to show what the appropriate functions for *amici curiae* are in relation to specific actors so as best to enhance the institution's legitimacy while also respecting key constraints. These chapters make a number of suggestions for the reform of the relevant framework, including the adoption of more specific criteria for *amici curiae* in certain circumstances. Other suggestions are contained in Annex C, a guide for practitioners.

Chapter eight reaffirms how use of the *amicus curiae* is linked to the legitimacy of international crimes tribunals and reflects larger issues concerning the representation, integrity, accuracy and fairness of international criminal proceedings. The book thus situates the *amicus curiae* in the context of debates about participation and representation in international criminal justice and the legitimacy of international criminal tribunals.

[104] The report from this workshop is confidential and on file with the authors. The executive summary is available here: 'The *Amicus Curiae* in International Criminal Justice' (18 January 2016) at http://michaelgkarnavas.net/files/ExecutiveSummaryAmicusCuriaeICJ.pdf.

[105] For a summary, see K Brimelow et al, 'Shaping the Law: Civil Society Influence at the International Courts' (*Chatham House,* 25 January 2016), available at www.chathamhouse.org/sites/default/files/events/160125-meeting-summary-shaping-law-civil-society-influence-international-criminal-courts.pdf.

[106] In relation to the various contested meanings of civil society, see J Keane, *Global Civil Society?* (Cambridge, CUP, 2003); N Roht-Arriaza, 'Civil Society in Processes of Accountability,' in M Cherif Bassiouni (ed), *Post-Conflict Justice* (Ardsley, New York, Transnational Publishers, 2002) 98; HK Anheier, M Glasius and M Kaldor, *Global Civil Society* (Oxford, OUP, 2001); G Baker, *Civil Society and Democratic Theory: Alternative Voices* (London, Routledge, 2003); M Kaldor, *Global Civil Society: An Answer to War* (Cambridge, Polity Press, 2003) ch 1; L Hovil and M Chrispus Okello, 'Editorial Note' (2011) 5(3) *IJTJ* 333; B Woodward, *Global Civil Society in International Lawmaking and Global Governance: Theory and Practice*, (Leiden, Martinus Nijhoff, 2010) 9.

2

The Amicus Curiae *in Comparative Perspective*

I. ADOPTING A FUNCTIONAL APPROACH

CHAPTER ONE INTRODUCED the three functions of the *amicus curiae* in international criminal tribunals: expertise; representative; and communicative. We suggested that each of these functions has a different rationale, although each contributes in its own way to enhancing the legitimacy of a tribunal. This chapter adopts a comparative approach to the *amicus curiae*, considering mechanisms for participation in national legal systems and regional and international institutions. The purpose of the comparative analysis was to explore the extent to which other systems recognise the *amicus curiae* mechanism and the functions we have identified. We also identified rules and practice that have informed our primary study of the *amicus curiae* in international criminal tribunals in the following chapters.

Our study of practice is not comprehensive. We considered practice in seven international institutions: the International Court of Justice (ICJ); the International Tribunal on the Law of the Sea (ITLOS); the World Trade Organisation (WTO); investor-state investment arbitration; the European Court of Human Rights (ECtHR); the Inter-American Court of Human Rights (IACHR); and the African Court of Human and People's Rights (African Court). These institutions do not exercise criminal jurisdiction; their focus is on state responsibility rather than individual criminal responsibility. Although these institutions may appear less relevant to a study of international criminal tribunals, they share a basis of state consent and the need to retain state support both for legitimacy and to operate. We therefore explore whether the focus on criminal responsibility in international criminal tribunals requires a different rationale for or approach to *amicus curiae* participation.

We have restricted our study of national legal systems to rules and practice in several selected jurisdictions (the United Kingdom;[1] the United States; Canada;

[1] We recognise that England and Wales have different rules to other parts of the UK, with Scotland, for example, having a civil law-based system. However, we focus on the UK Supreme Court.

Australia; South Africa;[2] Uganda; France; Germany; Indonesia; and Peru) with references to other jurisdictions as appropriate. We have attempted to include examples from common law and civil law systems, as well as to provide some regional diversity. Our focus is on criminal proceedings, although most participation at the national level does not arise in criminal proceedings but in 'higher' level courts, such as constitutional courts or superior courts.

Our study is not empirical, in the sense that we have not collated briefs and practice in the same way as for the Tribunals. Instead, we have relied on existing studies of international institutions, several of which are comprehensive and recent,[3] and supplemented those studies with our own research as necessary. At the national level, we have prepared overviews of rules and practice, drawing mainly on existing literature and studies where possible. Given the limited space available in this chapter, we have not been able to replicate the detail of our country studies; this chapter provides an overview only.

We adopted a functional approach to the comparative analysis, identifying the functions a mechanism is intended to fulfil, rather than whether a particular mechanism is labelled '*amicus curiae*'. The role of the *amicus curiae* in common law jurisdictions is linked to the concept of legal standing. Standing considers the relationship between the claimant and the claim raised by the litigation or the outcome of the litigation. Standing rules developed as a means to regulate who was entitled to commence legal proceedings and what constituted a sufficient interest to bring a claim. Standing rules are procedural in nature; however, such rules also have substantive impact as they determine which actors may participate in proceedings and the interests protected. There are four options for formal participation in legal proceedings in common law systems: standing to bring a claim; joinder; intervention, both as a party and 'third party' intervention; and the *amicus curiae*. This chapter considers these four options in relation to national and international legal systems, to situate the *amicus curiae* mechanism in its broader context. In particular, we explore the overlap between third party intervention and the *amicus curiae*, as the two mechanisms for participation perform similar functions in different systems. It is not unusual for applicants to apply both to intervene and to make submissions as an *amicus curiae* in the alternative, and some systems use the mechanisms almost interchangeably or define one mechanism by reference to the other.

[2] We also recognise that South Africa draws on civil law and is considered to be a mixed system. However, its approach to the *amicus curiae* is more clearly comparable with common law systems, so we have considered it as a common law system.

[3] In particular: N Bürli, *Third-Party Interventions before the European Court of Human Rights* (Cambridge, Intersentia, 2017); F El-Hosseny, *Civil Society in Investment Treaty Arbitration: Shifts and Prospects* (Leiden, Brill, 2018); A Wiik, *Amicus Curiae before International Courts and Tribunals* (Baden-Baden, Nomos, 2018); F Juaristi, 'The *Amicus Curiae* in the Inter-American Court of Human Rights (1982–2013)' in Y Haeck et al (eds), *The Inter-American Court of Human Rights: Theory and Practice, Present and Future* (Cambridge, Intersentia, 2015).

II. STANDING TO BRING A CLAIM

A. Standing Rules in International and Regional Institutions

Standing rules reflect the dominance of states in the international legal system. Under the rules on diplomatic protection, a state possessed international legal personality and would – at its discretion – espouse the interests of its nationals (both natural and legal) in international adjudication. Nationals did not have standing to bring a claim against a state at the international level. Several institutions still reflect that position. The ICJ, the principal judicial organ of the UN,[4] recognises that only member states can initiate proceedings.[5] The ITLOS determines disputes that arise from the application and interpretation of the UN Convention on the Law of the Sea (UNCLOS). In contentious proceedings, jurisdiction is open to states party to UNCLOS and entities other than states that have ratified or acceded to UNCLOS (namely, international organisations such as the European Union).[6] The WTO dispute settlement mechanisms, the Dispute Settlement Body (DSB) and the Appellate Body, responsible for determining disputes between member states arising from alleged violations of various trade-related agreements, are open only to WTO member states.[7] The ICJ, ITLOS and the WTO illustrate the traditional model of courts adjudicating concrete legal disputes between two or more states.

There has been some relaxation of formal standing rules for specific types of disputes. The loosening of standing rules in human rights institutions and investor-state investment arbitration developed partly in response to the failure of diplomatic protection to allow actors other than states to initiate claims. In investor-state investment arbitration, the investor may bring a claim against the host state pursuant to a general agreement or a specific bilateral investment treaty between the host state and its own state of nationality. While this still requires a violation of a core protection given by the host state to the investor in a treaty between two or more states, it allows actors other than states to commence claims. In human rights institutions, while states may initiate proceedings against another state (known as inter-state proceedings), victims can also initiate claims against a state, rather than rely on a state to bring their claim at the international level. At the ECtHR, for example, 'any person, nongovernmental organisation or group of individuals claiming to be a victim of a violation of the ECHR or its protocols' can initiate an individual petition. One distinction between the human rights institutions is whether standing is

[4] Charter of the United Nations (24 October 1945) 1 UNTS XVI, Art 92; Statute of the International Court of Justice (18 April 1946), Art 1.

[5] ICJ Statute, Art 34(1).

[6] Statute of the International Tribunal for the Law of the Sea (United Nations Convention on the Law of the Sea, 10 December 1982, Annex VI), Art 20.

[7] Understanding on Rules and Procedures Governing the Settlement of Disputes (Agreement Establishing the World Trade Organisation, 15 April 1994, Annex 2), Art 3(2).

limited to direct victims,[8] that is, those actors (including NGOs) who have *themselves* been a victim of a violation, or whether actors who are not themselves direct victims may bring 'representative' claims, that is on behalf of direct victims. At the ECtHR, applicants – including NGOs – must generally themselves be victims,[9] although they may bring a case on behalf of other victims in exceptional circumstances.[10] In contrast, in the Inter-American system, 'there is virtually no limit on who may file a petition with the Inter-American Commission', as the petitioner need not be the victim.[11] Yet, only a state party to the American Convention of Human Rights (the American Convention) or the Commission itself may submit cases to the Court, so there is a filter on claims progressing from the Commission to the IACHR. The African Court adopts a similar approach to standing, allowing any member state (including any state whose national is a victim of a violation), the Commission and any recognised African intergovernmental organisation to submit cases.[12] The African Court may also allow relevant NGOs with observer status before the Commission and individuals to institute cases directly before it, where the state has accepted the competence of the Court to do so.[13] Its practice suggests that this includes NGOs acting in a representative capacity.

Actors with standing to bring a claim participate as a party to proceedings and enjoy the full range of substantive and procedural rights available within that system. Such rights may include the right to: access to the case file and submissions of the parties; make written and oral arguments; tender evidence and examine witnesses; and appeal. A decision binds a party to the proceedings (but only in relation to that particular dispute).[14] The party must implement any measures adopted by the court or tribunal, although some systems, such as the WTO, require an additional step before a decision becomes binding.[15]

[8] European Convention for the Protection of Human Rights and Fundamental Freedoms (adopted 4 November 1950, entered into force 3 September 1953) ETS 5, Art 34.

[9] See (although it was decided before the 1998 amendment) *Betty Purcell v Ireland*, as to the Admissibility of App no 15404/89 (ECHR, 16 April 1991), in which the Court held that 'The fact alone that the trade unions consider themselves as guardians of the collective interests of their members does not suffice to make them victims within the meaning of Article 25'. See M Frigessi di Rattalma 'NGOs Before the European Court of Human Rights: Beyond *Amicus Curiae* Participation?' in T Treves et al, *Civil Society, International Courts and Compliance Bodies, Project on International Courts and Tribunals* (The Hague, TMC Asser Press, 2005).

[10] See *Centre For Legal Resources On Behalf of Valentin Câmpeanu v Romania*, App no 47848/08 (14 July 2014).

[11] D Shelton, 'The Jurisprudence of the Inter-American Court of Human Rights' (1994) 10 *American University International Law Review* 333, 342.

[12] Protocol to the African Charter on Human and Peoples' Rights on the Establishment of an African Court on Human and People's Rights (adopted 10 June 1998, entered into force 25 January 2004), Art 5.

[13] African Court Protocol, Art 5(3). See also Art 34(6).

[14] See eg ICJ Statute, Art 59.

[15] Decisions of WTO panels and Appellate Body are binding on parties to the dispute once adopted by the DSB: Dispute Settlement Understanding (DSU), arts 16.4 and 17.14.

These institutions, excluding the WTO and investor-state investment arbitration panels, also exercise advisory jurisdiction.[16] Advisory opinions are non-binding on states and can be requested by institutional actors, rather than states. For example, the General Assembly and Security Council may request an opinion from the ICJ on any legal issue,[17] while any subsidiary organ authorised by or in accordance with the UN Charter may request an opinion 'on legal questions arising within the scope of their activities'.[18] The ECtHR exercises advisory jurisdiction in limited circumstances, namely where a request is received from the Council of Ministers in respect of legal questions concerning the interpretation or scope of the ECHR or its protocols[19] (but not the scope of the rights or freedoms).[20] Following the entry into force of Protocol 16, the ECtHR can also give an advisory opinion when requested by the highest national court in a member state, but only in the context of a case currently before that national court.[21] The African Court does not limit standing to request advisory opinions only to institutional actors, but also allows member states and 'any African organization recognized by the AU' to file a request, thus in theory allowing civil society actors standing to initiate a request for an advisory opinion.[22]

B. Standing at the National Level

In non-criminal matters, most national common law systems require the applicant to have a directly affected interest to initiate a claim, with the rules of standing operating to restrict access to the courts to those with a legal interest or, for administrative actions, 'someone with a substantial interest in the matter before the Court'.[23] In some systems, standing rules have been relaxed at least in relation to certain types of proceedings, for example, judicial review or administrative procedures. Increasingly, standing rules recognise that actors – such as NGOs – may have standing to bring representational claims on behalf of direct victims or where it would be in the public interest for the claim to be brought.[24] In civil jurisdictions, standing rules tend to be more relaxed, and courts are open to third party participation, not requiring a legal interest for intervention, for example.[25]

[16] See American Convention on Human Rights, 'Pact of San Jose, Costa Rica' (adopted 22 November 1969, entered into force 18 July 1978), Art 64(1).

[17] UN Charter, Art 96(1).

[18] ibid, Art 96(2).

[19] ECHR, Art 47.

[20] ECHR, Art 47(2).

[21] Protocol No 16 to the Convention for the Protection for Human Rights and Fundamental Freedoms (adopted 2 October 2013, entered into force 1 August 2018) CETS 214, Art 1.

[22] ibid, Art 4.

[23] C Harlow, 'Public Law and Popular Justice' (2002) *MLR* 1, 4.

[24] For discussion of these developments in the UK, see ibid; C Harlow and R Rawlings, *Pressure Through Law* (London, Routledge, 1992). In the US, see B Tamanaha, *Law as a Means to an End: Threat to the Rule of Law* (Cambridge, CUP, 2009), particularly chs 5 and 9.

[25] S Kochevar, '*Amici Curiae* in Civil Law Jurisdictions' [2013] 122 *Yale LJ* 1653, 1668.

In criminal proceedings, the state is responsible for initiating criminal investigations and for prosecuting alleged offenders. In some systems, there is limited scope for victims to initiate criminal proceedings and for NGOs to initiate claims on behalf of victims based on private prosecution.[26] Other systems allow victims to file complaints and provide victims participatory rights in any investigation rather than standing to initiate and conduct the investigation. Therefore, in most instances, it is the state – acting through the prosecution service or investigating judge – that initiates and conducts a criminal trial. Systems differ as to the extent of discretion the prosecutor has to prosecute; in some states there is a duty to prosecute when the evidence suggests crimes have been committed, while in others, prosecutors can take into account a wider range of factors, including the public interest, and can decline to prosecute. The parties are the state (prosecution) and the accused, possibly with some participatory rights for victims. The prosecution represents the public interest in prosecuting and, in systems where victim participation is not recognised, the interests of victims.

III. JOINDER OF CLAIMS AND CASES

A potential claimant may have sufficient interest in proceedings to apply to join their claim to ongoing proceedings against the same respondent or to join related claims, a process known as *joinder*. Joinder brings two or more parties or claims together as they are related or the claims overlap. The emphasis is on the commonality of the facts, the parties and the claims. The rationale for joinder is the promotion of judicial economy and efficiency, as well as ensuring that related or similar cases are treated consistently. Where existing cases are joined, or where a claimant is joined to an ongoing proceeding, they are joined (or remain) as a party to proceedings and enjoy full procedural rights. We find joinder in both common law and civil law systems, for both civil and criminal proceedings, and in all international institutions studied here.[27] Joinder requires each of the parties to have standing to initiate the claim; it does not override standing rules but allows related or similar claims to be heard together.

[26] eg ss 7–8 of the Criminal Procedure Act 51 of 1977 (South Africa) allows private individuals (victims) to carry out prosecutions if the prosecuting authority declines to prosecute, and organisations to do so in particular circumstances.

[27] International Court of Justice, Rules of the Court (adopted 14 April 1978, entered into force 1 July 1978) r 47; DSU, Art 4(11) (joining consultations) and Art 9 (joining multiple complaints before one panel); International Tribunal for the Law of the Sea, Rules of the Tribunal (adopted 28 October 1997, as amended 17 March 2009) ITLOS/8, Art 47; European Court of Human Rights, Rules of Court (as amended 19 September 2016), r 42; Rules of Procedure of the Inter-American Court of Human Rights (1980, as amended 2009), Art 30; African Court on Human and Peoples' Rights, Rules of Court, r 54.

IV. INTERVENTION

Intervention enables an actor to intervene in ongoing proceedings. There are two key distinctions: (1) whether intervention is as of right or discretionary; and (2) whether the intervener becomes a party to proceedings or benefits from a lesser range of rights. Related questions are which actors may claim a right or request permission to intervene, and in which circumstances.

A. Intervention at the International Level

i. Intervention as of Right

At the international level, there are few examples of actors that may intervene as of right. One is Article 36(3) ECHR, which allows an institutional actor, the Council of Europe Commission for Human Rights, to participate in all cases. A state may intervene in certain circumstances, particularly where the state intervenes in support of a national that is participating in proceedings. For example, in ITLOS, the 'sponsoring state' has a right to participate in proceedings where one of its nationals (either natural or juridical) has initiated a dispute.[28] Similarly, at the ECtHR, where a national is an applicant in a case, the state of nationality has the right to submit written comments and take part in hearings.[29]

International institutions may also allow intervention as of right if the proceedings raise an issue of interpretation of a treaty to which that state is a party.[30] An example of this is Article 63 of the ICJ Statute, which provides that the Registry is to notify all states parties to a convention where the construction of that convention arises in proceedings, and states will have a right to intervene. The purpose of this form of intervention is not to protect a specific interest of that state, but rather recognises 'a general interest in the interpretation of a specific rule of a convention'.[31] If a state chooses to intervene, the construction of the convention given in the decision will bind the intervening state.[32]

ii. Intervention as a Matter of Discretion

International institutions recognise discretionary rights to intervene. In the ICJ, ITLOS and WTO, a state may apply to intervene where it has an interest of a

[28] United Nations Convention on the Law of the Sea (adopted 10 December 1982, entered into force 16 November 1994) UNTS 31363, Art 190.

[29] ECHR, Art 36(1).

[30] ICJ Statute, Art 63; ITLOS Statute, Art 32.

[31] P Palchetti, 'Opening the International Court of Justice to Third States: Intervention and Beyond' (2002) 6 *Max Planck Yearbook of United Nations Law* 139, 141.

[32] ICJ Statute, Art 63(2).

legal nature that may be affected by the decision of the Court.[33] Here, intervention reflects the principle that the Court cannot determine the rights and interests of a third state without its consent.[34] Allowing intervention therefore enables the participation – in a limited form – of a potentially affected third state. This provision leaves considerable discretion to the Court, and features several 'obscurities or ambiguities'.[35] The ICJ has held that the interest supporting intervention need not be a direct interest in the subject matter of the dispute, but 'may also relate to the reasons which constitute the necessary steps to the *dispositif*'.[36] However, where a state relies on an interest due to the reasoning the Court may adopt, it must show 'with adequate specificity' how a particular interpretation or application of a treaty may impact its claim.[37] Therefore, a general interest in the interpretation of particular instruments, or a concern that the decision may contain reasoning that is inconsistent with other claims the state may wish to make in future, is not sufficient for intervention.[38] Similarly, a political or economic interest in the subject matter will not support intervention. The state seeking to intervene need not show that the decision will affect the interest, only that the interest might possibly be affected.[39] A further issue is whether intervention requires a jurisdictional link between the parties and the intervening states. At the African Court, where a state party has an interest in a case, it may request permission to intervene, with the applicant state required to demonstrate a legal interest that has or will be affected by the case, the precise object of the intervention and the basis for jurisdiction it relies on.[40] Here, intervention is serving a representative function, and is linked to the protection – or at least preservation – of a specific legal interest. The ICJ, ITLOS and WTO permit intervention *only* by states, reflecting the dominance of states in terms of standing, the notion of diplomatic protection, and a sceptical approach to allowing broader participation in these institutions. Intervention is linked to a specific legal interest, not intervention to argue the public interest.

The IACHR does not include rules for intervention by states – or any actor – in contentious proceedings. Similarly, investor-state investment arbitration

[33] ibid, Art 62. Article 31(1) of the ITLOS Statute also refers to 'an interest of a legal nature'. At the WTO, 'a state having a substantial interest in a matter' and having notified that interest to the Dispute Settlement Body may seek to intervene under Art 10(2) of the DSU.

[34] This is known as the Monetary Gold Principle, drawing from the decision of the ICJ in *Monetary Gold Removed from Rome in 1943 (Italy v France, US and UK)* (Preliminary Question) [1954] ICJ Rep 19, 32. For discussion, see O Pomson, 'Does the Monetary Gold Principle Apply to International Courts and Tribunals Generally?' (2019) 10 *Journal of International Dispute Settlement* 88.

[35] MN Shaw, *Rosenne's Law and Practice of the International Court of Justice, 1920–2015*, 5th edn (Leiden, Brill, 2016) Volume III, 1496.

[36] *Sovereignty over Pulau Ligitan and Pulau Sipadan (Indonesia/ Malaysia)* (Application by the Philippines for Permission to Intervene, Judgment) [2001] ICJ Rep 596, para 47.

[37] ibid, para 60.

[38] ibid, para 83.

[39] *Territorial and Maritime Dispute (Nicaragua v Colombia)* (Application by Costa Rica for Permission to Intervene, Judgment) [2011] ICR Rep 420, 434, para 37.

[40] African Court Protocol, Art 5(2). Rule 53 governs the process.

tribunals, being based on principles of consent, do not recognise intervention by states – or other actors – other than by the state of nationality. There are no general rules governing intervention upon which to rely. In these two systems, states and other actors seeking to intervene whether to protect their own interest or the public interest must rely on the *amicus curiae* mechanism, discussed in section V.

At the ECtHR, states benefit from the general provision on intervention, which was introduced by amendments in 1998. Prior to 1998, there was no express provision detailing *amicus curiae* or other intervention in the ECHR or in the Rules of Procedure of the ECtHR. This did not preclude attempts at such intervention. The first attempt to do so was in 1978, in the case of *Tyrer v the United Kingdom*,[41] in which the National Council for Civil Liberties (now Liberty) wished to file observations, having represented the applicant before the Commission. The applicant withdrew the complaint, but the Commission referred the case to the Court, and Liberty sought to appear on behalf of the applicant's family, as an *amicus* or on any other basis. However, the Court found that it did not need to hear Liberty and rejected the request, seemingly on the basis that the submission would not be likely to assist.[42] The Court first granted third parties the ability to intervene in proceedings the following year in the *Winterwerp v The Netherlands* case, in which the United Kingdom was granted permission to submit comments.[43] The Court's rules were modified in 1983 to clarify that the President may invite or grant leave to any third party contracting state or 'any person concerned other than the applicant' to submit written comments.[44] While the Court began to accept further NGO interventions under this Rule, NGO participation in ECtHR cases remained relatively rare prior to 1998 – possibly amounting to only several dozen cases.[45]

The 1998 amendments introduced Article 36 of the Convention, which now forms the basis for intervention. This Article is supplemented by Rule 44 in the Rules of Procedure, which details many of the procedural requirements for third party intervention. The reforms in 1998 may be considered a 'constitutional' evolution for the Court and there has been enhanced recognition of the role the Court plays in the constitutional order of its member states and the demand for broader participation.[46]

In relation to states, Article 36(2) provides that 'any High Contracting Party which is not a party to the proceedings' may 'in the interest of the proper

[41] App no 5856/72 (25 April 1978).

[42] This was based on Art 38 of the Rules of the Court, which at the time allowed the Court to accept evidence or statements from a witness or expert where that would be likely to assist the Court.

[43] App no 6301/73 (24 October 1979). See Bürli (n 3), 4.

[44] ECtHR Rules, r 37, para 2.

[45] L Hitoshi Mayer, 'NGO Standing and Influence in Regional Human Rights Courts and Commissions' (2011) 36(3) *Brooklyn Journal of International Law* 911, 916.

[46] For further discussion, see Bürli (n 3), 4–6; H Nicols Haddad, *The Hidden Hands of Justice: NGOs, Human Rights and International Courts* (Cambridge, CUP, 2018) 55–83.

administration of justice' be invited to submit written comments or take part in hearings. This provision applies in both inter-state proceedings and individual complaints and does not require the intervening state to demonstrate it has a legal interest affected by the proceedings. In practice, many of the state interventions under Article 36(2) concerned the interpretation of the ECHR and allowed the ECtHR to see how its decision may have an impact in other states, beyond those states affected directly by the decision.[47] Judges see value, particularly in the human rights institutions, in permitting intervention by states on this basis. Bürli suggests that in the ECtHR, state interventions partly alleviate the tension between judicial 'law-making' and sovereignty hence building its legitimacy with states, allow the Court to receive assistance from states particularly about domestic systems and potential impact of decisions, and may enhance cooperation and implementation of decisions.[48]

Article 36(2) ECHR also enables 'any person concerned who is not the applicant' to 'in the interest of the proper administration of justice' be invited to submit written comments or take part in hearings. Thus, civil society actors may also seek to intervene in proceedings. Importantly, the ECtHR does not have a separate provision addressing *amicus curiae* participation; rather Article 36(2) provides the only option for participation in proceedings. Bürli suggests that the ECtHR recognises three 'types' of intervention in practice, if not formally in the rules.[49] First, interventions by individuals (or legal persons) who are implicated in the facts of the case, which is usually one of the parties to the claim at the national level. Bürli labels these third party interventions. The essential requirement is a legal interest that is, or could be, directly affected by the outcome. The rationale for third party intervention is the concept of due process or the right of everyone affected by a decision to be heard'.[50] Bürli suggests this requires being affected by *individual measures* arising from the decision (ie, due to execution of the judgment or reopening of national proceedings), and is more than the risk of the Court setting a future precedent. A second type of intervention is to advocate the perspective of a specific category of persons that has an interest that might be affected – albeit not directly – by the court's decision, for example, future victims. The final category Bürli identifies is intervention by individuals or organisations that have no direct legal interest in the case but who possess a special expertise or authority with regard to the issue before the Court. This latter category Bürli labels *amicus curiae* submissions, as this form of submission is closest to the role of the *amicus curiae* in many national systems. Interestingly, Bürli does not consider that the ECtHR practice supports intervention to argue the public interest, at least not without expertise (final category) or some form of representative claim (second category).

[47] Bürli (n 3), 153.
[48] ibid, 134–36.
[49] ibid, 6–9.
[50] ibid, 159.

The provision in the African Court is more general: where the Commission files the complaint with the Court, the Court can, if it feels it necessary, hear from the individual or NGO that communicated the case.[51] At the IACHR, the victims or their legal representatives participate in proceedings.[52] In both institutions, there are no other provisions regulating intervention – other actors would participate as *amici curiae*, discussed below, including those seeking to make public interest claims.

iii. Status and Rights of Interveners

In none of the international institutions studied does the intervener become a party to proceedings, regardless of whether intervention is as of right or by permission: this is the role of joinder, not intervention.[53] As the rights of third states are protected – to an extent – by the fact a decision is binding only on the parties, the purpose of intervention is not to realise or recognise the rights claimed. Instead, the purpose is to protect those rights by enabling the state to inform the Court of those rights and to allow the Court the opportunity to modify, if possible, its decision to leave the interest claimed unaffected by its decision. Where that is not possible, the intervener must join the claims (assuming a jurisdictional link exists) or the Court may be unable to issue a decision. Similarly, an intervening state at the WTO or ITLOS does not become a party, nor does a state in a human rights institution or investor-state investment arbitration panel, including where it intervenes to protect a national. Although they do not become parties to the dispute and are not bound by the decision or able to appeal, intervening states can be granted extensive participatory rights. For example, an intervening WTO member state 'shall have an opportunity to be heard by the panel and to make written submissions to the panel. These submissions shall also be given to the parties to the dispute and shall be reflected in the panel report'.[54]

iv. Participation in Advisory Proceedings

For those institutions that exercise advisory jurisdiction, there are rights of participation for states (and international organisations), although this is separate to, and distinct from, the provisions on intervention already discussed. Once the ICJ has received a request for an advisory opinion, the Court determines which states and international organisations 'are likely to furnish information on the question', and the Registry notifies the states and organisations identified through a 'special and direct communication' that it is willing to receive

[51] African Court Rules, r 29(3)(c).
[52] IACtHR Rules, Art 25.
[53] The exception to this is intervention under Art 63, as the intervening state is bound by the interpretation of a treaty adopted in the decision.
[54] DSU, Art 10(2).

submissions.[55] The Court is flexible as to the states identified and, depending on the legal question and context, the Court may invite all UN member states or member states of the body that initiated the request for an advisory opinion. Other states (those not receiving a direct notification) can apply to participate at the Court's discretion and, although not expressly stated, the Court has allowed other international organisations to participate. Therefore, Article 66 enables broader participation for states and international organisations in advisory proceedings than intervention allows in contentious proceedings.

For the Seabed Disputes Chamber of ITLOS, the Registrar notifies all states parties of the request and any state party may participate in proceedings; in contrast, the Chamber will decide which international organisations it will invite to furnish information.[56] At the IACHR, upon receipt of a request for an advisory opinion, the Secretariat must notify 'the Member States, the Commission, the Permanent Council through its Presidency, the Secretary General, and, if applicable, to the OAS organs whose sphere of competence is referred to in the request'.[57] These 'interested parties' may file comments, although the term 'interested' is not limited to states having a legal interest, more a general interest in the proceedings. At the ECtHR, member states receive notification of the request and may participate in proceedings.[58] At the African Court, states parties are notified of the request and may make written submissions. In addition, 'any other interested entity' may make submissions, but only with the permission of the Court.[59] Therefore, states – and in some circumstances international organisations or institutional actors – may participate as of right in advisory opinions, reflecting the non-binding nature of the proceedings and the often broader relevance and significance of the issue raised. However, with the exception of the African Court, none of the international institutions studied recognise participation by other actors or to protect a public interest.

B. Intervention in National Level Systems

i. Intervention as of Right

Two categories of actors may intervene as of right in national systems. The first category includes institutional and governmental actors, such as Attorneys-General, who may intervene where an issue of federal law, or a public or constitutional interest arises. The second category consists of actors that have an interest that may be directly affected by the outcome of the proceedings, which has

[55] ICJ Statute, Art 66(2).

[56] ITLOS Rules, Art 133.

[57] IACtHR Rules, Art 73(1).

[58] Rule 84 of the ECtHR Rules provides for written responses, with the possibility of participation in oral proceedings if held. Note that this does not extend to advisory proceedings under Protocol 16, which are regulated by rr 91–95 and do not permit states parties to participate.

[59] African Court Rules, rr 69, 70.

traditionally been focused on the protection of private, mainly property or financial, interests. Intervention as of right is often linked to standing; interveners have to establish a concrete interest that is affected by the proceedings, similar to an interest that would give rise to standing to initiate a claim. The rationale for intervention as of right to protect a legal interest is two-fold: first, allowing an actor whose interest is affected to intervene accords with principles of natural justice. Secondly, similar to joinder, intervention in such circumstances promotes judicial economy, by considering linked claims together. What is more controversial is whether a public interest in a particular issue is sufficient to support intervention as of right. While the US Supreme Court does not allow intervention as such,[60] other federal courts have adopted different views as to this question. Generally, though, the need to establish a concrete interest, usually of a legal nature, that is affected by the decision is challenging for a potential public interest intervener. For this reason, public interest interveners often rely on provisions allowing intervention, but only with the permission of the Court, discussed in the next section.

ii. *Intervention as a Matter of Discretion*

National legal systems allow intervention in proceedings as an exercise of the court's discretion. Some systems require government and institutional actors to seek permission to intervene for certain types of cases. For example, several statutes recognise that the Australian Human Rights Commission may intervene in proceedings with a connection to human rights, but only with the leave of the relevant court.[61] Aside from such actors, there are three main forms of discretionary intervention identified in national practice.[62] First, participation by civil society and other actors effectively equivalent to *amici curiae* in the traditional mode, namely, an intervention to assist the court on a point of law, with the intervener having no interest in the issue and neutral to the outcome of the case.

A second form of intervention allows those with their own (generally financial) interest in the proceedings to be heard and, more rarely, those seeking to represent those whose interests are affected (for example, an industry federation representing the interest of its members). This is similar to intervention by right, discussed in the previous section, in that it requires the intervener to have an interest close to that of a party; however, intervention requires the Court's permission.

The third category is known as 'public interest' intervention, although legal systems differ as to the extent to which intervention can be based on protecting a public interest and what type of public interest should support intervention. While there is no clear definition of 'public interest' intervention, it arises where a third party, with no direct interest in the proceedings, has a strategic interest in developing the law or its application in a particular way to achieve goals that are broader

[60] Intervention is pursuant to the rule on *amicus curiae*, which is discussed in section V.
[61] eg Australian Human Rights Commission Act 1986 (Cth), s 31(j).
[62] See S Hannett, 'Third Party Intervention: In the Public Interest?' [2003] *Public Law* 128, 130–31.

than those of the parties.[63] Public interest or strategic litigation perceives the courts as a forum for bringing about human rights or other social change. Given its implications for the role of the judiciary in a society, public interest intervention is controversial.[64] Hannett notes that an expansive public interest intervention regime 'shifts the court towards a legislative function, by allowing intervention to operate as one of several tactics in a campaign strategy and by permitting political battles lost elsewhere to be revisited'.[65] Moreover, it is very difficult to establish what the public interest is, and who is entitled to represent the public interest: 'What constitutes the public interest is contingent and contested'.[66]

Despite these concerns, many jurisdictions have seen an increase in the extent of public interest intervention, with the shift generally – although not always – linked to a 'constitutional moment'. For example, the increase in public interest intervention in the UK is often traced to the adoption of the Human Rights Act in 1998, which 'domesticated' the ECHR into UK law, and led to a relaxation of the rules on intervention, which previously required the intervener to be directly affected.[67] Shah, Poole and Blackwell found that third party interventions had increased since the adoption of the Human Rights Act, due largely to a rise in voluntary applications by NGOs[68] – often repeat NGO players working as a coalition. They also noted a corresponding significant fall in the number of *amicus curiae* briefs in the House of Lords in the same period.[69] The transition of the House of Lords into the UK Supreme Court in 2009, and the constitutional role of that body, also saw an increase in judicial review proceedings and requests for intervention in the public interest.[70] The UK Supreme Court rules allow any person, in particular 'any official body or non-governmental organisation seeking to make submissions in the public interest' to apply for permission to intervene in the appeal.[71] This rule does not define the public interest, and accords considerable discretion to the Court to determine when and for whom it should permit intervention.[72]

[63] Drawing from H Duffy, *Strategic Human Rights Litigation: Understanding and Maximising Impact* (Oxford, Hart Publishing, 2018) 3.

[64] Hannett (n 62); ibid, 4.

[65] Hannett (n 62), 129.

[66] ibid, 135.

[67] Harlow (n 23), 7; see also ibid, 128. Note, however, Shah, Poole and Blackwell, suggesting that the rules had already relaxed 'and the HRA added another layer to the already-well-established practice of third party interventions': S Shah, T Poole and M Blackwell, 'Rights, Interveners and the Law Lords' (2014) 34 *Oxford Journal of Legal Studies* 295, 300.

[68] Shah, Poole and Blackwell (n 67), 321–2.

[69] ibid, 322. The authors here use the term *amicus curiae* in the traditional sense – a neutral actor providing the court with legal arguments that would otherwise not be put before it: 297.

[70] L Neudorf, 'Intervention in the UK Supreme Court' (2013) 2 *Cambridge Journal of International and Comparative Law* 16.

[71] Supreme Court of the United Kingdom, The Supreme Court Rules 2009 No 1603 (L 17), r 26(1). For extensive discussion of the legal and practice aspects of third party intervention in UK Courts, see Justice, 'To Assist the Court: Third Party Interventions in the Public Interest' (2016), available at https://2bquk8cdew6192tsu41lay8t-wpengine.netdna-ssl.com/wp-content/uploads/2016/06/To-Assist-the-Court-Web.pdf.

[72] Neudorf (n 70), 23.

Canada sought to expand third party intervention from the mid-1970s,[73] with intervention codified in rule amendments in 1983. There was an increase in intervention following the addition of the Canadian Charter of Rights and Freedoms to the Constitution in 1982.[74] The Rules of the Supreme Court of Canada enable any person interested in making submissions in an appeal to apply to intervene. The application must identify that person's 'interest in the proceeding, including any prejudice that the person interested in the proceeding would suffer if the intervention were denied' as well as set out the questions on which they propose to intervene and the position and submissions they intend to make in relation to those questions.[75] Other Canadian jurisdictions have followed the development of intervener status by the Supreme Court. The rationale for allowing intervention was set out by the Supreme Court of Canada as such: 'The purpose of an intervention is to present the court with submissions which are useful and different from the perspective of a nonparty who has a special interest or particular expertise in the subject matter of the appeal'.[76] This form of intervention was developed in the Supreme Court jurisprudence specifically to facilitate interventions from public interest organisations, which had previously been precluded from participation as third party interveners and *amici curiae* due to the restrictive scope of those roles.[77] The Supreme Court and other Canadian courts[78] have emphasised that intervention is more likely to be granted in relation to public law issues and especially Charter issues, particularly to gather information as to the perspective of groups likely to be affected by the determination of Charter issues.[79] The Supreme Court Rules also retain the ability of the court to appoint an *amicus curiae*.[80] However, Canadian courts have tended to reject applications by NGOs for *amicus curiae* status on the basis that they sought to introduce partisan arguments in a manner that was inconsistent with the role of the *amicus*.[81] Thus, the role of the *amicus curiae* remains

[73] See BM Dickens, 'A Canadian Development: Non-Party Intervention' (1977) 40 *MLR* 666, 674.

[74] See B RD Alarie and AJ Green, 'Interventions at the Supreme Court of Canada: Accuracy, Affiliation, and Acceptance' (2010) 48 *Osgoode Hall Law Journal* 381.

[75] Rules of the Supreme Court of Canada, SOR/2002-156, rr 55, 57.

[76] *R v Morgentaler* [1993] 1 SCR 462.

[77] See Dickens (n 73); J Koch, 'Making Room: New Directions in Third Party Intervention' (1990) 48 *University of Toronto Faculty of Law Review* 151, 155–60.

[78] For discussion of the rules applicable to other Courts, see P Muldoon and D Scriven, 'Intervention as Added Party: Rule 13 of the Ontario Rules of Civil Procedure' (1985) 6(2) *The Advocate's Quarterly* 129, 131, noting that wider provisions on intervention incorporate intervention as an added party as well as traditional *amicus curiae* interventions.

[79] See, eg *Trinity Western University v Law Society of Upper Canada* 2014 ONSC 5541.

[80] Rules of the Supreme Court of Canada, r 92.

[81] See, eg *Re Clark and Attorney-General of Canada* (1977) 17 OR (2d) 593, 598, Evans CJHC rejecting an application for *amicus* status by the Canadian Civil Liberties Association: 'Subject to statutory or court-made rules, it is my view that intervention *amicus curiae* should be restricted to those cases in which the court is clearly in need of assistance because there is a failure to present the issues (as for example, when one side of the argument has not been presented to the court). When the intervention would only serve to widen the lis between the parties or introduce a new cause of action, the intervention should not be allowed'.

restricted to impartial submissions made to assist the court upon appointment by the tribunal in question; that is the traditional role of the *amicus curiae*.

Judges or legislators rarely articulate the rationale for allowing public interest intervention. The trend reflects the realisation that courts are taking decisions with broader impact than the parties, generally in areas concerning human rights and constitutional issues, in which the public has a genuine interest.[82] This shift recognises that government actors, such as the Attorney-General, that may intervene to protect the public interest may not always do so, or may have a different view as to what the public interest requires. Others have argued that the rise is a consequence of globalisation and internationalisation, with actors – particularly international NGOs – transferring the concept of third party intervention from one jurisdiction to another.[83]

Allowing broader participation through intervention enables more informed decisions, which take into account the perspectives of directly affected groups and the public interest and accord with natural justice and broader democratic values. Such decisions are more likely to be perceived as 'better' decisions and hence contribute to normative and sociological legitimacy. Neudorf suggests that interveners can provide social and economic data that make judges feel more comfortable in making determinations with competing policy dimensions; although noting that this raises concerns as to how courts assess the expertise, reliability and objectivity of such data.[84] Intervention may also address democratic deficits of courts: 'if courts are seen to be participatory and responsive, they too can claim a sort of democratic legitimacy'.[85] Attitudes towards intervention vary, and reflect the judicial culture in each system and the view taken of the respective roles of judges and the legislature. For example, Australia, which lacks a bill of rights, is not a member of a regional human rights mechanism and has few constitutionally protected rights, has a more conservative approach to public interest intervention. Although Australia, like Canada and the UK, recognises both third party intervention and the *amicus curiae*, its approach is influenced by 'the narrow perspective of adversarial litigation', which 'fails adequately to recognise the Court's law-making function' and 'the broader dimensions of constitutional litigation as public interest litigation affecting the wider community'.[86]

Rules on intervention tend to be widely drafted, leaving considerable discretion to judges. Enabling intervention at the Court's discretion, rather than by right, allows the Court greater flexibility as to whether to permit the intervention.

[82] See A Chayes, 'The Role of the Judge in Public Interest Litigation' 89 *Harvard Law Review* 1281, 1290.

[83] Harlow (n 23), 9.

[84] Neudorf (n 70), 24, 32.

[85] Harlow (n 23), 14.

[86] E Willheim '*Amici Curiae* and Access to Constitutional Justice in the High Court of Australia' (2010) 22 *Bond Law Review* 126, 126. See also G Williams, 'The *Amicus Curiae* and Intervener in the High Court of Australia: A Comparative Analysis' (2000) 28 *Federal Law Review* 365.

The Court may consider the increased burden on the parties, the consent of the parties, the risk that proceedings will be politicised as a result of the intervention and the extent to which the interest is raised by the issue before the Court or already 'represented' before the Court (including by actors such as the Attorney-General). The Court can assess the nature of the interest claimed, in particular whether it is a 'public interest' and the genuineness of those claiming to represent the public interest. Scholars have called for the development of specific criteria for intervention, including identifying when an actor is genuinely representing the public interest,[87] as well as for judicial restraint so that courts do not make determinations that are more appropriately made in other fora.[88] Hannett has highlighted the frequent failure of courts to identify the function to be served by an intervention, and urges judges to articulate the rationale for intervention and how an intervention is likely to be helpful in their leave to intervene decisions. This is a concern we raise in the context of international criminal tribunals, in chapter four.

Some governments have resisted public interest intervention, 'taking steps to protect [themselves] against the threat of future 'judicial interference' by changing the rules of the game in a restrictive fashion'.[89] This may include changes to the procedural rules, or changes to the funding regime, or both. One example of a restrictive practice is section 87 of the Criminal Justice and Courts Act 2015 (England and Wales),[90] which targeted financial arrangements for intervention by requiring judges to make cost orders against interveners where one of a number of circumstances apply. These circumstances include where the intervener: has functioned effectively as a party; has not 'been of significant assistance'; has made submissions, a significant part which related to matters it was unnecessary for the Court to consider; or has acted unreasonably. This amendment restricted judicial discretion and had a potentially chilling effect on potential public interest interveners, due to the increased financial risks associated with intervention.[91]

C. Rights Attached to Intervention

At the national level, the position is varied; however, rarely does the intervener become a party with the full range of procedural rights, including access to the case file, a right to appeal and being bound by the decision. Courts

[87] Hannett (n 62), 146–7.
[88] Harlow (n 23), 16–17.
[89] C Harlow and R Rawlings '"Striking Back" and "Clamping Down": An Alternative Perspective on Judicial Review' in J Bell et al (eds), *Public Law Adjudication in Common Law Systems: Process and Substance* (Oxford, Bloomsbury Publishing, 2016) 301.
[90] A number of restrictive measures were introduced: see ibid.
[91] M Moriarty and E Sibley, 'Counting the True Costs of Section 87 of the Criminal Justice and Courts Act 2015' (2015) 20(3) *Judicial Review* 147.

can control the nature, scope and extent of rights given to an intervener, and interveners are often given more limited rights, in particular the ability to make written and perhaps oral submissions to the court. Interveners may be permitted to receive copies of party filings and to respond to the arguments of others but generally do not have access to the full case file or the right to appeal (although they may be able to participate in any appeal brought by the parties). Public interest interveners may be given less extensive rights than those intervening to protect a specific interest, including the scope of their submissions being limited to a particular question or issue. The court will also attempt to balance the benefits of intervention with the likely burden on the parties and the court and the efficiency of proceedings. However, the rights attached to intervention are generally greater than those accorded to an *amicus curiae*, as we see below.

D. Intervention in Criminal Proceedings

This section addresses intervention in criminal proceedings at the national level, given that the international institutions studied above do not address individual criminal responsibility. The national practice reveals a cautious approach to permitting intervention in criminal proceedings. Many of the reforms of judicial procedures noted above in relation to intervention in civil or administrative claims were not extended to criminal proceedings. Where the accused is represented by counsel,[92] intervention is permitted only where there are overwhelming reasons to do so, generally where a broader public interest or constitutional issue arises. As expressed by the Supreme Court of Canada, 'While the Court is often reluctant to grant intervener status to public interest groups in criminal appeals, exceptions can be made under its broad discretion where important public law issues are considered'.[93] The Court in that case approved the intervention of several public interest groups in a prosecution concerning allegations of international crimes. However, courts have highlighted the need for caution when allowing intervention in criminal proceedings, with intervention potentially raising issues of fairness and equality of arms in criminal cases where the defendant already faces the resources of the prosecution. The Alberta Court of Appeal, for instance, has held in *R v JLA*:[94]

> Intervention by a third party in a criminal case is generally shunned by the courts for a variety of policy and prudential reasons. Without discussing all those reasons, it can be said that all necessary voices with proper standing will necessarily be heard through the traditional binary process. There is a risk that the hearing of

[92] See the discussion in the next section for use of *amicus curiae* where the accused is not represented.

[93] *R v Finta* [1993] 1 SCR 1138, 1142.

[94] *R v JLA* 2009 ABCA 324, paras 2–3.

> other voices can distort an appeal. The risk of distortion is of acute concern where the intervention might be directly or indirectly adverse to the defendant in the case. Where the defendant already faces the voice of the state, the courts must necessarily be concerned about introduction of any other voice that could hurt the defendant.
>
> As such, it is very unusual for the Court to consider interventions in sentence appeals in criminal cases. The issue in such cases is between an individual and the state. Here, both the individual and the state are very ably represented. The specific interests and circumstances of the individual are unique to him, and they are of great importance to him. He alone faces jeopardy to his liberty. The public interests involved are large and general. It is the function of the Crown counsel to speak to those interests and from the broad public perspective – although obviously the defendant is entitled to speak to them from his perspective. Only the individual and the Crown can properly speak to this outcome of the case.

In Australia, the Northern Territory Court of Criminal Appeal highlighted the role of the prosecution in representing the public interest:[95]

> There are significant reasons why this Court, in the absence of statutory authority, has no jurisdiction or power to permit an intervention in criminal proceedings. … When an accused is put on his trial in accordance with the time-honoured formula repeated in every criminal trial in the presence of a jury the issues are joined between the Sovereign and the accused. It is the Sovereign which represents all of the interests of the community including the individual interests of the victims of crime and no one else.

There is evidence that some national courts may be revisiting the cautious approach towards intervention in criminal proceedings. In a subsequent decision, the Alberta Court of Appeal reversed its position expressed in the *R v JLA* case above, admitting two NGOs as interveners in a criminal appeal to make submissions on issues such as the definition of consent in relation to sexual violence, and other related issues. One judge in *R v Barton* criticised the view that all relevant perspectives are represented in the traditional criminal process:[96]

> I say, with great respect, that judges are too quick to shun intervention by a third party in a criminal case. Watson JA has observed 'all necessary voices with proper standing will necessarily be heard through the traditional binary process' – but not always. In fact, I have a real concern that the focus on the risk that 'the hearing of other voices can distort an appeal,' cited theoretically as a basis to reject the intervention of a party who is perceived to lend support to the Crown's position, is then invoked far too frequently to deny the appropriate intervention of a party who might assist the court but whose submissions may also be helpful to the defendant in the case.

[95] *The Queen v GJ* [2005] NTCCA 20, para 54.

[96] *R v Barton* 2016 ABCA 68, Reasons for Decision of the Honourable Mr Justice Ronald Berger, para 10. For another decision of the Alberta Court of Appeal that reiterates the limited role of participation in criminal proceedings: see *R v Vallentgoed* 2016 ABCA 19.

However, permission to intervene is rare in criminal proceedings where the accused has legal representation, although it does happen on occasion and generally only in appellate proceedings.[97] The literature distinguishes between interveners that are neutral as to the outcome for the defendant and those that represent a particular perspective.[98] For example, interveners providing information on related legal issues, such as Liberty providing information and arguments in the public interest on the implications of Articles 8 and 13 of the ECHR in *R v Khan*, perform 'a function akin to the traditional *amicus curiae*'.[99] Loux suggests that the interests of justice require the courts be open to the specialist expertise human rights organisations might make available to it and which may be unavailable to counsel.[100] In contrast, NGO interveners in *R v Smith* sought to present the perspective of future victims, those women who are victims of domestic violence and ultimately kill their abusers, who were likely to be affected by the decision. Loux suggests that such perspective interventions make the court's decision better informed and more legitimate. There is, in her view, little point in distinguishing between civil and criminal proceedings for the purpose of intervention; rather the question should be what benefit the intervention will bring, in particular whether intervention will allow different voices to be heard and greater access to expertise.[101] However, the risks for the fair trial rights of the defendants in allowing intervention in either role are clear, as Loux acknowledges, in particular the risk that an intervener may 'hijack' a case to argue for a particular interest in line with their broader strategic agenda.[102] Hannett points to the example of *R v Khan* and the intervention by Liberty, which she suggests undermined the position of the appellant (the accused in the criminal proceedings), even though on its face it appeared to be neutral.[103] The practice therefore recognises intervention in criminal proceedings, but suggests that national courts adopt a cautious approach to such intervention so as to protect the rights of the accused. The following chapters show that similar considerations apply to participation in international criminal tribunals.

[97] eg, the Australian Human Rights Commission, although denied permission to intervene in *The Queen v GJ*, has been given permission to intervene in criminal proceedings, including in the High Court. See *Magaming v The Queen* [2013] HCA 40 (High Court, Mandatory Minimum sentence for people smuggling); *Karim v R; Magaming v R; Bin Lahaiya v R; Bayu v R; Alomalu v R* [2013] NSWCCA 23 (NSW CCA – mandatory minimum sentences – two overlapping provisions for sentences – whether minimum mandatory sentences valid); *R v Cheung* (Supreme Court of New South Wales, Badgery-Parker J, 26 November 1992, right to a fair trial); *Maloney v The Queen* [2013] HCA 28.

[98] See AC Loux, 'Hearing a "Different Voice": Third Party Intervention in Criminal Appeals' (2000) 53 *Current Legal Problems* 449.

[99] ibid, 455.

[100] ibid, 459.

[101] ibid, 462–63.

[102] ibid, 469.

[103] Hannett (n 62), 141.

V. THE *AMICUS CURIAE*: A FRIEND OF THE COURT

A. The Traditional *Amicus Curiae* Model

The *amicus curiae* enables actors who are not a party to proceedings to provide information that is relevant to the proceedings before a court, but which may not otherwise be brought before the court. The *amicus curiae* emerged as 'an early instrument of the common law' in England,[104] although its origins may lie in Roman law.[105] The *amicus curiae* traditionally provided assistance to judges by drawing attention to legal authorities, statutes or other relevant information not before the court and informing the judge of manifest errors. The understanding was that the *amicus* acted as an impartial servant of the court, 'he acts for no one, but simply seeks to give information to the court'.[106] The role of this bystander progressed from merely informing the court to acting in the interests of those not represented in proceedings, including minors, unrepresented defendants and third parties. The device was considered a partial solution to the problem of the representation of third parties in common law, adversarial proceedings which generally did not permit intervention by 'strangers' to the litigation.[107] The concept, at least as initially conceived, envisages the *amicus curiae* as a neutral, impartial actor, usually a lawyer with special knowledge. This traditional view of the *amicus curiae* featured an absence of formal rules, with the ability to accept or invite *amici curiae* within the discretion of the judge and falling within the judges' inherent power to regulate proceedings.

In the UK, the traditional notion of the *amicus* remains largely unchanged, with *amicus* participation limited to two circumstances: (1) an issue not fully litigated; and (2) an interest not fully represented in proceedings.[108] An *amicus curiae* is to assist the court, not the parties. Unlike with intervention, the focus is on the expertise, experience, independence (from the parties) and neutrality (as to the outcome) of the *amicus curiae* and ultimately how valuable the court believes the assistance offered by the *amicus curiae* will be to its decision-making. In England and Wales, where a court requires the assistance of an *amicus curiae*, the court sends a request to the Attorney-General, who may approve the request and ask the Treasury Solicitor to appoint and instruct counsel to act as an *amicus curiae*. There are no formal rules on *amicus curiae*

[104] S Krislov, 'The *Amicus Curiae* Brief: From Friendship to Advocacy' (1963) *Yale Law Journal* 694, 695.

[105] E Angell, 'The *Amicus Curiae*: American Development of English Institutions' (1967) 16 *ICLQ* 1017.

[106] *Campbell v Swasey*, 12 Ind 70, 72 (1859), quoted in Krislov (n 104), 697.

[107] Harlow and Rawling (n 24), ch 3, outline how the common law has traditionally had a problem with third parties supporting litigation, prohibited through concepts such as champetry and maintenance.

[108] For fuller discussion of these developments, see J Bellhouse and A Lavers, 'The Modern *Amicus Curiae*: A Role in Arbitration?' (2004) 23 *Civil Justice Quarterly* 187.

participation, although in 2001 a working group renamed the mechanism 'advocate of the court' and issued guidance to judges in the form of a memorandum.

B. Transplantation and Adaptation of the Traditional *Amicus Curiae*

This traditional model was transplanted as part of the English common law to other common law-based systems, and remains influential in other systems. The representative function of the *amicus* has become less significant as the function has been allocated to specific statutory or institutional actors, for example litigation friends for minors, or legal aid systems have developed to allow the appointment of counsel. However, the narrow and neutral role of the traditional *amicus curiae* is maintained in several systems: namely to provide assistance. The court sets out the circumstances and the point of law on which assistance is required and regulates the manner and scope of participation. Krislov notes that as the *amicus curiae* has always been 'a matter of grace rather than right, the courts have from the beginning avoided precise definition of the perimeters and attendant circumstances involving possible utilization of the device. This, of course, increases judicial discretion, which concomitantly maximises the flexibility of the device'.[109]

The flexibility and relative ambiguity of the mechanism has allowed the concept of the *amicus curiae* to be transplanted and adapted in several systems. The most oft-cited example is the US, where the role has expanded significantly beyond the traditional model, with a shift from neutral adviser to advocate and a blurring of the distinction between intervention and the *amicus curiae*.[110] In the US, the *amicus curiae* is a tool of strategic interest litigation; a lobbyist and an advocate in a cause,[111] often with a direct or indirect interest in the outcome.[112] The US Supreme Court 'makes no pretense of such disinterestedness on the part of its "friends"'.[113] *Amici* may have an unclear relationship with the parties, and may be approached by the parties to file a brief; for this reason, the USSC requires *amici* to disclose connections to the parties, including the source of funding for the brief and any research relied on in the brief. The volume of the practice has also expanded, with *amici* – often multiple *amici* – participating in most proceedings before the US Supreme Court. Government actors have

[109] Krislov (n 104), 695. See also MK Lowman, 'The Litigating *Amicus Curiae*: When does the Party Begin after the Friends Leave?' (1992) 41 *American University Law Review* 1243, 1247.

[110] For the history of this transformation, see Angell (n 105); Krislov (n 104); and Lowman (n 109).

[111] Lowman (n 109), 1245.

[112] M Rustad and T Koenig, 'The Supreme Court and Junk Social Science: Selective Distortion in *Amicus* Briefs' (1994) 72 *North Carolina Law Review* 91, 96; A Orr Larsen, 'The Trouble With *Amicus* Facts' (2014) 100 *Virginia Law Review* 1757.

[113] Krislov (n 104), 704. See also S Banner, 'The Myth of the Neutral *Amicus*: American Courts and Their Friends, 1790–1890' (2004) 20 *Constitutional Commentary* 111.

distinct rights, and constitute a significant part of *amicus* practice. Government actors may appear without requiring leave to argue governmental interests in a federal context, and, in some circumstances, to advance public interest arguments.

More striking has been the rise in the use of the mechanism by public advocacy groups and public interest litigation firms, both as part of the civil and minority rights movement from the 1970s and on behalf of organised financial, social and political groups such as trade associations.[114] US practice reflects a legal culture that is more accepting of judges engaging in policy-making than many systems. US courts, including the Supreme Court, require a two-stage approach to admissibility, with a request for leave filed. The consent of the parties is a relevant but not essential factor in determining admissibility and courts adopt a largely permissive approach to briefs, accepting a large proportion of briefs filed. In the US Supreme Court, the *amicus curiae* mechanism performs many of the functions third party intervention fulfils in countries like the UK and Canada. In fact, in the UK, the third party intervener is functionally equivalent to the *amicus curiae* as used in other jurisdictions, while Canadian decisions may use the terms interchangeably for the same functions. These functions include officials representing state, federal and institutional interests, actors seeking to protect a legal interest affected by proceedings, actors claiming to represent a particular affected group, actors seeking to provide expertise (which can include legal analysis, but also factual information and social science-based submissions)[115] and actors seeking to represent the public interest. The US model of the *amicus curiae* thus captures all of the functions we identified in chapter one: expertise; representative; and communicative (public interest). This, alongside a different legal culture, may partly explain why the US Supreme Court has the most expansive *amicus* practice: it is seeking to perform a range of functions, including those performed by intervention in other institutions, rather than the more narrow expertise or occasionally representative traditional role of the *amicus curiae*. There are concerns that an overly permissive approach to *amicus curiae* participation wastes resources, may not be helpful and risks overwhelming the court, particularly where the submissions are duplicative of party or other submissions or not on relevant issues. Collins suggests *amici curiae* may lead to more dissents or separate decisions, hence potentially causing uncertainty in the law.[116]

[114] Krislov (n 104); Harlow and Rawlings (n 24). Collins found that the most common *amici* in the US Supreme Court were trade associations (62%), state governments (41.5%), public advocacy groups (38.7%), public interest law firms (37.2% and the US Government (36.4%): P Collins, *Friends of the Supreme Court: Interest Groups and Judicial Decision Making* (New York, OUP, 2008) 48.

[115] For concerns regarding the impact of a lack of neutrality on data supplied to US courts, see Rustad and Koeing (n 112).

[116] Collins (n 114), 163; see also S Chandra Mohan 'The *Amicus Curiae*: Friends No More' (2010) 2 *Singapore Journal of Legal Studies* 352, 373.

Other systems have moved towards the political or modern *amicus*. For example, in South Africa, the *amicus curiae* mechanism has been a long-standing feature of judicial practice, transplanted as part of the British common law. However, *amicus curiae* practice was fairly limited. After the introduction of the 1996 Constitution, the role of the *amicus* was intentionally expanded to echo the prominent role *amici* play in the US Supreme Court.[117] Rule 10 of the Constitutional Court Rules allows for 'any persons interested in any matter before the Court' to apply to become an *amicus curiae*, in order to make submissions intended to influence the reasoning and outcome of a case.[118] This has led to a largely welcoming attitude towards the admission of *amici* at the Constitutional Court, generally also reflected in the lower courts. It is common for the Constitutional Court to admit several *amici* in individual cases. The Constitutional Court has explicitly justified the admission of *amici* in its proceedings as a method to increase representivity and participation in its decision-making, as an important aspect of constitutional democratic legitimacy. The Court justified its generous approach to admission of *amici* in *Koyabe*:[119]

> First, it reflects the underlying theme of participatory democracy in the Final Constitution. In matters of broad public interest, such as the interpretation of the Final Constitution, courts are more disposed towards listening the voices of persons other than the parties to a particular dispute. Secondly, it reflects the fact that constitutional litigation often affects a range of people and interests that go well beyond those of the parties already before the court.

The Court went on to hold that 'Amici curiae have made and continue to make an invaluable contribution to this Court's jurisprudence. Most, if not all, constitutional matters present issues, the resolution of which will invariably have an impact beyond the parties directly litigating before the Court. Constitutional litigation by its very nature requires the determination of issues squarely in the public interest, and insofar as amici introduce additional, new and relevant perspectives, leading to more nuanced judicial decisions, their participation in litigation is to be welcomed and encouraged'.[120]

Thus, the welcoming attitude to *amicus* applications relies on their contribution to issues of significant public interest, either matters relating to the interpretation or application of the constitution, or matters of such significance as to warrant consideration by appellate courts. Alongside these rules, a more traditional form of the *amicus curiae* persists that appears to rely on the inherent jurisdiction of the court in question. Such *amici* are appointed at the initiative

[117] See G Budlender, '*Amicus Curiae*' in S Woolman et al (eds), *Constitutional Law of South Africa* (Cape Town, Juta Law, 2008).

[118] Similar provisions are included in r 16A of the Uniform Rules of Court (15 January 1959, as amended 8 May 2009) (applicable to the High Court), and re 16 of the Rules Regulating the Conduct of the Proceedings of the Supreme Court of Appeal of South Africa (GNR 27 November 1998).

[119] *Koyabe and Others v Minister for Home Affairs and Others* (CCT 53/08) [2009] ZACC 23, fn 70, quoting Budlender (n 117).

[120] ibid, para 80.

of the court, rather than through the procedural rules cited above. In such cases, the role of the *amicus* is generally to advise the court on an impartial basis, or to represent an unrepresented party, and the conditions of the *amicus'* participation are set by the court in its invitation.[121]

We do not draw a conclusion as to whether the development of the modern form of the *amicus curiae* is desirable. Some systems may be more comfortable with these types of submissions and judges must always determine the weight, if any, to be given to submissions. Rather, this discussion has illustrated that there are different concepts of the *amicus curiae* in different legal systems, depending on the functions the mechanism is expected to perform and the interests it is supposed to protect, as well as how the *amicus curiae* intersects with other forms of participation, such as intervention. These different understandings account for some of the confusion as to the criteria that should be applied to *amici*, in particular the requirements of independence, impartiality and expertise. Subsequent chapters will explore the mechanisms for participation available and the notion(s) of the *amicus curiae* that have emerged in international criminal tribunals.

C. The *Amicus Curiae* in Civil Law Jurisdictions

So far we have focused mainly on practice in common law jurisdictions, reflecting in part the assumption that the *amicus curiae* is a common law device. However, there is another view that the *amicus curiae* originated from Roman law and is linked to the idea of appointing a group of distinguished advisers to assist magistrates (a *consilium*), thus becoming friends of the court or *amici curiae*.[122] Mohan argues that Roman *amici* were 'highly regarded for their legal knowledge and expertise' and that the 'giving of such legal advice is said to have remained the main feature of these jurists' work for more than four centuries'.[123] This alternative view of the origin of the mechanism may account for why the *amicus curiae* mechanism is found in several civil law systems such as France and, Mohan suggests, explains some of the features of the traditional model, including legal expertise, impartiality and appointment at the discretion of the Court.[124]

In addition to these possible origins, the concept of the *amicus curiae* has been transplanted to civil law systems in which the mechanism was not traditionally recognised and/or where there may not be a legal basis for accepting briefs.[125] This transplantation was due largely to the rise in strategic litigation

[121] See Budlender (n 117), 2–3.
[122] See Angell (n 105) and Krislov (n 104), mentioning this possible origin. For a more detailed explanation, see Mohan (n 116).
[123] Mohan (n 116), 362.
[124] ibid, 364–6.
[125] Kochevar (n 25).

at the national, regional and international levels. Western, particularly US and UK-based, 'repeat-player' NGO and other civil society actors have encouraged transplantation, through 'constructive litigation opportunism',[126] seeking to rely on the mechanism in civil law systems even in the absence of a provision on *amici curiae* or previous practice.[127] Such litigants have 'ventured to use *amicus* interventions increasingly, across legal systems, and through acceptance of such interventions on a case-by-case basis, they have come to constitute standard procedure in many systems'.[128] Transplantation has been multi-directional, for example, with UK practice influencing early submissions at the ECtHR and then UK actors, gaining experience in the ECtHR, seeking to intervene at the national level.[129] Similarly, the extensive *amicus curiae* practice at the IACHR is credited with the expansion of the *amicus curiae* mechanism in several member states,[130] while encountering briefs in investor-state investment arbitration has led to many states agreeing to *amicus curiae* provisions in subsequent investment treaties as well as amending national procedural law to recognise the mechanism.[131] The amendment of procedural rules to recognise the *amicus curiae* (or third party intervention) mechanism formally is important: Collins and McCarthy, in their comparative study of interest litigation in 11 countries, found that institutional design, including the availability of a bill of rights, judicial review and – most relevantly – the restrictiveness of procedural rules on third party participation, all impact engagement of third party actors.[132] Kochevar suggests that the *amicus curiae*, in national and international legal systems, is an 'evolving global procedural norm'.[133] Duffy situates the mechanism as one of the 'key prerequisites to effective litigation [that] are now in place, with the existence of adequate substantive law, legal mechanisms, engaged actors and a legal-cultural shift as part of the phenomenon of juridical globalisation'.[134]

Examples of transplantation include reliance on the *amicus curiae* mechanism in Peru, particularly within the Constitutional Court, over the past ten years. Submissions have been made by international and national NGOs, university centres (especially for the study of human rights) and the *Defensoria del Pueblo* (Ombudsman's Office). One author describing the work of the Ombudsman's

[126] Duffy (n 63), 62.

[127] ibid, 22, 62–3; Kochevar (n 25), 1664–5.

[128] Duffy (n 63), 62.

[129] See A Dolidze, 'Bridging Comparative and International Law: *Amicus Curiae* Participation as Vertical Legal Transplant' (2015) 26 *EJIL* 851. Arold observed that the experience of French actors in the ECtHR system as influencing development of the *amicus curiae* in French courts: N-L Arold, *The Legal Culture of the European Court of Human Rights* (Leiden, Brill, 2007); see also M de S-O-l'E Lasser, *Judicial Transformations: The Rights Revolution in the Courts of Europe* (Oxford, OUP, 2009); and Kochevar (n 25), 1665–6.

[130] Kochevar (n 25), 1666.

[131] Kochevar (n 25), 1666, refers to the example of Mexico's experience with investment arbitration.

[132] P Collins and L McCarthy, 'Friends and Interveners: Interest Group Litigation in a Comparative Context' (2017) *Journal of Law and Courts* 55, 75–6.

[133] Kochevar (n 25), 1669.

[134] Duffy (n 63), 22.

Office characterised the *amicus* as 'an extended figure of International Human Rights Systems'.[135] Indeed, the practice in Peru seems to have evolved from the use of the *amicus curiae* in other Latin American states such as Brazil, as well as at the IACHR.[136]

In Indonesia, the '*amicus curiae*' is known by that term, although it is often described, using English, as 'friend of the court', or sometimes as 'sahabat pengadilan' (friend of the court) or as an actor providing a letter of opinion.[137] The *amicus curiae* is yet to find much formal recognition in Indonesian courts, although NGOs have submitted *amicus curiae* briefs to Indonesian courts since the early 2000s. In 2006, the International Center for Transitional Justice prepared a brief contesting a law that aimed to establish a Truth and Reconciliation Commission in Indonesia, as it provided for amnesties,[138] although the Constitutional Court did not mention the brief in its decisions.[139] The practice of submitting *amicus curiae* briefs gathered pace from 2008, after a large group of organisations including Article 19, Dow Jones & Company, Human Rights Watch, *The Jakarta Post* and *The Economist* prepared a submission contesting the liability of *Time* magazine for defamation involving former President Suharto's family.[140] Following the submission of supportive *amicus* arguments, *Time* won its appeal in the Supreme Court. Since then, a range of actors (although predominantly international and Indonesian NGOs) have submitted *amicus curiae* briefs in Indonesian District Courts, the Supreme Court, and Constitutional Court, including in some criminal proceedings. *Amicus curiae* submissions tend to explain the role of the *amicus curiae* as having its roots in Roman law, but developed through common law systems, especially in England and the US Supreme Court. While there does not appear to be an explicit rule or procedure for *amici curiae* to participate, there are provisions in Indonesian law that support expert, or related or interested party participation. In particular,

[135] H Leon-Manco, 'Human Rights In Practice: The Work of the Peruvian Ombudsman – and how it Contributes to Legal Empowerment of the Poor', (ANLEP Working Paper No 3, December 2011), 20, available at http://lnweb90.worldbank.org/exteu/SharePapers.nsf/(ID)/FB647574177F9B1785257 9FE00075A5A/$File/human+rights+in+practice.pdf.

[136] A Fujimori, Sala Penal Especial de la Corte Suprema, 'Resolución del 1 de agosto del 2008, recaida en el proceso penal contra Alberto Fujimori por los crimenes de Barrios Altos y La Cantuta' (1 August 2008), para 2, available at http://historico.pj.gob.pe/CorteSuprema/spe/Documentos/SPE_RESOLUCION_CSJP_070808.pdf; see Defensoría del Pueblo, 'El *amicus curiae*: ¿qué es y para qué sirve? Jurisprudencia y labor de la Defensoria del Pueblo, Serie Documentos Defensoriales – Documento N° 8' ('The *amicus curiae*: what is it and what is it for? Jurisprudence and the work of the Ombudsman's Office, Ombudsman's Document Series – Document No. 8' (October 2009), available at www.corteidh.or.cr/tablas/26654.pdf.

[137] 'Surat pemberian pendapatan' – especially by the National Human Rights Institution Komnas HAM.

[138] International Centre for Transitional Justice, 'ICTJ Written Submission: Legality of Truth and Reconciliation Commission' (July 2006), available at www.ictj.org/publication/ictj-written-submission-legality-truth-and-reconciliation-commission.

[139] Putusan no 020/PUU-IV/2006 (7 December 2006) [Arukat Djaswadi et al]; Putusan no 006/PUU-IV/2006 (7 December 2006) [ELSAM, Kontras et al].

[140] *Time* had published allegations that former President Suharto's family had embezzled $15 billion during his regime.

nearly all briefs are justified with reference to judges' obligations under Indonesian law to explore, follow, and understand the values of law and sense of justice that lives in society.[141] This suggests that the *amicus* can provide a broader, perhaps more representative, range of interests and arguments to help support judicial decision-making – or even, 'participate in the realisation of a democratic legal state'.[142]

D. The *Amicus Curiae* in Criminal Proceedings

One traditional role of the *amicus curiae* was to 'represent' the interests of an unrepresented accused in criminal proceedings, which would fall within our representative function. In many legal systems, this function has become rare due to the introduction of legal aid arrangements that provide counsel to the accused, at least in serious proceedings. However, situations still arise where an unrepresented accused may appear before a court. In common law jurisdictions, *amici* have been permitted to make submissions on behalf of an accused who is otherwise unrepresented. For example, in *The Queen v GJ*, the Northern Territory Court of Criminal Appeal stated:[143]

> ... I accept this Court has power as well as jurisdiction to permit counsel to appear as *amicus curiae*. Indeed that frequently occurs in this Court, particularly in cases where a person who has been found guilty of an offence wishes to appeal and is unrepresented. In those circumstances it is the long standing practice of this Court to allow counsel to appear as *amicus curiae* and to put such arguments in favour of the appeal or the granting of leave to appeal as may have been put properly by the appellant or would be appellant had he been legally represented.

This practice can be a means of securing constitutionally protected fair trial rights. However, the practice of appointing an *amicus* to speak for an unrepresented accused has been criticised, as shifting the *amicus* from a friend of the court to an advocate directly representing one of the parties. The decision of the Canadian Supreme Court in *Ontario v Criminal Lawyers' Association of Ontario*[144] concerned four cases where *amici* had been appointed in cases of unrepresented/self-representing defendants, which was not necessary to secure fair trials but was done to maintain order and prevent delay in complex proceedings. In these cases, the *amici* had been given broad roles, including cross-examining witnesses, leading evidence, and a right of confidential communication

[141] Section 5(1) of Law 48 of 2009 on Judicial Power (29 October 2009).

[142] S Aminah, 'Menjadi Sahabat Keadilan: Panduan Menyusun *Amicus* Brief' ('Becoming a Friend of the Court: Guidelines for Preparing an Amicus Brief'), Indonesian Legal Resource Center (ILRC) and HiVOS (November 2014), 'Untuk berpartisipasi dalam mewujudkan negara hukum yang demokratis', 19, available at www.mitrahukum.org/wp-content/uploads/2015/02/Amicus-Brief.pdf.

[143] [2005] NTCCA 20, para 63.

[144] *Ontario v Criminal Lawyers' Association of Ontario* 2013 SCC 43.

with the defence. The essential factor distinguishing the *amici* from defence counsel in these cases was that they could act contrary to the accused's instructions, and could not be dismissed by the accused. The Supreme Court held that vesting *amici* with such rights and duties was problematic for several reasons, including that it may undermine the accused's constitutional right to self-representation, creates a potential conflict of interest between the *amicus*'s duties to the court and duties to the defence; and may undermine legal aid schemes by subverting a rejection of an application for publicly-funded counsel. Ultimately, the Court held that this practice unacceptably 'blurred the line' between defence counsel and the role of the *amicus*, and that an *amicus* vested with the responsibilities of defence counsel ceased to be an *amicus*.[145]

While the Supreme Court decision does not bar the appointment of *amici* to assist the Court in the case of an unrepresented or self-represented accused, it is clear that their role must be limited. We will explore the role of *amici* acting as surrogate defence counsel in international criminal tribunals in chapter six; however, we recognise here that many national systems appoint counsel where a defendant needs to be 'properly represented' rather than have their views presented by an *amicus curiae*.

Where the accused is represented, there is more flexibility in permitting *amicus curiae* participation in criminal proceedings than intervention, as it is a less intrusive mode of participation and therefore raises fewer risks for the accused. That said, permitting *amicus curiae* participation occurs less frequently in criminal proceedings than in other types of proceedings. We should also note that higher courts, where we tend to see more *amicus curiae* participation, do not hear criminal cases as such, but are restricted to appeals from trials before lower courts and generally only where the proceedings raise a constitutional or human rights issue. The High Court of Australia has permitted *amici* to appear in criminal proceedings on several occasions, mainly in an expertise function where the *amicus* is to address a particular legal issue. For example, in *Momcilovic v The Queen*,[146] the Human Rights Law Centre's submissions before the Victorian Court of Appeal were directly raised in the subsequent appellate proceedings and challenged by at least one of the parties. The Centre was accordingly granted leave to participate as an *amicus curiae* in proceedings before the High Court of Australia. The South African Constitutional Court has also permitted *amici curiae* in criminal proceedings,[147]

[145] 'Further, I agree with my colleague Fish J that "[o]nce clothed with all the duties and responsibilities of defence counsel, the *amicus* can no longer properly be called a 'friend of the court'" (para. 114)': ibid, para 49. See D Berg, 'The Limits of Friendship: the *Amicus Curiae* in Criminal Trial Courts' (2012) 59 *Criminal Law Quarterly* 67, 72–74.

[146] [2011] HCA 34.

[147] See, eg *Jezile v S and Others* (A 127/2014) [2015] ZAWCHC 31. Most recently, the Constitutional Court, acting on its own initiative, invited several individuals and organisations to make *amicus* submissions in the Okah appeal: *S v Henry Okah* (CCT315/16), directions dated 15 November 2017.

as well as in administrative law proceedings concerning international criminal law matters.[148] However, it cautioned against the risks of admitting *amici*:[149]

> As a general matter, in criminal matters a court should be astute not to allow the submissions of an amicus to stack the odds against an accused person. Ordinarily, an accused in criminal matters is entitled to a well-defined case emanating from the state. If the submissions of an amicus tend to strengthen the case against the accused, this is cause for caution. This, however, is not an inflexible rule. But it is a consideration based on fairness, equality of arms, and more importantly, what is in the interests of justice.

We will explore how similar considerations have influenced international criminal tribunals in their decision to admit *amici curiae* in proceedings.

E. The *Amicus Curiae* in International Institutions

The *amicus curiae* mechanism is also found at the international and regional level, although there is considerable variation in practice across institutions. The basic division is between those institutions that are 'open' to *amicus curiae* participation and those that are not.

i. Closed Institutions: The ICJ and ITLOS

The ICJ and ITLOS lie at the 'closed' end of the spectrum. Neither tribunal has a rule permitting *amicus curiae* participation in contentious proceedings and neither has relied on its inherent powers to accept *amicus curiae* briefs. Provisions in the instruments of each tribunal allow them to receive information from international organisations;[150] however, this provision is restricted to intergovernmental organisations,[151] which most likely includes hybrid organisations whose membership comprises mainly – but not exclusively – states.[152]

[148] See, eg *Minister of Justice and Constitutional Development and Others v Southern African Litigation Centre and Others* (867/15) [2016] ZASCA 17.

[149] *Ex Parte Institute for Security Studies: In re The State v Basson* (2006) (2) SACR 350 (CC), para 15.

[150] Art 34(2) of the ICJ Statute refers to 'public international organizations', while Art 84 of the ITLOS Rules refers to 'an appropriate international governmental organization'.

[151] Art 69(4) of the ICJ Rules specifies that the term applies only to organisations that 'are an international organisation of states'. For discussion, see L Bartholomeusz, 'The *Amicus Curiae* before International Courts and Tribunals' (2005) 5 *Non-State Actors and International Law* 209, 213.

[152] In 2010, the International Union for the Conservation of Nature, a hybrid organisation comprising states, NGO member organisations and volunteer scientists and experts, was permitted to provide submissions: *Responsibilities and Obligations of States Sponsoring Persons and Entities with Respect to Activities in the Area* (Advisory Opinion) ITLOS, Seabed Disputes Chamber, 1 February 2011, paras 5, 7; discussed in A Dolidze 'Advisory Opinion on Responsibility and Liability for International Seabed Mining (ITLOS Case No 17) and the Future of NGO Participation in the International Legal Process' (2013) 19 *ILSA Journal of International and Comparative Law* 379. Bartholomeusz (n 151), 22, concludes that hybrid organisations would also be permitted to furnish information under Art 66 of the ICJ Statute.

This has not prevented non-state actors from filing submissions, although they have not had much success. The one occasion on which the ICJ has given permission for an *amicus* submission by an NGO occurred in the proceedings concerning the 1950 Advisory Opinion on the International Status of South-West Africa.[153] The Court indicated that it would accept a written statement from the International League for the Rights of Man 'which was likely to assist the Court in its examination of legal questions'.[154] Yet, the League failed to meet the deadline for submission and therefore the Court took no notice of the submission.[155] The Court rejected subsequent attempts by the League and others to participate as *amici* in the 1971 advisory proceedings on Namibia, with the exception of the application of the Organization of African Unity.[156] The ICJ has also rejected requests by individuals, with the most highlighted instance being the inquiry by Michael Reisman as to whether he could make submissions as an *amicus* in the 1970 South-West Africa advisory proceedings.[157] The proceedings concerning the two requests for advisory proceedings from the ICJ on the legality of nuclear weapons, which partly resulted from a high profile campaign by NGOs, led to an influx of unsolicited NGO briefs, reports and petitions at the Court.[158] That material was placed in the Court's library and made available to judges, but was not accepted formally or made part of the case file.[159] The judges' opinions revealed different responses to the value and appropriateness of such material. Judge Weeramantry, for example, referred to the substance of NGO materials and considered the submissions as 'evidence of a groundswell of global public opinion which is not without legal relevance'.[160] In contrast, Judge Guillaume was opposed to the involvement of NGOs, urging international institutions 'to resist the powerful pressure groups which besiege them today with the support of the mass media'.[161]

The ICJ formalised this practice of receiving submissions in 2004 when it adopted a practice direction to address the situation where an international NGO submits a written statement or document in proceedings concerning an advisory opinion on its own initiative.[162] The practice direction 'formalizes the

[153] *International Status of South-West Africa* (Advisory Opinion of 11 July 1950) [1950] ICJ Rep 128; ICJ Pleadings, 324.

[154] *South-West Africa Advisory Opinion*, 130; ICJ Pleadings, 327.

[155] *South-West Africa Advisory Opinion*, 130. See R Clark, 'The International League for Human Rights and South West Africa 1947–1957: The Human Rights NGO as Catalyst in the International Legal Process' (1981) 3 *Human Rights Quarterly* 101.

[156] *Legal Consequences for States of the Continued Presence of South Africa in Namibia (South West Africa) Notwithstanding Security Council Resolution 276 (1970)* [1971] ICJ Pleadings, Vol II, 639–40.

[157] See discussion in Bartholomeusz (n 151), 224–5.

[158] *Legality of the Threat or Use of Nuclear Weapons* (Advisory Opinion of 8 July 1996) [1996] ICJ Rep 226.

[159] Ascensio, quoted in Bartholomeusz (n 151), 222, referring to a letter from the Registry.

[160] *Legality of the Threat or Use of Nuclear Weapons* (Advisory Opinion of 8 July 1996), [1996] ICJ Rep 226, Dissenting Opinion of Judge Weeramantry, 438.

[161] ibid, Separate Opinion of Judge Guillaume, para 2.

[162] ICJ Practice Direction XII (issued 30 July 2004), available at www.icj-cij.org/en/practice-directions.

Court's relationship with NGO's',[163] rather than precluding submissions. While such materials are not part of the case file, the Court makes them available to states and other participants in the case in the same way as other material that is in the public domain.[164] This means that participants (and presumably the judges) in advisory proceedings can access this material and refer to or incorporate it in their own submissions. Reaction to the adoption of this practice direction varied. Some commentators welcomed the development as signalling an increased recognition of the need to expand participation, at least in advisory opinions.[165] Others, such as Shelton, criticise the practice direction as being more restrictive than the Court's previous practice, noting that it only extends to 'international' NGOs, and would exclude national NGOs.[166] Ronen notes that the practice direction is 'a compromise procedure between proponents and opponents of NGO participation'.[167]

At the ITLOS, two NGOs – Greenpeace International and the World Wide Fund for Nature – applied to participate jointly as *amici* in the Seabed Disputes Chamber advisory opinion.[168] Both organisations are experienced *amici*, nationally and in other international fora, and enjoy observer status at relevant organisations, including the International Seabed Authority (ISA). Despite this, the President of ITLOS informed the applicant organisations that their statements could not be placed on the case file, as their acceptance was not in accordance with Rule 133.[169] The Chamber also subsequently formally declined the request to participate as *amici curiae*.[170] Yet the Registry transmitted the statement to states, intergovernmental authorities and the ISA. While the decision demonstrates that NGOs will not be considered as 'intergovernmental organisations' for the purpose of providing information in advisory opinions, Dolidze suggests that this was still a favourable consideration of the brief, as although ITLOS rejected the application, it facilitated the dissemination of the brief and therefore allowed the submissions to be taken into account by the parties in their own submissions.[171] The Registry displayed the submission on the ITLOS website, which allowed further discussion of the brief by scholars and other interested actors.

[163] Bartholomeusz (n 151), 223.

[164] ICJ Practice Direction, para 2.

[165] eg Bartholomeusz (n 151), 224 – a sign of the Court 'taking seriously its new openness to NGO briefs'.

[166] D Shelton, 'The International Court of Justice and Nongovernmental Organisations' (2007) 9(2) *International Community Law Review* 139.

[167] Y Ronen, 'Participation of Non-State Actors in ICJ Proceedings' (2012) 11 *The Law and Practice of International Courts and Tribunals* 77, 108.

[168] Petition of Stitching Greenpeace Council (Greenpeace International) and the World Wide Fund for Nature to be Granted *Amicus Curiae* Status (13 August 2010). See n 154 above for the opinion. For further discussion, see Dolidze (n 152).

[169] *Responsibilities and Obligations of States Sponsoring Persons and Entities with Respect to Activities in the Area* (Advisory Opinion) ITLOS, Seabed Disputes Chamber, 1 February 2011, para 13.

[170] ibid, para 14.

[171] Dolidze (n 152), 414–6.

Greenpeace was denied permission to participate as an *amicus curiae* in the *Arctic Sunrise Case*, a contentious proceeding that concerned the return by Russia of a vessel operated by Greenpeace and registered in the Netherlands.[172] ITLOS formally notified Greenpeace International that its submission would not be accepted and would not be placed on the case file. Unlike the submission by Greenpeace and WWF discussed above, while this brief was circulated to the parties and to the members of the Tribunal, it was not added to the case file and the ITLOS website, likely due to the contentious nature of proceedings.[173] The decision highlights the limited rights of participation given to actors other than states in the ITLOS system, particularly in contentious proceedings. Greenpeace International, as the operator of the vessel, employer of the crew and the entity effectively providing the financial guarantee for their release (it paid the bond that was provided by the Netherlands) had a significant and direct interest in the outcome of the proceedings, yet had no right to participate and certainly no right to intervene as a party. One of the traditional roles of the *amicus curia*e function is to represent otherwise unrepresented interests. Here, the state-centric focus of ITLOS relies on the notion of diplomatic protection, with the Netherlands as the flagship state the only entity able to represent Greenpeace International's interests in proceedings.

The legal instruments and practice of the ICJ and ITLOS reveal a limited role for *amicus curiae* 'type' participation. There is effectively no prospect of participation in respect of contentious proceedings. Advisory opinions offer greater, but still limited, potential for informal participation of at least international NGOs, but not local NGOs or individuals. There are two main reasons given for this restrictive approach. First, and most significantly, is the state-centric focus and tradition of these institutions, which are based on state consent, with the support of states essential to their legitimacy and operation.[174] This is particularly so in contentious proceedings, which are possible only where states have consented to the exercise of jurisdiction by the court and in which judgments are binding on states party to the proceedings. The restrictive approach to broader participation reflects the traditional view that ICJ proceedings, especially contentious proceedings, are fundamentally disputes between states. The ICJ has not been subject to the same pressures for democratisation and representation as other institutions, both nationally and internationally, due to its exclusive focus on inter-state disputes. In addition, the absence of a provision allowing broader participation serves as a prohibition on admitting information from other actors. Secondly, these institutions are – perhaps rightly – concerned about the number and range of actors that might seek to

[172] See A Dolidze, 'The Arctic Sunrise and NGO's in International Judicial Proceedings' (2014) 18(1) *ASIL Insights*.

[173] ibid.

[174] See discussion in GI Hernández, 'Non-state Actors From the Perspective of the International Court of Justice' in J d'Aspremont (ed), *Participants in the International Legal System: Multiple Perspectives on Non-state Actors in International Law* (Abingdon, Oxon, Routledge, 2011).

participate in proceedings, the range of competing interests and views they would present, and the impact this may have on the ability to operate efficiently and effectively. The ICJ is certainly wary about opening the floodgates and the risk of politicising proceedings before it. However, scholars argue that the benefits of participation – additional legal analysis, provision of detailed legislative or jurisprudential history and arguments the parties are not prepared to make, as well as expert assistance on novel issues – outweigh the potential impact on workload.[175] Moreover, allowing greater access to civil society may assist these institutions 'to protect the collective interests of the international community'[176] and recognises 'the impact that its decisions and pronouncements can have beyond the parties and the narrow issues before it'.[177]

ii. A Conflicted Position: The WTO

The DSU does not contain an express provision addressing other forms of participation, in particular as an *amicus curiae*. However, Article 13 DSU provides that each panel 'shall have the right to seek information and technical advice from any individual or body which it deems appropriate', provided that where that individual or body is within the jurisdiction of a member state it must inform the national authorities. Despite the absence of a specific legal provision, WTO panels and the Appellate Body have received unprompted requests to participate as *amici curiae* and the issue has attracted considerable attention. Panels and the Appellate Body have accepted submissions based both on their inherent power to manage proceedings and Article 13 DSU. In *US-Shrimps*, two environmental NGOs sought to file *amicus curiae* briefs before a panel considering a dispute concerning a US embargo on shrimp harvested by a method that caused harm to sea turtles. The Appellate Body rejected the Panel's 'unnecessarily formal and technical' reading of Article 13, instead viewing that provision as conferring broad powers of inquiry, including the discretion 'either to accept or to reject information and advice submitted to it whether requested by a panel or not'.[178] Article 13 DSU does not apply to appellate proceedings; however, the Appellate Body has relied on Article 17.9 DSU and Rule 16(1) of its working procedures to conclude that it has the legal authority to accept and consider *amicus* briefs where 'we find it pertinent and useful to do so'.[179] However, as individuals and organisations are not WTO member states, they

[175] See Shelton (n 166) 143.

[176] S Santivasa, 'The NGO's Participation in the Proceedings of the International Court of Justice' (2012) 5 *Journal of East Asia and International Law* 377, 400–01.

[177] D Shelton, 'The Participation of Nongovernmental Organizations in International Judicial Proceedings' (1994) 88 *AJIL* 611, 641.

[178] WTO, *United States – Import Prohibition of Certain Shrimp and Shrimp Products – Panel Report* (6 November 1998) WT/DS58R.

[179] WTO, *United States – Imposition Of Countervailing Duties On Certain Hot-Rolled Lead And Bismuth Carbon Steel Products Originating In The United Kingdom – Appellate Body Report* (7 June 2000) WT/DS138/AB/R, paras 37–42.

have no legal right to be heard and the Appellate Body has no legal duty to accept or consider unsolicited briefs.[180]

In a major development, in *EC-Asbestos*, the Appellate Body, recognising the general public interest in the dispute and the likelihood that submissions would be received, for the first time decided to invite briefs from all interested sources, relying on Article 16(1) of its working procedures.[181] To manage the process, the Appellate Body adopted an Additional Procedure, which set out a number of procedural conditions, including page limits, the requirement to explain briefly how its submissions would assist in deciding the case and to identify how the arguments go beyond those of the parties.[182] The applicants also had to disclose the nature of the entity applying for leave, any interest in the dispute and whether they received financing or support from a party to the dispute. While the Appellate Body received a number of submissions from environmental NGOs, victims' rights groups, the chemical trade industry, professional health organisations and academics, the final report indicated without explanation that of the 17 *amicus* briefs submitted, none had been accepted or taken into account in deciding the case.[183]

The Appellate Body has been criticised for 'caving in to political pressure' on the *amicus* issue.[184] The issuance of the Additional Procedure prompted WTO members to call a special General Council meeting on 22 November 2000 at which the majority of members clearly indicated their opposition to the admission of *amicus* briefs.[185] They argued that the Appellate Body had gone beyond its mandate and acted as a legislator in adopting the Additional Procedure, and that only member states could determine whether non-state actors should participate in proceedings. States also raised concerns as to the impact on politicisation of the proceedings, the potential delay and increased expense (particularly for developing countries). Umbricht argues that the Appellate Body placed itself in an untenable situation; it angered NGOs as it had encouraged participation and then not accepted any briefs, while also attracting the ire of member states due to the general opposition towards acceptance of *amicus* briefs.[186]

Since the decision in *Asbestos*, panels and the Appellate Body have received unsolicited submissions on several occasions, from a variety of actors,[187] and

[180] ibid, para 41.

[181] WTO, *European Communities – Measures Affecting Asbestos and Asbestos-Containing Products – Report of the Appellate Body* (12 March 2001) WT/DS135/AB/R, paras 50–51.

[182] The Additional Procedure was reproduced at ibid, para 52.

[183] ibid, paras 53–57.

[184] R Howse, 'Membership and Its Privileges: The WTO, Civil Society, and the *Amicus* Brief Controversy' (2003) 9 *European Law Journal* 496, 505.

[185] For an outline, see S Charnovitz, 'Judicial Independence in the World Trade Organization' in L Boisson de Chazournes, C PR Romano and R Mackenzie (eds), *International Organizations and International Dispute Settlement* (Ardsley, New York, Transnational Publishers, 2002) 219; discussed also in R Howse, 'The World Trade Organization 20 Years On: Global Governance by Judiciary' (2016) 27 *EJIL* 9.

[186] GC Umbricht, 'An "*Amicus Curiae* Brief" on *Amicus Curiae* Briefs at the WTO' (2000) 4 *Journal of International Economic Law* 773.

[187] A search of the WTO website reveals *amicus* submissions have been filed in at least eight further disputes.

have confirmed that there is a legal basis for them to do so.[188] While panels and the Appellate Body have maintained the right to receive *amicus* submissions in the face of opposition from many WTO members, the Appellate Body has never found it necessary to rely on any *amicus* brief submitted to it. Many reasons have been advanced to support enhanced participation in the WTO, including the provision of additional materials and perspectives that would improve the quality and representativeness of WTO decisions and processes, particularly when such perspectives are unlikely to be brought by governments. Greater participation is argued to enhance the transparency of a 'secret' organisation and – it is suggested – partly address its undemocratic structure. *Amicus* participation also permits transnational interests to be represented as well as participation by civil society, particularly where there is no open and democratic process at the national level in the member state. In these ways, allowing *amicus* participation will enhance the legitimacy of the institution and its decisions. Yet the WTO institutions have not addressed these justifications, restricting analysis almost exclusively to the legal basis upon which briefs may be accepted. Given the strength of such opposition amongst member states, it does not seem likely that a more welcoming stance will be adopted.

iii. Open Institutions: Investor-State Investment Arbitration Panels and Regional Human Rights Tribunals

Investor-state investment arbitration also faced pressure to address its transparency (or lack of). Zachariasiewicz states that in investor-state investment arbitration 'there is a fundamental tension between the consensual character of arbitration underlying a commercial dispute between two parties and an increasing need to offer transparent proceedings where a public interest is involved'.[189] Confidentiality and privacy of proceedings are key aspects of international commercial arbitration,[190] as is greater control of the proceedings, and reduced delay and expense in proceedings. However, investor-state investment arbitration disputes concern state measures that affect public policy and public sector services[191] and which have a significant impact on the economy, specific industries, natural resources, labour, environment or human rights.[192] Finally, awards

[188] See WTO, *European Communities – Trade Description of Sardines – Report of the Appellate Body* (23 October 2002) WT/DS231/AB/R.

[189] M Zachariasiewicz, '*Amicus Curiae* in International Investment Arbitration: Can it Enhance the Transparency of Investment Dispute Resolution? (2012) 29 *Journal of International Arbitration* 205, 205.

[190] K Fach Gomez, 'Rethinking the Role of *Amicus Curiae* in International Investment Arbitration: How to Draw the Line Favorably for the Public Interest' (2012) 35 *Fordham International Law Journal* 510.

[191] E Levine, '*Amicus Curiae* in International Investment Arbitration: The Implications of an increase in Third-Party Participation' (2011) 29 *Berkeley Journal of International Law* 200.

[192] E de Brabandere, 'NGOs and the "Public Interest": The Legality and Rationale of *Amicus Curiae* Interventions in International Economic and Investment Disputes' (2016) 12 *Chicago Journal of International Law* 85.

and orders made in investor-state investment arbitration generally impact the state, and its finances and therefore taxpayers, directly.[193] It is this public dimension of investor-state investment arbitration that has led to a shift from confidential and secretive proceedings to a more transparent decision-making process: 'the political legitimacy of the process is put at risk if genuine stakeholders cannot participate in decisions affecting their rights and interests'.[194] The *amicus curiae* mechanism is one way in which to enhance transparency and hence the legitimacy of investor-state investment arbitration.[195]

However, as with the ICJ and ITLOS, the relevant rules did not include a provision for broader participation. There has been a gradual shift from a closed approach to broader participation to the present, where El-Hosseny finds that 'the *amicus* procedure is now fully recognized in investor-state arbitration as a means to channel broader public interest concerns'.[196] This process is traced to the finding in *Methanex Corp v US*[197] that Article 15(1) of the UNCITRAL Rules provided an implied legal basis for the Tribunal to accept briefs. Article 15(1) is a general provision that authorises the Tribunal to conduct the arbitration 'as it considers appropriate'. A different NAFTA tribunal confirmed that decision later in 2001 in *UPS v Canada*.[198] In the International Centre for Settlement of Investment Disputes (ICSID), the Tribunal in *Aguas Argentinas et al v Argentine Republic*, where five NGOs had requested permission to file submissions, considered whether Article 44 of the Convention on the Settlement of Investment Disputes between States and Nationals of Other States (ICSID Convention) provided a legal basis to accept such submissions. Article 44 is a general provision that allows the Tribunal to determine any question of procedure that has arisen and the ICSID Convention or the Arbitration Rules do not address. The Tribunal held that the authority to accept *amicus* submissions was a procedural question and determined that it did in fact have the power to 'admit *amicus curiae* submissions from suitable non-parties in appropriate cases'.[199] The Tribunal discussed the role an *amicus* would play and justified its decision based on the practice in NAFTA tribunals (referring to the *Methanex* Tribunal decision discussed above), the WTO and the Iran-US Claims Tribunal. The approach of the Tribunal demonstrates that the decision to accept an *amicus* submission

[193] Gomez (n 190), 528.

[194] R Buckley and P Blyschak, 'Guarding the Open Door: Non-Party Participation Before the International Centre for Settlement of Investment Disputes' (2007) 22 *Banking and Finance Law* Review 353, 355.

[195] N Butler, 'Non-Disputing Party Participation in ICSID Disputes: Faux *Amici*?' (2019) 66 *Netherlands International Law Review* 143.

[196] El-Hosseny (n 3), 300.

[197] *Methanex Corporation v United States of America* (Decision of the Tribunal on Petitions from Third Persons to Intervene as *Amicus Curiae*) UNCITRAL NAFTA, 15 January 2001.

[198] *United Parcel Service of America Inc v Canada* (Decision of the Tribunal on Petitions for Intervention and Participation as *Amicus Curiae*) UNCITRAL NAFTA, 17 October 2001.

[199] *Suez, Sociedad General de Aguas de Barcelona, SA, and Vivendi Universal SA v The Argentine Republic*, ICSID Case No ARB/03/19, Order in Response to a Petition for Transparency and Participation as *Amicus Curiae*, 19 May 2005, para 16.

remained a discretionary one, and that it favoured a case-by-case approach. The Tribunal identified two criteria: the appropriateness of the case for acceptance of *amicus* submissions, which it emphasised required a significant public interest component,[200] and the suitability of the applicants, requiring that they possess 'the expertise, experience and independence to be of assistance in the case'.[201] In 2006, states amended the ICSID Arbitration Rules to include an additional paragraph in Rule 37. Paragraph 2 now provides that '[a]fter consulting both parties, the Tribunal may allow a person or entity that is not a party to the dispute … to file a written submission with the Tribunal regarding a matter within the scope of the dispute'.[202] Further amendments to the rules are currently under consideration that would insert additional criteria for admission and require disclosure of any affiliation with a disputing party or the receipt of any assistance in preparing the brief.[203]

In 2003, the NAFTA Free Trade Commission (FTC) issued a statement addressing the participation of non-disputing parties (as *amici* are referred to) that detailed several procedural provisions governing written submissions 'from a person or entity' that is not a disputing party.[204] The FTC Statement reiterates that acceptance of a submission does not require a panel to address that submission or entitle the non-disputing party to make further submissions at any point. The FTC Statement is non-binding, but provides guidance to panels and to *amicus* applicants. The UNCITRAL rules also contained no express provision for the submission of information by *amici curiae*, either under the 1976 version or the 2010 amendment. However, Article 4 of the UNCITRAL Rules on Transparency,[205] effective from 1 April 2014, provides for submissions by 'a person that is not a disputing party, and not a non-disputing Party to the treaty, that address a matter within the scope of the dispute'. The provision provides for a two-stage approach and requires the applicant to comply with a number of procedural requirements, including describing their organisation and disclosing any affiliations and financial support.[206] In determining whether to accept a brief, a tribunal must consider whether the applicant has a significant interest in the proceedings and 'the extent to which the submission would assist the arbitral tribunal in the determination of a factual or legal issue related to the arbitral proceedings by bringing a perspective, particular knowledge or insight that is

[200] ibid, paras 18–19, noting the relevance of participation to enhancing transparency.

[201] ibid, para 24.

[202] International Centre for Settlement of Investment Disputes, Arbitration Rules (adopted 25 September 1967, entered into force 1 January 1968), ICSID/15, Art 37(2).

[203] 'Proposals for Amendment of the ICSID Rules – Working Paper' (*ICSID Secretariat,* 2 August 2018), vol 3, available at https://icsid.worldbank.org/en/Documents/Amendments_Vol_3_Complete_WP+Schedules.pdf, discussed in Butler (n 195), 173–4.

[204] 'Statement of the Free Trade Commission on Non-disputing Party Participation' (2005) 44 *ILM* 796.

[205] UNCITRAL Rules on Transparency in Treaty-based Investor-State Arbitration, adopted by UN GA Res 68/109 (adopted 16 December 2013, entered into force 1 April 2014).

[206] ibid, Art 4(2).

different from that of the disputing parties'.[207] Many bilateral and multilateral investment treaties now include provisions on the *amicus curiae*.[208]

In summary, the development of the *amicus curiae* practice in investor-state investment arbitration tribunals is similar to that in other international institutions. In the absence of a specific provision providing the legal basis for *amicus curiae* submissions, the tribunals relied on general procedural and evidence-gathering powers to support their ability to accept submissions on a discretionary basis. Moreover, the drafters of the rules have established criteria and procedures for the acceptance of briefs, and the tribunals have provided detailed reasoning and guidance as to the criteria they are applying.[209] There is an insistence on the need for broader transparency where there is a public interest in the dispute (likely to be found in most investor-state investment arbitration disputes) and recognition that an actor may also have a separate, but also significant, interest in the dispute. The main role of *amici curiae* has been to show how obligations should be interpreted in light or other areas of international law, in particular environmental law, human rights and indigenous rights.

Turning now to human rights institutions, as discussed in section IV(A)(ii), a general provision on intervention was introduced to the Rules of the ECtHR in 1998. There is not a separate provision for *amicus curiae* participation, although Bürli identified *amicus curiae* type interventions as one of the three forms of intervention seen in the ECtHR's practice; namely, intervention by individuals or organisations with no direct legal interest in the case but who possess a special expertise or authority with regard to the issue before the Court.[210] In her examination of all ECtHR cases until 2016, Bürli finds that the vast majority of external interventions in proceedings (518 of 667) can be characterised as *amici curiae*, in that the interveners are non-state actors not directly involved in the dispute, even though the ECtHR does not typically use this term.[211] The *amici curiae* represent a concentration of (mostly British)[212] 'repeat player' NGOs, such as Liberty, Interights, and Amnesty International, with 82 per cent of briefs submitted by *amici* who participated more than once (between 1986 and 2013).[213] Yet the applicants are more diverse than those statistics might suggest; 71 per cent of *amici curiae* (until 2016) only intervened once, usually concerning an issue upon which they are especially focused.[214] Many NGOs submit joint *amicus curiae* briefs, which make up approximately a third of the submissions received by the ECtHR.[215]

[207] ibid, Arts 4(3)(a), (b).
[208] El-Hosseny (n 3), 93.
[209] C Knahr, 'Transparency, Third Party Participation and Access to Documents in International Investment Arbitration' (2007) 23 *Arbitration International* 327.
[210] See section IV(A)(ii).
[211] Bürli (n 3), 6.
[212] See L Van Den Eynde 'An Empirical Look at the *Amicus Curiae* Practice of Human Rights NGOs before the European Court of Human Rights' (2013) 31(3) *Netherlands Quarterly Human Rights* 271, 286.
[213] ibid, 285.
[214] Bürli (n 3), 7, 114.
[215] Van Den Eynde (n 212), 288.

It is difficult to identify the precise requirements for admitting *amicus curiae* briefs before the ECtHR. Article 36 specifies that interventions in ECtHR proceedings must be in the 'interest of the proper administration of justice'. Rule 44 of the Rules of Court sets out the procedural requirements. The President of the relevant Section or Chamber has discretion to decide whether an *amicus* or other intervener meets this requirement, although this involves 'at least a connection between the issues considered by the Court and the content of the intervention'.[216] Apart from these rules, the Court has significant discretion concerning the admission of interventions, including *amicus curiae* briefs, and has not set down further guidance in its decisions. While the Court has a practice of listing all interventions and summarising their arguments in judgments, it does not issue public decisions in response to applications to intervene in cases. Nor does it typically provide any rationale for accepting or refusing submissions, either in its judgments or in letters to applicants. Judgments do not usually indicate whether any applications have been rejected, although 46 per cent of applications were reportedly denied between 1990 and June 2012.[217] There is also no database on the Court's website providing all *amicus curiae* applications, decisions concerning them, or briefs. This means that there is minimal transparency concerning the parameters of acceptable intervention at the ECtHR. This may be deliberate. As Bürli observes, '[p]resumably the Court wants to keep a maximum of flexibility' by not establishing specific rules.[218]

Civil society has engaged with the ECtHR in a variety of ways that reflect the Court's significance and influence upon the protection and promotion of human rights in Europe.[219] Some of the aims of NGOs seeking to participate as *amici curiae* include to 'challenge national laws, practices and interpretations, to establish precedents, to inform and influence the Court and to extend the interpretation given to the Convention'.[220] The *amicus curiae* offers an important and relatively accessible avenue for potentially influencing the Court, given the restrictions upon NGOs bringing cases on behalf of other victims if they are not directly affected (see above). The practice of the ECtHR indicates that *amici curiae* need not be entirely neutral, but may have an indirect interest in the outcome of the case.

The American Convention and IACHR Statute[221] do not provide an explicit legal basis for *amicus curiae* submissions. However, the absence of an express rule has not prevented the Court developing an extensive *amicus* practice. In earlier contentious cases, the Court relied on Rule 34(1), which provided: 'The

[216] Bürli (n 3), 10; AA Mohamed, 'Individual and NGO Participation in Human Rights Litigation before the African Court of Human and Peoples' Rights: Lessons from the European and Inter-American Courts of Human Rights' (1999) 43 *Journal of African Law* 201, 208.

[217] Statistics on file with Bürli (n 3), 116; Van Den Eynde (n 212), 281.

[218] Van Den Eynde (n 212), 273.

[219] ibid.

[220] ibid, 275.

[221] Statute of the Inter-American Court (adopted by the General Assembly of the OAS at its Ninth Regular Session, held in La Paz Bolivia, October 1979) Res no 448.

Court may, at the request of a party or the delegates of the Commission, or *proprio motu*, decide to hear as a witness, expert, or in any other capacity, any person whose testimony or statements seem likely to assist in carrying out its function'. Although in these earlier years the Court did not address briefs within judgments,[222] the briefs favoured a 'liberal' approach to determining the Court's advisory jurisdiction, which the court ultimately adopted.[223]

The 2001 amendments to the Rules did not include a specific provision on *amicus* submissions, but Rule 45 on the Procedure for Taking Evidence gave a similar broad scope to that provided by Rule 34(1). Further amendments to the Rules in 2009 led to the adoption of a specific provision on *amicus curiae* submissions in contentious proceedings, which is currently Rule 44.[224] That rule provides that 'any person or institution seeking to act as *amicus curiae* may submit a brief to the Tribunal'. Article 2.3 defines '*amicus curiae*' as: 'the person or institution who is unrelated to the case and to the proceeding and submits to the Court reasoned arguments on the facts contained in the presentation of the case or legal considerations on the subject-matter of the proceeding by means of a document or an argument presented at a hearing'.[225]

Despite the civil law systems followed by many of the parties to the American Convention, and therefore the civil law background of many IACHR judges, the Court regularly – and increasingly – accepts *amicus curiae* briefs.[226] More than 500 briefs have been submitted to the Court. The IACHR allows *amici curiae* to provide 'reasoned arguments on the facts' or 'legal considerations on the subject-matter' of the case.[227] This suggests that briefs can address factual issues, although they have tended to offer legal analysis and have typically addressed legal, rather than political or factual, issues.[228] Most provide an analysis of the relevant human rights law, consistent with statistics from 1988 to 2013 showing that approximately 60 per cent of *amici curiae* at the IACHR have been human rights NGOs.[229] The remainder were 'academic institutions, private individuals, government officials or agencies, and corporations'.[230]

The IACHR has rarely refused *amicus* submissions, especially in its earlier years.[231] The position of the Court has been that, rather than declaring *amicus*

[222] Juaristi (n 3), 103.

[223] C Moyer, 'The Role of the *Amicus Curiae* in the Inter-American Court of Human Rights', 2, available at www.corteidh.or.cr/tablas/a11770.pdf.

[224] Article 74 of the Rules extends the rules on contentious proceedings to advisory opinions, to the extent the Court considers them to be compatible.

[225] IACHR Rules, Art 2.3, also introduced in 2009.

[226] Juaristi (n 3), 106–08; Moyer (n 223), 8.

[227] IACHR Rules, Art 2.3.

[228] Juaristi (n 3), 114 and fn 40; JM Pasqualucci, *The Practice and Procedure of the Inter-American Court of Human Rights*, 2nd edn (Cambridge, CUP, 2016) 159.

[229] Juaristi (n 3), 107, calculates that 58% of briefs came from NGOs and 24.5% from academic institutions between 1982–2013.

[230] ibid, 107–08.

[231] Shelton (n 11), 349, observed in 1994 that it 'does not appear that the Court has ever rejected an *amicus* filing'. However, Juaristi (n 3), 115, observes that the Court, since 2009, has become more willing to reject or at least discuss the admissibility of briefs.

submissions to be inadmissible, it evaluates the brief 'through the Court's estimation of the evidential or legal value of a particular brief'.[232] Unlike other international institutions discussed in this section, Rule 45 does not require the *amicus* to identify how its submissions will assist the Court, nor how those submissions will differ from those of the parties. *Amici* at the IACHR mostly submit written briefs, which are circulated to the parties, although oral observations are permitted and have increasingly been heard.[233] The admission of *amicus curiae* submissions is within the discretion of the Court and, while the views of the parties are sought in contentious proceedings, consent is not a prerequisite for acceptance, although it may influence the Court's evaluation of the brief. One observer argues that the perpetual underfunding of the Commission and IACHR, as well as the lack of a legal aid programme, has contributed to the significant engagement of NGOs with both institutions.[234] In summary, the *amicus curiae* mechanism is an important feature of the IACHR's activities and accepted as a mode for expanding the representativeness of the arguments heard by the Court.

None of the legal instruments establishing or regulating the African Court make explicit reference to *amici curiae*. However, a number of the Rules may give sufficient discretion to the Court to admit *amici* in both contentious and advisory proceedings.[235] In particular, rule 45(2) empowers the Court to 'ask any person or institution of its choice to obtain information, express an opinion or submit a report to it on any specific point'. The interpretation that such rules enable the admission of *amici* at the discretion of the Court is supported by the 2012 Practice Directions, which set out the procedure for a 'Request to act as *Amicus Curiae*', which can be either an 'individual or organization'.[236] The relevant provisions clarify that *amici* are to be admitted at the discretion of the Court, either at the invitation of the Court or on application by prospective *amici*. It appears that the Court has so far granted *amicus* status in two contentious cases: the *Libya* case,[237] in which the Pan-African Lawyers Union was the first *amicus* to be admitted at the Court, but which was eventually struck off the roll; and the *Lohe Issa Konate v Burkina Faso case*,[238] in which multiple

[232] A-K Lindblom, *Non-governmental Organisations in International Law* (Cambridge, CUP, 2005) 357.

[233] Juaristi (n 3), 122–3; Pasqualucci (n 228), 75–76.

[234] H Nichols Haddad, 'Judicial Institution Builders: NGOs and International Human Rights Courts' (2012) 11 *Journal of Human Rights* 126.

[235] See F Viljoen and A Kassie Abebe, 'Amicus Participation before Regional Human Rights Bodies in Africa' (2014) 58(1) *Journal of African Law* 22, 35; International Justice Resource Center, 'Advocacy before the African Human Rights System: A Manual for Attorneys and Advocates Preventing and Remedying Human Rights Violations through the International Framework' (November 2016), 123, available at https://ijrcenter.org/wp-content/uploads/2016/11/Advocacy-before-the-African-Human-Rights-System.pdf.

[236] African Court on Human and Peoples' Rights, Practice Directions (1–5 October 2012, 5th extraordinary session), paras 42–47.

[237] *African Commission on Human and Peoples' Rights v Libya*, App No 004/2011.

[238] *Lohe Issa Konate v Burkina Faso*, App No 004/2013.

amici were admitted,[239] and which has concluded with a final decision of the Court. In relation to advisory proceedings, Rule 70 arguably[240] allows the Court to receive *amicus* submissions by permitting the receipt of written submissions on legal matters by 'any interested entity'. From the Court's public records, it appears that *amicus* applications have been made in two advisory opinions.[241] The practice of the African Court in relation to *amici curiae* is thus far limited. *Amici* have only been admitted in a very small number of cases, and only a subset of those cases have reached a final decision. It is therefore very difficult to determine the legal basis on which *amici* will be admitted, the criteria that will be applied, the rationale for which *amicus* submissions are accepted, and the impact of these submissions on the decision-making of the Court.

F. Impact of the *Amicus Curiae*

Studies of the *amicus curiae* at the national and international levels face the same methodological challenges that we encountered (see chapter four and Annex A): it is difficult to determine the impact of *amicus* briefs on substantive outcomes. Many studies also focus on intervention, rather than the *amicus curiae*, and few consider the two mechanisms together. The influence of the *amicus curiae* has received the greatest attention in relation to the US Supreme Court, with numerous scholars undertaking quantitative studies. In the most comprehensive study, Collins concluded that *amicus* briefs do influence judicial law making on the US Supreme Court and that the attitudes and values of the judges do not dictate influence.[242] Interestingly, Collins found that *amicus* briefs 'are the single strongest predictor of increased variance in judicial decision making',[243] with briefs contributing to the decision as to whether to write or join a separate or dissenting decision.[244] Collins postulates that this is due to the approach to decision making adopted by judges, in that they search for the best legal answer, but become overwhelmed by numerous briefs containing different versions

[239] Centre for Human Rights, Comite Pour la Protection des Journalistes, Media Institute of Southern Africa, Pan African Human Rights Defenders Network, Pan African Lawyers' Union, Pen International and National Pen Centres (Pen Malawi, Pen Algeria, Pen Nigeria, Pen Sierra Leone and Pen South Africa), Southern Africa Litigation Centre and World Association of Newspapers and News Publishers – though it is unclear whether these organisations made joint or individual submissions.

[240] See Viljoen and Abebe (n 235), 36.

[241] *Request for Advisory Opinion by the Socio-Economic Rights and Accountability Project (SERAP),* App No 001/2013, Advisory Opinion, 26 May 2017, para 17 (the Centre for Human Rights at the University of Pretoria was admitted as *amicus curiae*); *Request for Advisory Opinion by The Centre for Human Rights of the University of Pretoria and the Coalition of African Lesbians*, App No 002/2015, Advisory Opinion, 28 September 2017, para 13 (rejected as the applicants (four NGOs) had not submitted the application themselves).

[242] Collins (n 114), 172–73, ch 4.

[243] ibid, 173, ch 5.

[244] ibid, 173.

of what that 'best' answer might be.[245] In a separate, subsequent study, using plagiarism software, Collins, Corley and Hamner found evidence that 'justices systematically incorporate language from *amicus* briefs into the Court's majority opinions'.[246] This judicial 'borrowing' is more likely to occur where the briefs are 'high quality' and rely on arguments advanced in other sources.[247]

A study of interventions in the Supreme Court of Canada found 'modest but significant impact of interveners on voting by the Court as a whole and by individual judges', with the Court using briefs 'to better understand the impact of its decisions' and more open to hearing from interveners 'if there is a possibility of gaining some valuable information'.[248] Shah, Poole and Blackwell found that intervention had no significant effect on whether judgments at the UK House of Lords were unanimous, majority or had dissenting or separate opinions.[249] Moreover, there was 'no statistical evidence to support the proposition that intervention in post-[Human Rights Act] human rights cases had an effect on the outcome of those cases'.[250] They concluded that '[T]hird party interveners do not appear to have had the kind of leverage that they might have hoped for'.[251] While there have been no comparable studies in South Africa, our own analysis suggests that *amicus* submissions have had some impact in a number of proceedings. This impact has been both explicit and implicit. In judgments such as *Carmichele*[252] and *Shilubana*,[253] the Court explicitly cites the *amici's* arguments and relies on them in the judgment of the Court. In other cases, there is no explicit citation of the *amicus* submissions, but comparison of the *amicus* brief with the content and format of the judgment reveal that the former had substantial influence on the judgment of the court.[254]

At the international level, as the ICJ does not accept briefs in contentious proceedings and only informally in advisory opinions, impact is negligible. ITLOS has a similarly restrictive approach; however, Wiik notes that the WWF brief in the Seabed Disputes Chamber advisory opinion,[255] which although not accepted had been made available publicly, had some influence on the Chamber

[245] ibid, 173–77.

[246] P Collins, P Corley and J Hamner 'The Influence of *Amicus Curiae* Briefs on US Supreme Court Opinion Content' (2015) 49 *Law & Society Review* 917, 938. This supports earlier studies that concluded that briefs influence the US Supreme Court, eg, JD Kearney and TW Merrill, 'The Influence of *Amicus Curiae* Briefs on the Supreme Court' (2000) 148 *University of Pennsylvania Law Review* 743.

[247] Collins, Corley and Hamner (n 246).

[248] B Alarie and A Green, 'Interventions at the Supreme Court of Canada: Accuracy, Affiliation, and Acceptance' (2010) 48 *Osgoode Hall Law Journal* 381, 409–10.

[249] Shah, Poole and Blackwell (n 67), 315–16.

[250] ibid, 319, although noting that this may be because the briefs did not address issues included in the ratio of the decision.

[251] ibid, 324.

[252] *Carmichele v Minister of Safety and Security* (CCT 48/00) [2001] ZACC 22, para 62.

[253] *Shilubana and Others v Nwamitwa* (CCT 03/07) [2008] ZACC 9.

[254] See, eg *National Commissioner of the South African Police Service v Southern African Human Rights Litigation Centre and Another* (CCT 02/14) [2014] ZACC 30.

[255] See section V(E)(i) above.

through references to the brief in the submissions of participating states and possibly because members of the Chamber had read the brief.[256] WTO panels and the Appellate Body even where they accept *amicus* briefs rarely mention the brief or rely on the brief to support their substantive conclusions, thus their direct impact is also minimal. In fact, Wiik concludes that 'the assertion of authority to admit *amici curiae* has been more symbolic than real. Submissions are only rarely considered in substance (or at least it is rarely made known when they are)'.[257] As with the ICJ and ITLOS, submissions may have more impact when they are adopted – in whole or in part – by the parties in their own submissions.

In investor-state investment arbitration, a study by Butler of non-disputing party participation in ICSID arbitrations concluded that, while there was evidence that tribunals had become more open to accepting *amicus* briefs,[258] 'even when *amicus* applications are granted, tribunals appear to ignore the content of *amicus* submissions'.[259] Butler found that only in six instances where an *amicus* had participated did the brief directly affect the outcome of the dispute (in the sense of the tribunal making explicit reference to the brief). In a further case, the brief affected the outcome both directly and indirectly (in the sense of having an influence on the decision in a way other than direct citation).[260] Given this, despite recognition that *amicus curiae* participation does contribute to transparency and legitimacy of international investment arbitration, Butler concludes that '*amicus* briefs are grossly underutilised'.[261] El-Hosseny also concluded that results were mixed, as it was hard to determine impact since '[O]nly those attending deliberations would be aware of what ultimately swayed a tribunal's decision in one direction or another'.[262] Other scholars have concluded that *amicus curiae* briefs do not have much influence, and tribunals rarely cite briefs in substantive decisions.[263] In particular, Wiik observed that '[W]hile tribunals often acknowledge a public interest in the arbitration, the arguments of *amici curiae* on the public interest engaged are not adopted'.[264]

In contrast, based on analysis of the ECtHR and IACHR, human rights courts rely more extensively on *amicus curiae* submissions.[265] In her study of ECtHR practice, Bürli found that state interventions received less space than

[256] Wiik (n 3), 442–3.
[257] ibid, 467–8.
[258] Butler (n 195), 172.
[259] ibid, 172.
[260] For Butler's definition of these terms, see 150. This study examined 11 cases in which *amici* had participated that had reached the stage of a final, published award. The study also excluded states as non-party participants.
[261] Butler (n 195), 172.
[262] El-Hosseny (n 3), 180.
[263] See, eg, N Blackaby and C Richard, '*Amicus Curiae*: A Panacea for Legitimacy in Investment Arbitration?', in M Waibel et al (eds), *The Backlash against Investment Arbitration* (Austin, Wolters Kluwer, 2010) 270; F Francioni, 'Access to Justice, Denial of Justice and International Investment Law' (2009) 20 *EJIL* 729, 741.
[264] Wiik (n 3), 478.
[265] Practice is too limited at the African Court to draw conclusions, as only two cases with *amici* participation have reached judgment.

amicus curiae submissions (in the sense that summaries where shorter), but decisions were more likely to refer to a state submission in its own reasoning. However, its engagement with state interventions was 'not as profound' as with *amici curiae*.[266] Similarly, third party interventions from those with an interest in proceedings 'do not play a crucial role in the reasoning of judgments', are usually summarised in a paragraph and 'the Court barely engages with the third party intervention'.[267] Yet, Bürli concludes that the evidence:[268]

> reveals that the Court's engagement with and reliance on *amici curiae* is profound. The Court not only cites *amicus curiae* interventions but frequently bases its reasoning on their arguments. In addition, many landmark decisions on the rights of detainees, LGBT people and Travellers were decided with *amicus curiae* interventions pushing for an evolutive interpretation of the Convention. Thus *amici curiae* have influenced the development and shaping of human rights protection.

By comparison, Haddad's study of NGO engagement at the ECtHR found low frequency and low impact of NGO *amicus curiae* briefs, at least relative to NGOs' role in supporting applicants.[269] Haddad suggests three reasons for this outcome. First, the ECtHR is well resourced when compared to other regional human rights mechanisms. Secondly, the institution developed its rules and practices at a time when there was not the same degree of civil society involvement, leading to historical exclusion and distrust of NGO actors. Finally, at least until recently, the ECtHR enjoyed high levels of support and cooperation from its member states, so it did not need to rely on NGOs to boost its legitimacy.[270]

There is no doubt that *amicus curiae* submissions have had significant impact at the IACHR. Judgments often mention *amicus curiae* submissions and occasionally to support judicial findings.[271] Still, the impact of *amicus curiae* briefs upon case outcomes is difficult to discern, since citations remain rare compared to the number of briefs and the Court does not publish submissions on the website.[272] Given the limited assessment of the 'helpfulness' of *amicus* briefs at the admissibility stage, it is hard to identify how the Court has assessed the value of a particular brief to the Court in reaching its decision. The high and increasing number of submissions, including from repeat submitters such as the International Human Rights Law Group and the Centre for Justice and International Law,[273] suggests that *amici* perceive some impact,[274] while the progressive rule

[266] Bürli (n 3), 152–3.
[267] ibid, 178.
[268] ibid, 129.
[269] Haddad (n 46), 50.
[270] ibid, 50–51.
[271] eg concerning 'femicide' in *Gonzalez et al ("Cotton Field") v Mexico* (Judgment) (16 November 2009), fn 134; the impartiality obligations of forensic doctors in *Caso Espinoza Gonzales v Peru* (Judgment) (20 November 2014), fn 437.
[272] Juaristi, (n 3), 109, also found it 'difficult to gauge' the influence of amicus briefs; see also see Shelton (n 11), 350.
[273] For a list of repeat submitters by 1994, see Shelton (n 11), 349.
[274] Juaristi (n 3), 109.

changes to facilitate *amicus* observations indicate that the Court also finds some value in receiving them.[275] Haddad concluded that there is both high frequency and high impact of NGO *amicus curiae* submissions at the IACHR,[276] highlighting that the Court needed such submissions due to its own under-funding, the absence of adequate research and legal assistance and the risk that member states may not be well-resourced and able to assist the Court.[277]

There is recognition of broader impact beyond citations and the outcome in an instant case, with the impact of some briefs much longer term. Duffy's study of effectiveness of strategic litigation notes the contribution *amicus curiae* submissions can make to developing the law – both procedural and substantive – in other fora, and for enhancing the understanding of the court and the public about the broader implications of a decision.[278] Bürli also found that such interventions have benefits beyond the decision, with *amici curiae* providing 'argumentative representation' that can help foster dialogue and debate.[279] *Amicus curiae* briefs can also be an important site of knowledge production in areas of expertise.[280] First, *amici* provide valuable arguments and legal analysis, particularly by compiling analysis on human rights law, international law, international humanitarian law and EU law.[281] Secondly, *amici* can assist the Court in contextualising a case, through their country-specific knowledge on either local laws or the context of an issue, information that can be factual or legal. Finally, *amici curiae* can lend credibility to certain arguments due to their acknowledged expertise, particular membership or representative authority, an effect multiplied by joint submissions.[282] By enhancing the quality of the Court's decisions (both legally and from a participatory perspective), *amici curiae* contribute to building legitimacy. Wiik recognises the contribution of the *amicus curiae* to addressing institutional and structural concerns, for example, improving transparency in investor-state investment arbitration.[283] However, Wiik suggests that, with the exception of human rights tribunals, the limited engagement with *amici's* submissions in substance means that 'the legitimizing effect of the instrument currently is aspirational rather than real .... There is a risk that lack of substantial consideration of *amicus curiae* briefs may actually

[275] Juaristi (n 3), 110–13.
[276] Haddad (n 46), 50.
[277] ibid, 86–87, 101, 107.
[278] Duffy (n 63) explores in detail the ways in which strategic litigation may have impact. While many of these may not be reasonable expectations of an amicus brief (eg, changes to institutions or legislation), the discussion of legal reforms and developments is relevant to the amicus. See also Open Society Justice Initiative, Strategic Litigation Impacts: Insights from Global Experience (2018), available at www.opensocietyfoundations.org/sites/default/files/strategic-litigation-impacts-insights-20181023.pdf.
[279] Bürli (n 3), ch 2, s 5.
[280] ibid, 46–53.
[281] ibid, 53–61.
[282] ibid, 61–64.
[283] Wiik (n 3), 43–62.

deepen legitimacy concerns regarding the WTO dispute settlement system and investor-state investment arbitration'.[284]

VI. RELEVANCE OF COMPARATIVE PRACTICE TO INTERNATIONAL CRIMINAL TRIBUNALS

What does this chapter mean for the rest of the study? International criminal tribunals have key structural differences from the national systems and international institutions studied in this chapter. First, in the absence of other specific rights to participate, the *amicus curiae* remains the main mechanism for states, victims and other actors to participate in proceedings. This means that the mechanism may be expected to fill the functions served at the national level by standing and intervention, as well as the more traditional role of the *amicus curiae*. This is why a functional approach has explanatory value: different approaches and inconsistent application may be partly explained by understanding the extent to which the *amicus curiae* mechanism is being expected to or should perform all three functions (expertise, representative and communicative), which have different rationale and criteria at the national level and in other international institutions.

Secondly, international criminal tribunals are not human rights institutions, engaging in conversations about the realisation of rights or the appropriate balance of rights in a constitutional order. Nor are they equivalent to superior courts at the national level,[285] called upon to decide issues of constitutional law and application of human rights on a national level. Similarly, they are not adjudicating bilateral disputes between states or assessing state responsibility, even though the conduct of a state may be implicated in the alleged crimes. Instead, despite the varied claims about their broader purposes, the primary function of international criminal tribunals is to determine the guilt or innocence of an individual accused. The focus on individual criminal responsibility means that participation must be managed so as not to undermine the fair trial rights of the accused and to respect the core judicial competence and roles of the parties. It is for judges to know the law and to decide the facts according to the law based on evidence and legal arguments provided by the parties. The national practice demonstrates that a more cautious approach is required in criminal proceedings, both for intervention and *amici curiae*. The national practice also highlights the role of the prosecution in representing the victims, state and the public interest.

[284] Wiik (n 3), 531.

[285] Collins and McCarthy (n 132) concluded that this is where most strategic litigation and intervention will occur, where courts are performing a role in relation to human rights and constitutional issues.

Thirdly, the comparative practice shows that the *amicus curiae* is a feature of many legal systems, yet their role is generally not set out in any detail;[286] it is often as if a judge 'knows an *amicus* when she sees one' or – more precisely, knows what an *amicus* is not. However, as Murray notes, 'What is clear is that the institution of *amicus curiae* is versatile, and the *amicus curiae* fulfils a wide range of diverse and important functions'.[287] These include the functions of the traditional *amicus curiae*, namely to provide impartial legal advice or information not otherwise available to the court. However, the mechanism now also, to varying extents, represents otherwise unrepresented interests affected by the case, advocates for particular developments in the law, informs the court of the potential broader impacts of a case (including provision of social science data) and, in certain systems, argues for the public interest in a particular issue. The functions formally ascribed to the *amicus curiae* mechanism in a particular system differ depending on how open standing rules are, the existence and scope of separate rights to intervene and the overlap between those provisions and the *amicus curiae* mechanism. Moreover, the legal culture in a particular system influences how responsive courts are to *amici*, and the functions they will permit an *amicus* to perform. It is evident that the traditional model of the *amicus curiae* is too narrow to fully capture the range of functions the mechanism performs in the comparative practice.

Fourthly, there are a number of rationales for permitting *amicus curiae* participation, which include: enhanced transparency; hearing from those with an interest in proceedings; judges reaching more accurate and more representative decisions; supplementing court resources and expertise; affiliating actors with the court through participation; aiding in compliance (participating actors are more likely to accept the decision); addressing democratic deficits in courts; and building legitimacy through engaging states and other stakeholders in conversations about the implications of decisions and developing the law.

Fifthly, another feature that emerges from national practice is the trend towards formal *amicus* rules. Most provisions on intervention and the *amicus curiae* are initially informal, entirely discretionary and based on the inherent power of the Court to manage its own procedures. In many systems, both common law and civil law, there is then a gradual shift to set down formal rules. A similar process is seen in those international institutions that allow *amicus curiae* participation: an early reliance on inherent powers or general provisions, followed by the inclusion of specific provisions and procedures. Chapter three therefore explores the history of the inclusion of *amicus curiae* provisions in international criminal tribunals. What is consistent across jurisdictions, even without formal rules, is the discretionary nature of the mechanism and the

[286] See C Murray 'Litigating in the Public Interest: Intervention and the *Amicus Curiae*' (1994) 10 *South African Journal on Human Rights* 240, 242.
[287] ibid, 242.

limited rights accorded to *amici curiae*, given the need to balance the benefits of participation against risks to the parties and the expeditiousness, efficiency and expense of proceedings.

Sixthly, and related to the fifth point, is the role of state consent in international institutions and the responsibility for drafting rules of procedure. In the ICJ, ITLOS and WTO, states have given consent for rights of intervention for states in specific circumstances. They have not consented to inclusion of a provision authorising intervention or *amicus curiae* participation by other actors. Where the WTO has relied on inherent and general powers to enable *amicus curiae* participation, several member states have asserted political control and have refused to endorse *amicus* participation. In contrast, where states feel there is a reason for allowing participation, for example to address calls for greater transparency in investor-state investment arbitration, or where states may also benefit from greater participation rights, as in the ECtHR, they have positively endorsed or at least not opposed the inclusion of additional provisions. Chapter three details the role of states in supporting inclusion of formal rules on the *amicus curiae* mechanism in the relevant instruments of international criminal tribunals.

Having now provided a comparative context for the *amicus curiae* in other institutions and jurisdictions, we turn to explore the inclusion and development of the mechanism in international criminal tribunals.

3

The Amicus Curiae *in International Criminal Tribunals: An Introduction*

I. OVERVIEW

CHAPTER TWO OUTLINED the comparative practice in national, regional and international tribunals. This chapter shifts the focus of inquiry to international criminal tribunals. It first outlines standing in international criminal tribunals (section II), before exploring the history of the inclusion of the *amicus curiae* mechanism in the legal frameworks of the international criminal tribunals (section III). Section IV examines the *amicus curiae* prosecutor and the potential role of the ICC Prosecutor as an *amicus curiae* (chapter six considers the *amicus curiae* as substitute defence counsel). Next, the chapter examines the limits on the use of the *amicus curiae* in the Tribunals, in particular the need to support, but not infringe upon, the core judicial competence of the Chambers, and to respect the right of the accused to a fair trial (section V). Finally, section VI places the *amicus curiae* in the context of other institutional mechanisms that may fulfil expertise, representative and communicative functions, the availability of which may replace or influence *amicus curiae* practice.

II. STANDING IN INTERNATIONAL CRIMINAL TRIBUNALS

A. Standing to Initiate an Investigation

States have no standing to initiate investigations for international crimes in international criminal tribunals. For tribunals other than the ICC, the founding instrument for the tribunal confers and sets the parameters of the tribunal's jurisdiction.[1] The decision to trigger an investigation is the responsibility of

[1] Statute of the International Criminal Tribunal for the Former Yugoslavia (adopted 25 May 1993) UNSC Res 827, Art 1; Statute of the International Criminal Tribunal for Rwanda (adopted 8 November 1994) UNSC Res 955, Art 1; Statute of the Special Court for Sierra Leone (adopted 16 January 2002) 2178 UNTS 145, Art 1; Agreement Between the United Nations and the Royal Government of Cambodia Concerning the Prosecution under Cambodian Law of Crimes Committed During the Period of Democratic Kampuchea (adopted 6 June 2003, entered into force 29 April 2005) 2329 UNTS 117, Art 2; Statute of the Special Tribunal for Lebanon (adopted 29 March 2006) UNSC Res 1757, Art 1.

the Prosecutor; even in the tribunals with a judge-led investigation phase, the introductory submission or indictment filed by the prosecution sets the scope of the investigation.[2] At the ICC, states can trigger ICC jurisdiction by referring a situation to the Court[3] or confer jurisdiction by filing a declaration accepting ICC jurisdiction on an *ad hoc* basis.[4] The Security Council can refer a situation to the ICC acting under Chapter VII of the UN Charter, including in relation to a state that is not party to the Rome Statute.[5] States can provide information to the Prosecutor, which may lead to the Prosecutor exercising her *proprio motu* jurisdiction.[6] However, regardless of the manner in which jurisdiction is triggered or conferred, the decision to open a preliminary examination, initiate an investigation and bring charges in specific cases remains for the Prosecutor alone. The judges of the ICC may exercise judicial review of key prosecutorial decisions in limited circumstances, namely where the Prosecutor must request authorisation to open an investigation under Article 15[7] and where the Prosecutor has declined to open an investigation based on the interests of justice criterion.[8] A state that refers a situation to the Court has standing to request judicial review of a decision *not* to proceed with an investigation, as does the Security Council where it has referred a situation.[9] A state may also request a deferral to national proceedings[10] and challenge jurisdiction or admissibility of a situation or case.[11] Although these rights give states some influence on the decision to prosecute, states do not have standing to initiate investigations. This distinguishes international criminal tribunals from other international institutions, where states initiate claims (see chapter two). Moreover, the absence of the state as a formal actor also distinguishes the Tribunals from criminal proceedings at the national level, where the state is responsible for bringing prosecutions, albeit acting through prosecution services or investigating judges (chapter two).

[2] At the ECCC, the co-prosecutors files an introductory submission that opens the judicial investigation: Extraordinary Chambers in the Courts of Cambodia, Internal Rules (12 June 2007, as revised on 16 January 2015) Rev 9, r 53. At the STL, the prosecution files the indictment for approval by the pre-trial judge: Special Tribunal for Lebanon, Rules of Procedure and Evidence (20 March 2009, as amended 8 February 2012) STL/BD/2009/01/Rev.4, r 68.

[3] Rome Statute of the International Criminal Court (adopted 17 July 1998, entered into force 1 July 2002) 2187 UNTS 38544, Arts 13(a), 14.

[4] ibid, Art 12(3).

[5] ibid, Art 13(b).

[6] ibid, Arts 13(c), 15.

[7] ibid, Art 15(3).

[8] ibid, Art 53(3)(b).

[9] ibid, Art 53(3)(a).

[10] Article 18 of the Rome Statute allows a state that is (or has) exercised jurisdiction to request the Prosecutor to defer the ICC investigation, unless the Pre-Trial Chamber authorises the investigation. The state can appeal the decision of the Pre-Trial Chamber.

[11] Articles 17 and 19 of the Rome Statute allow a state that has jurisdiction over a case (because it is (or has) investigating or prosecuting to challenge admissibility and jurisdiction. A state from which acceptance of jurisdiction is required under Art 12 may also challenge admissibility or jurisdiction.

As Mégret notes, international criminal law is the rare case of criminal law without a sovereign.[12]

The Prosecutor's exclusive responsibility for initiating investigations means that, as well as states, victims and civil society actors also lack standing in the traditional sense. This distinguishes the Tribunals from some national legal systems and from human rights and investor-state investment arbitration tribunals. As noted in chapter one, this reflects the Prosecutor's role in representing victims, states and the international community. Victims, states, international organisations, civil society and other actors can attempt to influence prosecutorial decisions by submitting information to the Office of the Prosecutor (OTP), including under Article 15, and the OTP has indicated it does consult during the investigation process. However, there is no means to compel the Prosecutor to act and, unlike states, victims do not have standing to initiate judicial review of prosecutorial decisions not to investigate.[13] Victims are given rights to participate in proceedings, explored in section VI(A) below.

The Tribunals do not exercise advisory jurisdiction. Drafters contemplated advisory jurisdiction for the ICC, but it was rejected by the International Law Commission and during the Rome negotiations as the:[14]

> function of the court is to try persons charged under the statute for crimes covered by article 20, including crimes contrary to the treaties referred to in article 20, subparagraph (e). In doing so it will necessarily have to interpret those treaties, but it does not seem appropriate to give it additional jurisdiction of an inter-State character under them. Many of the treaties have their own jurisdictional provisions, for example referring disputes over their interpretation or application to ICJ. There is no reason to displace this jurisdiction.

The Appeals Chamber has confirmed that it can only issue decisions in respect of concrete legal issues raised in the context of the proceedings[15] and must not issue *obiter dicta* statements or act as an advisory body.[16] Judge Perrin de Brichambaut in the *Myanmar/Bangladesh* proceedings was critical of the Chamber as acting ultra vires as 'to answer the Prosecutor's jurisdictional question at this stage would be an exercise in speculation tantamount to delivering a *de facto* advisory opinion'.[17]

[12] F Mégret, 'The Anxieties of International Criminal Justice' (2016) 29 *LJIL* 197, 206.

[13] Article 53 of the Rome Statute does not provide any rights to victims to seek review of prosecutorial decisions. See S Williams, 'Civil Society Participation in Preliminary Examinations' in M Bergsmo and C Stahn (eds), *Quality Control in Preliminary Examinations* (Torkel Opsahl Academic Epublisher, 2018).

[14] *Draft Statute for an International Criminal Court with Commentaries* (Report of the International Law Commission on the Work of its Forty-Sixth Session, 1994) 38.

[15] eg *Prosecutor v Katanga and Chui*, ICC AC, 25 September 2009, ICC-01/04-01/07-1497, para 38.

[16] eg *Situation in the Democratic Republic of the Congo*, ICC AC, 30 June 2008, ICC-01/04-503, para 30.

[17] *Request Under Regulation 46(3) of the Regulations of the Court*, ICC PTC I, 6 September 2018, ICC-RoC46(3)-01/18-37-Anx, para 4.

B. Joinder

The Tribunals have all conducted joint trials of multiple accused and most provide expressly for formal joinder.[18] The basic rule is that persons accused jointly should be tried together. There is a clear preference for joint trials, and perhaps even a presumption in favour of joint proceedings at the ICC.[19] The rationale for joinder is that it promotes the fairness of the proceedings, with all accused having the same rights as if they were tried separately, and improves judicial economy. Joinder avoids having witnesses testify more than once, which can prevent additional distress and inconvenience to witnesses as well as reducing the costs of multiple trips to the Court to testify. It minimises duplication of evidence and inconsistency in the presentation of evidence across different trials, which may prevent differential treatment of accused, inconsistent findings and allegations of conflicts of interest. Joinder may also reflect recognition that international crimes are often the outcome of collective action and allows a more detailed presentation of the evidence – thus aligning with broader goals of international criminal justice.[20] Joinder is at the discretion of the Chamber. The practice on joinder tends to focus on whether trials are connected, for example: whether the crimes were similar in nature, perpetrated as part of a plan or strategy, or there is a nexus between the acts of the individual accused. Chambers also consider whether joinder would adversely prejudice the fair trial rights of the accused, the expeditiousness of the trial or be contrary to the interests of justice, having regard to the complexity of the trial and the timing of the request.[21] Joinder serves a different function to the *amicus curiae* although, as is seen in chapter six, there may be overlap where accused in separate but related trials seek to present views as *amici*.

C. Intervention

The Tribunals do not recognise rights of intervention; their constituent instruments do not contain rules enabling states and other actors to intervene in proceedings, either as of right or with permission. The approach adopted is to allow actors *specific* participatory rights in certain contexts, for example, victim participation or the ability of states to challenge admissibility. The majority in

[18] Joinder here includes joinder of cases and charges. Also related to joinder is the concept of severance. See ICTY RPE, r 48; ICTR RPE, rr 48 and 48*bis*; SCSL RPE, rr 48 and 49; Rome Statute, Art 64(5); International Criminal Court, Rules of Procedure and Evidence (9 September 2002) ICC-ASP/1/3 and Corr.1, r 136; ECCC Internal Rules, r 89*ter*; STL RPE, r 70.

[19] *Prosecutor v Katanga*, ICC PTC I, 10 March 2008, ICC-01/04-01/07-257, 9. As Linton notes, this is 'the furthest that an international criminal court or tribunal has gone, but it is what is essentially being practiced, and is a justified reading of Rule 136(1)': S Linton, 'Joinder and Severance' in G Sluiter et al (eds), *International Criminal Procedure: Principles and Rules* (Oxford, OUP, 2013) 519.

[20] *Prosecutor v Kayishema*, ICTR TC I, 6 November 1996, ICTR-95-1-T-250, 3.

[21] See, eg *Prosecutor v Yekatom,* ICC PTC II, 20 February 2019, ICC-01/14-01/18-87, paras 8–14.

the *Myanmar/Bangladesh* proceedings relied on Article 119 of the Rome Statute as the legal basis for the Chamber to determine the Prosecutor's request.[22] That Article provides that 'any dispute concerning the judicial functions of the Court shall be settled by the decision of the Court', with the majority finding that the Court 'is clearly subject to a dispute with Myanmar'.[23] One NGO has suggested that the majority position potentially opened up standing. In January 2019, an Israeli-based NGO filed an application whereby it 'seeks to exercise the recently recognized right to intervene in a Situation by virtue of Article 119(1) of the Rome Statute' suggesting a dispute existed as to the Court's judicial functions in the Comoros situation.[24] It argued that 'any interested party' could bring a request to the Court under Article 119 to draw issues to the attention of the Chamber.[25] The OTP asked the Chamber to dismiss the application based on the lack of standing,[26] with the victims and the Government of Comoros supporting the OTP request. The Pre-Trial Chamber agreed and dismissed the application, stating that the decision in *Myanmar/Bangladesh* 'neither established a right for victims' intervention in the proceedings outside the Court's legal framework as suggested by the Applicants, nor has it provided for an automatic right of intervention by any interested entity beyond the scope of the Court's statutory documents'.[27] Instead, the Chamber confirmed that intervention was possible only as an *amicus curiae*. Therefore, in the absence of a specific right to participate, the *amicus curiae* mechanism is the main basis for participation in proceedings, and the mechanism to which we now turn.

III. HISTORY OF *AMICUS CURIAE* PARTICIPATION IN INTERNATIONAL CRIMINAL TRIBUNALS

A. Post WWII Institutions

The instruments establishing the International Military Tribunal (IMT) and the International Military Tribunal for the Far East (Tokyo Tribunal) permitted the judges of each tribunal to draft rules of procedure and evidence. However, the two tribunals operated with a limited set of procedural rules, which did not include a provision enabling the tribunals to receive *amicus curiae* submissions. The IMT and Tokyo Tribunals drew heavily on the adversarial form of trial and

[22] *Request Under Regulation 46(3) of the Regulations of the Court*, ICC PTC I, 6 September 2018, ICC-RoC46(3)-01/18-37-Anx.

[23] ibid, para 28.

[24] *Situation on Registered Vessels of the Union of the Comoros, the Hellenic Republic and the Kingdom of Cambodia*, ICC PTC I, 1 February 2019, ICC-01/13-82, Annex I, para 17.

[25] ibid, para 15.

[26] *Situation on Registered Vessels of the Union of the Comoros, the Hellenic Republic and the Kingdom of Cambodia*, ICC PTC I, 5 February 2019, ICC-01/13-83.

[27] *Situation on Registered Vessels of the Union of the Comoros, the Hellenic Republic and the Kingdom of Cambodia*, ICC PTC I, 14 February 2019, ICC-01/13-89, para 21.

the judges had broad discretion to manage the trial proceedings based on the inherent competence of a judicial organ to manage its own proceedings. This inherent power would also have provided a legal basis for *amicus curiae*, as seen in national and some international practice in chapter two.

B. ICTY, the ICTR and the SCSL

The United Nations Security Council adopted the statute of the International Criminal for the former Yugoslavia (ICTY). The Statute left the judges to draft the rules of procedure and evidence (RPE).[28] The judges of the ICTY were thus responsible for the inclusion of the first formal provision on *amicus curiae* submissions in an international criminal tribunal. Rule 74, which has remained unchanged, was included in the first iteration of the ICTY RPE. It is difficult to trace the history of the rule with no formal drafting record. However, the inclusion of Rule 74 is likely to have been drawn from US and UK experience of the *amicus curiae* (see chapter two), reflecting the heavy US/UK-influence particularly in the early days of the ICTY, including US assistance in drafting the RPE. Morris and Scharf suggest that judges included the *amicus curiae* mechanism in the ICTY RPE partly to address the absence of a mechanism for victim participation. They note: 'To the extent that a victim's interests are not considered to be adequately by the Prosecutor, it may be possible to bring such interests to the attention of the Trial Chamber or the Appeals Chamber with respect to relevant issues by means of an *amicus curiae* brief'.[29] Thus, drafters envisaged the *amicus curiae* as having some representative functions, as well as the provision of expertise.

The ICTR judges based the ICTR RPE on those of the ICTY and included an identical rule – Rule 74.[30] That rule has also remained unchanged since its adoption in 1995. The SCSL RPE, which drew from the procedural framework of the ICTR,[31] included an identical provision, Rule 74. There does not appear to have been discussion as to the inclusion of the *amicus curiae* mechanism in either the ICTR or SCSL RPE. States did not challenge the inclusion of a formal rule permitting *amici curiae* in the procedural frameworks of these tribunals, signalling their acquiescence if not positive consent to the mechanism. The Presidents[32] of the ICTY and the SCSL supplemented the brief formal rule

[28] ICTY Statute, Art 15.

[29] V Morris and MP Scharf, *An Insider's Guide to the International Criminal Tribunal for the Former Yugoslavia* (New York, Transaction Publishers, vol 1, 1995) 167. See also B McGonigle Leyh, *Procedural Justice? Victim Participation in International Criminal Proceedings* (Cambridge, Intersentia, 2011) 137–40.

[30] Drafters arrived at the ICTR RPE by adopting the ICTY RPE, and then allowing the ICTR judges to make necessary amendments: ICTR Statute, Art 14.

[31] Article 14 of the SCSL Statute provided that the judges should apply the ICTR RPE, amended appropriately where the rules do not govern a particular situation. Any amendments were governed by the relevant national criminal procedural code.

[32] The authority to do so stems from the RPE: ICTY RPE, r 19B; SCSL RPE, r 19(c).

on *amicus curiae* participation by practice directions adopted for the ICTY in 1997[33] and for the SCSL in 2004.[34] These practice directions allowed the judges to provide greater procedural content to the brief rule included in the RPE, as discussed further in chapter four. The intention appears to have been to assist potential *amici*, rather than setting out binding requirements. Judges revised the ICTY practice direction in 2015.[35] The ICTR did not adopt a similar practice direction. The RPE adopted for the Residual Mechanism for Criminal Tribunals included a provision identical to Rule 74,[36] but judges have not adopted a practice direction.[37] Similarly, a provision on the *amicus curiae* was included in the RPE for the Residual Special Court for Sierra Leone.[38]

C. International Criminal Court

States established the ICC by treaty and, consequently, there is more information concerning the drafting history of the Rome Statute and the ICC RPE. Unlike the position at other tribunals, the member states drafted the ICC RPE, rather than the judges.[39] This reflects the reduced role given to the ICC judges to develop the legal and procedural framework of the ICC.[40] Australia and the Netherlands produced a draft set of the RPE ahead of negotiations in Rome in 1998, including a provision based on Rule 74 of the ICTY RPE.[41] However, states did not address the RPE in detail until the 1999 preparatory commission, where some states made proposals that addressed the *amicus curiae* mechanism. Costa Rica, for example, noted that 'It is important that the proposed Rules recognize the Court's authority to request or receive reports from States, organizations or individuals in the capacity of *amicus curiae* at any stage of the proceedings, and not only during the trial or the appeal'.[42] A Working Group of the American Bar

[33] International Criminal Tribunal for the Former Yugoslavia, Information Concerning the Submission of *Amicus Curiae* Briefs under Rule 74 (27 March 1997) IT/122.

[34] Special Court for Sierra Leone, Practice Direction on filing *Amicus Curiae* applications pursuant to Rule 74 of Rules of Procedure and Evidence of the Special Court for Sierra Leone (20 October 2004) SCSL-2004-16-T.

[35] Revised 16 February 2015 (IT/122/Rev.1).

[36] Mechanism for International Criminal Tribunals, Rules of Procedure and Evidence (8 June 2012) MICT/1, r 83.

[37] *Amici curiae* are included in the general Practice Direction on Filings made before the Mechanism for International Criminal Tribunals (14 December 2012) MICT/7, but there are no provisions specific to the *amicus curiae*.

[38] Residual Special Court for Sierra Leone, Rules of Procedure and Evidence, r 74.

[39] Rome Statute, Art 51.

[40] See D Hunt, 'The International Criminal Court: High Hopes, "Creative Ambiguity" and an Unfortunate Mistrust in International Judges' (2004) 2 *JICJ* 56; A Appazov, 'International Criminal Court and the Decision-Making Heritage of the Ad Hoc Tribunals: A Study of Judicial Activism' (2016) 3 *Journal of Global Justice and Public Policy* 1, 2.

[41] Draft Set of Rules of Procedure and Evidence for the International Criminal Court, Working Paper by Australia and the Netherlands (17 July1996) A/AC.249/L.2, r 96.

[42] Proposal by Costa Rica concerning the Rules of Procedure and Evidence (24 February 1999) PCNICC/1999/WGRPE/DP.2, para 5.

Association recommended inclusion of a rule permitting *amicus curiae* submissions based on Rule 74 of the ICTY RPE.[43]

A July 1999 discussion paper prepared by the Coordinator for the second session of the preparatory commission included a provision on the *amicus curiae* and other forms of submissions that was more detailed than Rule 74.[44] The proposed rule (Rule 6.6) formed the basis of what eventually became Rule 103. Croatia filed a proposal concerning *amicus curiae* submissions, suggesting that the proposed rule include the statement 'The Chamber shall in every case grant leave to a State to submit orally or in writing its observation concerning issues related to its national interest'.[45] As is discussed further in chapter seven, this proposal reflects Croatia's experience with the ICTY and its failed attempts to secure greater rights of participation in ICTY proceedings where the accused was a Croatian national. Spain and Colombia objected to Croatia's proposal, with Colombia noting that the proposed wording suggested that the Court 'might be ordered to accept the intervention of an *amicus curiae*, a situation that would contradict the principle of discretion on the part of the Court in respect of evidence'.[46] Costa Rica repeated its request for the inclusion of 'at any stage of proceedings' to draft Rule 6.[47] A significant change was the removal of the right of victims and their legal representatives to respond to *amicus curiae* submissions, with this right limited in Rule 103 to the Prosecutor and the defence.[48] However, this amendment occurred in response to revisions to the provisions regulating victim participation more broadly, thus it appears that the right for victims to respond was removed as it was subsumed within broader rights of participation for victims set out elsewhere.

The history of Rule 103 and its inclusion in the ICC RPE is significant for several reasons. First, this is the first instance of states parties drafting an instrument for an international criminal tribunal that expressly incorporates the *amicus curiae*; at other institutions, judges drafted the rules and included provisions on the *amicus curiae*. Rule 103 is therefore a strong signal of state support for the *amicus curiae* mechanism, particularly when contrasted with the opposition of

[43] Draft Rules of Procedure and Evidence for the International Criminal Court Prepared by a Working Group of the American Bar Association Section of International Law and Practice (11 February 1999), available at www.legal-tools.org/doc/6d651c/.

[44] Discussion Paper proposed by the Coordinator, Part 6 of the Rome Statute: The Trial (1 July 1999) PCNICC/1999/WGRPE/RT.5.

[45] Proposal Submitted by Croatia Concerning the Rules of Procedure and Evidence, Rule 6.6 *Amicus Curiae* and Other Forms of Submission (27 July 1999) PCNICC/1999/WGRPE/DP.23.

[46] Proposal submitted by Colombia concerning the Rules of Procedure and Evidence: Comments on the Coordinator's Proposal (29 July 1999) PCNICC/1999/WGRPE/DP.24.

[47] Revised Discussion Paper Proposed by the Coordinator, Part 6 of the Rome Statute: The Trial (6 August 1999) PCNICC/1999/WGRPE/RT.5/Rev.1/Add.1.

[48] A 23 June 2000 Coordinator's Discussion Paper set out proposed rules on victim participation, allowing victims to present their views and concerns to the Chamber and to attend and participate in proceedings under certain conditions. The paper then referred to subsequent amendments required 'as a consequence' of those proposals. See Discussion Paper Proposed by the Coordinator Regarding Rules of Procedure and Evidence Relating to Part 6 of the Rome Statute, Concerning the Trial (23 June 2000) PCNICC/2000/WGRPE(6)/RT.11, 14–16.

states to the mechanism in other regimes explored in chapter two (in particular, the WTO). This includes states with civil law, common law and mixed systems at the national level. We suggest that the limited participatory rights granted to states in the Rome Statute partially explains this strong level of state support. States viewed the *amicus curiae* mechanism as an important procedural mechanism from which they, and not just civil society actors, might benefit.

Secondly, the inclusion of the mechanism reflects the experiences of civil society actors with the *amicus curiae* mechanism at other tribunals, particularly the ICTY and the ICTR, and the increased role of civil society in the Rome negotiations and with the Rome Statute framework generally.[49] As Haddad notes, the Rome Statute system incorporates an unprecedented range of roles for civil society actors.[50] Prominent NGOs have commented that inclusion of a right to participate in proceedings as an *amicus curiae* was a priority for them at Rome and during the drafting of the RPE. For example, Chappell writes that one of the priorities for the Women's Caucus at Rome was to 'embed victim participation and representation provisions at all "appropriate stages of the proceedings"'.[51] As part of this strategy, the Caucus supported the inclusion of an *amicus curiae* provision because such 'submissions provide the court with additional contextual information about the case before it and, as the ICTY and ICTR experience showed, can prove critical to the representation and recognition of the interests of gender and sexual violence victims'.[52] Such actors, then, clearly saw the *amicus curiae* as having a representative as well as an expertise function.

Thirdly, Rule 103 developed in parallel with the rules on victim participation. The broader rights of participation given to victims in the Rome Statute and the RPE removed the need to include specific rights of victims to appear as *amici curiae* or to respond to submissions by *amici*. This thus signalled a shift from the *ad hoc* tribunal approach, where drafters considered the *amicus curiae* mechanism a partial substitute for victim participation. We explore the link between victim participation and the *amicus curiae* mechanism further in section VI(A) below and in chapter five.

Fourthly, the Assembly of States Parties (ASP) offers a different, arguably more transparent, drafting process for the RPE than drafting by the judges. However, it also means that, while the ICC judges can suggest rule changes or additions, the ASP controls amendment of the RPE, including Rule 103. Any amendment of Rule 103 will require political support. This also means that the ASP could

[49] For discussion of the role of civil society in the Rome negotiations, see BN Schiff, *Building the International Criminal Court* (Cambridge, CUP, 2008); M Glasius, *The International Criminal Court: A Global Civil Society Achievement* (Milton Park, Routledge, 2006); and HN Haddad, *The Hidden Hands of Justice: NGOs, Human Rights and International Courts* (Cambridge, CUP, 2018).

[50] Haddad ibid.

[51] L Chappell, *The Politics of Gender Justice at the International Criminal Court: Legacies and Legitimacy* (Oxford, OUP, 2016) 60, quoting Women's Caucus for Gender Justice, Submission to the Standing Committee on Foreign Affairs and International Trade (9 June 1998) 5–6.

[52] ibid, 60; see further 63 referring to Rule 103 as an example of 'how representation is to be performed'.

vary rules in a manner contrary to the wishes of judges. While this may seem of limited concern in relation to the *amicus curiae* mechanism, one need only look to some of the efforts by states at the national level to manage 'strategic litigation' by civil society actors – so-called 'lawfare' – to see the potential risk. Such measures may include limiting standing for certain types of actors or introducing a risk of costs orders imposed against *amici*.[53] If member states were to become disillusioned with the level, form or content of civil society involvement in formal proceedings, one way to restrain such participation would be to amend Rule 103 in a restrictive manner, for example to exclude certain types of actors (NGOs) or to impose express criteria for the admission of *amici curiae*. This would be controversial, particularly as the right to admit *amici curiae* is long established as part the discretionary powers of the judges. Judges and civil society would likely view moves to vary Rule 103 as an attack by the ASP on judicial independence. Given the conservative practice of the Tribunals towards *amici* so far, it also seems unlikely. However, the resistance of states within the WTO to the *amicus curiae* demonstrates there is a chance that states may try to control what is considered to be an unwarranted opening of proceedings to civil society.

The ICC President has not adopted a practice direction on the *amicus curiae*; in fact, the ICC does not issue practice directions. Instead, the ICC judges have adopted regulations of the Court intended to deal with mainly administrative matters.[54] The regulations do not address the *amicus curiae* directly. The judges have also adopted the Chambers practice manual,[55] which captures best practice and guidance for judges to improve consistency in processes between Chambers.[56] While the legal status of the Chamber's Manual is uncertain,[57] and its provisions do not presently address the *amicus curiae* mechanism, the Chambers Practice Manual could offer scope for greater guidance or regulation of the *amicus curiae*, if desirable.

D. STL and ECCC

As with the ICTY, ICTR and SCSL, the STL judges were responsible for drafting the RPE of the STL.[58] The ECCC judges did not have an express power to adopt

[53] eg, in 2015, Parliament in the UK intervened for the first time to deal specifically with certain aspects of third party intervention in judicial review proceedings, with s 87 of the Criminal Justice and Courts Act 2015 providing that, in certain circumstances, the court may order a third party intervener to pay to the parties the costs associated with the intervention. This change was met with dismay by the NGO sector and the judiciary, with many NGOs predicting it would have a chilling effect on intervention and impact the quality of judicial decisions.

[54] Rome Statute, Art 52; International Criminal Court, Regulations of the Court (26 May 2004, as amended on 12 November 2018) ICC-BD/01-05-16.

[55] International Criminal Court, Chambers Practice Manual (February 2016, as updated May 2017).

[56] Y McDermott, 'The International Criminal Court's Chambers Practice Manual: Towards a Return to Judicial Law Making in International Criminal Procedure?' (2017) 15 *JICJ* 873.

[57] ibid.

[58] STL Statute, Art 18.

rules; however, in 2007 the ECCC judges – rather controversially – adopted a document labelled Internal Rules.[59] However, while the judges of the STL and ECCC could draw on international standards when drafting the rules, they were also required to take into account the code of criminal procedure in Lebanon and Cambodia respectively.[60] As both Lebanon and Cambodia are civil law jurisdictions, the STL and the ECCC incorporated significant features not found in previous tribunals, including a role for investigating judges and victim participation. This resulted in procedural rules that differed in substantial ways from those adopted for the ICTY, ICTR and SCSL, although they still reflected an adversarial influence at the trial stage.[61] However, both tribunals were able to have regard to 'other reference materials' reflecting the highest standards of international criminal procedure.[62] As indicated by the President of the STL, this enabled the judges to take account of the RPE of other international criminal tribunals when drafting the rules. He noted that judges 'carefully considered the emerging procedural practice of these other courts and tribunals, and the lessons learned from their experience in conducting international criminal proceedings'.[63]

Both tribunals incorporated a procedural rule recognising the *amicus curiae* mechanism in the first iteration of their respective RPE. In the STL, the provision is Rule 131, while in the ECCC it is Rule 33 of the Internal Rules. Neither the STL Explanatory Memorandum nor the public statements concerning the ECCC Internal Rules expand upon the inclusion of these provisions. However, given the absence of this mechanism in the domestic legal systems of Lebanon and Cambodia,[64] it is reasonable to assume that the judges drew these provisions from the RPE of other institutions, all of which included a formal rule addressing *amicus curiae* participation.[65] Both provisions have remained unchanged

[59] Under the Cambodian Constitution, the Assembly is the only actor capable of adopting laws, so scholars have argued the Internal Rules were adopted *ultra vires*. See, eg G Acquaviva, 'New Paths in International Criminal Justice? The Internal Rules of the Cambodian Extraordinary Chambers' (2008) 6 *JICJ* 129; S Starygin, 'Internal Rules of the Extraordinary Chambers in the Courts of Cambodia (ECCC): Setting an Example of the Rule of Law by Breaking the Law?' (2011) 3 *Journal of Law and Conflict Resolution* 20.

[60] Agreement Between the United Nations and the Royal Government of Cambodia Concerning the Prosecution under Cambodian Law of Crimes Committed During the Period of the Democratic Kampuchea (adopted 6 June 2003), Art 4 – shall apply procedural rules that 'are in accordance with Cambodian law'; STL Statute, Art 28(2) – the judges 'shall be guided by' the Lebanese Code of Criminal Procedure.

[61] M Gillet, and M Schuster, 'The Special Tribunal for Lebanon Swiftly Adopts its Rules of Procedure and Evidence' (2009) 7 *JICJ* 885, 887.

[62] STL Statute, Art 28. Article 12(1) of the ECCC Agreement allows guidance to be sought in international standards where Cambodian law is silent, its interpretation or application is uncertain, or there is a concern that the local law is inconsistent with international standards. See G Sluiter, 'Due Process and Criminal Procedure in the Cambodian Extraordinary Chambers' (2006) 4 *JICJ* 314.

[63] Special Tribunal for Lebanon, Explanatory Memorandum by the Tribunal's President (5 June 2009) para 1.

[64] See Starygin (n 59) for specific discussion of the *amicus curiae* in the Internal Rules.

[65] See Gillet and Schuster (n 61), 887: the STL RPE 'draw heavily on analogous instruments' like the ICC and ICTY/R. Starygin (n 59) also suggests that this internal rule is derived from the practice of other tribunals.

in subsequent revisions of the rules, although judges did supplement the STL provision with a practice direction.[66] At the ECCC, a further reference to *amici curiae* was included in the first revision of the Internal Rules, on 1 February 2008, which empowered the co-investigating judges to make decisions in the Closing Order regarding sealed items and 'for this purpose' the co-investigating judge may 'grant leave or invite the submission of *amicus curiae* briefs'.[67] A similar reference to the *amicus curiae* was included in Rule 99, where the Chamber can make decisions as to sealed documents following a final judgment.[68] The ECCC has not adopted a tribunal-wide practice direction concerning *amici curiae*; however, the Supreme Court Chamber has provided general guidance to potential *amici*,[69] while the co-investigating judges and other Chambers have done so in specific instances (see chapter four).

E. Other Hybrid and Internationalised Courts

It is not our intent to survey here the practice of the increasing number of hybrid and internationalised tribunals; our focus is limited to the above six tribunals. However, we have included details of the availability of the mechanism in other institutions to identify whether there is a uniform approach to the *amicus curiae* and the possible transplantation of the concept between the international and national level. The institutions largely reflect a distinction between civil law and common law, although as the extent of internationalisation increases, so does the likelihood an *amicus curiae* provision is included. Inclusion of an *amicus curiae* provision is also more likely the more recent a tribunal is or where lawyers from common law systems or with previous experience at the Tribunals have been involved in drafting the rules of procedure and evidence.

Several institutions did not contain a provision concerning the *amicus curiae* in their founding instruments. The specialist mixed panels for Timor Leste and Kosovo were both based on civil law systems and did not introduce a provision on *amici curiae*, although the instruments for the SPSC drew heavily on the Rome Statute. Similarly, the Bosnian War Crimes Chamber, CAR Specialist Chamber and the Extraordinary African Chambers (EAC), all embedded in a national civil law legal system, did not include a provision on the *amicus curiae*. As we saw in chapter two, the absence of a formal provision does not necessarily preclude the tribunal accepting *amicus curiae* submissions. For example, a number of academics and gender advocates submitted a brief on sexual and

[66] Special Tribunal for Lebanon, Practice Direction on *Amicus Curiae* Submissions Before the Special Tribunal for Lebanon (23 February 2012) STL/PD/2012/05.

[67] ECCC Internal Rules, r 67, added in Revision 1 to the Internal Rules (1 February 2008).

[68] ibid, r 99, introduced in Revision 1 to the Internal Rules (1 February 2008).

[69] Extraordinary Chambers in the Courts of Cambodia, Information Concerning the Submission of *Amicus Curiae* Briefs to the Supreme Court Chamber of the ECCC (7 March 2011).

gender-based violence to the Trial Chamber of the EAC.[70] Consistent with the absence of an articulated legal basis for accepting the brief and the uncertainty of its status, the Chambers did not formally accept the brief, although the President of the Chambers acknowledged receipt. The brief was available to the parties, who referred to its contents. In the absence of rules addressing the ability to file *amicus* submissions, the legal status of the brief was uncertain and the Chamber did not invoke its inherent powers to accept the brief. However, the brief appeared to have some impact, with the Trial Chamber re-characterising the charges to include sexual and gender-based violence, with parts of the judgment clearly influenced by the brief.[71]

Several tribunals do include provisions recognising *amici curiae*. The International Crimes Division (ICD) of the High Court of Uganda adopted its own rules of procedure and evidence in 2016, which includes a provision allowing the Trial Chamber to accept briefs from *amici curiae* 'if necessary'.[72] In 2017, a team from Berkeley University's International Human Rights Law Clinic, professors from Makerere University, and Richard Goldstone (a former ICTY and ICTR Prosecutor and South African Constitutional Court judge) prepared an *amicus curiae* brief addressing the ICD's potential reliance upon customary international law in the *Thomas Kwoyelo* case.[73] This is consistent with national practice: as a common law jurisdiction, the *amicus curiae* procedure has been available to Ugandan courts for many years.[74]

The RPE for the Iraqi Higher Tribunal (IHT) provided a Chamber could accept submissions from interveners 'if it considers it desirable for the proper determination of the case'.[75] The inclusion of this provision is perhaps unsurprising given the influence of the ICTY RPE and the level of US legal assistance provided to the IHT, including in drafting the statute and RPE.[76] There is an

[70] *Prosecutor v Habré* (Rape and Other Forms of Sexual Violence as Crimes Against Humanity, War Crimes and Torture Under Customary International Law, *Amicus Curiae* Brief of the Human Rights Center at the University of California, Berkeley, School of Law, and International Experts on Sexual Violence Under International Criminal Law) (8 December 2015), available at www.law.berkeley.edu/wp-content/uploads/2015/04/MICUS-CURIAE-BRIEF-OF-THE-HUMAN-RIGHTS-CENTER-AT-THE-UNIVERSITY-OF-CALIFORNIA-BERKELEY-SCHOOL-OF-LAW-AND-INTERNATIONAL-EXPERTS-ON-SEXUAL-VIOLENCE-UNDER-INTERNATIONAL-CRIMINAL-LAW-Eng.pdf.

[71] S Williams, 'Hybrid Courts and *Amicus Curiae* Briefing' in S Weill, KT Seelinger and KB Carlson (eds), *Prosecuting the President: The Trial of Hissen Habré* (Oxford, OUP, forthcoming 2019).

[72] The Judicature (High Court) (International Crimes Division) Rules, SI 2016 No 40, r 25(2).

[73] KT Seelinger, 'Uganda's Case of Thomas Kwoyelo: Customary International Law on Trial' (2017) 8 *Californian Law Review* 19, 19.

[74] See J Oloka-Onyango and C Mbazira, 'Befriending the Judiciary: Behind and Beyond the 2016 Supreme Court *Amicus Curiae* Rulings in Uganda' (2016) 1 *African Journal of Comparative Constitutional Law* 1.

[75] Iraqi High Criminal Court Rules for Proceedings and Evidence Gathering (18 October 2005), r 46; the earlier version of the rules for the Iraqi Special Tribunal included a similar provision: Iraqi Special Tribunal Rules of Procedure and Evidence (31 December 2003), r 70.

[76] MP Scharf, 'The Iraqi High Tribunal A Viable Experiment in International Justice?' (2007) 5 *JICJ* 258, 259; M Newton and M Scharf, *Enemy of the State: The Trial and Execution of Saddam Hussein* (New York, St Martin's Press, 2008).

example of at least one request for intervention, with Louise Arbour as UN High Commissioner for Human Rights requesting leave to intervene in the sentencing of Taha Yassin Ramadan.[77] It is not clear what happened to that brief, although it did not have any obvious impact on the outcome as Ramadan was executed.

In drafting the RPE of the Kosovo Specialist Chambers,[78] the judges were to be 'guided by the Kosovo Criminal Procedure Code 2012',[79] although they were influenced by the rules at the international tribunals.[80] The RPE incorporate a provision addressing *amici curiae* in similar terms to Rule 103 ICC RPE.[81] The KSC RPE also introduces for the first time an institutional actor able to act as an *amicus curiae*: the Ombudsperson of the Specialist Chambers (OSC). Under the RPE, the OSC 'shall act independently to monitor, defend and protect the fundamental rights and freedoms enshrined in Chapter II of the Constitution of persons interacting with the Specialist Chambers and Specialist Prosecutor's Office in accordance with the Law and the Rules'.[82] The inclusion of this office was required as both the KSC and the Specialist Prosecutor's Office have been established under the law of Kosovo and are public authorities for the purpose of the Constitution.[83] The Ombudsperson does not have a general right to intervene, but may do so when given permission to participate as an *amicus curiae*.[84]

Adaptation of the *amicus curiae* mechanism is also evident in other contexts. The Special Jurisdiction for Peace (JEP) in Colombia, established pursuant to the Final Peace Agreement,[85] initially included foreign lawyers alongside domestic counterparts.[86] While Colombian judges would have been in the majority, the Colombian Revolutionary Armed Forces-Popular Army (FARC) and the government supported the inclusion of international judges as a way of ensuring the

[77] *In the Matter of Sentencing of Taha Yassin Ramadan*, Application for Leave to Intervene as *Amicus Curiae* and Application in Intervention as *Amicus Curiae* of United National Commissioner for Human Rights (8 February 2007), available at http://online.wsj.com/public/resources/documents/tribunal20070207.pdf.

[78] For an overview of the Specialist Chambers, see S Williams, 'The Specialist Chambers of Kosovo: The Limits of Internationalization?' (2016) 14 *JICJ* 25.

[79] Law on Specialist Chambers and Specialist Prosecutor's Office (2015) Law No 05/L-053, Art 19(2).

[80] For further discussion, see A Heinze, 'The Kosovo Specialist Chambers' Rules of Procedure and Evidence A Diamond Made Under Pressure?' (2017) 15 *JICJ* 985.

[81] Rules of Procedure and Evidence Before the Kosovo Specialist Chambers (17 March 2017), r 67. The rules also include an *amicus curiae* provision for proceedings before the Specialist Chamber of the Constitutional Court: KSC RPE, Part II, r 16.

[82] KSC RPE, Art 28.

[83] KSC Law, Art 34(9). See E Cimiotta, 'The Specialist Chambers and the Specialist Prosecutor's Office in Kosovo: The "Regionalization" of International Criminal Justice in Context' (2016) 14 *JICJ* 53.

[84] KSC RPE, Art 29(1).

[85] Final Agreement to End the Conflict and Establish a Stable and Long-lasting Peace (24 November 2016), available at www.altocomisionadoparalapaz.gov.co/procesos-y-conversaciones/Documentos%20compartidos/24-11-2016NuevoAcuerdoFinal.pdf. For an overview, see H Olasolo and JMF Ramirez Mendoza, 'The Colombian Integrated System of Truth, Justice, Reparation and Non-Repetition' (2017) 15 *JICJ* 1011.

[86] Joint Communiqué # 60 Regarding the Agreement for the Creation of a Special Jurisdiction for Peace (adopted 23 September 2015), para 3; see Olasolo and Mendoza (n 85), 1027.

tribunal would issue case law consistent with international standards. However, due to opposition, drafters removed the requirement for international judges, replaced by a requirement to appoint foreign lawyers as *amici curiae*.[87] The *amici curiae* are appointed in advance to specific chambers, but will participate only where invited to do so by the Chamber. They are then able to participate in deliberations in a similar manner to the judges, but without the right to vote. This model is different to the traditional notion of the *amicus curiae* and the mechanism as seen in the Tribunals to date. While the function of the *amici curiae* in the JEP remains that of providing expert assistance to the judges, their participatory role and the potential influence they are able to exert goes beyond anything we see in our study. The *amici curiae* are more similar to embedded legal experts or consultants, appointed by the body responsible for judicial appointments, and actively involved in judicial decision-making. In practice, it may be that the *amici* act in a more limited fashion, much closer to the traditional model, but having been appointed through a more extensive and thorough selection process and with institutional standing. Regardless, the creation of a model for institutionalising the *amicus curiae* function may provide a useful precedent for other tribunals.

F. Conclusion

This analysis of the history of the *amicus curiae* mechanism demonstrates that judges, states and civil society recognise the power of judges to accept submissions from *amici curiae*. Even though this power was not used at the IMT and IMTFE, the power was gradually formalised, most likely due to the influence of UK and US lawyers and judges drafting the ICTY RPE, which then provided the basis for the RPE of the ICTR and SCSL and influenced the adoption of the STL RPE and the ECCC Internal Rules. Importantly, states did not object to the inclusion of a provision for *amici curiae*, other than to argue it should give wider rights for states. States formalised this tacit consent when they adopted Rule 103 of the ICC RPE. It is evident that inclusion of a provision enabling *amicus curiae* participation has become 'best practice' in international criminal procedure, with such provisions found in the procedures of hybrid and internationalised criminal tribunals. Moreover, even tribunals that do not expressly include a provision on *amici curiae* – for example the EAC – have engaged with *amici* to an extent.

This leads to four important conclusions. First, the *amicus curiae* mechanism – at least at present – functions both as part of the inherent powers of

[87] Final Agreement, para 65. For a more extensive discussion of this mechanism, see: K Ambos and S Adoueldahab, 'Foreign Jurists in the Colombian Special Jurisdiction for Peace: A New Concept of *Amicus Curiae*?' (*EJIL: Talk!*, 19 December 2017), available at www.ejiltalk.org/foreign-jurists-in-the-colombian-special-jurisdiction-for-peace-a-new-concept-of-amicus-curiae/.

the tribunal and on the basis of state consent. This wide acceptance by states of the mechanism contrasts to the position in other international institutions, in particular the ICJ and WTO. Secondly, if the UK and US legal systems and regional human rights mechanisms influenced early adoption of the *amicus curiae*, the mechanism is now well-established in international criminal procedure. Thirdly, there is limited information available in the drafting histories of the provisions addressing *why* the provision has been included. The drafting history of Rule 103 ICC RPE suggests that both state and civil society actors supported its inclusion, which indicates that these actors see some value in the mechanism. Similarly, judges at other tribunals have incorporated the provision into the RPE, so judges must see a role for the mechanism; however, it is rare for judges to comment on the normative basis for the inclusion of the rule. Fourthly, the consistency in the inclusion of a provision on *amici curiae* in the instruments of the Tribunals suggests that the *amicus curiae* mechanism as initially envisaged in Rule 74 has emerged as 'best practice'. In contrast, we see more variation and local adaptation concerning the *amicus curiae* in hybrid and internationalised tribunals, which is not surprising given the closer links to the national legal systems and procedures.

IV. THE *AMICUS CURIAE* PROSECUTOR AND THE PROSECUTOR AS *AMICUS CURIAE*

A. The *Amicus Curiae* Prosecutor

The RPE of three of the Tribunals include the mechanism of the *amicus curiae* prosecutor in relation to contempt proceedings.[88] For example, where a Chamber considers that the Prosecutor may have a conflict of interest with respect to the relevant conduct, Rule 77 of the ICTY RPE provides for the Chamber to direct the Registrar to appoint an *amicus curiae* 'to investigate the matter and report back to the Chamber as to whether there are sufficient grounds for instigating contempt proceedings'. Where the Chamber considers there are sufficient grounds to proceed against a person for contempt, one option is for it to direct the *amicus curiae* to prosecute the matter. Chambers have appointed *amicus curiae* prosecutors in contempt proceedings on several occasions.[89]

In contrast, the ICC RPE are silent as to the appointment of *amicus curiae* prosecutors, with Rule 165 permitting the Prosecutor to investigate contempt proceedings under Article 70 on his or her own initiative. This suggests that the Prosecutor has the primary responsibility for initiating contempt investigations,

[88] STL RPE, r 60*bis*; ICTR RPE, r 77; ICTY RPE, r 77.

[89] See *Prosecutor v Hartmann*, IT-02-54-R77.5; *Prosecutor v Maglov*, IT-99-36-R77; *Prosecutor v Šešelj* IT-03-67-R77.2 (no 1), IT-03-67-R77.3 (no 2).

although the Chamber must retain residual jurisdiction as part of its inherent jurisdiction to manage its own proceedings. The Code of Conduct for the Office of the Prosecutor requires the Prosecutor to disclose and manage potential conflicts of interest within the Office, which would presumably extend to making the Chamber aware of any conflicts in relation to contempt proceedings.[90] The Chamber should manage any likely conflicts concerning the role of the OTP in contempt proceedings, which could extend to the appointment of an *amicus* prosecutor. In the proceedings concerning Kenya, defence counsel for Mr Ruto requested the Trial Chamber appoint 'an *amicus* prosecutor to investigate, with a view to initiating criminal prosecution, OTP witnesses, OTP intermediaries, and possibly ICC staff members, for offences against the administration of justice, contrary to Article 70'.[91] While the Trial Chamber ultimately declined to exercise jurisdiction on the merits of the application, the Chamber did not reject the argument that it had jurisdiction to consider allegations of misconduct on the part of the Prosecution or prosecution witnesses and, if appropriate, to appoint an *amicus curiae* prosecutor.[92]

The use of the term *amicus curiae* in this context is confusing and, we argue, a misuse of the term. Applying a functional approach, the *amicus* prosecutor does not perform any of the functions we have identified *amici* as performing. At best, the *amicus curiae* prosecutor could be characterised as representing the broader institutional and stakeholder interest in the proper functioning of the Court and its proceedings. We recommend that a different term should be preferred to distinguish this role properly from that of the *amicus curiae*, particularly as there is no normative justification for using the term *amicus curiae*. This was the approach adopted in the RPE of the SCSL, with the equivalent provision referring to the appointment of 'an experienced independent counsel' rather than an *amicus curiae*.[93] Accordingly, we have excluded the appointment of *amicus curiae* prosecutors from this study.

B. The Prosecutor as *Amicus Curiae*

The Prosecutor is a party to proceedings and does not need to rely on the *amicus curiae* to participate. There are two exceptions to this: first, where the prosecution may seek to participate in reparations proceedings at the ICC[94] and, secondly, in contempt proceedings. For example, the SCSL admitted the prosecution as an *amicus curiae* at the sentencing phase of contempt

[90] International Criminal Court Office of the Prosecutor, Code of Conduct for the Office of the Prosecutor (5 September 2013), s 9.

[91] *Prosecutor v Ruto and Sang*, ICC TC V(A), 2 May 2016, ICC-01/09-01/11-2028-Red, para 1.

[92] *Prosecutor v Ruto and Sang*, ICC TC V(A), 2 June 2016, ICC-01/09-01/11-2034.

[93] SCSL RPE, r 77(c)(iii).

[94] The Prosecutor is not a party in reparations proceedings, although may participate under r 103: see ch 4, s VII.

proceedings concerning interference with prosecution witnesses during trial. The prosecution based its request on its 'strong interest' in the matter given that 'these proceedings are inextricably linked to the continuing need to protect witnesses who bore testimony' and that its submissions on sentencing practices would assist the contempt judge.[95] In approving the request, the contempt judge specifically noted the interest of the prosecution and the assistance the submissions would offer, although the judge precluded the prosecution from addressing the particular circumstances of the case.[96] Thus, it appears that in this instance, the OTP was acting in a combined representative and expertise role.

Although the Rome Statute, the RPE and the OTP Regulations do not provide any express legal basis for the ICC Prosecutor to make submissions before other institutions, there is one example of the ICC Prosecutor filing a brief as an *amicus curiae* in a national jurisdiction. In September 2017, the President of the Constitutional Court of Colombia invited the ICC Prosecutor as an *amicus curiae* to present her opinion of the legislation that implemented the Special Jurisdiction for Peace (JEP) (see above), which was the subject of constitutional review.[97] The Prosecutor submitted her brief in October 2017, stating:[98]

> In light of the close working relationship that the Office of the Prosecutor has with the Colombian State and its national authorities, the Prosecutor presents, through this document, the points of view of the Office of the Prosecutor on certain aspects of the JEP, hoping that the information will be useful for the Constitutional Court. The presentation of the Prosecutor's Office is aimed at contributing to the analysis of national legislation by the Constitutional Court, insofar as it raises issues of consistency and compatibility with customary international law and the Rome Statute.

The Prosecutor's submission addressed four key aspects of the JEP: 'the definition of command responsibility; the definition of grave war crimes; the determination of "active or determining participation" in the crimes; and the implementation of sentences involving the "effective restriction of freedoms and rights"'.[99]

The Constitutional Court issued its decisions on the constitutionality of the JEP in 2018, finding the laws constitutionally valid. While the Constitutional Court addressed three of the issues raised by the Prosecutor in her brief – command responsibility, the definition of grave war crimes and sentencing – it did

[95] *Prosecutor v Senessie*, SCSL TC II, 22 June 2012, SCSL-11-01-T-014, para 3.

[96] *Prosecutor v Senessie*, SCSL TC II, 25 June 2012, SCSL-11-01-T-015.

[97] International Criminal Court Office of the Prosecutor, 'Report on Preliminary Examination Activities 2017' (4 December 2017) paras 152–53, available at www.icc-cpi.int/itemsDocuments/2017-PE-rep/2017-otp-rep-PE_ENG.pdf.

[98] ibid, para 153. See International Criminal Court Office of the Prosecutor, 'Escrito de *Amicus Curiae* de la Fiscal de la Corte Penal Internacional Sobre la Jurisdicción Especial Para la Paz: Ante la Corte Constitucional de la República de Colombia,' (18 October 2017), para 1, available at http://cr00.epimg.net/descargables/2017/10/21/17135b6061c7a5066ea86fe7e37ce26a.pdf?int=masinfo (unofficial translation, original in Spanish).

[99] ibid, para 2.

not directly endorse the Prosecutor's arguments.[100] The Prosecutor has noted that constitutional challenges, as well as legislative and other initiatives at the national level, 'that could result in delays in bringing perpetrators to account, restrict the scope and thoroughness of investigations into complex crimes and, overall, call into question the genuineness of the proceedings, are of great interest to the Office to the extent it may impact on the admissibility of potential cases pertaining to state agents'.[101] Therefore, we may see the Prosecutor participating as an *amicus curiae* in future national proceedings. However, we suggest that the Prosecutor should exercise care in doing so, and should do so only by invitation and within areas of particular expertise (that is, the Prosecutor should fulfil an expertise function only). Otherwise, there is a risk that such submissions may politicise the *amicus curiae* role and be perceived as the Prosecutor trying to force particular views on national jurisdictions. There may also be an implication for the resources if the OTP is to file *amicus curiae* briefs regularly in national proceedings.

V. LIMITS ON *AMICUS CURIAE* PARTICIPATION

There are two essential limits to the admission of *amici curiae* that flow from the criminal nature of proceedings before the Tribunals – the requirement that *amicus curiae* participation must not interfere unduly with: (1) the core judicial competence of the tribunal; and (2) the right of the accused to a fair and expeditious trial. We outline these criteria briefly here, while chapter four considers the extent to which the criteria applied by Chambers when admitting *amici curiae* reflect these limits.

A. Core Judicial Competence

As indicated in the comparative practice discussed in chapter two, the purpose of the *amicus curiae* is to assist the judges in reaching their decision by providing expertise or by representing interests that would not otherwise be before the Court. The *amicus curiae* clearly relates to the core functions of the judges. In civil law systems, this inherent judicial competence is referred to as '*jura novit cura*'. In common law systems, while there is no equivalent term, we expect judges to be able to follow the arguments of the parties and to identify and apply the law.[102] Judges at the Tribunals should fulfil two core judicial

[100] International Criminal Court Office of the Prosecutor, 'Report on Preliminary Examination Activities 2018' (5 December 2017), paras 153–59, available at www.icc-cpi.int/itemsDocuments/181205-rep-otp-PE-ENG.pdf.

[101] ibid, para 159.

[102] See discussion in C Davidson, 'Explaining Inhumanity: The Use of Crime-Definition Experts at International Criminal Courts' (2015) 48 *Vanderbilt Journal of Transnational Law* 359, 363.

competencies: to know the relevant law and – in the absence of juries – to determine the individual criminal responsibility of an accused.

The qualifications required for judges recognise these two core competencies. The Rome Statute is the most prescriptive in terms of requiring specific expertise in judicial appointments and provides for a balance of judges selected from two 'lists'. List A includes judges with 'established competence in criminal law and procedure, and the necessary relevant experience, whether as judge, prosecutor, advocate or in other similar capacity, in criminal proceedings'. List B comprises judges with 'established competence in relevant areas of international law such as international humanitarian law and the law of human rights, and extensive experience in a professional legal capacity which is of relevance to the judicial work of the Court'.[103] Drawing on the experience of the ICTY and the ICTR, the Rome Statute prioritises judges with criminal trial experience, rather than expertise in relevant areas of international law. Although drafters recognise the need for both forms of competence, criminal experience is considered more useful. As Bohlander states: 'This shows … a common-sense approach to the necessities of judging in the international arena: Trial experience cannot be gained from reading, knowledge of international law can and, if need be, from hearing experts as *amicus curiae*'.[104]

Judges at the Tribunals are required to know (or to be able to ascertain) the law, including with the help of the parties, institutional actors and research assistants. The Tribunals draw on a different, although sometimes overlapping, body of applicable law to their international – and national – counterparts: international criminal law and procedure; international humanitarian law; public international law; human rights law; and general principles of criminal law. The Tribunals deal with specific international crimes: war crimes, crimes against humanity, genocide and aggression that have specific contextual elements, requiring an assessment of a broader range of contextual evidence than is normally required in a criminal trial at the domestic level. Moreover, the substantive crimes may raise novel legal issues, either because judges have not previously considered these issues, or because significant issues remain unresolved.[105] Modes of liability are particularly significant in the Tribunals, due to the focus on senior leaders and those most responsible for the commission of international crimes, whereas national courts tend to focus on direct perpetrators. The Tribunals must develop and apply complex and often unfamiliar principles to establish liability,

[103] Rome Statute, Art 36(3)(b).

[104] M Bohlander, 'The International Criminal Judiciary: Problems of Judicial Selection, Independence and Ethics' in M Bohlander (ed), *International Criminal Justice: A Critical Analysis of Institutions and Procedures* (London, Cameron May, 2007) 356.

[105] For discussion of the role of tribunals in clarifying international law, see M Cupido, 'Facing Facts in International Criminal Law: A Casuistic Model of Judicial Reasoning' (2016) 14 *JICJ* 1; R Aloisi and J Meernik, *Judgment Day: Judicial Decision Making at the International Criminal Tribunals* (Cambridge, CUP, 2017). In relation to specific crimes, see, eg WA Schabas, 'Judicial Activism and the Crime of Genocide' in S Darcy and J Powderly (eds), *Judicial Creativity at the International Criminal Tribunals* (Oxford, OUP, 2010).

including indirect perpetration, command and superior responsibility and joint criminal enterprise.[106] The temporal jurisdiction of some international criminal tribunals, particularly those considering 'historic' violence or in situations where the violence has been ongoing for several decades requires an assessment of the legality of conduct at the national and international level often several decades previously to satisfy the principle of *nullum crimen sine lege*.

International crimes generally occur in a complex context, with historical, social and political dimensions. The crimes will have been committed in the territory of a state, and most – if not all – of the judges will have no experience of or familiarity with the context or the national legal system.[107] Judges may therefore need educating about the relevant national legal, social and political systems and structures that may be relevant to their judicial determination, both as to the substantive crimes but also concerning related issues such as cooperation, jurisdiction and admissibility. Judges are called upon to consider aspects of national law (whether of one state or of national legal systems), in particular national criminal law and procedure. The procedural framework is also a unique blend of adversarial and inquisitorial approaches, which may require judges to apply national procedural law, only referring to international rules where national law is silent or inconsistent. Many introduce unfamiliar mechanisms, for example, the need to incorporate victim participation and to design and implement reparations mandates. These are all new challenges, the resolution of which may go well beyond the normal 'comfort' zone of judges and personnel and may require additional sources of expertise.

The need for assistance may also be linked to the resources available to judges. While judges at the ICC have access to research and drafting support in Chambers, and the OTP has access to resources and experts,[108] there is still a clear role for the *amicus curiae* to play in terms of assisting judges to know the law. In other tribunals, particularly the hybrids, where support for both parties and Chamber was lower, there may be more of a need for judges to receive assistance from external actors as *amici curiae*.[109] The SCSL Appeals Chamber indicated that:[110]

> Sitting as we do in Freetown, albeit with the benefit of the Internet and of capable resident lawyers, we can nevertheless be assisted by outside counsel provided at its own expense by an organization with a legitimate interest in the subject matter of our hearings.

[106] For how judges have approached these issues, see R Cryer, 'The Ad Hoc Tribunals and the Law of Command Responsibility: A Quiet Earthquake' in S Darcy and J Powderly (eds), *Judicial Creativity at the International Criminal Tribunals* (Oxford, OUP, 2010); M Shahabuddeen 'Judicial Creativity and Joint Criminal Enterprise' in S Darcy and J Powderly (eds), *Judicial Creativity at the International Criminal Tribunals* (Oxford, OUP, 2010).

[107] This excludes, of course, national judges sitting on hybrid tribunals such as the SCSL, STL and ECCC.

[108] Rome Statute, Art 42(9).

[109] S Williams and H Woolaver, 'The Role of the *Amicus Curiae* before International Criminal Tribunals' (2006) 6(2) *ICLR* 151.

[110] *Prosecutor v Kallon*, SCSL AC, 1 November 2003, SCSL-2003-07-PT-128, para 5.

We explore the *amicus curiae* practice in chapter four to examine the extent to which – and how – *amici curiae* have assisted the tribunals to 'know the law'.

The second core competence of international criminal judges is to act as a trier of fact, to assess the evidence presented impartially and independently and determine the individual criminal responsibility of the accused. This is an important limit on *amicus curiae* participation. This is not to say that judges do not require expert advice concerning evidence. As a criminal tribunal, like their national criminal counterparts, the Tribunals require factual evidence (detailed witness and documentary evidence) and scientific evidence, for example forensic evidence, that the parties should provide to the Chamber. However, the Tribunals also require knowledge and evidence from the social sciences: historians; anthropologists; military experts; political scientists; journalists; occasionally lawyers; and increasingly experts in social media and data. Such evidence may be required to establish the broader context to the crimes, including the contextual elements of the crimes themselves (eg, the existence of an armed conflict or the widespread or systematic nature of an attack against a civilian population). It may also be required to demonstrate elements of the crimes, for example, whether a target group is an ethnic group and therefore protected under the definition of genocide. Evidence may address the individual responsibility of the accused; for example, a military adviser may provide details as to command and control models to establish command responsibility. The Tribunals require access to a broad range of knowledge and expertise including from *amicus curiae* submissions that would assist the Chamber with accessing or interpreting these additional forms of expertise. It will usually be for the parties to provide this expertise to the Chamber, including by relying on their own experts and calling expert witnesses (see section VI(C)). In criminal proceedings, the submissions of *amici curiae* should not constitute evidence against the accused or make submissions on the facts or on issues directly relevant to the individual criminal responsibility of the accused. However, it should also be recalled that that the Tribunals, sitting without juries, employ professional judges, with many having experience in criminal trials. Rules on the admissibility of evidence are more flexible than in many national systems, with evidence being admissible but the judges left to determine the probative value of evidence and to decide what weight, if any, to accord to it.[111] Similarly, a Chamber can accept an *amicus curiae* submission, even if it addresses responsibility, but is under no obligation to consider or to give the submission any weight.

B. Defence Rights: The Counterbalance to Participation

As a criminal institution, as with their national counterparts, the Tribunals must protect and respect the fair trial rights of the accused. Fair trial rights

[111] See, eg Rome Statute, Art 69.

include the right to: a public hearing; a fair hearing conducted impartially; to be tried without undue delay; to be informed about the charges; to have adequate time and facilities to prepare a defence; to be present at trial and to conduct the trial in person or with legal assistance; to examine witnesses; appropriate translation and interpretation facilities; the presumption of innocence; not to be compelled to testify and with no inferences drawn from choosing to remain silent; to make an unsworn statement; and not to face any reversal of the burden of proof.[112] Chapter two showed that national jurisdictions are cautious in permitting participation by actors other than the parties (and sometimes victims) in criminal proceedings, particularly at the trial phase, due to the risks this raises for the fair trial rights of the accused. As detailed in chapter four, the provisions addressing *amicus curiae* participation do not specifically refer to fair trial rights. However, judges have specific obligations to protect fair trial rights that would also affect the admission of *amici curiae*.[113] Chapter four explores how Chambers have managed the risk to fair trial posed by *amicus curiae* participation.

VI. THE *AMICUS CURIAE* AND OTHER MECHANISMS FOR EXPERTISE, REPRESENTATION AND COMMUNICATION

We have already mentioned the ability of actors, including NGOs, states and individuals to provide information to the Prosecutor under Article 15 of the Rome Statute.[114] Although an Article 15 communication creates no participatory rights, the organisation submitting the communication will at a minimum have the communication acknowledged and will be notified of the outcome of the Prosecutor's consideration of the material. Article 15 therefore remains an important mechanism for getting information, including legal expertise, to the Prosecutor.[115] In addition, the Prosecutor may appoint 'advisers with legal expertise on specific issues'.[116] This section discusses some of the other specific mechanisms for participation that exist alongside the *amicus curiae*: (1) victim participation; (2) representations in reparations proceedings at the ICC; (3) expert witnesses; and (4) institutional actors. We discuss rights of participation for states in jurisdiction, admissibility and non-cooperation proceedings in chapter seven. We have not identified any mechanisms that perform a communicative function. The closest mechanisms we can identify are Article 15 communications and the role of the Assembly of States Parties at the

[112] This list draws from Arts 66 and 67 of the Rome Statute.
[113] eg Rome Statute, Art 64(2).
[114] ICTY Statute, Art 18; ICTR Statute, Art 17.
[115] Williams (n 13).
[116] Rome Statute, Art 42(9). For discussion of this power, see A Overton and D Rothe, 'The International Criminal Court and the External Non-Witness Expert(s), Problematic Concerns: An Exploratory Endeavour' (2010) 10(3) *ICLR* 345.

ICC (ASP); however, neither gives rise to rights to participate in proceedings. Chapter seven discusses the ASP as an alternative forum for states to raise legal and institutional concerns, rather than attempting to do so through *amicus curiae* submissions.

A. Participation of Victims

i. Overview

The IMT, Tokyo tribunal, the *ad hoc* tribunals and the SCSL applied an instrumental approach to participation, with victims involved in proceedings only as witnesses and only when called by one of the parties. As noted in section III(B), drafters of the ICTY RPE viewed the *amicus curiae* as a possible mechanism for victims wishing to place their particular perspective before the Chamber. Yet, victims generally did not apply directly as *amici curiae* at the ICTY, ICTR or SCSL. Nor did civil society actors, particularly NGOs, regularly seek to represent particular victims or groups of victims directly as *amici curiae*. Therefore, at the ICTY, ICTR and SCSL, the prosecution largely represented the interests of victims.

The Rome Statute adopts a more rights-based approach, and incorporates a shift towards specific rights and procedures for victim participation.[117] The ECCC[118] and the STL[119] also incorporate rights for victims to participate in proceedings, both influenced by their grounding in the civil law systems of Cambodia and Lebanon, which recognise participation by civil parties. Although the legal framework and modalities of participation vary between each of these institutions, this suggests an emerging consensus that victims should have a right to participate in proceedings in international criminal tribunals, rather than relying on general mechanisms, in particular the *amicus curiae*. There remains some overlap between the two mechanisms, and the discussion of victim participation assists in appreciating the scope remaining for the *amicus curiae* to represent victims' interests. Here we highlight key aspects of the legal framework of those institutions that permit victim participation (ICC, STL and ECCC). In chapter five, we explore how the two mechanisms – victim participation and *amici curiae* – have interacted in practice.

[117] For more detailed discussion see B McGonigle Leyh (n 29); L Moffett, *Justice for Victims before the International Criminal Court* (Milton Park, Routledge, 2014).

[118] See, eg D Boyle, 'The Rights of Victims: Participation, Representation, Protection, Reparation' (2006) 4 *JICJ* 307. For a detailed study of victim participation at the ECCC, see R Killean, *Victims, Atrocity and International Criminal Justice: Lessons from Cambodia* (Milton Park, Routledge, 2018).

[119] For discussion, see H Morrison and E Pountney, 'Victim Participation at the Special Tribunal for Lebanon' in A Alamuddin, NN Jurdi and D Tolbert (eds), *The Special Tribunal for Lebanon: Law and Practice* (Oxford, OUP, 2014).

ii. Victim Participation at the ICC

The Rome Statute recognises three specific rights of participation for victims, as well as a general right to participate. First, under Article 15(3), victims may make representations to the Pre-Trial Chamber where the Prosecutor has sought authorisation to open an investigation *proprio motu*. Secondly, Article 19(3) provides that in proceedings 'with respect to jurisdiction or admissibility' victims may submit observations to the Court. Finally, victims have specific rights in reparations proceedings.[120] These specific rights address phases where proceedings are most likely to engage the interests of victims: the opening of an investigation; the exercise of jurisdiction; determining whether the ICC or a national system should hear a case; and identifying appropriate reparations. Victims also have a general right to participate 'where the personal interests of the victims are affected' in accordance with Article 68(3). This right is managed by the Chamber: 'the Court shall permit their views and concerns to be presented and considered at stages of the proceedings determined to be appropriate by the Court and in a manner which is not prejudicial to or inconsistent with the rights of the accused and a fair and impartial trial'.[121]

Victims wishing to participate in proceedings face a two-stage process. First, they must qualify as a victim. Rule 85 defines victims as 'natural persons who have suffered harm as a result of the commission of any crime within the jurisdiction of the Court'. Where a victim satisfies this legal definition, they must then demonstrate that they have a specific right to participate at that stage of proceedings or that their participation is appropriate at the stage of proceedings and their personal interests are affected. The practice of Chambers on when participation is appropriate varies, with some Chambers adopting a systematic approach – identifying on which issues victims have a core interest and then allowing participation whenever those interests are affected. Other Chambers have adopted a piecemeal approach, deciding that although victims share common interests, Article 68(3) requires that issues affected specific, personal interests of victims at that stage of proceedings.[122] There is also inconsistency as to how 'personal' the interests need to be to support participation, with Chambers recognising that indirect victims may be able to participate.[123] This divergence in approach means that there is a lack of certainty and clarity as to when victims may participate under Article 68(3).

As with the *amicus curiae*, the modalities of participation are at the discretion of individual Chambers. The main limiting factor is the need to ensure a fair and expeditious trial, with Chambers particularly concerned that victims do not become a second 'accuser'.[124] Participating victims are not parties and have

[120] Discussed further in s VI(A) and ch 4, s VII.
[121] Rome Statute, Art 68(3).
[122] McGonigle Leyh (n 29), 257–61.
[123] ibid, 247–48.
[124] Article 68(3) of the Rome Statute stipulates this requirement.

more limited rights and scope of participation. Chambers require legal counsel to represent victims, usually on a collective basis.[125] The modalities of victim participation may include: (1) access to the public record and certain documents and filing (this tends not to include access to confidential filings); (2) access to hearings, status conferences and trial, as well as to file written submissions and oral submissions; (3) making opening and closing statements; (4) the ability to initiate procedures by filing applications and requests; and (5) the ability to respond to submissions of other parties and participants, including, on occasion, *amici curiae*. Victims are not entitled to file appeals concerning the decision to admit them as victims (they can instead refile a fresh application).[126] Other than reparations decisions, victims do not have standing to appeal judgments (including sentencing) or decisions.[127] Participation in appeals is regulated by Article 68(3) and, for interlocutory appeals, victims must seek leave to participate.[128] However, Chambers have permitted victims to participate in an appeal where they participated in the proceedings below.[129]

We should also mention Regulation 93, which creates a general right of a Chamber to request submissions from victims at any stage. This regulation provides: 'A Chamber may seek the views of victims or their legal representatives participating pursuant to rules 89 to 91 *on any issue*, inter alia, in relation to issues referred to in rules 107, 109, 125, 128, 136, 139 and 191. In addition, a Chamber may seek the views of *other victims*, as appropriate'. This is not a right to participate; rather the Chamber invites victims to make observations at its discretion. This provision is broad and offers a potential alternative to the *amicus curiae* for victims, including those not formally participating in proceedings.

iii. Victim Participation – The ECCC and STL

The arrangements for victim participation at the ECCC and STL are different to those at the ICC, and from each other. The constituent instruments for the ECCC, the UN Agreement and the ECCC Law do not mention participation of victims in proceedings. However, as noted above, the Internal Rules draw on Cambodian criminal procedural law, which recognises the role of civil parties. A victim is 'a natural person or legal entity that has suffered harm as a result of the commission of any crime within the jurisdiction of the ECCC'.[130]

[125] Rome Statute, Art 68(3); discussed in McGonigle Leyh (n 29), 326–29.

[126] *Situation in Democratic Republic of the Congo*, ICC PTC I, 10 December 2007, ICC-01/04-418, paras 16–17; *Prosecutor v Lubanga*, ICC TC I, 18 January 2008, ICC-01/04-01/06-1119.

[127] Article 82(4) of the Rome Statute permits victims (via their legal representative) to file an appeal an order under Art 75. However, otherwise, Art 82 limits appeals to a 'party'.

[128] *Prosecutor v Lubanga*, ICC AC, 16 May 2008, ICC-01/04-01/06/1335, paras 12–13.

[129] There is some variation here: some judges on the Appeals Chamber require victims to apply for leave to participate and to establish how their interests are affected, while others consider that they should be permitted to participate based on reg 65(5) as they participated in the proceedings leading to the appeal: see McGonigle Leyh (n 29), 305–6.

[130] ECCC Internal Rules, glossary.

To gain participatory rights, a victim must be recognised as a civil party and the Co-Investigating Judges or Pre-Trial Chamber find the request admissible.[131] Unlike the ICC, civil parties are party to proceedings and are not limited to participating where their personal interests are engaged. Civil parties are required to participate in support of the prosecution,[132] although the judges have recognised that this does not amount to a second Prosecutor or 'confer a right of equal participation with the Co-Prosecutors'.[133] Participatory rights also allow the civil parties to seek reparations.[134] Where participation does not relate to these two aims, Chambers have refused to recognise participatory rights, for example in submissions regarding sentencing.[135] Chambers recognise the need to maintain the right of the accused to a fair and expeditious trial and to bring hearings to conclusion within a reasonable time.[136]

The status as a party does not mean that civil parties receive the same participatory rights as parties, although the rights they do enjoy are greater than at the ICC.[137] Civil parties may participate in the initial hearing, but only to provide a specification of the reparations awards they intend to seek.[138] Civil parties do not make opening statements,[139] but can access the case file,[140] question the accused[141] and all other witnesses with the permission of the President,[142] make written statements,[143] request witnesses,[144] and make closing and rebuttal statements at the close of proceedings.[145] A lawyer must represent civil parties from the issue of the closing order, which may be on a collective basis.[146] Following amendments to the Internal Rules, Lead Co-Lawyers are responsible for the in-court presentation of the interests of all civil parties, with the support of other civil party lawyers.[147] Civil parties also have limited appeal rights and may only appeal decisions on reparations and, where the prosecution has also appealed, appeal a verdict but not a sentence.[148]

The RPE of the STL also include victim participation, through a legal representative assigned by the Registry. As at the ICC, victims are not parties.

[131] ibid, glossary, r 23*bis*.
[132] ibid, r 23(1).
[133] *Co-Prosecuors v Duch*, ECCC TC, 9 October 2009, 001118-07-2007/ECCC/TC-E72/3, para 5.
[134] Internal Rules, r 23(1).
[135] *Co-Prosecutors v Duch*, ECCC TC, Transcript, 27 August 2009, 41–42.
[136] Internal Rules, r 21.
[137] Participatory rights also changed between Case 001 and Case 002. For further discussion, see McGonigle Leyh (n 29); Killean (n 118).
[138] Internal Rules, r 80*bis*.
[139] ibid, r 89*bis*.
[140] ibid, r 86.
[141] ibid, r 90.
[142] ibid, r 91.
[143] ibid, r 92.
[144] ibid, r 139.
[145] ibid, r 94.
[146] At the investigation stage, victims participate on an individual basis: ibid, rr 23(3), 23*ter*.
[147] ibid, rr 12*ter*, 23*ter*, adopted in Rev 6 (February 2010).
[148] ibid, r 105(1)(c).

The RPE allows for participation by victims following the issue of an indictment. Article 17 of the Statute provides for victim participation 'where the personal interests of the victims are affected'. As with the ICC, participation is limited to victims presenting 'their views and concerns' at appropriate stages of the proceedings and so as not to prejudice or be inconsistent with the rights of the defence.[149] Judges retain discretion regarding the modalities of participation.[150] Victims have certain potential rights during the pre-trial phase, including suggesting witnesses and evidence they would like the pre-trial judge to admit into evidence and to receive copies of documents filed by parties.[151] During the trial phase, victims can request permission to call and question witnesses and may, where authorised, examine witnesses,[152] present evidence and file written submissions.[153] Victims have an express right to make an opening statement,[154] to request questions be put to an accused,[155] to make closing arguments[156] and to be present at judgment[157] and sentence.[158] In sentencing, victims are limited to providing submissions as to the impact of the crimes.[159] Victims cannot appeal judgment or sentence,[160] but may be permitted to participate by the Appeals Chamber in accordance with Article 17 (ie, where personal interests are affected). Similarly, victims may participate in interlocutory appeals in accordance with Article 17, and may be able to appeal from a decision directly affecting their participation (eg, denial of victim status).[161]

iv. Conclusion: Victim Participation and the Amicus Curiae

This brief overview shows that where victims would previously have had to rely on the *amicus curiae* mechanism, we now see a range of specific and general rights to participate. As with *amici curiae*, a key challenge for the Tribunals is enabling victim participation while not adversely affecting the fair trial rights of the accused or the expeditiousness of proceedings. Even where given party status (at the ECCC), Chambers do not accord victims the full range of participatory rights given to parties. Importantly, victim participation at these tribunals performs a representative function, since victims are participating with a particular purpose and *because* their interests are affected.

[149] STL Statute, Art 17. See STL RPE, r 86 for the admissibility procedure.
[150] STL RPE, r 87.
[151] ibid, r 86.
[152] ibid, r 145.
[153] ibid, rr 87(B),146.
[154] ibid, r 143.
[155] ibid, r 144, although questions are to be asked through the judges.
[156] ibid, r 147.
[157] ibid, r 168.
[158] ibid, r 145.
[159] ibid, rr 87(c), 171(b).
[160] ibid, r 177.
[161] ibid, r 86.

The legal framework for victim participation creates some gaps where victims, or actors seeking to represent victims, may rely on the *amicus curiae* mechanism. There is also a representative function in an *amicus curiae* presenting the views of victims who have chosen not to participate formally as victims. The scope for this is greater at the ICC and the STL, given the more expansive rights as civil parties accorded at the ECCC. However, where the victims' personal interests are engaged, specific rights to participate should be utilised, rather than the general discretion of the *amicus curiae*, for two reasons. First, victim participation provides more extensive and systematic rights. Secondly, it better reflects the representative function required. We consider the interaction between victim participation and the *amicus curiae* in chapter five, in the context of civil society actors.

B. Representation in Reparations Proceedings at the ICC[162]

Article 75 of the Rome Statute creates a framework for the award of reparations to victims.[163] Chambers order reparations against the convicted person, and the reparations phase follows conviction (and any appeal).[164] Where the convicted person does not have sufficient assets to meet the costs of reparations, the Chamber can request an institutional actor, the Trust Fund for Victims (TFV), to meet the cost of all or some of the reparations ordered by the Chamber. The TFV, as an independent actor, will then make a decision as to whether to do so.[165] The TFV also has a separate assistance mandate under Article 79 of the Statute. However, this mandate is not linked to judicial proceedings against an individual accused, so we do not consider it further here.

For present purposes, the relevant provision is Article 75(3), which provides that 'Before making an order under this article, the Court may invite and shall take account of representations from or on behalf of the convicted person, victims, other interested persons or interested States'. As noted above, this is one of the specific rights of victim participation contained in the Rome Statute. Victims are given additional rights concerning reparations for example, victims can appeal a reparations order but not the conviction,[166] and limits on victims questioning witnesses do not apply to reparations proceedings, where victims can, with permission, question witnesses, experts and the persons concerned.[167]

[162] This issue is particular to the ICC, as the ICTY, ICTR and SCSL did not have a mandate to order reparations, while the ECCC incorporates reparations into the trial process and does not have a separate phase of proceedings.

[163] For more specific discussion, see Moffett (n 117); C McCarthy, *Reparations and Victim Support in the International Criminal Court* (Cambridge, CUP, 2012).

[164] *Prosecutor v Lubanga*, ICC AC, 3 March 2015, ICC-01/04-01/06-3129.

[165] ibid.

[166] Rome Statute, Art 82(4).

[167] ICC RPE, r 91(4).

Article 75(3) is available to actors other than victims and appears to establish a separate participatory regime than for other stages of proceedings. This signals the shift from the trial, which focuses on the criminal responsibility of the accused, to the reparative phase, where the focus is on the harm to the victims and how best to redress that harm. As reparations are a key aspect of victim participation, it is not surprising that victims have participatory rights here – their interests are directly affected by proceedings and should be represented. As reparations arise from the guilt of the accused and his or her liability and ability to pay, the convicted person's direct interest in the proceedings is also clear. The language of 'interested' persons and 'interested' states suggests that other actors participating in this stage, at least under this article, should have a similar 'interest' in the reparations proceedings, although there is no guidance as to what an interest may be in this context. This also suggests that participation in reparations proceedings under Article 75(3) performs a representative function, allowing those with an interest affected by the proceedings to put their position before the Chamber. In contrast, those without an interest affected by proceedings would need to seek permission to make submissions as *amici curiae*. Both mechanisms are discretionary, although Article 75(3) suggests the Chamber will initiate the process (the Court *may* invite). Importantly, Article 75(3) suggests that where a Chamber receives representations it must consider them ('the Court ... *shall take into account*'). This is different to *amici curiae*, where the Chamber is under no obligation to accept or to consider the submissions. In chapter four, we consider the practice in reparations practice at the ICC to explore whether the practice reflects the apparent distinctions between these two mechanisms.

C. Expert Witnesses

i. Appointing Expert Witnesses

Judges have the power to admit expert witnesses, although the procedures vary across the Tribunals.[168] At the ICTY, ICTR and SCSL, the adversarial nature of the trial proceedings meant that it was the responsibility of the parties to call expert witnesses, provided the procedural requirements had been satisfied, although the ultimate decision to admit the expert testimony rested with the Trial Chamber.[169] At the ECCC, based on the inquisitorial system at the national level, the Chamber is responsible for calling expert witnesses, although generally based on a request from the parties.[170] Neither the Rome

[168] For more detailed discussion, refer to S Linton, 'Testimony of Expert Witnesses, Journalists, ICRC, and UN staff' in G Sluiter et al (eds), *International Criminal Procedure: Principles and Rules* (Oxford, OUP, 2013).

[169] The instruments of these tribunals did not include a provision addressing expert witnesses, although Rule 94*bis* in the RPE for each tribunal regulates the procedural aspects for testimony by expert witnesses. Chambers can also summon an expert witness: see ICTY RPE, rr 54, 98.

[170] ECCC Internal Rules, r 31. The position is similar for the STL: see STL RPE, r 161.

Statute nor the RPE contain a specific provision on expert witnesses. Instead, the ICC adopts a different approach, moving from party-led appointment of experts to a list of standing experts compiled and maintained by the Registry that must be available to all Court organs and participants in proceedings.[171] Regulation 44 provides for the joint instruction of experts by the parties.[172] The Chamber may appoint an expert *proprio motu*[173] and issue orders as to 'the subject of an expert report, the number of experts to be appointed, the mode of their instruction, the manner in which their evidence is to be presented and the time limits for the preparation and notification of their report'.[174] There is thus greater judicial control over the process at the ICC, with Chambers preferring joint instruction of experts.[175]

Chambers have used different language to describe the function of an expert witness. In general, the expert witness is to provide some specialised knowledge or skill or training to assist the Chamber, as the trier of fact, to understand the evidence and to make its primary determination on the guilt or innocence of the accused.[176] An expert witness must respect the core judicial competence of the Chamber and should not give legal advice, nor purport to apply the law to the facts, make a 'judicial' type determination on the facts or opine as to the individual criminal responsibility of the accused.[177] In *Stakić*, the Trial Chamber decided it did not require the assistance of a legal expert to determine legal issues, as this was within the competence of the Chamber.[178] Those issues 'were (1) whether or not the principle of command responsibility embodied in Article 7(3) of the Statute enjoyed the status of customary international law in 1992; and (2) whether application of these principles would amount to a retroactive application of substantive criminal law'.[179] The Appeals Chamber agreed, finding that 'there was no justification for the introduction of expert testimony as to issues of international criminal law; the Trial Chamber was perfectly competent to pronounce on such issues without the assistance of a legal expert'.[180] It is clear, however, that admission of expert testimony is a matter of discretion, and the Chamber retains the power to accept expert witness testimony and to

[171] ICC Regulations, reg 44(1).
[172] ibid, reg 44(2).
[173] ibid, reg 44(4).
[174] ibid, reg 44(5). In Lubanga, the Trial Chamber issued specific instructions on expert witnesses, which were subsequently applied in Bemba: *Prosecutor v Lubanga*, ICC TC I, 10 December 2007, ICC-01/04-01/06-1069; *Prosecutor v Bemba*, ICC TC III, 12 February 2010, ICC-01/05-01/08-695, para 4.
[175] ICC Regulations, reg 44(2); Linton (n 168), 916.
[176] See *Prosecutor v Brđanin*, ICC TC II, 3 June 2003, IT-99-36-T-11073, citing *Prosecutor v Galić*, ICTY TC, 3 July 2002, IT-98-29-T-5849. See also *Semanza v Prosecutor*, ICTR AC, 20 May 2005, ICTR-97-20-A-5874/H, para 303.
[177] Linton (n 168), 886, quoting *Prosecutor v Hadžihasanović* ICTY TC II, 11 February 2004, IT-01-47-T-6/7923*bis*, citing an oral decision in *Prosecutor v Kordić & Čerkez*, ICTY TC, Transcript, 28 January 2000 13306-7.
[178] *Prosecutor v Stakić*, ICTY TC, Transcript, 25 November 2002, 9440.
[179] *Prosecutor v Stakić*, ICC AC, 22 March 2006, IT-97-24-A, para 163.
[180] ibid, para 164.

determine its value. The Chamber is not bound to adopt the conclusions of the expert or arguably even to consider them. This requires the Chamber to assess the reliability and probative value of the testimony or report, as it does with any other evidence. Thus, similar to the *amicus curiae*, even where an expert does impinge on the core competence of the Chamber, the Chamber can disregard such statements and draw its own conclusions.

ii. Who is an Expert Witness?

The RPE of the various tribunals do not provide a definition of an expert witness, and practice has varied. The ICTY has indicated that an expert is a 'person who by virtue of some specialised knowledge, skills or training can assist the trier of fact to understand or determine an issue in dispute'.[181] At the ICTR, guidelines on remuneration define an expert as 'Anyone with specific and relevant information on and/or knowledge of the matter brought before the Tribunal. Such specific information or knowledge which qualifies an individual to appear as an expert witness may have been acquired through training or actual studies, special aptitudes, experience or some reputation in the field or through any other means considered by the party calling the witness to give testimony as being necessary and sufficient to qualify him as an expert witness'.[182] The SCSL defined an expert as having 'special knowledge, skills, experience or training'.[183]

The jurisprudence suggests a number of criteria for determining who is an expert, all of which aim at ensuring the reliability of the evidence provided and its usefulness to the Chamber.[184] First, the expert should establish their expertise or experience, based on their qualifications, including their CV, scholarly and other publications and other available information. Chambers also require material to be produced by the expert themselves, using their specialised knowledge, and will be reluctant to accept as expert evidence collations of NGO reports for example, without more, particularly where material would otherwise be publicly available. Secondly, Chambers expect experts to present their testimony and draw conclusions in an independent and impartial manner. This means that experts should be independent from the parties. The primary role of the Chamber as the trier of fact means that Chambers have been somewhat flexible in considering what amounts to independence for an expert witness. For example, having worked for or with a party does not necessarily preclude use of the evidence; rather, this would affect the weight given to the evidence. Thirdly, the witness's expertise must be relevant to the issues raised in the proceedings,

[181] Linton (n 168), 882, quoting *Brđanin* (n 176), citing *Galić* (n 176).

[182] International Criminal Tribunal for Rwanda, Guidelines on the Remuneration of Expert Witnesses appearing before the International Criminal Tribunal for Rwanda, available at www.legal-tools.org/en/doc/983aa0/.

[183] Headquarters Agreement Between the Republic of Sierra Leone and the Special Court for Sierra Leone (21 October 2003), Art 1(f).

[184] See discussion in Linton (n 168), 882-884 (ICTY), 893-896 (ICTR), 900-902 (SCSL).

and their proposed testimony must fall within the scope of the witness's expertise and the parameters set by the Chamber and therefore assist the Chamber.

At the ICC, Regulation 56 of the Registry regulations sets up a formal, institutional procedure.[185] This requires prospective experts to apply for entry into a list of approved experts available to Chambers. Experts can be both natural persons and expert organisations. The criteria applied equate to those identified in the jurisprudence of the other tribunals. The Registry invites applications from experts having a minimum of nine years of relevant experience, or seven years with an advanced university degree; fluency in either English or French; and with expertise in either a general area (ballistics, finance, forensic medicine, graphology, psychology and reparations) or in an area relevant to a specific situation (history, judicial systems, military science, policing, politics and geopolitics and linguistics). The list of expertise types corresponds to the need for range of expertise discussed in section V(A) above. All ICC experts must maintain high standards of professional and personal integrity and show strict respect of confidentiality.[186] The application forms contain detailed questions regarding potential conflicts, including affiliation with states.[187] ICC Chambers may also initiate a separate process for the appointment of experts. For example, in the *Al-Mahdi* reparations proceedings, the Chamber initiated a separate call for experts concerning cultural heritage, assessment of damage and reparations for crimes against cultural heritage.[188]

iii. Expert Witnesses and the Amicus Curiae

Commentators have noted that 'The ICC approach seems to be moving the expert witness and *amicus curiae* closer together'.[189] The potential overlap between the two mechanisms is evident, particularly concerning the expertise function of the *amicus curiae*. For instance, one of the first expert witnesses to appear in the *Lubanga* case, Radhika Coomaraswamy, the UN Special Representative for Children and Armed Conflict, initially sought to participate in proceedings as *amicus curiae*.[190] The Trial Chamber invited her to submit observations as an *amicus curiae*;[191] however, in May 2009 Coomaraswamy requested a change in status to an expert witness.[192] Coomaraswamy appeared before the Chamber as

[185] See also International Criminal Court, 'Experts', available at www.icc-cpi.int/get-involved/Pages/experts.aspx.

[186] This is a note on the Registry website, although the legal basis for this statement is not provided; however, experts are not subject to the Code of Conduct for Counsel.

[187] See application form for natural persons, available at International Criminal Court (n 185).

[188] *Prosecutor v Al-Mahdi*, ICC TC VIII, 29 September 2016, ICC-01/12-01/15-172.

[189] Linton (n 168), 906.

[190] *Prosecutor v Lubanga*, ICC TC I, 18 March 2008, ICC-01/04-01/06-1229.

[191] *Prosecutor v Lubanga*, ICC TC I, 18 February 2008, ICC-01/04-01/06-1175.

[192] The transcript refers to her request for a formal change in status: *Prosecutor v Lubanga*, ICC TC I, Transcript, 7 January 2010, 3, 7. However, the discussion as to why this change was requested and approved is confidential: *Prosecutor v Lubanga*, ICC TC I, Transcript, 19 May 2009.

an expert, but the Chamber limited her testimony to the two issues it had given permission for her proposed *amicus curiae* submission to address.[193]

In general, though, the key points of distinction are as follows. First, with expert witnesses, there is specific consideration of the expertise, qualifications, reliability, independence and impartiality of the expert. The ICC regulates the appointment (and removal) of experts through a formal application and listing procedure. In contrast, with *amicus curiae* submissions, as is seen in chapter four, few *amici* identify their expertise in any detail and Chambers make little effort, if any, to verify the expertise of the *amici*, even when performing an expertise function. As explored in chapter four, the approach to identifying appropriate expertise for expert witnesses may offer useful guidance to Chambers assessing whether a potential *amicus curiae* has sufficient and relevant expertise to perform an expertise function. Secondly, experts usually appear in person, under oath, whereas *amici* generally make written submissions only (see chapter four). This means that the Chamber and the parties can examine and test the expert's qualifications, independence and impartiality, as well as the findings and methodology used. Therefore, the parties and the Chamber can test expert witnesses more extensively in comparison to *amici curiae*. Thirdly, Chambers tend to give experts longer to prepare and more time (and pages) to present their expert report. Fourthly, there may only be one jointly appointed expert, so this minimises costs and delay and does not impact on the fair trial rights of the accused, whereas multiple *amici* may appear in one stage of proceedings. Fifthly, the ICC Code of Conduct for counsel does not apply to expert witnesses but does apply to *amici curiae*. Sixthly, similar to *amici*, Chambers may appoint experts at any phase of the judicial proceedings, including pre-trial, trial, sentencing and reparations. Seventhly, expert witnesses receive remuneration, whereas *amici curiae* generally do not (see chapter four).

Finally, the expert witness does not overlap with but complements the core judicial competence: as noted above, experts should assist the Chamber in explaining the evidence and should not provide legal submissions or make statements as to criminal responsibility. Their role also recognises the parties bear the primary responsibility for presenting the evidence to the Chamber. While *amici curiae* must also avoid statements as to criminal responsibility, as discussed in chapter four they are limited in most circumstances to providing legal information and should not present evidence. Therefore, one specific form of expert witness that raises particular issues of overlap with the *amicus curiae* is the so called 'crime-definition expert'. Davidson uses this term to refer to those experts who have provided evidence on the legal elements of a crime or the accused's criminal responsibility.[194] She notes that 'Crime-definition experts have given testimony and submitted expert reports … on the concepts of genocide, forced marriage, and conscription – and enlistment – of child soldiers in prosecutions

[193] *Prosecutor v Lubanga*, ICC TC I, Transcript, 7 January 2010, 3, 7.
[194] Davidson (n 102).

of these crimes',[195] thus they 'testify about the contours and elements of the very crimes with which the accused stands charged'.[196] Davidson illustrates her analysis by referring to the testimony of Radhika Coomaraswamy in *Lubanga* mentioned above.[197] Davidson argues that the evidence by Ms Coomaraswamy 'very directly tackled legal aspects of recruiting child soldiers, not merely the factual context of the phenomenon'.[198] As Davidson notes, this is likely because Coomaraswamy was initially to participate as an *amicus curiae*, so had been directed to address legal issues.[199] We support the distinction established in the ICTY and ICTR stipulating that expert witnesses should provide factual material and non-legal expertise (or legal expertise only on peripheral issues), while legal submissions should be the role of the parties or, where there are novel legal issues, by *amici curiae* acting in the expertise function. However, as discussed in chapters four and seven, there are circumstances in which Chambers do require factual material from *amici*, particularly states.

D. Institutional Actors

The legal framework of the ICC enables a range of institutional actors to provide expertise to Chambers or parties or to participate in proceedings on a limited basis. This is limited largely to the Registry and its divisions and to the TFV in the context of reparations proceedings. As noted above, the ASP established the TFV under Article 79 of the Rome Statute 'for the benefit of victims of crimes within the jurisdiction of the Court, and of the families of such victims'. Where the Court has ordered an award of reparations, the TFV must approve a plan for implementation of that award (subject to the terms of the order itself),[200] which is submitted to the Chamber for its approval. The TFV must then 'consult' the Chamber 'on any questions that arise in connection with the implementation of the award'[201] and provide updates to the Chamber (as ordered by the Chamber) and a final report at the end of the implementation period.[202] The TFV may consult victims or their legal representatives, or victims' families, as well as interested persons, interested states and any competent expert or expert organisation in developing options for reparations.[203] Therefore, the TFV has limited participatory status in reparations proceedings. Chapter four, section VII explores the role of the TFV in reparations proceedings.

195 ibid, 361.
196 ibid, 362.
197 ibid, 393–403. Davidson also considered the evidence provided to the SCSL by Ms Bangura, an expert on the phenomenon of forced marriage, who, Davidson argues, despite her testimony being largely non-legal in nature, helped to define the crime of forced marriage: 382–91.
198 ibid, 395.
199 ibid, 395.
200 ICC Regulations, regs 54, 55.
201 ibid, reg 57.
202 ibid, reg 58.
203 ibid, reg 60(c).

Chambers may invite the Registry to provide specific information or take certain actions in accordance with a Chamber's order and to report to the Chamber. The Registry also performs a role in communicating to the Chamber the views of victims at the very early stages, before participating victims and lawyers are appointed.[204] The Registry may appoint experts to its staff in the victims and witnesses unit.[205] As is considered in more detail in chapter seven, the Registry communicates with states and other actors on behalf of the Chamber.[206] However, beyond this administrative role, the Registry rarely participates formally in proceedings.[207]

The Regulations of the Court create the Office of Public Counsel for Victims (OPCV)[208] to represent victims where the interests of justice require, usually when victims are not otherwise represented by counsel.[209] Here, the OPCV performs a representative function and is subject to the same participatory framework as outlined in section VI(A). A Chamber can also invite the OPCV to make submissions on particular issues where there may not otherwise be a right to participate and to assist Chambers on specific issues.[210] This recognises both a potential representative function, where a Chamber appoints the OPCV to represent the interests of non-participating victims, for example. It also recognises an expertise function for the OPCV, based on the expertise of the OPCV in legal issues particularly concerning victims and reparations. The OPVC may separately perform a support role, providing advice and expertise to legal representatives for victims, which it tends to do based on a request from counsel.[211] As explored further in chapter five, the availability of the OPCV means that Chambers do not need to rely on civil society and other actors to represent victims' interests. However, such actors may still provide expertise, as the OPCV is not the only recognised source of expertise on victims' issues.

The Office of Public Counsel for the Defence (OPCD) for the ICC is an independent office located for administrative purposes in the Registry. The OPCD has several roles: (1) to represent the rights of the defence during the early stages of proceedings; (2) to provide general support and assistance to counsel and the accused entitled to legal assistance, including providing legal research and advice and, on the instruction or with the leave of the Chamber, assisting with detailed factual context of the case; (3) 'appearing, on the instruction or with the leave of the Chamber, in respect of specific issues'; (4) 'Advancing

[204] For the role of the Registry see ICC RPE, rr 16, 17.
[205] ibid, r 19.
[206] ibid, r 13.
[207] Rome Statute, Art 43 refers to the Registry as responsible for the non-judicial aspects of the administration of the Court.
[208] The ECCC Victim Support Service and the STL Victim Participation Unit play a similar administrative role, assisting victims to communicate with counsel, and supporting counsel. However, they do not participate in proceedings as counsel or otherwise, but will arrange representation.
[209] ICC Regulations, regs 80, 81.
[210] ibid, reg 81(4).
[211] ibid, reg 80(4)(a).

submissions, on the instruction or with the leave of the Chamber, on behalf of the person entitled to legal assistance when defence counsel has not been secured or when the mandate of temporary counsel is limited to other issues'; (5) acting as duty counsel, defence counsel or standby counsel; and (6) assisting or representing defence counsel or witnesses in Article 70 proceedings.[212] As explored in chapter six, the participation of the OPCD – and defence offices at other tribunals – may serve as a substitute for defence-aligned *amici*.

VII. CONCLUSION

This chapter has established the grounding for the consideration of practice in the next four chapters. Section II explored rules on standing in the Tribunals. Section III traced the development of the *amicus curiae* mechanism in international criminal tribunals from the post-World War II institutions to current institutions, suggesting that the *amicus curiae* is now best practice when designing tribunals. Section IV briefly outlined the role of the *amicus curiae* prosecutor, concluding that this is a misuse of the term. That section also introduced the potential of the ICC Prosecutor to participate as an *amicus curiae* in proceedings. Section V identified two key limits on the *amicus curiae* in the Tribunals: the core competence of the judges and the need to protect fair trial rights. We explore the extent to which these limits are reflected in the practice of the Tribunals in chapter four. Finally, section VI outlined mechanisms and institutional actors other than the *amicus curiae* that may perform expertise and representative functions, allowing us to explore the interaction between these mechanisms and institutional actors and *amici curiae* in the study of practice in the next chapter.

[212] ibid, reg 70.

4

The Amicus Curiae *in International Criminal Tribunals in Practice*

I. INTRODUCTION

THIS CHAPTER DRAWS on our empirical study of the *amicus curiae* in the Tribunals as well as the legal framework for participation, introduced in chapter three. The review of *amicus curiae* practice produced approximately 408 applications, including responses to invitations or calls, across the six tribunals studied, with 247 accepted submissions. Figure 4.1 shows the breakdown of applications and acceptances by tribunal.

Figure 4.1 Acceptance of *Amicus Curiae* Submissions by Participation Avenue

Acceptances	**ICC**	**ICTY**	**ICTR**	**ECCC**	**SCSL**	**STL**	**Total**
Applications	48	16	36	1	9	0	110
Open calls	22	22	0	37	0	21	102
Direct invitation*	8	14	4	3	5	1	35
	78	52	40	41	14	22	247
Overall Acceptance Rate	50%	68%	56%	72%	78%	79%	61%
Acceptance Rate	ICC	ICTY	ICTR	ECCC	SCSL	STL	All
Applications	38%	39%	54%	6%	69%	0%	41%
Open calls	100%	100%	0%	100%	0%	88%	97%
Direct invitation*	80%	100%	100%	100%	100%	100%	95%

*Includes direct invitations that did not receive a response and one where the route was unclear, but likely via invitation.

Invitations without response are not counted as having then been 'accepted' (hence < 100% of direct invitations accepted at the ICC).

In sections II and III we discuss who can apply to be an *amicus curiae*, and when they may apply. Section IV then explores the procedural arrangements for *amicus* participation in more detail, including the process and modes of participation and how Chambers manage the *amicus* function and the rights, status and duties of *amici*. In section V, we analyse the general criterion for *amicus curiae* participation – that the submissions will assist in the proper determination of the case or issues before the Chamber – and the additional criteria for admission of *amici curiae* applied by judges or suggested in the literature. Section VI considers how *amicus curiae* submissions may have an impact on the outcome of proceedings and beyond. Finally, in section VII, we explore the practice in reparations at the ICC, in particular the relationship between Rule 103 submissions and those under Article 75(3), which, as we indicated in chapter three, creates a separate mechanism for participation in reparations proceedings. This chapter therefore provides the basis for the following chapters, which analyse the Tribunals' practice by reference to key stakeholders: civil society, the defence and states.

II. WHO CAN PARTICIPATE AS AN *AMICUS CURIAE*?

As shown in Annex B, the provisions on the *amicus curiae* are broad in terms of the types of actors that may appear as *amici curiae*. With the exception of the ECCC,[1] *amici* may be states, organisations and individuals. There are no other requirements. For example, the state need not be a state party to the tribunal's statute, nor are organisations and individuals required to be based in an affected state or an ICC member state. Thus it is clear that the mechanism is intended to be a tool not only of NGOs, but is available to a wide range of actors. These provisions do not mention the prosecution, defence and victims specifically. This reflects their status ordinarily as parties or with other legal bases for participation. However, as shown in this study, there may be situations in which these actors may seek to rely on the *amicus curiae* mechanism.[2]

Figure 4.2 Proportion of Applicants by Type

	ICC	ICTY	ICTR	ECCC	SCSL	STL	All
NGO	39%	21%	42%	30%	33%	11%	33%
Academic	15%	26%	1%	46%	22%	14%	19%
Government	15%	23%	25%	0%	0%	0%	15%
Legal	10%	16%	25%	7%	22%	29%	15%
Other	21%	14%	6%	16%	22%	46%	18%

Note: Individual figures rounded.

[1] Rule 33 does not include a reference to states, unlike the provision in other tribunals, suggesting that state *amici* are not permitted.

[2] For further discussion, see ch 3, s IV (prosecution); ch 3, s VI(A); ch 5, s IV (victims); and ch 6 (defence).

Figure 4.2 shows the range of actors that have sought to appear as *amici curiae* before the tribunals. The largest group, around a third, can be categorised as NGOs. As discussed further in chapter five, these include large human rights organisations such as Amnesty International or Human Rights Watch, as well as relatively 'specialist' groups such as Women's Initiatives for Gender Justice, or Redress, which has a particular focus on victims' interests. There have also been a number of applications from smaller nationally based NGOs or victims' groups. The next major group of prospective *amici curiae* consists of academics and international criminal law and public international law experts, who may seek to provide submissions individually, in groups, or through their university centres. A third group includes 'legal' organisations, including bar associations. Fourthly, states have attempted to intervene in proceedings in a manner analogous to parties to the case and as *amici curiae*. Fifthly, other categories of *amicus curiae* applicants include individuals and international organisations or other international actors, as well as accused persons from other cases who have sought to appear as *amici*.

There is no restriction as to the number of times an *amicus curiae* can participate or apply to participate in proceedings or before particular institutions. While some *amici* are 'repeat players', most are not.[3] Similarly, there is no limit as to how many *amici* can be admitted to participate in a particular phase of proceedings (as opposed to how many may be signatories to a joint *amicus curiae* brief, which is discussed below). In some jurisdictions, such as the US, multiple *amici curiae* are often admitted to participate in proceedings. In contrast, while Chambers do admit multiple *amici*, particularly where there has been an open call, the number admitted in each phase of proceedings tends to be relatively low, although there are some exceptions.[4]

III. WHEN CAN AN *AMICUS CURIAE* PARTICIPATE?

A. 'At any Time of Proceedings'

The Tribunal Rules do not specify the stage of proceedings at which *amici curiae* may participate. Importantly, the *amicus curiae* is a friend of the court and is given leave by a Chamber, so it is a mechanism within the discretion of the

[3] At the ICC, approximately 80% of applications were 'first time'; this figure was higher at other tribunals except the ICTR and ECCC, where there were relatively more with 'repeat' applications (more than one).

[4] eg, as discussed in s VII below, in the implementation phase of reparations in *Lubanga*, the Trial Chamber accepted 14 *amici*, as well as submissions from the government: *Prosecutor v Lubanga*, ICC TC II, 4 October 2016, ICC-01/04-01/06-3240-tENG (with 13 submissions as annexes). In the *Jordan* non-cooperation proceedings, the Chamber received 11 submissions from academics and two from international organisations.

judges, rather than other actors within the court. To illustrate, a decision by the President of the STL to issue an invitation to the United Nations to appear as an *amicus curiae* was overturned, as the President did not have the authority to invite *amici*; only the relevant Chamber could do so.[5]

Under Rule 103 ICC RPE an *amicus* submission can occur 'at any stage in proceedings', thus judicial proceedings must have been initiated before an *amicus curiae* can participate. This raises the question as to when judicial proceedings commence. In tribunals, such as the ECCC and the STL, that are based on civil law systems and have judicial investigations, the rules make clear that the investigating judges are also able to accept *amicus* submissions during the judicial investigation phase.[6] In the ICC, in the context of victim participation, the Appeals Chamber has held that proceedings is 'a term denoting a judicial cause pending before a Chamber', while 'an investigation is not a judicial proceeding but an inquiry conducted by the Prosecutor'.[7] Thus, the *amicus curiae* mechanism is not generally available during the preliminary examination and investigation phases. Instead, the Appeals Chamber has stated that 'there is ample scope within the statutory scheme of the Statute for victims and anyone else with relevant information to pass it on to the Prosecutor without first being formally accorded "a general right to participate"'.[8] Therefore, although actors may be dissatisfied with the actions of the Prosecutor, rather than a Chamber, the *amicus curiae* mechanism is not particularly effective to influence the Prosecutor in the absence of judicial proceedings.[9]

Judicial proceedings can be triggered, and *amici curiae* participate, in pretrial phases. For example, Pre-Trial Chamber I invited Louise Arbour and Antonio Cassese to provide information to the ICC about their investigations into events in Darfur in Sudan, in their capacities as High Commissioner of the Office of the United Nations High Commissioner for Human Rights and Chairperson of the International Commission of Inquiry on Darfur, respectively.[10] There is also no reason why *amici curiae* would be precluded from seeking to make submissions in proceedings where the Prosecutor has requested authorisation to open an investigation. Two academics sought to participate as *amici* in the Article 15 proceedings in the Kenyan situation, arguing that the novel nature of the issues to be determined and the effectively *ex parte* nature of the proceedings warranted the Chamber hearing from *amici*.[11] The Chamber rejected the

[5] *Prosecutor v El Sayed*, STL AC, 8 November 2010, CH-AC-2010-01, paras 29–34.

[6] eg, r 33 of the ECCC Internal Rules specifically mentions Co-Investigating Judges.

[7] *Situation in the Democratic Republic of the Congo,* ICC AC, 19 December 2008, ICC-01/04-556, paras 45, 51.

[8] ibid, para 53.

[9] S Williams, 'Civil Society Participation in Preliminary Examinations' in M Bergsmo and C Stahn (eds), *Quality Control in Preliminary Examination* (Torkel Opsahl Academic Epublisher, 2018).

[10] *Situation in Darfur, Sudan,* ICC PTC I, 24 July 2006, ICC-02/05-10.

[11] *Situation in Kenya*, ICC PTC II, 11 January 2010, ICC-01/09-8.

application on the basis that the proposed submissions would not help it to 'reach a proper determination on the Prosecutor's Request'.[12] As discussed further in chapter six, one of the suspects ultimately charged by the Prosecutor, William Ruto, also sought to appear as an *amicus curiae* via his legal counsel after the Pre-Trial Chamber had authorised the Prosecutor to open the investigation, arguing that he could provide a different perspective on the investigation and that he had been misrepresented in key sources relied upon by the Prosecutor in the Article 15 request.[13] The Chamber rejected the request, arguing that a suspect under investigation is not a category of person able to submit observations as an *amicus curiae*, as Rule 103 refers to the right of the defence to respond to any observations.[14]

Similarly, actors should in principle be able to seek leave to participate as *amici* in proceedings for review by a Pre-Trial Chamber of a decision *not* to open an investigation. In the Pre-Trial Chamber's review of the Prosecutor's decision in the *Comoros* situation, one civil society organisation, the European Centre for Law and Justice sought leave to submit submissions as an *amicus curiae* in the initial appellate proceedings, in support of the Prosecutor's request to appeal.[15] The proposed submissions, which were appended to the request for leave, concerned the issue of jurisdiction in respect of nationals of a state that is not a party to the Rome Statute, the basis of the Pre-Trial Chamber's review of the Prosecutor's evidence, and the proper role of review under Article 53 of the Rome Statute. As the Appeals Chamber ultimately rejected the Prosecutor's appeal, the request to participate as an *amicus curiae* was never finally determined.[16] This shows that there is potential for *amici curiae* to participate in proceedings under Article 15 and reviews under Article 53. Most recently, the judicial proceedings in relation to *Myanmar/Bangladesh* show that *amici curiae* may be able to participate at very early stages. Those proceedings arose following a request by the Prosecutor for a preliminary ruling on jurisdiction before a preliminary examination has been opened,[17] with the Pre-Trial Chamber admitting several *amici*.[18]

[12] *Situation in Kenya*, ICC PTC II, 3 February 2010, ICC-01/09-14, para 8.

[13] International Criminal Court, Pre-Trial Chamber II, *Situation in Kenya,* ICC PTC II, 21 December 2010, ICC-01/09-32. See ch 6, n 37.

[14] International Criminal Court, Pre-Trial Chamber II, *Situation in Kenya,* ICC PTC II, 18 January 2011, ICC-01/09-35.

[15] *Situation on Registered Vessels of the Union of the Comoros, the Hellenic Republic of Greece and the Kingdom of Cambodia*, ICC AC, 7 August 2015, ICC-01/13-44.

[16] *Situation on Registered Vessels of the Union of the Comoros, the Hellenic Republic of Greece and the Kingdom of Cambodia*, ICC AC, 14 August 2015, ICC-01/13-46.

[17] *Request under Regulation 46(3) of the Regulations of the Court,* ICC PTC I, 9 April 2018, ICC-RoC46(3)-01/18-1.

[18] The Pre-Trial Chamber accepted five amici (including one join submission): see *Request under Regulation 46(3) of the Regulations of the Court,* ICC PTC I, 6 September 2018, ICC-RoC46(3)-01/18-37, para 8.

B. *Amicus Curiae* Practice Over the Life of an Institution

We have previously suggested that *amicus curiae* participation may be more prevalent during the early existence of an institution or when a new process is introduced.[19] This is due to the novelty of the proceedings and the issues raised, the absence of well-developed jurisprudence and the need to develop new proceedings and substantive law.

As seen in Figure 4.3, our analysis did not show a clear pattern toward declining numbers of *amicus curiae* briefs over time.[20] In fact, there are often 'spikes' in *amicus curiae* participation later in an institution's life. However, when these spikes are analysed further, it is apparent that the increase is caused by a number of briefs on one particular issue, which is generally associated with a novel phase of proceedings or procedure. For instance, most briefs at the ECCC initially concerned provisional detention. As proceedings commenced both at the ECCC and ICC there were briefs on victim participation and – later again – reparations. Similarly, there was an increase in the number of *amicus curiae* briefs later in the life of the ICTR, which was associated with the referral of cases to Rwanda.[21]

Figure 4.3 Number of Amicus Applications by Year and Court from 2003

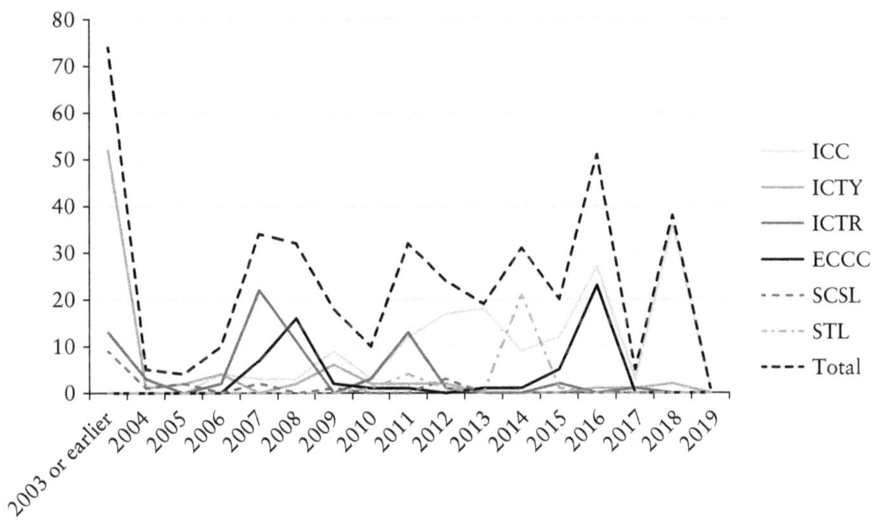

[19] S Williams and H Woolaver, 'The Role of the *Amicus Curiae* before International Criminal Tribunals' (2006) 6(2) *ICLR* 151.

[20] The initially high numbers are because the table includes the total number of briefs prior to 2003 to begin with.

[21] See discussion in ch 7, s IV(B).

IV. HOW DO *AMICI CURIAE* PARTICIPATE?

The rules on the *amicus curiae* provide few details as to the modalities for application, approval and participation of *amici*, as well as the rights, obligations and status of *amici*. Consequently, through the adoption of practice directions, specific orders and decisions, judges have developed more detailed rules and practice (see chapter three). This section considers how Chambers have approached these aspects of *amicus curiae* participation.

A. Process for Admission of *Amici Curiae*

i. Invitations, Open Calls and Voluntary Applications

The Tribunals engage with potential *amici curiae* in three ways. First, Chambers have invited specific *amici curiae* to make submissions, including states, those affected by an issue before the Court and named or groups of individuals. Secondly, Chambers have issued 'open calls' – invitations to potential *amici* to make submissions on specific issues or addressing questions generally listed in the call for submissions. Such calls can be truly open, that is with no target audience indicated. On other occasions, the call is limited to particular categories of potential *amici*, for example states, international organisations and academics. Thirdly, Chambers may receive unsolicited applications from potential *amici*, which we refer to as 'voluntary applications'. Figure 4.4 shows the breakdown of how the Tribunals have engaged *amici* through these different methods. It shows that the majority of applications arise from voluntary applications across the total of all Tribunals (65 per cent). It also demonstrates that the practice of the Tribunals varies, with the STL and the ECCC receiving the highest proportion of responses to open calls.

Figure 4.4 Attempted Participation Avenue (%)

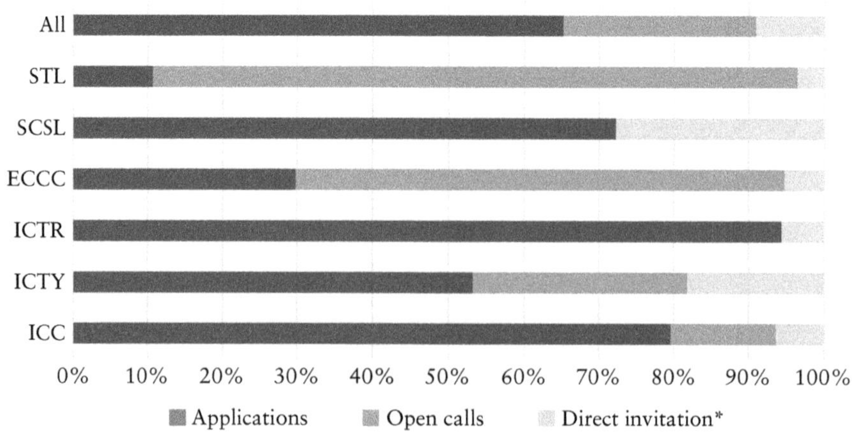

All of the Tribunals rely upon a two-stage approach to admission of *amici curiae* for voluntary applications and sometimes for open calls and particular types of actors. For voluntary applications, applicants are required to submit a request for leave to appear as an *amicus curiae* to the relevant Chamber. The Chamber (or a designated judge) considers the request and makes a decision granting or denying the request. This two-stage approach provides a valuable filtering mechanism for voluntary applications and, as explored below, allows the Chamber to consider the merits of accepting a particular *amicus curiae* submission, the potential impact on the proceedings and, we suggest, the function to be performed by the applicant. One area where there is inconsistency is whether applicants are required, permitted or precluded from attaching their proposed brief to the request for leave, with the ECCC Supreme Court Chamber indicating the brief should be attached where possible, the SCSL and STL practice directions indicating that the brief 'may' accompany an application, but other tribunals generally discouraging this practice.[22] The ICC Appeals Chamber has indicated that 'the submission of substantive observations is only permissible after a Chamber has decided to invite or grant leave to do so';[23] however, individual Chambers have accepted observations attached to a request 'on an exceptional basis'[24] or required potential *amici* to make 'summary initial observations' with their request.[25]

For invited *amici*, including states, generally the Chamber stipulates a deadline for submission and accepts the submissions without the need for a formal leave process. The practice varies for open calls, and may differ depending on the actors targeted by the call. For example, where a call addresses civil society actors, ICC Chambers usually adopt a two-stage process, requiring potential *amici* to apply for leave to participate.[26] This has also been the case for calls made to states generally, although on some occasions open calls allow states and international organisations to file submissions without first seeking approval.[27] We suggest that Chambers should adopt a two-stage process for *amici* responding

[22] Extraordinary Chambers in the Courts of Cambodia, Information Concerning the Submission of *Amicus Curiae* Briefs to the Supreme Court Chamber of the ECCC (7 March 2011), para 3; Special Court for Sierra Leone, Practice Direction on filing *Amicus Curiae* applications pursuant to Rule 74 of Rules of Procedure and Evidence of the Special Court for Sierra Leone (20 October 2004) SCSL-2004-16-T, Art 3; Special Tribunal for Lebanon, Practice Direction on *Amicus Curiae* Submissions Before the Special Tribunal for Lebanon (23 February 2012) STL/PD/2012/05, Art 3(2).

[23] *Prosecutor v Bemba*, ICC AC, 9 November 2009, ICC-01/05-01/08-602, para 9.

[24] eg, in *Ruto and Sang*, the Trial Chamber noted that substantive submissions should not normally be made in the request, but allowed those submissions from the Government of Kenya on an exceptional basis: *Prosecutor v Ruto and Sang*, ICC TC V(A), 5 May 2014, ICC-01/09-01/11-1291, para 35.

[25] *Prosecutor v Al-Bashir*, ICC AC, 29 March 2018, ICC-02/05-01/09-330, para 4.

[26] See, eg the call issued to 'professors of international law' in the *Jordan* non-cooperation proceedings: ibid, para 4.

[27] eg, in the *Jordan* non-cooperation proceedings, states (other than Sudan) had to indicate their interest in applying, while international organisations could make submissions without requiring permission: see ibid, paras 3 and 2 respectively.

to an open call; such calls can produce a large number of potential *amici*, often with overlapping submissions. A permissive approach to *amici curiae*, that is accepting all submissions without a filtering process, risks overwhelming the Chamber and the parties and affecting the fair trial rights of the accused and the expeditiousness of proceedings and is therefore inappropriate for an institution primarily concerned with individual criminal responsibility. Moreover, accepting a number of briefs that are not actually helpful and are therefore ignored appears tokenistic, wastes resources of the Chamber, parties and the *amici* and may undermine support of the institution from *amici* in future. The practice also identifies a tension between inviting specific *amici*, a process that may not be transparent or representative, and open calls, which are more open and transparent but may overburden the parties and waste resources. We explore this tension in further chapters.

Figure 4.1 (set out above) also shows the acceptance rates overall and for each tribunal based on the method used to engage potential *amici*. In terms of acceptance rates, the overall acceptance rate across the Tribunals for all three methods is 61 per cent. There is a marked difference in the acceptance rate for voluntary applications (41 per cent overall), compared to open calls (97 per cent) and direct invitations (95 per cent, though 100 per cent would likely have been accepted – these statistics count only briefs actually submitted: the 5 per cent included for instance a non-response to an invitation). Again, the practice varies across the Tribunals, with the SCSL more likely to accept voluntary applications (69 per cent) compared to the ECCC (6 per cent), the latter making much more use of open calls.

ii. Role of the Parties in the Approval Process

Unlike in some national jurisdictions, the Tribunals do not require the parties to consent to the admission of *amici curiae*[28] – admission is within the discretion of the Chamber alone. Further, the rules do not grant parties or other participants the right to be heard on the admission of potential *amici*. Therefore, while some Chambers have allowed the parties an opportunity to comment before making the admissibility decision, others have not. Where parties do comment on admissibility, Chambers appear to take the position of the parties into account; however, the position of the parties is not definitive and Chambers have admitted *amici* in the face of opposition from one or more parties. Nor does the *amicus curiae* have the right to respond to the objections of the parties to its participation. Where possible, we suggest that it is good practice to allow the parties to comment on the admissibility of *amici curiae*.

[28] eg, r 37(2) of the Rules of the US Supreme Court provides that a brief can be filed with the written consent of the parties or with the permission of the Court.

Once an *amicus curiae* has received leave to participate, the ICC and the STL RPE explicitly provide for the Prosecutor and defence to respond to *amicus* submissions.[29] The ICC Appeals Chamber has held that failure to do so is a procedural error that could constitute a ground of appeal where it materially affected the relevant decision.[30] The Appeals Chamber suggested that this requires a Chamber to render a separate decision on the admission of the *amicus curiae*, rather than leaving this to the substantive decision.[31] However, Chambers, including the Appeals Chamber, do not always follow this requirement, particularly where an *amicus curiae* is rejected, rather than admitted.[32] Even in the absence of a formal requirement, other tribunals have allowed the parties and occasionally other participants (including other *amici*, particularly state *amici*) to submit observations regarding *amicus curiae* briefs.[33]

B. Modes of *Amicus Curiae* Participation

An *amicus curiae* will generally indicate in their request for leave the mode in which they wish to participate, although the call or invitation may specify the proposed mode of participation. This may include filing written submissions, presenting oral submissions or both. The decision on the admissibility request then indicates how the *amicus curiae* is to participate. The vast majority of *amici* participate by way of written submissions only. This is consistent with the more document-driven aspects of international criminal proceedings with many stages and issues, particularly for pre-trial issues, being resolved without oral hearings. There are examples of *amici* presenting submissions orally. For example, scholar Diane Orentlicher provided both written and oral submissions on the issue of amnesties at the SCSL.[34] Two civil society actors participated in oral proceedings concerning the implementation of reparations in *Lubanga*,[35]

[29] Special Tribunal for Lebanon, Rules of Procedure and Evidence (20 March 2009, as amended 8 February 2012) STL/BD/2009/01/Rev.4, r 131(B). The ECCC Rules provide that copies of the observations will be filed with the parties: Internal Rules (12 June 2007, as revised on 16 January 2015) Rev 9, r 33(2).

[30] *Prosecutor v L Gbagbo*, ICC AC, 12 December 2012, ICC-02/11-01/11-321, para 43–45, although in this instance the error did not have a material effect.

[31] ibid, para 43.

[32] For example, in an appeal of the order for reparations in Lubanga, the Appeals Chamber decided not to admit two civil society amici only in the judgment: *Prosecutor v Lubanga*, ICC AC, 3 March 2015, ICC-01/04-01/06-3129, paras 248–51.

[33] eg, International Criminal Tribunal for the Former Yugoslavia, Information Concerning the Submission of *Amicus Curiae* Briefs under r 74 (adopted 27 March 1997) IT/122, ss 5(c), (e); SCSL, *Amicus* Practice Direction, Art 6; STL, *Amicus* Practice Direction, Art 7 allows the Chamber to 'give other Participants an opportunity to be heard on the matter'.

[34] *Prosecutor v Kallon*, SCSL AC, 27 October 2003, SCSL-2003-06-PT-1815; *Prosecutor v Kallon,* SCSL AC, Transcript, 3 November 2003.

[35] *Prosecutor v Lubanga*, ICC TC II, 6 October 2016, IC-01/04-01/06-3245-tENG. See *Prosecutor v Lubanga,* ICC TC, Transcript, 11 October 2016.

alongside submitting written observations. In September 2018, several *amici* appeared in person during appellate proceedings concerning Jordan's failure to comply with a request to arrest and surrender President Bashir of Sudan.[36] Yet *amici* making oral submissions remain the exception.

C. Managing *Amicus Curiae* Participation

Chambers include limits on *amicus curiae* participation to manage the impact of the *amici* on the parties, the defendant's fair trial rights and the expeditiousness and efficiency of proceedings. First, Chambers impose restrictions on time, with deadlines for filing of submissions and, where an *amicus curiae* appears in person, limiting the time available to present oral submissions. Secondly, Chambers impose limits on the content of *amicus curiae* submissions. This includes limits as to volume, with page limits imposed and strictly enforced for written submissions. Chambers also restrict the focus of *amicus curiae* submissions to the matters on which the Chamber wishes to hear submissions. These may be the issues identified in the open call or invitation, listed in the application or stipulated in the admissibility decision. Thirdly, formal requirements will also apply to the written submissions in the same way as other submissions filed with that institution, for example, the language of submission, the format and presentation of the submission, the need for signature, and requirements to attach case lists and bibliographies.

This raises the question of what happens when an *amicus curiae* does not comply with these requirements. The Tribunals are strict with missed filing deadlines and reject late submissions, although this does not mean the Chamber does not see or take the submission into account.[37] Some Chambers have been more flexible with briefs that do not comply with formal requirements than for non-compliant filings by parties. Similarly, where *amici* provide oral submissions, they are expected to adhere to the time allocated. Where *amici* do not comply with content restrictions, there is usually a more subtle approach. As a Chamber is under no obligation to consider the submissions, the judges can simply ignore the entire submission or the parts that do not comply.

Managing the participation process is an important aspect of the Chamber's obligation to secure a fair and expeditious trial. It is also essential that Chambers

[36] Hearings were held from 10 to 14 September 2018: see, eg *Prosecutor v Al-Bashir,* ICC AC, Transcript, 10 September 2018, 105 onwards.

[37] Professor Ben Saul sought to file a brief in response to an open call issued by the STL, yet his request was rejected as he narrowly missed the deadline for filing: see B Saul, 'Legislating from a Radical Hague: The United Nations Special Tribunal for Lebanon Invents an International Crime of Transnational Terrorism' (2011) 24 *LJIL* 677, introductory note. Professor Saul subsequently published the rejected brief along with criticism of the Appeal Chamber's decision: B Saul, '*Amicus Curiae* Brief on the Notion of Terrorist Acts Submitted to the Appeals Chamber of the Special Tribunal for Lebanon Pursuant to Rule 131 of the Rules of Procedure and Evidence' (2011) 22 *Criminal Law Forum* 365.

treat *amici* in a fair, consistent and transparent manner, or they risk undermining any potential legitimacy benefits allowing *amicus curiae* participation may provide. However, our study shows that Chambers rarely explicitly consider the function an *amicus curiae* is to perform (expertise, representative or communicative) and how it might affect the modes of participation and any additional rights that the Chamber may be warranted in extending to particular *amici*. Subsequent chapters explore how Chambers may make such distinctions in practice, particularly by actor and function.

Chambers should continue to impose limits – both time and word or page restrictions – on all *amici curiae*. *Amici* indicated that Chambers had in the past set very short deadlines, which made it difficult for potential *amici* to apply and then meet filing deadlines.[38] Practice shows that some Chambers have set generous deadlines, which has been more successful in attracting a number of applications.[39] While Chambers must balance the time allowed for potential *amici curiae* to respond against the need to maintain expeditious proceedings, we suggest that where a Chamber views it as desirable to hear from a range of actors with particular expertise, that is more likely to occur when a reasonable time is allowed for application and filing of submissions (other than for urgent applications). Moreover, if the Chamber desires well-considered and thorough submissions, placing unrealistic time demands on potential *amici* risks undermining the quality of submissions. It may also disadvantage local actors who might not have the resources to 'drop everything' for a brief, have less experience in drafting briefs or lack a large staff to write the brief.

The steps taken to publicise calls for *amicus curiae* submissions are also relevant, as often the call is located within a scheduling order or issued orally at a status conference, so that only those following proceedings closely or notified by informal channels are aware of the call.[40] This means potentially valuable *amici curiae* learn of the call too late to apply or not at all, which may perpetuate the perception that certain actors, particularly larger international NGOs with a history of support for the Court, are privileged in participating in proceedings. Better-publicised calls with adequate time to respond may allow more collaborative submissions, which will reduce the burden on the Court and potentially improve the quality of the submission. One example is the open call issued by the international co-investigating judge in the ECCC in Case 003,[41] which allowed

[38] Professor Saul commented that the deadline set for the open call by the STL Appeals Chamber was not publicised: see Saul, 'Legislating from a Radical Hague' (n 37). Moreover, the deadline was very short. The President of the Appeals Chamber issued an invitation, in an oral decision, on Monday, 7 February 2011, inviting any amici to submit observations by that Friday: *Prosecutor v Ayyash et al*, STL AC, Transcript, 7 February 2011, 6, lines 13–21.

[39] eg in the *Jordan* non-cooperation proceedings, state and academic *amici* were allowed from 29 March to 30 April to file their request, and those *amici* approved were given from 21 May to 18 June to file observations.

[40] See eg the call by the STL, discussed at n 38 above, which was made in an oral decision.

[41] *Co-Prosecutors v Meas (Case 003)*, ECCC OCIJ, 19 April 2016, 003/07-09-2009-ECCC-OCIJ-D191.

one month for submissions[42] and was published on the website and through a range of other channels, including blog posts and international criminal law mailing lists.[43] It attracted a high number of applications, including a number of submissions made jointly.[44] At a minimum, Chambers should ensure that open calls are made available on the Tribunal website (in a visible and easy to locate position) and circulated through other channels, including social media or mailing lists. For open calls issued to states, Chambers will request the Registry to circulate the call to ICC states parties, a practice that should become standard. Moreover, the ICC and possibly future tribunals may wish to consider appointing an *amicus curiae* officer, either within the Registry or within the Chambers, to disseminate open calls and to manage requests and submissions. This role could also include designing guidance for potential *amici*, as well as maintaining the website so that information concerning past submissions and decisions is easily available.

Where reasonable deadlines are set, the Chamber should accept late applications or submissions only where there are exceptional grounds to justify the delay and the delay will not seriously impact the accused or the expeditiousness of proceedings. Of course, some Chambers may have deliberately set a short deadline so as to dissuade potential *amici* or *amici* they have not specifically informed about the opportunity.[45] We argue that this practice should be avoided: where a Chamber wishes to hear from a particular actor, it should invite them directly, explaining their reason for doing so.[46] If a Chamber does not wish to receive submissions or has no intention of relying on submissions it receives, it should not call for or accept submissions, as to do so wastes the resources of *amici*, potentially leads to frustration and may undermine the commitment to the institution and willingness of such actors to participate in future.

D. Status, Rights and Responsibilities of the *Amicus Curiae*

i. Status and Rights of the Amicus Curiae

The rules and practice make clear that the *amicus curiae* is not a party to proceedings, which is consistent with the practice in all international institutions and in national legal systems (see chapter two). A number of consequences for the

[42] ibid, para 12, which allowed from 19 April to 19 May 2016.

[43] The International Co-Investigating Judge requested 'the Office of the Administration to publish this call for submission on the ECCC's website and to take any other measure suitable to disseminate it among persons and organisations operating in the field of international criminal law': ibid, para 15.

[44] Eleven requests were received from academic and civil society actors: see *Co-Prosecutors v Meas (Case 003)*, ECCC OCIJ, 7 February 2017, 003/07-09-2009-ECCC-OCIJ-D306-17.1, para 4.

[45] We cannot know what the Chamber intended, but a possible example of this may be the invitation to *amici* in Lubanga reparations appeals, which allowed only 3 days, see *Prosecutor v Al Mahdi*, ICC AC, 7 November 2017, ICC-01/12-01/15-246. Similarly, this may lie behind the short deadline for the STL open call, discussed in n 38.

[46] eg, the specific invitation to Arbour and Cassese, see n 10 above.

rights of the *amicus curiae* follow from this limited status. First, an *amicus curiae* has no right to participate; participation is always only with the leave of the Chamber. This also means that there is no right to appeal a Chamber's decision *not* to admit an *amicus curiae*. *Amici* have no right to receive detailed reasons (or any reasons) for a decision to allow, or not to allow, participation. Secondly, as participation is discretionary, *amici curiae* have no right to have their submissions – whether oral or in writing – considered by the Chamber. The Chamber is free to ignore or give less weight to the submissions of *amici*. Thirdly, *amici* have no right to appeal the decision arising from the proceedings in which they participated (although note the position of certain *amici* as substitute defence counsel discussed in chapter six). Nor does an *amicus curiae* have a right to appear at subsequent phases of the proceedings and must apply for leave to participate at each stage. Some Chambers take a generous view and may invite or allow those *amici* participating at previous stages to participate in subsequent proceedings. Fourthly, *amici* do not have formal access to the case file or evidence held by the Chamber or the parties. Unlike institutions like the WTO and investor-state investment arbitration tribunals, where material on the case file is confidential, this may not be such an issue in the Tribunals, where most material is made publicly available via the tribunal's website (although case files during judicial investigations and in preliminary examinations and investigations at the ICC are confidential). However, there may be a delay in making this material available. This makes it challenging for an *amicus* seeking to access material for the purpose of making submissions, which is important given the requirement that submissions not duplicate those of the parties (see section V(D) below). Moreover, it is clear that *amici* do not have access to confidential filings or evidence or often the parties' proposed submissions.

Fifthly, *amici* are not parties and have no right to participate in hearings, respond to the submissions of the parties, question or call witnesses (including expert witnesses), present evidence or respond to party submissions or those of other participants (including other *amici*).[47] Further, *amici* are not considered witnesses and unlike expert witnesses cannot be examined by the parties.[48] Their submission, if accepted by the Chamber, will generally form part of the case file and will be made available to the parties and publicly via the tribunal website, although in some tribunals this has taken some time and the practice has not been uniformly followed. Oral submissions will ordinarily be in public session and will form part of the transcript of the proceedings. For those *amici* who apply, but are not granted leave to participate, their application will form

[47] Although note the position of *amici* as substitute counsel discussed in ch 6 and additional rights sometimes given to state *amici* discussed in ch 7.

[48] See ICTY *Amicus* Information, s 5(e); ECCC *Amicus* Information, s 5(d); STL *Amicus* Practice Direction, Art 8 – though this matter is not addressed in the SCSL *Amicus* Practice Direction. For example, regarding standing, see *Prosecutor v Prlić et al*, ICTY AC, 4 July 2017, IT-04-74-A-22158.

part of the case file but any submissions they may have already prepared will not, although the *amicus* can make the submissions available via their own dissemination mechanisms. The exception is where the brief is annexed to the request for leave.

Sixthly, the *amicus* must bear his or her own costs and generally has no right to benefit from costs orders against the parties or to receive financial assistance towards the costs of preparing submissions or, if permitted, appearing in person.[49] This is in contrast to the accused and victims, who receive financial and legal assistance, and experts, who receive remuneration for their services. There have been some exceptions to this approach: unusually, a Chamber may allow reimbursement of expenses where the *amicus curiae* was specifically invited.[50] There is also no support fund for *amici* from developing states. However, unlike some national systems, there is no provision for the *amicus curiae* to be ordered to pay costs either for impact on the Chamber or on the parties. For a Chamber to introduce an obligation for costs would be inconsistent with the notion of *amici* appearing either at the invitation of, or with leave from, that Chamber.

ii. Duties of the Amicus Curiae

As a non-party, *amici curiae* are not bound by the decision reached by the Chamber, even where they have participated in proceedings, therefore they have no duty to comply with a decision. While this may appear to be irrelevant given the primary function of the Tribunals is individual criminal responsibility, this may be significant, particularly for two categories of *amici*. First, states may seek to participate in proceedings concerning issues such as cooperation or jurisdiction, where the outcome may have broader implications. State *amici* would not be bound by a determination by the Chamber. However, as is considered further in chapter seven, state submissions may contribute to establishing practice for the ICC, or to the formation of customary international law, or be applied in proceedings in other tribunals. Secondly, for accused in linked trials as discussed in chapter six, while they are not formally bound, the decision may contribute to establishing a 'judicial fact' of which judges take notice, lead to jurisprudence that other chambers apply, or lead to *res judicata* findings in subsequent hearings.

As noted above, *amici* are usually not entitled to receive confidential filings or evidence or to participate in closed sessions. However, *amici* should be subject to provisions in the legal frameworks of the Tribunals regarding confidentiality, non-publicity and the protection of victims and witnesses.

[49] See, eg STL Practice Direction, Art 9.

[50] ICTY *Amicus* Information, s 5(f); ECCC *Amicus* Information, s 5(e); SCSL *Amicus* Practice Direction, Art 7; STL *Amicus* Practice Direction, Art 9(2).

V. SUBSTANTIVE CRITERIA FOR ADMITTING *AMICI CURIAE*

A. The General Criterion for Admission

As outlined in chapter three, admission of *amici curiae* is a matter of procedure. Although the wording differs slightly across the Tribunals, the general criterion is that admission of the *amicus curiae* must be 'desirable for the proper determination of the case'.[51] However, Chambers have varied in the test applied. For example, the ICTY and ICTR have commonly considered whether submissions 'would assist'[52] or 'may also assist'[53] the Chambers. Thus, it appears that the essential criterion is that the submissions must be helpful to the Chamber. Chambers have occasionally used a higher test, for example, stating that the submissions must be essential to reach a decision or that *amici* participate only on an exceptional basis. One example of this, discussed further in chapters five and six, is in *Ntaganda*, where the Chamber stated that 'the Chamber will resort, at its discretion, to *amicus curiae* observations **only on an exceptional basis**, when it is of the view that such observations providing specific expertise are needed on particular topics'.[54] Other Chambers have articulated a more flexible test for admission of *amici curiae*. Of particular note is that advanced by the Appeals Chamber of the SCSL, which provides:[55]

> The issue is whether it is desirable to receive such assistance, and desirable does not mean 'essential' (which would be over-restrictive) nor does it have an over-permissive meaning such as 'convenient' or 'interesting'. The discretion will be exercised in favour of an application where there is a real reason to believe that written submissions, or such submissions supplemented by oral argument, will help the Court to reach the right decision on the issue before it.

The use of this broad criterion – being helpful to the Chamber – accords with the discretion the relevant rules give to Chambers. Applying too high a threshold for the admission of *amici* is inconsistent with the wording of the provisions and unduly restricts the Chamber's discretion to accept submissions. The flexibility of the criterion has led Chambers to develop specific criteria, but on an *ad hoc* basis. This section examines the criteria Chambers have applied in practice to determine whether admitting *amicus curiae* will be helpful.

[51] This is the wording for the rule at the ICTY, ICTR, ICC and SCSL. The ECCC refers to the 'adjudication' of the case, while the STL uses the phrase 'would assist the proper determination of the case'.

[52] eg, *Prosecutor v Nahimana, Barayagwiza and Ngeze*, ICTR AC, 12 January 2007, ICTR-99-52-A-9702/H, 3.

[53] *Prosecutor v Hategekimana*, ICTR TC, 20 March 2008, ICTR-00-55B-I-377, para 21.

[54] *Prosecutor v Ntaganda*, ICC PTC II, 18 February 2014, ICC-01/04-02-06-259, para 3, citing *Prosecutor v Ruto, Kosgey and Sang*, ICC PTC II, 12 April 2011, ICC-01/09-01/11-49, para 14 (emphasis added).

[55] *Prosecutor v Kallon*, SCSL AC, 1 November 2003, SCSL-2003-07-PT-2386, para 5 (emphasis in original).

Chambers sometimes make decisions on admission of *amici* orally or there is no record of a decision being taken at all. On occasion, the decision to reject or accept a request is contained in the decision arising from the proceedings in which the *amicus* sought to participate. Where written decisions are issued, they are usually brief and may not indicate clearly why a particular application was accepted or rejected. This 'means the conditions under which *amici* are granted leave to submit observations remain opaque'.[56] It also makes determining the Chambers' reasoning and view of the role of the *amicus curiae* mechanism challenging and may lead to different treatment of an *amicus curiae* or class of *amici*. This undermines the transparency, consistency and predictability of the process for the parties and potential *amici* and may affect the legitimacy of the institution in the eye of certain stakeholders. NGOs appearing before the ICC, for example, 'have expressed concerns regarding the lack of clarity that characterizes the Court's practice in this respect'.[57] Therefore, while admission of *amici* is within the discretion of the Chamber, we consider a failure to give adequate reasons as poor judicial practice. We recommend that Chambers should provide reasons that allow an *amicus curiae* to understand on what basis their application has been accepted or rejected, beyond merely saying submissions will or will not be of assistance. Although admissibility decisions do not need to be extensive, the decisions should as a minimum address the function the *amicus* will be fulfilling (ie, why it will be of assistance to the tribunal) and the criteria that are relevant to that function (see below). Failure to do so is inconsistent with principles of transparency and equal treatment of *amici curiae* across Chambers and makes it challenging for *amici* to know how to meet the Chamber's expectations in future.

Despite the challenges in identifying judicial reasons, we have advanced a number of substantive criteria for admission of *amici*, which are set out in Table 4.1, against the three functions we have identified. Table 4.1 also identifies additional criteria drawn from the literature but that have not yet featured in judicial decisions. The criteria we have identified are not determinative; rather, they are factors we suggest a Chamber should consider when assessing whether a submission will be helpful. Many of the criteria are connected; for example, concerns regarding delay may be addressed by the criteria of duplication and requiring submissions only on novel issues. As we explore in the next three chapters, these criteria may apply differently to various categories of stakeholders and depending on the function the *amicus curiae* is to perform. Ultimately, given the discretion under the relevant rules, the Chamber has considerable flexibility. Moreover, the Chamber remains the decision-maker and is able to accept submissions regardless of these criteria, but may then assess their probative value and determine the weight – if any – given to such submissions in reaching a decision.

[56] MS Ellis, 'NGO Intervention in Court Proceedings Through *Amicus Curiae* Briefs' in LE Carter, MS Ellis and C Chernor Jalloh (eds), *The International Criminal Court in an Effective Global Justice System* (Cheltenham, Edward Elgar, 2016) 327.

[57] ibid, 285. Our own interviews supported this statement.

Table 4.1 Suggested Criteria for Accepting *Amici Curiae*

Criteria	Description	Expertise function	Representative function	Communicative function
General criterion: Useful/ of assistance to the Chamber	This is the general requirement for an *amicus curiae* to be accepted. The proposed submissions must assist the Chamber in reaching a proper determination of the issue or case; that is, the submissions must be **helpful** to the Chamber.	Yes.	Yes.	Yes.
Fair Trial	Acceptance of an *amicus curiae* must not unduly impact the right of the accused to a fair trial, in particular the right to trial without undue delay and equality of arms and, in some circumstances, the right to self-representation. *Amici curiae* should not put forward a substitute line of defence without input from or the full agreement of the accused.	Yes.	Yes.	Yes.
Expeditious and efficient proceedings	Generally increasing the burden on the Chamber or delaying proceedings. The *amicus curiae* must remain the friend of the Court and must not become a substitute counsel for the accused.	Yes.	Yes.	Yes.
Duplication	Submissions should not duplicate those of the parties and other participants, the core competence of the judges or expertise/submissions otherwise available to the Chamber (ie, repeat information already in public domain).	Yes.	Yes.	Yes.
Timeliness	*Amici curiae* must meet any deadlines for applying and filing. Submissions must not be filed after the determination has already been made or the relevant proceedings held (ie, if Chamber has heard from parties and has retired to reach a decision).	Yes.	Yes.	Yes.

(continued)

Table 4.1 *(Continued)*

Criteria	Description	Expertise function	Representative function	Communicative function
The stage of proceedings	*Amici curiae* must participate at the right stage of proceedings, where their submissions are relevant. The Chamber may consider the stage of proceedings, and the extent to which defence rights are engaged, when determining whether *amicus* participation is appropriate.	Yes.	Yes.	Yes.
The impact of *amicus curiae* participation on the parties	The participation of *amici* should not have a disproportionate impact on the parties, in the sense of creating additional burdens for the parties, for example excessive submissions to review or introducing additional arguments that have not been raised by the parties or are not necessary to consider in the proceedings.	Yes.	Yes.	Yes.
Legal or factual submissions	*Amici* should normally provide legal submissions, not factual submissions.	Yes.	Yes – although *amici* may be required to give factual information in certain circumstances due to their particular interest.	Yes.
Relevance	The submissions must be relevant to the issues to be determined by the Chamber. This means the submissions must: (1) be relevant to the stage of proceedings (ie, submissions re sentencing not relevant re pre-trial); (2) address legal (and exceptionally factual) issues that are ***raised directly*** by the proceedings at hand not unrelated or speculative issues.	Yes.	Yes.	Yes.

(continued)

Table 4.1 *(Continued)*

Criteria	Description	Expertise function	Representative function	Communicative function
Nature, novelty and importance of the issues raised	**Novel issue:** legal provision, rule or procedure has not been previously applied or interpreted or there is ambiguity/ uncertainty in its interpretation or application, seeking to declare or develop customary international law. **Importance:** the issue is of broader importance than the outcome in a particular proceeding and goes to the efficacy of the institution/ system.	Yes.	No – those affected by a decision should be able to participate regardless of the issue.	Not typically – while communicative function submissions will almost certainly need to address novel and important issues if they are provided, this function should be limited to situations where novel and important issues arise, normally for states in non-cooperation proceedings.
Independence	This means independent from the Court and the parties and – for actors other than states – the state: in the sense of not having an on-going or previous relationship with the Court or its personnel, or an affected state.	Yes.	Yes – except where the *amicus curiae* representing the interests of defence, victims, or others directly interested in proceedings that do not have an alternative avenue for participation.	Yes.
Impartiality and the presence or absence of an interest	An interest of a legal nature that is directly affected by the proceedings or their outcome. A general interest in the development of the law, the institution or the issue before the Chamber should not be considered an interest that is directly affected by proceedings.	No – *amici curiae* acting as experts should not have a direct interest in proceedings.	Yes – an interest is required for the representative function.	No – *amici curiae* acting in the communicative function should not have a direct interest.
Expertise and experience	*Amici curiae* should demonstrate expertise and experience relevant to their proposed submissions and the issues before the Chamber.	Yes – it is vital that an *amicus curiae* demonstrate a specific expertise not otherwise available to the Chamber and relevant to issues raised.	No – although submissions must still be legally sound, professional and competent.	No – although submissions must still be legally sound, professional and competent.
Availability of alternative avenues	Where a state, victim, defence or other actor has a specific right of standing/participation under the statute, that should be preferred to Rule 103.	Yes.	Yes.	Yes.

(continued)

Table 4.1 *(Continued)*

Criteria	Description	Expertise function	Representative function	Communicative function
Professionalism and ethics	The *amicus curiae* is able to assist the Chamber in a professional and ethical manner and to meet any ethical/professional standards expected of *amici*.	Yes.	Yes.	Yes.
Representativeness and plurality of voices	To what extent does *amicus curiae* participation allow broader representation and plurality in proceedings?	Yes – the Chamber should consider, where possible, the diversity of *amici curiae* and where appropriate try to encourage participation from groups that are under-represented.	Yes – the Chamber should consider any claims to represent an interest-holder. The Chamber should consider whether any affected actors have not participated and, where it would be appropriate to do so, consider calling for submissions.	No – it is not possible for *amici curiae* to represent the diversity of public interests in criminal proceedings.

B. Fair Trial

As noted in chapter three, section V(B), the Tribunals must protect the rights of the accused to a fair trial. We argue that this should also extend to how a Chamber approaches its *amicus curiae* practice. Our study shows that three fair trial rights have particularly been implicated in *amicus curiae* decisions: the right to trial without undue delay, the principle of equality of arms, and the right of self-representation. We discuss here the first two principles, while we consider the right of self-representation in chapter six.

i. Trial Without Undue Delay

The right of the accused to trial without undue delay is explicitly protected in the statutes of all of the Tribunals.[58] The concept of undue delay is also related to a tribunal's duty to ensure 'fair and expeditious' proceedings.[59] Therefore, the prevention of delay is not only an aspect of fair trial, but also an institutional

[58] See Rome Statute, Art 67(1)(c); SCSL Statute, Art 17(4)(c); STL Statute, Art 16(4)(c); ICTY Statute, Art 21(4)(c); ICTR Statute, Art 20(4)(c).

[59] See Rome Statute, Arts 64(2) and 64(3).

interest of the Tribunals (see below).[60] The Tribunals often do not explicitly distinguish between the tribunal's interest in expediency and the accused's right to trial without undue delay in their reasoning, making an assessment of the balancing of the different interests made by the Tribunals difficult. Both concepts, of delay and expediency, are implicated in *amicus curiae* practice. Chambers commonly cite the risk of causing delay to proceedings as a reason to deny applications. For example, ICC Pre-Trial Chamber II rejected an *amicus* application by Amnesty International stating: 'the desirability and appropriateness of allowing submissions under rule 103(1) of the Rules has to be assessed against the duty of the Chamber to ensure the expeditiousness of the proceedings as a fundamental tenet of their fairness'.[61] Secondly, the defence often objects to the admission of *amicus* submissions on the basis of delay. In both the *Lubanga*[62] and *Ntaganda*[63] cases, the defence opposed the admission of *amici* due to the prolongation of proceedings that their participation would cause, arguing that this would constitute a violation of the accused's right to trial without undue delay.[64]

The question of whether admitting *amici* is 'desirable' requires Chambers to consider the impact on the length of the proceedings. Nonetheless, it is rare that delay to proceedings is cited as the sole reason for denying an *amicus* application. The decisions indicate that delay becomes more concerning to the Tribunals when the submissions are likely to be duplicative of submissions made by the parties or other *amici*. Furthermore, the reasoning of the Chamber in these decisions generally does not distinguish between delay as a risk to the accused's right to a fair trial, and the tribunal's institutional interest in expediency. As noted above, this lack of specificity makes it difficult to assess how the Tribunals have balanced the different interests involved. This is particularly problematic in cases where Chambers cite delay to reject *amicus curiae* briefs that would align with the defence, or where, *a fortiori*, the defence supports admission of the *amicus* brief.[65] We explore this issue further in chapter six.

ii. Equality of Arms

Although the principle of equality of arms is not explicitly protected in the statutes of the Tribunals, judicial decisions have confirmed that this

[60] The ICTY TC held 'the Tribunal has a legitimate interest in ensuring that the trial proceedings in a timely manner without interruptions, adjournments or disruptions'. *Prosecutor v Šešelj*, ICTY TC II, 9 May 2003, IT-03-67-PT.

[61] *Prosecutor v Kony et al*, ICC PTC II, 10 November 2008, ICC-02/04-01/05-342.

[62] *Prosecutor v Lubanga*, ICC AC, 9 April 2013, ICC-01/04-01/06-3013.

[63] *Prosecutor v Ntaganda*, ICC TC VI, 23 September 2014, ICC-01/04-02/06-375.

[64] Both applications were also opposed by the defence in the two cases on the basis that the *amici* sought to make factual rather than legal submissions.

[65] See, eg *Prosecutor v Bemba*, ICC AC, 9 November 2009, ICC-01/05-01/08-602.

principle is part of the fair trial rights of the defence, and particularly the right to adequate time and resources for the preparation of the defence case.[66] The prosecution, as well as the defence, may benefit from the principle of equality of arms.[67] The admission of *amici* can exacerbate concerns as to equality of arms. An influx of *amicus* submissions increases the already large amount of material that the defence must address, and can further augment the structural imbalance against the accused. This is particularly so if the *amicus* submissions align with the prosecution, as the defence will be required to carefully review and respond to such submissions alongside those of the prosecution. Further, at tribunals that provide for victim participation, such as the ICC and ECCC, the defence is already tasked with responding to two parties' submissions, which are likely to align against defence interests. Logically, therefore, the equality of arms principle must also require that *amicus* admission decisions be considered in light of the additional burden it may cause for the defence.

Defence submissions have highlighted equality of arms objections to several applications for *amicus curiae* status. For instance, counsel for Nuon Chea and Khieu Samphan at the ECCC objected to the admission of an *amicus* on the basis that 'abuse of *amici curiae* poses threats to equality of arms'. The defence argued:[68]

> *[A]mici curiae* should not be lightly resorted to as it may easily affect the proper balance between the parties to a case. The arguments that the Applicants seek to make clearly benefit the Co-Prosecutors and the Civil Parties to the present case. In such a circumstance, if the *Amicus Curiae* Brief is admitted, the Defence will effectively have to respond to three counterparts: the Co-Prosecutors, the Civil Parties, and the *amici curiae*. This undermines the fundamental principle of equality of arms, unfairly increases the burden of the Defence, and will eventually infringe upon the rights of Mr Nuon Chea.

Such arguments have generally not been persuasive and Chambers have not rejected *amici* expressly based on the equality of arms. However, while the ECCC Trial Chamber admitted the briefs in question, it appeared to recognise the *possibility* that partisan, pro-prosecution *amicus* briefs may create an 'imbalance of resources' between prosecution and defence and therefore may hypothetically violate the principle of equality of arms.[69] Some

[66] See, eg *Prosecutor v Banda, Nourain and Jerbo*, ICC AC, 28 August 2013, ICC-02/05-03/09-501, para 34.

[67] *Prosecutor v Chui*, ICC AC, 27 February 2015, ICC-01/04-02/12-271-AnxA, para 6.

[68] *Co-Prosecutors v Nuon and Khieu (Case 002)*, ECCC TC, 4 July 2016, 002/19-09-2007-ECCC/TC-E418/1, para 18. See also *Prosecutor v Lubanga*, ICC TC I, 18 February 2008, ICC-01/04-01/06-1175, para 3.

[69] *Co-Prosecutors v Nuon and Khieu (Case 002)*, ECCC TC, 13 September 2016, 002/19-09-2007/ECCC/TC-E418/3, para 14.

domestic courts have recognised the risk to the principle of equality of arms posed by *amici*. For example, the South African Constitutional Court recognised that *amicus curiae* participation possibly infringes the equality of arms principle:[70]

> As a general matter, in criminal matters a court should be astute not to allow the submissions of an *amicus* to stack the odds against an accused person. Ordinarily, an accused in criminal matters is entitled to a well-defined case emanating from the state. If the submissions of an *amicus* tend to strengthen the case against the accused, this is cause for caution. This, however, is not an inflexible rule. But it is a consideration based on fairness, equality of arms, and more importantly, what is in the interests of justice.

The principle of equality of arms is therefore a factor the Chamber should consider when determining whether to admit an *amicus curiae*. Particularly where multiple *amici* seek to participate, Chambers can minimise the impact on the defence by managing the process carefully, preferably by setting a single deadline for submission of briefs (on clearly defined questions and with word/page limits), therefore allowing the defence and the prosecution to make a single combined response to the submissions. The Chamber should also allow the parties a reasonable time within which to review and respond to submissions. However, the practice at the Tribunals does not suggest that *amicus* participation has been impacting significantly on equality of arms. As discussed above, Chambers do not admit a large number of *amici* in a given stage of proceedings, particularly during the trial phase. The main exceptions usually arise in the context of state cooperation, thus not directly raising fair trial concerns, for example, the Jordan non-cooperation proceedings and the *Blaškić* ICTY subpoena proceedings, both discussed in chapter seven.

Another measure that provides further data on whether *amicus* participation unduly affects the equality of arms is to consider the apparent alignment of the *amicus curiae* with the parties and other participants. This can be challenging, as *amici curiae* do not typically profess their alignment and, where *amici* are rejected, we do not have the benefit of the submission to assess the alignment of the arguments. However, with this caveat, most briefs align with those of the prosecution, defence or victims. As shown in Figure 4.5, across the tribunals around a third of applicants support the defence, with a similar proportion of 15–20 per cent of applicants favouring each of the prosecution, victims, government, or seeming to focus only on 'legal' analysis (or undetermined). This suggests that, at the very least, *amici curiae* do not exclusively buttress the arguments of an already relatively better resourced prosecution.

[70] *Ex Parte Institute for Security Studies: In re The State v Basson* (2006) (2) SACR 350 (CC), paras 14–15. For further comment on this decision see J Brickhill, 'The Intervention of *Amici Curiae* in Criminal Matters: *S v Zuma* and *S v Basson* Considered' (2006) 123 *South African Law Journal* 391.

However, of accepted *amicus curiae* observations, the proportions allocated to each of these categories of alignment are much more similar, suggesting that defence-oriented applicants are more likely to be rejected. Thus, as outlined in chapter six, equality of arms may be a factor in favour of admitting defence-aligned briefs.

Figure 4.5 Proportion of Applicants by Apparent Alignment

	ICC	ICTY	ICTR	ECCC	SCSL	STL	All
Defence	31%	23%	52%	19%	11%	64%	33%
Prosecution	18%	3%	6%	40%	44%	0%	16%
Victims	30%	10%	10%	11%	6%	4%	17%
Legal/Other	9%	36%	6%	26%	39%	14%	18%
Government	10%	22%	25%	0%	0%	11%	13%
Unknown	2%	5%	1%	4%	0%	7%	3%

Note: Individual figures rounded.

C. Expeditious and Efficient Proceedings

As indicated in the previous section, *amicus curiae* participation may impact the institutional interest in maintaining expeditious proceedings. In the face of budgetary pressures, and the introduction of completion strategies at the *ad hoc* tribunals, expeditiousness is increasingly a focus of international criminal proceedings.[71] This institutional interest is distinct from the obligation to ensure the accused is tried without undue delay. The institutional interest in expediency and efficiency at times may pull in a different direction from the rights of the defence.[72] Moreover, Kent and Trinidad comment that while the:[73]

> management of third-party *amicus* participation before international courts and tribunals is often presented as a trade-off between legitimacy and efficiency ... The more nuanced reality is that, depending on how third-party *amicus* participation is managed, it has the potential to enhance or undermine both the efficiency and the legitimacy of the proceedings.

[71] See R Clements, 'From Bureaucracy to Management: The International Criminal Court's Internal Progress Narrative' (2019) 32(1) *LJIL* 149.

[72] See G-J Alexander Knoops, 'The Dichotomy between Judicial Economy and Equality of Arms within International and Internationalized Criminal Trials: A Defense Perspective' (2004) 28 *Fordham International law Journal* 1566, 1568, noting the tension between 'judicial economy' – an aspect of the expediency of proceedings – and the principle of equality of arms displayed in recent practice at the ICTY (giving the example of Art 73ter of the ICTY RPE, allowing limitations on the time and number of defence witnesses).

[73] A Kent and J Trinidad, 'The Management of Third-party Amicus Participation before International Criminal Tribunals: Juggling Efficiency and Legitimacy' (2017) 17 *ICLR* 728, 729.

The practice suggests that Chambers do consider the extent to which admitting *amici curiae* leads to delays from an institutional perspective. However, the Chamber balances the potential benefit of the submission against the likely delay and the measures it can adopt to minimise delay. Chambers appear to be managing consequences for delay: the practice does not reveal examples of significant delay to proceedings caused by participation of *amici curiae*. As chapter six discusses, Chambers may use *amici* as substitute counsel to encourage expeditiousness where an accused is uncooperative, although this too has not proved to be successful.[74]

D. Duplication

Submissions are unlikely to assist a Chamber if they duplicate the submissions that the parties or other participants have made or are likely to make (including other *amici* or experts)[75] or repeat submissions that the applicant has made at an earlier stage.[76] Similarly, submissions that present material that is otherwise available to the Chamber, particularly information already in the public domain, are unlikely to be accepted, although this does not include information that would only be available to the Chamber through excessive effort or expense. A Chamber may also decline to admit *amici curiae* when it considers that 'sufficient information has been provided to the Chamber to enable it to reach an informed decision'.[77]

Chambers can take steps to minimise potential duplication by stipulating questions on which they require submissions in open calls and managing the approval process so that *amici* cover different questions, linked to their expertise or experience, rejecting *amici* that will make submissions that clearly duplicate other participants and/or encouraging *amici* to submit coordinated or collaborative submissions.

There are a number of challenges for Chambers and *amici* in this process. First, potential *amici* may not have access to the full case file, particularly the filings of the parties, or know which arguments the parties will be submitting. Similarly, *amici* usually are not aware of which other *amici* may be considering applying, which makes collaboration and avoiding duplication challenging. Secondly, particularly for voluntary applications, Chambers often accept the first

[74] See ch 6, s IV(C).

[75] eg *Prosecutor v Bemba*, ICC AC, 9 November 2009, ICC-01/05-01/08-602, para 11: the Appeals Chamber finds that the observations that Aprodec wishes to make 'would serve merely to repeat submissions already provided by the parties and participants'.

[76] eg *Prosecutor v Munyakazi*, ICTR AC, 15 July 2008, ICTR-97-36-R11*bis*-82/H, 2: 'the issues that the ICDAA submits that it would address as *amicus curiae* before the Appeals Chamber are the same as those it addressed in its submissions before the Trial Chamber'.

[77] *Prosecutor v Lubanga*, ICC TC I, 12 December 2011, ICC-01/04-01/06-2832, para 5.

amicus curiae to apply and then reject subsequent *amici* as likely to duplicate. This is not the best way to make sure the Chamber receives the most suitable submissions from the most qualified experts, nor is it a fair and consistent process. Instead, where a Chamber wishes to have assistance from *amici curiae*, or the issues are such that voluntary submissions are likely, better practice would be to issue an open call with a reasonable deadline for applications and then to consider the applications together to identify the *amici* most likely to be helpful, rather than accepting the first to file.

E. Timeliness

A related matter is the timeliness of the proposed brief. As noted above, Chambers require *amici* to meet any deadlines for applying and filing of submissions and can reject applications or submissions received after the deadline.[78] The application must be made at the appropriate time, namely when the issue is actually under consideration. Chambers will generally refuse leave where the application is premature, has been filed after the relevant proceedings have been held, the Chamber has already heard from the parties on the issue, or the determination is already made or is pending. The *amicus curiae* must be applying to participate in the right stage of proceedings, for example, if an issue is relevant to a subsequent phase of proceedings or is now on appeal, the Chamber will not grant permission to participate, as the submissions will not be relevant to an issue currently before the Chamber.

F. The Stage of Proceedings

Chambers also consider the stage of proceedings as a possible factor when determining whether to admit *amici*. As discussed in section III(A) above, there is no restriction as to the type or phase of judicial proceedings in which *amicus curiae* participation can occur. *Amici* can participate in the pre-trial and trial phase and in appellate proceedings (including interlocutory appeals) and during sentencing. *Amici* have also participated in proceedings concerning challenges to admissibility and jurisdiction and state cooperation, as well as reparations proceedings (where separate to the trial). We expected to see fewer briefs accepted during trial (and confirmation of charges), sentencing and appellate proceedings concerning conviction. These phases directly concern the core competence of the judges – determining the individual criminal responsibility of the accused – and have a greater focus on evidence and factual submissions,

[78] eg Saul, 'Legislating from a Radical Hague' (n 37).

therefore presenting the biggest potential risk to the fair trial rights of the accused. As the SCSL Appeals Chamber noted:[79]

> The Rule [Rule 74] may, however, be approached differently in the Trial Chamber as distinct from the Appeals Chamber. What is desirable in the latter may be most undesirable in the former where the equality of arms principle may require that the parties engage in an adversarial exercise untrammeled by interventions from third parties, however well-intentioned. The overriding need to get on with the trial, without disruption and fairly both to prosecution and defence, may well make it undesirable to grant leave …

We also expected to see more briefs at the pre-trial phase (including interlocutory appeals) and in novel phases, such as reparations. Based on the literature concerning judicial decision-making that suggests judges at the appellate level are more likely to face novel and important issues,[80] we also anticipated a higher number of briefs in appellate chambers.

The practice partly realises these predictions. Figure 4.6 shows the breakdown of *amicus curiae* participation by stage of proceedings across all of the Tribunals and within each of the tribunals. It shows that the largest proportion of *amicus* applications have occurred at the pre-trial stage. However, when broken down by tribunal, the practice at the ECCC and STL skews this result, due to the submission of a number of pre-trial briefs addressing issues such as jurisdiction, provisional detention, preliminary legal matters and civil party participation. The balance between the trial and pre-trial stage favours the pre-trial stage at the ICC as well, when issues of state cooperation, jurisdiction and admissibility are included. The practice concerning reparations at the ICC, discussed separately at section VII below, does show a higher number of briefs accepted. In contrast, at the ICTR and SCSL *amici* participated almost exclusively during the trial phase. However, this impression is somewhat misleading, given the absence of comparable pre-trial procedures at these institutions. When we examine the substance of the briefs, the ICTR and the SCSL *amici* were often addressing issues that in other tribunals are pre-trial issues, including jurisdiction, head of state immunity and the effect of amnesties and, for the ICTR, proceedings concerning referral to national jurisdictions (see chapter seven). What is clear is that *amici* admitted in trial proceedings very rarely address issues directly concerning criminal responsibility, with the exception of *amici* as substitute defence counsel, discussed in chapter six (and not included in the data mentioned here).

[79] *Prosecutor v Kallon*, SCSL AC, 1 November 2003, SCSL-2003-07-PT-2386, para 6.

[80] eg Aloisi and Meernik suggest that judges will be more likely to exercise judicial creativity at the appellate level, which we thought may lead appellate judges to accept more briefs: R Aloisi and J Meernik, *Judgment Day: Judicial Decision Making at the International Criminal Tribunals* (Cambridge, CUP, 2017).

Figure 4.6 Applications (including for Calls/Invitations) by Stage of Trial (%)

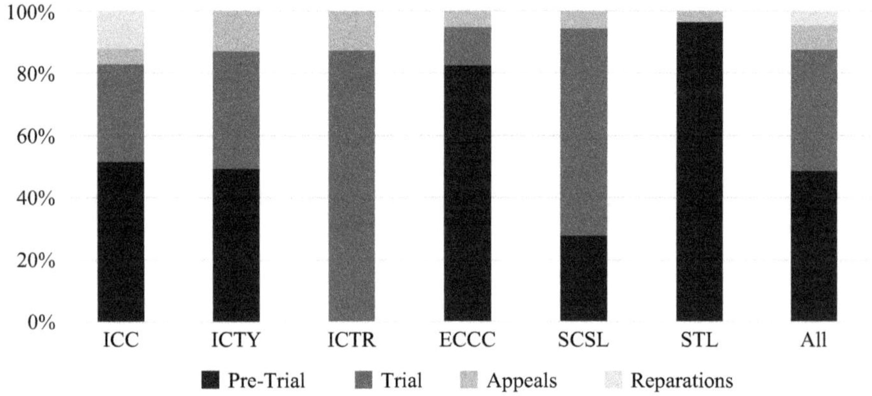

In relation to a more flexible approach to *amici* at the appellate level, the practice does not support this prediction, as shown in Figure 4.7. The ICC Appeals Chamber has accepted 22 *amici*, giving it an approximately 56 per cent approval rate, which is higher than the overall approval rate for the ICC of 48 per cent (not including invitations).[81] However, this statistic is dominated by *amici* participating in interlocutory appeals, with the proceedings in the *Jordan* non-cooperation proceedings pursuant to the open call causing a spike in both application and admission rates. Otherwise, the ICC Appeals Chamber only received one application in relation to a substantive appeal from conviction, which it rejected,[82] and approved two requests in appeals from reparations proceedings (both concerning the TFV, see section VII). With the exception of the *Jordan* non-cooperation proceedings, the Appeals Chamber has not adopted a noticeably more permissive approach to *amicus curiae* participation; in fact, the data suggests the opposite.

Figure 4.7 Acceptances by Chambers and Stage of Trial

	No.	Proportion %	Acceptances	Acceptance Rate (%)
Pre-Trial Chamber	98	24%	58	59%
Trial Chamber	170	42%	106	62%
Appeals Chamber	108	26%	61	56%
Other*	32	8%	22	69%
	408	100%	247	

* eg Contempt Judge, Single Judge, Specially Appointed Chamber or Unknown.

[81] This figure is based on the number of accepted applications from voluntary applications and open calls, but excludes invitations, in contrast to Figures 4.6 and 4.7, which include all avenues of participation.

[82] *Prosecutor v Lubanga*, ICC AC, 16 August 2013, ICC-01/04-01/06-3044.

At the ECCC, the practice is more complex as, in addition to the appellate role of the Supreme Court Chamber (SCC), the Pre-Trial Chamber hears appeals from decisions of the co-investigating judges and from the issue of closing orders. The SCC did not receive many applications (one from an interlocutory matter and four in substantive appeals) and rejected them all. The Pre-Trial Chamber was more liberal in its approach, accepting 37 briefs from 44 applications or responses to calls; however, most of these concerned preliminary issues (appeals from decisions on provisional detention and on civil party participation) and were in response to open invitations. The Pre-Trial Chamber accepted only three briefs in relation to 'substantive' appeals from a closing order, but those three *amici* had been directly invited.[83] The SCSL Appeals Chamber did adopt a flexible approach to *amici* at the appellate stage, accepting 11 from 13 applications (two of which were directly invited); however, these all concerned interlocutory appeals and it did not admit *amici* in relation to substantive appeals. The ICTY Appeals Chamber admitted only one brief in a substantive appeal that advanced legal arguments concerning the *mens rea* requirement for aiding and abetting under customary international law,[84] although it admitted several in interlocutory proceedings, mainly in the *Blaškić* proceedings (see chapter seven). The ICTR and STL Appeals Chambers also had modest practice, with no briefs admitted in substantive appeals and only a few in interlocutory appeals.

This is contrary to what the literature would suggest and, with a few key exceptions, does not show appellate judges engaging in conversations with stakeholders regarding the development of the law or seeking stakeholder 'support' for more liberal interpretations of the law. The low number of applicants at the appellate stage may reflect that interested actors have already offered submissions at previous stages or the issues on appeal may be quite narrow and technical. Alternatively, it may also evidence a more cautious attitude from appellate judges to *amici*, other than where the judges issue an open call (eg, in the *Jordan* non-cooperation proceedings and *Blaškić*). The practice does suggest that, with the exception of the SCSL, appellate judges tend not to admit *amici* in appeals from substantive judgments.

G. The Impact of *Amicus Curiae* Participation on the Parties

Chambers consider the impact of *amicus curiae* submissions on the parties. Permitting *amici curiae* risks broadening the scope of the issues beyond those

[83] In case 001, the Pre-Trial Chamber invited 3 *amici* (Professor Antonio Cassese and members of the Journal of International Criminal Justice, Professor Kai Ambos and McGill Centre for Human Rights and Legal Pluralism) to make submissions on joint criminal enterprise: *Co-Prosecutors v Duch (Case 001)*, ECCC PTC, 23 September 2008, 001/18-07/2007-ECCC/OCIJ (PTC 02)-D99/3/12; *Co-Prosecutors v Duch (Case 001)*, ECCC PTC, 25 September 2008, 001/18-07/2007-ECCC/OCIJ (PTC 02)-D99/3/13; *Co-Prosecutors v Duch (Case 001)*, ECCC PTC, 25 September 2008, 001/18-07/2007-ECCC/OCIJ (PTC 02)-D99/3/14.

[84] *Prosecutor v Šainović et al*, ICTY AC, 7 September 2010, IT-05-87-A-11133.

intended or desired by the parties and may result in lines of argument and evidence that the parties omitted or deliberately avoided introducing. Thus, for the parties, *amicus curiae* participation creates a risk of loss of control of the proceedings and issues raised. Further, particularly where numerous *amici* respond to open calls, it may impose additional burdens on the parties in terms of time, delay in proceedings, and resources. Parties and other participants have raised concerns that hearing from *amici* has increased the burden on parties and has moved the issues away from those the parties had raised. As discussed in section V(B), while this has particular significance for the defence, it may also affect other parties. For example, Jordan complained that the participation of several *amici curiae* in the appellate proceedings concerning its non-cooperation extended the legal issues argued before the Chamber well beyond the three points of appeal raised.[85]

H. Legal or Factual Submissions

As discussed in chapter three, section V(A), the focus on determining individual criminal responsibility has an important consequence for *amicus curiae* participation: *amici* should focus on providing legal analysis rather than factual evidence that may go towards the elements of the crime charged. It is the parties or (where relevant) the investigating judges that are primarily responsible for presenting the evidence. Reflecting this key role, the ICTY, STL and ECCC require applicants to specify the nature of their proposed submissions and restrict submissions to questions of law only unless the Chamber indicates otherwise.[86] Judicial statements also support the view that *amici* would not normally present factual materials.[87] One situation where factual submissions might be accepted is where particular *amici curiae* hold information that would otherwise not be available to the Chambers. Examples include when ICC Pre-Trial Chamber I invited Antonio Cassese and Louise Arbour to provide information to the ICC about their investigations into events in Sudan,[88] or where the Government of Kenya provided information about its cooperation with the ICC Prosecutor.[89]

[85] *Prosecutor v Al-Bashir*, ICC AC, Transcript, 10 September 2018, 25–26.

[86] STL Practice Direction, Arts 3(f), 4; ECCC Amicus Information, paras 2(b), 5(b); ICTY *Amicus* Information, paras 4(b), 9(b). The SCSL Practice Direction requires applicants to indicate the nature of the submissions: Art 2(d).

[87] Chambers have restricted briefs to legal questions. See eg regarding Art 28, superior responsibility, *Prosecutor v Bemba,* ICC PTC II, 9 April 2009, ICC-01/05-01/08-401, para 12, where Amnesty 'must confine its submissions to the legal aspects outlined in the Request' rather than their connection to facts in the case; at the ICTY, *Prosecutor v Prlić et al*, ICTY AC, 18 July 2016, IT-04-74-A-21059, paras 7–8; *Prosecutor v Hartmann*, ICTY AC, 5 February 2010, IT-02-54-R77.5-A-3299; at the ICTR, *Prosecutor v Semanza*, ICTR TC III, 9 February 2001, ICTR-97-20-T-4702; at the STL, *Prosecutor v Al Jadeed SAL and Khayat,* STL AP, 25 November 2015, STL-14-05/A/AP-R000696, para 7, citing Art 4 of the Practice Direction at fn 18.

[88] *Situation in Darfur, Sudan*, ICC PTC I, 24 July 2006, ICC-02/05-10.

[89] *Prosecutor v Ruto and Sang*, ICC TC V, 8 April 2013, ICC-01/09-01/11-670.

Amici have also sought to address a range of miscellaneous topics where factual and legal elements overlap. Chambers are more likely to accept or even request such submissions where they do not relate directly to the trial process and the responsibility of the accused, particularly on issues of national law, reparations (see section VII) and state cooperation (see chapter seven). The practice evidences the strong preference for legal, not factual, analysis, with Figure 4.8 showing that the vast majority of submissions across the tribunals are legal in nature (82 per cent).

Figure 4.8 Broad Topic or Content to Be Addressed (%, Law vs Fact)

	ICC	ICTY	ICTR	ECCC	SCSL	STL	All
Legal Questions							
Legal Analysis	27%	51%	16%	72%	50%	93%	41%
Defence Rights	6%	12%	72%	7%	6%	0%	18%
Procedural Issue	9%	9%	1%	9%	22%	4%	8%
Victims	29%	4%	1%	12%	6%	0%	14%
Contempt	0%	1%	0%	0%	11%	0%	1%
Factual Questions							
Historical Background	3%	3%	1%	0%	0%	4%	2%
Ascertain Facts	5%	6%	0%	0%	0%	0%	3%
Other/Mixed	21%	14%	8%	0%	6%	0%	13%
Legal Questions	71%	77%	90%	100%	94%	96%	82%
Factual Questions	29%	23%	10%	0%	6%	4%	18%
	100.0%	100.0%	100.0%	100.0%	100.0%	100.0%	100%

I. Relevance

The relevance of the proposed *amicus curiae* observations is a crucial factor across the Tribunals.[90] As stated by ICC Pre-Trial Chamber I 'the first and

[90] *Prosecutor v Kenyatta*, ICC TC V(B), 6 November 2014, ICC-01/09-02/11-971, para 5. See eg where the matters 'are *not related* to the Prosecutor's appeal', *Prosecutor v L Gbagbo*, ICC AC, 16 September 2013, ICC-02/11-01/11-505, para 10; or 'the issues raised by the applicant are not live issues', *Prosecutor v Ongwen*, ICC PTC II, 15 April 2015, ICC-02/04-01/15-221, para 2. At the ICTR: 'the issues … are relevant to the determination of the appeal', *Prosecutor v Munyakuzi*,

foremost factor for leave to be granted pursuant to rule 103 of the Rules is whether the relevant application relates to an issue that is actually before the competent Chamber'.[91] This means the submissions must: (1) be relevant to the stage of proceedings (ie, submissions regarding sentencing will not relevant at a pre-trial hearing); and (2) address legal and exceptionally factual issues that are *raised directly* by the proceedings at hand, and do not concern unrelated or speculative issues, for example, issues that are beyond the scope of the charges in the indictment.

Chambers can assist *amici* to provide relevant submissions in several ways, thus minimising their own burden and that of the *amici*. First, in any open calls or invitations, the Chamber should indicate the issues on which the Chamber requires assistance, including where possible questions they would like *amici* to address. Secondly, the Chamber should require potential *amici* to demonstrate the relevance of their proposed submissions, for example, by indicating which of the questions they intend to address and, where seeking to provide expertise, how their expertise relates to those issues. Thirdly, where a Chamber receives a voluntary application and approves participation, it should restrict the *amicus curiae's* submissions to (a) particular issue(s) where it believes the *amicus* can be of assistance. Finally, Chambers should be strict in rejecting applications that do not address relevant issues. Similarly, Chambers should reject submissions that do not comply with the Chambers' directions, for example, those that do not answer the questions indicated or address additional issues. While the Chamber could also indicate in its decision that it did not find those submissions helpful, we believe that it is better to be firm than to accept irrelevant briefs or briefs that the Chamber does not actually find useful. We do not advocate a permissive approach to *amici* as seen in other institutions, particularly the US Supreme Court, where briefs are routinely accepted but may not be considered. In addition to such an approach being inappropriate for a criminal tribunal, this also risks the legitimacy of the institution's *amicus curiae* practice. Particularly where the briefs go beyond the legal issues raised and introduce new legal submissions, accepting irrelevant briefs, even if not used, still impacts upon the parties, which must consider and respond to those briefs. It also renders the sources the Chamber has taken into account less transparent.

J. Nature, Novelty and Importance of the Issues Raised

The rules do not limit the substantive content of *amicus curiae* submissions, referring to submissions addressing 'any issue'. Contrary to the wording of

ICTR AC, 18 July 2008, ICTR-97-36-R11*bis*-86/H, 2; the 'application does not raise any issue of relevance that may guide it in resolving the present matter', *Prosecutor v Nahimana, Barayagwiza and Ngeze*, ICTR, 12 January 2007, ICTR-99-52- A-9702/H, 3.

[91] *Situation in Darfur, Sudan*, ICC PTC I, 4 February 2009, ICC-02/05-185, para 8.

the rules, the issues do not have to be specified by the Chamber, but can be suggested by the *amici*, although they are ultimately approved by the Chamber. The practice shows that topics addressed by *amicus curiae* applications or briefs vary widely and they may consider several topics in one brief. However, it is clear that *amicus* participation reflects the core competencies of the Tribunals. Most admitted *amici* addressed the following topics: national law, particularly criminal law; comparative law; public international law; international criminal law; human rights law; defence or fair trial matters; victim participation and reparations; process or evidence matters (including processes for state cooperation or witnesses); and historical or other information, such as updates on related domestic proceedings (see Figure 4.9). Most briefs addressed more than one of these topics. They therefore fall within the range of areas we expected to see addressed before the Tribunals (see chapter three, section V(A)).

Figure 4.9 Subject Matter Addressed in Submissions

	No. addressed	Percentage*
ICL/Modes of Liability	52	21%
IHL	1	0%
Human Rights	26	11%
General/Public International Law	121	49%
Procedure/Evidence	108	44%
Defence Rights	65	26%
Victims/Reparations	40	16%
Facts/Background	15	6%
Gender	6	2%

* Percentage of accepted briefs (n=247).

Note: More than one subject matter per brief/submission.

Some questions have attracted such a significant number of *amicus curiae* applicants so as to alter the relative balance between *amicus* topics. For instance, an ECCC open call attracted a large number of briefs on the nature of crimes against humanity committed against an accused's own forces, which, alongside *amici* addressing joint criminal enterprise, led international 'legal analysis' to account for the vast majority of ECCC *amici curiae* applicants.[92] A similar preponderance of briefs relating to amnesties under the Lomé Accord[93] and

[92] In response to *Co-Prosecutors v Meas (Case 003)*, ECCC OCIJ, 19 April 2016, 003/07-09-2009-ECCC-OCIJ, attracting 11 submissions then duplicated for each Case 003 and 004 to amount to 22 in our analysis.

[93] *Prosecutor v Kallon*, SCSL AC, 1 November 2003, SCSL-2003-07-PT-2386.

head of state immunity[94] mean a majority of SCSL applications also address legal questions. In contrast, there have been slightly more applications related to victims' issues than other legal matters at the ICC, whereas at the ICTR a large proportion of briefs about the transfer of cases to Rwanda were categorised as relating to defence issues, making this the most frequent category of *amicus curiae* submissions.

Chambers also consider whether the *amici* propose to address issues that are novel and/or important. Where an issue is novel, Chambers may welcome additional submissions to help inform their decision. We consider an issue to be novel where it concerns a provision, rule or procedure that has not previously been applied, on which there is no established jurisprudence or ambiguity, uncertainty or disagreement as to its interpretation or application. A novel issue also arises where a Chamber is called upon to declare or develop customary international law. Other studies have shown that where an issue is novel or the law is in a state of transition, judges have the greatest potential to exercise judicial creativity (or activism) and to develop the law or its application.[95] *Amici* may assist the Chambers to reach informed decisions and – in the long-term – develop better law, by allowing the Chamber to draw from a wider range of arguments and expertise than provided by the parties. This in turn enhances the legitimacy of the institution, in both a normative and sociological sense. While we have not separately quantified briefs as raising 'novel or important issues', an examination of the practice reflects the openness of Chambers to *amici* for novel issues, particularly where the issue is important beyond the outcome in the particular proceedings and goes to the efficacy of the institution. This is where we are most likely to see Chambers issue an open call or direct invitations and to engage *amici* in a communicative function.

K. Independence

Wiik notes that in other international institutions the *amicus curiae* is not intended to be 'a tool of parties in the adversarial process'.[96] In contrast, the practice found in some national systems, in particular the US, is for extensive

[94] *Prosecutor v Taylor*, SCSL AC, 20 November 2003, SCSL-2003-01-I-2835; *Prosecutor v Taylor*, SCSL AC, 23 October 2003, SCSL-2003-01-I-1669; *Prosecutor v Taylor*, SCSL AC, 23 October 2003, SCSL-2003-01-I-1643.

[95] See, eg Aloisi and Meernik (n 80); P Webb, *International Judicial Integration and Fragmentation* (Oxford, OUP, 2013) referring to the law of immunities (at 100) and use of force (at 140); S Darcy and J Powderley (eds), *Judicial Creativity at the International Criminal Tribunals* (Oxford, OUP, 2010).

[96] A Wiik, *Amicus Curiae before International Courts and Tribunals* (Baden-Baden, Nomos, 2018) 129.

collaboration between a party and an *amicus*, with parties approaching *amici* to file briefs supportive of their position.[97] We argue that an *amicus curiae* in the Tribunals should be independent, with independence in this context meaning not having an on-going or previous relationship with the Court or its personnel, the parties or an affected state. The possible exception to this is where certain actors are acting in a representative function and the value of the information may outweigh the risks created by the lack of independence.

Although there has been inconsistency as to what independence means and decisions tend to link independence and impartiality (discussed below), in general, Chambers are concerned about a close or direct relationship with the Tribunal or trial process, including the parties and other participants. For example, the ECCC Supreme Court Chamber found that *amici curiae* 'should be unaffiliated with the court or any of its offices'.[98] Moreover, since 'an *amicus curiae* is traditionally an independent and impartial adviser to the court whose role is simply to inform and not to advocate' – where the *amicus curiae* is 'affiliated with the court or its offices [they] cannot be considered impartial and independent advisers'.[99] Institutional actors may seek to participate as *amici*, for example, the OPCV or the TFV. However, such actors are generally acting in an expertise function or representing specific interests and their institutional connection to the Court is evident.[100]

Chambers are, we suggest, rightly concerned with undisclosed links to parties. Some tribunals require potential *amici* to disclose contacts or relationships the applicant has had or may have with a party and, for the STL, other participants.[101] The ICC Code of Conduct for Counsel, which applies to *amici*, requires counsel to remain independent rather than requiring potential *amici* to disclose links that might affect their independence. We suggest that judges should clarify what they expect of potential *amici* in terms of disclosure of contacts and relationships and establish a formal disclosure requirement for all *amici*. This should explicitly include funding arrangements, which would make it easier for a Chamber to detect where *amici* have financial links to relevant actors. We explore what independence means for different actors and for the functions of the *amicus curiae* in subsequent chapters.

[97] See, eg MK Lowman, 'The Litigating *Amicus Curiae*: When Does the Party begin After the Friends Leave?' (1992) 41 *American University Law Review* 1243.

[98] The SCC dismissed requests by the Defence Support Section and counsel for an accused twice: *Co-Prosecutors v Duch (Case 001)*, ECCC SCC, 9 December 2010, 001/18-07-2007-ECCC/SC-F7/2, para 9; see also *Co-Prosecutors v Duch (Case 001)*, ECCC SCC, 3 March 2011, 001/18-07-2007-ECC/SC-F16/3.

[99] *Co-Prosecutors v Nuon and Khieu (Case 002)*, ECCC TC, 4 June 2014, 002/19-09-2007/ECCC/TC-E306/3/1, para 5.

[100] See, in the context of reparations, the discussion at s VII below.

[101] ICTY *Amicus* Information, s 4(g); ECCC *Amicus* Information, s 2(f); SCSL *Amicus* Practice Direction, Art 1(f); STL *Amicus* Practice Direction, Art 3(i).

L. Impartiality and the Presence or Absence of an Interest

As discussed in chapter two, in many domestic and international jurisdictions, courts grant leave to actors with an interest in the case to submit their views through a separate avenue such as third-party intervention, which requires the existence of a legal interest directly affected by the proceedings. Where such an interest is not present, participation is as an *amicus curiae*. Some jurisdictions recognise that *amici* may have an interest in proceedings, but require disclosure of the interest, while others adhere to the traditional view of the *amicus curiae* as *not* having an interest in the proceedings. The rules for the Tribunals do not provide a general right of intervention where an actor has a legal interest, and are silent as to whether an interest is required for or precludes participation as an *amicus curiae*.[102] This has led to some confusion and inconsistency in the practice, with the presence of an interest often argued to preclude participation, yet Chambers have on occasion accepted briefs from interested actors. We suggest that Chambers should not *require* an *amicus curiae* to establish a legal interest directly affected by proceedings to participate. The practice of the Tribunals reflects this approach.

What is more challenging is whether *amici curiae* must have *no* interest in the proceedings; that is, an actor must be disinterested to participate. This issue has arisen mainly in two contexts. First, where an actor (usually a civil society NGO) has a general interest in the development of the law, the institution itself or the specific issue before the Chamber or argues that they represent a public interest in proceedings. As we explore further in chapter five, we argue that an interest of a general nature should not preclude an actor from participating in the expertise function. However, similar to expert witnesses (chapter three, section VI(C)), *amici* relying on their expertise as the basis for participation should not have a direct interest in proceedings. On the rare occasions where the *amicus curiae* serves a communicative function, the existence of an interest should not preclude participation; however, the *amicus* should disclose the nature of the interest to the Chamber to allow the Chamber to weigh the material accordingly.

The second context in which impartiality has arisen is where an actor – which may be a state, an accused in a related trial or an NGO seeking to represent victims' interests – claims that they should participate *because* they have an interest in proceedings, that is they seek to perform a representative function. While the existence of an interest should not create a *right* to participate as an *amicus curiae*, the existence of an interest should not *preclude* an actor from participating within this function, provided the submissions may assist the Chamber in its decision. A number of Chambers have recognised this approach.[103]

[102] See Annex B.

[103] eg, in *Prosecutor v Kallon*, SCSL AC, 1 November 2003, SCSL-2003-07-PT-2386, para 5, the Chamber focused on how the submissions will assist, not the interest the *amicus* may have.

As is shown in subsequent chapters (see chapters five, six and seven), submissions of *amici* may be useful precisely *because* the actor has an interest.

As with independence, there is an obvious connection between the criterion of impartiality and disclosure regimes. Only three of the Tribunals require potential *amici* to disclose 'the applicant's interest in the case'.[104] As the term 'interest' is not defined, it is unclear in what sense 'interest' is used, although practice shows it is broader than a legal interest. The ICC Code of Conduct for Counsel applies to *amici*, but does not include a comparable disclosure requirement. Some *amici* provide such information in their applications (eg, Human Right Watch generally includes a statement of interest in its applications), but many do not. Chambers have on occasion invited potential *amici* to indicate their interest in applying, for example, the open call issued by the ICC Appeals Chamber in the *Jordan* non-cooperation proceedings required states wishing to participate as *amici* to indicate their interest in the proceedings.[105] We suggest that the ICC (and other tribunals) should require *amici* to disclose any interest in the proceedings or in the issues raised.

M. Expertise and Experience

Chambers have considered the expertise and experience of *amici curiae* as one factor in determining whether to admit an *amicus*. If the admission of *amicus curiae* submissions contributes to legitimacy by improving the quality of judicial decision-making, it is essential that *amici* are actually experts in relevant areas or are otherwise providing valuable information. Moreover, to maximise legitimacy, institutions and individual Chambers should indicate clear, accessible, predictable and justifiable criteria to assess expertise of individual *amici* and apply those criteria in a consistent and transparent manner. Only three of the Tribunals require potential *amici* to specify their qualifications in the application, but then do not provide further guidance or requirements.[106] Many *amici* address this requirement briefly or not at all in their applications.

Our first observation is that expertise and experience is only an essential requirement for *amici* seeking to fulfil an expertise function, although submissions by *amici* in other functions must of course be competent, accurate and professional. The practice shows that the issue of expertise and experience has mainly arisen in relation to civil society applicants, discussed further in chapter five, section III. It is harder to characterise state actors as 'experts', although it is perhaps easier when state *amici* are addressing national law, institutions

[104] STL *Amicus* Practice Direction, Art 3(d); ECCC *Amicus* Information, s 2(a) – also includes interest in the issues; ICTY *Amicus* Information, s 4(a).

[105] *Prosecutor v Al-Bashir*, ICC AC, 29 March 2018, ICC-02/05-01/09-330, para 3.

[106] STL *Amicus* Practice Direction, Art 3(g); ICTY *Amicus* Information, s 4(c); ECCC *Amicus* Information, s 2(c).

and procedures (see chapter seven, section III). In any event, Chambers have not required state *amici* to demonstrate expertise in the same way as civil society actors.

Secondly, there are currently no requirements or guidance as to what constitutes sufficient expertise or experience, although individual Chambers have attempted to establish such standards. We argue that where Chambers admit *amici* based on their expertise, assessing that expertise should be key. The ICC and other tribunals should firstly indicate the general standards of expertise required of *amici*, which should take the form of general, minimum level requirements such as those in the ICC framework for expert witnesses. In most instances, given the focus of *amici* on legal submissions (see section V(H) above), this would be relevant legal expertise. However, as with expert witnesses, other forms of expertise may be relevant, particularly in related phases of proceedings such as reparations (see section VII below). Chambers should establish NGO and academic expertise through a combination of academic qualifications, professional qualifications, publications and a number of years of experience in a relevant role or context. The general requirements should be easily accessible via the institution's website so that potential *amici* can consult these requirements during the application process. *Amici* submitting in response to an open call or on a voluntary basis should be required to address these requirements when applying for leave so that the Chamber can make an informed decision as to whether the *amici* meets these general requirements. Where a Chamber invites an *amicus curiae* to participate on the basis of their expertise, in the interests of consistency and transparency, the Chamber should specify on which grounds they consider the *amicus* to be an expert, including by reference to the general requirements. One suggestion to institutionalise requirements for expertise in *amici* is to establish a list of recognised, 'pre-approved' *amici curiae*, similar to that for expert witnesses at the ICC, whereby potential *amici* may apply, with evidence of their expertise, to be included in this list. However, Chambers should not be limited to admitting only those *amici* included in the list. Even where an *amicus curiae* is 'pre-approved' in this sense, they would still need to demonstrate that their expertise is relevant to the issue before the Chamber on a case-by-case basis.

In addition, individual Chambers should seek particular forms of expertise in open calls or, if appropriate, through invitations to specific *amici* (although note our reservations concerning specific invitations, discussed further in chapter five). So as to ensure the Chamber receives the benefit of submissions from *amici* with the expertise it needs, it should specify in the call the nature of the expertise it requires, reiterating the general requirements for all *amici* or indicating additional or alternative requirements. However, a Chamber should retain the flexibility to vary or waive the general requirements in certain circumstances. For example, as section VII shows, in the reparations implementation phase, expertise was needed from those organisations with experience of implementing projects either for the types of crimes or in the situation context and may warrant a more flexible approach. Similarly, where *amici* will provide information, rather than expertise, a Chamber may relax the general requirements.

One issue that has arisen is if previously being accepted as an *amicus curiae*, whether in the same institution or in other fora, is of itself sufficient to establish expertise or experience. There is no requirement that *amici* be 'experienced' in the sense of having previously submitted briefs, so *amici* with no prior experience should not be precluded from participating, which may be more relevant to local actors. Some *amici* have asserted prior experience as a factor justifying admission. We suggest that previous experience, without more, should not justify admitting an actor as an *amicus curiae*. It also means that experienced or regular *amici curiae* cannot be assured that their applications will be approved but must establish their expertise each time they apply. That said, the knowledge of experienced *amici* of the process is likely to assist them in many respects, particularly in how to formulate the application and submissions, and may make it more likely they will assist a Chamber, with some Chambers noting favourably an applicant's previous experience as an *amicus curiae* when accepting their submissions. However, this should be one factor to consider and not the only basis for admission.

This is reflected in the practice. Some organisations, for example Redress and Human Rights Watch, are 'regular' users of the *amicus curiae* process, while states affected by proceedings frequently apply to participate, such as the Republic of Rwanda at the ICTR. However, the vast majority of *amicus curiae* applicants are indeed 'one time' applicants: around 80 per cent at the ICC, two-thirds at the ICTR, and closer to 90 per cent at the STL, SCSL and ICTY.[107] At the ICC, those who have applied as an *amicus* have on average had a higher percentage of acceptances the more times they applied. However, applicants can apply multiple times without ever receiving permission to act as *amicus curiae* – for example, Moraa Gesicho applied on three occasions (in five applications across both Kenya cases) without success. The relationship between the number of applications and average success rate is less clear at the other tribunals.

Another possible indicator of expertise or experience may be the number of individuals or organisations signing joint submissions. There is no limit or minimum requirement for the number of organisations or individuals that can participate jointly as *amici curiae*. *Amicus curiae* submissions can involve multiple organisations or individuals, either with one actor acting 'on behalf of' others, or by a number of co-signatures upon the application and brief. This practice has been most prevalent for academic submissions and at the ICTY, where there have been a number of *amicus curiae* briefs co-signed by multiple

[107] Closer to half of applicants at the ECCC attempted to intervene more than once, but the statistics are skewed by the large number of submissions concerning crimes against humanity that were filed in both Cases 003 and 004, in response to *Co-Prosecutors v Meas (Case 003)*, ECCC OCIJ, 19 April 2016, 003/07-09-2009-ECCC-OCIJ-D191.

academics (up to 34).[108] However, the average number of signatories per *amicus curiae* application across the Tribunals is 1.5 (not including Article 75 representations). Across the Tribunals, there is not a notable difference between the average number of co-signatories for accepted versus rejected applications as a whole. This suggests that Chambers are not necessarily more willing to accept applications that have a higher number of signatories. The Tribunals have also not tended to cite the number of authors as a reason for or against receiving the submissions.

N. Availability of Alternative Avenues

Where an actor has a specific right to participate under other provisions, the actor should rely upon that right rather than the *amicus curiae* provision. Alternative avenues of participation include: specific rights for states to challenge jurisdiction or admissibility and to participate in non-cooperation proceedings (chapter seven); the rights of victims to participate in proceedings (chapter three, section VI(A)); expert witnesses (chapter three, section VI(C)); reliance on institutional actors (chapter three, section VI(D)); or providing information directly to the parties. However, the ICC Appeals Chamber has confirmed the role of Rule 103 as governing participation in the absence of a specific right to participate. The Pre-Trial Chamber had allowed observations from Cote d'Ivoire in proceedings arising from a challenge to jurisdiction by the accused. Although the state did not have a specific right to participate, the Pre-Trial Chamber relied on Rule 58(2) ICC RPE, which provides that where a Chamber received a challenge to jurisdiction, 'it shall decide on the procedure to be followed and may take appropriate measures for the proper conduct of the proceedings'. Noting that Rule 58(2) provides a Chamber with broad discretion, the Appeals Chamber found that:[109]

> such discretion is not unlimited. It has to be exercised in conjunction with other relevant legal provisions … The Appeals Chamber therefore finds that rule 58(2) of the Rules of Procedure and Evidence has to be applied by the pre-Trial Chamber in conjunction with rule 103 of the Rules of Procedure and Evidence, if it decides to hear States that may have an interest in jurisdiction proceedings, but does not have a right to participate in the proceedings pursuant to article 19(3) of the Statute.

The Appeals Chamber found that the failure to refer to Rule 103 did not negate the legal basis for the submissions, which was Rule 103; however, the Pre-Trial Chamber should have expressly applied Rule 103, including the requirement for a separate decision on admissibility and allowing the parties to respond to the

[108] eg, *Prosecutor v Brđanin and Talić*, ICTY AC, 17 August 2002, IT-99-36-AR73.9-502(34 co-signatories); *Prosecutor v Bemba*, ICC PTC II, 28 August 2009, ICC-01/05-01/08-488, para 18.
[109] *Prosecutor v L Gbagbo*, ICC AC, 12 December 2012, ICC-02/11-01/11-321, para 39.

submissions.[110] This decision indicates that, even where Chambers may benefit from discretion in terms of how they conduct proceedings, where they accept or invite submissions from participants that do not have an express right to participate, the legal basis for doing so is Rule 103 and Chambers must meet its requirements.

O. Professionalism and Ethics

One factor that we suggest should be relevant to whether an *amicus curiae* is likely to assist a Chamber is whether they will act in a professional and ethical manner and meet expected standards. No Chamber has expressly considered this as a factor,[111] although this criterion is linked to others, such as independence, impartiality and expertise. Although the ICC Code of Conduct applies to *amici curiae*, the professional and ethical standards for *amici* remain unclear. Particularly the ICC, as a permanent body, should clarify expectations of *amici* and any potential sanctions for unacceptable conduct by *amici*. Past experience may be relevant, as previous misconduct of an *amicus*, for example, where an *amicus* has previously filed misleading material, should be a factor a Chamber can consider in deciding whether to admit that *amicus curiae* in subsequent or separate proceedings.

P. Representativeness and Plurality of Voices

If the *amicus curiae* mechanism is a means to boost legitimacy through allowing stakeholders access to proceedings to engage in a conversation with judges, then one must consider the extent to which a particular *amicus curiae* represents a stakeholder or other interest group. This issue arises in several ways. First, for *amici* performing – or claiming to perform – a representative function, how can Chambers validate their claims to represent a holder of a particular interest? For example, where an NGO purports to 'represent' the interests of victims in proceedings, should the NGO be required to establish its authority to do so, and to clarify and identify which victims it seeks to represent? As is explored further in chapter five, civil society actors make claims to represent victims and affected communities, but Chambers do not question these representational claims. This may raise issues where international NGOs seek to represent victims groups

[110] ibid, paras 41–42.

[111] One possible example is the ICTY Trial Chamber dismissing one of the three *amici* appointed to assist Milosevic because one of the *amici* had given interviews that could indicate bias against the accused: *Prosecutor v Milošević*, ICTY TC, 10 October 2002, IT-02-54-T-D12126 (Judge May). However, that situation is unusual, as the *amici* were appointed as quasi-counsel (see ch 6).

with which they may have no connection. As Kent and Trinidad note 'claims by *amici* that they are giving voice to the interests of affected communities should not be accepted at face value', or this may 'fuel a "representativeness deficit"'.[112] For us,[113] this potential for a representativeness deficit is a challenge with both the representative function and recognising a communicative function for *amici* in the Tribunals, as it would be difficult for Chambers to verify claims to be legitimately representing a broader interest or constituency.

Another question is whether the *amici* participating in proceedings represent the array of interests and perspectives that exist or the range of arguments that may be made on a particular issue? Or do certain interests or actors remain excluded from the proceedings, for example, perspectives of particular national groups? There is some evidence that Chambers try to hear the perspectives of key stakeholders, although this tends to concern states. As seen in chapter seven, Chambers have invited affected states to participate as *amici curiae* on several occasions. Chambers have also permitted institutional actors, in particular the Office of Public Counsel for Victims, to represent the interests of non-participating victims. However, in general, Chambers do not seek to ensure that all possible interests and perspectives are represented in the proceedings. In particular, as noted in chapter one, the practice of the Tribunals is criticised for under-representation of the perspective(s) of local constituencies, with the *amicus curiae* a possible mechanism for addressing this imbalance.

Kent and Trinidad considered practice in the ICTY, ICTR and ICC as revealing 'a significant (though not overwhelming) proportion of third-party *amicus curiae* interventions are by foreign actors', but noted that this is 'certainly not sufficient to disclose the existence of a representativeness deficit'.[114] Figure 4.10 reveals that applications from international actors constituted 57 per cent of all applications across the Tribunals, whereas applications from national actors constituted 38 per cent, with the remainder mixed or not able to be ascertained. Chambers accepted 70 per cent of applications from international actors, compared to 47 per cent from national actors. At the ICC (see Figure 4.11), 56 per cent of applications were from international *amici*, with 55 per cent of those accepted, compared to 41 per cent applications from national actors, of which 42 per cent were accepted. These figures overstate the proportion of national participation, as our data categorised submissions by states as national actors. The practice therefore reveals an apparent gap in terms of both the number of applications from national actors, as well as the acceptance rate of briefs. The gap is more pronounced in the ICC.

[112] Kent and Trinidad (n 73), 736.

[113] Kent and Trinidad support public interest amici as a means of boosting legitimacy through broader participation (n 73). As noted in ch 1, we generally do not consider a communicative role appropriate for a criminal tribunal.

[114] Kent and Trinidad (n 73), 742.

Figure 4.10 Origin of *Amicus Curiae* – All Tribunals

	No. (All Tribunals)	% (All Tribunals)	Proportion Accepted by Category (%)	Accepted (No.)	Not Accepted (No.)	Acceptance Rate
National	154	38%	30%	73	81	47%
International	231	57%	65%	161	70	70%
Mixed	22	5%	5%	12	10	55%
Other or N/A*	1	0%	0%	1	0	100%
Total	408	100%	100%	247	161	

* One open call accepting briefs but with no briefs located.

Figure 4.11 Origin of *Amicus Curiae* – ICC

	No. (ICC)	% (ICC)	Proportion Accepted by Category (%)	Accepted (No.)	Not Accepted (No.)	Acceptance Rate
National	65	41%	35%	27	38	42%
International	88	56%	62%	48	40	55%
Mixed	4	3%	4%	3	1	75%
Total	157	100%	100%	78	79	

Finally, representativeness issues may arise in relation to the expertise function in terms of the plurality of actors appearing as *amici curiae*, looking at criteria such as gender, geographical distribution, and different legal systems, similar to the criteria applied to facilitate representativeness of judges at the ICC. Chambers do not explicitly consider any of these dimensions of representativeness in their admission decisions and *amicus* practice is not representative in this sense. The closest we have been able to find to a Chamber explicitly considering such factors is the comment by the Appeals Chamber in the *Jordan* non-cooperation proceedings that, when selecting which academic *amici* to admit, it had tried to invite a cross-section of applicants.[115]

Is it realistic to require *amici* to be representative (in these different senses) in international criminal tribunals? It is a challenging criterion for Chambers to satisfy, for several reasons. First, Chambers are limited by the voluntary nature of *amicus* participation; even when specifically invited, *amici* are not obliged to participate and Chambers rely on *amici* that voluntarily decide to participate. Secondly, claims to represent actors in international criminal proceedings are challenging, and many actors, including the Tribunals themselves, make

[115] *Prosecutor v Al-Bashir*, ICC AC, Transcript, 10 September 2018, 6–7.

representational claims in a broader sense.[116] Thirdly, for expert *amici*, the need to obtain the necessary expertise should be the primary concern. Fourthly, given the focus on criminal responsibility, it is not feasible, nor desirable, to ensure that each interest and perspective is represented in proceedings. However, Chambers could do more to enhance representativeness through using open calls, disseminating those calls widely, encouraging joint submissions and considering representativeness when inviting and admitting *amici*. Institutionally, the Court or other actors may wish to establish some form of capacity building or legal support for prospective *amici*; as discussed in chapter five, a number of international NGOs have attempted to build capacity among local actors to submit briefs in future, including as a partner with and training those actors in writing applications and submissions. In addition, Chambers should seek further information from *amici* making vague claims to represent particular groups or interests as a standard part of the application process or on an *ad hoc* basis in response to particular applications. Finally, as we suggested in chapter one, Chambers should be wary of accepting *amici* operating only in the communicative function, particularly where they claim to represent the public interest.

Q. Background of the Judges

One factor that may influence admission of *amici curiae* is the background of the judges. As discussed in chapter three, section V(A), judges at the Tribunals come from a range of backgrounds. This will include whether they are from common law or civil law systems, with the ICC judges selected with reference to the 'representation of the principal legal systems of the world'.[117] Selection of judges 'adopts a laissez faire approach to stipulating the level of experience and what constitutes "expertise", deferring to the qualifications required for high judicial office in national legal systems'.[118] This means that judges come from different professional backgrounds, including criminal judges or lawyers, academics, and former diplomats. As a result, 'the level of experience and expertise of ICC judges as appointed is variable'.[119] We predicted that this variation may influence *amicus curiae* practice, with certain judges potentially being more inclined to accept or to use briefs.

[116] See, eg S Kendall and S Nouwen, 'Representational Practices at the International Criminal Court: The Gap Between Juridified and Abstract Victimhood' (2013) 76 *Law & Contemporary Problems* 235; F Mégret, 'In Whose Name? The ICC and the Search for Constituency' in C De Vos, S Kendall and C Stahn (eds), *Contested Justice: The Politics and Practice of International Criminal Court Interventions* (Cambridge, CUP, 2015).

[117] Rome Statute, Art 36(8)(a)(i). States parties must also consider equitable geographical representation and a fair representation of male and female judges.

[118] H Mistry, 'The Significance of Institutional Culture in Enhancing the Validity of International Criminal Tribunals' (2017) 17 *ICLR* 703, 711.

[119] ibid.

It was challenging to extract data concerning the influence of judicial background on *amicus curiae* participation particularly as judges sit in Chambers of three or five judges, with the composition of chambers changing. In addition, applications did not spread equally amongst Chambers. We had initially expected that, as the *amicus curiae* was initially a common law mechanism, we might observe that common law judges were more willing to accept briefs. However, the data does not support this. There does not seem to be an observable distinction between common law and civil law judges, although there is some evidence that there may be a slightly lower proportion of civil law judges sitting in Chambers that accept briefs than overall, at least at the ICC and ECCC. However, Chambers tend to have more civil law judges overall and there were other factors potentially at play – for instance, a large number of single judge decisions regarding *amici curiae* at the STL, while national Cambodian judges always sit at the ECCC, which skews the results (see Figure 4.12). The STL and SCSL have the highest, and very similar, acceptance rates of the Tribunals, yet one has had predominantly civil law judges and the other common law judges. A review of the *amicus* data looking at decisions on admissibility by ICC judges did reveal that certain judges were more often involved in cases concerning *amici*, but it was not possible to show causation, as these judges participated in Chambers that received the most requests.

Figure 4.12 Judges' Backgrounds

	ICC	ICTY	ICTR	ECCC	SCSL	STL
Average % Civil Law Judges per Bench – All Applications	74%	42%	51%	60%	20%	97%
Average % Civil Law Judges per Bench – Approved Briefs*	71%	43%	55%	47%	18%	95%
Overall Acceptance Rate	50%	68%	56%	72%	78%	79%

*Excludes briefs approved with particular conditions attached.

Note 1: ECCC has fixed proportions of national judges from the Cambodian civil law system.

These observations align with studies on judicial culture in the Tribunals and in other international institutions, which suggest judicial background does not significantly influence decision-making.[120] Instead, judges appreciate that they serve an international institution, with its own procedures and legal culture, and will adjust to the cultural practices of the institution rather than insist on the practices with which they are most familiar, particularly where judges sit in panels. Mistry concludes that the ICC, as a relatively young institution, may not

[120] See, eg N-L Arold, *The Legal Culture of the European Court of Human Rights* (Leiden, Brill, 2007) 159; N Schlesinger, 'Making International Criminal Law: Factors Influencing Judicial Behaviour at the ICTY and ICTR' (PhD thesis, the University of Melbourne) 246–50; J Meernik, K Lynn King and G Dancy, 'Judicial Decision Making and International Tribunals: Assessing the Impact of Individual, National and International Factors' (2005) 86 *Social Science Quarterly* 683.

yet have a 'robust institutional culture',[121] which may account for some of the inconsistency concerning the *amicus curiae* mechanism.

R. The Function an *Amicus Curiae* Will be Performing

As indicated in chapter one, we suggest that *amici curiae* in international criminal tribunals perform one – or a combination – of three functions: expertise, representative or communicative. As we explore in subsequent chapters, the function is relevant to the criteria the Chambers should apply when assessing whether to admit a particular *amicus*. However, the practice shows that Chambers rarely consider explicitly the function an *amicus* will perform, although we have tried to identify the function by studying the application, decision and the submission itself. It is challenging and somewhat imprecise, as several briefs may be fulfilling a number of functions.

As Figure 4.13 shows, across the Tribunals, Chambers appeared to consider that the largest proportion of applicants sought to perform the expertise function (32 per cent). This figure increased to almost 56 per cent when aggregated with *amici* seeking to perform a combined expertise/representative function (7 per cent) and expertise/communicative function (17 per cent). At the ICC, as shown in Figure 4.14, most actors (52 per cent) were treated as performing an expertise function, increasing to 61 per cent when aggregated with combined expertise/representative function and expertise/participatory function (both 4.5 per cent). Therefore, most *amici* perform an expertise function, whether exclusively or in combination with another function. Chambers considered 36 per cent of accepted briefs to be providing expertise, increasing to 67 per cent when including expertise in combination with another function. Subsequent chapters explore these functions by reference to a type of actor.

Figure 4.13 Function by Actor Type (All Tribunals)

	Academic (%)	Government (%)	Legal (%)	NGO (%)	Other (%)	All (%)
Information/Expertise (Info.)	41%	8%	15%	47%	27%	32%
Representation (of specific/ direct interests) (Rep.)	0%	48%	20%	10%	32%	19%
Communicative (Comm.)	22%	20%	15%	18%	7%	16%
Combined Info/Rep	3%	22%	8%	5%	4%	7%
Combined Info/Comm	34%	0%	23%	11%	19%	17%
Combined Rep/Comm	0%	0%	8%	2%	4%	2%
All evident	1%	0%	2%	2%	1%	1%
Unclear	0%	2%	10%	5%	7%	5%

[121] Mistry (n 118), 727.

Figure 4.14 Function by Actor Type (ICC)

	Academic (%)	Government (%)	Legal (%)	NGO (%)	Other (%)	All (%)
Information/Expertise (Info.)	83%	13%	20%	61%	55%	52%
Representation (of specific/direct interests) (Rep.)	0%	50%	27%	15%	27%	22%
Communicative (Comm.)	0%	33%	7%	8%	9%	11%
Combined Info/Rep	4%	4%	13%	3%	3%	4%
Combined Info/Comm	13%	0%	0%	5%	3%	4%
Combined Rep/Comm	0%	0%	33%	2%	0%	4%
All evident	0%	0%	0%	3%	0%	1%
Unclear	0%	0%	0%	3%	3%	2%

VI. IMPACT OF *AMICUS CURIAE* SUBMISSIONS

This section analyses the influence of *amicus curiae* submissions in the Tribunals. As described in Annex A, this research combined a number of methods to assess the impact of the *amicus curiae*, including qualitative comparisons of the structure and content of *amicus* briefs and related judicial decisions, as well as a general assessment of whether the judicial outcome was 'similar' or 'different' to that proposed by the *amicus*. We consider impact by key stakeholder in subsequent chapters; here, we provide an overview.

A. Minimal Influence

Most voluntary *amicus curiae* applications are rejected (59 per cent, Figure 4.1 above), meaning that they are unlikely to have a direct impact on proceedings. It is possible that Chambers are influenced by applications, especially those with annexed submissions, even where they are rejected or not formally admitted. For example, a brief concerning sexual and gender-based violence appears to have influenced proceedings at the Extraordinary African Chambers, despite not formally having been admitted.[122] However, courts often fail to mention *amicus*

[122] *Prosecutor v Habré* (Rape and Other Forms of Sexual Violence as Crimes Against Humanity, War Crimes and Torture Under Customary International Law. *Amicus Curiae* Brief of the Human Rights Center at the University of California, Berkeley, School of Law, and International Experts on Sexual Violence Under International Criminal Law) (8 December 2015), available at www.law.berkeley.edu/wp-content/uploads/2015/04/MICUS-CURIAE-BRIEF-OF-THE-HUMAN-RIGHTS-CENTER-AT-THE-UNIVERSITY-OF-CALIFORNIA-BERKELEY-SCHOOL-OF-LAW-AND-INTERNATIONAL-EXPERTS-ON-SEXUAL-VIOLENCE-UNDER-INTERNATIONAL-CRIMINAL-LAW-Eng.pdf. For discussion, see S Williams, 'Hybrid Courts and *Amicus Curiae*

curiae applications. Even accepted briefs or *amicus curiae* responses to open calls or invitations may not have much, or any noticeable, impact upon proceedings. Chambers are increasingly mentioning briefs in the procedural history;[123] however, the Chamber may then decide that the submissions were not useful or relevant and not consider them further. For instance, the ICC Appeals Chamber noted that observations by the Africa Centre for Open Justice, which addressed Kenyan law and cooperation with the ICC in the *Kenyatta* case, were 'outside the scope of the issues certified on appeal'. It decided that they 'are therefore unhelpful for the proper determination of the present appeal. Under these circumstances, the Appeals Chamber will not address the submissions made in the *Amicus Curiae* Observations or in the responses thereto'.[124] However, this does raise the question why the Chamber accepted the brief in the first place.

B. Moderate Influence

In many instances where a Chamber accepts a brief, the decision will refer to the submission in the procedural history, may include a brief summary of the submission or note that the submission was interesting or helpful. However, the decision does not rely upon the *amicus curiae* submission to support its reasoning, that is in the substantive part of the decision. This may reflect judicial citation practices in international criminal tribunals, which tend not to cite *amicus* briefs or academic commentary directly, instead citing primary instruments, their own jurisprudence or, less frequently, that of other tribunals. On some occasions, the judgment may appear to address similar arguments and draw similar conclusions, relying on the same primary sources, which suggests there has been some influence. In other instances, a Chamber has used the same argument and phrasing as an *amicus* in its decision, but did not cite or refer to the brief.[125] For novel issues (which is when *amici* are more likely to participate), there may be several possible interpretations of or ways of applying the law, all of which are reasonable, and the Chamber must decide which it considers the most appropriate. The submissions may have been useful to the Chamber in setting out different interpretations and arguments, and drawing the Chamber's attention to suitable sources and literature, which has assisted the Chamber to arrive at its own conclusion. We recommend that where a Chamber has found a brief useful it should acknowledge this expressly, as failing to do so undermines transparency, does not recognise the contribution of the *amici*, and makes it

Briefing' in S Weill, KT Seelinger and KB Carlson (eds), *Prosecuting the President: The Trial of Hissen Habré* (Oxford, OUP, forthcoming 2019).

[123] eg *Prosecutor v Katanga*, ICC TC II, 24 March 2017, ICC-01/04-01/07-3728-tENG.

[124] *Prosecutor v Kenyatta*, ICC AC, 19 August 2015, ICC-01/09-02/11-1032, para 28.

[125] Referred to in Ellis (n 56), 268, citing an example provided by Anne Heindel of the Cambodian Documentation Centre.

difficult for *amici* and others to measure influence, thus lessening the legitimacy of the judicial decision-making process.[126]

However, it is clear that an absence of references to *amicus* submissions in a judgment does not necessarily mean the absence of influence. One example of moderate influence concerned the ECCC's potential application of the doctrine of joint criminal enterprise. This issue had attracted significant attention from prospective *amici curiae* at the ECCC, including from defendants in other cases, but the focus here is upon the first group of relevant *amici*. In 2008, the ECCC Co-Prosecutors appealed the Case 001 Closing Order and requested that joint criminal enterprise be included as a mode of criminal responsibility.[127] The accused in Case 002 attempted to make submissions on this topic as an *amicus curiae* in Case 001, on the basis that the ECCC's findings in Case 001 regarding joint criminal enterprise would also affect their case. Separately, the Pre-Trial Chamber invited submissions from Kai Ambos, Antonio Cassese and the Centre for Human Rights and Legal Pluralism of McGill University (McGill) on the development of the theory of joint criminal enterprise and whether it could be applied by the ECCC, given that it was focused on crimes committed between 1975 and 1979.

The invited *amici curiae* agreed that the first form of joint criminal enterprise (JCEI, based on perpetrators holding basic or shared intent) had grounding in customary international law, representing a form of commission or co-perpetration. This arose from the cases following World War II and therefore could be considered a relevant form of criminal responsibility for crimes committed by 1975. However, the *amici* differed as to the other forms of joint criminal enterprise. Ambos argued that the second form of joint criminal enterprise ('JCEII' or systemic JCE) could narrowly be considered as representing a variation of JCEI where the accused participated in operating a system, such as a concentration camp, that is managed with a common purpose of which the accused was aware. However, if understood more broadly to encompass mere membership of a common enterprise, this would be more akin to the third form of joint criminal enterprise ('JCEIII' or extended JCE), which extends liability to the co-perpetrators for acts that are a 'natural and foreseeable consequence' of their plan. For Ambos, this wider conception of JCEII would not amount to the commission of a crime, but a form of accomplice liability. Further, he argued that the identification of JCEIII in the ICTY's *Tadic* case had insufficient grounding in customary international law, meaning that it could not have formed an applicable mode of liability in international criminal law by 1975.[128]

[126] Ellis also reached this conclusion, based on interviews with NGO *amici* (n 56 at 268).

[127] *Co-Prosecutors v Duch (Case 001)*, ECCC PTC, 5 September 2008, 001/18-07-2007-ECCC/OCIJ (PTC 02)-D99/3/3.

[128] *Co-Prosecutors v Duch (Case 001)*, ECCC PTC, 27 October 2008, 001/18-07-2007-ECCC/OCIJ (PTC 02)-D99/3/27.

In contrast, McGill argued that '[w]hile the post-Second World War jurisprudence cited in *Tadic* is less conclusive than national jurisprudence, each of the three categories of JCE finds some support amongst the World War Two military tribunals' jurisprudence'.[129] Cassese argued that the 'principles of JCE as a mode of criminal liability crystallized after World War II and were customary rules of international criminal law by 1975',[130] though he agreed that JCEII was 'essentially a variant of the first' form of JCE.[131]

The Pre-Trial Chamber referred to the *amicus curiae* briefs in its decision on the appeal against the Closing Order,[132] but decided that joint criminal enterprise had not formed 'part of the factual basis for the investigation' and so should not be added to the Closing Order, meaning that it did not address the status of this doctrine in customary international law.[133] However, the Co-Prosecutors continued to request that the Chambers employ joint criminal enterprise and, in June 2009, the Trial Chamber gave notice to the accused that it would consider the applicability of this doctrine in the trial judgment.[134] In the Case 001 judgment, the Trial Chamber decided that it would not breach the accused's fair trial rights to re-characterise the charges to include joint criminal enterprise.[135] It addressed the scope of joint criminal enterprise in customary international law without citing the *amicus curiae* briefs, but with reference to many of the sources they cited and to reach similar conclusions regarding the derivation of JCE from the post-World War II cases.[136] For example, using Cassese's language, the Chamber agreed that JCE II was 'a variant of the basic form' of JCE,[137] which corresponded to Ambos' analysis. Consistent with all three *amici curiae*, the Trial Chamber found that 'the systemic form of joint criminal enterprise, along with the basic form from which it derives, were part of customary international law during the 1975 to 1979 period'.[138] However, as the Co-Prosecutors only relied upon the basic and systemic forms (JCEI and JCEII), the Chamber determined that 'it need not generally pronounce on the customary status of the third extended form of joint criminal enterprise during the 1975 to 1979 period'.[139]

[129] *Co-Prosecutors v Duch (Case 001)*, ECCC PTC, 27 October 2008, 001/18-07-2007-ECCC/OCIJ (PTC 02)-D99/3/24, para 15.

[130] ibid, para 20.

[131] ibid, para 24.

[132] *Co-Prosecutors v Duch (Case 001)*, ECCC PTC, 5 December 2008, 001/18-07-2007-ECCC/OCIJ (PTC 02)-D99/3/42, para 136.

[133] ibid, paras 141–42.

[134] *Co-Prosecutors v Duch (Case 001)*, ECCC TC, 26 July 2010, 001/18-07-2007-ECCC/TC-E188, para 501.

[135] ibid, para 503.

[136] ibid, paras 504–15.

[137] ibid, para 509.

[138] ibid, para 512.

[139] ibid, para 513.

Thus, it seems likely that the *amicus curiae* briefs had an indirect influence upon the Trial Chamber judgment in Case 001. The issue of whether joint criminal enterprise was applicable for the ECCC arose subsequently in Case 002. The Case 002 Pre-Trial Chamber[140] and Trial Chamber[141] found, following similar reasoning to that provided by Ambos and involving a comparable review of the post-World War II jurisprudence, that JCEIII was not a recognised mode of responsibility in customary international law by 1975.[142] Thus, Ambos' *amicus curiae* brief may have had a belated influence upon subsequent proceedings as well, even though the Chambers did not overtly rely upon the briefs.

C. Significant Influence

Amicus curiae briefs can have a significant influence, although this is relatively rare in international criminal tribunals. The SCSL was willing to rely upon *amicus* submissions to a considerable degree. For example, in the *Kallon Decision* the Appeals Chamber summarised and made extensive reference to the written and oral *amicus curiae* observations provided by Redress, Lawyers Committee for Human Rights and the International Commission of Jurists, as well as by Dianne Orentlicher. The Chambers found that it 'is not difficult to agree with the submissions made by the *amici curiae*, Professor Orentlicher and Redress' that amnesties included in the Lomé Agreement did not preclude the SCSL from prosecuting international crimes. Similarly, the Appeals Chamber summarised the arguments of three *amici curiae* in deciding that Charles Taylor could not benefit from immunity as a Head of State,[143] finding that 'it is not difficult to accept and gratefully adopt' Professor Sands' argument in finding that the SCSL is an international tribunal.[144] The SCSL Appeals Chamber also set out in detail and placed significant reliance upon *amicus curiae* submissions provided by the University of Toronto Human Rights Clinic and UNICEF – and especially to a UN report referred to in the UNICEF brief. The Chambers agreed with the *amici* that the recruitment of child soldiers was an established crime in customary international

[140] *Co-Prosecutors v Ieng, Ieng and Khieu (Case 002)*, ECCC PTC, 20 May 2010, 002/19-09-2007-ECCC-OCIJ (PTC38)-D97/15/9.

[141] *Co-Prosecutors v Nuon et al (Case 002)*, ECCC TC, 12 September 2011, 002/19-09-2007-ECCC-TC-E100/6, paras 30–38.

[142] The International Co-Investigating Judge has since confirmed that he 'will not apply JCE III in Case 003, but that this determination may change subject to the outcome of the JCE III Appeal': *Co-Prosecutors v Meas (Case 003)*, ECCC OCIJ, 7 March 2016, 003/07-09-2009-ECCC-OCIJ-D87/2/1.15/1, para 11.

[143] In *Prosecutor v Taylor*, SCSL AC, 31 May 2004, SCSL-2003-01-I-3014 the Chambers address Professors Sands and MacDonald's brief (at para 17), Diane Orentlicher's brief (at para 18) and they provide a short outline of African Bar Association's relevant submissions (at para 19).

[144] *Prosecutor v Taylor*, SCSL AC, 31 May 2004, SCSL-2003-01-I-3014, para 41.

law before the accused's indicted actions,[145] even though the UN report was not produced until after the relevant period.[146]

Thus, while *amicus curiae* briefs may not always be accepted, or have a significant influence upon proceedings where they are admitted, there are instances in which *amici curiae* arguments have had an important bearing on international crimes cases. The influence may not be restricted to the immediate proceedings, but may contribute to the development of international criminal law. For example, the decision of the SCSL Appeals Chamber in Taylor was influential in the decision of the ICC Appeals Chamber in holding that no immunity existed in customary international law to preclude prosecution of President Al-Bashir of Sudan before the ICC.[147]

Amici may also influence the Prosecutor, as seen in the well-known example of the *amicus curiae* brief that the Coalition for Women's Human Rights in Conflict Situations sought to file before the ICTR Trial Chamber in *Akayesu*.[148] That brief aimed to persuade the Chamber to call on the Prosecutor to amend the indictment to include charges of sexual violence. The Chamber accepted the brief, placed it on the case file and served it on the parties.[149] The Prosecutor subsequently sought to amend the indictment to include sexual violence, although the Prosecutor claimed that the brief was not the impetus for this change.[150] The Prosecutor suggested that it had already been considering evidence of sexual violence and reconsidered the charges based on further evidence that emerged during testimony linking the accused to crimes of sexual violence.[151] The Chamber granted leave to amend the indictment. Further factual allegations concerning sexual violence were incorporated into the amended indictment and three additional charges – of rape and other inhumane acts as crimes against humanity and outrages upon human dignity in particular rape, degrading and humiliating treatment and indecent assault as a war crime – were included.[152] Sexual violence then became a prominent feature of the prosecution case, ultimately leading to conviction of Akayesu for rape and other inhumane acts as crimes against humanity and genocide, with the judgment specifically recognising that acts of rape and sexual violence could

[145] *Prosecutor v Norman*, SCSL AC, 31 May 2004, SCSL-2004-14-AR72(E)-7383.

[146] *Prosecutor v Norman*, SCSL AC, 31 May 2004, SCSL-2004-14-AR72(E)-7413, para 42.

[147] *Prosecutor v Al-Bashir*, ICC AC, 6 May 2019, ICC-02/05-02/09-397-Corr, paras 109 and 113.

[148] *Prosecutor v Akayesu*, ICTR TC, 17 June 1997, ICTR-96-4-I. For further discussion, see B van Schaak, 'Engendering Genocide: The Akayesu Case before the ICTR' in DR Hurwitz, ML Satterthwaite and D Ford (eds), *Human Rights Advocacy Stories* (New York, Thomson Reuters/ Foundation Press 2009) 198–200.

[149] As detailed by van Schaak (n 148), 202.

[150] *Prosecutor v Akayesu,* ICTR TC, Transcript, 17 June 1997, 8.

[151] ibid, 6; van Schaak (n 148), 202. This claim was also evident in a 2016 film outlining the history of the *Akayesu* case, which interviewed key prosecution officials: see *The Uncondemned* (2016), available at www.theuncondemned.com/.

[152] *Prosecutor v Akayesu*, ICTR, 17 June 1997, ICTR-96-4-1.

constitute prohibited acts for genocide, particularly where rape may impact upon births within the group.[153]

Despite the prosecution's assertion to the contrary, it is probable that the *amicus* brief did have some influence. The Chamber referred to the brief in its decision 'noting the interest shown in this issue by non-governmental organizations, which it considers as indicative of public concern over the historical exclusion of rape and other forms of sexual violence from the investigation and prosecution of war crimes'.[154] Certainly, key gender advocates and commentators considered the brief to have been significant in changing the outcome of the trial.[155] The resulting Trial Chamber judgment in *Akayesu* significantly developed the law concerning sexual violence, recognising for the first time that sexual violence can be prosecuted as constituting part of genocide and highlighting the links between sexual violence and torture.[156]

It is hard to predict when an *amicus curiae* submission is likely to have a significant impact, as the majority do not. Tentatively, we can say that significant influence is more likely where the *amicus curiae* is: (1) directly invited; (2) performing an expertise function; and (3) offers relevant and focused submissions on a novel legal issue on which there might be a number of possible, but reasonable, views of the law. More procedural rights do not necessarily lead to greater influence; for example, in the *Jordan* non-cooperation proceedings, *amici* participated more extensively, but did not have a significant impact on the decision. The following chapters explore influence by actor.

VII. PARTICIPATION IN ICC REPARATIONS PROCEEDINGS

Chapter three highlighted how Article 75(3) of the Rome Statute has created an additional mechanism for participation in the reparations phase of proceedings in the ICC. A preliminary analysis of *amicus curiae* practice suggested that there are distinctions between the practice in other stages of proceedings and in reparations proceedings, including greater acceptance rates and influence of

[153] *Prosecutor v Akayesu*, ICTR TC I, 2 September 1998, ICTRY-96-4-T, paras 507, 508.

[154] ibid, para 417.

[155] AM de Brouwer, *Supranational Criminal Prosecution of Sexual Violence: The ICC and the Practice of the ICTY and the ICTR* (Oxford, Intersentia, 2005); Coalition on Women's Human Rights in Conflict Situations, 'RWANDA: Akayesu Sentencing a Victory for Women's Rights', available at www1.essex.ac.uk/armedcon/story_id/000054.pdf; van Schaak (n 148).

[156] *Prosecutor v Akayesu*, ICTR TC I, 2 September 1998, ICTRY-96-4-T. See further V Oosterveld, 'Gender-sensitive Justice and the International Criminal Tribunal for Rwanda: Lessons Learned for the International Criminal Court' (2005) 12 *New England Journal of International and Comparative Law* 119; KD Askin, 'Prosecuting Wartime Rape and Other Gender-Related Crimes Under International Law: Extraordinary Advances, Enduring Obstacles' (2003) 21 *Berkeley Journal of international Law* 288; de Brouwer (n 155); R Copelon, 'Gender Crimes as War Crimes: Integrating Crimes Against Women into International Criminal Law' (2000) 46 *McGill Law Journal* 217, 225–26.

submissions. Consistent with the approach adopted throughout this study, we have applied a functional approach to this phase of proceedings, exploring the different participants and functions performed by participants, not only looking at actors labelled formally as *amicus curiae*. This section has three aims. First, to explore the function(s) performed by the *amicus curiae* in the reparations phase. Secondly, to analyse the extent to which there are key differences in the *amicus curiae* practice in this stage. Finally, to explore the interaction between Article 75(3) 'representations', *amicus curiae* submissions under Rule 103 and any other participatory mechanisms in reparations proceedings.

A. The Nature of Reparations Proceedings and Identifying the Parties

Reparations are a distinct phase of proceedings that follows the conviction of an accused.[157] Moreover, the reparations phase remains criminal in nature as reparations orders potentially directly affect the accused and his or liability for reparations.[158] Even where an accused is indigent and is not financially affected by an order (because the TFV is meeting the costs of reparations), reparations have a symbolic value and affect the accused. Consequently, Chambers must continue to protect the rights of the accused during the reparations phase.[159] The Appeals Chamber has indicated that the reparations phase comprises two stages. The first involves the proceedings up to the issue of a reparations order (and any appeal) while the second stage concerns the implementation of the reparations order.[160] We consider practice in both stages, although noting that the practice is limited: only three cases have resulted in the issue of a reparations order and reached the implementation phase (*Lubanga*, *Katanga* and *Al Mahdi*); reparations proceedings in *Bemba* ceased following the accused's acquittal.[161]

Recognising that reparations concern victims, while also engaging the interests of the defence, the parties to reparations proceedings are the victims and the defence.[162] This includes the right to appeal a reparations order.[163] Victims participate as of right and do not need to establish that the proceedings engage their personal interests.[164] The definition of victim for the purposes

[157] See, eg *Prosecutor v Lubanga*, ICC AC, 14 December 2012, ICC-01/04-01/06-2953, para 70.
[158] ibid, paras 65–66.
[159] *Prosecutor v Lubanga*, ICC TC I, 29 August 2012, ICC-01/04-01/06-2911, para 23.
[160] *Prosecutor v Lubanga*, ICC AC, 14 December 2012, ICC-01/04-01/06-2953, paras 53–55.
[161] *Prosecutor v Bemba*, ICC TC III, 3 August 2018, ICC-01/05-01/08-3653.
[162] *Prosecutor v Lubanga*, ICC TC I, 7 August 2012, ICC-01/04-01/06-2904, para 267.
[163] Rome Statute, Art 82(4); *Prosecutor v Lubanga*, ICC TC I, 29 August 2012, ICC-01/04-01/06-2911; *Prosecutor v Lubanga,* ICC AC, 14 December 2012, ICC-01/04-01/06-2953, paras 65 and 67.
[164] *Prosecutor v Lubanga*, ICC AC, 14 December 2012, ICC-01/04-01/06-2953, para 67.

of participation may be broader at the reparations stage, not limited to those victims actively participating in the trial phase, but including victims seeking to participate in the reparations phase and victims that may benefit from collective or symbolic reparations, but who remain unidentified.[165] Although victims participate, they do so through legal representation, in particular the LRV. The OPCV can represent those participating victims not allocated legal representation.[166] Trial Chamber I also permitted the OPVC to represent the interests of non-participating victims who had not submitted applications but may benefit from an award for collective reparations.[167] However, the Appeals Chamber confirmed that non-participating victims do not have a right of appeal as they are unidentified, although the OPVC can seek leave to represent their interests in appellate proceedings.[168] In sum, of the actors mentioned in Article 75(3) as able to make representations, two – the victims and the convicted person – are recognised as parties to the reparations proceedings and thus do not need to rely on Article 75(3) to participate.

B. Institutional Participants

Other institutional actors, such as the prosecution, TFV and Registry, as well as the state concerned, are not parties to proceedings but may participate. In its decision on reparations in *Lubanga*, Trial Chamber I indicated that the OTP was also a party, alongside the defence and victims.[169] Yet, the practice of the ICC does not reflect this statement. In all four cases, the Trial Chamber has invited the OTP to file observations on the relevant reparations principles and procedures.[170] However, the OTP is not a party to proceedings and may only make submissions when invited to do so.[171] Without leave, the OTP does not have standing to respond to the submissions of others or to make final submissions, or to receive filings marked for the parties only, which includes expert reports[172] and confidential decisions.[173] The OTP recognises its secondary role

[165] ibid, paras 69–70.

[166] *Prosecutor v Lubanga*, ICC TC I, 5 April 2012, ICC-01/04-01/06-2858, para 12.

[167] ibid. Confirmed by the Appeals Chamber as appropriate, given their interest: *Prosecutor v Lubanga*, ICC AC, 14 December 2012, ICC-01/04-01/06-2953, para 71.

[168] ibid, para 72.

[169] *Prosecutor v Lubanga*, ICC TC I, 7 August 2012, ICC-01/04-01/06-2904, para 267.

[170] See, eg *Prosecutor v Lubanga*, ICC TC I, 14 March 2012, ICC-01/04-01/06-2844, para 3.

[171] In *Al Mahdi*, the OTP was invited to file observations on identification of experts: *Prosecutor v Al Mahdi*, ICC TC VIII, 29 September 2016, ICC-01/12-01/15-172, para 2(ii).

[172] eg, the OTP as a non-party, would not have received the expert reports in *Al Mahdi*: see *Prosecutor v Al Mahdi*, ICC TC VIII, 17 August 2017, ICC-01/12-01/15-236, para 7.

[173] eg in *Katanga*, the OTP had to request access to a confidential decision: *Prosecutor v Katanga*, ICC TC II, 21 August 2018, ICC-01/04-01/07-3806-tENG.

in the reparations phase and makes limited submissions.[174] The Appeals Chamber has confirmed that the OTP is not a party to appellate proceedings and has no right to make submissions on appeals from reparation proceedings, although indicating it could request permission to make submissions.[175] Prosecution submissions generally refer only to the invitation extended by the Trial Chamber, not to any particular legal basis, meaning they could be pursuant to the Chamber's inherent powers, Article 75(3) or Rule 103.

The Registry plays an important institutional role in managing applications for reparations. Trial Chambers have invited the Registry to make initial submissions on reparations principles in each of the four cases.[176] The Registry may also play a role in the appointment of experts[177] and file a response to submissions of others during proceedings,[178] at the discretion of the Chamber. In addition to its role in representing victims (where it is considered a party to proceedings), Trial Chamber I in *Lubanga* recognised that the OPCV can also perform an expertise function[179] as 'an expert body within the Court [established] in order to efficiently and timely address victims' issues'.[180] In this role, the OPCV is a participant and not a party, with permission to participate under a specific provision (Regulation 81(4)(b)) but in a similar manner to *amici*. In *Bemba*, the Chamber asked the OPCV to make submissions on proposed experts and consequential submissions following the accused's acquittal, although it did not indicate on what basis, potentially for its expertise or on behalf of victims.[181]

The institutional actor that has been the most extensively involved in reparations proceedings is the TFV, having participated in all cases and at the trial and appellate stages. Submissions from the TFV have indicated the roles it plays in reparations, and the functions its submissions perform.[182] The TFV has described its relationship with the ICC as a partnership that during reparations proceedings has three dimensions, depending on the stage of proceedings and the needs of the Chamber. In the phase leading up to the issue of a reparations order (and any appeal), the TFV functions mainly as an expert advisory body

[174] *Prosecutor v Al Mahdi*, ICC TC VIII, 6 December 2016, ICC-01/12-01/15-192-Red, recognising the primary role of the victims, deferring to the views of the LRV and the TFV and submitting only that collective and symbolic reparations would be better suited to this case.

[175] *Prosecutor v Lubanga*, ICC AC, 14 December 2012, ICC-01/04-01/06-2953, para 74.

[176] *Prosecutor v Lubanga*, ICC TC I, 14 March 2012, ICC-01/04-01/06-2844, para 9.

[177] eg, in *Bemba*, the Registry was invited to comment on proposed experts: see *Prosecutor v Bemba*, ICC TC III, 2 June 2017, ICC-01/05-01/08-3532-Red, para 1, noting an invitation extended on 21 February 2017.

[178] In *Katanga*, the Registry was permitted to file a full response to the submissions of the parties and other participants: see *Prosecutor v Katanga*, ICC TC II, 1 April 2015, ICC-01/04-01/07-3532-tENG.

[179] *Prosecutor v Lubanga*, ICC TC I, 5 April 2012, ICC-01/04-01/06-2858, para 11, although linked to interests of potential beneficiaries of collective reparations.

[180] *Prosecutor v Lubanga*, ICC TC I, 28 March 2012, ICC-01/04-01/06-2848, para 9.

[181] *Prosecutor v Bemba*, ICC TC III, 2 June 2017, ICC-01/05-01/08-3532-Red.

[182] See *Prosecutor v Al Mahdi*, ICC TC VIII, 2 December 2016, ICC-01/12-01/15-187, paras 7–15.

offering expertise and experience to the Chamber, not submissions on specific issues raised by the case, which should be the domain of the parties. Following the order for reparations, the TFV functions as the implementing agency (post-order) and a funding body (once the Trial Chamber has determined the accused's liability for reparations). In the implementation phase, the TFV functions mainly as an interested actor, although it will also raise potential challenges for implementation pre-order. The TFV has stressed that it has a unique institutional relationship with the ICC and is not a party to proceedings.[183]

The practice reflects these distinct roles. Each Chamber has invited the TFV to make observations in the first stage of reparations as to the relevant principles and procedures. During this phase, the TFV may respond to the submissions of others and make final observations, although the practice is not consistent across Chambers.[184] The TFV has made submissions on other issues that may arise. In *Katanga*, the Chamber invited the TFV to make observations on monetary value of liability 'in view of its extensive knowledge of the context in Ituri'.[185] The observations reflect the scope of this permission, interpreting this to be providing context on Ituri only, such as the cost of daily life, and not on specific amounts.[186] In *Bemba*, the TFV made submissions following the acquittal.[187] In pre-order proceedings and related appeals, the TFV functions as an expert body to assist the Trial Chamber with developing the principles and procedures. Given the limited number of cases so far, it has also assisted the Chamber to see how reparations principles may apply to different types of charges: use of child soldiers (*Lubanga*), sexual violence (*Katanga* and *Bemba*) and destruction of cultural heritage (*Al Mahdi*). As the practice grows, its role as an expert body may become less significant. The legal basis for the TFV's participation is not always evident or consistent: sometimes referring only to the Chamber's invitation, and occasionally referring to either Article 75(3) or Rule 103.[188] In appellate proceedings, the position is clear, as Article 75(3) does not concern appeals. Consistent with this, the Appeals Chamber considered the TFV able to participate only pursuant to Rule 103, even where specifically invited to do so.[189] The Appeals Chamber has also on occasion required the

[183] ibid.

[184] eg in *Katanga* the Chamber did not ask the TFV to file a response, while in *Al Mahdi*, after raising the issue in its submissions, the TFV was permitted to do so: *Prosecutor v Al Mahdi*, ICC TC VIII, 19 January 2017, ICC-01/12-01/15-203-Red.

[185] *Prosecutor v Katanga*, ICC TC II, 15 July 2016, ICC-01/04-01/07-3702-tENG.

[186] *Prosecutor v Katanga*, ICC TC II, 30 September 2016, ICC-01/04-01/07-3714-Red, paras 7–8.

[187] *Prosecutor v Bemba*, ICC TC III, 13 June 2018, ICC-01/05-01/08-3639, para 2; *Prosecutor v Bemba*, ICC TC III, 6 July 2018, ICC-01/05-01/08-3648.

[188] In *Katanga*, the Trial Chamber specifically mentioned Art 75(3): *Prosecutor v Katanga*, ICC TC II, 15 July 2016, ICC-01/04-01/07-3702-tENG; in other decisions, no legal basis is mentioned.

[189] In addition to the three appeals from the reparations order, the Appeals Chamber also invited the TFV to make submissions in an appeal concerning the monetary liability of Mr Lubanga for reparations: *Prosecutor v Lubanga*, ICC AC, 21 September 2018, ICC-01/04-01/06-3419.

TFV to seek leave so the Chamber can determine whether the proposed submissions would be helpful.[190]

The TFV's role in the implementation phase is quite different. While the Trial Chamber remains ultimately responsible for the implementation of its order, the TFV is the primary actor. It drafts the implementation plan for comments from the parties and participants and eventual approval by the Chamber.[191] Consequently, the TFV participates almost as a party in implementation proceedings. For example, in *Lubanga*, the TFV participated in oral hearings and responded to submissions by others, including *amici*, both in oral submissions and in writing.[192] In the implementation phase, submissions by the *amici* tend to become more practical concerning specific projects or types of projects. Chambers have indicated that it is not their role to consider all these suggestions; rather, it is the role of the TFV to take such suggestions into account when designing and implementing projects.[193] Thus, in this stage, *amici* seek to assist or influence the TFV as the implementing body, in addition to (or possibly instead of) the Trial Chamber.

C. Legal Basis for Participation by Other Actors: Article 75(3) or Rule 103?

Other actors have participated in reparations proceedings. Although states are not victims under Rule 85, and thus cannot participate as such, states have participated in reparations proceedings but only in the implementation phase and it appears only under Rule 103. In *Lubanga*, the Trial Chamber invited the authorities of the Democratic Republic of Congo (DRC) as well as the UN and its agencies to provide submissions as *amici curiae*, seeking information about projects already in place in the DRC.[194] The UN mission in the DRC (MONUSCO) submitted observations as *amici curiae*[195] and the DRC sent observations on a confidential basis.[196] After the order approving symbolic reparations, the Chamber invited the DRC to provide information regarding the participation of child soldiers in demobilisation programmes in Ituri.[197]

[190] See, eg *Prosecutor v Katanga*, ICC AC, 7 August 2017, ICC-01/04-01/07-3752; *Prosecutor v Katanga*, ICC TC II, 25 August 2017, ICC-01/04-01/07-3755.

[191] eg *Prosecutor v Lubanga*, ICC AC, 3 March 2015, ICC-01/04-01/06-3129-AnxA, para 77, recognising that before the implementation plan is approved the parties and other interested parties may make submissions to the Chamber.

[192] See *Prosecutor v Lubanga,* ICC TC II, Transcript, 11 October 2016; *Prosecutor v Lubanga,* ICC TC II, Transcript, 13 October 2016.

[193] See, eg *Prosecutor v Al Mahdi*, ICC TC VIII, 4 March 2019, ICC-01/12-01/15-324-Red, paras 14 and 17.

[194] *Prosecutor v Lubanga*, ICC TC II, 15 July 2016, ICC-01/04-01/06-3217-tENG, paras 7–8.

[195] *Prosecutor v Lubanga*, ICC TC II, 30 September 2016, ICC-01/04-01/06-3240-Anx15.

[196] *Prosecutor v Lubanga*, ICC TC II, 21 October 2016, ICC-01/04-01/06-3253-tENG.

[197] *Prosecutor v Lubanga*, ICC TC II, 22 November 2016, ICC-01/04-01/06-3260-tENG.

The DRC provided this information[198] as well as formal observations on the proposed collective reparations projects.[199] In *Al Mahdi*, Trial Chamber VIII included the Malian authorities in its initial invitation for submissions on the reparations principles and procedure, but the government elected not to participate.[200] The Chamber invited Mali to participate in the implementation phase, referring to Rule 103.[201] Mali submitted observations in January 2019 on a confidential basis.[202] The victims in *Katanga*, supported by the defence, requested the Chamber to facilitate the participation of the DRC in proceedings, although what form of participation was proposed was not clear from the application.[203] The Chamber did not respond to this request and did not invite the DRC to participate, nor did the DRC seek leave to do so.

In *Lubanga*, the Trial Chamber invited other individuals or interested parties to seek leave to make submissions on the principles or the procedure to be followed.[204] It did not indicate a legal basis for such submissions. Five organisations sought leave: Women's Initiatives for Gender Justice (WIGJ);[205] International Centre for Transitional Justice; UNICEF; *Avocats Sans Frontières* (ASF) jointly with four other organisations; and the *Fondation Congolaise pour la Promotion des Droits humains et la Paix* (FOCDP). Most requests did not refer to the legal basis for submissions, referring only to the scheduling order, although the ASF request referred to Rule 103. The defence objected to the requests, arguing that their participation is only possible under Rule 103, which it argued should only be used exceptionally, and that none of the applicants had the required expertise or experience.[206] In its decision, the Trial Chamber referred to Article 75 as well as Rule 103 and stated that the 'central matter to be determined … is whether the Chamber will be assisted in its proper determination of the issues identified in the Scheduling Order by receiving submissions from the five organisations'.[207] The Chamber also indicated that it did not accept the defence submissions that the organisations could only participate as *amici curiae*, noting that the 'proceedings set out in Article 75(3) of the Statute are distinct from those provided for in Rule 103(2) and (3) of the Rules', which perhaps implied that they considered these interventions were made

[198] Submissions were sent on 24 January 2017 from the government authority in charge of the DDR programme: *Prosecutor v Lubanga*, ICC TC II, 21 December 2017, ICC-01/04-01/06-3379-Red-Corr-tENG, para 12.

[199] *Prosecutor v Lubanga*, ICC TC II, 20 February 2017, ICC-01/04-01/06-3274-tENG.

[200] *Prosecutor v Al Mahdi*, ICC TC VIII, 29 September 2016, ICC-01/12-01/15-172, para 2(iii); *Prosecutor v Al Mahdi*, ICC TC VIII, 17 August 2017, ICC-01/12-01/15-236, para 4.

[201] *Prosecutor v Al Mahdi*, ICC TC VIII, 5 November 2018, ICC-01/12-01/15-293.

[202] *Prosecutor v Al Mahdi*, ICC TC VIII, 8 January 2019, ICC-01/12-01/15-312. Submissions were confidential as the implementation plan was itself confidential.

[203] *Prosecutor v Katanga*, ICC TC II, 24 March 2016, ICC-01/04-01/07-3674.

[204] *Prosecutor v Lubanga*, ICC TC I, 14 March 2012, ICC-01/04-01/06-2844, para 10.

[205] *Prosecutor v Lubanga*, ICC TC I, 28 March 2012, ICC-01/04-01/06-2853.

[206] *Prosecutor v Lubanga*, ICC TC I, 16 April 2012, ICC-01/04-01/06-2862-Red.

[207] *Prosecutor v Lubanga*, ICC TC, 20 April 2012, ICC-01/04-01/06-2870, para 17.

under the former process.[208] The Chamber highlighted that Article 75(3) says that the Court 'shall take into account' representations, which is 'not specifically provided for' in regards to the *amicus curiae*.[209] In approving the requests, the Chamber did not refer to *which* legal basis it was relying on: Article 75(3) or Rule 103. However, it appeared to be applying the test for *amici curiae*, and clearly saw the organisations as providing expertise.[210] None of the *amici* mentioned a legal basis when filing observations, referring only to the decision giving permission[211] and the cover sheet to the Trial Chamber decision listed the organisations as 'Other' and not *amici*.[212] In contrast, during the implementation phase, when Article 75(3) is no longer applicable as a reparations order has already been issued, the Trial Chamber issued an 'Order under Rule 103' encouraging organisations to submit observations.[213] Therefore, despite the comment that Article 75(3) constitutes a separate procedure, Trial Chamber I in *Lubanga* either relied on Rule 103 or adopted an approach to participation closely modelled on it.

In *Katanga*, Trial Chamber II had a different approach, inviting submissions from interested persons 'pursuant to Article 75' but requiring applicants to seek leave and to specify their expertise and the issues they proposed to address.[214] The four applicants all referred to Article 75(3) as the basis for their application, and set out their expertise as requested.[215] The order granting leave for the four organisations to participate referred to Article 75(3) in the title, although the text of the order also mentioned Rule 103.[216] The Chamber satisfied itself as to the expertise of the applicants and the relevance of their submissions, before finding that receiving the 'representations is in the interests of the administration of justice',[217] a different test to that for the *amicus curiae* at the ICC. The order uses the word 'representations' which is the term used in Article 75(3). Three of the four organisations referred to Article 75(3) as the basis for their submissions, with two organisations and the Trial Chamber judgment listing these organisations as 'other participants' rather than *amici*

[208] ibid, paras 11, 20.

[209] ibid, para 21.

[210] The Chamber considered whether it would be assisted in the proper determination of the issues: see ibid, paras 17–21.

[211] *Prosecutor v Lubanga*, ICC TC I, 10 May 2012, ICC-01/04-01/06-2876; *Prosecutor v Lubanga*, ICC TC I, 10 May 2012, ICC-01/04-01/06-2877; *Prosecutor v Lubanga*, ICC TC I, 10 May 2012, ICC-01/04-01/06-2870; *Prosecutor v Lubanga*, ICC TC I, 10 May 2012, ICC-01/04-01/06-2879.

[212] *Prosecutor v Lubanga*, ICC TC I, 7 August 2012, ICC-01/04-01/06-2904.

[213] *Prosecutor v Lubanga*, ICC TC II, 15 July 2016, ICC-01/04-01/06-3217-tENG.

[214] *Prosecutor v Katanga*, ICC TC II, 21 January 2015, ICC-01/04-01/07-3516, para 10.

[215] *Prosecutor v Katanga*, ICC TC II, 2 February 2015, ICC-01/04-01/07-3517; *Prosecutor v Katanga*, ICC TC II, 2 February 2015, ICC-01/04-01/07-3519; *Prosecutor v Katanga*, ICC TC II, 13 February 2015, ICC-01/04-01/07-3253; *Prosecutor v Katanga*, ICC TC II, 12 February 2015, ICC- 01/04-01/07-3521-Conf.

[216] *Prosecutor v Katanga*, ICC TC I, 1 April 2015, ICC-01/04-01/07-3533-tENG, preamble.

[217] ibid, para 16.

in the cover page.[218] This suggests that participation in Katanga relied on Article 75(3) rather than Rule 103. The Appeal Chamber confirmed that the organisations participated pursuant to Article 75(3).[219]

In *Bemba*, Trial Chamber III mentioned both Article 75(3) and Rule 103 in its call for submissions from 'organisations interested in making submissions'.[220] Of the four organisations who responded to the call, the Human Rights Centre at Queen's University Belfast (QUB) referred to Article 75 and the scheduling order,[221] Redress referred to both Article 75 and Rule 103, but seemed to rely primarily on Article 75(3) as the basis for its request,[222] the UN relied on both provisions[223] and the International Organisation for Migration (IOM) appeared to rely on both.[224] However, when approving participation, the Chamber referred *only* to Rule 103 and applied the test for admission of *amici curiae*, that is: the Chamber considered it desirable for the proper determination of a case.[225] In filing submissions, the organisations inconsistently referred to the legal basis: QUB and the IOM referred to Article 75(3) in the title of their filing, the UN referred only to Rule 103, while Redress referred to both Article 75(3) and Rule 103.[226] In its final decision on reparations, Trial Chamber III acknowledged the contribution of *amici curiae*, thus the Chamber clearly considered these organisations as admitted under Rule 103, not Article 75(3).[227]

Finally, in *Al Mahdi*, Trial Chamber VIII referred specifically to Rule 103 in its invitation for submissions.[228] The three organisations who sought leave all referred to both Rule 103 and Article 75(3) in their requests.[229] In its decisions on the requests, the Chamber referred to Rule 103, satisfied itself as to the organisations' expertise and experience and applied the 'will assist in determination of reparations test'.[230] Thus, Trial Chamber VIII viewed these submissions as from

[218] Redress and Queen's University of Belfast's Human Rights Centre and University of Ulster's Transitional Justice Institute, with the UN referring to Art 75 as the legal basis: *Prosecutor v Katanga*, TC II, 24 March 2017 ICC-01/04-01/07-3728-tENG.
[219] *Prosecutor v Katanga*, ICC AC, 8 March 2018, ICC-01/04-01/07-3778-Red, para 11.
[220] *Prosecutor v Bemba*, ICC TC III, 22 July 2016, ICC-01/05-01/08-3410, para 8.
[221] *Prosecutor v Bemba*, ICC TC III, 8 August 2016, ICC-01/05-01/08-3420.
[222] *Prosecutor v Bemba*, ICC TC III, 10 August 2016, ICC-01/05-01/08-3421.
[223] *Prosecutor v Bemba*, ICC TC III, 15 August 2016, ICC-01/05-01/08-3422.
[224] *Prosecutor v Bemba*, TC III, 16 August 2016, ICC-01/05-01/08-3425-Conf-AnxI.
[225] *Prosecutor v Bemba*, ICC TC III, 25 August 2016, ICC-01/05-01/08-3430.
[226] *Prosecutor v Bemba*, ICC TC III, 17 October 2016, ICC-01/05-01/08-3444; *Prosecutor v Bemba*, ICC TC III, 17 October 2016, ICC-01/05-01/08-3447; *Prosecutor v Bemba*, ICC TC III, 17 October 2016, ICC-01/05-01/08-3448; *Prosecutor v Bemba*, ICC TC III, 17 October 2016, ICC-01/05-01/08-3449.
[227] *Prosecutor v Bemba*, ICC TC III, 3 August 2018, ICC-01/05-01/08-3653, para 8.
[228] *Prosecutor v Al Mahdi*, ICC TC VIII, 29 September 2016, ICC-01/12-01/15-172, para 2(iii).
[229] *Prosecutor v Al Mahdi*, ICC TC VIII, 20 October 2016, ICC-01/12/-01/15-175; *Prosecutor v Al Mahdi*, ICC TC VIII, 21 October 2016, ICC-01/12-01/15-176; *Prosecutor v Al Mahdi*, ICC TC VIII, 28 October 2016, ICC-01/12-01/15-179.
[230] *Prosecutor v Al Mahdi*, ICC TC VIII, 25 October 2016, ICC-01/12-01/15-178; *Prosecutor v Al Mahdi*, ICC TC VIII, 31 October 2016, ICC-01/12-01/15-180.

amici curiae, rather than relying on some separate legal basis, referring to them as *amici curiae* in its decision on reparations.[231]

There is evident confusion and inconsistency across Chambers and applicants as to the basis on which organisations and individuals participate in reparations proceedings, whether this is Article 75(3) or Rule 103. Article 75(3) does not set out a test for participation, although it refers to 'interested' states and persons (which clearly includes organisations), so we suggest that the test may well be that the actor has an 'interest' in the outcome of reparations. However, no Chamber has applied this test. Chambers have not admitted an organisation based on having an interest in the outcome, in the sense we have used elsewhere in this study, that is, a specific interest that is directly affected by the proceedings, although we note that UNESCO was ultimately the beneficiary of a symbolic reparation, a payment of one euro in the *Al Mahdi* case.

Instead, Chambers have effectively used the same approach to participation under Article 75(3) as for the *amicus curiae* under Rule 103, looking to whether the submissions will assist in their determination, considering in particular the expertise and experience of the actor and the relevance of the proposed submission. The organisations admitted are fulfilling an expertise function, not a representative one, a finding we explore in the next section. Moreover, no Chamber has indicated it is bound to take into account representations in reparations proceedings in a way it is not for *amici*. Although the Trial Chamber hinted at this in *Lubanga*, the practice shows no discernible difference in the way Chambers consider submissions depending on whether the submissions are under Rule 103 or Article 75(3). Similarly, while there are suggestions that Article 75(3) envisages a more permissive approach to representations, as is shown below, Chambers approach submissions more permissively in this phase generally, regardless of the legal basis for the submission. Therefore, Article 75(3) has not created a significant new mechanism that has substantially altered participation. Instead, we suggest that as a matter of principle Chambers should continue to invite and to admit organisations to participate as *amici curiae* under Rule 103, as these actors are not 'interested' in a strict legal sense (certainly not in the same way as the victims or a convicted person) and will most likely be offering expertise. Rule 103 offers an existing framework and body of jurisprudence for Chambers to consider whether to accept submissions. Affected states, however, may be better characterised as 'interested', in that they may benefit from or be required to cooperate with reparations projects, so it may be preferable to characterise them as participating under Article 75(3). In practice, however, states have more often been providing information, rather than representing an interest, so the *amicus curiae* role may also be appropriate.

[231] *Prosecutor v Al Mahdi*, ICC TC VIII, 17 August 2017, ICC-01/12-01/15-236, paras 3–4.

D. Differences in Practice in Reparations Phase

i. Rates of Acceptance and Variations in Procedure

There certainly appears to be a higher acceptance rate in reparations proceedings than the acceptance rate for other stages combined. Of the four trial chambers that have considered reparations, all issued a call for *amici curiae* or Article 75(3) submissions on reparations once a conviction had been entered (ie, at the pre-reparations order stage). All Chambers adopted a two-step approach, requiring a request for leave before submission. Excluding institutional actors, 16 organisations applied. The Chambers approved all requests,[232] although one organisation ultimately did not submit observations. At the implementation phase of the reparations order, only the Trial Chamber in *Lubanga* issued an invitation for *amicus curiae* submissions,[233] recognising that it would be helpful for it to have additional information and local expertise. The Chamber adopted a one-step process (ie, a separate approval process was not required), asked the Registry to publicise the call as widely as possible and indicated that *amici* could seek leave to participate in oral proceedings as well as to make written submissions. In addition to authorities from the DRC, 14 other actors made submissions, including the UN mission in DRC.[234] Two *amici*, WIGJ and Child Soldiers International, participated in the first oral hearings held by any Chamber during the reparations phase.[235] Across the reparations order and implementation phase, Trial Chambers have admitted 30 organisations to participate and no request or submission has been rejected, equating to a 100 per cent acceptance rate.[236]

The picture in proceedings before the Appeals Chamber is different. In proceedings concerning the appeal of the reparations order in *Lubanga*, the Appeals Chamber invited those *amici* who had participated in the Trial Chamber proceedings to seek leave to appear as *amici curiae*.[237] Two organisations, WIGJ and a coalition of NGOs led by ASF, sought leave.[238] The Chamber rejected both organisations on the basis that the issues the submissions proposed to address were no longer relevant.[239] In the appellate

[232] This figure does not count organisations making joint submissions separately.

[233] *Prosecutor v Lubanga*, ICC TC II, 15 July 2016, ICC-01/04-01/06-3217-tENG.

[234] *Prosecutor v Lubanga*, ICC TC II, 4 October 2016, ICC-01/04-01/06-3240-tENG (with 13 submissions as annexes); *Prosecutor v Lubanga*, ICC TC II, 30 September 2016, ICC-01/04-01/06-3234-tENG (actually a submission by Cooperazione Internazionale).

[235] *Prosecutor v Lubanga*, ICC TC II, 6 October 2016, ICC-01/04-01/06-3245-tENG. See *Prosecutor v Lubanga*, ICC TC II, Transcript, 11 October 2016.

[236] Again, this counts only submissions (ie, does not count each organisation separately where there is a joint submission).

[237] *Prosecutor v Lubanga*, ICC AC, 14 December 2012, ICC-01/04-01/06-2953, para 77.

[238] *Prosecutor v Lubanga*, ICC AC, 8 March 2013 ICC-01/04-01/06-2993; *Prosecutor v Lubanga*, ICC AC, 8 March 203, ICC-01/04-01/06-2994-tENG.

[239] *Prosecutor v Lubanga*, ICC AC, 3 March 2015, ICC-01/04-01/06-3129, paras 248–51.

proceedings in *Katanga* and *Al Mahdi*, the Appeals Chamber set a short deadline (rather than a call) for receipt of requests to appear as an *amicus curiae*, requiring potential *amici* to indicate the issues on which they would make submissions.[240] No organisations submitted a request in either case. The different approach in the Appeals Chamber may reflect several factors. First, *amici* have already made any relevant submissions in the Trial Chamber. Secondly, the deadlines for filing a request and then the submissions tend to be short, making it challenging to respond in time. Finally, the issues on appeal (with the exception of the appeal from the reparations decision in *Lubanga*) tend to concern narrow and technical issues.

In addition to the confusion regarding the legal basis for submissions, the discussion of practice in this section reveals some differences in procedures, as well as a level of consistency in terms of which actors are able to participate regularly. Variations include the use of open calls or specific invitations, and whether a Chamber applies a two-stage process or directly accepts submissions. It is clear that, as with *amicus* submissions generally, a two-stage approach is more effective at managing the volume and quality of submissions. However, as we discuss below, where local knowledge and content is the primary objective, a simple and more inclusive process may be required.

ii. What Functions are Amici Curiae *Performing?*

Our analysis of the practice suggests that the parties and certain institutional actors, particularly the OPCV, represent those with a legal interest in proceedings. *Amici curiae* (including under Article 75(3)) are performing an expertise function. However, the nature of the expertise is somewhat different from other phases. The expertise is in three areas: expertise concerning reparations and transitional justice; expertise in reparations for or generally in relation to the crimes for which the accused is convicted (eg, cultural heritage in *Al Mahdi*, child soldiers in *Lubanga*); and contextual expertise, that is experience operating in and preferably delivering programmes in the country or region where reparations will be implemented. This different focus for expertise has a number of implications. First, the *amicus* submissions, particularly at the implementation phase, have a higher factual content, with most providing factual information rather than or in combination with legal analysis. As with submissions on national legal systems in other phases, this may be the only way the Chamber can obtain such information, at least without expending considerable time and effort. As the accused is convicted, there may be more flexibility in accepting factual material at this stage, although decisions at the reparations stage still impact the accused's liability and rights, and testing of

[240] *Prosecutor v Katanga*, ICC AC, 7 August 2017, ICC-01/04-01/07-3752 (allowing just over 2 weeks); *Prosecutor v Al Mahdi*, ICC AC, 7 November 2017, ICC-01/12-01/15-246 (allowing 3 days).

evidence is still important. This leads to a related issue – the overlap between *amicus curiae* submissions and expert witnesses, where we see different practice across Chambers, with two Chambers having appointed experts (*Bemba* and *Al Mahdi*). It is difficult to assess this overlap, as the identity and reports of experts are often confidential. At the implementation stage, the effect of submissions by *amici* or experts may be to modify the implementation plan, which is also confidential.

Secondly, given the increasing need for local implementation, Chambers often equate expertise to local knowledge or experience. This has led to more local actors participating in reparations proceedings than at other stages. Many of the international organisations are also relying on their 'in country' experience, contacts and programme offices to establish the relevance of their participation to the Chambers. This in part speaks to concerns regarding the balance between local and international participation in proceedings. However, the reparations practice shows that many local actors face significant security risks from participating, leading to a number of submissions being filed on a confidential basis. The practice also shows that, in terms of international actors, two NGOs – QUB and Redress Trust – have dominated submissions in reparations.

Thirdly, the reparations practice shows that Chambers may be adopting a more flexible approach to independence in the context of reparations proceedings. Many of the actors have long-standing associations with the Court, including in the situation country (being local). They have been intermediaries, supported victims in the process and may already work with the TFV in delivering assistance programmes or programmes for other funders. Some suggest specific projects for consideration by the TFV or the Chamber. Yet, Chambers have held that this does not preclude participation, finding that Chambers in considering the weight given to the submissions can disregard anything inconsistent with being fair to the accused or the victims.[241] Importantly, these actors are not seeking to represent the victims directly, but are passing on their knowledge from interactions with often a much broader range of victims and affected communities than those participating in the ICC proceedings.

Fourthly, while the submissions in reparations proceedings have been quite wide-ranging, given the novelty of this process for the Court, Chambers have appointed *amici* in the pre-order phase as experts, not to represent the public interest as part of a communicative function. It is harder to assess the role in the implementation phase given the confidential status of many submissions; however, the information sought seems to be limited to specific issues and submissions arising from expertise and particularly experience in the affected area, rather than a communicative function.

[241] *Prosecutor v Lubanga*, ICC TC I, 20 April 2012, ICC-01/04-01/06-2870, paras 18–21.

iii. Influence of Submissions in Reparations Proceedings

As noted elsewhere in this study, identifying direct influence of submissions on judicial decisions is challenging. The same challenges apply in the reparations phase. However, the qualitative analysis of decisions shows that submissions in reparations proceedings appear to have greater influence than in other phases, particularly the submissions before the Trial Chamber in *Lubanga*. The Chamber noted the significance of this decision, as the first decision on reparations by the Court.[242] It indicated that it had reviewed all submissions, including those of the NGOs and set out detailed summaries of the *amicus* submissions alongside those of the parties and other participants for each key issue.[243] Although the Chamber did not refer to the submissions in the substantive part of the judgment, where it set out principles and procedures for reparations, it referenced many of the concepts, instruments and jurisprudence those submissions relied upon, for example, the notion of transformative reparations. However, given the absence of specific citation to any of the submissions, we cannot prove influence on the Trial Chamber's decision. To the extent these submissions did impact the Chamber's decision, they have broader influence, as the Trial Chamber's decision, as amended by the Appeals Chamber, has become the point of departure for reparations orders in other cases. Trial Chamber II also relied upon the submissions of the participants in *Katanga*, particularly concerning the modalities of reparations and the issue of whether awards should be collective or individual.[244] In *Al Mahdi*, Trial Chamber VIII included references to the submissions of the *amici* throughout the decision, including expressly agreeing with submissions made by *amici*.[245] The Chamber also relied heavily on the experts' reports, raising again the issue of the interaction between expert reports and *amicus* submissions.

VIII. CONCLUSIONS

This chapter has set out the results of our empirical assessment of the *amicus curiae* practice across the Tribunals. It has established who can act as an *amicus curiae*, when, and how Chambers manage *amicus curiae* participation. The data confirms the wide discretion accorded to judges to invite, to accept and to manage *amici curiae*. The chapter also explored in detail the general criterion for admission – that the proposed submissions must be helpful in the determination of the issue or the case – and how Chambers have used additional criteria to

[242] *Prosecutor v Lubanga*, ICC TC I 7 August 2012, ICC-01/04-01/06-2904, para 20.
[243] ibid.
[244] *Prosecutor v Katanga*, ICC TC II, 24 March 2017, ICC-01/04-01/07-3728-tENG. See, eg, the discussion and pages 93–102.
[245] *Prosecutor v Al Mahdi*, ICC TC VIII, 17 August 2017, ICC-01/12-01/15-236. See, eg, fn 105.

assess the potential benefit of submissions, which must be balanced against the rights of the parties, in particular the accused. The practice suggests that Chambers have been fairly conservative in their *amicus curiae* practice, and have not adopted an overly permissive approach. This is appropriate for an institution that is primarily concerned with individual criminal responsibility, and reflects the caution seen in criminal proceedings at the national level.

The practice does reveal areas of inconsistency in the criteria applied and the procedural aspects of *amicus curiae* participation. To ensure transparency, predictability, consistency and fair treatment of *amici* (and the parties) across different Chambers, we have made a number of recommendations for how the practice could be improved, both in this chapter and in the practice guidance in Annex C. These suggested reforms would maximise the legitimacy benefits that can be realised from allowing *amicus curiae* participation.

In particular, we have highlighted that the function to be performed by an *amicus curiae* differs, and is a relevant criterion when assessing whether or not to invite or admit an *amicus curiae*. Moreover, the type of actor and the function to be performed should influence how other criteria (eg, independence, expertise and impartiality) apply. The following three chapters therefore disaggregate the practice of the Tribunals first by key stakeholder, namely: civil society (chapter five); defence and defence-aligned actors (chapter six); and states and international organisations (chapter seven). Within each chapter, we consider how the three functions we have identified – expertise, representative and communicative – operate in distinct ways for each actor and may require variations in how admissibility criteria are applied, as well as how the process is managed.

5

Civil Society Actors as Amici Curiae

I. INTRODUCTION

ALL OF THE Tribunals enable civil society actors to participate as *amici curiae*: as outlined in chapter three, both states and civil society actors supported the inclusion of Rule 103 in the ICC RPE. In fact, civil society actors are the largest group of applicants for *amicus curiae* status at the International Criminal Court (see chapter four, Figure 4.2). It is therefore important that we examine the participation of these actors in international criminal proceedings – both from the perspective of the Tribunals, and from the civil society actors themselves. As seen in chapter two, civil society actors have played significant roles in human rights institutions, including bringing claims on their own behalf, representing the claims of victims and the public interest and providing particular expertise to the chambers as *amici curiae*. These actors have featured to a lesser extent in international investment tribunals and in the WTO, and rarely – if at all – in the ICJ and ITLOS. Civil society actors have been active in driving strategic litigation at the national level, including in relation to proceedings concerning international crimes.[1]

Civil society actors also play an important role in the Tribunals, in particular the ICC. The involvement of civil society in the adoption of the Rome Statute was 'unprecedented',[2] and drew on the experiences of civil society with the ICTY and ICTR.[3] This early involvement in the adoption of the Rome Statute and the establishment of the ICC 'conferred on NGOs legitimacy and name recognition as well as facilitated relationships with stakeholders that eased formal and informal participatory access at the Court and the ASP'.[4] Moreover, many civil society actors have a longstanding commitment to the ICC and the capacity for participatory engagement. Combined with the ICC's limited resources and struggle to maintain state support, these factors led Court officials to allow 'NGO participation because NGOs help it to fulfil its

[1] H Duffy, *Strategic Human Rights Litigation: Understanding and Maximising Impact* (Oxford, Hart Publishing, 2018).

[2] M Glasius, *The International Criminal Court: A Global Civil Society Achievement* (Milton Park, Routledge, 2006) xiii.

[3] For further discussion, see Glasius ibid.

[4] H Nichols Haddad, *The Hidden Hands of Justice: NGOs, Human Rights, and International Courts* (Cambridge, CUP, 2018) 116.

mandate through information sharing, expertise, investigative and operational assistance'.[5] From the Rome negotiations on, 'the relationship between the ICC and the NGOs has probably been closer, more consistent, and more vital to the Court than have analogous relations between NGOs and any other international organisation'.[6] Schiff traces how NGOs in particular 'have moved from being crucial to the Court's creation to being vital to its operations'.[7] Haddad, in her study of NGO involvement with the ICC, identified ten participatory roles for NGOs including Court and state-directed advocacy or consultative roles, information sharing and operational support roles and formal roles in trials (the *amicus curiae*).[8] The extensive roles performed by civil society, in particular NGOs, have led to civil society becoming 'critical players' at the ICC, with civil society an important stakeholder, almost as vital to the Court's legitimacy and success as states.[9] Other tribunals have also been heavily reliant on civil society actors to assist in achieving core mandates; for example, the ECCC depended on civil society for key outreach, victim participation and reparations functions,[10] while the establishment and operation of the EAC was driven largely by civil society actors.[11]

Civil society in the context of the Tribunals is not homogenous and comprises a diverse group of actors, with varied memberships, issue-focus and mandates and different funding and priorities. Some long-standing NGOs, many of whom played key roles at Rome, have a well-established relationship with the ICC, and have more international criminal law specific expertise and insider knowledge than some states. Such 'insider-track' NGOs tend to be large, international NGOs, and have become repeat-submitters, including Amnesty International, Human Rights Watch, Redress and FIDH. Such organisations have extensive, pre-existing expertise and experience in the international context in which the Court must operate.

Given the ICC's relationship to national legal systems, as explored in chapter one, there is also a 'local' civil society constituency. Many actors located within the relevant national systems may seek to participate in or support the ICC. There may be distinct views between insider track actors and those with a more local focus, with international actors tending to conceive of justice narrowly, as criminal trials, while local actors may have a broader view. As noted in chapter one, there needs to be a two-way communication between the Court and those based within the places it is investigating, including engaging with state and non-state actors. The Tribunals also know that with these diverse mandates and priorities, it is impossible to keep all civil society actors happy at the same

[5] ibid, 117.
[6] B Schiff, *Building the International Criminal Court* (New York, CUP, 2008) 144.
[7] ibid.
[8] Haddad (n 4), 112, Table 4.1 in particular.
[9] ibid, 113; Schiff (n 6), ch 5.
[10] C Sperfeldt, 'Cambodian Civil Society and the Khmer Rouge Tribunal' (2012) 6 *IJTJ* 149.
[11] C Sperfeldt, 'The Trial Against Hissène Habré: Networked Justice and Reparations at the Extraordinary African Chambers' (2017) 9 *International Journal of Human Rights* 1.

time – which may support why the Tribunals want to hear a range of their views, even if they do not decide in one or another's favour.

It is also common for civil society actors to work in collaboration with other actors in both their *amicus* practice as well as other international criminal justice activities. This may be in informal groupings, such as in an *amicus* submission jointly signed by several NGOs or academics, or formal and long-standing collaborations. A key example of the latter is the Coalition for the International Criminal Court, a network of more than 2500 NGOs working on ICC matters around the globe. It operates as a quasi-institutional actor by coordinating activities of NGOs on international criminal justice, especially at the Court.[12] The CICC engages largely on matters of overarching policy, administration and strategy, rather than on particular cases.[13] While the CICC does not itself make *amicus* submissions, its work has included enabling and coordinating members to submit *amicus* briefs, individually or jointly with other members.[14] The CICC therefore operates as a facilitator in terms of its members' *amicus* activity and may advise as to the coordination of this activity within the larger strategy and aims of the Coalition.

Despite such examples of collaboration, it is well accepted that civil society is fragmented and heterogeneous,[15] while even frequently aligned organisations may compete or take different positions on some matters. NGOs, academics and other influential actors often rely upon funding from donors with certain goals or performance criteria, or have political or personal interests.[16] NGOs make up only one component of civil society, but even NGOs do not always favour the norms of international criminal justice, or may promote alternative responses to serious violence, perhaps drawing on local expertise.[17] Further, civil society is not necessarily a 'force for good'. It has been noted that 'Although this has not occurred in all transitional contexts, it is vital to be brutally honest about civil society and recognize that its veneer of civility is often painfully thin'.[18] For many actors, the ICC (or criminal justice) is one part of a broader strategy, with litigation pursued in other fora, other cases, balancing long term as against short term strategies.[19] Civil society actors can be critical as well as supportive

[12] See K Lohne, 'Global Civil Society, the ICC, and Legitimacy in International Criminal Justice' in N Hayashi and CM Bailliet (eds), *The Legitimacy of International Criminal Tribunals* (Cambridge, CUP, 2017) 452–53.

[13] See Haddad (n 4), 153.

[14] Interview H8_CI_WP_150522_0057, 11.

[15] N Roht-Arriaza, 'Civil Society in Processes of Accountability', in M Cherif Bassiouni (ed), *Post-Conflict Justice* (Ardsley, New York, Transnational Publishers, 2002) 98; Haddad (n 4), 3.

[16] L Hovil and MC Okello, 'Editorial Note' (2011) 5 *IJTJ* 333, 339; J Dosch, 'The Role of Civil Society in Cambodia's Peace-Building Process: Have Foreign Donors Made a Difference?' (2012) 52 Asian Survey 1067.

[17] AP Boesenecker and L Vinjamuri, 'Lost in Translation? Civil Society, Faith-Based Organizations and the Negotiation of International Norms' (2011) 5 *IJTJ* 345, 347.

[18] Hovil and Okello (n 16), 336; C Mercer, 'NGOs, Civil Society and Democratization: A Critical Review of the Literature' (2002) 2(1) *Progress in Development Studies* 5, 10–11.

[19] Duffy (n 1).

of the Tribunals. However, criticism of the Tribunals by insider track organisations in particular tends to be done through informal methods, so as not to provide ammunition to opponents of the Tribunals.

This study focuses on the *amicus curiae*, although we recognise that this is only one, quite limited, participatory role for NGOs and other civil society actors. We recognise Haddad's point that focusing on the *amicus curiae* may skew analysis of the nature, breadth and depth of civil society interaction with the Tribunals and may understate the actual influence of such actors on process, outcomes and the institution itself.[20] However, it is also useful to understand how the Tribunals and civil society actors are using the *amicus curiae* mechanism and the impact it has had and may have for legitimacy.

As with their engagement with the Tribunals generally, this diverse group of actors has a variety of aims, functions, and interests when seeking to make *amicus curiae* submissions. These can include: providing factual information to the Tribunal; contributing legal expertise and analysis in terms of a particular dispute or influencing the development of the law more generally; making submissions in the interests of victim communities or others affected by the international crimes under examination; giving voice to wider debates in and perspectives of the international community; or seeking to increase accountability of individuals, states, or the institution itself. It can be seen then that these different civil society actors, depending on the aims and content of the submissions, can echo all three of the modes of the *amicus curiae* that we have identified: the expertise, representative, and communicative functions. Further, civil society actors, like other *amici*, can simultaneously act in more than one of these modes in their submissions. For example, an NGO may aim both to provide a novel legal argument, while also advocating for the interests of victims in the proceedings. By fulfilling these different functions, as we have previously established in chapter one, civil society *amicus* submissions can contribute to both the normative and sociological legitimacy of the Tribunals by potentially contributing to core values of transparency, accountability and engagement with perspectives of stakeholders and affected communities.

However, civil society's participation through the *amicus curiae* mechanism also comes with particular risks and concerns for the Tribunals. As will be discussed below, these include the possible negative effect on fair trial rights and the proper allocation of tribunal resources, concerns regarding the use of tribunal processes as a tool for 'lawfare' by NGOs and other civil society actors, and the misrepresentation, whether intentional or unintentional, of the interests, such as those of communities affected by international crimes, that the civil society actor claims to represent. Given these concerns, the practice of civil society *amici* makes us consider the scope and content of the requirements of independence and impartiality, how the Tribunals should identify and test the

[20] Haddad (n 4), 4.

expertise of potential *amici*, and the value of a communicative or discursive approach to *amicus* participation.

Nonetheless, if these risks are properly managed by the Tribunals, as noted earlier, civil society acting as *amici* can potentially make significant contributions to the quality of decision-making at the Tribunals and represent important interests that would otherwise be absent from the proceedings. This chapter analyses the practice of civil society *amicus* participation in international criminal tribunals, examining the ways in which the Tribunals have managed the potential contributions and risks of such participation, as well as making normative suggestions for how this might be improved. Given the wide range of aims, functions, and interests of different members of civil society, and the particular considerations that attach to each, the chapter is structured around the most significant categories of civil society actors that we have identified in terms of *amicus curiae* practice: NGOs, academics, agencies of inter-governmental organisations, and individuals. The analysis is disaggregated into each of the three functions we have identified, assessing the potential role, contribution and risks of civil society actors as *amici* in the expertise, representative and communicative functions. The practice demonstrates that there are different considerations and limitations that should be applied by the Tribunals in admitting and considering civil society *amicus* submissions, depending on the type of civil society actor in question, and the purpose of the submission that is sought to be made. We aim to assess the extent to which civil society *amici* may contribute to the normative and sociological legitimacy of the proceedings in question, and how this contribution can be maximised while reducing the attendant risks of civil society participation through this mechanism.

II. OVERVIEW OF CIVIL SOCIETY ACTORS AT INTERNATIONAL CRIMINAL TRIBUNALS

A. Non-Governmental Organisations

NGOs represent one of the largest categories of *amicus curiae* applicants (see chapter four, Figure 4.2) at the Tribunals, and thus have significant potential to affect, whether positively or negatively, the legitimacy of the Tribunals. NGOs account for the greatest number of civil society *amicus curiae* applications at the ICC, as well as at most other international criminal tribunals. The large majority (currently 73 per cent) of NGOs' applications are voluntary, rather than in response to an invitation by a tribunal. This indicates that NGOs view this as a valuable tool to achieve their mandates. Moreover, the substantial number of *amicus* applications by NGOs that are admitted suggests that the Chambers themselves value the contributions of NGOs – though, as discussed below, their rate of acceptance is lower than most other categories of civil society actors.

The NGOs that have applied to act as *amici* before the Tribunals are diverse in terms of their size, geographical location, mandate, and available resources. They include small and large organisations, local and international bodies, and organisations with broad human rights mandates as well as those focusing on a single conflict or single issue. NGOs may have explicit mandates to advocate for judicial outcomes, such as to 'pressure those with power to respect rights and secure justice',[21] uphold 'the whole range of human rights',[22] or help survivors of violence to 'obtain justice and reparation'.[23] Frequently, NGOs represent victims' groups or individual victims, and may seek to make submissions on their behalf, at times alongside formal victims' representatives (at tribunals where such representation is provided). Others might represent lawyers (such as the International Criminal Defence Attorneys Association, ICDAA), or typically undertake domestic human rights or development activities. Some NGO *amicus* applicants might argue against prosecutions, perhaps with strong (suspected) government affiliations, as did the Sudan Workers Trade Union Federation and Sudan International Defence Group,[24] or have aims less related to international criminal convictions, such as a concern about the human rights implications of disclosing information sources.[25] Thus, perhaps more than any other kind of actor, the reasons for which NGOs seek to make *amicus* submissions vary widely, as do the potential benefits, contributions, and risks to the Tribunals arising from their participation.

Despite the high number of applications for *amicus* status made by NGOs at the Tribunals, their acceptance rate is relatively low, especially at the ICC and the ICTR. Our analysis, set out in Figure 5.1, indicates that NGO *amici* have an overall acceptance rate of 56 per cent across all Tribunals, falling to 54 per cent at the ICC and 47 per cent at the ICTR. This can be compared with their higher acceptance rates at other tribunals: 63 per cent at the ICTY, 67 per cent at the SCSL, and a high of 71 per cent at the ECCC. This is significantly lower than some other categories of civil society actors, such as academics, though not as low as for 'legal' applicants, which include defence lawyer associations and lawyers acting for other parties, or individuals. As discussed further below, this reflects the Tribunals' preference for civil society *amici* that act within the expertise function, rather than those that seek to use the mechanism as an opportunity for public interest advocacy or the representation of particular interests, as well as their method of admission predominantly through voluntary applications rather than through open calls or direct invitations.

[21] Human Rights Watch, 'About Us', available at www.hrw.org/about-us.
[22] Amnesty International, 'What We Do', available at www.amnesty.org.au/what-we-do/.
[23] Redress, 'Who We Are', available at www.redress.org/about-redress/who-we-are.
[24] *Situation in Darfur, Sudan*, ICC PTC I, 11 January 2009, ICC-02/05-170, para 47.
[25] eg as attempted by the human rights and media rights organisation Art 19: *Prosecutor v Taylor*, SCSL TC II, 3 February 2009, SCSL-03-01-T-24033.

Figure 5.1 Acceptance Rate of Applicants by Type (No. approved/No. not approved, %)

	ICC	ICTY	ICTR	ECCC	SCSL	STL	All
NGO	54%	63%	47%	71%	67%	67%	56%
Academic	54%	80%	0%	100%	100%	50%	77%
Government	58%	72%	94%	0%	0%	0%	73%
Legal	45%	64%	25%	10%	50%	100%	52%
Other	20%	50%	44%	50%	100%	63%	46%

Given the diversity of NGO applicants, and the range of expertise needed to fulfil the Tribunals' mandates,[26] it is unsurprising that these organisations have sought to make *amicus* submissions on a wide variety of topics before the Tribunals, which align with different interests in the proceedings. Our analysis indicates that the most frequent topics addressed by NGO *amicus curiae* applicants are as follows: victims' issues (32 per cent), legal analysis (28 per cent), and defence representation and defence rights (19 per cent) (see Figure 5.2). The statistics remain very similar in relation to those NGO submissions that are successfully admitted.[27] However, while the topics addressed by NGOs are diverse, as discussed below, the repeat acceptance of certain 'insider track' NGOs leads to concerns about possible Western dominance and the marginalisation of views of other communities, including those of the regions in which the crimes being prosecuted at the Tribunals are committed.

Despite their lower acceptance rate, there are a significant number of NGOs that have been admitted as *amici*, some of whom have had a discernible impact on the decision-making at the Tribunals. In the sections below, we analyse the practice of NGOs acting as *amici* in relation to each of the three functions that we had identified. In our view, the Tribunals have, in general, managed this practice effectively, in order to increase the benefits of NGO participation as *amici* while reducing the associated risks. In the following sections we discuss how this is done by taking a restrictive approach to the admission of NGO *amicus* submissions, commonly emphasising the need for NGOs to bring additional legal expertise to proceedings in order to be admitted as *amici* – that is, prioritising the first function in our typology – rather than opening the door to wide-ranging public interest-oriented submissions without a clear benefit to a tribunal's decision-making process. However, as we discuss below, more consideration is needed as to how NGOs' contributions are assessed as justifying admission and reliance by the Tribunals in light of the criteria set out in chapter four, particularly in relation to their expertise, independence, and claimed representation of the actors and interests for whom they propose to speak.

[26] See discussion in ch 3, s V(A).

[27] Victims Issues (37%), legal analysis (29%), defence representation and rights (20%), evidentiary issues (3%).

Figure 5.2 Topics Addressed by NGOs – All Tribunals

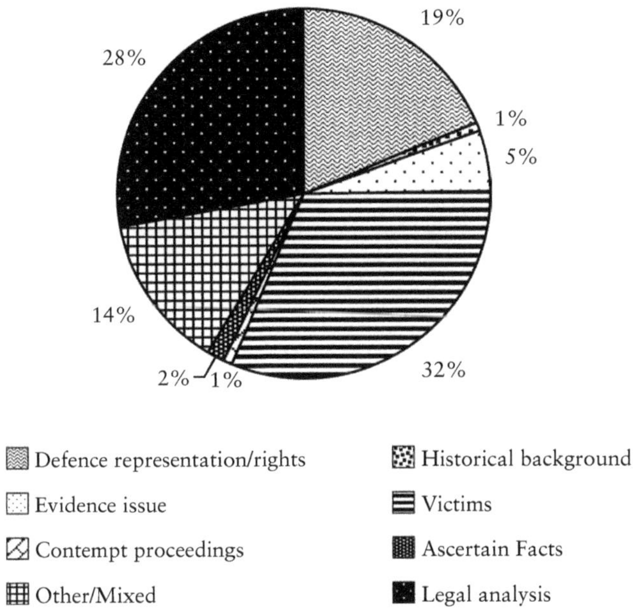

B. Academics

Academics also frequently act as *amici curiae* before international criminal tribunals. Academics from legal disciplines dominate the *amicus* practice at the Tribunals: the large majority of these proposed *amici* are legal academics, while all those admitted have been legal academics, or had at least one legal academic in the group of authors.[28] This is consistent with the primary focus on admitting civil society *amici* that provide additional legal expertise, which will most often be legal knowledge and analysis, as we discuss in chapter four.[29] Academics from other disciplines, especially historians, are generally admitted as expert witnesses rather than *amici* at the Tribunals.[30]

As with NGOs, there are many different academic *amici*. The most typical is the individual or small group of academics employed at a university, but academic *amici* have also included legal clinics and research units within academic institutions, as well as independent research organisations outside of universities, and some individual academics without institutional affiliation. There are instances where multiple and/or different kinds of academic actors collaborate in making *amicus* submissions.

[28] There appears to be one exception where a group of academics without a single legal expert was admitted as *amici*: see *Prosecutor v Lubanga*, ICC TC II, 30 September 2016, ICC-01/04-01/06-3240-Anx9.

[29] See discussion of expertise in ch 4, s V(M).

[30] See, eg Alison des Forges at the ICTR, Elizabeth Becker at the ECCC.

In contrast to NGOs, academic *amici* are most frequently admitted in response to Tribunals' calls for *amicus* submissions, or direct invitations rather than voluntary applications.[31] Tribunals' calls for submissions have been of differing scope.[32] These calls may apply only to academics, or include a variety of civil society actors depending on the expertise sought. For instance, the ECCC issued an open call for 'any qualified person or organisation to submit *amicus curiae* briefs' concerning whether soldiers *hors de combat* constitute 'civilian populations' for the purposes of crimes against humanity, which attracted a large number of academic submissions.[33] In contrast, the ICC Appeals Chamber took a more exceptional approach, issuing a targeted call inviting 'Professors of International Law' to apply to be admitted as *amici*.[34] In addition, at times, the Tribunals have invited specific academics to make submissions on particular issues, such as when the ECCC invited *amicus curiae* briefs from Antonio Cassese and Kai Ambos addressing the principle of 'joint criminal enterprise', as discussed in detail in chapter four, section VI(B). As discussed below, these different approaches have implications for how expertise is identified as being worthy of admission by the Tribunals. Further, as with NGOs, academic *amici* (both applicants and those admitted) largely stem from Western institutions, meaning that academic perspectives from other regions may be underrepresented. As discussed in chapter four, section V(P) and further below this limited representativeness is a factor that should be considered by international criminal tribunals in shaping their *amicus* practice.

This greater tendency of the Tribunals to directly invite academic *amici*, as opposed to specific other civil society actors (except for representatives of international organisations), indicates an assumption that they can be relied on to provide valuable legal expertise that can assist in their decision-making. As discussed in more detail below, this in turn seems to indicate that the Tribunals consider that academic submissions are not skewed by vested interests in the outcome or decision. However, some of these academic actors, particularly some legal units and clinics, like NGOs, are funded by external donors, and operate with the purpose of contributing to and influencing the development of global human rights mechanisms, including by acting as *amici curiae* in international criminal tribunals.[35] In addition, individual academics working at universities may be motivated, at least in part, by ulterior considerations such as political convictions, a desire to further the influence of their scholarship and academic status (and perhaps also to meet promotion criteria that increasingly

[31] Currently, 43% of academics' *amicus* applications are unsolicited, compared to 73% of NGOs.

[32] See further discussion in ch 4, s IV(B).

[33] *Co-Prosecutors v Meas (Case 003)*, ECCC OCIJ, 19 April 2016, 003/007-09-2009-ECCC-OCIJ-D191.

[34] *Prosecutor v Al-Bashir*, ICC AC, 29 March 2018, ICC-02/05-01/09-330.

[35] See, eg the Canadian Partnership for International Justice amicus application in Myanmar/Bangladesh: *Request Under Regulation 46(3) of the Regulations of the Court*, ICC PTC I, 25 May 2018, ICC-RoC46(3)-01/18-6, sec V; Queen's University Belfast Human Rights Centre, 'Supporting Human Rights Globally', available at www.law.qub.ac.uk/schools/SchoolofLaw/Research/HumanRights/?fbclid=IwAR3kk99URGP76pXWpvh9v1b0LiwVKQzpLIbhyTKShKZnEANGRaof1yhE6Bs.

require evidence of 'impact').[36] It is also possible that academic *amici* may act as legal counsel in other cases before the same tribunal, as was the case with one *amicus* admitted in the *Jordan* proceedings.[37] Further, in many contexts, academic independence from government is not guaranteed. Thus, it cannot be assumed that academic *amici* will not have an agenda beyond providing neutral legal expertise.[38] These considerations should influence how the Tribunals regulate the admission and influence of these *amici*, and the weight given to them, particularly in terms of the requirements of independence and impartiality.

Sometimes groups of academics co-sign *amicus curiae* applications or briefs in order to contribute arguments concerning the development of international criminal law – and possibly to demonstrate or promote their expertise.[39] Group submissions have also been provided by research units and legal clinics at university centres – such as the Queen's University of Belfast, which has contributed several thorough briefs concerning reparations issues to the ICC (see chapter four, section VII).[40] Some academics hesitate to join large group academic submissions, as it may be difficult to ensure that the entirety of the brief represents their views,[41] and may result in 'compromise' or generalised submissions.[42] These group submissions also raise questions concerning the identification of expertise, the overlap with previously published work of those in the group (an issue which also arises with individual academic briefs), and whether every member of the group must qualify individually as an expert on the issues. One NGO representative with academic experience noted her 'inherent dislike for the practice of American universities submitting briefs and getting like 50 million people to sign onto them',[43] although this appears to occur more often in US domestic proceedings than before the Tribunals. Nonetheless, as we discuss in chapter four, section V(M) such groupings may influence whether a submission will be accepted or used, by showing that the views expressed therein are shared by multiple experts. Further, this may be a useful strategy to avoid duplication and avoid unnecessary waste of time and resources spent addressing numerous similar submissions.

Academics have a relatively high success rate in their applications for *amicus* status, particularly in comparison to NGOs. Currently, 77 per cent of academic

[36] See R Fallon, 'Scholars' Briefs and the Vocation of Law Professors' (2012) 4 *Journal of Legal Analysis* 223; P Horwitz, 'Is Fallon's Article a No-Brainer?' (*PrawfsBlawg*, 31 October 2011), available at https://prawfsblawg.blogs.com/prawfsblawg/2011/10/is-fallons-article-a-no-brainer.html.

[37] See *Prosecutor v Al-Bashir*, ICC AC, 30 April 2018, ICC-02/05-01/09-350.

[38] See A Kent and J Trinidad, 'International Law Scholars as *Amici Curiae*: An Emerging Dialogue (of the Deaf)?' (2016) 29 *LJIL* 1081, 1085.

[39] eg *Prosecutor v Gabgbo*, ICC AC, 9 October 2013, ICC-02/11-01/11-534.

[40] *Prosecutor v Katanga*, ICC TC II, 14 May 2015, ICC-01/04-01/07-3551; *Prosecutor v Bemba*, ICC TC III, 17 October 2016, ICC-01/05-01/08-3444. See also *Co-Prosecutors v Duch (Case 001)*, ECCC PTC, 27 October 2008, 001/18-02-2007-ECCC/OCIJ (PTC 02)-D99/3/25; *Prosecutor v Norman*, SCSL AC, 29 October 2003, SCSL-2003-08-PT-3268.

[41] Interview HG10.

[42] See Kent and Trinidad (n 38), 1085.

[43] Interview CT1.

applicants have been admitted. However, these figures reflect the high numbers of academics who apply and are admitted in response to direct invitations, and targeted and open calls. Only 53 per cent of voluntary academic applications have been admitted – though this remains significantly higher than the acceptance rate of unsolicited NGO applications (40 per cent).

Reflecting the almost exclusive admission of legal academics, academic applicants overwhelmingly sought and were admitted to make submissions providing expert legal analysis,[44] with a small number addressing victims' issues[45] and even fewer on defence rights or representation.[46] This is strikingly different from NGO *amici*, who, as noted above, most frequently made submissions on victims' issues. Academic submissions therefore predominantly fall within the expertise function. Unlike NGOs, subject to some exceptions discussed below, it is rare that academics will seek to act within the representative or communicative functions, and even rarer for them to be admitted on this basis. However, the emerging practice of NGO-like units and clinics, mentioned above, may alter the predominance of the expertise mode academic *amicus*.

Factors that are likely to be relevant for academics and academic institutions in determining whether to act as *amici* include their expertise in relation to the specific legal issue, the perceived importance of the proceedings for developing jurisprudence in that area, potential reputational effects of acting as an *amicus*, and time and resource requirements. In many cases, publishing academic views in a journal article that the parties and/or the judges may read might be just as influential. Indeed, we may question why an academic would choose to draft an *amicus* submission, particularly regarding matters on which she has previously published, when the parties and/or the judges can access her published research. It is our view that the latter would often be preferable, as it would reduce the time and resources consumed in obtaining academics' views, which would commonly also have been subject to peer review and so provide some measure of quality control. However, in the case of novel issues, or issues on which little has been written, it may be valuable to obtain academic submissions crafted specifically to the issues at hand. Further, obtaining *amicus* submissions from the academic will increase the transparency of the influences on judicial decision-making, particularly given the paucity of citations to academic literature in the Tribunals' decisions.

As with NGOs, the Tribunals are in general managing academic *amicus* applicants and submissions appropriately. It is obvious that the expertise function is that best suited to academic submissions, though, as discussed below, the manner in which tribunals solicit and define academic expertise, as well as concerns regarding the independence of academic *amici*, require further consideration.

[44] 85% of applications, 89% of admitted submissions.
[45] 6% of applications, 8% of admitted submissions.
[46] 1% of applications, 2% of admitted submissions.

C. International Organisations

International organisations or their representatives, such as United Nations (UN) bodies or UN Special Rapporteurs, have occasionally acted as *amici curiae*, usually to contribute their expertise on a matter as part of their role for the development or maintenance of a particular body of law, such as UNICEF in relation to international law on children's rights or UNESCO regarding cultural heritage. International organisations have at times also acted as *amici* in a representative capacity when their institutional interests are directly affected by the proceedings.[47] Here, we include only those that are acting as independent representatives of the organisation itself, rather than where an *amicus* should be seen as representing its member states. We address further practice of international organisations in chapter seven on states as *amici curiae*.

There are a small, but influential, number of such interventions. Like academics, these international organisations' representatives often gain admission in response to a direct invitation or an open call from the tribunal. For example, as discussed in chapter four, ICC Pre-Trial Chamber I invited Louise Arbour and Antonio Cassese to provide information to the ICC about their investigations into events in Darfur in Sudan.[48] What the Chamber did not mention in its invitation was that Arbour was a former ICTY Prosecutor and Cassese the first President of the ICTY Chambers. Here, arguably, it was hoped that their expertise might facilitate progress in the Prosecutor's stalled investigations.[49] This practice illustrates that judges may instrumentalise the *amicus curiae* to achieve their own ends, even if the reasons for inviting (or proposing) civil society *amicus curiae* submissions may not always be apparent from the call or decision allowing their observations.

International organisations have also applied to act as *amici curiae* in a small number of proceedings, as well as to provide their views concerning the ICC's reparations awards.[50] As discussed in chapter three, the Special Representative for Children, Radhika Coomaraswamy (at her own application) provided both written and oral submissions, first as an *amicus* and later as an expert witness, concerning the definition of 'conscripting or enlisting' children and the interpretation of 'using them to participate actively in hostilities'.[51] UNICEF submitted observations concerning the reparations awarded in the *Lubanga* case under Article 75(3) of the Rome Statute, having argued that its experience working

[47] See, eg ICRC's *amicus* submissions in the *Simić* case concerning the Tribunal's jurisdiction to compel their former employees to provide testimony in proceedings: Ex parte and Confidential Submission by the ICRC Concerning the Proposal to Call a Former Employee of the ICRC as a Prosecution Witness, 13 April 1999, cited in *Prosecutor v Simić et al*, ICTY TC II, 17 October 2003, IT-95-9-T, fn 2428.

[48] See ch 4, s III(A).

[49] LS Sunga, 'How Can UN Human Rights Special Procedures Sharpen ICC Fact-Finding?' (2011) 15 *International Journal of Human Rights* 187.

[50] See discussion of reparations practice in ch 4, s VII.

[51] See ch 3, s VI(C)(iii).

with children and communities affected by armed conflict may assist the Court in its considerations.[52] Similarly, a group of UN agencies submitted Article 75(3) observations in *Katanga*[53] and the Office of the High Commissioner for Human Rights and Office of the Special Representative of the United Nations Secretary-General on Sexual Violence in Conflict successfully sought 'to share their experiences and expertise on the issue of reparations for victims' under both Rule 103 (ie, as an *amicus curiae*) and Article 75(3) in *Bemba*.[54] UNESCO also provided submissions after applying for *amicus* status under Rule 103 in the *Al Madhi* reparations proceedings, in response to an open call.[55]

The approval rate of these *amici* is very high (approximately 92%). However as noted above, the number of these interventions is small, and frequently in response to an invitation by a tribunal. Participation as an *amicus* is of course voluntary, and some organisations have declined to participate even when specifically invited. This includes examples where organisations have been invited to make submissions on questions that may affect their own legal interests. For instance, the UN, the EU and the Organization of American States declined an invitation to make submissions under Article 103 on matters concerning head of state immunity of those subject to ICC arrest warrants, even though this could in future affect their ability to hold meetings.[56] Further, some international organisations as a rule do not provide *amicus* submissions. The ICRC, for instance, does not engage in *amicus* practice (except where their own interests were directly implicated in proceedings) due to the confidentiality of its work, and does not collaborate with NGOs in order to maintain their neutrality and independence. The participation of such international bodies (or lack thereof) can be assumed to involve a range of strategic considerations, including an assessment of their ability to contribute important expertise, whether they were invited, internal policy requirements, time, resource considerations and other priorities, the availability of alternative avenues for influencing proceedings, and the potential to coordinate the submissions of a range of internal agencies.

While most submissions by international organisations have provided legal expertise, some have addressed factual information, particularly in reparations proceedings. UNESCO, for instance, sought to 'address the importance of international cultural heritage generally and the harm to the international community caused by its destruction'.[57] As a result, there is an overlap between the *amicus* submissions of international organisations and those usually made by expert witnesses – as demonstrated by the change in status of Ms Coomaraswamy from the former to the latter over the course of proceedings. From the perspective of

[52] *Prosecutor v Lubanga*, ICC TC I, 10 May 2012, ICC-01/04-01/06-2878.

[53] *Prosecutor v Katanga*, ICC TC II, 14 May 2015, ICC-01/04-01/07-3550.

[54] *Prosecutor v Bemba*, ICC TC III, 15 August 2016, ICC-01/05-01/08-3422, para 17; *Prosecutor v Bemba*, ICC TC III, 17 October 2016, ICC-01/05-01/08-3449.

[55] *Prosecutor v Al Mahdi*, ICC TC VIII, ICC-01/12-01/15-180.

[56] *Prosecutor v Al-Bashir*, ICC AC, 29 March 2018, ICC-02/05-01/09-330.

[57] *Prosecutor v Al Mahdi*, ICC TC VIII. 28 October 2016, ICC-01/12-01/15-179, 4.

the Tribunals, the key benefit has generally been to provide expert knowledge on the areas of the organisation's operations, and thus falls within the expertise function.

D. Individuals

A small number of individuals independent of an organisation or government has also applied for *amicus* status at the Tribunals (individual academics are excluded from this category). These individuals have had a range of motivations and interests in seeking to intervene as *amici*, though most frequently have been linked to the defence in some way. Given the small number and variety of these applicants, it is difficult to generalise about this practice. Overall, such applications are not generally successful, with the lowest acceptance rate of any group of actors at approximately 30 per cent.

These individual applicants are often lawyers seeking to represent the defence or other actors in the proceedings. For instance, Philip-Jan Schüller and Goran Sluiter applied to provide submissions in the ICC's *Katanga* and *Lubanga* cases in relation to the asylum proceedings of several witnesses from the Democratic Republic of the Congo.[58] As discussed in chapter six, defence lawyers have also attempted to provide submissions in related cases on behalf of their clients,[59] but may also seek to provide legal arguments in their personal capacity.[60] Individual lawyers have tended to have their applications to act as *amici* rejected, whereas submissions from legal organisations, such as bar associations, have been admitted especially where they have addressed fair trial issues.[61]

Private persons may also have reason to provide *amicus curiae* submissions, in particular where they have personal links to the defence but lack other available avenues to provide information or arguments to the Court. For example, Mishana Hosseinioun submitted five *amicus curiae* applications before being allowed to inform the ICC about steps taken to obtain legal representation for Saif Gaddafi.[62] She explained that she was 'in a unique position to offer observations to the Chamber as she is a very close friend and confidant who is requesting to have access to Saif Gaddafi to assist in the appointment of legal counsel and to safeguard his rights'.[63] Similarly, Gaddafi's sister, Aisha, also (unsuccessfully) sought to act as an *amicus* to 'protect the interests of her brother'.[64]

[58] Two briefs were accepted: *Prosecutor v Lubanga*, ICC TC I, 23 November 2011, ICC-01/04-01/06-2827; *Prosecutor v Katanga*, ICC TC II, 14 March 2013, ICC-01/04-01/07-3358.

[59] eg in Cases 003 and 004 before the ECCC: *Co-Prosecutors v Nuon and Khieu (Case 002)*, ECCC SCC, 8 April 2015, 002/19-09-2007-ECCC/SC-F20/1, para 9, emphasis added.

[60] eg *Prosecutor v Bemba et al*, ICC TC VII, 31 August 2015, ICC-01/05-01/13-1205.

[61] See discussion in ch 6, ss III–IV.

[62] Her fifth application was approved, see *Prosecutor v Gaddafi and Al-Senussi*, ICC AC, 15 August 2013, ICC-01/11-01/11-404.

[63] ibid, para 10.

[64] *Prosecutor v Gaddafi and Al-Senussi*, ICC PTC I, 31 January 2012, ICC-01/11-01/11-47, para 1.

Such personal motivations may be less affected by time or resource priorities, which helps to explain why Dr Hosseinoun was patient enough to continue to submit applications, despite her initial lack of success.

Notably, these actors most frequently apply to make submissions representing specific interests in the proceedings, rather than to provide additional expertise or to make public interest oriented submissions as is more common with other kinds of civil society *amici*. As noted above, though, admission rates of individuals are low – which is again consistent with the general practice of the Tribunals' prioritisation of the expertise function for civil society actors.

III. THE EXPERTISE FUNCTION AND CIVIL SOCIETY ACTORS

As we have argued throughout this study, the expertise function constitutes an important way for *amici* to augment the legitimacy of international criminal proceedings. The expertise provided by civil society actors, in particular NGOs and academics, in the Rome negotiations was evident.[65] As we discuss in this section, civil society actors are most often admitted to make submissions that fall within the expertise function. This can be contrasted with other actors, particularly states, in which the representative *amicus* function appears to be more widely accepted by the Tribunals. As we discuss in more detail in section IV below, the appropriate scope for representative submissions by NGOs and other civil society actors is limited by several factors, including the existence of institutional actors to represent constituencies whose interests are implicated in proceedings, such as victims' groups. In our view, largely restricting civil society *amici* to the provision of legal expertise on novel and relevant matters is correct since this maximises the utility of these submissions, while also limiting the risks to the integrity of the proceedings and fair trial rights of the accused. Restricting civil society *amici* to this role minimises the possibility that *amicus* submissions will directly address the guilt or innocence of the accused, and the introduction of parallel lines of argument that may conflict with the submissions of the prosecution, defence or the victims' formal representatives. Nonetheless, the Tribunals must carefully consider how they test and identify the expertise of civil society actors.

While NGOs are often perceived as focusing on public interest advocacy,[66] which falls primarily within the communicative function, they have an important role to play within the expertise function. NGOs may have considerable expertise on legal issues that are relevant to the proceedings. In particular, many NGOs have sophisticated legal knowledge of international criminal law, acquired through decades of involvement in international criminal proceedings.

[65] Glasius (n 2).
[66] See, eg Kent and Trinidad (n 38), 1082.

Furthermore, many NGOs work closely with communities of victims of international crimes and on issues of human rights in relation to international criminal proceedings. By sharing this knowledge, NGOs may add significant valuable expertise to international criminal trial and reparations proceedings.

The Tribunals' practice reflects this position. As noted above in section II(A), approximately half of NGO *amicus* applications are rejected at the ICC; those that are successful are almost always admitted on the basis of the additional expertise that the submissions will provide, perhaps in combination with the representative or communicative function. Thus, it is as an expert rather than an advocate that the Tribunals have most often considered NGO submissions to be able to assist their judicial determinations. The ICC practice in particular has emphasised the need for NGO *amici* to bring additional expertise to the proceedings in order to justify their admission. Indeed, the ICC has held NGO *amici* to a more restrictive requirement of defined and novel expertise than other *amicus* applicants, especially states. When considering *amicus* applications submitted by an individual and an NGO, Pre-Trial Chamber II adopted a strict test of accepting '*amicus curiae* observations *only on an exceptional basis*, when it is of the view that such observations providing *specific expertise are needed* on particular topics', which was drawn on in some subsequent decisions on other NGO applicants.[67] As discussed in chapter four, we do not consider such a strict test to be appropriate, as it may exclude useful civil society expert perspectives, and has the implicit effect of privileging the views of states over civil society.[68] Nonetheless, this articulation of a requirement of novel expertise is a welcome recognition of the expertise function within the Tribunals' *amicus* practice.

While this restrictive threshold has not consistently been applied to all NGO *amicus* applications, the Chambers' emphasis on new and relevant expertise or information that would not otherwise be available to the tribunal is widespread in the ICC decisions on civil society *amicus* applications. For instance, the Pre-Trial Chamber admitted both the International Commission of Jurists and the Canadian Partnership for International Justice as *amici* in referral proceedings to consider whether the Court could exercise jurisdiction over crimes of deportation of Rohingya from Myanmar to Bangladesh.[69] Both of these applicants had emphasised their extensive expertise in international criminal law in their applications and their submissions, as had the Chamber in justifying their admission. Similarly, in admitting *amicus* applications by victims' organisations,

[67] *Prosecutor v Muthaura, Kenyatta and Ali*, ICC TC II, 12 April 2011, ICC-01/09-57; *Prosecutor v Ruto, Kosgey and Sang*, ICC PTC II, 12 April 2011, ICC-01/09-56, para 15, emphasis added; and see the subsequent decisions, *Prosecutor v Ruto, Kosgey and Sang*, ICC PTC II, 11 May 2011, ICC-01/09-01/11-84, para 8; *Prosecutor v Ruto, Kosgey and Sang*, ICC PTC II, 13 June 2011, ICC-01/09-01/11-124; *Prosecutor v Muthaura, Kenyatta and Ali*, ICC PTC II, 13 June 2011, ICC-01/09-02/11-118, para 7; *Prosecutor v Ntaganda*, ICC PTC II, 18 February 2014, ICC-01/04-02/06-259, para 3.

[68] See further discussion in ch 4, s V(A).

[69] See *Request Under Regulation 46(3) of the Regulations of the Court*, ICC PTC I, 6 September 2018, ICC-RoC46(3)-01/18-37, fns 33, 86, 87, 90, 93, 98, 103, 104, 106, 120.

ICC Chambers have emphasised that 'the most desirable aspect of the proposed submissions … consist[ed] of the factual information they may be in possession of and therefore able to provide to the Chamber',[70] and rejected those without such expertise or information.[71] *Amicus* status, therefore, was not granted for the representative value of giving voice to communities affected by the alleged crimes. The ICTR has also rejected NGOs seeking to make submissions focusing on victims' issues due to their lack of expertise, or where other actors are better placed to provide the expertise they claim, even though victims' participation mechanisms were not otherwise provided at the Tribunal.[72] This practice indicates that without contributing demonstrable expertise or otherwise unavailable information, merely providing views on relevant community interests, or even the additional perspective of those whose interests are directly implicated in the proceedings, is unlikely to make the submissions sufficiently beneficial to the tribunal to justify their admission.

As noted above, other civil society actors are also primarily admitted within the expertise function. Academics, in almost every instance, both apply and are admitted in order to provide additional expertise to the Tribunals' proceedings. While international organisations' numbers of representative briefs are higher than NGOs or academics, they too most frequently apply and are admitted within the expertise function. The preference for the expertise function is seen even in the case of individuals, who most frequently apply to make submissions representing defined interests, but are most commonly admitted when the Tribunals consider that they have additional expertise or information to contribute. This focus on obtaining additional expertise supports the normative legitimacy of the proceedings, deepening tribunals' consideration of relevant matters with a potentially positive impact on the quality of the decisions made.

A. Legal or Factual Expertise?

While academics have almost exclusively contributed legal expertise, primarily in areas of international criminal law and public international law, NGOs and international organisations' representatives have given factual as well as legal

[70] *Prosecutor v Kony et al*, ICC PTC II, 18 November 2008, ICC-02/04-01/05-353, para 13.

[71] eg contrast ICC Trial Chamber V's rejection of the first application by Kituo Cha Sheria with the admission of the second: *Prosecutor v Muthaura and Kenyatta*, ICC PTC V, 13 September 2012, ICC-01/09-02/11-484; *Prosecutor v Ruto and Sang*, ICC TC V, 13 September 2012, ICC-01/09-01/11-456; cf *Prosecutor v Muthaura and Kenyatta*, ICC TC V, 15 November 2012, ICC-01/09-02/11-532.

[72] See, eg the ICTR Trial Chamber rejecting an NGO *amicus* application because 'the survivor's organizations do not suggest why they are well placed to provide the Chamber with information on these issues. The Chamber is of the view that the Rwandan Government is better placed to provide this information': *Prosecutor v Hategekimana*, ICTR TC, 20 March 2008, ICTR-00-55B-I-377, para 27. In contrast, in the same decision, *amici* including HRW and the Kigali Bar Association were admitted where the Chamber was convinced they could provide useful information or expertise, at paras 18 and 29. See also the admission of Human Rights Watch: *Prosecutor v Kanyagurika*, ICTR TC, 22 February 2008, ICTR-02-78-I-1361.

submissions. Such factual submissions have included matters such as knowledge of domestic criminal justice systems,[73] the factual context of allegations of crimes within the jurisdiction of the Court[74] or of non-compliance by states parties.[75] This practice then is not consistent with our view, already set out, that *amici* should generally be restricted to legal expertise, and should have a limited role in relation to providing factual information.[76] However, the Tribunals regularly accept the provision of information on local law, as it does not address criminal responsibility of the accused, and may be considered a mixed issue of fact and law.

This is not to say that civil society *amici's* role in providing *legal* expertise should be unlimited; the criteria of novelty and non-duplication provide important constraints.[77] As discussed further below, the practice regarding civil society has indeed indicated that in order to qualify for admission within the expertise function, the expertise must be distinctive; that is, the *amicus* must contribute expertise or information that is not provided by the submissions of other parties or participants on the proceedings – including those of other *amici* – and does not overlap with the core judicial functions of the tribunal.[78] As a result, matters on which expertise may most often be valuable are those such as analysis of national law, comparative approaches between different national and international jurisdictions, or assessment of the status of a new or developing rule of customary international law – all of which are complex legal issues that may fall outside of the parties' submissions and the knowledge of the judges.

In addition, a form of 'expertise' that is increasingly cited by civil society *amicus* applicants, including NGOs and academics, and the Tribunals themselves to justify the admission of *amici* is that the applicant has previously acted as an *amicus* in proceedings before the tribunal, or before other international tribunals.[79] As we discuss in chapter four, section V(M), in our view this in and of itself is not a form of expertise justifying *amicus* status, though it may be that such experience may make the brief better drafted and contribute to the unified development of international criminal law, which can again improve the quality of the tribunal's decision-making. Further, relying on this form of expertise would lead to the repeated admission of certain civil society actors, and the resulting risk that these actors are privileged and subjected to less scrutiny of their subject-matter expertise than those who have not previously acted as

[73] eg, *Prosecutor v Al-Bashir*, ICC PTC II, 10 March 2017, ICC-02/05-01/09-288.

[74] eg *Situation in Darfur*, ICC PTC I, 24 July 2006, ICC-02/05-10; *Request Under Regulation 46(3) of the Regulations of the Court*, ICC PTC I, 18 June 2018, ICC-RoC46(3)-01/18-21.

[75] *Prosecutor v Al-Bashir*, ICC PTC II, 10 March 2017, ICC-02/05-01/09-288.

[76] See ch 4, s V(H).

[77] See discussion of these criteria in ch 4, s V(J) and (D), respectively.

[78] eg contrast ICC Trial Chamber V's rejection of the first application by Kituo Cha Sheria with the admission of the second: *Prosecutor v Muthaura and Kenyatta*, ICC PTC V, 13 September 2012, ICC-01/09-02/11-484; *Prosecutor v Ruto and Sang*, ICC TC V, 13 September 2012, ICC-01/09-01/11-456; cf *Prosecutor v Muthaura and Kenyatta*, ICC TC V, 15 November 2012, ICC-01/09-02/11-532.

[79] eg *Request Under Regulation 46(3) of the Regulations of the Court*, ICC PTC I, 29 May 2018, ICC-RoC46(3)-01/18-8, para 7; *Prosecutor v Kanyarukiga*, ICTR TC, 22 February 2008, ICTR-02-78-I-1361, para 7; *Prosecutor v Bemba*, ICC TC III, 26 August 2016, ICC-01/05-01/08-340, 8.

amici, thereby reducing the opportunity for contributions from a more diverse range of *amici*. However, this should be distinguished from instances where the NGO or other civil society actor has been involved in related national proceedings, which may indeed provide valuable expertise and information that could not otherwise be obtained. For instance, the Southern Africa Litigation Centre was admitted as an *amicus* in the non-cooperation proceedings relating to South Africa's failure to arrest former President Bashir of Sudan during his visit to the country.[80] The NGO had been one of the parties in the domestic proceedings in which the government's actions were held to be unconstitutional.[81] As a result, their extensive involvement in the national proceedings provided an important source of expertise on the issues for the Pre-Trial Chamber's determination.

B. Identification of Expertise of Civil Society *Amici*

Given the focus on the expertise function in relation to civil society *amici*, it is notable that the Tribunals have not clearly and consistently articulated how they identify and test such actors' expertise – a gap which is pervasive in the Tribunals' practice in relation to all potential *amici*, as discussed in chapter four, section V(M). As noted above, NGO *amici* have been rejected when the Tribunals thought another actor would be better placed to provide the information they proposed to submit, and also where the Chamber is not convinced that an NGO possesses the expertise that it has claimed in its application.[82] However, it is not clear how the Tribunals are making these determinations – for instance, whether they are simply relying on the organisational and biographical information in the application (if any), or whether they are undertaking independent measures to determine the NGO's area of expertise. This stands in contrast to the standards established for the appointment of expert witnesses (and counsel), which are detailed and controlled by the Tribunals.[83]

Similarly, more clarity is needed as to how academics' expertise on a matter is tested. While their higher admission rate in comparison to NGOs indicates that their claims of expertise are more often accepted, the Tribunals have applied various approaches that have not been consistently successful in identifying the most useful academic expertise. For instance, the ICC Appeals Chamber restricted its first open call for submissions to address the immunity of heads of state of non-party states to 'Professors of International Law', and required that 'any such request for leave shall be accompanied by summary

[80] *Prosecutor v Al-Bashir*, ICC PTC II, 28 February 2017, ICC-02/05-01/09-283.

[81] See *The Minister of Justice and Constitutional Development v The Southern African Litigation Centre and Others* (867/15) [2016] ZASCA 17.

[82] eg *Prosecutor v Lubanga*, ICC AC, 8 March 2013, ICC-01/04-01/06-2995; *Prosecutor v Lubanga*, ICC AC, 16 August 2013, ICC-01/04-01/06-3044, para 11: the 'issues upon which Child Soldiers International wishes to make observations are of an essentially legal nature, whereas Child Soldiers International is a "research and advocacy organisation"'.

[83] See discussion of standards for expert witness in ch 3, s VI(C).

initial observations ... describing the particular expertise of the Professor in the legal question presented, as well as summary conclusions as to those questions'.[84] While the requirement to detail the applicant's expertise on the matters in question was a positive innovation, the limitation to 'Professors' was counterproductive. This requirement was likely intended as a proxy for academic standing, seniority and high-quality submissions, but ultimately led to a formalistic litmus test in which only those employed with the title of 'full professor' were admitted.[85] This resulted in the rejection of certain applicants who, though not 'Professors', were leading academic experts in the legal issues under consideration, and the admission of others with less expertise in the area. This test, therefore, arguably did not succeed in obtaining the most valuable expertise, limiting the contribution that the *amici* could make to the quality of the Chamber's decision-making. A preferable approach may have been to invite 'scholars' or 'university academics' to make submissions, and then for the Appeals Chamber to examine the actual expertise of each applicant, and the relevance thereof to the issues for determination, regardless of their title.

The Tribunals' practice also illustrates different approaches taken to try to ensure that civil society *amicus* submissions provide expertise that is distinct from the parties and other *amici* so as to avoid duplication. ICC Chambers have frequently narrowed the scope of NGOs' *amicus* submissions to those issues on which the Chamber considers that it can provide distinct expertise or information.[86] Similarly, when admitting academic *amici*, the ECCC emphasised that there were 'relatively few submissions' from the parties on the issue addressed by the *amicus* and so 'the Chamber would benefit from further submissions on this topic'.[87] In the same vein, the ICC rejected academic *amicus* submissions that were 'expected to overlap with the [*amicus*] submissions for which the Chamber has already granted leave. Accordingly, the Chamber considers that ... [the] observations are not desirable for the proper determination of the Prosecutor's Request, within the meaning of rule 103 of the Rules'.[88]

While Chambers should certainly not waste time and resources on receiving submissions that do not yield distinct expertise, this practice does highlight a flaw in the process of *ad hoc* applications. If the aim is to obtain the best and

[84] *Prosecutor v Al-Bashir*, ICC AC, 29 March 2018, ICC-02/05-01/09-330, 3. See also Yau for further discussion of this amicus practice: SSM Yau, 'Academic *Amici* and the Legitimacy of International Criminal Court: Some Reflections on the Al Bashir Appeal' (*Cambridge International Law Journal Blog*, 2018), available at http://cilj.co.uk/2018/11/19/academic-amici-and-the-legitimacy-of-international-criminal-court-some-reflections-on-the-al-bashir-appeal/.

[85] *Prosecutor v Al-Bashir*, ICC AC, 21 May 2018, ICC-02/05-01/09-351; International Criminal Court, 'Q&A Regarding Appeals Chamber's 6 May 2019 Judgment in the Jordan Referral re Al-Bashir Appeal' (May 2009), available at www.icc-cpi.int/itemsDocuments/190515-al-bashir-qa-eng.pdf.

[86] See, eg *Prosecutor v Muthaura and Kenyatta*, ICC TC V, 15 November 2012, ICC-01/09-02-11-532.

[87] *Co-Prosecutors v Nuon and Khieu (Case 002)*, ECCC TC, 13 September 2016, 002/19-09-2007-ECCC-TC-E418/3, 13.

[88] *Request under Regulation 46(3) of the Regulations of the Court*, ICC PTC I, 7 June 2018, ICC-RoC46(3)-01/18-12.

most useful expertise, instead of simply admitting the first *amicus* that proposes submissions on a topic, as we have discussed in chapter four, section V(D), it would be preferable to issue an open call (using a two-stage process) where possible. The ICC recently issued its first open call in the *Jordan* proceedings, discussed above, though other tribunals made more frequent use of this tool. Open calls also increase the transparency of the proceedings, and the equality of opportunity to make *amicus* submissions, and may then encourage submissions from a more diverse range of civil society sources – though this has not generally been the result of these calls thus far. Both academic and NGO submissions made in response to these calls have largely originated from the same regions, and in some cases the same individuals or organisations, as unsolicited applications. It would be possible for tribunals to target actors from particular regions in their calls for submissions, but this has not yet been attempted. Thus, while open calls may be a potential tool not only to identify more relevant expertise, but also to increase the diversity of the actors providing *amicus* submissions, the latter has not yet proven to be the case.

As noted above, another method used by the Tribunals has been to invite specific academics to act as *amici*, based on their prior academic reputation and published work.[89] The same has been done for certain representatives of international organisations.[90] While this may ensure that the actor's expertise is relevant for the tribunal, it is potentially problematic from the perspective of privileging certain voices and seeming to indicate a predetermined decision – that the tribunal is seeking out support for their preferred approach from an *amicus* whose views are already known, rather than using the submissions of the parties and *amici* to come to a decision on the issues. Such an approach, it is submitted, is detrimental both to normative and sociological legitimacy, as it not only misses an opportunity to obtain expertise from academics that may not be known to the tribunal, but also may lead to a perception of a biased decision-making process, undermining trust in the judicial determinations of the tribunal. Further, if a tribunal is already convinced of the value of the views of a particular academic, it can always rely on her written work on the matter, or on published reports of NGOs. Indeed, if tribunals can access the expertise through published sources, this should generally be preferred for the sake of efficiency and to avoid duplication.

C. Independence and Impartiality of Civil Society *Amici* in the Expertise Function

The prevalence and potential impact of civil society submissions admitted within the expertise function highlights the importance of impartiality and

[89] Section II(B) supra.
[90] Section II(C) supra.

independence of these *amici*. As we have already discussed, the Tribunals have applied these criteria to varying degrees when deciding applications for *amicus* status.[91] It is our view that neutrality as to the outcome of proceedings or a lack of interest in the broader impact or development of the law should not be expected of *amici*. However, independence – in the sense of having no pre-existing relationship with a party – and impartiality – in terms of a lack of direct legal interest in the proceedings – can be crucial criteria, depending on the function(s) that *amici* seek to fulfil. In particular, these are important requirements for *amici* acting within the expertise function, as the tribunal is allowing the submissions in order to glean new and reliable information and knowledge to influence its reasoning.

These concerns about independence and impartiality are particularly pressing in relation to civil society actors. In contrast to *amici* such as states or accused individuals, these actors' identity and interests may be unclear. Without information, for example, as to who is funding and influencing NGO *amici*, it can be difficult to determine whether the organisation has a vested interest in a particular outcome. NGOs, for instance, may claim to be independent, but have strong ties to victims, the government or the accused.[92] More generally, NGOs' strategic aims and priorities, and those of their donors, may result in selectivity in terms of the sources or arguments cited in their submissions. Similarly, as noted above, academic *amici* may also have close ties with government, the parties and other participants (including as counsel in other cases), or rely on donor funding with specific strategic aims, which may undermine their independence.

In order to assist the verification of the identity and interests of those making civil society submissions, we propose the introduction of requirements that the funding of all *amici* and potential conflicts of interest be disclosed as part of the application for *amicus* status, similar to the requirements at the US Supreme Court.[93] The danger of admitting and relying on biased expertise is particularly acute in the case where the *amicus* is providing the tribunal with factual information, and even more so where that is being relied on as evidence of the guilt of the accused. However, as we have already argued, determinations of criminal responsibility are made by professional judges at the Tribunals, who can be expected to appreciate the particular focus or perspective of *amici* and to give the brief appropriate weight. As put by Schiff, 'ICC officials recognize that NGOs pursue their own agendas, and that they will seek to pressure the ICC in the direction of their own priorities rather than necessarily understanding or being fully sympathetic to the myriad constraints and pressures under which

[91] See ch 4, ss V(K) and V(L).

[92] See, eg discussion of the Sudan Workers Trade Union Federation and the Sudan International Defence Group and possible links with former President Bashir and the state of Sudan in ch 6, s IV(B).

[93] See further discussion in ch 2, s V(B).

the Court operates'.[94] Nonetheless, if it is clear that submissions will be biased and so will be of limited or no value to the tribunal, they should generally be excluded in the interests of fairness and expediency.

IV. REPRESENTATION OF INTERESTS BY CIVIL SOCIETY AS *AMICI CURIAE*

For many commentators, a significant reason that NGO and other civil society participation, in international criminal law generally, and as *amici curiae* specifically, is valued, is their perceived ability to give voice to a variety of interests and perspectives that may not otherwise be represented in international criminal proceedings. This echoes the justifications for NGO participation in human rights tribunals discussed previously.[95] As indicated by the figures quoted above, the largest group of civil society applications seek to address victims and defence issues, which are two of the groups, alongside states, that most commonly have interests directly affected by the proceedings. Indeed, given the criminal nature of the proceedings, it is rare that other actors' interests will be sufficiently directly affected to require representation in the proceedings. Within civil society, it is NGOs and legal organisations that most commonly apply to make such submissions. NGOs play a crucial role in supporting victims locally, and several representative briefs by NGOs and other civil society actors have sought to make submissions addressing victims' interests. NGOs, legal organisations and a small number of individuals have also sought to act as *amici* focusing on defence interests. *Amicus* submissions on behalf of these directly-implicated interests fall within the representative function that we have identified. A small number of representative submissions have also been proposed by international organisations, when their own interests have been implicated in proceedings.[96]

As previously argued, those actors whose interests are directly implicated in proceedings should, in general, have an opportunity to contribute thereto. This is important so that such interests are not unfairly compromised, and to ensure that all relevant considerations are before the tribunal. This is required to satisfy key values of representation, participation and transparency, as well as to ensure that a correct decision is reached.[97] Depending on the tribunal and the stage of proceedings, the *amicus* mechanism may be the only possibility for representation of interests of victims or the accused. Thus, such *amicus* representation may be necessary for the legitimacy of the proceedings.

However, two important caveats are necessary, indicating that the appropriate scope for civil society *amici* to act within the representative function on

[94] Schiff (n 6), 162.

[95] See ch 2, s IV(A).

[96] We have also identified one academic application by Professors T Zwart and GGJ Knoops who sought to make submissions partly in the representative mode, but it was rejected: *Prosecutor v L Gbagbo*, ICC PTC I, 4 June 2014, ICC-02/11-01/11-653.

[97] See ch 1, s III.

behalf of victims' or defence interests is much more limited than that within the expertise function. First, we must distinguish between direct representation of individual actors with interests, such as identified victims, as opposed to a more general, discursive claim to represent 'victims' interests'.[98] At the ICC, though NGOs initially had a role in the victim participation process,[99] this process is now managed by formal victims' representatives and through the OPCV; NGOs cannot directly represent individual victims at the ICC, unlike at certain human rights tribunals.[100] Thus, it is only in terms of more abstract representation of victims' interests that NGOs are engaged as *amici*. These more abstract claims of representation by NGOs or other civil society actors are questionable. It is no straightforward task, for instance, to identify the 'victim's voice'. One interviewee experienced with NGO and academic partnerships in an ICC situation country suggested:

> I would love to see … if there is an *amicus curiae* process [where] they were forced to say … 'Who exactly are you speaking on behalf of? Like what groups? Where's the geographic location?' but not just like, 'We're an organisation that's dealt with X, Y and Z and we're saying victims want this.' That's so broad. And it won't represent everybody. So that's a huge problem.[101]

Similar concerns apply to submissions of NGOs or legal organisations that claim to speak on behalf of defence interests, claiming that these organisations' views represent those of all, or even a subset of defendants before the Tribunals – as opposed to direct representation of the accused by counsel or the OPCD at the ICC. As discussed further in chapter six, such *amicus* submissions in fact run the risk of contradicting the defendant's own arguments in the case. In addition, the opacity of the funding and goals of some NGOs make it difficult to identify precisely whose interests are being represented by these organisations. Tribunals must therefore carefully consider the link between the organisation in question and the interests that they claim to represent, and should also require disclosure of any links between the *amicus* and the parties, and other interested actors such as states.[102] This abstract form of representation has less potential to create the legitimacy benefits set out above, which will only accrue if the *amicus* truly represents those actors whose interests are directly affected by the proceedings. Often, NGOs' and other civil society actors' claims to representation of broad interests will not be sufficient to justify admission within the representative function.

[98] See S Kendall and S Nouwen, 'Representational Practices at the International Criminal Court: The Gap Between Juridified and Abstract Victimhood' (2013) 76 *Law & Contemporary Problems* 235.

[99] FIDH filed the first application for victims' participation at the ICC, this was later taken over by the OPCV.

[100] See discussion in ch 2, s II(A).

[101] Interview CT3.

[102] Article 3 of the Practice Direction on *Amicus Curiae* Submissions before the Special Tribunal for Lebanon is an example of such disclosure requirements. See Annex B.

Secondly, the value of any representative briefs by NGOs or other *amici* is negated when those with affected interests have alternative modes of participation in the proceedings. If these interests are represented through other procedural mechanisms, *amicus* submissions on their behalf are duplicative and unnecessary, creating unjustified risk to the expeditiousness of the proceedings and the fair trial rights of the accused. For instance, victim participation is already provided for in pre-trial, trial, appeal, and reparations proceedings at the ICC, as well as at certain other tribunals, and through institutional actors such as the OPCV, meaning that *amicus* submissions addressing the same interests are not needed. In contrast, as discussed in chapter three, section VI(A), such submissions may be necessary at other tribunals where victims have no standing in the proceedings, or in stages of proceedings where victim participation in not guaranteed. In deciding whether to admit proposed *amici* coming within the representative function, then, the tribunal should consider whether the interests at play may already be represented in the proceedings through another means. This discussion has implications for the use of the *amicus curiae* mechanism by victims, and indicates a very limited role for NGOs or other civil society actors in this regard.

We foresee three situations where victims may seek to rely on the *amicus curiae* as a 'stop-gap' measure whenever victim participation is not available. First, where there is no right for victims to participate: examples may include in non-cooperation proceedings, where victims have been denied standing to participate in an appeal, or where the Chamber has determined that victims' personal interests are not affected by the decision. Secondly, where victims are uncertain as to the existence or scope of a right to participate as victims at a particular stage. In this circumstance, victims seek to participate as victims and in the alternative as *amicus curiae* under the relevant *amicus curiae* rule. For example, in 2018 the ICC Prosecutor sought a ruling from the Pre-Trial Chamber under Article 19(3) as to whether the Court could exercise jurisdiction in relation to crimes alleged to have occurred in Myanmar (a non-party state) where at least one element of the crime had occurred on the territory of Bangladesh (a state party). In her request, the Prosecutor noted that as a situation did not exist at this stage, 'it appears that no State or participating victim is formally entitled to file additional observations on this matter under Article 19(3)'. However, the Prosecution noted that the Pre-Trial Chamber could allow submissions from the OPCD and OPCV, as well as states and victims as *amicus curiae*. Several NGOs sought leave to appear as *amici curiae* under Rule 103. Two observations were filed on behalf of victims: one filed on behalf of victims from Tula Toli by a legal representative, claiming to be based on Article 19(3); the other by an NGO, Global Rights Compliance, on behalf of 400 victims under Article 19(3) or alternatively Article 68(3). Given the uncertainty as to the process and whether victims could participate at this very early stage, Global Rights Compliance sought in the alternative to be an *amicus curiae*. Although the Chamber found that the victims had standing by virtue of Article 68(3), this shows how victims may rely on the *amicus* mechanism when standing for victims is uncertain. Thirdly, victims who have chosen not to participate as victims in the proceedings may seek to use the *amicus curiae* mechanism as a means to alert the Court to their interests and views. However, this has risks, as it enables victims to participate without the admissibility criteria required for formal participation, so it should be carefully managed by the Chambers and limited to specific issues. This could be particularly significant where it may lead to submissions that conflict with those victims who have chosen to participate. As discussed in chapter three, sections VI(A) and (B), the OPCV may be asked to represent the interests of non-participating victims, in particular those that may decide to seek reparations at a later stage.

Does it matter then which provision is relied upon to allow victims to participate? Where victim participation is available, that should be the preferred option for participation, for two reasons. First, victim participation provides more extensive and systematic rights. Secondly, it accords most closely with the representative function. If victims' interests are not sufficiently affected so as to justify participation under Article 68(3) then, according to our typology, the representative function of the *amicus curiae* would also not be engaged. Alternatively, Chambers should rely on Regulation 93 to seek submissions from victims (see chapter three, section VI(A)(ii)). This does not preclude NGOs or other actors participating as *amici curiae* in the expertise function; however, this should be limited to drawing on their expertise or experience to address general questions of law or procedure concerning victims and not advancing the views or interests of specific, identifiable victims in the case at hand.

In relation to defence interests, the defendant has a right of participation and representation by counsel and, at the ICC, the OPCD has a responsibility to make whatever submissions on defence interests it considers necessary. In addition, all Chambers, as well as the Prosecutor, have a duty under the Rome Statute to protect the rights of the accused. Tribunals should therefore generally be wary of admitting civil society representative submissions speaking to defence interests – particularly given the risk that such submissions will actually undermine the defence's own arguments. However, as discussed in chapter six, there may be instances in which such submissions will be appropriate in pre-trial or other non-trial proceedings, such as during the investigatory phase or in non-cooperation hearings at the ICC. Further, it is possible that defendants in other cases, or unindicted perpetrators, will be affected by legal determinations in the proceedings, in which case representation may be necessary – though in such cases it would be preferable to give procedural rights of participation to these actors, or to formally join the cases, rather than a discretionary power to admit *amicus* submissions on their behalf.[103]

In keeping with this analysis, the practice of the Tribunals, and especially the ICC, largely demonstrates a conservative approach in this regard, frequently

[103] See further discussion in ch 6, s IV(A).

rejecting civil society *amicus* submissions seeking to play a purely representative function on behalf of victims or defence. This is particularly so when the proposed *amici* were not also able to show that they could bring novel expertise to the proceedings. For instance, Trial Chamber VI rejected an application by the Redress Trust and Avocats san Frontières, in which the NGOs 'propose[d] to bring to the Chamber's attention relevant factual information regarding victims' communities' experiences with the new application system implemented at trial in the Kenya cases; the Observations would also highlight practical issues, based on consultations with victims, [and] affected communities … that may impact on modalities for a possible tiered application and participation process'.[104] The Chamber rejected the application on the basis that the views of the victims had already been submitted through the Legal Representative for Victims, and so 'in this case the Chamber is not persuaded that the proposed observations of the Applicants would assist it with the proper determination of issues related to the victims' application process and the modalities of their participation'.[105] In addition, the ICC has also emphasised the fact that applicants would *not* play a representative role as a positive factor favouring their admission. For instance, Pre-Trial Chamber I in part justified the admission of Lawyers for Justice in Libya and the Redress Trust in the *Gaddafi and Senussi* proceedings, because 'the Applicants do not purport to speak on behalf of specific victims, victim-applicants, etc'.[106] We have in fact only identified one successful civil society application to make purely representative submissions at the ICC, in which Kenyan NGO Kituo Cha Sheria was admitted. In its decision, the ICC Trial Chamber emphasised the NGO's direct contact with the victims in holding that, due to its 'specialised knowledge and experience … Kituo is an appropriate organization to submit observations as *amicus curiae* in relation to the implementation of the system of victims' representation and participation'.[107] Nonetheless, the Chamber sought to restrict these submissions quite narrowly to ensure that there was no duplication resulting from these submissions, ordering that Kituo exclude, inter alia, submissions concerning the appointment of the common legal representation.

This is of course not to say that civil society *amicus* submissions that seek to provide the perspective of victims or defence should or will always be rejected. Indeed, some influential NGO *amicus* briefs have done just that. For instance, two joint NGO briefs in the *Al Mahdi* case sought to provide information concerning victims' interests in reparations proceedings. Queen's University Belfast Human Rights Centre and Redress sought to directly represent views of certain victims, writing that, inter alia, their 'submission would address … the impact of the destruction of cultural property on affected communities and individual victims, … appropriate measures to address the victims'

[104] *Prosecutor v Ntaganda*, ICC TC VI, 29 August 2014, ICC-01/04-02/06-359.
[105] *Prosecutor v Ntaganda*, ICC TC VI, 24 September 2014, ICC-01/04-02/06-377.
[106] *Prosecutor v Gaddafi and Al-Senussi*, ICC PTC I, 18 May 2012, ICC-01/11-01/11-153.
[107] *Prosecutor v Ruto and Sang*, ICC TC V, 15 November 2012, ICC-01/09-01/11-473.

psychological, moral and economic harm as a result, [and] … appropriate apologies and acknowledgements of responsibility, given representations by the victims that they are not satisfied with Mr Al Mahdi's apology and expression of remorse'.[108] However, in this case, submissions concerning the interests of the victims were made in combination with contributing significant novel legal and factual expertise and information. It was this expertise that was cited as the primary motivation both for the *amici*'s applications, and their 'relevant expertise' was the sole reason given for their admission by the ICC Trial Chamber.[109] Further, it was their submissions presenting their expert knowledge of the regulation and significance of cultural heritage – rather than those claiming to represent the views of victims – that were cited by the Chamber to support aspects of its reparations order.[110] The representative function, then, appropriately was supplementary to the primary contribution of expertise.

V. THE COMMUNICATIVE FUNCTION AND CIVIL SOCIETY

Civil society participation in international criminal tribunals, as with other international bodies such as regional human rights courts, is often praised for its potential to facilitate the inclusion of public interests and community perspectives that are otherwise absent in the adversarial format. Along with representation of those with interests directly affected by the proceedings, as discussed in the preceding section, it is often claimed that NGOs in particular can and should contribute more general, public interest-oriented submissions in international criminal tribunals. For instance, one civil society actor, based in Nigeria, argued:

> [T]he fact that more and more Africans are involved is going to legitimise the operation of the ICC itself. And perhaps validate the concept of international criminal justice on the continent. So … the more involvement of Africans and African professionals and African CSO's, [suggests] that international criminal justice is not a European concept, it's not an imposed concept, it is a concept that Africans promote the concept, that Africans subscribe to.[111]

As we discuss in chapter one, such statements posit that generous *amicus* participation of NGOs or other civil society actors in this manner will contribute to the sociological legitimacy of the Tribunals. The submission of *amicus* briefs that speak to these broader public interests reflects the communicative function of the *amicus curiae* mechanism that we have identified.

There is a significant number of examples of civil society actors of all kinds applying to make submissions that would come within the communicative

[108] *Prosecutor v Al Mahdi*, ICC TC VIII, 20 October 2016, ICC-01/12-01/15-175, para 9.
[109] *Prosecutor v Al Mahdi*, ICC TC VIII, 25 October 2016, ICC-01/12-01/15-178.
[110] eg *Prosecutor v Al Mahdi*, ICC TC VIII, 17 August 2017, ICC-01/12-01/15-236, fns 38, 39, 44.
[111] Interview CT4.

function, or in combination with the representative or (more commonly) the expertise function. However, generally, the practice of the Tribunals reflects concerns regarding the value of admitting *amicus* applicants solely to make submissions speaking to the public interest or indirect interests in the proceedings, especially when the applicants do not have particular expertise to contribute. The ICC has consistently rejected applications by civil society actors, namely NGOs and academics, that have sought to make submissions focusing on public or community interests implicated in the proceedings. For instance, Pre-Trial Chamber I rejected the proposed *amicus* submissions of the Sudan Workers Trade Unions Federation and Sudan International Defence Group, which sought to oppose the issuance of an arrest warrant for President Bashir because:[112]

> issuing such warrants would have grave implications for the peace building process in Sudan and that deference must be given to considerations of national interest and security; (2) that the interests of justice will not be served particularly in light of the Prosecutor's conduct in bringing these applications; (3) that such warrants could entrench the negative perceptions of the ICC and thus contribute to a deterioration of the situation in Sudan; and, (4) that alternative means of transitional justice and resolution are being and will pursued without the need for any consideration of involvement of the ICC at this stage.

The Chamber held that these were not issues that were relevant for their determination.[113] Similarly, Pre-Trial Chamber II rejected an application by No Peace Without Justice to address 'desirability and feasibility of conducting the confirmation of charges hearing … on the territory of the Republic of Kenya', including consideration concerns relating to in situ proceedings and the impact on affected communities.[114] The Chamber held that the absence of specific expertise meant that the submissions would not assist its determination.[115] Furthermore, it has admitted no academic *amici* to make public interest submissions even in combination with the expertise function, and has only very rarely admitted NGO *amici* to do so.[116]

Other tribunals have been slightly more receptive to these submissions, with a small number of communicative submissions from NGOs, academics and legal organisations having been approved at the ECCC[117] and the ICTY.[118] Almost all were admitted in response to an open call or direct invitation, which may have influenced the Tribunals' openness to such submissions. When the civil society

[112] *Situation in Darfur, Sudan*, ICC PTC I, 11 January 2009, ICC-02/05-170, para 8.

[113] *Situation in Darfur, Sudan*, ICC PTC I, 4 February 2009, ICC-02/05-185.

[114] *Prosecutor v Ruto, Kosgey and Sang*, ICC PTC II, 10 June 2011, ICC-01/09-01/11-119.

[115] *Prosecutor v Ruto, Kosgey and Sang*, ICC PTC II, 13 June 2011, ICC-01/09-01/11-124.

[116] *Prosecutor v Al-Bashir*, ICC PTC II, 10 March 2017, ICC-01/05-01/09-288.

[117] *Co-Prosecutors v Ieng*, ECCC PTC, 19 February 2008, 002/19-09-2007-ECCC-OCIJ (PTC 03)-C22/1/14; *Co-Prosecutors v Ieng*, ECCC PTC, 19 February 2008, 002/19-09-2007-ECCC-OCIJ (PTC 03)-C22/1/13; *Co-Prosecutors v Duch*, ECCC PTC, 27 September 2007, 002/14-08-2006-ECCC/PTC-C5/10.

[118] See admission of multiple civil society *amici* in *Prosecutor v Blaškić*, ICTY AC, 29 July 1997, IT-95-14-AR108*bis*-D15.

amici have combined public interest argument with the provision of expert legal analysis, their rate of admission increased significantly at the ECCC, ICTY, ICTR, SCSL and STL – though again largely in response to open calls and direct invitations rather than voluntary applications. For instance, in *Al Jadeed*, the STL made an open call and ultimately admitted 18 submissions from NGOs, academic and media organisations concerning the tribunal's jurisdiction over corporations in a contempt proceeding. In her decision, the Contempt Judge emphasised the public and discursive value of *amicus* participation, emphasising that the briefs would be available on the tribunal's website and accepting the submissions even when they did not comply with formalities.[119] At the same time, the decision also sought to ensure that the submissions would contribute some expertise, specifically inviting certain kinds of actors, and specifying the subject on which submissions would be accepted. This approach is consistent with the civil society practice here, demonstrating that communicative submissions are most likely to be admitted when combined with the expertise function, and when made in response to an open call or direct invitation from the Chamber.

Haddad has argued that institutions may seek to draw more on NGOs and other civil society actors to bolster their legitimacy in the face of crises.[120] Given the considerable challenges facing the ICC at this stage of its development, one might therefore expect to see greater receptivity to civil society submissions within the communicative function at the Court. However, the practice does not indicate such a shift. While the ICC has issued its first open call to civil society actors – though limited to academics – in the *Jordan* non-cooperation proceedings discussed above, as we have already set out, the resulting *amici* were selected on the basis of their legal expertise and standing. Though the oral hearings with the academic *amici* did address wider implications of the decision on immunity, these focused on the consequences for the interests of states and international organisations in their ability to invite foreign leaders for diplomatic meetings.[121] Further, in the recent decision refusing the Prosecutor's request to open an investigation into alleged crimes in Afghanistan, the Pre-Trial Chamber did not seek civil society submissions, despite this being the first decision in which ICC Chambers sought to define the meaning of the 'interests of justice' within the Rome Statute.[122]

There are several considerations that support this restrictive approach to the admission of *amici* whose proposed submissions fall within the communicative function. First, scepticism as to the benefit of NGO representation of broad and abstract interests via the *amicus* mechanism is warranted. It is difficult to maintain that NGOs are neutral representatives of public interests, given their own mandates, political aims, donor priorities, and resource limitations. Increasingly,

[119] See *Prosecutor v Al Jadeed SAL and Khayat*, STL, Transcript, 12 May 2014, 20, referred to in *Prosecutor v Al Jadeed SAL and Khayat*, STL, 16 May 2014, STL-14-05/PT/CJ-R000238.

[120] Haddad (n 4).

[121] *Prosecutor v Al-Bashir*, ICC AC, Transcript, 10 September 2018, 114.

[122] *Situation in Afghanistan*, ICC PTC II, 12 April 2019, ICC-02/17-33, paras 87–96.

civil society actors are funded specifically to make 'strategic interventions' such as *amicus* briefs in the Tribunals, highlighting the potential of this tool to achieve strategic aims.[123] In any event, as we have discussed, the determination of the 'public interest' is highly contested, and the Tribunals should be wary of accepting one organisation's perspective as to what this might be.[124] Further, given the discretionary and *ad hoc* nature of both applications for and approval of *amicus curiae* status, the mechanism can only broaden the accessibility of international criminal tribunals to a certain extent. As a result, it cannot be relied on to provide the full range of views on public interests involved in international criminal proceedings, but will instead always represent a narrow, and perhaps somewhat random, selection of perspectives, favouring those with the knowledge of the proceedings and the means to intervene. The *amicus curiae* is therefore inherently not a pluralist mechanism, but is only one narrow procedural mechanism for participation. Instead, alternative mechanisms are better suited to these discussions. In particular, the Assembly of States Parties can be utilised by NGOs and other civil society actors, which provides for extensive civil society participation and engagement on such issues.[125]

In addition, as discussed previously, the proper role of the public interest must be significantly more limited in international criminal tribunals than in international human rights or domestic constitutional proceedings, given that the primary aim is to determine individual criminal responsibility of the accused.[126] The focus of the proceedings must always be the successful discharge of the tribunal's core judicial mandate to determine the guilt or innocence of the accused while respecting the defence's right to a fair and expeditious proceeding – accordingly, civil society *amicus* submissions that potentially distract from that goal by addressing only broader considerations must be limited, if not excluded entirely. An exception may be appropriate for civil society *amicus* submissions addressing public interest arguments in combination with providing novel expertise or information to the tribunal – that is, in combination within the expertise function. For instance, a number of academic briefs were admitted in response to the open call by the ECCC, discussed above, to address whether soldiers' *hors de combat* constitute civilian populations for the purposes of the definition of crimes against humanity. Interestingly, in justifying the admission of these academic *amici*, the Chamber emphasised both the benefit to the legal determinations in the case at hand, and that the submissions 'will benefit international criminal law as a whole'. This represents an appropriate use of the communicative function, as it was combined with providing distinctive legal expertise on a specific and novel question of the interpretation of international criminal law that was necessary for the case at hand.

[123] See, eg Canadian Partnership for International Justice, 'Our Research' (2017), available at https://cpij-pcji.ca/about-our-research/.

[124] See ch1, s IV.

[125] See ch 7.

[126] See ch 3, s V.

It should also be noted that while large, international NGOs are granted admission more often than local organisations as *amici* before the Tribunals, the former may have a weaker connection to issues and interests affected by and at stake in the proceedings, thus potentially undermining the justification for their admission. In light of this, an important practice has emerged in which international NGOs partner with local organisations in situation countries, potentially increasing the participatory value of the *amicus* submissions in question. For example, London-based Redress partnered with Uganda Victims Foundation to provide an *amicus curiae* brief to the ICC concerning the admissibility of cases in the Uganda situation, including in relation to the experiences of victims.[127]

Collaborations of this kind might be of particular benefit to the international NGO, since local groups often have important domestic contacts and relationships, and actual expertise on the matters.[128] Further, in some situations, local organisations might add rhetorical force to the arguments of a New York or London based organisation. One actor observed that in broader international criminal justice advocacy, 'we knew at the outset that we were not going to carry a lot of weight in a debate that's about international justice being in the neo-colonialist, western, dominated [environment] … So for me local partners are … really at the core of the work'.[129] In this situation, where the partnership may aim to support the credibility of one partner, *amici* may need to consider 'who are we trying to advocate on behalf of, really?'[130] The participants will need to consider what the goals of the partnership are and what arguments the *amicus curiae* brief should therefore address. This may also affect the choice of partner, which may depend on 'who you're targeting' or hoping to support with the *amicus*: the Court's legitimacy, governments in the relevant country or elsewhere, the parties, or particular victims.[131]

Thus, for another representative, a local partner's potentially significant contributions mean that for larger organisations deciding to collaborate, rather than 'dominating' or leading the process, 'it's important that we identify what we're contributing, what's our value – whether it's our international membership, our access at the UN, our legal expertise on particular issues'.[132] For instance, international NGOs may be able to assist smaller organisations that have not submitted an *amicus curiae* application to an international criminal tribunal (or any international legal mechanism) before regarding the process or appropriate style, or

[127] *Prosecutor v Kony et al*, ICC PTC II, 18 November 2008, ICC-02/04-01.15-142.

[128] eg 'If we're working with civil society partners who already have those relationships, then is there a need for us to establish those direct relationships ourselves?' Interview SY7.

[129] Interview CT2.

[130] Interview CT3.

[131] eg speaking generally in relation to international criminal justice partnerships in Uganda, Interview CT3 said: 'I'm not saying it's not strategic to partner but it depends who you're targeting. And, if you want to win the hearts and minds of government officials, sure; you want to deal with the Kampala-based organisations. But, if it's the communities, you want access to victims and witnesses, etc, then you need to deal with those local organisations …'.

[132] Interview SY7.

provide access to resources, including legal advice, to prepare their submissions.[133] It may therefore be easier for a national or community organisation to be accepted when they act in partnership with an international group. Increased participation of local actors may be enabled if Chambers issued guidance as to the appropriate issues and procedures for *amicus* participation targeted at these actors. The value of such partnerships could reach beyond the ICC, with benefits for local capacity building also at the national level, and lessons for the international NGOs.

Tribunals may have scope to be more generous concerning the admission of communicative submissions in stages of proceedings where fair trial rights would be less impacted, for example in pre-trial or reparations phases. All of the communicative briefs admitted at the ECCC, ICTY and ICTR noted above were admitted in pre-trial or, less frequently, appeals proceedings – and almost always when invited by the tribunal. But even in these non-trial stages, tribunals should consider what value is served through these submissions. The Tribunals' practice indicates that submissions focusing on public and general interests, rather than providing expert advice and information addressing relevant and complex issues in the proceedings, will generally not be of sufficient aid to the legal determinations the tribunal must make to justify their admission. This is emphasised by the apparent lack of impact of the few communicative submissions by civil society actors that have been admitted by the Tribunals.

Thus, given the fair trial concerns and limited tribunal resources, an approach that excludes civil society *amici* solely acting within the communicative function is appropriate. The perspectives of civil society actors on these larger public interests involved in international criminal trials are important, but should rather be presented through alternative mechanisms to which these actors have access. In particular, as noted above, the ICC Assembly of States Parties is better suited to accommodating these wider discussions. Taking such discussion out of the criminal trial context enables wider participation and transparency without compromising the fairness and expediency of the proceedings, which is preferable for the legitimacy of the institution as a whole.

VI. IMPACT OF CIVIL SOCIETY *AMICUS CURIAE* SUBMISSIONS

As with all *amicus* submissions, it is possible for civil society briefs to be influential in a range of ways. These include directly influencing the decision of the tribunal, including either in the judicial reasoning or the outcome, but could also influence other actors at the tribunal, such as the Prosecutor's decisions on charges.[134] NGOs' briefs may also have indirect influence outside of the particular proceedings in which they were submitted. Along with the expertise function

[133] S Williams and E Palmer, 'Civil Society and *Amicus Curiae* Interventions in the International Criminal Court' in S Williams and H Woolaver (eds), *Civil Society and International Criminal Justice in Africa: Challenges and Opportunities* (Cape Town, Juta Law, 2016).

[134] See discussion in ch 4, s VI(C).

being the most likely to lead to a successful application for admission as an *amicus* for civil society applicants, it is also the mode in which these submissions are most likely to influence the Tribunals. However, despite the numerous cases in which NGOs, academics, and other civil society actors have been successfully admitted in international crimes proceedings, overall, their submissions have not had substantial direct influence in the Tribunals, when measured by citations or quotation of such briefs in judicial decisions. While there appears to be a perception that NGOs' *amicus* submissions had a 'degree of super-influence' at the ICTY and ICTR,[135] in contrast to lesser influence at the ICC, this is a misconception. Evidence of such direct influence is rare, across all the Tribunals.

In the instances where there is evidence that civil society *amicus* submissions have had moderate or significant influence on the tribunal, as in the examples discussed in chapter four, section VI, it is most often when the civil society actor has provided specific information or expertise that the tribunal would otherwise not have had access to. Further examples can be found in the impact of submissions from legal organisations such as bar associations, which have influenced proceedings at the ICTR, especially where they have addressed fair trial issues, as discussed in chapter six. In *Hategekimana*, the *amicus* submissions provided by the ICDAA, in which they had emphasised their independence from the accused and expertise on the legal issues at play,[136] were referred to by the Trial and Appeals Chamber in the 11*bis* referral decision.[137] There are also instances in which NGO *amicus* submissions have been cited or quoted by the ICTR, but where the Tribunal held against their submissions.[138] Nonetheless, even though the outcome was contrary to the views of the *amici*, the reliance on their submissions indicates that they played some part in the judicial decision-making process.

More recently, in the ICC, submissions provided by the International Commission of Jurists and the Canadian Partnership for International Justice were cited relatively extensively by the Pre-Trial Chamber in their reasoning when deciding that the Court could exercise jurisdiction over crimes of deportation of Rohingya from Myanmar to Bangladesh.[139] As discussed above,

[135] '[I]f you look at the ICTR or the Yugoslavia tribunal, and all the amazing work that was done on promoting gender crimes and like the really massive influence that was had in those very early briefs, I don't see that our briefs are having that same degree of super-influence. It doesn't mean they're not having influence … But, on the gender-specific issues, you wouldn't have been able to have the amicus the same way as you did in Rwanda or the Yugoslavia because of the Court's own reasoning as to who is standing before the confirmation of charges hearing'. Interview CT1.

[136] *Prosecutor v Hategekimana*, ICTR TC III, 3 April 2008, ICTR-00-55B-I-429.

[137] *Prosecutor v Hategekimana*, ICTR AC, 4 December 2008, ICTR-00-55B-R11*bis*, paras 15, 21, 41. See also Palmer on the significant influence of the amici in these decisions. N Palmer, 'Transfer or Transformation?: A Review of the Rule 11*bis* Decisions of the International Criminal Tribunal for Rwanda' (2012) 20(1) *The African Journal of International and Comparative Law* 1, 10.

[138] See, eg *Prosecutor v Uwinkindi*, ICTR, 11 March 2011, ICTR-01-75-I-2774; *Prosecutor v Uwinkindi*, ICTR, 28 June 2011, ICTR-2001-75-R11*bis*.

[139] See *Request under Regulation 46(3) of the Regulations of the Court*, ICC TC I, 6 September 2018, ICC-RoC46(3)-01/18-37, fns 33, 86, 87, 90, 93, 98, 103, 104, 106, 120.

both of these civil society applicants had emphasised their extensive expertise in international criminal law in their applications and their submissions, as had the Chamber in justifying their admission. The *amicus* submissions in the *Jordan* non-cooperation proceedings in the *Al-Bashir* case also appeared to have a degree of impact on the Appeals Chamber's decision, though to a lesser extent.[140] This limited impact is striking, given that the *amicus* submissions were made in response to the Chamber's targeted call for academic analysis of the issues at play, and, unusually, substantial time was devoted to oral hearings of the submissions of the admitted 'Professor' *amici* rather than limiting them to written submissions. The *amici* were also granted an opportunity to make supplementary submissions after the hearing. Despite giving extensive summaries of these submissions, alongside those of the parties, most did not appear to influence the Chamber's reasoning.[141] However, one set of submissions did seem to have impact on the issue of whether Jordan's non-cooperation should be referred to the ASP or the Security Council. The Chamber, echoing arguments made by the *amicus* submissions of Robinson et al, upheld Jordan's appeal against the Pre-Trial Chamber's decision to refer to matter to the ASP.[142]

It would be reasonable to expect that tribunals would rely more heavily on *amicus* submissions where they have specifically asked for submissions on particular issues, and (perhaps) even more so, when they have asked for submissions from specific actors. In such cases, the tribunal is often explicitly seeking specific information or expertise that is not being provided by the parties. The view that briefs that are invited and related specifically to the organisation's expertise might be more influential is shared by at least some civil society representatives. As one invited *amicus* explained:

> I thought [our submissions were] incredibly effective … I guess that probably is the perfect confluence of events that would make an *amicus* spot-on … we are one of the key beneficiaries and key experts to weigh in, have unusual experience and expertise on that issue. We were the right people to offer information that the court would not otherwise have. And it would be information … that they couldn't easily find by doing a legal search …[143]

However, the greater impact of the civil society submissions in the *Myanmar/Bangladesh* proceedings compared to those in the *Jordan* proceedings, with the ICC specifying the type of civil society actor and issues on which they required assistance in the latter, indicates that the method of admission does not necessarily correlate with the influence of the submissions. Nonetheless, citation may not indicate actual influence on the tribunal's decision-making, but instead the use of these briefs to justify their pre-existing views – particularly where specific

[140] *Prosecutor v Al-Bashir*, ICC AC, 6 May 2019, ICC-02/05-01/09-397-Corr.

[141] Though the Chamber did note that 'In determining these issues, the Appeals Chamber has carefully considered the submissions it received from all parties and participants, including the *amici curiae*, even though it will not address all arguments made': ibid, para 99.

[142] See ibid, para 180 onwards.

[143] Interview CT2.

actors with well-known views on certain issues are directly invited to act as *amici*. In addition, tribunals may be influenced by certain submissions that they do not cite in their reasons.

Civil society *amicus* submissions have also at times had impact other than on judicial decision-making. In these cases of 'alternative' forms of impact, the *amicus* again acted most often in the expertise mode. As we have discussed in chapter four, section VI(C), one of the most frequently mentioned cases of NGO *amicus curiae* influence concerned the sexual violence charges prosecuted by the ICTR in *Akayesu*, which in turn impacted upon proceedings.[144] Arguably, gender organisations – particularly the Coalition for Women's Human Rights in Conflict Situations and Women's Initiatives for Gender Justice (WIGJ) – have strongly influenced the approaches of the ICTY, ICTR and ICC in relation to prosecuting sexual and gender-based violence, even though the Coalition's *amicus curiae* applications were not always accepted.[145]

VII. CONCLUSION

This chapter has argued that civil society *amici* are most valuable in assisting a tribunal's decision-making when they are acting at least predominantly in the expertise function, and are generally limited to providing legal expertise and information that does not directly address the culpability of the accused. While there is a role for representative and communicative submissions, given the focus on individual criminal responsibility, this must be restricted and carefully justified by the Tribunals. The practice echoes this view, demonstrating that civil society actors are most likely to be successfully admitted and have impact when providing distinctive, relevant and useful legal expertise to the tribunal.

This in turn leads to further indicators of when such submissions are most valuable. First, we suggest that novel topics might allow greater scope for influencing international criminal proceedings than areas where the law is more settled, and where the tribunal and parties are more likely to have the necessary expertise to decide the issues without the assistance of *amici*. Secondly, *amici* have more impact where they have direct experience and access to information that is relevant to issues being addressed by the Court, and where their submissions correspond to their areas of expertise, but are independent from the outcome in the proceedings at hand. Cooperating with other NGOs or academic

[144] AM de Brouwer, *Supranational Criminal Prosecution of Sexual Violence: The ICC and the Practice of the ICTY and ICTR* (Cambridge, Intersentia, 2005); R Copelon, 'Gender Crimes as War Crimes: Integrating Crimes Against Women into International Criminal Law' (2000) 46(1) *McGill Law Journal* 217, 225.

[145] eg *Prosecutor v Ntagerura, Bagambiki and Imanishimwe*, ICTR TC III, 24 May 2001, ICTR-99-46-T-2470; E Haslam, 'Subjects and Objects: International Criminal Law and the Institutionalization of Civil Society' (2011) 5 *IJTJ* 221. See also the coalition's request for a review in *Prosecutor Ntagerura, Bagambiki and Imanishimwe*, ICTR TC III, 24 September 2001, ICTR-99-46-T-2470.

groups that provide complementary insights or resources may enhance this potential. Thirdly, open calls for submissions provide a mechanism for tribunals to specify the expertise or information that will be of most assistance, which in turn increases the opportunity to influence the judicial decision-making. They may also enhance the transparency of the proceedings and increase the equality of opportunity for civil society actors to make *amicus* submissions at tribunals – though thus far, such calls have not significantly increased the diversity of the *amici*. Fourthly, tribunals are justified in being more generous with admitting representative or communicative submissions in non-trial proceedings, where fair trial concerns are not as pressing. Nonetheless, the manner in which civil society can best contribute to the quality of a tribunal's decision-making – and thus its normative legitimacy – is through the provision of additional and relevant expertise on complex legal questions, again emphasising the chief role of the expertise function. Further, representation of directly affected interests and communication of public interest concerns are usually best accomplished through mechanisms other than the *amicus* – the former through guaranteed rights of participation and the latter in fora other than criminal proceedings themselves.

Overall, though, as noted above, cases where NGO and other civil society *amici* have had clear and demonstrable impact, either on the Tribunals' decision-making or in other ways, are significantly outweighed by those instances where admitted briefs showed no impact. This raises the question of why the ICC and other tribunals continue to admit civil society actors as *amici*. While this apparent lack of impact may be explained in part by the Tribunals' style of judicial decision writing which tends not to cite influential sources other than their own institution's jurisprudence, it may also reflect the concerns we have set out above about the effectiveness of the Tribunals' approaches to identifying and testing expertise and independence of civil society actors. Enacting certain reforms that we have proposed may facilitate the submission of more relevant and useful expertise for the questions on which tribunals require assistance, perhaps leading to greater impact. These proposed reforms include clearer and more consistent identification of the expertise function as the focus of civil society's *amicus* participation and appropriate application of the criteria that we had identified for such participation, including novelty, relevance, non-duplication of party submissions or the core judicial competence of the Tribunals, impartiality and independence. We have also proposed the increased use of open calls on specified questions to enable consideration of all expert submissions before admission decisions are made rather than simply accepting the earliest submission. In addition, requiring greater transparency regarding the affiliation and funding of *amici* would have benefits for identifying impartial and independent expertise.

This practice may also indicate the Tribunals' appreciation for the more diffuse benefits of civil society participation. Even if the expertise is not being explicitly harnessed in their judicial determinations, and thus is not making substantial contributions to the normative legitimacy of the judicial decision, the legitimacy of the tribunal, and perhaps specifically its *sociological* legitimacy may be improved by facilitating the consideration of a wide range of expert views through the *amicus curiae* function. Facilitating the contribution of different views, information, and expertise, is in itself seen as valuable by stakeholders – regardless of impact – and may contribute to the values of participation, representation, accountability, and transparency. However, it is questionable whether civil society participation is indeed improving a 'democratic deficit', given the limited plurality and diversity in views that we have seen thus far, and the lack of a clear representative link between affected communities and many of the civil society actors claiming to speak to these interests.[146] Further, the potential benefits of civil society participation must be managed against the fairness of the proceedings, another key basis for legitimacy. Restricting civil society submissions to those that provide distinctive and valuable legal expertise, rather than opening participation to civil society actors in order to address abstract public interest issues or indirect representative claims, assists the Tribunals in striking this delicate balance.

[146] See discussion in ch 1, s III.

6

The Amicus Curiae *and the Defence*

I. INTRODUCTION

THE USE OF the *amicus curiae* in international criminal tribunals raises significant challenges and distinctive issues in relation to the defence. On the one hand, *amicus* submissions can be disadvantageous for the accused. The admission of *amici* can potentially undermine the fair trial rights of the accused, for example, by overburdening the defence, undermining the principle of the equality of arms, and causing undue delays to the trial.[1] On the other hand, the use of the *amicus curiae* also provides an opportunity to enhance the position of the defence, by, inter alia, enabling submissions by external actors that support the defence or provide additional perspectives on defence-related issues, and perhaps providing additional opportunities for the defence to participate in stages of proceedings where they otherwise have no right to participate. Given that the most basic function of an international criminal tribunal is to conduct a fair trial of the accused, the role of the *amicus* in relation to the defence warrants careful consideration.

Unlike the other actors whose *amicus* practice we examine, namely civil society (chapter five) and states (chapter seven), the defence is a party to the proceedings, with a right to participate as soon as charges have been laid against the accused. One may therefore assume that the defence would have limited use for the *amicus* mechanism. However, the practice of the Tribunals includes a significant number of *amicus* applications and submissions made by the defence, or by actors whose submissions support the defence position. In this chapter we discuss the practice relating to *amicus* submissions that are made directly by the accused, or by the accused's legal counsel, as well as those actors whose submissions we have classified as aligning with defence interests. As we discuss in more detail elsewhere,[2] we determined 'alignment' with the defence by making a general qualitative assessment of the main arguments put forward by the *amici* and assessing that they were in favour of defence interests. These 'defence-aligned' submissions at times explicitly supported the defence position,

[1] See discussion in ch 4, s V(B).
[2] See discussion of methodology in Annex A.

for instance by stating that the purpose of the submission was to advocate for an outcome in favour of the defence, while at other times the alignment was more subtle based on the substance of the brief. Overall, the rates of admission of *amicus* applications by the defence and defence-aligned actors are very low in comparison to those by *amici* whose submissions support the interests of the prosecution, victims, or states at the Tribunals. In addition, the success rate varies widely between the Tribunals. This reveals inconsistencies in how Chambers conceive the role of the *amicus*, and particularly tensions between the view of the *amicus* as an impartial adviser to the court, or partisan advocate for particular interests. This practice also reveals the complex relationship between the defence use of the *amicus* and the Tribunals' duty to ensure the fairness and expediency of the proceedings.

The low rate of admission is also attributable in part to the fact that *amicus* submissions by the defence, or in support of defence interests, will frequently overlap with defence submissions or address matters, such as fair trial rights, that may fall within the core judicial competence of the tribunal. There is a need for the Tribunals to ensure that admitting such *amicus* submissions does not introduce parallel lines of defence, which may undermine rather than support the accused's chosen defence. Further, as we have argued throughout, the presentation and assessment of evidence or matters directly addressing the accused's criminal responsibility must be reserved for the parties and the Chambers. Thus, in order to avoid duplication, and risks to fairness and efficiency, the appropriate scope for such *amicus* submissions is limited. However, in this chapter, we argue that there is nonetheless a valuable role for the provision of expertise and representation of defence interests through *amicus* submissions, as long as the suggested criteria are applied appropriately with consideration for the function played by *amici*.

As we discuss in this chapter, the practice demonstrates considerable confusion in the application of these criteria to defence-aligned *amici*, with unfortunate consequences for the defence. These include unduly restricting *amicus* submissions which would provide additional legal expertise to support the position of the defence, which we argue is a missed opportunity to redress the inequality of arms between the prosecution and defence. In addition, at other times, the Tribunals have been too ready to admit *amici* to represent the accused's interests. This is particularly so when states have acted as *amici*, or in cases where the Tribunals have used *amici* as a 'creative solution' to protect fair trial rights in the case of proceedings carried out *in absentia* or with a self-representing accused. The practice concerning the defence use of the *amicus* that we discuss in this chapter indicates that more coherent and effective use of the *amicus* mechanism could be achieved if Chambers had greater appreciation that the criteria we have identified may apply differently depending on the function that the *amicus* is admitted to play. In so doing, the Tribunals could better ensure fairness and efficiency, with benefits for the normative and sociological legitimacy of the international criminal proceedings.

II. OVERVIEW OF DEFENCE *AMICUS CURIAE* PRACTICE

A range of actors has sought to use the *amicus* mechanism to support the defence position at the Tribunals. Such submissions have been made both by those directly representing the accused, and by those actors whose submissions align with defence interests. These include submissions made by the legal representatives of the accused; defence associations and other civil society actors whose submissions are, either implicitly or explicitly, sympathetic to the defence;[3] institutional actors within the tribunal whose mandate is to represent defence interests, such as the Defence Office at the SCSL, and the Defence Support Service at the ECCC;[4] states whose nationals are subject to proceedings at the Tribunals;[5] and lawyers invited by the tribunal to represent the accused's interests, as a form of substitute defence counsel for self-representing accused. As discussed below, associations of defence counsel are important 'repeat players' here, having made numerous applications especially at the ICTY, ICTR and ICC. Defence-aligned potential *amici* most frequently apply to fulfil a representative function, though they are most successful in gaining admission, and having influence on the Tribunals' decisions, when acting within the expertise function. These applications and briefs primarily address legal questions concerning the rights of the defence and other fair trial issues.

Interestingly, and perhaps surprisingly, as set out in chapter four, Figure 4.5, the most common alignment of all proposed *amicus* submissions across the Tribunals is with defence interests.[6] In contrast, alignment of applications with victims, prosecution, and government is considerably lower.[7] Defence-aligned submissions, however, have been admitted at a significantly lower rate – indeed, less than half as frequently – than those aligned with other interests.[8] As a result of their greater number of applications, but lower rates of admission, the percentage of admitted *amicus* submissions that align with the defence is approximately equal to those that align with the victims, prosecution, and government, at approximately 20 per cent each aggregated across all of the Tribunals (see Figure 6.1 below). Further, most defence-aligned *amici* apply for admission through voluntary applications,[9] rather than via open calls[10] or, even fewer, direct invitations.[11] As discussed further below, this is likely a significant factor in their low rates of admission.

[3] See also discussion in ch 5, s IV.

[4] See also overview of institutional organs in ch 3, s VI(D).

[5] See also ch 7.

[6] Currently 33% of all proposed *amicus* submissions.

[7] Impartial legal advice at 18%, victims at 17%, prosecution at 16%, government at 13%, and other at 3%.

[8] Currently only 39% of defence-aligned applications made in all tribunals are approved, in stark contrast to the admission rates for victim-aligned submissions at 63%, prosecution-aligned submissions at 81%, and government-aligned submissions at 81%.

[9] Currently 86% of defence-aligned applications are made via voluntary applications.

[10] Currently 12% of defence-aligned applications.

[11] Currently 2% of defence-aligned applications.

Figure 6.1 Proportion of Accepted Submissions by Apparent Alignment – All Tribunals

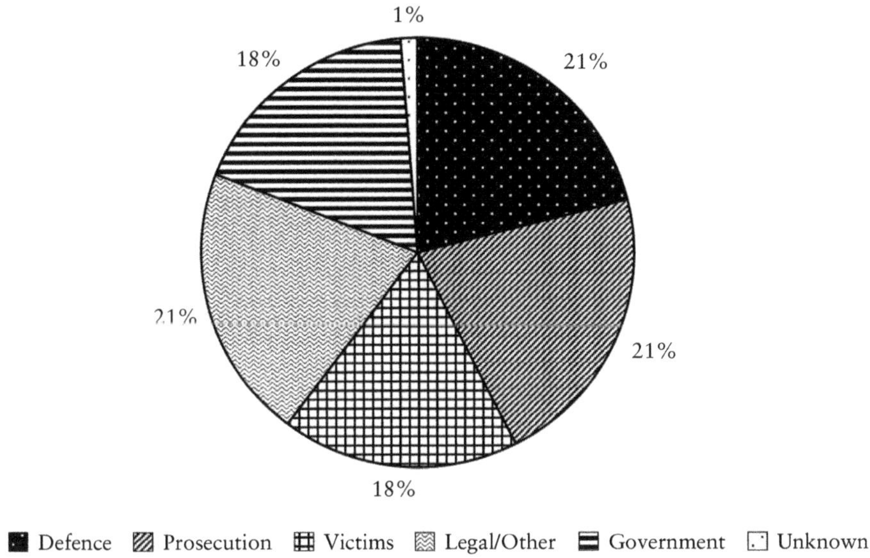

Another important consideration highlighted by the practice is that many of these proposed submissions address issues that come within the core judicial competence of the Tribunal, or overlap with defence submissions. Thus, submissions touching on these matters have often been – and should generally be – rejected. As one of its core duties, Chambers will ordinarily not require assistance from *amici* to analyse fair trial and defence rights issues, particularly given the extensive jurisprudence on these matters from both criminal and human rights tribunals. Further, as we have argued throughout, *amicus* submissions should not be used to directly address criminal responsibility, especially by making factual or evidentiary argument, as this is primarily the responsibility of the parties, including through the use of expert witnesses. In addition, there is a risk that submissions promoting defence interests will introduce parallel or alternative defence arguments, which may conflict with the accused's chosen defence. As discussed in the following sections, this has mostly, though not always, been reflected in the Tribunals' practice. Such considerations regarding fair trial, duplication and core judicial competence are likely factors in the low rates of admission of defence-aligned submissions.

The figures however reveal a large disparity in the admission rates of defence-aligned submissions between the Tribunals. At the ICC, 31 per cent of all applications have been aligned with defence interests (see chapter four, Figure 4.5), compared with only 14 per cent of admitted submissions: an approval rating of 22 per cent. Further, every defence-aligned submission was made through voluntary application. The ICTY's rate of admission of such submissions was slightly higher at 33 per cent. In contrast, the STL had the highest rate of admission, accepting 83 per cent of such submissions, followed by a rate of 51 per cent at the ICTR. At the lowest end of the spectrum, only 9 per cent of defence-aligned submissions were admitted at the ECCC, and the SCSL has admitted no defence-aligned *amicus* submissions, though only two such applications were made at that tribunal.

Why such a significant disparity? The factor that seems to hold considerable explanatory power is the method of application. The high acceptance rate at the STL stems from a single open call, in which all defence-aligned *amici* who responded were admitted. All other defence-aligned applications at the STL, of which there were only two, were made by voluntary application, and were rejected. Indeed, across the Tribunals, 100 per cent of applications by defence counsel or defence-aligned actors that were made in response to an open call or direct invitation were admitted – though it should be noted that the number of such applications is small, consisting only of those already mentioned at the STL, one application in response to an open call at the ECCC, and two direct invitations at the ICTY. In comparison, less than one-third of submissions by the defence or actors aligned with the defence via voluntary application were admitted.[12] This striking disparity strongly illustrates the value of tribunals using open calls and direct invitations to specify the issues regarding which assistance is most needed (and at times the individuals from whom they consider they will receive the greatest assistance). Below we discuss the possible factors contributing to the low numbers of open calls attracting submissions by defence-aligned actors.

Apart from the method of admission, it is difficult and speculative to explain the differential outcomes between the Tribunals. The varying rates of admission will turn, at least to a certain extent, on the quality of the applications received. It might be thought that tribunals without organs dedicated to protecting defence interests and assisting defence counsel might rely more on *amici* to do so. However, the tribunals with both the highest and lowest rates of admission, the STL and the SCSL respectively, have dedicated Defence Offices, and the ICC's Office of Public Counsel for the Defence (OPCD) has a similar role. Only the ICTR and ICTY do not have such dedicated units, and, as noted above, they have significantly different rates of admission. Though, at least part of the variation between the ICTR and ICTY is accounted for by practice related to 11*bis* transfers at the two tribunals. The focus of such proceedings on defence rights matters has attracted a high number of defence-aligned *amici*, predominantly defence associations. As the ICTR has heard more such proceedings than the ICTY, this has resulted in significantly more defence-aligned applications, and admitted *amici* at the former.

[12] Currently at a rate of 28%.

As already noted, across the Tribunals, applications aligned with defence interests most commonly sought to make submissions within the representative function alone or in combination with another function (39 per cent of defence-aligned applications across all Tribunals, 51 per cent at the ICC). However, such applications were the least frequently admitted. In fact, the expertise function, alone or in combination, had the highest rate of admission across the Tribunals (63 per cent), followed by the communicative function (53 per cent), and then the representative function (17 per cent). At the ICC, the rates of admission have been lower and relatively even for all defence-aligned submissions, with only 24 per cent of proposed defence-aligned submissions involving the representative and communicative modes admitted, and 20 per cent of those in the expertise function.

A significant set of practice concerns the use of *amici* at the ICTY in proceedings against defendants that asserted their right to self-representation, as in the *Milošević* and *Krajišnik* cases. Here, *amici* were directly invited to participate by Chambers in order to make submissions in the interests of the defence, due to concerns that the self-representing accused may not present an adequate defence without the aid of legal assistance. Such use of the *amicus* mechanism is unique in comparison to the other practice that we discuss in this study, as *amici* were used as quasi-counsel to the accused, given more extensive rights of participation than 'normal' *amici*, and appointed for participation in the proceedings on an ongoing basis, rather than for an individual hearing. Because of the unusual character of this practice, we have excluded it from our statistical analysis; inclusion of this practice would have significantly skewed the data, given the high numbers of hearings in which these *amici* participated over the course of the proceedings against the accused in question. This practice, which is discussed in detail in relation to the representative function below, also pushed (and arguably exceeded) the appropriate boundaries of the *amicus* as a partisan actor at the Tribunals.

As will be discussed in the following sections, the link between the *amicus* and defence in all the practice analysed in this chapter underscores the ambiguities concerning the need to be independent and/or impartial when acting as an *amicus curiae*, and the proper role, if any, of *amici* that explicitly advocate for the interests of a party. Associations of defence counsel, for instance, have in some instances been admitted as *amici*, though they have more frequently been denied *amicus* status due to Chambers deciding that they are insufficiently impartial. Further, while *amicus* submissions can be a valuable tool to augment the position of the defence, particularly in light of their lesser resources in comparison to the prosecution,[13] this potential is currently underused. As a result, this practice demonstrates the need for greater acknowledgement that the nature and purpose of *amicus* submissions may require differential application

[13] See discussion of equality of arms principle in ch 4, s V(B)(ii).

of criteria when assessing *amicus* applications and briefs at the Tribunals, as we have proposed. The practice of the defence use of the *amicus* in each of the functions of the *amicus* that we have proposed is discussed below.

III. THE DEFENCE AND THE PROVISION OF EXPERTISE THROUGH THE *AMICUS CURIAE*

While defence-aligned actors have most commonly sought to make *amicus* submissions to represent the accused's interests (as discussed in the following section), several have applied to make submissions that we consider to fall within the expertise function – and in fact had the highest admission rate within this function. The largest number of these submissions has been at the ICTR, with a significant number also at the ICC and SCSL, and fewer at the ICTY. Most commonly, such submissions have been proposed by associations of defence counsel or other defence-friendly NGOs, seeking to make legal submissions focusing on the defendant's fair trial rights, or fair trial issues more generally in international criminal proceedings. Less frequently, such applications have been made by individuals, academics, or states whose nationals are the subject of prosecutions.

We have earlier defined the expertise function as those *amicus* submissions that seek to provide additional expert knowledge or information to the proceedings, which would otherwise be unavailable to the tribunal. We emphasised that for *amici* to fulfil this expertise function effectively, they should generally be independent and impartial, in the sense of having no pre-existing relationship with the parties or the tribunal, and not having a direct legal interest in the outcome of the proceedings. These criteria are impossible for defence counsel themselves to meet, and may also be difficult for *amici* with strong sympathies for the defence to satisfy. This is reflected in the absence of *amicus* submissions providing legal expertise by defence counsel.[14] On the other hand, we have argued that a general sympathy for the interests of the defence (or another party), rather than a formal link with the defence, should not of itself disqualify a potential *amicus* from acting within the expertise function, if they are providing otherwise unavailable legal knowledge or information on relevant issues that will assist the tribunal. Given the greater resources available to the prosecution than the defence in most international criminal proceedings, legal expertise provided by *amicus* submissions that favour the defence may be a valuable tool

[14] Only one example of submissions providing legal expertise by defence counsel can be found, in which Mucić's defence counsel provided oral *amicus* submissions in the hearing concerning the power of the ICTY to subpoenas against a state. While the submissions were not explicitly framed as representing the defence interests in the matter, given the *amicus'* status as defence counsel, we consider these to be better qualified as representative submissions, and discuss them in the following section. See *Prosecutor v Mucić et al*, ICTY TC, Transcript, 15 October 1997.

to lessen this inequality of arms. However, in order to realise this potential, tribunals must properly consider the requirements of impartiality and independence, and not too readily exclude proposed expertise submissions merely due to a sympathy for defence interests. At the same time, Chambers must be mindful not to threaten the expediency of proceedings by admitting submissions that duplicate those of the parties, or that may conflict with the accused's chosen defence nor intrude on the core judicial competence of the tribunal itself.

The Tribunals' practice has generally been consistent with this approach to independence and impartiality. The practice of associations of defence counsel acting as *amici* is illustrative. These include applications by the International Criminal Defence Attorneys Associations (ICDAA), an NGO engaged with defence interests across the international criminal tribunals, as well as the Association of Defence Counsel for the International Criminal Tribunal for Yugoslavia (ADC-ICTY) and the Association of Defence Counsel for the International Criminal Tribunal for Rwanda (ADAD).[15] Such organisations have applied for *amicus* status most frequently at the ICTR, with fewer applications at the ICC and ICTY. These proposals largely sought to make legal submissions concerning fair trial rights, the procedural rights of the defence, modes of liability, and standards governing transfer of accused to national courts for prosecution. The bulk of these applications have been rejected. Indeed, thus far, all applications by defence associations at the ICC have been rejected, and the ICTY has only admitted two such applications. The ICTR has admitted the highest number of these applications for *amicus* status – as noted above, many in 11*bis* transfer proceedings. The defence associations have had the highest rate of admission when their proposed submissions at least partly sought to provide legal expertise (all such admitted submissions were at the ICTR). In contrast, all

[15] The International Criminal Court Bar Association (ICCBA) may play a similar role in the future. The ICCBA was established in July 2016 as an independent association to present the views of independent counsel and support staff that represent defendants, victims and other actors in proceedings before the ICC. The ASP formally recognised the establishment of the ICCBA in November 2016. The ICCBA is independent of the ICC and its organs, and works without prejudice to the roles played by the OPCV and OPCD. Its objectives include to 'enhance the quality of justice at the ICC required under the provisions of the Rome Statute and other recognized texts' through providing support to counsel, including providing advice on ethical issues, boosting capacity of counsel in advocacy, procedural and substantive law and advocating in respect of issues confronting counsel. Most relevant to our study is the declared intent of the ICCBA to 'advocate on behalf of its members with respect of issues of collective concern', including through the submission of *amicus curiae* briefs in legal proceedings. The institutional framework of the ICCBA includes the creation of an *amicus curiae* committee as an organ of the ICCBA, comprising five elected members and reporting to the Executive Council. The ICCBA is independent of the ICC, although it maintains close relationships with Court actors and the ASP. It has no legal status or rights under the Rome Statute framework and would be subject to the same procedures and requirements applied to other actors seeking to participate as *amicus curiae* (ie, r 103). As at May 2019, the ICCBA has not submitted briefs to the judicial chambers of the ICC, which means no conclusions can be drawn as to its likely practice or potential contribution in future. See Constitution of the ICCBA, available at www.iccba-abcpi.org/home.

of the associations' applications which sought to advocate explicitly for defence interests (that is, within the representative function) were rejected, as were the majority of their proposed submissions addressing general public interest issues (falling within the communicative function).

In light of their clear institutional sympathy for defence interests, Chambers frequently cited independence and impartiality, or the lack thereof, as factors both in favour of and against *amicus* applications by defence associations to provide legal expertise. In *Munyakazi*, for instance, ICDAA was admitted to provide *amicus* submissions on Rule 11*bis* transfer standards in the following terms:

> In light of ICDAA's submissions on their experience with the issues to be determined, as well as their *objectivity as an amicus, specifically their lack of affiliation with any party in the case, including the Accused*, the Chamber is of the view that granting the ICDAA leave to file an *amicus* brief will assist it in a proper determination of the case.[16]

Thus, the absence of either any formal link to the defence or direct interest in the outcome of the case at bar was essential to the success of ICDAA's application in this and other cases,[17] alongside their provision of valuable legal expertise concerning matters for determination by the tribunal. In contrast, the ICTR rejected ADAD's *amicus* application in 11*bis* transfer proceedings in cases such as *Kayishema* on the basis of a perceived lack of impartiality and a formal link with the accused.[18] ADAD challenged this decision, arguing that impartiality is not a requirement of *amicus* status. In its decision on ADAD's motion for reconsideration, the Trial Chamber agreed that strict neutrality between the parties is not required of *amici*. However, the Chamber made clear that the formal link between ADAD and the defendants at the ICTR was a factor militating against their admission as *amici*, emphasising that 'ADAD presents itself as "the only entity charged with representing the collective voice of the Defence Counsel"', and that 'its members are defence counsel who are assigned to represent the interests of individuals who have been indicted by the Tribunal'.[19]

Chambers, then, have not denied defence associations' applications purely for their sympathy to defence interests (which would had led to their rejection in all cases), but instead have focused on the lack of a legal interest in a particular case and/or formal affiliation with a party as the litmus test within this function. Chambers have also indicated that such submissions must provide

[16] *Prosecutor v Munyakazi*, ICTR TC III, 6 December 2007, ICTR-97-36-I-359, para 13 (emphasis added).

[17] See, eg *Prosecutor v Kayishema* ICTR TC III, 6 December 2007, ICTR-01-67-I-496; *Prosecutor v Kanyarukiga*, ICTR TC, 22 February 2008, ICTR-02-78-I-1364.

[18] See, eg *Prosecutor v Kayishema*, ICTR TC III, 13 December 2007, ICTR-01-67-I-507. See also *Prosecutor v Munyakazi*, ICTR TC III, 13 December 2007, ICTR-97-36A-I-365.

[19] *Prosecutor v Munyakazi*, ICTR TC III, 13 December 2007, ICTR-97-36A-I-365.

legal expertise rather than factual submissions, and must not duplicate parties' submissions nor impede on core judicial competence by making submissions directly relevant to the responsibility of the accused. In *Kayishema*, the Chamber noted that ADAD's proposed submissions were seeking to directly represent the accused's interests, and thus 'due to [ADAD's] interests in the case, and due to the fact that the Accused has defence counsel assigned to fulfil the same role, [ADAD] could not assist the Chamber in a proper determination of the case'.[20] In *Kamuhanda*, on the other hand, the ICTR admitted ADAD and ADC-ICTY as *amici*, emphasising that their proposed submissions concerned 'issues … of a general nature and not linked to facts particular to Kamuhanda's case', and the absence of established jurisprudence on these matters.[21] Chambers have also rejected applications by other defence-aligned *amici* on the basis that they sought to make evidentiary submissions, rather than provide legal expertise. For instance, the ICC Pre-Trial Chamber rejected proposed *amicus* submissions by Moraa Gesicho, a Kenyan national, in the Ruto case because 'evaluation of evidence is primarily a function of the Chamber itself'.[22]

These factors – independence, impartiality, novel legal expertise, and respect for tribunals' core judicial functions – are, as we have noted above, particularly important when assessing proposed defence-aligned *amicus* submissions, which could overlap with submissions by defence counsel and may therefore undermine the accused's chosen defence. The cumulative effect of these factors may explain the higher rate of success of the ICDAA's *amicus* applications than those of the ADC and ADAD at the ICTR. While the institutional aims of the former clearly aligns it with defence interests, it is not formally linked to any parties before the Tribunals, and is repeatedly described by Chambers as an 'independent NGO', whereas the ADC and ADAD are composed of and explicitly act for the interests of those representing the accused at the Tribunals in question. Notably, ADC-ICTY and ADAD have only been admitted as *amici* where they seek to make submissions of a general nature, rather than concerning the case at bar, as in the *Kamuhanda* decision discussed above.[23]

Overall then, we consider that Chambers have applied the criteria of independence and impartiality appropriately in this practice. The potential utility of such submissions in redressing the inequality of arms, mentioned above, also calls for a balanced, rather than overly restrictive, approach to

[20] *Prosecutor v Kayishema*, ICTR TC III, 1 July 2008, ICTR-01-67-I-716, para 14.

[21] *Prosecutor v Kamuhanda*, MICT, 13 August 2015, MICT-13-33-548, 10.

[22] *Prosecutor v Ruto and Sang*, ICC TC V(A), 8 October 2013, ICC-01/09-01/11-1020, para 4.

[23] This may also indicate that the ICCBA will be more readily accepted as sufficiently impartial to act as *amici*, given their objective to speak to a variety of interests, including those of both defence and victims (see n 15). However, it will depend on the nature of their proposed submissions and their intended function.

admission of these *amici*. Other aspects of the Tribunals' practice, though, indicate an unduly cautious and inconsistent approach to defence-aligned submissions seeking to provide legal expertise. First, as with the practice discussed in chapter five, section III(B), there is a lack of clarity as to how the Tribunals are testing the expertise of potential *amici*, and the form of expertise that is required. The ICC in particular has applied varying thresholds to different kinds of defence-aligned *amici*, which has favoured states over civil society organisations. The Pre-Trial Chamber rejected another application by Ms Gesicho, who in this application sought to share her knowledge of the context of the crimes in the *Ruto* case. It held 'that the Chamber will resort, at its discretion, to *amicus curiae* observations *only on an exceptional basis*, when it is of the view that such observations providing *specific expertise* are needed on particular topics'.[24] While we agree that the ICC must carefully consider whether the proposed *amicus* brings additional and valuable expertise – which did not appear to be so in this case – such a restrictive standard is inappropriate,[25] and, when applied to defence-aligned *amici*, limits the potential for the *amicus* mechanism to assist in rebalancing the inequality of arms between prosecution and defence at the Court. Further, this is a notably more stringent test than that applied when admitting the Kenyan Government to make legal submissions in the proceedings against both President Kenyatta and Deputy President Ruto. The Trial Chamber approved both applications without interrogating the expertise that would be provided, nor the obvious pro-defence partiality of the submissions.[26] In the *Ruto* case, the Chamber simply stated that the submissions 'may be of assistance'. As we discuss in chapter seven, it would be preferable to recognise a distinct role for state *amici* whose legal interests are directly implicated in the proceedings – as, arguably, Kenya's were here – rather than giving states unacknowledged preferential treatment.

Secondly, as noted above, overall, the number of defence-aligned expertise submissions admitted is low, in comparison to those aligned with other parties or interests. This has arguably unnecessarily limited the scope of valuable expertise that has been received by the Tribunals, and also the potential to strengthen the relatively weaker position of the defence. One reason for this is that the Chambers have made very infrequent use of open calls and direct invitations for *amicus* submissions on fair trial issues and other issues that concern defence interests. In fact, only two open calls have been responded to by any defence-aligned *amici*, only one of which resulted in submissions providing expertise supporting the defence; and only two direct invitations have been made to *amici* supporting the defence position. Both of these direct invitations were made by

[24] *Prosecutor v Ruto and Sang*, ICC PTC II, 12 April 2001, ICC-01/09-01/11-49, 8.

[25] See discussion in ch 4, s V(A).

[26] *Prosecutor v Ruto and Sang*, ICC TC V(A), 15 October 2013, ICC-01/09-01/11-1043; *Prosecutor v Kenyatta*, ICC TC V(B), 12 February 2014, ICC-01/09-02/11-901.

ICTY Chambers, and neither were to provide expertise.[27] While, as we have noted, the overlap with Chambers' core competence, and submissions of the defence and institutional actors such as the OPCD do restrict the matters on which additional expertise may be useful, we argue that there are some defence rights issues of considerable importance that would have benefited from a greater range of expertise. These include novel legal issues such as the requirement of the accused's presence in ICC proceedings, the applicable legal standards in 11*bis* transfers at the ICTY and ICTR, and proceedings in which knowledge of domestic legal standards was required. Such matters were usually addressed only by state *amici*, or by defence associations. A wider array of expertise, particularly from local civil society actors, may have been obtained had open calls on defence rights and related topics been utilised.

This is illustrated in the one open call that resulted in expertise provided by defence-aligned *amici*, issued by the STL in the Al-Jadeed case. The Contempt Judge requested submissions on the novel issue of the STL's jurisdiction over corporations, in relation to contempt proceedings against a media organisation.[28] Several defence-aligned actors, including journalists and media organisations, responded to the call, all of whom proposed submissions that can be categorised as coming within the expertise function, and all were successful in gaining *amicus* status. The Trial Chamber's decision relied heavily on the resulting submissions to justify its conclusion that there was no jurisdiction to hear the case[29] – though the Appeals Chamber ultimately overturned this decision, without making reference to the *amicus* submissions.[30] This shows the potential, and underused value, of open calls to facilitate tribunals' consideration of otherwise absent legal knowledge and information that favour defence interests, thereby assisting in improving the equality of arms at international criminal tribunals and the quality of tribunals' decisions. This exceptional instance of clear and demonstrable impact by the *amicus* submissions also suggests that such impact (which, as discussed throughout this study is usually difficult to detect) may be maximised when tribunals are proactive and precise about the expertise that would be of value to their determinations, including through the use of open calls inviting submissions on particular issues or by particular actors.

[27] The ICTY Trial Chamber invited Tadić's national defence counsel to make submissions representing his interests in the hearing of the motion for deferral concerning Tadić's indictment in Germany: see *Prosecutor v Tadić*, ICTY TC I, Transcript 8 November 1994. Also, the ICTY Appeals Chamber invited ADC-ICTY to address the interests of 'future defendants' on the definition of joint criminal enterprise in its proceedings (discussed in s V below): see *Prosecutor v Brđanin*, ICTY AC, 5 May 2005, IT-99-36-A.

[28] *Prosecutor v Al Jadeed SAL and Khayat*, STL, 16 May 2014, STL-14-05/PT/CJ-R000238.

[29] *Prosecutor v Al Jadeed SAL and Khayat*, STL, 24 July 2014, STL-14-05/PT/CJ-R001208, 4-8.

[30] *Prosecutor v Al Jadeed SAL and Khayat*, STL AP, 2 October 2014, STL-14-05/PT/AP/AR126.1.

IV. THE USE OF THE *AMICUS CURIAE* TO REPRESENT THE INTERESTS OF THE DEFENCE

A variety of actors have sought to act as *amici curiae* to represent the interests of the defence, that is, within the representative function. As noted above, this is the function within which most defence-aligned *amici* have sought to make submissions, but also the function within which the rate of admission is lowest. These applicants have included defence counsel, both representing the accused in the case at bar, as well as the accused in linked cases,[31] defence associations (whose practice falling within the expertise function is discussed above), and states whose nationals are the subject of proceedings (also discussed in chapter seven). In addition, Chambers have used the *amicus* mechanism as a form of substitute defence submissions in some prominent cases where the accused is absent or has chosen to assert the right of self-representation. This section discusses the practice of each of these variations on the use of the *amicus* to represent defence interests.

As we have proposed in this study, the representative function is an appropriate function of the *amicus curiae* when there is an actor with direct legal interests in the proceedings that would otherwise be unrepresented. When acting within the representative rather than the expertise function, it should not be expected that *amici* will be impartial, as the purpose of the submissions is to represent particular interests – here, those of the defence. Thus, a lack of impartiality should not disqualify *amici* from acting in the representative mode. While some aspects of the Tribunals' practice has reflected this approach,[32] there are several instances in which proposed representative briefs addressing defence interests have been rejected due to a lack of impartiality.[33] We suggest that in such cases, the Chambers have erred by applying this criterion to such submissions, as the criterion should be confined to those submissions under the expertise function.

However, that is not to say that the Tribunals should be ready to accept all *amici* seeking to represent defence interests. Instead, as we have already argued concerning the use of civil society submissions to represent the interests of victims,[34] the appropriate scope for *amicus* submissions to represent defence interests at international criminal tribunals is narrow. This is due to several considerations. Most importantly, given that the accused is a party with full rights of participation in the proceedings, defence interests are generally represented without the need for intervention by *amici*. Thus, to admit *amici*

[31] See discussion of what we consider to be a 'linked case' below in s IV(A).

[32] See, eg the use of *amici* in Milošević as substitute defence, discussed below, where impartiality was not required.

[33] See, eg the ECCC decisions discussed in s IV(A) below.

[34] See ch 5, s IV.

for this purpose is often duplicative and unnecessary. Such submissions also risk introducing arguments that may conflict with the accused's chosen defence, thus posing a threat to fair trial rights, even if the asserted purpose is to advance defence interests. Further, we have previously argued that independence – that is, the lack of a formal relationship with any party to the proceedings – remains an important consideration under the representative function. In addition, several of the Tribunals have organs whose institutional responsibility is to assist defence teams and to make submissions on behalf of unrepresented accused, such as the OPCD at the ICC, and the Defence Support Service ('DSS') at the ECCC. At the ICC, the Registry is also obliged to provide a wide range of support, assistance, and information to defence counsel.[35] In most instances, then, there is no need for *amicus* submission to represent the interests of the defence, and indeed allowing such submissions introduces risks to the efficiency and fairness of the proceedings.

While the reasoning of the Tribunals does not always cite these justifications, the very low acceptance rates of proposed defence-aligned representative mode submissions across all the Tribunals, set out above, are consistent with these considerations. For instance, every application in which the defence has sought to make *amicus* submissions in their own case has been rejected[36] – consistent with the position that *amici* should generally be independent from the parties in the proceedings. However, notably, the Tribunals did not reject the submissions on the basis that defence counsel do not have standing to act as an *amicus* in their own case. Instead, Chambers rejected the submissions simply on the basis that they would not assist in the proper determination of the case, seemingly leaving open the possibility that an accused could perhaps make *amicus* submissions in future.

However, an ICC Pre-Trial Chamber established reasoning that appears to disqualify defence counsel from acting as an *amicus* in their own proceedings. Counsel for Mr Ruto applied for *amicus* status to make submissions to counter adverse statements made against their client by the Prosecutor during the investigatory stage of the Kenya situation.[37] The Pre-Trial Chamber rejected the application, holding that counsel for individuals under examination did not have standing to make *amicus* submissions under Rule 103:[38]

> If rule 103 of the Rules was meant to permit a person under the Court's investigation to submit *amicus curiae* observations, it would have excluded him or her from responding to his or her own observations. The core rationale underlying an

[35] See International Criminal Court, Rules of Procedure and Evidence (9 September 2002) ICC-ASP/1/3 and Corr.1, r 20.

[36] See *Prosecutor v Banda and Jerbo*, ICC TC IV, 9 March 2012, ICC-02/05-03/09-307; *Prosecutor v Karadžić*, ICTY AC, 21 September 2012, IT-95-5/18-AR98*bis*.1-57.

[37] *Situation in the Republic of Kenya*, ICC PTC II, 21 December 2010, ICC-01/09-32.

[38] *Situation in the Republic of Kenya*, ICC PTC II, 18 January 2011, ICC-01/09-35 (emphasis added).

> *amicus curiae* submission is that the Chamber be assisted in the determination of the case by an *independent and impartial intervener having no other standing in the proceedings*.

Thus, independence from the parties and the lack of alternative rights to participate in proceedings were the key tests in rejecting this application. This supports our suggestion that the representative function is only appropriate where the interests in question are not already represented, given the duplication that would otherwise result.

Similar considerations justify the rejection of several defence associations' applications where they sought not to provide additional legal expertise or analysis, but rather to directly promote the interests of the accused. For instance, in *Munyakasi*, the ICTR Trial Chamber rejected ADAD's application to make *amicus* submissions 'in opposition to' the Prosecutor's application to transfer the accused's trial to Rwanda:[39]

> In this case, the Chamber found that ADAD, as an organisation consisting of Defence counsel who represent the interests of accused persons before this Tribunal, would not bring value to the process of determining the issues herein, and would further be duplicating the role of defence counsel.

Thus, in such instances the Tribunals have appropriately rejected representative briefs on behalf of the defence, whose interests are already represented through counsel. This avoids unnecessary duplication, introduction of conflicting lines of defence, and prevents needless waste of resources and prolongation of proceedings.

There are also instances in which actors have sought *amicus* status to make submissions representing defence interests concerning what they claim to be significant issues neglected by defence counsel. In such cases, despite the participation of the accused's counsel in the proceedings, the *amici* have argued that there is no substantive duplication between the *amicus* and defence submissions. While most such applications have been rejected, the ICC exceptionally granted *amicus* status to the International Criminal Bar (ICB) in the *Lubanga* case where it sought to address issues concerning the prosecution's obligation of disclosure to the defence:[40]

> … which are not raised in the pleadings by the parties … which will impact upon all future cases and which are central to maintaining the independence of defence counsel and a correct balance in the relationship between the parties and the Trial Chamber, as well as achieving equality of investigative arms.

While the Appeals Chamber simply stated that the submissions 'may assist' its determinations without giving further reasons, it is likely that the novelty

[39] *Prosecutor v Munyakazi*, ICTR TC III, 13 December 2007, ICTR-97-36A-I-365, para 15; see further *Prosecutor v Munyakazi*, ICTR TC III, 26 November 2007, ICTR-01-36A-I-620.

[40] *Prosecutor v Lubanga*, ICC AC, 10 April 2008, ICC-01/04-01/06-1273, para 11.

and import of the issue that was not dealt with by the parties was significant. Further, the Appeals Chamber noted that neither the defence nor the prosecution objected to the submissions.[41]

Submissions that address an issue of consequence to the interests of the accused that has not been dealt with by counsel, and which is of importance to future cases, may assist in improving a tribunal's decision-making and strengthening the defence position. However, even in such cases, such submissions should not be admitted too readily. Where the accused is participating in the proceedings, as in the *Lubanga* case, as we have already noted, Chambers must be careful not to admit *amici* that put forward a separate line of defence, which may conflict with that chosen by the accused. For this reason, the standard established by the ICTR – duplication of the *role* of the defence counsel, rather than the individual *submissions* of counsel – should generally be preferred. The risk of undermining the chosen defence is lessened if the accused has an opportunity to comment on proposed *amici*, as in *Lubanga*, though it is the judges and not the parties that exercise the discretion to admit *amici*.[42]

These concerns have been cited by the ECCC to reject *amicus* applications by the DSS, which sought to make submissions in the appeal against the Trial Chamber's judgment in the *Duch* case. The DSS's reasons supporting their admission echoed those of the ICB in *Lubanga*, namely that there were crucial issues that would not be addressed by the submissions of defence counsel, which were 'novel and complex international criminal law issues [to] be argued and determined for the first time: the final judgement will set precedents that will influence all future trials at the ECCC'.[43] The Supreme Court Chamber, however, rejected the proposed submissions:[44]

> The Supreme Court Chamber agrees with the Co-Prosecutors that 'it is not the role of DSS to serve as a substitute for international counsel through the submission of an *amicus curiae* brief.' … The Supreme Court Chamber finds that, since the Accused is represented by two national Co-Lawyers, the only appropriate capacity in which the DSS may fulfil its mandate is by offering legal assistance and support to the Accused and his Co-Lawyers in accordance with Internal Rule 11(2)(j). The Accused, through his Co-Lawyers, has the right to accept or decline the DSS' offer of legal assistance and support.

In a subsequent application by the DSS in the same appeal, the SCC held that it 'must respect the appeal strategy chosen by the two national Co-Lawyers … [and] must respect the Accused's right to have the appeal proceedings "brought to a conclusion within a reasonable time"'. Thus, rather than admitting *amici* to 'supplement' defence counsel's submissions, which risks duplication, waste of

[41] ibid, para 8.
[42] See further discussion in ch 4, s IV(A)(ii).
[43] *Co-Prosecutors v Duch (Case 001)*, ECCC SCC, 9 December 2010, 001/18-07-2007-ECCC/SC-F7/2 para 5.
[44] ibid paras 8–9.

time and resources, and may threaten the accused's right to choose his defence, it would generally be preferable for these *amici* to give assistance and support directly to the defence counsel, enabling them to choose whether or not to adopt the submissions.

Generally, then, *amicus* submissions representing defence interests should not be admitted, given the defence right to participate in proceedings. This position is, with some exceptions, reflected in the Tribunals' practice. However, as we have argued in relation to civil society *amici* representing the interests of victims, where the accused's interests are not effectively represented through another mechanism, there remains some scope, though limited, for the appropriate admission of representative submissions on behalf of the defence. There are three main instances in which this may be the case: when the accused has no right of participation in proceedings which may impact on his legal interests; in the case of proceedings *in absentia*; and in the case of an accused who has asserted the right of self-representation.

A. Where the Accused has no Right to Participate

First, it is possible that there are proceedings in which the defence's interests are directly affected, but the accused has no right of participation. For instance, at the ICC it does not appear that the accused has a right to participate in Article 87(7) proceedings against states who fail to comply with requests for cooperation pertaining to their case.[45] However, such proceedings may have a direct impact on the accused's legal interests. An example is the non-cooperation proceedings against states that failed to arrest President Al-Bashir of Sudan, in which the key legal issue was whether Al-Bashir benefited from head of state immunity. This determination has a significant impact on Al-Bashir's legal position in any proceeding against him. In such proceedings, then, it would be appropriate to admit defence counsel as an *amicus* to represent defence interests (if the accused, unlike Al-Bashir, had elected to participate in the proceedings). The ICTY previously admitted *amici* to represent defence interests in analogous circumstances, including admitting the accused's national legal representatives as *amici* in deferral proceedings in the *Tadić* case, and the accused's counsel in proceedings regarding the issuance of a subpoena to the state of nationality in the *Mucić* case.[46] In such proceedings, which are related to the prosecution against the accused, and implicate defence interests, but where the accused has no right of participation, it is appropriate to permit representative submissions

[45] International Criminal Court, Regulations of the Court (26 May 2004, as amended on 12 November 2018) ICC-BD/01-05-16, reg 109(3) only states that 'Before making a finding in accordance with article 87, paragraph 7, the Chamber shall hear from the requested State'.

[46] *Prosecutor v Mucić et al*, ICTY TC, Transcript, 15 October 1997.

by *amici* on behalf of the defence. Such submissions are indeed necessary to ensure that the Chamber considers all relevant interests.

The second instance in which representative submissions on behalf of the defence may be appropriate is in proceedings against accused in linked cases. By this, we mean cases in which legal determinations in proceedings against another accused will affect the defence's interests, for instance by establishing a legal precedent, or an evidentiary finding that will then be applied in the defendant's own case. Several applications have been made by defence counsel to act as *amici* in such cases, though all have thus far been rejected. The ECCC has received the largest number of these types of *amicus* applications, where defence counsel have repeatedly applied for *amicus* status in other cases being heard by the tribunal prior to their own, arguing that they should have input in the proceedings so as to be able to contribute to the development of legal principles that will be applied in their client's case. For instance, defence counsel from *Case 002* applied for *amicus* status in *Case 001* to make submissions on the legal definition of joint criminal enterprise.[47] The *Case 002* defence counsel argued that since the judicial decision on this matter in *Case 001* would affect the scope of this mode of liability in *Case 002*, they had a direct legal interest in the judicial determinations, and so should be admitted as *amici* to make submissions on the issue. Similar applications were also made by defence counsel in *Case 003* and *Case 004*[48] in cases being heard prior to the proceedings of their own trials.

The ECCC has rejected all of these applications, citing the lack of impartiality and independence of the defence counsel as justification. In rejecting the application by the defence counsel of the accused in *Case 003* and *Case 004* to make *amicus* submissions in *Case 002* on the admissibility of evidence acquired by torture, the Tribunal held:[49]

> An *amicus curiae* is traditionally an independent and impartial adviser to the court whose role is simply to inform and not to advocate. … The Chamber considers that, as Case 003 Application and Case 004 Applicant are affiliated with the court or its offices by virtue of their roles as defence counsel in Case 003 and Case 004, they cannot be considered impartial and independent advisers to the Chamber.

Subsequently, the Supreme Court Chamber recognised that the case law is inconsistent on the required impartiality of *amicus* submissions. Nonetheless, the application in question – an *amicus* application made by *Case 003* defence in

[47] *Co-Prosecutors v Duch (Case 001)*, ECCC PTC, 6 October 2008, 001/18-07-2007-ECCC/OCIJ (PTC 02)-D99/3/19; *Co-Prosecutors v Duch (Case 001)*, ECCC PTC, 5 November 2008, 001/18-07-2007-ECCC/OCIJ (PTC 2)-D99/3/31.

[48] *Co-Prosecutors v Nuon Chea and Khieu Samphan (Case 002)*, Extraordinary Chambers in the Courts of Cambodia, Supreme Court Chamber, Decision on Requests to Intervene or Submit Amici Curiae Briefs in Case 002/01 Appeal Proceedings, 8 April 2015, 002/19-09-2007-ECCC/SC-F20/1.

[49] *Co-Prosecutors v Nuon and Khieu (Case 002)*, ECCC TC, Memorandum, 23 June 2015, E350/7, para 5.

Case 002 on modes of liability – was rejected due to the interest defence counsel had in the legal question. The Chamber held that though '"absolute impartiality" is practically unattainable', 'it is still preferable that person's or entity's motives in making submissions lie rather in an *abstract interest* in a particular question than in promoting or producing any particular outcome in relation to the criminal case'.[50] This requirement of impartiality, or at least an absence of direct interest in the legal determination on which submissions were sought to be made, was also relied on to reject the other similar applications.[51]

A small number of *amicus* applications have also been made by defence counsel at the ICC, which have also been rejected.[52] Interestingly, the ICC did not cite the requirement of independence or impartiality as the reason for rejecting these applications – even in relation to an application by defence counsel to submit an *amicus* brief in proceedings against their client's co-perpetrator.[53] Rather, these applications were refused on the standard basis that they would not assist in the determination of the cases at hand without greater specificity being given.

In our view, despite the lack of independence of the proposed *amici* in these cases (that is, they will be affiliated with a party before the tribunal), contrary to the ECCC practice, there should be no blanket prohibition on such applications. Depending on the tribunal, and particularly the rules of judicial precedent and *res judicata* that are applied, it may well be the case that legal determinations in one case will have a significant impact on other cases. This could result either from decisions that do not deal specifically with the case of the other accused, for instance by the judicial establishment of definitions of crimes or modes of liability which will be applied in the other accused's proceedings, or rulings that have specific bearing on the linked case for instance from judicial findings of a conspiracy or group responsibility for crimes. As a result, a failure to allow for the representation of the interests of the accused in the linked case may mean that all relevant considerations have not been presented. This may not only

[50] *Co-Prosecutors v Nuon and Khieu (Case 002)*, ECCC TC, Memorandum, 4 June 2014, E306/3/1 (emphasis added).

[51] *Co-Prosecutors v Nuon and Khieu (Case 002)*, ECCC SCC, 8 April 2015, 002/19-09-2007-ECCC/SC-F20/1; *Co-Prosecutors v Nuon and Khieu (Case 002)*, ECCC SCC, 11 December 2015, 002-19-09-2007-ECCC/SC-F31/11; *Co-Prosecutors v Nuon and Khieu (Case 002)*, ECCC TC, Memorandum, 23 June 2015, E350/7; *Co-Prosecutors v Duch (Case 001)*, ECCC PTC, 6 October 2008, 001/18-07-2007-ECCC/OCIJ (PTC 02)-D99/3/19.

[52] The STL also considered appointing an *amicus* to represent the interests of an alleged member of a conspiracy that had died. See *Prosecutor v Ayyash et al*, STL TC, 22 September 2016, STL-11-01/T/TC-R287985.

[53] See *Prosecutor v S Gbagbo*, ICC PTC I, 17 December 2013, ICC-02/11-01/12-25; see also *Prosecutor v Blé Goudé*, ICC PTC I, 24 September 2014, ICC-02/11-02/11-167. A similar unsuccessful request was made at the SCSL by the Fofana defence counsel in the *Norman* case, but to intervene as an 'interested party' rather than *amicus curiae*: *Prosecutor v Norman*, SCSL AC, 20 October 2003, SCSL-2003-11-PT-1022.

negatively impact the quality and consistency of a tribunal's decision-making, but may also violate principles of natural justice and fair trial rights.

At the same time, tribunals must not threaten the integrity of the proceedings and the fair trial rights of the accused in the case at bar by unnecessarily admitting *amici* representing defendants in other cases who may put forward multiple, and possibly conflicting, lines of defence. Much will turn, then, on the nature of the interest of the accused in the linked case. If the finding of responsibility of the one accused will necessarily result in a finding against the other, then joinder is likely the most appropriate option, rather than allowing *amicus* submissions from the other accused.[54] The nature of this interest would justify a guaranteed *right* to participate fully in the proceedings, rather than discretionary intervention as an *amicus*. If, on the other hand, the other accused has a direct but more general interest, for instance because of being charged with the same category of crime, which is being defined for the first time by the tribunal and setting a new precedent in that regard, then it may be appropriate to allow representation of the other accused's interests via the *amicus* mechanism – particularly at appellate level, where the decision may have binding force. However, if the other accused has no real legal interest in the determination in the 'linked' case, for instance because there is no system of precedent applied at the tribunal and so the decision will not have legal consequence in the other proceedings, then, generally, *amicus* submissions by accused in other cases should be refused. Given that the accused's arguments can be presented in his or her own trial, it is unnecessary to permit duplicate arguments to be made in another accused's trial – which are also likely to duplicate at least in some respects the arguments of the defence in the case at bar – with the attendant risks to fair trial rights and expeditiousness that might entail. Further, there is a risk that allowing *amicus* submissions from the other accused will overburden the prosecution, forcing it to face multiple potential defences.

B. Proceedings *in Absentia*

Secondly, there are instances where the accused is not represented in proceedings as a result of a refusal to participate, rather than due to a lack of procedural rights at a particular stage of proceedings. *Amicus curiae* submissions have been employed as a method to mitigate problems caused by carrying out pre-trial proceedings *in absentia* at the ICC. Here, the *amicus* has been granted leave to make submissions due to a perceived overlap between the proposed submissions and defence interests. In such instances, in contrast to other practice discussed previously, the partiality of the *amicus* submissions, explicitly favouring the defence, has not been a bar to admission.

[54] See discussion in ch 3, s II(B) on joinder.

The clearest example of such a use of the *amicus curiae* is in the *Al-Bashir* case, in which the accused, then-President Al-Bashir of Sudan, remained at large and refused to participate in the proceedings. In the Pre-Trial Chamber proceedings considering the Prosecutor's request for addition of charges of genocide to Al-Bashir's first arrest warrant for charges of war crimes and crimes against humanity, an application for *amicus* status was received from the Sudan Workers Trade Union Federation and the Sudan International Defence Group.[55] Though the groups claimed to be independent of the Government of Sudan, it is unclear whether this was so.[56] In any event, the applicants overtly sought to make submissions in favour of defence interests, to support the earlier majority PTC decision rejecting the application for charges of genocide, which they submitted was desirable in light of the absence of argument from the defence:[57]

> There is no party in the present appeal to argue in support of the Majority [Pre-Trial Chamber decision rejecting charges of genocide]. … Rule 103 permit[s] the Appeals Chamber to receive observations from participants or *amici curiae* at any stage of the proceedings if it deems that such submissions could assist the Chamber in its deliberations. … In the absence of argument from any other party, the Appeals Chamber could benefit from submissions contrary to the Prosecution's arguments which seek, in an adversarial setting, to highlight the flaws in the Prosecution's submissions. It could not be sensibly suggested that it would undermine or harm the proceedings for the alternative view to be put, to which the Prosecution would be entitled to respond.

The prosecution opposed the application on several grounds, including that the *amici* sought to act as a substitute for defence counsel, which the prosecution argued was impermissible: 'the Application proposes to present the adversary position of the defendant, President Omar Al-Bashir, without legally representing him …' and '[t]hey are, in effect, seeking to replace the Defence'.[58] As put by the prosecution, '[r]eliance on *amicus* counsel or on the subterfuge of an *amicus* as a front for the accused himself is not necessary or desirable'.[59] The prosecution argued that, instead of appointing an *amicus* to play this role, the Chamber could appoint counsel to represent the interests of an absent accused if it was in the interests of justice to do so.

Despite the objections of the prosecution, however, the Appeals Chamber granted leave to the applicant to submit an *amicus* brief in the proceedings under Rule 103(1). The Chamber justified this decision in effect by recognising

[55] *Prosecutor v Al-Bashir*, ICC AC, 20 July 2009, ICC-02/05-01/09-27. These groups had made a previous, unsuccessful, application to appear as *amici* in relation to the first applications for arrest warrants against Al-Bashir: *Situation in Darfur, Sudan*, ICC PTC I, 4 February 2009, ICC-02/05-185.

[56] The applicants rejected the prosecution's allegation that they were in fact linked to the accused and therefore not independent.

[57] *Prosecutor v Al-Bashir*, ICC AC, 20 July 2009, ICC-02/05-01/09-27, paras 15–16.

[58] ibid, para 5.

[59] ibid, para 25.

that the *amicus* submissions would partially address the gap left by the defence's failure to participate in the proceedings:[60]

> [T]he Appeals Chamber noted that the Applicants proposed putting forward another view to that of the Prosecutor who was the only participant to have made submissions before the Appeals Chamber on the merits of the appeal. In light of the issue on appeal, the Appeals Chamber considered it desirable for the proper determination of this appeal to grant the Applicants leave to submit observations.

Clearly, therefore, the partial nature of the proposed submissions, as well as the express declaration of an intention to argue for the position of one of the parties, was not seen as a barrier to the admission of the *amici* in this case by the Appeals Chamber. Rather, the Chamber cited that partiality as a reason *in favour of* granting *amicus* status – contrary to other decisions of the ICC requiring *amicus* impartiality.

The submissions of the *amici*[61] were given detailed considered by the Appeals Chamber in its decision on the Prosecutor's appeal. The Appeals Chamber summarised the *amicus* submissions alongside those of the prosecution, without commenting on the relationship between these submissions and the defence. However, the Appeals Chamber's judgment upheld the Prosecutor's appeal, agreeing with the prosecution that the standard of proof applied by the Pre-Trial Chamber to the confirmation of charges of genocide was incorrect. As such, the *amicus* submissions did not appear to influence the Appeals Chamber's decision. It is possible, though, that they were influential in relation to the relief ordered. The Appeals Chamber decided to remand the decision back to the PTC, in line with the *amicus* submissions, and in contrast to the prosecution's submission that the Appeals Chamber could itself apply the correct standard of proof to the previously presented evidence to confirm or reject charges of genocide. The Appeals Chamber did not cite the *amicus* brief in support of this decision, nor any other source. After the appeal was upheld, the PTC applied the standard of proof as set out by the Appeals Chamber, and confirmed charges of genocide against President Al-Bashir. Ultimately, then, it does not appear that the *amicus* submissions had a significant impact on the judicial decision-making in this instance.

There are several important points to be drawn from this set of decisions. First, it provides a clear example of the ICC's support for the representative function of the *amicus*, by admitting *amici* explicitly to represent interests or actors that are implicated in the proceedings, and that would otherwise not be represented. Further, the ICC did not apply a requirement of impartiality to these applications, which it had established in certain other Rule 103 applications, in which it was asserted that impartiality was a universal requirement

[60] *Prosecutor v Al-Bashir*, ICC AC, 9 November 2009, ICC-02/05-01/09-51, para 9.
[61] *Prosecutor v Al-Bashir*, ICC AC, 25 September 2009, ICC-02/05-01/09-44.

for *amici*. This acknowledgement of differential criteria for *amici* dependent on the nature and purpose of their submissions should be adopted more widely throughout the ICC's *amicus* practice, which would help to clarify the appropriate standards to apply to *amici* fulfilling different functions. However, this decision also illustrates the dangers of using an *amicus* to represent the accused without a clear link between them. It is the right of the accused to choose his legal representatives, whereas here the Chamber is in effect appointing an *amicus* to speak for the defence without the consent of or consultation with the defence. There is no real basis on which to accept the *amicus* submissions as a proxy for the views of the accused. In such instances, it is unclear how the *amicus* submissions could be of assistance to the Appeals Chamber in making its legal determination on the appeal, other than to provide a superficially adversarial process with the *amicus* submissions seemingly filling the *lacuna* left by the absence of the accused. In this case, the *amicus* is arguably being used to provide a veil of legitimacy to adversarial proceedings carried out in absentia. In fact, rather than effectively representing the accused's interests, the accused's fair trial rights are threatened by assuming an identity of views with the *amicus*.

Given these concerns, if a tribunal considers it necessary to obtain argument on behalf of an accused who refuses to participate, and if reliance on submissions through organs such as the OPCD are deemed insufficient (indeed, it is unclear why the OPCD did not provide submissions in this case), it would be preferable to use an alternative mechanism such as a stand-by counsel. This was the solution adopted by the ECCC when a defence counsel boycott resulted in the absence of the accused in trial proceedings, instead of the appointment of an *amicus* as suggested by the Prosecutor.[62] This solution at least establishes a clear relationship with the accused, and a duty on behalf of the stand-by counsel to represent the accused's interests directly, providing greater fair trial safeguards.

C. Self-Representing Accused

The most extensive use of *amici* to represent the interests of the defence was seen at the ICTY in cases of accused who had asserted their right to self-representation, refusing to appoint defence counsel. Interestingly, as seen in chapter two, the *amicus* was used historically in certain jurisdictions to represent accused who did not have counsel in criminal proceedings.[63] This practice, however, has largely been replaced at the domestic level by the creation of legal

[62] *Co-Prosecutors v Nuon and Khieu (Case 002)*, ECCC TC, 5 December 2014, 002/19-09-2007/ECCC/TC-E321/2.

[63] See MS Chandra, 'The *Amicus Curiae*: Friends no More?' (2010) *Singapore Journal of Legal Studies* 352, 370.

aid schemes for indigent accused, the appointment of court-assigned counsel, and stand-by counsel.[64] These mechanisms are used to various extents in the different international criminal tribunals.[65] The ICTY, however, rejected the use of assigned and stand-by counsel in prominent cases of self-representing accused. Instead, in certain cases the Tribunal explicitly tasked *amici* with representing defence interests, raising submissions to support the defence case, and the *amici* were given procedural rights normally reserved to parties, such as filing appeals. Here, then, the *amici* were almost wholly transformed into partisan defence counsel.

In the *Milošević* and *Krajišnik* cases, the accused had refused representation by counsel, in both cases choosing to exercise his right to self-representation under Article 21 of the ICTY Statute.[66] The relevant Trial Chambers sought to alleviate concerns that the defence case presented without assistance of counsel may be inadequate by appointing *amici curiae* to address issues that the accused might have missed and otherwise seek to ensure that the Tribunal had access to the fullest and most expertly presented defence submissions possible in the circumstances. The Chambers also used *amici* to try to facilitate the continuation of proceedings where the self-representing accused refused to participate or acted in a disruptive manner, causing extensive delays to proceedings.

In contrast to other tribunals, which have assigned counsel against the wishes of accused,[67] the ICTY Trial and Appeal Chambers were remarkably reluctant to impose counsel on unwilling accused, despite the disruption, delay, and abuse of proceedings caused by their behaviour.[68] This reluctance largely stemmed from having held that Article 21 of the ICTY Statute and customary international law gives a 'presumptive right' to self-representation without the imposition of counsel.[69] Some commentators welcomed this as a desirable development in international criminal procedure, arguing that this approach

[64] See D Berg, 'The Limits of Friendship: The *Amicus Curiae* in Criminal Trial Courts' (2012) 59 *Criminal Law Quarterly* 67.

[65] See JT Tuinstra, 'Assisting an Accused to Represent Himself' (2006) 4 *JICJ* 47; MP Scharf 'Self-Representation Versus Assignment of Defence Counsel Before International Criminal Tribunals' (2006) 4 *JICJ* 31; CC Jalloh, 'Self-Representation and the Use of Assigned, Standby and Amicus Counsel' in L Carter and F Pocar (eds), *International Criminal Procedure: The Interface of Civil Law and Common Law* (Cheltenham, Edward Elgar, 2013) 127–28 for an overview of the different roles of stand-by vs assigned counsel.

[66] Statute of the International Criminal Tribunal for the Former Yugoslavia (adopted 25 May 1993) UNSC Res 827, Art 21.

[67] See, eg *Prosecutor v Barayagwiza*, ICTR TC I, 2 November 2000, ICTR-99-52-T-3937; *Prosecutor v Norman, Fofana and Kondewa*, SCSL TC, 8 June 2004, SCSL-04-14-T-167; *Prosecutor v Norman, Fofana and Kondewa*, SCSL TC, 1 October 2004, SCSL-04-14-T-217.

[68] Boas points to 'the inevitable use of self-representation of senior political accused of their pro se status to peddle a political agenda and obstruct the proper conduct of the criminal proceedings' as a key reason justifying the assignment of defence counsel rather than allowing accused at the tribunals to self-represent with the assistance of *amici*. G Boas, 'Self-Representation before the ICTY: A Case for Reform' (2011) 9 *JICJ* 53, 77.

[69] *Prosecutor v Milošević*, ICTY TC, Status Conference 30 August 2001, IT-02-54-T; *Milošević v Prosecutor*, ICTY AC, 1 November 2004, IT-02-54-AR73.7.

protects the fairness of the trial by presenting a fuller defence than would be possible only through the accused's own submissions, while still preserving the accused's right to self-representation. These commentators argue that the imposition of stand-by or assigned counsel would be contrary to the right of self-representation.[70] This approach necessarily involves acknowledging that these *amici* are not impartial (nor in some cases independent), as their role here is to advocate for defence interests. As with the ICC practice in the *Al-Bashir* case, discussed above, then, these cases again evidence recognition of the possible use of *amici* for the representative function. However, in our view, this practice also demonstrates that attempts to use *amici* as quasi-defence counsel do not facilitate the effective representation of defence interests, nor preserve the right to self-representation.

In the *Milošević* case, the Registrar appointed three '*amici*' upon invitation by the Trial Chamber after Milošević refused to appoint counsel, and sought to represent himself throughout the trial proceedings.[71] After reaffirming the accused's right to represent himself, and holding that imposing counsel on the accused would violate the statutory and customary international law right to self-representation,[72] the Trial Chamber noted its obligation under Article 20 of the ICTY Statute to ensure that the trial is fair and conducted in full respect of the accused's rights. The Trial Chamber justified the appointment of the *amici* as follows:[73]

> [The Chamber] considers it desirable and in the interests of securing a fair trial that an *amicus curiae* be appointed as permitted by the Rules of Procedure and Evidence, not to represent the accused but to assist in the proper determination of the case, pursuant to Rule 74.

The Chamber insisted that the *amici* were not being appointed to act as a substitute for defence counsel, and distinguished the functions of the *amici* from that of the defence counsel: 'the amicus is not there to represent [the accused] but to assist the Court … And what the amicus cannot do is put forward a positive Defence case. That would be the role of Defence counsel or the accused'.[74]

However, the Chamber then set out the functions that were to be carried out by the *amici* in the proceedings: making any submissions properly open to the accused by way of preliminary or other pre-trial motion; making any submissions or objections to evidence properly open to the accused during the trial proceedings and cross-examining witnesses as appropriate; drawing to the attention of the Trial Chamber any exculpatory or mitigating evidence; and

[70] See, eg Jalloh (n 65), 158–159; Tuinstra (n 65).

[71] *Prosecutor v Milošević*, ICTY TC, Order Inviting the Designation of *Amicus Curiae*, 30 August 2001, IT-02-54-T.

[72] *Prosecutor v Milošević*, ICTY TC, Status Conference, 30 August 2001, IT-02-54-T.

[73] *Prosecutor v Milošević*, ICTY TC, Order Inviting the Designation of *Amicus Curiae*, 30 August 2001, IT-02-54-T.

[74] *Prosecutor v Milošević*, ICTY TC, Transcript, 30 August 2001, 18.

acting in any other way which designated counsel considers appropriate in order to secure a fair trial.[75]

Thus, despite the protestations of the Trial Chamber, the *amici* were clearly intended to represent the accused's interests, even if they did not formally represent the accused in the sense of sharing a lawyer-client relationship, and were granted certain procedural rights normally reserved for the parties for this purpose. These functions were later expanded in subsequent orders of the Trial Chamber, so that the *amici* had the right to: draw any possible defences open to the accused on the evidence to the attention of the Trial Chamber;[76] make submissions on the relevance to the defence of the NATO air campaign in Kosovo;[77] identify witnesses to be called by the Trial Chamber;[78] carry out confidential communication with the accused;[79] file a motion of acquittal;[80] and receive remuneration from the Tribunal. The Chamber also repeatedly stated that the *amici's* functions were wider than those they had explicitly enumerated, since they had been empowered to 'act in any way which they consider appropriate in order to secure a fair trial'. The totality of these functions means that ultimately there was very little difference between the role of the *amici* and that of court-assigned defence counsel.

That the *amici* essentially filled the function of defence counsel, and were vested with legal standing approximating that of a party to the case, was highlighted by the decision to permit the *amici* to file an appeal against an order of the Trial Chamber, requesting more time for the defence to present its case. Rule 73 stated that only a 'party' could file appeals at the ICTY, which clearly excludes *amici*. Both the Trial and Appeals Chamber acknowledged this. Nonetheless, both Chambers upheld the admissibility of the appeal filed by the *amici*. The Trial Chamber's reasoning turned on the broad mandate given to the *amici* to ensure a fair trial for Milošević: they 'consider[ed] that the *Amici Curiae* are mandated by the Trial Chamber to, *inter alia*, act in any way which they consider appropriate in order to secure a fair trial, and that this request falls within that mandate'.[81] The Trial Chamber also, somewhat ambiguously, seemed to indicate that in this instance, contrary to their many previous assertions, the *amici* could be said to be acting directly on behalf of the accused, holding that the *amici's* appeal 'could be construed as a request for certification from the Accused's application for a two-year continuance'.[82]

The Appeals Chamber's decision rested on different but similarly unpersuasive reasoning. It emphasised that *amici* are not parties to the proceedings and

[75] *Prosecutor v Milošević*, ICTY TC, Order Inviting the Designation of *Amicus Curiae*, 30 August 2001, IT-02-54-T.
[76] *Prosecutor v Milošević*, ICTY TC, 11 January 2002, IT-02-54-T.
[77] ibid.
[78] ibid.
[79] *Prosecutor v Milošević*, ICTY TC, 6 October 2003, IT-02-54-T.
[80] *Prosecutor v Milošević*, ICTY TC, 27 June 2003, IT-02-54-T.
[81] *Prosecutor v Milošević*, ICTY TC, 25 September 2003, IT-02-54-T.
[82] ibid.

do not represent the accused, and therefore cannot file an appeal per Rule 73. The Appeals Chamber held that the Trial Chamber was incorrect to find that the *amici's* broad mandate to pursue a fair trial empowered them to bring an appeal under this Rule on behalf of the accused. Nonetheless, the Appeals Chamber held that the 'identity of interests' between the *amici* and the accused in this case rendered the appeal admissible.[83] Shahabuddeen noted in his dissenting opinion that this reasoning is unsatisfactory – the appeal was brought solely by the *amici curiae*, and if, as recognised by the Appeals Chamber, *amici* do not have the standing to do so, then there was no appeal that could be considered by the Chamber. The majority decision ultimately dismissed the appeal, holding that the Trial Chamber had correctly exercised its discretion regarding the presentation of the defence case.[84]

A similar use of the *amicus curiae* to act as quasi-defence counsel for a self-representing accused occurred in the *Krajišnik* case. Mr Krajišnik had been represented by counsel during trial, but sought to represent himself during appellate proceedings. The Appeals Chamber approved his request for self-representation, and decided to appoint an *amicus curiae* to 'complement Krajišnik's self-representation'.[85] Mr Colin Nicholls QC, who had represented the accused at trial, was appointed to this role. As in the *Milošević* proceedings, the Chamber held that the role of the *amicus* was to act in the interests of justice, to ensure the fairness of the proceedings by representing defence interests, but not to directly represent the accused. Nonetheless, the *amicus* was given a broad mandate to represent the interests of the defence, including to make submissions to counter the Prosecutor's grounds of appeal, and to make submissions in a format similar to those of a party, but, curiously, with two thirds of the word limit available to the defendant. Perhaps most importantly, the *amicus curiae* was given the power to put forward new grounds of appeal for the defence, though these would formally be considered to be raised by the Chamber *proprio motu*, rather than by the *amicus*. In Shahabuddeen's separate concurring opinion, the distinction between assigned counsel and the *amicus* was emphasised: 'The power of the Appeals Chamber to decide an issue raised by *amicus curiae* does not convert *amicus* in a *de facto* defence counsel. He does not represent the accused; he is a friend of the court'.[86] Judge Schomburg argued in a strident dissenting opinion that the *amicus's* role in this case greatly exceeded that provided in the Statute, and raised problems of conflicts of interest in seeking to represent both the interests of the Tribunal and those of the defence.[87]

[83] *Prosecutor v Milošević*, ICTY TC, 20 January 2004, IT-02-54-AR73.6.

[84] ibid, Separate Concurring Opinion of Judge Shahabuddeen.

[85] *Prosecutor v Krajišnik*, ICTY AC, 11 May 2007, IT-00-39-A-1322.

[86] ibid, para 34.

[87] Schomburg reiterated and expanded on these views extra-curially: 'In sum, the misuse of *amicus curiae* as a kind of mediator between the bench and the accused has proven to be a fundamental mistake. The true purpose of *amici curiae* is to submit arguments of states or others who do not have standing at trial, but nevertheless want judges to hear their perspective. *Amici curiae* cannot

It does appear that the Appeals Chamber in *Krajišnik* heeded the inflated role of the *amici* in the *Milošević* case, and consequently imposed some limitations on the *amicus's* functions, seeking to distance the *amicus* from the defence. For instance, the Appeals Chamber rejected a request from the *amicus* to undertake new factual investigations to support the grounds of appeal he raised.[88] It held that the *amicus* was limited to assessing evidence on the record, and to allow him to initiate his own factual investigations would exceed the 'carefully calibrated mandate for *amicus curiae*', such that the '*amicus curiae's* role would become essentially equivalent to that of a defence counsel rather than limited to helping the Appeals Chamber assess whether the Trial Judgement and other relevant rulings of the Trial Chamber are fair to Mr Krajišnik in light of the evidence at trial and the applicable law'.[89] Further, unlike in the case of *Milošević*, the *amicus* was barred from communicating with Krajišnik.[90] While these limitations were seemingly intended to bring the *amicus* back towards a role where independence, if not impartiality, was maintained, if anything, it simply made it more difficult for the *amicus* to play the representative function that was expected of him. Indeed, the Appeals Chamber stated that the purpose of the *amicus* participation here was 'to assist the Appeals Chamber by arguing in favour of Mr Krajišnik's interests'.[91] Additionally, despite the statements of the Tribunal that the *amicus* was not empowered to raise grounds of appeal, and the statutory limitation of such a power to parties to the proceedings, in its judgment, the Appeals Chamber did indeed consider in detail the grounds of appeal raised by the *amicus*, upholding several of these grounds.[92]

It is clear from this practice that the *amici's* role went beyond that which is accepted in the Tribunal's statute and the criteria that we have suggested in several ways. First, the *amici* were empowered to make submissions directly going to the accused's criminal responsibility, and made extensive factual as well as legal arguments. Secondly, the *amici* were vested with broad procedural rights normally reserved for parties, some of which were plainly contrary to the statutory provisions, such as making appeals. Thirdly, there was confusion about the requirement of independence and impartiality here. While the *amici* were encouraged to argue on behalf of the accused's interests, they were sometimes permitted and at other times barred from communicating with the accused. Further, one of the *amici* in the *Milošević* case was dismissed for an apparent lack of impartiality, after making statements in the press that it was unlikely that

serve both as pseudo-counsel for an accused pursuant to Article 14(3)(d) of the ICCPR and as pseudo-assistants to the bench. The conflict of interests in such circumstances is blatantly obvious'. W Schomburg, 'The Role of International Criminal Tribunals in Promoting Respect for Fair Trial Rights' (2009) 8 *Northwestern University Journal of International Human Rights* 1, 18.

[88] *Prosecutor v Krajišnik*, ICTY AC, 20 July 2007, IT-00-39-A-1837.

[89] ibid, para 8.

[90] *Prosecutor v Krajišnik*, ICTY AC, 11 June 2008, IT-00-39-A-5470.

[91] ibid.

[92] *Prosecutor v Krajišnik*, ICTY AC, 17 March 2009, IT-00-39-A.

Milošević would be acquitted of all charges. The Appeals Chamber held that 'In the circumstances, the Chamber cannot be confident that the *amicus curiae* will discharge his duties (which include bringing to its attention any defences open to the accused) with the required impartiality'.[93] This points to a different understanding of impartiality, which would be more akin to an ethical obligation on the part of the *amicus* in his representation of the accused's interest approximating that of counsel, though the Chamber did not discuss this in detail.

These decisions then illustrate the difficulty of using *amici* as a substitute for defence counsel submissions to protect the fairness and expediency of the proceedings and represent the accused's interests.[94] The *amici* are thrust into a hybrid role, with, on the one hand, the responsibility to represent defence interests and right to a fair trial without undue delay, while, on the other hand, not being vested with the formal authority and powers to do so effectively. The result is not only that the Chambers are required to act ultra vires the provisions of the Statute. Perhaps more significantly, it is impossible for an *amicus* to put forward an effective defence without guarantees of all the rights and duties of defence counsel, such as privileged communication with the accused, full access to the case records, investigative powers, procedural rights to present evidence and appeals, and clear ethical and professional duties to the defendant. Instead, in these cases, the Chambers grant such privileges in a piecemeal and inconsistent manner, which undermines any contribution to the fairness of the proceedings that the *amicus* can make. These decisions also starkly illustrate the concerns we have previously noted about using the *amicus* mechanism to represent interests when there is no clear relationship between the *amicus* and the actor whose interests are at stake. In such cases, then, the *amicus* is being used to give some protection for the legitimacy of the proceedings, which ultimately is superficial. Certainly, the use of *amici* in these cases did not result in expedient proceedings. The extreme delays in Milošević's trial despite the extensive engagement of the *amici*, ending with his death in custody in 2006, is illustrative.

Further, it is not clear that using *amici* in this way is in fact less restrictive of the right of self-representation than the imposition of assigned counsel – which, as noted above, is often the main justification for the practice by the Chambers and in academic commentary. While the ICTY repeatedly emphasised that the *amici* were not representing the accused, and could not act on his behalf, this is belied by the record. The Trial and Appeals Chamber both repeatedly accepted *amicus* submissions essentially as submissions of the defence – a prime example being the admission of grounds of appeal raised only by the *amici* in the *Krajišnik* judgment. Indeed, when discussing the modalities of assigning counsel in *Milošević*, Judge Kwon stated 'the amici have been playing a role that is similar

[93] *Prosecutor v Milošević*, ICTY TC, 10 October 2002, IT-02-54-D12126.

[94] See Boas (n 68); Scharf (n 65); J Williams, 'Slobodan Milosevic and the Guarantee of Self-Representation' (2006) 3(2) *Brooklyn Journal of International Law* 553.

to that of a Defence counsel already, so it may be a matter of nomenclature'.[95] It seems disingenuous then to maintain that the *amici* were not representing the accused in these cases. There is a significant risk that parallel, and potentially conflicting, defence strategies will be run by *amici* and the accused in such cases – particularly if the accused later wishes to appoint counsel and introduce new lines of argument that are counter to the prior submissions by the *amici*. Using *amici* in this way may well undermine the case presented by the defence, and undercut the right to self-representation, as significantly as if counsel had been assigned to the accused. In fact, it may be more problematic given the ambiguous relationship between the submissions of the *amicus* and the accused, and because it allows the circumvention of the formal criteria that are applied in the case of appointed and stand-by counsel.

We therefore welcome the Tribunals' practice which favours assigning counsel or using stand-by counsel in such cases, rather than using *amici* in this manner. Other tribunals have consistently rejected the path taken by the ICTY, which refused to appoint counsel even in the face of extensive delays caused by self-representing accused – indeed, the President of the STL explicitly referenced the 'recent unfortunate experiences at the ICTY' regarding Milošević's continued disruption of the trial and the use of *amici* instead of assigning counsel in that case as a reason for the adoption of Rule 59(F) of the STL RPE allowing for the imposition of counsel against the wishes of the accused.[96] The SCSL and ICTR Rules both long permitted the imposition of counsel in the interests of justice, and this is also provided for in Articles 55 and 67 of the Rome Statute.[97] Even at the ICTY, after four years of the *amici* acting as quasi-counsel to a self-represented Milošević, the Trial Chamber resorted to the assignment of counsel due to the extreme delays caused by Milošević's poor health,[98] with the approval of the Appeals Chamber.[99] Subsequently, the ICTY also assigned counsel in other cases where the accused had sought to assert his right to self-representation.[100] Ultimately, in 2008 Rule 45 ter of the ICTY RPE was introduced, which states 'the Trial Chamber may, if it decides that it is in the interests of justice, instruct the Registrar to assign a counsel to represent the interests of the accused'. The Tribunals, then, have ultimately concluded that the right to self-representation can be limited in the interests of justice. As a result, it is clear that the right of

[95] *Milošević*, ICTY TC, Transcript, 2 September 2004, 32388.

[96] Special Tribunal of Lebanon, 'Explanatory Memorandum on the Rules and Procedures of Evidence by the Tribunal's President' (25 November 2010), available at www.stl-tsl.org/en/documents/rules-of-procedure-and-evidence/explanatory-memoranda/216-rules-of-procedure-and-evidence-explanatory-memorandum-by-the-tribunal-s-president-25-november-2010.

[97] See also ICC Regulations, reg 76.

[98] *Prosecutor v Milošević*, ICTY TC, 22 September 2004, IT-02-54-T.

[99] *Milošević v Prosecutor*, ICTY AC, 1 November 2004, IT-02-54-AR73.7.

[100] See, eg *Prosecutor v Šešelj*, ICTY TC II, 9 May 2003, IT-03-67-PT; *Prosecutor v Šešelj*, ICTY TC I, 27 November 2006, IT-03-67-T-15840; *Prosecutor v Janković and Stanković*, ICTY TC, 19 August 2005, IT-96-23/2-PT; *Prosecutor v Karadžić*, ICTY TC, 15 April 2010, IT-95-5/18-T-34821.

self-representation is not absolute in customary international law.[101] It is thus likely that alternative mechanisms such as assigned or stand-by counsel will be used, replacing this controversial form of representative *amici*. As noted above, this parallels developments in national systems, institutionalising and clarifying one of the historical functions of the *amicus*.[102]

V. THE COMMUNICATIVE FUNCTION AND THE DEFENCE

We have argued throughout this study that, given the Tribunals' focus on individual criminal responsibility, the admission of *amicus* submissions that seek to address general public interest issues implicated in the proceedings is generally inappropriate. One of the primary reasons for this view is the possible negative effect on fair trial rights which may result from admitting unnecessary submissions by external actors. However, we argue that even in the case of communicative submissions that favour the defence, international criminal tribunals should take a restrictive approach when assessing such potential *amici*. Generally, the Tribunals' practice has supported this approach, approving only 35 per cent of such submissions. Nonetheless, there have been several instances in which *amici* have been admitted to address public interest concerns that extend beyond the matters directly at issue in the trial, which, as discussed below, we consider to be potentially damaging to the fairness and efficiency of the proceedings. These risks, in our view, outweigh the potential benefit to sociological legitimacy that may be achieved by widening stakeholder participation through the communicative function.

Defence-aligned communicative submissions have been proposed by a variety of actors, including defence counsel, defence associations, states (including those whose nationals are being tried in the proceedings in question), and NGOs – most of which have been rejected. Several such proposed submissions have been rejected precisely because they sought to address wider matters, rather than legal questions raised directly in the proceedings. For instance, in the *Al Jadeed* proceedings at the STL the Committee to Protect Journalists sought to make *amicus* submissions on several issues concerning the relationship between 'the imperatives of protection of the integrity of the Tribunal's proceedings with the fundamental right of freedom of the press'.[103] However, the Tribunal held that these matters were not raised by either party: 'the Appeals Panel is of the view that the matters identified by the Applicant do not address the substantive legal questions which are raised on appeal and that, in any event,

[101] See Boas (n 68), 77; Scharf (n 65), 36.
[102] See Berg (n 64).
[103] *Prosecutor v Al Jadeed SAL and Khayat*, STL AP, 9 November 2015, STL-14-05/A/AP-R000445, para 10.

the Application lacks specificity on how these matters would assist'.[104] This rejection stands in contrast to the admission of several defence-aligned *amici* who sought to provide expertise on relevant legal issues, as discussed above in section III. Similarly, in *Milutinović*, the Appeals Chamber rejected the application by ADC-ICTY to make submissions on the ICTY's new legal aid scheme, holding that this was a 'larger issue' that would not assist the determination of the appeal.[105] A final example is the ICTR's rejection of the proposed *amicus* submissions by ADAD in *Bagosora*, when Peter Erlinder, defence counsel for Ntabakuze, one of the defendants in the case, had been arrested by Rwandan authorities. ADAD sought to make *amicus* submissions on the impact of the arrest on the position of defence counsel at the ICTR.[106] The Appeals Chamber, however, held that 'considering the proposed submissions of ADAD would focus on the effect of Mr Erlinder's arrest on other Defence counsel appearing before the Tribunal, and that ADAD fails to appreciate that … the Appeals Chamber is only seized with the Bagosora et al case and not the general situation of Defence counsel in Rwanda or other proceedings before the Tribunal … [the submissions] would not assist the Appeals Chamber'.

This exclusion of *amicus* submissions that would address general public or indirect interests is the correct approach, even if the proposed submissions would seemingly favour the defence. There is a significant risk that proceedings will be delayed and possibly derailed if tribunals allow submissions of external actors to address issues beyond those directly relevant to the accused's trial. Such submissions do not assist with, and indeed distract from the primary and most important task of the tribunal, which is to determine the accused's guilt or innocence. Further, even if the submissions appear to align with defence interests, the defence (as well as the Prosecutor and the victims) is still required to allocate likely scarce resources to considering and addressing such submissions. In addition, even apparently neutral submissions may (inadvertently) undermine the defence case in criminal proceedings.[107] Thus, defence-aligned communicative submissions may still undermine the fairness and expediency of the proceedings, without giving substantial assistance to a tribunal's decision-making and should not be admitted more readily than other submissions seeking to address wider public interests.

[104] *Prosecutor v Al Jadeed SAL and Khayat*, STL AP, 25 November 2015, STL-14-05/A/AP-R000696, para 10.

[105] *Prosecutor v Milutinović, Ojdanić and Šainović*, ICTY AC, 13 November 2003, IT-99-37-AR73.2-222.

[106] *Bagosora, Ntabakuze and Nsengiyumva v Prosecutor*, ICTR AC, 29 June 2010, ICTR-98-44-A-2316/H.

[107] See, eg Hannett, arguing that Liberty's 'neutral' public interest submissions addressing the interpretation of Art 8 of the European Convention of Human Rights in *R v Khan* undermined the position of the appellant: S Hannett, 'Third Party Interventions: In the Public Interest?' [2003] *Public Law* 128, 141.

However, there are a small number of defence-aligned communicative submissions that have been admitted at the Tribunals. First, *amicus* submissions have been admitted to address the interests of abstract classes of possible defendants – rather than to represent the interests of specific accused – at the ICTY and ICTR. For instance, the ICTY Appeals Chamber directly invited ADC-ICTY to act as an *amicus* in the *Brđanin* appeal to make submissions concerning aspects of joint criminal enterprise as a mode of liability. The Tribunal held that this invitation was justified because the issue in question was one on which the defence would not make legal submissions. Interestingly, though, the ADC was tasked not with representing the interests of the accused in this case, but rather those of *possible future defendants* concerning a legal issue which 'is of considerable significance to the [ICTY's] jurisprudence as it affects every case employing a JCE theory'.[108] The Tribunal reasoned that:[109]

> [B]ecause the parties agreed on the issue before the Trial Chamber and because the Defence no longer has an incentive to contest the matter, no full adversarial argumentation on this issue will have taken place at any stage of the proceedings in this case unless the possible point of view of future defendants before the International Tribunal is otherwise represented during these appeal proceedings.

ADC-ICTY then applied for, and was unusually granted, a right to make oral submissions alongside their written submissions. In approving this request, the Appeals Chamber again emphasised that the *amicus* was not representing the accused's interests, holding that 'the Association would be arguing on an issue in which M Brđanin has no interest in the outcome'. Rather, the *amicus* submissions would 'reflect[] the interests of potential future defendants'.[110]

Another category of defence-aligned communicative submissions that have been admitted are those that address the interests of states in the interpretation of provisions of the Rome Statute at the ICC. As discussed in more detail in chapter seven, the Appeals Chamber admitted a number of state and international organisations (on behalf of their member states) as *amici* in the *Ruto* proceedings, first to address the requirement of the accused's presence under Article 63 of the Statute and Rule 134 *quarter*, and secondly to obtain their views on the ASP's retrospective application of the amendment of Rule 68 that permitted the admission of prior recorded testimony.[111] None of the state or international organisation *amici* had legal interests directly implicated in the proceedings in which they had been admitted to provide submissions, and indeed some of the *amici* were not even party to the treaties in question. Despite this, they were permitted to give their opinion on how these treaty provisions should be interpreted, indicating the Chambers' acceptance of a communicative role for these state *amici*.

[108] *Prosecutor v Brđanin*, ICTY AC, 5 May 2005, IT-99-36-A.
[109] ibid.
[110] *Prosecutor v Brđanin*, ICTY AC, 7 November 2005, IT-99-36-A.
[111] See discussion in ch 7, s V.

In our view, as discussed throughout this study, such uses of the *amicus curiae* to play a communicative role, even if aligned with defence interests, should be avoided. As already noted, and in fact recognised in the above-cited decisions rejecting certain proposed communicative submissions, such submissions take the scope of the trial beyond those issues which are raised by the parties, undermining the fairness and expediency of the proceedings. It is the Tribunals' independent duty to protect fair trial rights and prevent undue delay, and this duty should not be abdicated in the case of *amici* that (at least superficially) support the defence position. There are alternative and more appropriate ways to address the issues raised by the *amici*. In the case of abstract classes of actors, such as 'future defendants', it is our view that such interests should be raised if and when they arise in proceedings, by the actual interest-bearer or by organisations with whom they have a substantiated link, rather than pre-emptively, and speculatively by an *amicus*. As discussed in chapter five, it is difficult to claim that any organisation, even those with the extensive experience of defence associations, can effectively determine and communicate public interests – particularly of an undefined and hypothetical group such as 'possible future defendants'. Alternatively, it may be appropriate to admit an *amicus* to address the possible legal impact of a decision, but this would be better done through submissions providing expertise on this precise question, rather than a discussion of abstract interests. Further, states' interests of the kind addressed in the *Ruto amicus* submissions, as discussed in chapter seven, should be addressed in the ASP or perhaps non-cooperation proceedings, rather than in the context of an active trial, with the effect of hijacking the proceedings to facilitate discussion of states' views of treaty interpretation.[112]

Though there have been a small number of defence-aligned communicative submissions admitted at the Tribunals, some of these have had significant impact on the Tribunals' decisions. In the *Brđanin* case, while the Appeals Chamber's judgment ultimately decided against the position adopted by the *amici*, the Chamber set out an extensive summary of the *amicus* submissions alongside those of the parties,[113] considered the case law raised by the *amici*, and also 'briefly reiterated' the elements of joint criminal enterprise in light of concerns expressed by the ADC that the doctrine constituted 'guilt by association'.[114] Similarly, in the *Ruto* proceedings, the state *amicus* submissions were summarised by the Appeals Chamber, and were cited by the Chamber in justifying aspects of their judgments. This seems to bear out concerns that the admission of communicative submissions, perhaps in an attempt to boost

[112] Though see AC Loux, 'Hearing a "Different Voice": Third Party Interventions in Criminal Appeals' (2000) 53 *Current Legal Problems* 449, who argues that this 'hijacking' is justified despite the fair trial risks, to facilitate 'perspective interventions' by constituencies possibly affected by the decision in the future, so as to improve the legitimacy of the decision.

[113] *Prosecutor v Brđanin*, ICTY AC, 3 April 2007, IT-99-36-A, paras 372–76.

[114] ibid, para 428.

sociological legitimacy, will divert tribunal and party resources away from the issues directly relevant to the determination of the case within the parameters set by the parties, and so compromise other important aspects of legitimacy, including the integrity, efficiency, and fairness of the proceedings.

VI. CONCLUSION

The defence use of the *amicus curiae* mechanism is distinct from the practice discussed in other chapters due to the party status of the accused. It is also the actor with the lowest rate of admission of *amicus* submissions at the Tribunals. While this is explained in part by the defence's wide right of participation in proceedings, and the need to protect the core judicial competence of the Tribunals from intrusion, we have argued that this also stems from problematic and inconsistent decisions of the Tribunals concerning *amicus* submissions by the defence and other defence-aligned actors. In particular, confusion persists concerning the appropriate role for the criteria of independence and impartiality in admitting *amici*, and the need to consider the impact – whether positive or negative – of *amicus* participation on the fairness and expediency of the proceedings. The absence of clarity of these criteria has meant that the potential utility of the *amicus* as a tool to augment the position of the defence relative to the prosecution has been under-utilised. The lack of open calls and direct invitations targeted at defence-aligned *amici* has likely impeded the Tribunals' ability to receive additional legal expertise and information that would redress the inequality of arms at the Tribunals. The Tribunals could improve in this regard by clarifying the application and scope of the requirements of impartiality and independence and actively seeking a wider range of novel legal expertise, perhaps through targeted calls to pro-defence local actors. Provided that the other criteria that we have suggested for the expertise function – including non-duplication of parties' submissions and avoidance of evidentiary matters – are respected, that could augment both the quality of the decision-making and the position of the defence, with significant benefits for normative legitimacy.

The confusion concerning the requirement of impartiality has also been apparent in the very high rate of rejection of proposed *amicus* submissions that seek to represent defence interests explicitly, that is, to act within the representative function. While at times the Tribunals have admitted such *amici*, despite their partiality, other decisions have inappropriately indicated that such *amici* must be disqualified on this basis. This chapter has argued that, notwithstanding the wide rights of participation enjoyed by the defence, there is a limited scope within which it is desirable and appropriate for defence interests to be represented by *amici* in light of the principles of fairness and natural justice. This is particularly so in stages of proceedings where the accused's legal interests are at stake, but the rules do not provide a right to the accused participate. Such instances may include proceedings in a linked case, or at pre-trial stages of proceedings. Tribunals have been reluctant to admit such representative *amicus* submissions, largely due to a misapplication of the impartiality and independence criteria. However, in contrast, the ICC and especially the ICTY have dispensed completely with these criteria in the case of absent or self-representing accused, where there is an extensive practice of attempting to use *amici* as a substitute for legal submissions by defence counsel. In such cases, we argued that the fair trial rights of the accused, including the right to choose one's own defence, and the integrity, efficiency, and legitimacy of the Tribunals' proceedings would be better served by appointing counsel or using stand-by counsel, which is made possible by the rules of all the Tribunals. In order to protect the fairness of the proceedings, it is crucial that *amici* are not permitted to make submissions going directly to the accused's criminal responsibility. This limit has not been consistently observed in the Tribunals' practice that we have discussed.

Finally, the overlap between the interests of states whose nationals are being prosecuted at the Tribunals and of the accused himself has been apparent from the practice discussed in this chapter. This is particularly so when the accused is a high-ranking government member, as in the *Kenyatta* and *Ruto* cases. However, it is our view that tribunals should not equate the interests of the defence in such cases with state interests too readily. In particular, the unrestricted admission of state *amici* – or indeed any *amicus* whose interests align with the defence – will not necessarily benefit the defence. The use of the *amicus* mechanism as a tool to engage stakeholders and to discuss general public interest matters will divert time and resources of the tribunal and parties away from the issues and interests directly relevant to the judicial determination of the accused's guilt or innocence. This risks undercutting the position of the defence, and negatively impacting the fairness and expediency of the proceedings. As a result, any benefit to sociological legitimacy through increased participation is outweighed by the risks to other key measures of the legitimacy of the proceedings. Thus, while there is a valuable role for *amicus* submissions by the defence and defence-aligned actors within the expertise and representative functions, any communicative role should be restricted to non-trial proceedings.

7

Representing State Interests

I. INTRODUCTION

THE ESTABLISHMENT OF the Tribunals, in particular the ICC, reflects a normative commitment on the part of states parties to end impunity for international crimes.[1] States are one of the most important – if not the main – stakeholders for these tribunals. Yet, as chapter one explained, there is a paradox in that international criminal tribunals need to retain the support of states, while at the same time seeking to regulate the behaviour of state actors and officials. How well a tribunal manages this paradox, pushing forward with prosecutions while maintaining state support, will affect its effectiveness and legitimacy. Ideally, the ICC wishes to retain and engage states within the legal and political framework of the Court, not withdrawing from that system, failing to cooperate or actively working to undermine the Court. The ICC also wishes to expand its membership. To do so, the Court needs to demonstrate to states its effectiveness, efficiency and legitimacy, including through how it uses discretionary powers such as Rule 103 to facilitate transparency, draw on expertise for its decisions and enable representation of state interests.

Despite the vital role of states in the operation of the Tribunals, as explored in chapter three, section II, states enjoy limited rights of standing to initiate or to intervene in proceedings. These rights reflect the few points on which the interests of states, other than directly affected states (situation countries), intersect with the mandates of the Tribunals.[2] These points of intersection relate mainly to jurisdiction, admissibility and (non-)cooperation. States may also have particular points of intersection (and rights of participation) as host states or pursuant to other agreements, such as sentence enforcement agreements.[3] Like other stakeholders, states are not a homogenous body, and may have different views and interests, which may change as they interact with the tribunal. The interests of states vary depending on whether they are party to the tribunal's

[1] BN Schiff, *Building the International Criminal Court* (Cambridge, CUP, 2012) ch 6.

[2] ibid.

[3] The host state is often given specific rights to be heard concerning certain issues, which may include being invited to participate as *amicus curiae*. For example, the Netherlands was invited to participate as an *amicus curiae* in proceedings concerning the provisional release of Blagojević, see *Prosecutor v Blagojević et al*, ICTY TC II, 25 November 2002, IT-02-60-PT-D7753; *Prosecutor v Blagojević et al*, ICTY TC II, Transcript, 27 November 2002.

legal instrument or not, whether an investigation concerns their territory or nationals, and whether a tribunal seeks the cooperation of that state. The interaction with the tribunal will therefore fluctuate over time. Moreover, we cannot assume that the views of a state align with that of its nationals, whether as defendants or victims. Consistent with the functional approach adopted in other chapters, this chapter explores the means through which states may participate formally in judicial proceedings, as opposed to political processes, including as *amici curiae*.

The state *amicus curiae* practice shows that states are more likely to fulfil a representative function, although often in combination with the expertise function or communicative function. As shown in Figure 4.13 in chapter four, 48 per cent of all applications made by states across the Tribunals can be characterised as being representative, compared to 14 per cent for other actors. This chapter explores the types of interest states seek to represent and the nature of their participation. The dominance of the representative function affects the criteria Chambers should consider when deciding whether to accept state *amici curiae*; as outlined in chapter four, the existence of an interest in the proceedings is often used to oppose admitting certain actors, the suggestion being that they lack impartiality and independence. However, as we suggested in chapter four, the existence of an interest in proceedings does not automatically preclude *amici curiae*. In fact, this chapter demonstrates that states are often invited or given leave to participate as *amici curiae* precisely ***because*** they have an interest in proceedings. This interest makes the state uniquely placed to provide particular information or requires their participation so that the Chamber has heard all views necessary to its determination. Therefore, hearing from states as *amici curiae* boosts normative legitimacy as it improves the quality of judicial decision-making. It may also improve sociological legitimacy in that states that have been heard are more likely to accept the decision and, hopefully, to cooperate and remain within the system, rather than withdrawing. However, we argue that the *amicus curiae* is a limited mechanism that should be used cautiously given the need to maintain the tribunal's independence and fair trial rights of the accused.

This chapter also considers the *amicus curiae* practice of certain intergovernmental organisations, those organisations composed of member states. This includes the UN itself (as distinct from UN agencies and office holders like special rapporteurs, which are considered in chapter five), and organisations such as the African Union, European Union, League of Arab States and NATO.[4]

[4] Given the unique international status of the International Committee of the Red Cross (ICRC), its close link to states and unique mandate in international humanitarian law, we include it in this chapter rather than as an NGO. Due to its commitment to confidentiality, the ICRC does not submit *amicus curiae* briefs unless its own interests are directly affected, so in this respect it behaves more like a state.

II. OVERVIEW OF STATE AND INTERNATIONAL ORGANISATION *AMICUS CURIAE* PRACTICE

This section makes some initial points that frame the discussion that follows. First, as outlined in chapter four, in each of the Tribunals the test for admission of *amici curiae* is the same for states as for other actors: the submissions must assist the Chamber in the proper determination of the issue or dispute. Secondly, the practice concerning states is comparatively small, particularly relative to civil society: states account for approximately 15 per cent of applications compared to 52 per cent for civil society (academics 19 per cent and NGOs 33 per cent) (see chapter four, Figure 4.2). Several factors may contribute to the less extensive state practice. These include: (a) the limited intersection between state interests and judicial proceedings; (b) the decision by some states not to engage with judicial proceedings (or the tribunal itself) and to use other fora, for example the ASP, diplomatic means or the media to engage with the Court; (c) a reluctance by some states to be seen to be 'interfering' in judicial proceedings and undermining judicial independence; and (d) limited resources or expertise devoted to international criminal justice issues.

Thirdly, there is considerable variation in the practice across the Tribunals, with the STL, SCSL and ECCC having no state *amicus* practice at all. This is not surprising for the ECCC, as Rule 33 does not include states as potential *amici*. Issues of non-cooperation are addressed through political fora in these tribunals. Given the absence of practice, we do not consider these three institutions further in this chapter. Fourthly, for the ICTY, ICTR and ICC, the practice tends to cluster around certain issues and states. We explore below how this reflects the impact of particular rules, legal and practical issues that arise. Some states are more willing to use the mechanism as part of their legal strategy, often in support of a defendant (eg, Croatia in the ICTY and Kenya in the ICC).

Fifthly, we have classified an *amicus* as 'state' where the filing is made on behalf of the government and not by former officials or national actors, for example, members of parliament;[5] these submissions are considered civil society submissions for data analysis purposes, although their submissions may align with government interests. This also raises the issue of which actor is entitled to represent the state. For example, in 2014, President Morsi and the Freedom and Justice Party of Egypt filed an application requesting judicial review of the Prosecutor's decision not to open a preliminary examination in

[5] The STL received a number of letters and submissions from members of parliament and other national entities in relation to the contempt proceedings, which the Chamber considered as *amicus curiae* submissions but we have not included as government submissions in our data as they were not provided on behalf of the state. See, eg *Prosecutor v Al Jadeed SAL and Khayat*, STL, 18 June 2014, STL-14-05/PT-CJ-R001058.

respect of the situation in Egypt or, alternatively, leave to appeal that decision.[6] ICC Pre-Trial Chamber II dismissed the application on the basis that a state could not request a review where the Prosecutor was operating based on the *proprio motu* power.[7] However, the application also raised the question of whether the applicant was entitled to represent the state and had standing.[8] The Chamber declined to address this question, but noted that its decision should not be 'construed as an acknowledgement that the Applicant enjoys *locus standi* in these proceedings'.[9] Similarly, in admissibility proceedings in *L Gbagbo*, confusion arose as to which counsel were entitled to file submissions on behalf of the Côte d'Ivoire.[10] Further, there have been examples where the link between a state and a civil society actor is not clear, for example NGOs that seek to appear as *amici curiae*, but which the government controls or funds.[11] Similarly, as noted in chapter six, there are instances where the connection between the state and the accused is not evident. As with other *amici*, Chambers should require states, parties and other participants to disclose collaboration and links, for example, a state funding a defence counsel. For our data, we have included as state submissions only those submissions accepted as made on behalf of a state.

Sixthly, there is some overlap between submissions made on behalf of the state and those of other actors, particularly the accused, but also victims and civil society actors, which are nationals of or have links to a particular state and seek to make submissions that duplicate or align closely with those of the government. We explore this connection below; however, we do not consider these to be state submissions for data analysis purposes.

Finally, the practice suggests that state *amici* may have higher acceptance rates, with Chambers accepting approximately 77 per cent of state applications[12] compared to 58 per cent of applications from other actors (including both open calls and specific invitations) and perhaps more favourable treatment

[6] *Request Pursuant to Regulation 46(3) of the Regulations of the Court,* ICC PTC II, 1 September 2014, ICC-RoC46(3)-01/14-2.

[7] *Request Pursuant to Regulation 46(3) of the Regulations of the Court,* ICC PTC II, 12 September 2014, ICC-RoC46(3)-01/14-3, para 9.

[8] See the Request, which mentions that President Morsi, as the head of a democratically elected government, should be considered as effectively the state: *Request Pursuant to Regulation 46(3) of the Regulations of the Court,* ICC PTC II, 1 September 2014, ICC-RoC46(3)-01/14-2-AnxA, para 14.

[9] *Request Pursuant to Regulation 46(3) of the Regulations of the Court,* ICC PTC II, 12 September 2014, ICC-RoC46(3)-01/14-3, para 11.

[10] *Prosecutor v L Gbagbo,* ICC PTC I, 15 August 2012, ICC-02/11-01/11-212.

[11] Although this issue was not formally raised in admissibility proceedings, this appeared to be the suggestion concerning one request in the *Myanmar/Bangladesh* proceedings, the request by the Thayninga Institute for Strategic Studies: *Request Under Regulation 46(3) of the Regulations of the Court,* ICC PTC I, 6 August 2018, ICC-RoC46(3)-01/18-34; and in relation to the Sudan Workers Trade Unions Federation and Sudan International Defence Group: see *Situation in Darfur, Sudan,* ICC PTC I, 11 January 2009, ICC-02/05-170.

[12] See Figure 5.1, ch 5.

procedurally. The method of admission does not explain this variation in acceptance rates; although there have been more calls and specific invitations aimed at states than other actors, of state applications, 63 per cent were voluntary applications compared to 66 per cent for other actors. Therefore, states are not meaningfully more likely than other actors to participate via open calls or a specific invitation. Moreover, where states do apply on a voluntary basis, they are more likely to be accepted (61 per cent approved for states compared to 41 per cent approved for other actors).

For international organisations, there is even less practice. Across the Tribunals, there have been fewer than ten *amicus curiae* applications by international organisations. Therefore, rather than analyse this practice separately, we have incorporated it into the broader discussion of state *amici*. Chambers generally invite international organisations to participate, which explains a higher acceptance rate. One issue is whether an international organisation is representing its own particular interest, the interest of its member states (and whether it should be assumed that the interests will always coincide) or a broader constituency (eg, the African Union's claim to act on behalf of 'African citizens' that may end up as accused before the ICC). There is insufficient practice to draw conclusions; however, we highlight relevant examples where possible. The next sections disaggregate state and international organisation *amicus curiae* practice according to our typology of functions: expertise, representative and communicative.

III. STATE AND INTERNATIONAL ORGANISATION *AMICI* PROVIDING EXPERTISE

States and international organisations may provide information, often as to the national context, including national laws, the national legal system and relevant national proceedings. This role is the focus of this section. There is no requirement in the ICTY, ICTR and ICC for judges of the nationality of the affected state (both territorial and nationality of the accused) to be in a Chamber.[13] One function of the national judge in human rights institutions is to explain points of national law, procedure or practice relevant to the decision. This means that at the ICTY, ICTR and ICC, there is usually no judicial expertise in or familiarity with the local context, including the local laws and legal system. The ICC may feel the absence of national judges more keenly than the ICTY and ICTR, as there is a wider range of situation countries and closer engagement between the ICC and national jurisdictions, particularly concerning complementarity and cooperation. There are several examples of state *amici curiae* providing information to Chambers concerning their national laws and procedure. In this sense, the state is fulfilling an expertise function. However, this information is mainly

[13] Ch 3, s V(A).

provided in association with what we categorise as a representative function, as there is some direct legal effect for the state as a result of the Chamber's decision. For example, a Trial Chamber permitted Kenya to submit observations as to the implications of its potential withdrawal from the Rome Statute where the accused are its nationals.[14] The need for a state to participate as an *amicus curiae* to fulfil this role is relatively rare since, as detailed below, affected states have specific participatory rights that enable the provision of this information to the Chamber directly. Moreover, states may give information directly to the OTP during consultations in the preliminary examination or investigation phase or to the defence during trial.

Two questions arise from states performing an expertise function. First, is the state the *only* actor that can provide information on national legal systems or can other actors also fulfil this role, perhaps to provide competing interpretations of national law? In proceedings concerning South Africa's failure to arrest and surrender President Al-Bashir of Sudan, the Pre-Trial Chamber admitted a national NGO as an *amicus*, despite the strong opposition of the government,[15] to provide submissions on national law and South Africa's obligations under national law.[16] In the ICTR, the Referral Chamber prioritised *amicus curiae* submissions by Rwanda on domestic law issues over submissions from civil society actors, including the Kigali Bar Association, on the basis that the government is best placed to make submissions on many legal issues.[17] The civil society *amici* were limited to specific issues that would supplement, rather than duplicate, the government's submissions.

These examples indicate that, while Chambers have recognised that the government is often the most appropriate actor to provide such information, it is not the only actor capable of doing so, nor is the state's interpretation of national law the only one. Admitting other *amici* as well as the state may be a way of countering the problem of potential bias in the information provided by states. However, this is not a particularly useful approach where there are disputed understandings of national law, as *amici* generally cannot respond to submissions of the parties or other *amici*.[18] For example, in *Uwinkindi*, Rwanda sought unsuccessfully to respond to submissions by other *amici* that it suggested were 'largely speculative and rely on incorrect information regarding the functioning of the Rwandan judicial system' and 'distort available facts and information',

[14] *Prosecutor v Ruto and Sang*, ICC TC (VA), 8 October 2013, ICC-01/9-01/11-1021, para 7, recognising that submissions on the possible impact of resolutions regarding withdrawal from the Rome Statute, particularly as regards witnesses to testify in the case, would 'be desirable for the proper administration of the issues under consideration'.

[15] *Prosecutor v Al-Bashir,* ICC PTC II, 27 February 2017, ICC-02/05-01/09-281.

[16] *Prosecutor v Al-Bashir,* ICC PTC II, 27 January 2017, ICC-02/05-01/09-275; *Prosecutor v Al-Bashir,* ICC PTC II, 28 February 2017, ICC-02/05-01/09-283.

[17] *Prosecutor v Hategekimana*, ICTR TC, 4 December 2007, ICTR-00-55B-I-84; *Prosecutor v Hategekimana*, ICTR TC, 20 March 2008, ICTR-00-55B-I-377.

[18] Note that the state participating in non-cooperation proceedings is considered a participant and can respond to submissions by *amici* on its legal system: see s IV(B)(ii)(b) below.

particularly around issues such as judicial independence, corruption and political interference.[19] The shift to specific participatory rights where Chambers are likely to require certain information from states may partly address this problem.

A second issue is whether submissions on national law constitute factual or legal information, or a combination of both. *Amici curiae* should generally provide submissions on legal issues to maintain the distinction between the *amicus curiae* and the presentation of evidence, which is for the parties and expert witnesses.[20] That said, submissions concerning national legal systems have included mixed issues of law and fact, with information such as existence of crimes in local law, prosecution or conviction rates and details of victim and witness protection schemes, for example, being considered as factual submissions rather than legal. Information concerning national legal systems is unlikely to implicate the individual criminal responsibility of the accused and arises mainly in relation to admissibility or cooperation. Accordingly, in this context, the provision of mixed legal and factual or purely factual information by *amici curiae* is appropriate, provided the parties are able to respond to the submissions. However, where such material strays into issues where there may be disagreement, for example the fairness or independence of local proceedings, the Chamber may wish to supplement such material by specific submissions from the parties and the state concerned, as well as additional, non-state *amici* so as to increase the range of perspectives heard.

IV. THE STATE OR INTERNATIONAL ORGANISATION *AMICI* REPRESENTING AN INTEREST

The practice suggests two types of 'interest' that states may seek to protect. First, states may seek to intervene on behalf of nationals. Secondly, states make seek to intervene to protect a legal interest the state has in the outcome of the proceedings. This section will therefore explore how states have relied upon the *amicus curiae* and other mechanisms to protect these interests.

A. Representation of Nationals

The Tribunals do not recognise a right for a state to represent nationals directly or to intervene on their behalf.[21] This applies regardless of whether the national is a victim or an accused. Given the provisions on assignment of legal counsel

[19] *Prosecutor v Uwinkindi,* ICTR TC II, 4 April 2011, ICTR-01-75-PT-3761; *Prosecutor v Uwinkindi,* ICTR TC II, 8 April 2011, ICTR-01-75-PT-3787.

[20] Ch 4, s V(H).

[21] ICC regulations do recognise the right of the state of nationality to offer diplomatic or consular assistance to the accused: see International Criminal Court, Regulations of the Court (26 May 2004, as amended on 12 November 2018) ICC-BD/01-05-16, reg 98.

to all accused, and availability of additional defence expertise, there is no need for states to represent the interests of a national accused of committing crimes. The state can assist a national informally, including through directly engaging lawyers or providing financial and other assistance to defence teams. This is particularly likely where the accused is an incumbent senior state official and less likely where the accused is a former official and there has been a change in power or where the accused is an opponent of the current government. There is a risk, however, that a state 'managed' defence may be inconsistent with the provision of proper legal assistance to the accused, particularly where the state interest may conflict with the best strategy for an individual accused. For example, the state may wish to deny the existence of a state policy, while the best strategy for an accused may be to accept the existence of the policy but to deny his or her role in achieving that policy through the commission of crimes.

Despite this clear position, there are examples of states seeking to intervene as *amici curiae* on behalf of nationals, mainly by suggesting that intervention is necessary to protect the fair trial rights of the national. For example, Croatia sought to intervene in ICTY cases on behalf of nationals, namely senior officials and military personnel, that it argued were 'unindicted accused'; that is, individuals that are likely to be implicated in judicial findings, for example being named as part of a joint criminal enterprise, but are not or not yet the subject of prosecution.[22] In *Prlić*, Croatia sought to represent the interests of three deceased nationals found in the trial judgment to have been participants in the joint criminal enterprise.[23] Croatia argued that this violated the presumption of innocence, as the officials would never have an opportunity to refute the finding.[24] The Appeals Chamber rejected the *amicus* application, noting that the findings in the judgment were binding only on the accused in that case.[25] Similarly, Kenya and the African Union have sought to make submissions as *amici* partly based on the implication of the decision for the fair trial rights of their nationals (Kenya)[26] or for 'African suspects' (African Union).[27] While the Appeals Chamber rejected Kenya's request, it permitted the African Union to participate;[28] however, as discussed in section V, the African Union brief was fulfilling more of a communicative function than representative.

With respect to victims, the Prosecutor and legal representatives of victims (LRV) represent the interests of victims, not the state of nationality. There are examples of states seeking to represent their nationals as victims of crimes,

[22] This distinguishes unindicted co-perpetrators from accused in other cases, discussed in ch 6.
[23] *Prosecutor v Prlić et al*, ICTY AC, 18 July 2016, IT-04-74-A-21059 [3].
[24] ibid [4].
[25] ibid [9].
[26] See *Prosecutor v Ruto and Sang*, ICC AC, 23 September 2015, ICC-01/09-01/11-1972, para 15: 'may have a significant impact on the fundamental human rights of the accused persons who are citizens of the Republic of Kenya'.
[27] *Prosecutor v Ruto and Sang*, ICC AC, 5 October 2015, ICC-01/09-01/11-1983-Anx, para 25.
[28] *Prosecutor v Ruto and Sang*, ICC AC, 12 October 2015, ICC-01-09-01/11-1987.

particularly in the ICTR where victim participation was not available. Both Rwanda and Belgium applied to appear as *amici curiae* in ICTR proceedings on behalf of their nationals. Rwanda sought to make submissions in relation to restitution of property taken by the accused.[29] Belgium sought to make submissions concerning the existence of ICTR jurisdiction to prosecute the accused for the deaths of ten Belgian peacekeepers and to present the Belgian authorities who had investigated alleged crimes in Rwanda as witnesses. Further, Belgium argued that its participation would enable nationals harmed to appear 'as plaintiffs and not as mere witnesses' in relation to sentencing and compensation.[30] Based on their national civil law systems, both states attempted to persuade the Chamber to allow the state to represent the victims effectively as civil parties with broader participatory rights, including the ability to call witnesses and to adduce other evidence, via the *amicus curiae* mechanism. The respective Chambers rejected the applications.[31] Rwanda's request was rejected on the basis it was premature (separate proceedings would be held for restitution, after any conviction).[32] The Chamber noted that the request effectively sought provisional measures and the right to produce evidence during trial, for which Rule 74 does not provide.[33] After having heard oral submissions from the parties and the representative of Belgium,[34] the Chamber rejected Belgium's second request, as the presentation of witnesses is a matter for the parties and not *amici curiae*, and the third request as not being ripe for consideration, as there had not been a conviction.[35] However, the Chamber permitted Belgium to make submissions as to jurisdiction to prosecute the accused for the deaths of the ten Belgian peacekeepers, as the 'clarification of issues centering on Crimes Against Humanity, as it relates to the Bagosora matter, will be an important technical question in the proper determination of the present case'.[36]

This is an example where a Chamber has allowed a state to make legal submissions based on its nationals being victims of the crimes before the Chamber. However, Chambers should be cautious when admitting states as *amici curiae* to represent their nationals, as other mechanisms are available. We suggest that the Chamber was too permissive in this instance, and the more appropriate mechanism was for Belgium to provide any evidence and legal arguments to the Prosecutor, rather than as an *amicus curiae*, as the legal analysis was likely to be directly relevant to the criminal responsibility of the accused. In any event, as Belgium had not filed its submissions by the conclusion of the

[29] *Prosecutor v Bagosora et al*, ICTR TC, 20 April 1998, ICTR-96-7-I-315.

[30] The request by Belgium is not publicly available, so the requests are taken from the admission decision: *Prosecutor v Bagosora et al*, ICTR TC II, 6 June 1998, ICTR-96-7-T.

[31] *Prosecutor v Bagosora et al*, ICTR TC I, 13 October 2004, ICTR-98-41-T-22076.

[32] ibid, para 6.

[33] ibid, para 7.

[34] *Prosecutor v Bagosora et al*, ICTR TC II, Transcript, 13 March 1998.

[35] *Prosecutor v Bagosora et al*, ICTR TC II, 6 June 1998, ICTR-96-7-T.

[36] ibid.

trial, and the prosecution had led substantial evidence regarding the deaths of the Belgian peacekeepers, the Chamber reconsidered its decision and found that *amicus curiae* submissions from Belgium would no longer be of assistance.[37]

B. Representing a *State* Interest

Rights of intervention in other international institutions require the proceedings or the outcome of the proceedings to affect a *legal* interest of the state (see chapter two, section IV(A)). Given the focus on individual criminal responsibility, it is difficult to envisage how a judgment of an international criminal tribunal could directly affect a legal interest of a state. However, we distinguish here between two types of proceedings: the 'core' proceedings, namely trials; and related, but distinct, proceedings concerning the obligations or rights of states. We consider these distinct types of proceedings separately, although we recognise they overlap in the sense that decisions concerning cooperation will influence trial proceedings, including whether a trial can happen at all. There is also often overlap between representing a state protecting the interests of its nationals (see above) and protecting its own interests.

i. State Interests Arising in Trial Proceedings

Trial proceedings do not draw conclusions as to the responsibility of the state for violations of international law or apply principles of state responsibility.[38] Legally, the trial judgments of the Tribunals are not directed at nor binding upon states. Nor are they binding on other tribunals, either internationally or nationally, although they may form a subsidiary source of international law under Article 38(1)(d) of the ICJ Statute. That said, in the course of individual criminal proceedings, the Tribunals make conclusions concerning the role of the state and state actors in the commission of crimes. Trial judgments potentially influence proceedings for state responsibility in other international fora or national proceedings directed at reparations. For example, Bosnia, Croatia and Serbia faced the prospect that findings made in the ICTY might influence judicial proceedings before the ICJ.[39] While some states attempt to rebut arguments regarding potential state responsibility through the legal arguments

[37] *Prosecutor v Bagosora et al*, ICTR TC I, 13 February 2007, ICTR-98-41-T-32407, para 6.

[38] The potential exception here is the crime of aggression, which overlaps with state responsibility for violating the prohibition on aggression. Given the absence of practice, as the Court has not yet exercised jurisdiction in respect of aggression, we have not considered this further. However, see S Williams, 'Aggression, Affected States, and a Right to Participate: A Response to Koh and Buchwald' (2015) 109 *AJIL Unbound* 246.

[39] See eg *Application of the Convention on the Prevention and Punishment of the Crime of Genocide* (*Croatia v Serbia*) (Merits) [2015] ICJ Rep 5.

of the accused (see above), states have also sought to participate as *amici curiae* to protect their own 'interest' in trial proceedings. States have also claimed that they, as distinct from the accused, are entitled to 'fair trial rights' which include more extensive rights of participation.[40]

The most obvious example of this is Croatia's attempts to intervene in several cases before the ICTY. In addition to raising the interests of its nationals, Croatia asserted that there was a distinct *state* interest the trial would affect. Croatia signalled its intent as early as April 1996, when the government wrote to the President of the ICTY requesting that Croatia be given leave to appear as an *amicus curiae* 'in all matters involving its responsibility, rights and legal interests'.[41] While the President did not (and could not) grant that blanket request, the government sought permission from Trial Chamber II to appear as an *amicus curiae* in the Rule 61[42] proceedings in *Rajić*. Croatia sought to make submissions as to the nature of the armed conflict, particularly by giving notice of facts that would give rise to a competing view of the nature of the conflict to that offered by the Prosecutor.[43] Croatia noted that its 'sole interest' was to present 'its views and supporting evidence related to the character of the conflict'.[44] The prosecution objected, arguing that this request was a challenge to a substantive issue of fact, which are to be determined at trial and not during the Rule 61 proceedings, which are *ex parte*, and that at this stage of proceedings Croatia had no standing to submit a brief or to appear as an *amicus curiae*. Moreover, Croatia should pass any evidence in its possession to the prosecution.[45] The Presiding Judge, apparently based on the prosecution submissions, rejected the request, although without prejudice to a further request at trial.[46]

Croatia again sought to appear as an *amicus curiae* in *Gotovina et al* in 2006. Croatia indicated that the brief 'would assist in the determination of truth regarding the allegation [...] that the then state and military leadership of the Republic of Croatia participated in the joint criminal enterprise, which was crucial for the accurate determination of the broader context of the events to which the Indictment relates ... and the role, conduct and criminal responsibility of the Accused'.[47] Croatia also asserted that its arguments would assist 'in the interpretation of historical and political facts' and in 'a reliable historical and political record of events, as well as a legal record of events surrounding

[40] See the discussion concerning Croatia, below and *Prosecutor v L Gbagbo*, ICC AC, 8 October 2012, ICC-02/11-01/11-258-tENG, para 3.

[41] Letter from Ambassador of the Republic of Croatia to President Cassese (10 April 1996, on file with author).

[42] Rule 61 requires the Prosecutor to establish a prima facie case.

[43] *Prosecutor v Rajić*, ICTY TC II, 30 April 1996, IT-95-12-R61-D556.

[44] ibid.

[45] *Prosecutor v Rajić*, ICTY TC II, 15 May 1996, IT-95-12-R61-D568.

[46] *Prosecutor v Rajić*, ICTY TC II, 24 May 1996, IT-95-12-R61-D571.

[47] *Prosecutor v Gotovina et al*, ICTY TC II, 18 October 2006, IT-06-90-PT-284, 1.

international crimes committed'.[48] The Prosecutor opposed the request, while the defence supported it. The Chamber rejected Croatia's request as the proposed submissions 'appear to deal essentially with questions of fact, such as the existence and scope of the alleged joint criminal enterprise and the broader historical and political context'.[49] It reiterated that parties should address factual matters during the trial and Croatia should provide the relevant material to the parties.[50] Croatia subsequently sought a review of this decision under Rule 108*bis* (see below), in which Croatia sought to clarify that its *amicus curiae* submission would be providing 'argumentation regarding legal construction of the joint criminal enterprise' as advanced by the prosecution. While the Chamber had not raised Croatia's interest as a barrier to participation as an *amicus* in its initial decision, the prosecution had.[51] In its application for review Croatia challenged the notion that having an interest in proceedings precluded *amicus curiae* participation, referring to the US practice where *amici* may have 'strong, maybe even partial positions'.[52] The Chamber did not engage with these submissions as it rejected the request.[53]

In the *Prlić et al* proceedings, Croatia sought to participate as an *amicus curiae*, suggesting that its brief would rely on several experts to help to clarify 'issues on the participation of the political and military leaders in the joint criminal enterprise'.[54] Trial Chamber III rejected this request on the basis it would address mainly factual issues, but also because the intended submissions went beyond the scope of the indictment.[55] Moreover, unlike in *Gotovina*, Trial Chamber III linked the rejection to Croatia's partiality: 'it would not be in the interests of justice to authorise a State, whose former political and military leaders are mentioned in the Indictment as being participants in a joint criminal enterprise, to appear in the proceedings as *amicus curiae*'.[56]

In 2012, Croatia sought to participate in the appellate stage of the *Gotovina et al* proceedings by filing a confidential 'Motion to Intervene and Statement of Interest'.[57] Croatia argued that the Appeals Chamber should recognise a right for states to intervene or to file a statement of interest, particularly given the development of the doctrine of joint criminal enterprise. It suggested that the Trial Chamber 'effectively held Croatia liable for the crimes encompassed by the joint criminal enterprise' and 'where a state is found to have participated in a crime

[48] ibid, 2.
[49] ibid.
[50] ibid, 3.
[51] *Prosecutor v Gotovina et al*, ICTY TC II, 2 October 2006, IT-06-90-PT, paras 20–26.
[52] *Prosecutor v Gotovina et al*, ICTY AC, 25 October 2006, IT-06-90-AR108*bis*.1-5, para 3.
[53] *Prosecutor v Gotovina et al*, ICTY AC, 13 December 2006, IT-06-90-AR108*bis*.1-41.
[54] *Prosecutor v Prlić et al*, ICTY TC III, 11 October 2006, IT-04-74-T-26753, 2 (the original request is not available).
[55] ibid, 4.
[56] ibid, 5.
[57] The motion is not available, but was filed on 16 December 2001, and its contents are described in *Prosecutor v Gotovina et al*, ICTY AC, 8 February 2012, IT-06-90-4-k557.

by reason of actions taken by individual members of that state's government, the state should have "at least" a limited right to intervene and explain its interest'.[58] Moreover, Croatia asserted that customary international law recognises intervention to protect the interests of third parties. Its interests were directly affected and distinct from the accused, namely as the decision negatively impacts its office holders' ability to perform foreign policy decisions, harmed Croatia's legitimacy in international institutions, and was being used as a negative precedent in cases against Croatia in other international and national courts.[59]

The Appeals Chamber rejected the motion, distinguishing its mandate and rules from those of other institutions that allow intervention and statements of interest. Importantly for our purposes, the Chamber stated that the suggestion 'that individual criminal trials and appeals become a forum for exposition and consideration of state interests different from accused individuals, would both expand the Tribunal's jurisdiction beyond the limits set in the Statute and detract from the Tribunal's focus on individual criminal responsibility'.[60] The Chamber also rejected the alternative request to appear as an *amicus curiae*, not being satisfied that submissions would assist it in its determination of the issues.[61]

In the *Prlić* appeal proceedings, the Appeals Chamber denied a further request by Croatia, emphasising that in no way did a finding regarding the criminal responsibility of the accused pursuant to a joint criminal enterprise 'constitute findings of responsibility on the part of the state of Croatia'.[62] When Croatia sought reconsideration of that decision, and asked for the statement as to no liability against Croatia to be included in the judgment, the Appeals Chamber found that Croatia had no standing to file a motion regarding the content of a judgment.[63]

This is not to say that state interests will never support participation during trial. As noted above, Rwanda sought to intervene in ICTR proceedings to seek restitution of state property misappropriated or destroyed by the accused. The Chamber rejected this request as not being relevant to the stage of proceedings, but did not reject the notion of participation.[64] Belgium was able to file submissions regarding the ICTR's jurisdiction to prosecute the deaths of its nationals.[65] In *Semanza*, Belgium was given leave to file submissions regarding the 'scope of Common Article 3 and Additional Protocol II', which it suggested had been interpreted too restrictively in previous ICTR jurisprudence.[66] Belgium's request noted Belgium was 'affected particularly by the events in Rwanda' and had a

[58] ibid, para 9.
[59] ibid, para 10.
[60] ibid, para 15.
[61] ibid, para 21.
[62] *Prosecutor v Prlić et al*, ICTY AC, 18 July 2016, IT-04-74-A-21059, para 9.
[63] *Prosecutor v Prlić et al*, ICTY AC, 4 July 2017, IT-04-74-A-22158, 2.
[64] *Prosecutor v Bagosora et al*, ICTR TC I, 13 October 2004, ICTR-98-41-T-22076.
[65] *Prosecutor v Bagosora et al*, ICTR TC II, 6 June 1998, ICTR-96-7-T.
[66] *Prosecutor v Semanza*, ICTR TC III, 9 February 2001, ICTR-97-20-T-4702.

'special interest in following certain cases before the Tribunal'.[67] The Chamber did not engage with this 'special interest', but we presume this was its former colonial status and the presence of its peacekeepers in Rwanda; unlike in other cases in which Belgium sought to intervene, this case did not directly concern the death of Belgian peacekeepers. The Chamber permitted Belgium to make submissions after the presentation of evidence and before closing statements,[68] despite the objections of the defence.[69] Belgium provided a written brief but indicated that it would not participate in oral submissions.[70] We suggest that the Chamber's approach to Belgium's participation in these cases as an *amicus curiae* was too permissive and not justified by a particular state interest directly affected by proceedings. However, interestingly, *Semanza* is an example of a state advancing a more expansive interpretation of the law, suggesting states participating as *amici curiae* will not necessarily seek to limit the development of international law.[71]

The ICC has permitted a state to appear as an *amicus curiae* during the trial where its state interest is affected. In the Kenyan cases, Kenya sought leave to appear as an *amicus curiae* to respond to statements the OTP had made in formal pleadings as well as in the media concerning Kenya's cooperation with the Prosecutor.[72] Kenya sought recognition of a right to respond based on the *audi ateram partem* principle or, in the alternative, as an *amicus curiae*, and emphasised the need for cooperation based on a dialogue between state parties and the Court that takes into account the role of national law in this framework. Trial Chamber V in both cases gave permission to Kenya to appear as an *amicus curiae* 'given the desirability of fully understanding the status of cooperation between organs of the Court and the Government'.[73] The issues concerning Kenya's cooperation continued to escalate, with Kenya claiming that it was unable to comply with a request for it to compel witnesses to appear before the ICC. Both the Trial Chamber[74] and the

[67] ibid, para 1.

[68] ibid.

[69] The defence objected to the brief and submitted a response to the substantive brief. It relied on the Chamber's failure to make a finding on the brief and the defence's response as a ground of appeal, but this was not upheld by the Appeals Chamber as there was no evidence that this led to unfairness or bias: *Semanza v Prosecutor,* ICTR AC, 20 May 2005, ICTR-97-20-A-5874/H, paras 52 and 53.

[70] The brief is not publicly available, so this is based on the judgment: *Prosecutor v Semanza,* ICTR TC III, 15 May 2003, ICTR-97-20-T-7494, para 27 and fn 11.

[71] Bürli notes that briefs by states in the ECtHR tend to be arguing for a restrictive interpretation of the law: N Bürli, *Third-Party Interventions Before the European Court of Human Rights* (Cambridge, Intersentia, 2017) 134–38. However, she also finds that state briefs have little impact on decisions, and the data suggested that restrictive state briefs impact on the case law has not been vast: 152.

[72] See *Prosecutor v Kenyatta*, ICC TC V, 8 April 2013, ICC-01/09-02/11-713; *Prosecutor v Ruto and Sang*, ICC TC V, 8 April 2013, ICC-01/09-01/11-670.

[73] *Prosecutor v Kenyatta*, ICC TC V, 24 April 2013, para 2.

[74] *Prosecutor v Ruto and Sang,* ICC TC V (A), 29 January 2014, ICC-01/09-01/11-1165, noting that the prosecution had made Kenyan national law 'an important component of the present litigation' (para 8), and giving leave to Kenya to file observations and to participate in a status conference.

Appeals Chamber[75] continued to permit Kenya to participate as an *amicus curiae*, particularly as to national law. Kenya's intervention occurred during the trial phase and had a real impact on the conduct of the trial (the case subsequently collapsed). It also raised a significant and novel legal issue for the ICC. However, these proceedings essentially concerned non-cooperation. Arguably, this disagreement between the Prosecutor and Kenya as to the scope of the Court's powers and the interaction with Kenya's national law should have been resolved in separate non-cooperation proceedings, rather than in the trial proceedings themselves. Both Chambers effectively acted as if Kenya, as the state party who would be required to comply with the decision, was a party to proceedings, allowing rights not normally accorded to *amici* and dedicating considerable space in the eventual decisions to considering Kenya's submissions.[76] The Chamber eventually considered the overall issue of Kenya's non-cooperation in separate proceedings under Article 87(7) (see below).

International organisations have participated as *amici curiae* to represent their interests potentially affected by proceedings. The UN has appeared as an *amicus curiae* in the context of the immunity of UN personnel from testifying[77] and the inviolability of UN premises and documents.[78] The ICRC also sought to appear as an *amicus curiae* before an ICTY Chamber to make submissions regarding testimony by ICRC personnel.[79] ICC Chambers have invited the Security Council or the UN to appear to represent the interest of the Security Council in non-cooperation and admissibility proceedings where the Council referred the situation; the UN has declined the invitation.[80]

ii. State Interests Arising in Related Proceedings

Outside of trial proceedings, Chambers affect states' legal interests in three main ways.[81] First, by dictating whether a tribunal has jurisdiction and whether

[75] *Prosecutor v Ruto and Sang*, ICC AC, 10 June 2014, ICC-01/09-01/11-1350, giving permission for Kenya to make submissions as to whether a state party 'is under an obligation to cooperate with the Court to serve summonses and assist in compelling the appearance of witnesses subject to a subpoena' (para 7).

[76] *Prosecutor v Ruto and Sang*, ICC AC, 9 October 2014, ICC-01/09-01/11-1598.

[77] eg, in *Akayesu*, a representative of the United Nations Secretariat was invited to appear before the Trial Chamber as an *amicus curiae* 'to make a statement on the lifting of the immunity of Major-General Dallaire': *Prosecutor v Akayesu*, ICTR TC I, 12 February 1998, ICTR-96-4-T; *Prosecutor v Akayesu*, ICTR TC I, Transcript, 25 February 1998.

[78] See *In the Matter of El Sayed*, STL AC, 10 November 2010, CH/AC/2010/02.

[79] Ex parte and Confidential Submission by the ICRC Concerning the Proposal to Call a Former Employee of the ICRC as a Prosecution Witness, 13 April 1999, cited in *Prosecutor v Simić et al*, ICTY TC II, 17 October 2003, IT-95-9-T, fn 2428.

[80] See, eg *Prosecutor v Gaddafi*, ICC PTC I, 5 April 2019, ICC-01/11-01/11-662, para 9, inviting the Security Council to submit observations on the admissibility challenge; *Prosecutor v Al-Bashir*, ICC PTC II, 8 December 2016, ICC-02/05-01/09-274. The United Nations also declined an invitation from the Trial Chamber in *Tadić* to appear to represent the interest of the Security Council.

[81] Other issues where the state may participate include proceedings concerning provisional release, the transfer of witnesses or the legality of detention and transfer to the tribunal.

proceedings will occur at the national or international level, the Chamber is engaging state obligations either to prosecute itself or to surrender an accused to the tribunal. This decision also has practical implications for the state. Secondly, by directing a state to cooperate with a request for cooperation, the Chamber is creating a binding international obligation for the State. Thirdly, by determining that a state has failed to comply with its obligations to cooperate, a Chamber is finding a violation of international law, from which legal consequences will flow. It is therefore not surprising to see states predominantly involved in proceedings concerning jurisdiction, admissibility and cooperation.

a. Jurisdiction and Admissibility

The rules on deferral and referral of cases do not envisage participation for the state concerned, with one exception. Article 11 of the ICTY Statute, which concerns failure to comply with deferral requests, notes that the Trial Chamber can only proceed with a finding of non-cooperation where 'the State fails to file a response which satisfies the Trial Chamber that the State has taken or is taking adequate steps to comply with the request'. This provision relates to proceedings for non-cooperation with a deferral request, not the deferral proceedings. However, the limited practice on deferral demonstrates that the deferral state as well as the state of nationality of the accused (if different) was informed of their 'right to apply for leave to appear as *amicus curiae*' in deferral proceedings.[82]

Neither the ICTY nor ICTR Statute and RPE gave the potential state of referral (referral state) standing to initiate referral proceedings[83] or the right to be heard.[84] Despite this, both tribunals permitted the referral state to participate in proceedings, both in writing and orally. However, they did so on different legal bases. The ICTY specifically invited the referral state to make submissions, recognising that the Chamber would benefit from submissions from the referral state.[85] This also extended to any other state to which it might consider referring a case.[86] The Chamber invited the referral state to make submissions on the criteria for referral (gravity and seniority) as well as the competence of the

[82] See *Prosecutor v Tadić*, ICTY TC, 12 October 1994, IT-94-1-D-D58 (addressed to the Government of Germany); *Prosecutor v Tadić*, ICTY TC, 1 November 1994, IT-94-1-D-D65 (addressed to the Government of the Federal Republic of Yugoslavia). Similarly, Bosnia and Herzegovina relied on r 74 to participate in deferral proceedings concerning Karadžić, Mladić and Stanišić: see *Prosecutor v Karadžić, Mladić and Stanišić*, ICTY TC, 21 April 1995, IT 95-5-D-D25.

[83] See, eg, *Prosecutor v Janković*, ICTY AC, 15 November 2005, IT-96-23/2-AR11*bis*.2, para 23, confirming that neither Bosnia nor Serbia had standing to file a request for referral.

[84] Referral proceedings were heard by a separately constituted Chamber, the Referral Bench at the ICTY and the Referral Chamber at the ICTR. Exception is where a referral to that state is going to be revoked, either on request of the OTP or by tribunal itself.

[85] See, eg, *Prosecutor v Stanković*, ICTY TC, 9 February 2005, IT-96-23/2-PT.

[86] Serbia was given permission to participate both in writing and orally in several proceedings where it sought to have a case referred to its courts, rather than those of Bosnia.

national legal system to meet the requirements of Rule 11*bis*.[87] Referral states responded to specific questions on the national legal system and thus provided expertise (see section III above). While the referral state(s) did not appear in appellate proceedings, the Appeals Chamber referenced their submissions to the Referral Bench. The Chamber did not invite the referral state to make submissions as an *amicus curiae*, although other actors did participate as *amici curiae* in referral proceedings.[88] However, the Chamber adopted a similar test to that for *amici*, namely that it would be beneficial for it to hear from referral states.[89] The Chamber also recognised the referral state(s) as specially affected, thus justifying the need for their submissions.

The ICTR Referral Chamber allowed referral states to participate but did so using the *amicus curiae* mechanism. This practice was established before Rule 11*bis* was included in its rules, with the Chamber in *Ntuyahaga* allowing Belgium to appear as an *amicus curiae* in proceedings concerning the withdrawal of the indictment, linked to the potential transfer of the accused to Belgium to be prosecuted for the deaths of Belgian peacekeepers. The Chamber recognised Belgium as having an interest due to the nationality of the victims and as the state that was most likely to exercise jurisdiction.[90] The practice in referral proceedings dominates the state *amicus curiae* practice at the ICTR and, as with the ICTY, includes states other than Rwanda as potential referral states.[91] In accordance with 'normal' approaches to *amicus* participation, referral states sought leave to appear or the Chamber specifically invited states to participate. State *amici* made written submissions, responding to specific questions posed by the Chamber (addressing similar issues to referral states in the ICTY) and participated in oral proceedings.[92] The Referral Chamber recognised that state *amici* were distinct from other *amici*; referral states were specially affected by the decision. Specifically, if the Chamber referred the case, the decision created obligations for the referral state to assume responsibility for the prosecution, as well as to report to the Chamber and allow OTP monitoring of the national proceedings.[93]

[87] This was often done by posing specific questions to the referral state: eg, *Prosecutor v Janković*, ICTY TC, 15 April 2005, IT-96-23/2-PT.

[88] eg, two Croatian academics, Professor Mirjan Damaška and Professor Davor Krapac, participated as *amicus curiae* in the Ademi and Norac referral proceedings, their submissions aligning with the government.

[89] See, eg *Prosecutor v Stanković*, ICTY TC, 9 February 2005, IT-96-23/2-PT.

[90] *Prosecutor v Ntuyahaga*, ICTR TC I, 18 March 1999, ICTR-98-40-T; see also *Prosecutor v Ntuyahaga*, ICTR TC I, Transcript, 16 March 1999. The formal decision to admit Belgium, as well as the brief itself, are not publicly available.

[91] Due to the concerns with the suitability of the Rwandan legal system for trials, in particular the availability of the death penalty, cases were considered for referral to states such as the Netherlands and Norway. See, eg Michel Bagaragaza, which was eventually referred to the Netherlands for trial: *Prosecutor v Bagaragaza*, ICTR TC III, 13 April 2007, ICTR-05-86-I-875.

[92] See, eg *Prosecutor v Bagaragaza*, ICTR TC III, 31 January 2007, ICTR-05-86-11*bis*-769.

[93] See, eg, in *Prosecutor v Hategekimana*, ICTR AC, 4 December 2008, ICTR-00-55B-R11*bis*-165/H.

This special interest led to additional rights at the discretion of the Chamber.[94] For example, referral states participated in appellate proceedings, but first had to seek leave from the Appeals Chamber.[95] Chambers granted leave only if the state would be addressing additional issues not raised at the initial stage.[96] Chambers allowed state *amici* to respond to submissions by the parties and other *amici*, although Rule 74 did not provide for this right,[97] and to have access to documents on the case file that would be required for the state to discharge its mandate as an *amicus*.[98] Both tribunals therefore allowed the referral state to represent its interest before the Chamber. Chambers clearly valued the information provided, recognising the unique position of the state to provide it. The expertise role may well have been more important than the representative function: in later referral decisions, Rwanda did not apply as an *amicus curiae* and the Chamber did not invite Rwanda to do so. This suggests that once the Chamber was familiar with the legal system it did not require further assistance or for Rwanda to represent its interest.[99]

A further issue was whether the different legal basis in each tribunal mattered. The practice was more consistent in the ICTY while the use of the *amicus curiae* mechanism in the ICTR was often state-initiated, more flexible and led to small variations in practice. The ICTR practice also enabled greater participatory rights for some states. This supports our suggestion that where there is an institutional need for state participation it should be done through the adoption of a specific mechanism, rather than relying on the more discretionary *amicus curiae*. This will better facilitate equal and consistent treatment of actors, and will allow states to enjoy the type and extent of rights appropriate.

A shift to specific participatory mechanisms is evident in the ICC framework. As described in chapter three, when drafting the Rome Statute and RPE states had greater control of whether or not to include mechanisms for participation than for the *ad hoc* tribunals. Given the permanent nature of the ICC and its wider global reach, there was also greater potential for engagement of state interests. As the negotiating history of Rule 103 revealed, states were concerned to make sure that they could participate in proceedings as *amici*. However, rather than rely only on a discretionary mechanism, states incorporated specific

[94] In *Kayishema*, the Referral Chamber recognised that 'the Referral State has a unique position as an *amici*': *Prosecutor v Kayishema,* ICTR TC III, 1 July 2008, ICTR-2001-67-I-722.

[95] The Appeals Chamber accepted Norway as an *amicus curiae* in the appellate proceedings in Michel Bagaragaza: *Prosector v Bagaragaza,* ICTR AC, 30 August 2006, ICTR-05-86-AR11*bis*, para 7.

[96] eg, *Prosecutor v Kanyarukigia*, ICTR AC, 1 September 2008, ICTR-2002-78-R11*bis*.

[97] See *Prosecutor v Kayishema*, ICTR TC III, 1 July 2008, ICTR-2001-67-I-722, para 17, allowing Rwanda to respond to a brief submitted by Human Rights Watch. Contrast *Prosecutor v Uwinkindi*, ICTR TC II, 8 April 2011, ICTR-01-75-PT-3787, finding that as an *amicus*, Rwanda had no standing to respond to submissions by the defence or other *amici* and should provide its view to the prosecution.

[98] *Prosecutor v Uwinkindi*, ICTR TC II, 18 January 2011, ICTR-01-75-I-2226.

[99] See, eg *Prosecutor v Ntaganzwa*, ICTR TC, 8 May 2012, ICTR-96-9-R11*bis*-1226.

rights of standing and participation in relation to jurisdiction and admissibility, recognising that these areas have the greatest potential to impact on states' legal interests. This extends to rights of standing for states parties to 'trigger jurisdiction' by referring a situation to the ICC and, as a referring state, to request a review of a prosecution decision not to proceed with an investigation.[100] States participate effectively as parties in review proceedings they initiate, including having the right to appeal. These rights are, however, more limited in relation to other trigger mechanisms, with states having no standing to participate in Article 15 proceedings, where the Prosecutor requests authorisation from the Pre-Trial Chamber to open an investigation.[101]

Once an investigation is open, the Rome Statute confers standing on certain states to bring a challenge to the exercise of jurisdiction by the ICC and the admissibility of cases.[102] The scope of participatory rights states may enjoy under these provisions is wide, with states effectively parties, and include the ability to make oral and written submissions and to appeal. Our aim here is not to analyse this practice in detail; rather the move towards specific participatory rights for states in the Rome Statute means that we should generally not expect to see affected states participating as *amici* in proceedings concerning jurisdiction and admissibility. The creation of specific rights to address a systematic need for participation should be preferred, with the *amicus curiae* remaining a discretionary mechanism whenever specific rights are not available. One example of where it may be appropriate to use the *amicus curiae* is at the stage before an investigation is open, where participatory rights do not exist for states. In the *Myanmar/Bangladesh* proceedings, the Pre-Trial Chamber invited Bangladesh to submit observations as an *amicus curiae*, recognising that as the state where the cross-border crime of deportation was completed, the decision would specially affect Bangladesh.[103] Another example is where a challenge to admissibility or jurisdiction is brought by the accused or another state. The Appeals Chamber has confirmed that where a state does not initiate a challenge to admissibility or jurisdiction, it does not otherwise have standing and must rely on the *amicus curiae* mechanism.[104] As seen in admissibility proceedings concerning Saif Al-Islam Gaddafi, initiated by the defence,[105] the Chamber required information from Libya concerning the national prosecutions. Inviting Libya as an

[100] Rome Statute, Art 53(3)(a). In the first review request, the requesting state, Comoros filed submissions: *Situation on the Registered Vessels of the Union of the Comoros,* ICC PTC I, 16 July 2015, ICC-01/13-34 and was able to respond to the Prosecutor's appeal: *Situation on the Registered Vessels of the Union of the Comoros,* ICC AC, 6 November 2015, ICC-01/13-51.

[101] *Situation in Burundi,* ICC PTC III, 25 October 2017, ICC-01/17-9-Red, para 8.

[102] eg, Art 19 allows a state having jurisdiction over a case or a state from which acceptance of jurisdiction is required, to challenge admissibility and/or jurisdiction.

[103] *Request Under Regulation 46(3) of the Regulations of the Court,* ICC PTC I, 7 May 2018, ICC-RoC46(3)-01/18-3, para 6.

[104] *Prosecutor v L Gbagbo,* ICC AC, 12 December 2012, ICC-02/11-01/11-321, paras 37–45.

[105] *Prosecutor v Gaddafi,* ICC PTC I, 5 June 2018, ICC-01/11-01/11-640.

amicus curiae could have been an option for receiving such information, and the Chamber received a joint submission from two NGOs as *amici*: Redress and Lawyers for Justice in Libya, addressing issues concerning national law and the relevant proceedings.[106] However, rather than invite Libya to participate, the Chamber relied on information provided by Libya to the OTP in response to requests for cooperation.[107]

b. Cooperation and Non-cooperation Proceedings

For many states, the only occasion on which they will interact with an international criminal tribunal is where the state receives a request to cooperate by providing evidence or arresting and surrendering an accused present on their territory. Requests to cooperate and decisions as to non-compliance directly engage the legal interest of the requested state. The instruments of the ICTY, ICTR and ICC create a number of rights concerning cooperation, including rights of notification and consultation, as well as obligations for states to consult the tribunal where cooperation may not be possible. Rights to appear before a Chamber are less common. The ICTY and ICTR provision on non-cooperation[108] does not contain a right to appear before the determination of non-cooperation or the decision to refer non-compliance to the Security Council. Both tribunals adopted an ambiguous position; some states were able to make submissions, others were not.

In *Blaškić*, the Trial Chamber confirmed the binding nature of a subpoena issued by the ICTY to Croatia and its officials and directed Croatia to appear.[109] While Croatia had participated in proceedings concerning the legality of the order,[110] there was no basis for it to seek review of the decision, as Rule 108 provided that only a party had standing to do so. However, the ICTY judges quickly moved to adopt Rule 108*bis* of the RPE[111] in 1999 to 'address a perceived lacuna ... namely that a State whose interests were intimately affected by a Decision of the Trial Chamber could not request that decision to be submitted to appellate review'.[112] Rule 108*bis* provides that 'A State directly affected by an

[106] *Prosecutor v Gaddafi*, ICC PTC II, 28 September 2018, ICC-01/11-01/11-654.

[107] *Prosecutor v Gaddafi*, ICC PTC I, 5 April 2019, ICC-01/11-01/11-662, paras 49–50.

[108] International Criminal Tribunal for the Former Yugoslavia, Rules of Procedure and Evidence (11 February 1994, as revised 8 July 2015) IT/32/Rev.50, r 7*bis*; International Criminal Tribunal for Rwanda, Rules of Procedure and Evidence (29 June 1995) ITR/3, r 7*bis*.

[109] *Prosecutor v Blaškić*, ICTY TC, 18 July 1997, IT-95-14.

[110] Croatia had signalled its objection to the legal authority of the Tribunal in a letter dated 10 February 1997. For history of Croatia's involvement see *Prosecutor v Blaškić*, ICTY TC, 18 July 1997, IT-95-14, paras 3–13. Croatia appeared to participate not as an *amicus curiae* but by invitation of the Chamber.

[111] The STL RPE has an equivalent provision, presumably drawn from Rule 108*bis*, but no state has yet invoked this right.

[112] *Prosecutor v Blaškić*, ICTY AC, 29 July 1997, IT-95-14, para 6.

interlocutory decision of a Trial Chamber may, within fifteen days from the date of the decision, file a request for review of the decision by the Appeals Chamber if that decision concerns issues of general importance relating to the powers of the Tribunal'. The Appeals Chamber confirmed that Croatia was 'clearly "directly affected"' by the decision to produce documents and that the issue was clearly of sufficient importance; 'indeed it relates to the Tribunal's very competence'.[113] Interestingly, Croatia relied on Rule 108*bis* to seek review of decisions not to admit the government as an *amicus curiae* in *Gotovina et al* in 2006 (discussed above). In granting the prosecution's motion to strike out the request for review, the Appeals Chamber emphasised that the decision 'did not impact upon Croatia's legal rights .... A state has no legally cognizable interest in providing assistance to the Trial Chamber as *amicus curiae*, let alone in doing so in respect of an issue of its choice. Hence, a state that is denied the opportunity to participate as an *amicus* is not directly affected by that decision within the meaning of Rule 108*bis* and thus has no standing to challenge the merits of that decision'.[114]

The judges of the ICC appear to have learned from the inconsistent practice of the ICTY and ICTR. ICC regulations provide that before a Chamber may make a judicial finding as to non-cooperation, 'the Chamber *shall* hear from the requested State'.[115] This regulation creates a *right* for the affected state. As the Pre-Trial Chamber in the South African non-cooperation proceedings noted, non-cooperation proceedings are fundamentally different to other proceedings: 'Proceedings under article 87(7) indeed fall under Part 9 of the Statute (entitled "International cooperation and judicial assistance") which concerns the relationship between the Court, on the one hand, and a State, on the other hand, and fundamentally differ from the criminal proceedings before the Court'.[116] Accordingly, the Chamber held that the affected state is the only essential participant, generally alongside the Prosecutor as the party whose request to cooperate has triggered the proceedings.[117] The state can make written submissions and participate in oral proceedings if held,[118] as well as responding (with leave) to applications of *amici* and submissions of other participants.[119] This right also extends to whether the Chamber refers any finding of non-cooperation to the

[113] ibid, para 13.

[114] *Prosecutor v Gotovina*, ICTR AC, 13 December 2006, IT-06-90-AR108*bis*.1-41, paras 7–8. The same position was adopted in relation to a request to review the decision not to admit Croatia as an *amicus curiae* in the *Prlić* proceedings: *Prosecutor v Prlić et al*, ICTY AC, 13 December 2006, IT-04-74-AR108*bis*.1-36, paras 8–9.

[115] International Criminal Court, Regulations of the Court (26 May 2004, as amended on 12 November 2018) ICC-BD/01-05-16, reg 109, emphasis added.

[116] *Prosecutor v Al-Bashir*, ICC PTC II, 9 March 2017, ICC-02/05-01/09-286, para 5.

[117] ibid, para 6.

[118] eg, South Africa participated in oral proceedings before the Pre-Trial Chamber on 7 April: *Prosecutor v Al-Bashir*, ICC PTC II, Transcript, 7 April 2017.

[119] eg, South Africa was given leave to respond to proposed submissions by *amici* in non-cooperation proceedings.

ASP or the Security Council.[120] The state can also initiate and participate in appeals from non-cooperation proceedings.[121] Importantly, this is a right to an *opportunity* to be heard, which a Chamber may consider exhausted where a state fails to file submissions at all or on time or otherwise in a form required by the Chamber.[122]

As with jurisdiction and admissibility, the creation of a specific right enables participation by the affected state and, given the significance of non-cooperation decisions and some of the ambiguities raised, is consistent with principles of natural justice. Again, we suggest that the adoption of a specific mechanism, rather than the more flexible and discretionary mechanism of the *amicus curiae*, allows states to be treated fairly and consistently by different Chambers. This in turn facilitates legitimacy, ensuring equal and fair treatment and transparency. States that have had an opportunity to participate are more likely to accept the decision even if it is against their interest. However, states not directly affected by non-cooperation proceedings should rely on the *amicus curiae* mechanism (as discussed in section V below).

c. Head of State Immunity

Chamber decisions concerning head of state immunity specifically affect the state. Without wishing to delve into arguments concerning immunity before the ICC, many non-cooperation proceedings have arisen from the failure of states parties to arrest and surrender President Al-Bashir of Sudan. The immunity of President Al-Bashir as head of state of Sudan (a non-party state) is at the heart of these proceedings. As the immunity is that of the state, these decisions directly implicate Sudan's legal interest. The Appeals Chamber recognised this interest when it invited the Government of Sudan, as well as counsel for Al-Bashir, for the first time to submit observations as *amici curiae* in proceedings concerning Jordan's non-cooperation.[123] While Sudan chose not to participate,[124] which is unsurprising given its consistent refusal to engage or to cooperate with the ICC, in the absence of any other participatory mechanism, inviting Sudan to participate as an *amicus curiae* is appropriate for transparency and natural justice

[120] eg, South Africa made submissions in writing and orally as to both issues.

[121] In proceedings concerning Kenya's non-cooperation, the Trial Chamber initially considered Kenya as an *amicus curiae* in the leave to appeal stage, rather than as a party: see *Prosecutor v Kenyatta*, ICC TC V(B), 10 December 2014, ICC-01/09-02/11-986. The Appeals Chamber indicated that this was incorrect and Kenya is a party to the appeal proceedings due to Regulation 109: *Prosecutor v Kenya,* ICC AC, 27 March 2015, ICC-01/09-02/11-1010, para 5. Jordan subsequently appealed a finding of non-cooperation against it: *Prosecutor v Al-Bashir,* ICC PTC II, 21 February 2018, ICC-02/05-01/09-319.

[122] *Prosecutor v Al-Bashir,* ICC PTC II, 26 March 2013, ICC-02/05-01/09-151.

[123] *Prosecutor v Al-Bashir,* ICC AC, 25 May 2018, ICC-02/05-01/09-352. See also *Prosecutor v Al-Bashir,* ICC AC, 20 September 2018, ICC-02/05-01/09-386, 3, inviting Sudan to make submissions on issues raised during the appellate proceedings.

[124] *Prosecutor v Al-Bashir,* ICC AC, Transcript, 10 September 2018, 9, noting that no response had been received.

reasons. As members of the Appeals Chamber noted, Sudan's participation in the appeal would have 'assist[ed] the Chamber to better understand its perspectives in the case'.[125] As explored further below, it also has the benefit of allowing a mechanism by which to bring disagreement and legal arguments within the Court's formal processes, which may be more constructive than engaging in such disputes in the media or political fora.

ICC proceedings have also recognised the interest of international organisations in non-cooperation decisions concerning state immunity. As noted above, international organisations have appeared as *amici curiae* to represent the immunity of their personnel, premises and documents. In addition, international organisations – as hosts of international meetings – have a direct interest in how institutions such as the ICC interpret and apply international rules on immunity. A decision finding that states must enforce ICC arrest warrants regarding heads of state attending those meetings may impede the organisation's ability to arrange future meetings. That decision may also place the host state in a position of conflict between its obligations to the ICC and those set out in the constituent instrument of the international organisation, other agreements on immunity and the host state agreement. To illustrate, Al-Bashir was in South Africa to attend an African Union meeting, while he was in Jordan to attend a meeting of the League of Arab States.

This intersection between obligations to international organisations and to the ICC has featured in several proceedings.[126] Recognising that its decision may have a direct legal and practical impact on the operations of international organisations, the Appeals Chamber invited a number of international organisations, including the African Union and the League of Arab States, to participate in proceedings concerning Jordan's non-cooperation.[127] Both organisations participated as *amici* and advanced submissions addressing the impact of immunity on their ability to hold meetings and a proposed exception to ICC obligations where a head of state was travelling to an international meeting.[128] In this sense, these organisations were representing their own legal interest, distinct from or in addition to the more general interest of their members in the application of rules concerning immunity.

V. STATE *AMICI* PERFORMING A COMMUNICATIVE FUNCTION

Provisions such as Article 63 of the ICJ Statute allow states that are party to a treaty to intervene in proceedings raising the interpretation or application of

[125] *Prosecutor v Al-Bashir,* ICC AC, 6 May 2019, ICC-02/05-01/09-397, para 427.

[126] eg, this issue was considered in both the South African and *Jordan* non-cooperation proceedings.

[127] *Prosecutor v Al-Bashir,* ICC AC, 29 March 2018, ICC-02/05-01/09-330.

[128] *Prosecutor v Al-Bashir,* ICC AC, 13 July 2018, ICC-02/05-01/09-370; *Prosecutor v Al-Bashir,* ICC AC, 16 July 2018, ICC-02/05-01/09-367. See also *Prosecutor v Al-Bashir*, ICC AC, Transcript, 12 September 2018.

that treaty (see chapter two, section III). Palchetti has suggested that Article 62 of the ICJ Statute, which allows a state to apply to intervene where its legal interests are affected, creates a right to intervene where a state has a general interest in the interpretation of an instrument or rule of customary international law by the Court.[129] The state's interest may be the future effect of the precedent set by the decision or the rule of customary international law recognised. However, as indicated in chapter two, the practice of the ICJ establishes that this type of general interest does not support intervention.

The legal frameworks of the Tribunals do not recognise either a specific right to intervene where the Chamber will interpret or apply the relevant treaty or a more general interest in the development or application of the law. This is appropriate, as the primary role of the Tribunals is to determine individual criminal responsibility and not to resolve legal disputes *between* states. The Chambers are responsible for determining any issues concerning its judicial functions. The absence of advisory jurisdiction also mitigates against allowing states to present views on general questions of international law or treaty interpretation in judicial proceedings, as does the number of treaties that the ICC might interpret or apply as part of its applicable law.[130]

Despite this, states have sought to provide arguments concerning the interpretation of particular treaties or customary international law rules. One example is the submissions by the US in the *Tadić* proceedings before the ICTY. The US brief made submissions 'with respect to the validity of the action of the Security Council in creating the Tribunal and the interpretation of the jurisdictional provisions of the Statute'.[131] The US relied 'specifically on its *special interest and knowledge* as a Permanent Member of the UN Security Council and its substantial involvement in the adoption of the Statute of the Tribunal'.[132] The Trial Chamber granted leave to the US to appear as an *amicus curiae* on the issue of jurisdiction, but did not engage with how or why it thought the submission would assist. The main US submission was that the ICTY could not review the validity of the Tribunal's establishment; instead, this was a political question best referred to the Security Council. The US also engaged with the substance as to whether the Council could validly create the ICTY, detailing its understanding of the Council's powers, mandate and practice. Given the US based its submission on its special knowledge due to its role on the Council, this also has elements of the expertise function. Another example is the permission given to Belgium to make submissions regarding the interpretation of Common Article 3 in the *Semanza* proceedings.[133]

[129] P Palchetti, 'Opening the International Court of Justice to Third States: Intervention and Beyond' (2002) 6 *Max Planck Yearbook of United Nations Law* 139.

[130] Rome Statute, Art 21.

[131] *Prosecutor v Tadić*, ICTY AC, 17 July 1995, IT-94-1-T, 1.

[132] ibid, emphasis added.

[133] *Prosecutor v Semanza*, ICTR TC III, 9 February 2001, ICTR-97-20-T-4702.

One example of a communicative function is the ICTY in *Blaškić*. The Appeals Chamber invited member states – as well as NGOs and individuals – to submit *amicus curiae* briefs on the issue of whether the Tribunal could issue a legally binding subpoena to states.[134] The Tribunal justified its invitation to states by the importance of the issue, noting the link to maintaining the cooperation of states and the effectiveness of the Tribunal. States had an indirect interest in that they too could be the subject of an order from the Tribunal. Five states chose to participate, mostly adopting different positions as to the key legal questions posed by the Chamber, and not necessarily supporting the arguments of the state directly affected, Croatia (see above).[135] The diversity of the briefs shows that state views are not homogenous and they will not always make submissions that seek to restrict the scope of provisions.[136] All states made some mention of the need for the ICTY to recognise legitimate state interests. In contrast to other *amici*, to which the Chamber referred, the Chamber did not expressly consider the state briefs and the decision is contrary to the submissions of the states in several respects.[137] The Chamber did not consider the states to be experts; rather, the use of the state *amici* appears to have served a communicative function, to hear the views of state stakeholders as to how the Tribunal should interpret key provisions and powers of the ICTY that ultimately flow from the UN Charter.

ICC proceedings also include examples of state *amici* acting in a communicative function. Five states sought to appear as *amici curiae* in proceedings concerning whether the accused Ruto – a senior government official – could be excused from appearing at certain stages of his trial.[138] The Chamber had to interpret Article 63 of the Statute, which requires a trial to take place in the presence of the accused, and Rule 134*quater*. In their requests, the states highlighted the importance of the issue for state cooperation and fair trial concerns,[139] while Rwanda, a non-state party, indicated that the decision would have implications for states joining the Rome Statute in future.[140] All states emphasised the need to balance the requirement for the accused to be present with the demands of those in high office and several expressly noted that the Court should accommodate 'the rights of other interested constituencies'.[141] The decision did not directly affect these states; Kenya, the state directly affected, did not seek to participate. Therefore, in seeking to provide their views to the Chamber on how to interpret

[134] *Prosecutor v Blaškić*, ICTY AC, 29 July 1997, IT-94-14, para 16.

[135] New Zealand and Canada (joint submission), China, Netherlands and Norway.

[136] eg, China argued that the ICTY could not issue a subpoena and should respect the national interest of states, while New Zealand and Canada supported the ICTY's powers.

[137] *Prosecutor v Blaškić*, ICTY AC, 29 October 1997, IT-94-14. The Chamber did not accommodate state national interests to the extent sought by some state *amici*; while indicating that it should not be unmindful of legitimate state concerns regarding national security, it upheld the principle that states could not withhold information based on national security: para 67.

[138] Eritrea, Rwanda, Uganda, Burundi and Tanzania.

[139] eg, *Prosecutor v Ruto and Sang*, ICC TC V, 9 September 2013, ICC-01/09-01/11-928-Anx1.

[140] *Prosecutor v Ruto and Sang*, ICC AC, 6 September 2013, ICC-01/09-01/11-921-Anx1, para 5.

[141] *Prosecutor v Ruto and Sang*, ICC TC V, 9 September 2013, ICC-01/09-01/11-928-Anx1, para 5.

Article 63, the states were seeking a right of intervention similar to that provided by Article 63 of the ICJ Statute. The defence supported intervention by the states, while the prosecution argued such intervention went beyond the narrow legal point raised by the proceedings.[142] The Appeals Chamber, by majority, permitted the states to intervene given the circumstances of the case and the novelty of the issue.[143] However, in a strongly worded dissent, Judge Ušacka argued that the submissions 'appear to be aimed at highlighting the impact of judicial decisions of the Court in terms of encouraging or discouraging State cooperation' and that the intervention 'of the nature proposed endangers the risk of distorting the judicial process or, at a minimum, creating the appearance that States have inappropriately encroached upon the functions of the judiciary'.[144] Following this decision, Nigeria and Ethiopia also sought to participate and were rejected on the basis their submissions would be duplicative.[145] Judge Ušacka reiterated her view that the Chamber should not permit state *amici* to make this type of submission.[146] We agree with Judge Ušacka: given the absence of a right equivalent to Article 63 of the ICJ Statute, the Chamber should not accept 'interpretative' submissions from states, particularly when the submissions raise issues that are not relevant to the Chambers' determination. These proceedings directly related to the trial phase and concerned a vital element of trial procedure. Moreover, given that Kenya and other states had already pushed in the ASP for an amendment to Rule 134, the Chamber should not further privilege the position of those states.[147]

A second example concerns requests by several states and the African Union to participate as *amici curiae* before the Appeals Chamber to communicate their understanding of what the ASP had intended regarding the retrospective application of the amendment of Rule 68, the rule permitting the admission of prior recorded testimony. How the Chamber interpreted this rule would govern the admission of evidence during the trial and was therefore directly linked to the individual criminal responsibility of the accused. In the initial proceedings before the Trial Chamber, Kenya sought to appear as an *amicus curiae* citing its special knowledge based on its role in the negotiation of the rule amendment in the ASP, and certain assurances it claimed ICC officials had made concerning retrospective application of the rule in the cases in the Kenyan situation.[148] The Trial Chamber rejected the application, finding it was neither necessary

[142] *Prosecutor v Ruto and Sang,* ICC AC, 12 September 2013, ICC-01/09-01-11-932; *Prosecutor v Ruto and Sang,* ICC AC, 12 September 2013, ICC-01/09-01/11-934.

[143] *Prosecutor v Ruto and Sang,* ICC AC, 13 September 2013, ICC-01/09-01/11-942, para 10.

[144] *Prosecutor v Ruto and Sang,* ICC AC, 13 September 2013, ICC-01/09-01/11-942-Anx, paras 4 and 5.

[145] *Prosecutor v Ruto and Sang,* ICC AC, 25 September 2013, ICC-01/09-01/11-988.

[146] *Prosecutor v Ruto and Sang,* ICC AC, 25 September 2013, ICC-01/09-01/11-988-Anx.

[147] See H Woolaver and E Palmer, 'Challenges to the Independence of the International Criminal Court from the Assembly of States Parties' (2017) 15(4) *JICJ* 641.

[148] *Prosecutor v Ruto and Sang,* ICC TC V(A), 27 May 2015, ICC-01/09-01/11-1891.

nor appropriate to receive submissions from Kenya on the interpretation and application of Rule 68 to the instant case.[149]

Before the Appeals Chamber, Kenya,[150] Uganda[151] and Namibia,[152] as well as the African Union,[153] sought to participate as *amici curiae* to make submissions as to the context of the rule amendment. The African Union encouraged the Chamber to adopt a 'more flexible, open-door approach to Rule 103(1) requests on weighty issues … This more compelling approach takes seriously the centrality of States in the adoption of the RPE at the ICC as well as amendments to them'.[154] It argued that its submissions would help the Chamber reach the 'correct decision by better discernment of the original intention of states parties',[155] particularly as the defendant was not at the ASP and could not communicate the same information.[156] The African Union highlighted the novelty of the issue, its importance for fair trial rights, the significant impact the decision would have on the outcome of trials and on judicial economy, as well as the need to strengthen AU-ICC cooperation.[157] The request then explicitly links the proposed submission with a communicative function, emphasising that the intervention offers 'the prospect of a constructive dialogue on a novel and important legal question of apparent interest and far reaching implications' for African states, both parties and non-parties to the ICC.[158] The African Union recognised the submissions as a way 'to work constructively within the legal framework of the ICC system to channel its views'[159] and urged the Chamber 'to avoid the appearance of exclusion of the legitimate interests and legal views of the ICC's sovereign African State Parties'.[160] Rejecting the Prosecutor's request to respond to the request, the Appeals Chamber permitted the African Union to provide written submissions (but not oral submissions), to which the parties could respond, but rejected the state *amici* as duplicative of the African Union submissions.[161]

The decision raises four interesting points. First, the Chamber's assumption is that the submissions of an international organisation will always align with that of its member states. Secondly, there is recognition – if not tacit endorsement – of the intention of the African Union to use the *amicus curiae* mechanism to influence judicial proceedings concerning African nationals.[162] Thirdly, the Chamber

[149] *Prosecutor v Ruto and Sang*, ICC TC V(A), 29 May 2015, ICC-01/09-01/11-1893.
[150] *Prosecutor v Ruto and Sang*, ICC AC, 23 September 2015, ICC-01/09-01/11-1972.
[151] *Prosecutor v Ruto and Sang*, ICC AC, 5 October 2015, ICC-01/09-01/11-1938-Red.
[152] *Prosecutor v Ruto and Sang*, ICC AC, 5 October 2015, ICC-01/09-01/11-1938-Corr-Red2.
[153] *Prosecutor v Ruto and Sang*, ICC AC, ICC-01/09-01/11-1983-Anx, 5 October 2015.
[154] ibid, para 23.
[155] ibid, para 26.
[156] ibid, para 30.
[157] ibid, para 25.
[158] ibid, para 10.
[159] ibid, para 33.
[160] ibid, para 33.
[161] *Prosecutor v Ruto and Sang*, ICC AC, 12 October 2015, ICC-01/09-01/11-1987, paras 16 and 17.
[162] ibid, para 17, referring to the AU decision directing states to request leave to submit *amicus curiae* observations.

failed to articulate why the submissions would be helpful, instead stating only that the submissions 'may be desirable', without further elaboration.[163] The decision suggests some discomfort with accepting the submissions, signalling that the decision to accept the submissions was 'without prejudice to the weight to be given, if any'.[164] Finally, the Chamber appears to have endorsed a communicative role, at least for state *amici* and organisations with state membership. Despite this, in its substantive decision, although the Appeals Chamber set out the main points from the African Union submissions, the Chamber ultimately rejected arguments based on the interpretation adopted by the ASP in favour of a textual analysis.[165] This suggests that even if the Chamber did recognise a communicative role, the Chamber independently assessed the submissions and felt able to reach a different conclusion (the decision was partly reversed but for different reasons). Again, we have serious misgivings as to the Chamber's decision to accept the African Union submissions here, particularly given the involvement of several AU member states and the organisation itself in the decisions taken at the ASP.[166]

Two other examples of communicative state *amici* have arisen in the series of non-cooperation proceedings regarding President Al-Bashir of Sudan. As noted above, the state alleged to have failed to cooperate by arresting Al-Bashir is a party to these proceedings. Until the proceedings concerning South Africa, non-cooperation proceedings had not involved a hearing. The Pre-Trial Chamber in the South Africa proceedings announced it would hold a public hearing, and, as noted above recognised South Africa, the OTP and the United Nations as desirable participants. Recognising that the issue before it was of general importance, the Chamber invited 'all interested States Parties to the Statute to provide any relevant submission as *amicus curiae*' and adopted a one-step process, that is, states did not need to seek leave to participate.[167] As the representative of South Africa noted in the oral proceedings, this was the first time a Chamber had invited other actors to participate in non-cooperation proceedings.[168] Belgium, the only state to respond, made submissions particularly from its perspective as host state to a number of international organisations.[169] What is interesting, given that Al-Bashir was in South Africa to attend a meeting of the AU, was that the Chamber did not invite the African Union to participate, nor did the organisation apply to do so.

The Pre-Trial Chamber recognised the importance of the issue of head of state immunity, while stressing that the proceedings were non-criminal in nature

[163] ibid, para 16.
[164] ibid.
[165] See *Prosecutor v Ruto and Sang*, ICC AC, 12 February 2016, ICC-01/09-01/11-2024.
[166] Woolaver and Palmer (n 147).
[167] *Prosecutor v Al-Bashir*, ICC PTC II, 8 December 2016, ICC-02/05-01/09-274, para 17.
[168] *Prosecutor v Al-Bashir*, ICC AC, Transcript, 7 April 2017, 10.
[169] *Prosecutor v Al-Bashir*, ICC PTC II, 23 February 2017, ICC-02/05-01/09-277. The UN declined to participate.

and more concerned with the law applicable between states.[170] Judge Perrin de Brichambaut captured neatly why the issue was so significant:

> the question of Omar Al-Bashir's immunity is situated at the crossroads of different legal principles, regimes, and goals: from State sovereignty, to the role and powers of the UN Security Council and the commitment to ending impunity for the most serious crimes, which is the primary purpose behind the establishment of this Court ... Accordingly, the legal basis for the Chamber's determination is of paramount significance in these circumstances.[171]

However, while the Chamber set out Belgium's submissions in the decision, it did not expressly rely on those submissions for its substantive findings.[172]

In the appellate proceedings concerning Jordan's non-cooperation, the Appeals Chamber invited states parties to the Rome Statute to apply as *amici curiae*, requiring each state to indicate in its application their interest in doing so.[173] The process was therefore somewhat different to that adopted by the Pre-Trial Chamber in the South Africa proceedings, which did not require a two-stage application process for state *amici*. Mexico was the only state to apply to the Appeals Chamber, indicating that its interest arose due its status as a party to several treaties dealing with immunity, its support for immunity in bilateral relations in the region, and its support for international criminal justice.[174] Mexico highlighted the implications of the decision for the Court's effectiveness and cooperation, as well as the desire to see that the proceedings reflected views from all regions and legal systems.[175] However, despite having leave to file written submissions and to participate in hearings,[176] Mexico evidently chose not do so.

The Appeals Chamber also invited certain international organisations to appear as *amici curiae*, namely the United Nations, the European Union, the AU and the League of Arab States, as well as professors of international law (discussed in chapter five),[177] the state of Sudan (see above) and counsel for the accused.[178] Mexico's comment on regional inclusion may have been a response to this limited list of organisations. Unlike states parties and professors of international law, the Chamber directly admitted the invited organisations without a two-stage application process.[179] However, only the AU and League of

[170] *Prosecutor v Al-Bashir,* ICC PTC I, 8 December 2016, ICC-02/05-01/09-274. See also *Prosecutor v Al-Bashir,* ICC PTC II, 9 March 2017, ICC-02/05-01/09-286, paras 5 and 6, finding that victims did not have a right to participate in non-cooperation proceedings.

[171] *Prosecutor v Al-Bashir,* ICC PTC II, 6 July 2017, ICC-02/05-01/09-302-Anx, paras 2–3.

[172] *Prosecutor v Al-Bashir,* ICC PTC II, 6 July 2017, ICC-02/05-01/09-302.

[173] *Prosecutor v Al-Bashir,* ICC AC, 29 March 2018, ICC-02/05-01/09-330, para 2.

[174] *Prosecutor v Al-Bashir,* ICC AC, 27 April 2018, ICC-02/05-01/09-342, paras 3–5.

[175] ibid, paras 6–7.

[176] *Prosecutor v Al-Bashir,* ICC AC, 21 May 2018, ICC-02/05-01/09-351, para 1.

[177] *Prosecutor v Al-Bashir,* ICC AC, 29 March 2018, ICC-02/05-01/09-330, paras 1 and 3.

[178] *Prosecutor v Al-Bashir,* ICC AC, 25 May 2018, ICC-02/05-01/09-352.

[179] *Prosecutor v Al-Bashir,* ICC AC, 29 March 2018, ICC-02/05-01/09-330, para 1. Contrast paras 2 and 3.

Arab States participated, filing written submissions[180] and participating in oral hearings,[181] with the Chamber giving the organisations preferential treatment compared to the academic *amici*.[182] The non-cooperation decisions on immunity potentially directly affected these organisations as the hosts of international meetings and their submissions concentrated mainly on the impact on international organisations and the possibility of recognising an exemption for officials travelling to such meetings.[183]

Both the Pre-Trial Chamber in the South African proceedings and the Appeals Chamber in the proceedings concerning Jordan recognised that immunity was an issue of fundamental importance for the relationship between states and the Court. There was conflicting jurisprudence from different Chambers, competing views in the academic literature and inconsistent state practice, with many states including states parties to the Rome Statute having refused to arrest President Al-Bashir. The issue had been one of the most contentious and potentially destabilising challenges for the Court. Both Chambers realised that they had an opportunity to engage with states, to show they were listening to state perspectives and concerns. Therefore, we suggest that the *amicus curiae* mechanism predominantly served a communicative function in these proceedings, although there were aspects of the representative function in the submissions of the two international organisations.

As is evident throughout this study, we have serious reservations about use of the *amicus curiae* mechanism to fulfil a communicative function in the Tribunals, given the focus on individual criminal responsibility. As we observed in chapter five in the context of civil society actors, there are particular issues as to which community interests *amici* should represent and which actors are best placed to represent them in judicial proceedings. In assessing the state *amicus* practice for this chapter, we have struggled as to whether the key role of states in the creation and operation of tribunals justifies a communicative role for states, but not other actors. There are several risks with recognising such a communicative role. First, Chambers must carefully manage participation of this type, including by ensuring submissions are not duplicative, are directed at key legal issues that the Court must address and the parties are not exposed to unreasonable additional burdens. Jordan (the appellant) complained that the Appeals Chamber used the *amicus curiae* submissions to broaden the issues in dispute beyond the grounds of appeal it had raised.[184] We have some sympathy with

[180] *Prosecutor v Al-Bashir,* ICC AC, 13 July 2018, ICC-02/05-01/09-370; *Prosecutor v Al-Bashir,* ICC AC, 16 July 2018, ICC-02/05-01/09-367.

[181] *Prosecutor v Al-Bashir,* ICC AC, 27 August 2018, ICC-02/05-01/09-379.

[182] The organisations immediately followed *Jordan* and the Prosecutor, and were given more time than the academic *amici* to present their submissions: see ibid.

[183] *Prosecutor v Al-Bashir,* ICC AC, 13 July 2018, ICC-02/05-01/09-367; *Prosecutor v Al-Bashir,* ICC AC, 13 July 2018, ICC-02/05-01/09-370; *Prosecutor v Al-Bashir*, ICC AC, Transcript, 12 September 2018.

[184] *Prosecutor v Al-Bashir,* ICC AC, Transcript, 10 September 2017, 25–26.

Jordan here; the written submissions and discussions during the oral hearings canvassed a range of legal, political and practical issues well beyond the points raised by the appeal and more closely approximated proceedings in an advisory opinion. This is inconsistent with the ICC's lack of advisory jurisdiction and raises similar concerns advanced regarding the advisory type jurisdiction the Pre-Trial Chamber exercised in the *Myanmar/Bangladesh* proceedings.[185] It is also arguably inconsistent with the notion that the *amicus curiae* should not be a vehicle for introducing new legal arguments to proceedings (see chapter four). That said, the benefit of allowing participation by states in a communicative function may be warranted where the issue is novel and significant, and the risks of such participation are managed.

Secondly, state *amici*, as with other *amici*, should not make submissions that directly concern or introduce evidence in relation to the international criminal responsibility of the accused, which is the core function of the judges and the parties. The interventions discussed above concerning Article 63 and Rule 68 occurred during trial proceedings and related to the trial function (admissibility of evidence and presence of the accused during the trial). In such circumstances, the risks to fair trial rights are great and must be carefully managed. This means that it is less likely that a communicative function will be appropriate. Cooperation issues arising during the trial are more challenging: failure to cooperate can have serious implications for criminal responsibility, in that a failure to arrest and surrender an accused precludes a trial occurring at all (as per Al-Bashir) or failure to provide evidence can lead to a trial collapsing (as seen in the Kenyan cases). However, non-cooperation proceedings are distinct in the sense that they concern *state* responsibility and are not criminal proceedings. This is even clearer in relation to non-cooperation proceedings under Article 87(7), which are separate from the trial process and do not engage fair trial concerns. Therefore, there may be some scope for a communicative function in non-cooperation proceedings.

The nature of the issue and proposed submission is also relevant. Submissions should be legal and not factual, and addressed to points of international law, not the specifics of any case or situation. States should not be able to use the *amicus curiae* mechanism to communicate their understanding of negotiations at Rome or of amendments or discussions during the ASP, which are otherwise discoverable by the parties and the Chamber and do not necessarily bind the Chamber's interpretation. Great care should be taken so that discussions in the ASP, particularly when initiated or led by directly affected states such as Kenya or South Africa, are not able to influence judicial proceedings, otherwise the Court's independence is threatened. As two of us have written elsewhere, discussion of issues by the ASP and rule amendments already allows 'a forum for individual States Parties, or the ASP as a whole, to attempt to control judicial

[185] Discussed in ch 3, s II.

interpretation of the Rules'.[186] Having enabled this via the ASP, to allow states to make submissions about their understanding and interpretation would be a further incursion into judicial independence. Similarly, the ICC should resist initiatives that would instrumentalise the *amicus curiae* to achieve a political outcome, for example, the AU encouraging all AU member states to seek to participate as *amici curiae* in certain cases. Moreover, recognising a communicative function for states, but not other actors, privileges states and their interests above those of other, equally valid stakeholder interests. Therefore, any possible communicative function for states must involve a novel issue that is of importance to and has implications for *states*, most likely to be limited to the context of cooperation.

The practice suggests that there are different approaches between Chambers. It has predominantly been the Appeals Chamber that has invited state *amici* to perform a communicative function, but only in interlocutory appeals or non-cooperation proceedings (*Jordan, Ruto, Kenyatta*). The fact that the Appeals Chamber only hears appeals that raise an important issue 'that would significantly affect the fair and expeditious conduct of the proceedings or the outcome of the trial'[187] may explain its willingness to engage states, as it is more likely that these will be novel issues on which there is no consensus. The Appeals Chamber may be more willing to engage in judicial creativity and to address controversial issues or gaps in the legal framework.[188] Ultimately, the submissions must still be relevant to the issues and helpful to the judges in their decision, rather than a conversation with no substantive content that is purely intended to engage states and to appear responsive to state concerns. It is not evident how helpful judges have found communicative submissions, with many decisions not fully engaging with the submissions (or engaging at all). For example, the Appeals Chamber indicated in the *Jordan* proceedings that the submissions of the *amici curiae* and the wide-ranging discussion were helpful.[189] The decision set out the submissions of the two international organisations, along with other *amici curiae*, and acknowledged that it considered all submissions.[190] However, the submissions did not seem to have much discernible impact, with a few references in footnotes. The decision adopted reasoning largely contrary to the submissions advanced by the international organisations as *amici*. This suggests that the Chamber perhaps invited briefs to create an impression of greater engagement with key actors.

It is also significant that few states, excluding those directly affected, have taken up opportunities to participate in a communicative function. Even in the

[186] Woolaver and Palmer (n 147), 646.

[187] Rome Statute, Art 82(1)(d).

[188] R Aloisi and J Meernik, *Judgment Day: Judicial Decision Making at the International Criminal Tribunals* (Cambridge, CUP, 2017).

[189] *Prosecutor v Al-Bashir*, ICC AC, Transcript, 14 September 2018, 107–08.

[190] *Prosecutor v Al-Bashir,* ICC AC, 6 May 2019, ICC-02/05-01/09-397-Corr, paras 80–82 (AU), para 83 (League of Arab States) and para 99.

face of the AU decision that its member states should seek to appear as *amici*, only a few member states sought to do so. In the open calls made in the South African and *Jordan* proceedings, only two states, Belgium and Mexico, applied and only Belgium made submissions. There appears to be little interest from states to use the *amicus curiae* mechanism for a communicative function. Factors such as lack of interest or resources may explain this tendency; however, it may also reflect the view that such submissions are not useful to Chambers and may not be appropriate given the Court's role in determining its judicial functions and the need to maintain judicial independence. States may consider the ASP a better venue for broader conversations about the Court. In the South African proceedings, Judge Perrin de Brichambaut suggested another possible explanation: where the law is contested or undecided with significant implications for states, states will be reluctant to commit to a legal position as *amici curiae*.[191] The risk for states is that other states or fora will consider those legal arguments to comprise state practice or *opinio juris* and as evidence of customary international law, which may operate against the state's interests in future proceedings. This suggests that a communicative role may not be particularly effective – or representative of state views – anyway.

Chambers do not invite communicative submissions for all novel and significant issues. For example, the Pre-Trial Chamber in the proceedings concerning *Myanmar/Bangladesh*, which raised a novel and significant issue concerning jurisdiction, did not seek submissions from states other than directly affected states. Again, this shows that the *amicus curiae* mechanism is not suited to address a systemic demand, namely, the need to engage states. Other fora, particularly the ASP, are better suited to a broader conversation as to key challenges and states' concerns.

Finally, states have objected to an expansive use of the *amicus curiae* as undermining legitimacy, particularly for civil society actors. As noted above, Jordan complained that the use of academic *amici* expanded the scope of the appellate proceedings, while Myanmar criticised the Pre-Trial Chamber for having 'permitted organizations to file *amicus curiae* submissions without consideration of their identity or the beneficial scope of their proposed contributions'.[192] South Africa and Kenya both objected – unsuccessfully – to submissions by *amici* in proceedings concerning cooperation.[193] While this criticism relates to civil society *amici*, it demonstrates that states consider that the *amicus curiae* mechanism has limits. If the ICC were to adopt a communicative function,

[191] *Prosecutor v Al-Bashir,* ICC PTC II, 6 July 2017, ICC-02/05-01/09-302-Anx, para 91.

[192] Government of the Republic of the Union of Myanmar, Press Release (9 August 2018), para 14, available at www.president-office.gov.mm/en/?q=briefing-room/statements-and-releases/2018/08/09/id-8937.

[193] As noted above, South Africa objected to submissions by SALC: *Prosecutor v Kenyatta*, ICC AC, 21 May 2015, ICC-01/09-02/11-1030.

similar to that seen in some respects of the *Jordan* non-cooperation proceedings, it may be controversial and encounter resistance from states and other actors.

VI. THE CHALLENGE OF ENGAGING RELUCTANT OR RESISTANT STATES

This discussion has assumed that states *wish* to participate in proceedings. Of course, participation as an *amicus curiae* is voluntary and many states may elect not to participate, as is seen in the relatively low response rates to open calls to states. Even where given permission to participate as an *amicus curiae*, a state may still decide not to file a brief (eg, Mexico in the *Jordan* proceedings). Therefore, it is not surprising that we see participation generally only where a state's interests are directly affected. There may also be occasions where hearing from an affected state would be beneficial for the legitimacy of the institution, both for improving the quality of its decisions and engaging states, and potentially promoting cooperation. Key examples are states that are not state parties, but which are subject to the jurisdiction of the Court, whether by a Security Council referral (Sudan) or on some other jurisdictional basis. Possible examples of the latter are cross-border crimes (Myanmar) or actions of nationals in the territory of a state party (potentially Russia regarding Ukraine). Such states are unlikely to accept the exercise of ICC jurisdiction, including by participating formally in proceedings.

The non-participation of an affected state may not be such an issue for the ICC as for other international tribunals, where the state is the respondent and a party to proceedings. Even in tribunals resolving legal disputes between states, absent states have not precluded proceedings from continuing. The ICJ, for example, has concluded both contentious and advisory opinions without the participation of key states.[194] For a case to proceed at the ICC, there must be an accused in the presence of the Court, so some evidence and legal argumentation will be provided by the accused (which may well align with state views). It is unlikely that an uncooperative state will provide information to the Prosecutor. Thus, in pre-trial and related proceedings like non-cooperation proceedings, the accused may not participate and the views of the state and the valuable information it could provide will not be available to the Court, which undermines the quality of the decision reached. An absent state may also signal lack of authority and support for the Court, which affects its legitimacy. The *amicus curiae* may be one way of enabling the state to engage without conceding jurisdiction.

[194] See, eg *Case Concerning Military and Paramilitary Activities in and Against Nicaragua (Nicaragua v United States of America)* (Merits) [1986] ICJ Rep 14; *Legal Consequences of the Construction of a Wall in the Occupied Palestinian Territory* (Advisory Opinion) 2004, available at www.icj-cij.org/files/case-related/131/131-20040709-ADV-01-00-EN.pdf.

Yet, as members of the Appeals Chamber noted in the *Jordan* proceedings, not participating as an *amicus curiae* is often a reflection of a state's general non-cooperation so a non-cooperative state may be equally unlikely to participate as an *amicus curiae*.[195]

The attempt to engage Myanmar as an *amicus curiae* proved fruitless and, we suggest, led instead to a worrying method of engaging with a non-participating state. Instead of participating as an *amicus curiae*, Myanmar released two statements on its website effectively responding to the Prosecutor's request and setting out its legal position regarding the exercise of jurisdiction by the Court.[196] The Prosecutor drew the statements to the Chamber's attention.[197] The Chamber did not disregard the statements as not being part of the file (as requested by the Prosecutor)[198] or reiterate that Myanmar should submit the statements as an *amicus curiae* if it wished the content to be taken into account. Rather, the Chamber held that as the prosecution had attached the statements to its filing, the statements formed part of the record.[199] The majority judgment then proceeded to spend considerable time responding to the arguments of Myanmar, and footnoted both statements in their entirety.[200] While the Pre-Trial Chamber was seeking to engage and communicate with Myanmar, we suggest it should not do so by engaging with a state that has refused to avail itself of the procedural mechanism offered to it and has chosen to respond by a public statement. This, we argue, is actually counter-productive to encouraging a state to participate in judicial proceedings.

A related issue is the ability of Chambers to accept submissions from states on a confidential basis. As noted in chapters one and two, one claimed benefit of the *amicus curiae* is transparency in that the interests the Chamber is taking into account are clear, applicants are treated consistently and we can see what arguments are influencing the Chambers. Having states provide *amicus curiae* briefs is certainly more transparent than making informal representations to judges, lobbying in the public sphere or not engaging at all. However, there are examples of Chambers accepting submissions from states as *amici curiae* on a confidential basis. Croatia filed its motion to intervene in *Gotovina* in confidence in December 2011 (see above) although the Chamber was quick to remove this

[195] *Prosecutor v Al-Bashir,* ICC AC, 6 May 2019, ICC-02/05-01/09-397-Anx Separate opinion, para 427.

[196] The main statement is found at: Government of the Republic of the Union of Myanmar, Minister of the Office of the State Counsellor, Press Release (8 September 2018), available at www.statecounsellor.gov.mm/en/node/2084.

[197] *Request under Regulation 46(3) of the Regulations of the Court,* ICC PTC I, 17 August 2018, ICC-RoC46(3)-01/18-36.

[198] ibid, para 2.

[199] *Request under Regulation 46(3) of the Regulations of the Court,* ICC PTC I, 6 September 2018, ICC-RoC46(3)-01/18-37, para 23.

[200] ibid, nn 54 and 55.

classification. More recently, the Pre-Trial Chamber in the *Myanmar/Bangladesh* proceedings allowed Bangladesh to file on a confidential basis and offered to allow Myanmar to do the same.[201] Given the wide discretion accorded to the Chambers by Rule 103, judges are not precluded from accepting or inviting submissions on a confidential basis. However, it is at odds with the principle that proceedings should be in public and there is no justification for creating special status for state *amici*. Our view is that Chambers should only permit states acting as *amici curiae* to file briefs on a confidential basis when required to protect victims and witnesses[202] or, at the request of a state or international organisation, for 'the protection of its servants or agents and the protection of confidential or sensitive information'.[203] It is not evident from the Chamber's decision why the information provided by Bangladesh was sensitive or confidential, and Myanmar objected to the filing of the submission on a confidential basis.[204] There may be justification for this protection – it has been suggested that the submissions remained confidential so as not to affect sensitive resettlement negotiations with Myanmar – but the blanket protection without justification undermines the transparency of the Court's 'conversation' with an affected state and the representation of that interest to the Chamber. Moreover, there was no explanation as to why a redacted version would not suffice to protect sensitive information. Chambers should resist this practice unless exceptional reasons exist for it, as it privileges states and risks undermining rather than enhancing legitimacy through 'secret' filings. The reverse of this statement is also true; namely that state *amici curiae* should not receive access to confidential filings. While states have on occasion complained that not having access to all submissions interferes with their ability to participate fully,[205] Chambers must comply with obligations to protect witnesses, victims and confidential material.

VII. CONCLUSION

The state *amicus curiae* practice is not as extensive as that of the civil society actors explored in chapter five. There is even less practice concerning international organisations. Most state *amici* use the mechanism to perform a

[201] *Request Under Regulation 46(3) of the Regulations of the Court,* ICC PTC I, 7 May 2018, ICC-RoC46(3)-01/18-3, para 7; *Request Under Regulation 46(3) of the Regulations of the Court,* ICC PTC I, 21 June 2018, ICC-RoC46(3)-01/18-28, para 6.

[202] Rome Statute, Art 68(1).

[203] Rome Statute, Art 68(6).

[204] See Government of the Republic of the Union of Myanmar (n 191), para 13, citing this as a lack of transparency and preventing Myanmar from making an informed response.

[205] eg, Côte d'Ivoire suggested that not having full access to submissions of the parties impacted the ability to participate: *Prosecutor v L Gbagbo,* ICC AC, 8 October 2012, ICC-02/11-01/11-258-tENG, para 3.

representative function, seeking to participate to represent the interests of their nationals or state interests. However, the creation of specific participatory rights in the Rome Statute framework in proceedings concerning jurisdiction, admissibility and non-cooperation provides an alternative, and preferred, mechanism for an affected state to participate and provides more procedural rights for the state. Host states and states of provisional release also enjoy specific participatory rights. What is evident is that the representative function should not enable an affected state to participate in trial proceedings to support its nationals or to challenge findings on responsibility.

Even where there is no alternative mechanism, the practice demonstrates that Chambers require state *amici*, like other actors, to satisfy the Chamber that their submissions will be of assistance. Chambers therefore apply the same criteria identified in chapter four to states and will reject submissions where they would not be relevant, duplicate other submissions, address factual rather than legal issues or seek to address the individual criminal responsibility of the accused. However, there are five key differences in the application of these criteria to states and in the procedure adopted. First, the existence of an interest in proceedings does not preclude the state appearing in a representative function or in the expertise function where the subject of expertise is the national context and legal system. The interest of the state may actually increase the value of the submissions. However, Chambers should vary the weight, if any, given to the submissions, recognising that there may be partiality. Chambers can also invite other actors to provide different perspectives on national laws or state actions. Secondly, while normally *amici curiae* do not make factual submissions, Chambers should allow more flexibility to accept submissions that address factual aspects of the national system, often alongside legal analysis. Thirdly, where no other participatory rights apply, Chambers are perhaps more likely to invite affected states to participate as *amici* and affected states may face a one-stage admission process. Fourthly, issues of independence do arise, with states accused of colluding with the defence and the prosecution. Chambers should require states, parties and other participants to disclose collaboration and links, for example, a state funding a defence counsel. Finally, although it is hard to draw conclusions based on the limited practice, there is evidence that – when admitted – state *amici* have more impact than other actors, and their submissions are relied on to a greater extent, particularly where they are providing information about the national system. The practice therefore suggests that there appears to be – in some circumstances – preferential treatment of state *amici*.

As with other actors, although recognising the special place of states in relation to international law and their essential role in supporting the Tribunals, we have concluded that the ICC should in general not recognise or encourage a communicative function for state *amici*. Although a few of the instances discussed in this chapter have communicative aspects, we do not think this is appropriate for a criminal tribunal. Other fora, such as the ASP, are better sites for more general conversations with states and other actors. Moreover, to accord such a function to states preferences the views of states over other actors, and risks undermining legitimacy. However, where proceedings concern an issue of key importance to states and do not concern findings on criminal responsibility, most likely only in non-cooperation proceedings, exceptionally a Chamber may invite communicative submissions from states. The Chamber must closely manage this process and should consider whether it should also invite other actors to participate.

8

Conclusion

THIS STUDY HAS focused on a narrow procedural mechanism – the *amicus curiae* – but one that we have argued can have a substantial impact on the legitimacy of international criminal tribunals. The Tribunals have faced challenges due to their perceived selectivity, and lack of independence and effectiveness. The ICC, as the first permanent international criminal tribunal, is particularly subject to these criticisms, though earlier tribunals encountered similar critiques. These criticisms often relate to the Courts' normative legitimacy, which derives from the 'rules, process and outputs of a particular institution',[1] its sociological legitimacy, which concerns the attitudes and beliefs of key constituents and actors toward and about that institution, or both. Given the contested international political environment in which the Tribunals operate, the range of relevant stakeholders, and the need both to rely on state cooperation as well as to regulate state behaviour, their normative and sociological legitimacy are critical to their success. The *amicus curiae*, as the main mode of participation of non-parties within the Tribunals' proceedings, can be an important source of support for, or equally may undermine, legitimacy.

We consider that legitimacy is socially constructed, dynamic, and contested. However, in chapter one, we identified certain key elements of both the normative and sociological legitimacy of the Tribunals. Legality is one, but not the only, basis for the normative legitimacy of international criminal tribunals. The fairness of trials is also a key factor in building normative legitimacy. In addition, the independence and impartiality of courts' decision-making is another contributor to normative legitimacy. Nonetheless, the Tribunals do need to engage with various stakeholders to carry out their work. Democratic principles are also sometimes considered to be an important source of normative legitimacy, requiring institutions to exhibit representative participation. However, this is not necessarily possible nor appropriate for international criminal tribunals, whose focus is the determination of individual criminal responsibility. Further, stakeholders engaging with the Tribunals should not be assumed to be 'democratic'. On the other hand, engagement and communication with those stakeholders through the institution's formal structures and institutions, when subject to suitable limits, is likely to enhance normative legitimacy, as well

[1] A Buchanan and RO Keohane, 'The Legitimacy of Global Governance Institutions' (2006) 20 *Ethics & International Affairs* 405.

as sociological legitimacy (see below), by fostering values including accuracy, accountability and transparency. Therefore, normative legitimacy is complex, but relies upon aspects of legality, fairness, independence, impartiality, and some communication and representation of different views. None of these alone is sufficient, and this book showed that the *amicus curiae* process can contribute to each of them; at the same time, some of these factors also operate as constraints on the appropriate scope of *amicus* participation.

Many of these same factors will be relevant for different individuals or groups' perceptions of an institution. Stakeholders of international criminal tribunals include states, but also various elements of civil society, including NGOs and other organisations, victims and victim groups, academics, judges, lawyers and legal associations, as well as the accused persons that may be tried and even – the Rome Statute preamble perhaps suggests – all of 'humanity'. Schlesinger argues that participation in processes may generate a 'voice effect' that enhances support for the outcome, whatever it is.[2] Considering sociological legitimacy can focus attention toward the changing, plural and heterogeneous nature of these stakeholders and their potential perspectives of the Tribunals' legitimacy. It also directs attention toward the ways in which the Tribunals can represent and offer discursive processes for building their own legitimacy. Through its analysis of the *amicus curiae* mechanism, this book shows how the Tribunals can provide mechanisms for contesting and debating international criminal law practices, allowing for forms of communication that enhance perceptions of the legitimacy of the institution.

We have argued that the *amicus curiae* can and should have a substantial positive impact on these markers of legitimacy, depending on how the Tribunals admit and use *amicus* submissions in their practice. In chapter two, we situated the *amicus curiae* in comparative perspective, seeking to illustrate both a core understanding of its functions, as well as the distinct characteristics of international criminal tribunals that justified our focussed study. We drew on studies of other international tribunals including the ICJ, ITLOS, WTO dispute settlement mechanisms, investment arbitration panels, and regional human rights tribunals (the ECtHR, the African Court and the IACHR), as well as selected national jurisdictions. Our functional approach led us to analyse not only interventions labelled as '*amicus curiae*' in these jurisdictions, but also related doctrines and other procedures or modes of participation that filled a similar role(s) as the *amicus*. These included rules on standing, joinder and intervention, particularly third-party intervention. This comparative analysis revealed three underlying themes. First, the *amicus* is a discretionary, flexible mechanism, which is found in almost all international dispute settlement regimes as well as widely in both common and civil law national jurisdictions. The flexibility of the mechanism has facilitated its horizontal and vertical transplantation, and

[2] N Schlesinger, 'Making International Criminal Law: Factors Influencing Judicial Behaviour at the ICTY and ICTR' (PhD thesis, the University of Melbourne) 172.

reliance on the mechanism is increasing in both international and national jurisdictions. Secondly, the flexibility of the *amicus* also leads to differences between jurisdictions in the criteria for admission and functions of *amici curiae*, allowing its parameters to adjust to fill gaps in non-party participation not otherwise provided for. A key distinction that we have seen between jurisdictions is whether the *amicus* is required to act impartially, or whether it has developed an advocacy function – which often depends on the existence of other mechanisms such as intervention, comprehensive legal aid, or broad rules on standing. Thirdly, in international jurisdictions, we observe that differences between institutions in relation to the provision for the *amicus curiae* can be attributed at least in part to the dependence on state consent. It is notable that the *amicus* has been included in all international criminal tribunals, both where the rules of procedure were determined by judges and where drafted by the state parties. State support for the *amicus* is also demonstrated by states' use of the mechanism to themselves act as *amici* in the Tribunals. As we argue in chapter three, the inclusion of the *amicus curiae* is therefore best practice for international criminal tribunals, including for future tribunals.

This comparative analysis also highlighted the characteristics of international criminal tribunals that require a distinct approach to the *amicus curiae* mechanism. Unlike other international tribunals, the focus on individual criminal responsibility has important implications for the appropriate scope of *amicus* participation, requiring that fair trial rights always operate as a check on the Tribunals' practice. This concern is also reflected in national practice of criminal courts, which tend to adopt a more conservative approach to *amicus* participation than in activities such as constitutional adjudication. In addition, again unlike other international tribunals, the main parties in international criminal tribunals are the prosecution and defence, rather than states. However, unlike in most national criminal proceedings, a variety of interests of different states may be implicated, both because the nature of the crimes often involves high-level state policy and actors, but also because their jurisdiction includes certain stages that directly adjudicate on the legality of state action, including non-cooperation proceedings at the ICC. Further, the nature of the subject matter, dealing with the 'most serious crimes of concern to the international community as a whole',[3] means that there are potentially wide-ranging state and non-state interests implicated in the proceedings. Thus, as noted above, the unique range of stakeholders, interests, mandate and goals of international criminal tribunals calls for a distinct approach to the *amicus* mechanism.

We have argued in this study that the *amicus curiae* mechanism is most able to contribute to the legitimacy of the Tribunals when the Tribunals and *amici* themselves clearly identify the function that their participation would seek to fulfil, in the context of the general requirement seen in all Tribunals that *amici* should 'assist' the Chamber in making its determinations. We have

[3] Rome Statute, preamble.

identified three potential functions that reflect the predominant purposes of *amicus* participation: the expertise, representative and communicative functions (see Table 1.1, chapter one). This typology is both descriptive and normative. It is descriptive in the sense that we have drawn these three functions from the comprehensive analysis of *amicus* practice at the Tribunals in this study. However, these functions are usually implicit in the practice, with only a small number of instances where the *amicus* and/or the tribunal has expressly acknowledged the function that the particular *amicus* intervention seeks to play. We set out the details and key findings of this study in chapters three and four. A wide range of actors have applied and have been admitted as *amici* before all the Tribunals and at all stages of proceedings. Most *amici* apply to participate, though Tribunals (and some more than others) may invite *amici* or issue 'open calls' for submissions. The Chambers do not always apply consistent criteria to the admission of *amici*, though relevance, timing, impartiality, independence, fair trial issues, and avoiding duplication are key factors. The vast majority of *amici* address legal questions, often of a novel character, and most perform an expertise function, sometimes in combination with other functions. *Amici* are relatively evenly aligned between victims, prosecution, defence or governments, but are much more likely to come from countries outside of those where the alleged crimes were committed. In proceedings concerning reparations orders at the ICC, there seems to have been some confusion surrounding the distinction between the *amicus curiae* and interventions under Article 75(3), which should be resolved. The practice also reveals inconsistency in the treatment of *amicus* invitations, applications and submissions, regarding which we make further suggestions in the Practice Guide in Annex C. We have argued that a key source of this inconsistency is a lack of appreciation of the distinct functions that can be played by *amici* at the Tribunals.

Our typology is also normative in the sense that we consider that there are certain functions that the *amicus* ***should*** fulfil. We further suggest that more widespread and deliberate recognition of these distinct functions in the *amicus* practice could have significant benefits for both normative and sociological legitimacy of the Tribunals. We consider this to be the case for several reasons. First, as argued in chapter four, it is our view that these three functions are not equally appropriate for *amicus* participation in international criminal proceedings. We have argued that it is through only the expertise and representative functions that *amici* can make the most substantial contributions to the legitimacy of the Tribunals, without incurring significant costs in terms of threatening the fair trial rights of the accused, overburdening the parties or the Chamber, or intruding on the Tribunals' core judicial competence or the role of the parties. In contrast, the communicative function is generally inappropriate, since the determination of public interests is not directly relevant to the adjudication of individual criminal responsibility, and indeed can distract from that primary function of the Tribunals. This is demonstrated both in our overview of practice in chapters three and four, and in our discussion of the most significant actors in the Tribunals' *amicus* practice in chapters five to seven (civil society, the defence, and states). In contrast, the appropriate functions of *amici curiae* may be different at international institutions with other mandates and jurisdictional scope. For instance, the communicative function may be crucial to the legitimacy of international and regional human rights tribunals, whose focus is not on individual criminal responsibility, but rather measures with broad human rights and/ or constitutional implications. Thus, it is only if the Tribunals recognise these potential functions that they can identify *amici* most likely to fulfil a function appropriate to the goals and functions of the tribunal in question.

The recognition of these distinct functions is also important because they contribute to different aspects of the legitimacy of the Tribunals, though we recognise that these do overlap. As a result, we have argued that the type of actor and the function to be performed should influence how other criteria (eg, independence, expertise and impartiality) apply. Within chapters five to seven, we have considered how the three functions operate in distinct ways for each actor and may require variations in how admissibility criteria are applied, as well as how the process is managed.

The expertise function particularly serves the values of accuracy, transparency and legality. This is done by seeking to obtain *amicus* submissions that will contribute predominantly legal expertise on novel and important issues that would otherwise be unavailable to the Chamber, in order to improve the quality of the judicial decisions – and thus the normative legitimacy of tribunals. This is the function within which civil society actors, including NGOs and academics, should most often be admitted (see chapter five), though there is also a role for defence-aligned actors and states within this function (see chapters six and seven). The criteria of independence and impartiality are of special importance for the expertise function. In order for the expertise and information to be reliable and so contribute to the quality of decision-making, efforts should be made to ensure that *amicus* submissions are not skewed by direct interests in the proceedings, nor by a relationship with the parties. However, as we have argued in chapter four and in relation to the actors in chapters five to seven, this does not require *neutrality* of the *amici*, and a sympathy for or alignment with the position of a party should not, of itself, disqualify an *amicus* from providing expertise. Indeed, in chapter six, we have proposed that the Tribunals could enhance the position of the defence and redress the inequality of arms by issuing more invitations or open calls to *amici* to address defence rights issues within the expertise function. Confusion concerning the requirement of independence and impartiality is pervasive throughout the practice, and we argue clarification of the content and appropriate scope of application of these criteria could lead to greater consistency in admissions decisions and the use of admitted *amicus* submissions.

In addition, the expertise function requires the Tribunals to identify useful and relevant expertise that is distinct from the parties and the Tribunals' core judicial functions – without which *amicus* submissions will not benefit the quality of decision-making, waste time and resources of the Chambers and the parties, and may threaten fair trial rights, especially if *amicus* submissions directly concern the criminal responsibility of the accused. We argue that this is another area where improvement could be made, and suggest certain reforms, including the increased use of well-publicised open calls to specify the matters on which tribunals require assistance, and then assessing which submissions to accept (a 'two stage' approach) – rather than simply accepting the first in time; as well as to actively seek expertise from more diverse regions and actors; a general restriction to legal rather than factual expertise; and improved practices to identify and test expertise based on relevant experience and not merely formal titles or unfounded claims of expertise. These reforms would augment the contribution to both normative and sociological legitimacy made through this function.

In contrast, the representative function primarily furthers the values of participation, transparency and fairness at the Tribunals, by facilitating the representation of interests directly affected by the Tribunals' decisions. This function is crucial for normative legitimacy because high-quality decision-making requires consideration of all relevant interests directly affected by the decision. It is also crucial for sociological legitimacy, since those whose interests are affected by a legal determination are more likely to respect a judicial outcome if they have had an opportunity to be heard. In relation to this function, the criteria of independence and impartiality should not be required of *amici*, since it is precisely because of their interest in the proceedings that their submissions are valuable. Again, we argue that this confusion is at the root of much of the inconsistent judicial practice that we have discussed. We argue that different actors might be 'directly affected' in different ways. In chapters five to seven, we suggest that this might include victims of international crimes, the accused in related proceedings, states and international organisations. However, whether *amicus* submissions within the representative function are required will depend on whether the actor with a directly affected interest may participate through another mechanism. Thus, in chapter five, we consider that the need for NGO representation of victims' interests through *amicus* submissions is limited in tribunals, such as the ICC, where victims' participation is formally provided. We also suggest that caution is required when assessing the representative claims of many civil society actors, who may not have a substantiated representative relationship with the interests in question. It may also be generally more appropriate for actors to give information to the parties where their interests coincide. Similarly, as set out in chapter six, the defence's wide rights of participation will mean *amicus* submissions representing the accused's interests are merely duplicative of the defence's role, and may be incompatible with the right to choose one's own defence, except in stages of proceedings where the defence has no guaranteed right of participation. In addition, chapter seven demonstrates that states will normally not have interests that are directly affected in proceedings because of the focus on individual criminal responsibility except, perhaps, in cases concerning state cooperation in non-trial proceedings. Further, when actors do have a right of participation through another mechanism, such as victim participation or procedures for states to participate in certain stages (as the ICC does for admissibility and jurisdiction), this should be preferred to *amicus* submissions. The latter, as a discretionary mechanism, is not well-suited to the purpose of representing interests directly affected in proceedings and should only be used where there is no other accessible avenue for doing so.

The communicative function is fulfilled by *amicus* submissions that seek to address broad public interests relevant to the proceedings, or to make indirect representative claims on behalf of victims or other actors. Unlike the first two functions, we have argued that this is generally not an appropriate role for *amici* at international criminal tribunals, unless performed in combination with the expertise or representative function. While this function may appear to serve the value of representativeness and sociological legitimacy more broadly, we have argued that this function risks undermining the legitimacy of the criminal proceedings as it threatens the key values of fair trial, legality and independence. While public interests are certainly implicated in international criminal prosecutions, and are central to the international criminal justice project more generally, the Tribunals should not become a forum for such broad conversations, which may threaten the core function of determining individual criminal responsibility through fair trials. The lack of advisory jurisdiction at the Tribunals, in contrast to other international courts, emphasises the need to focus on matters directly implicated in the proceedings. In addition, there are significant difficulties for Tribunals in determining what constitutes the 'public interest' and identifying *amici* who can authoritatively speak to such interests. Rather, as set out in chapters five to seven, actors seeking to address broader interests may utilise other mechanisms to do so, which do not threaten the fairness, efficiency and expediency of criminal proceedings. At the ICC, these include participation in the ASP, which is open to states (both ICC member and non-member states) as well as civil society actors, and Article 15 representations to the Prosecutor. However, in chapter seven, we have considered a limited exception for states addressing novel and complex issues in the context of non-cooperation proceedings, which may be appropriate given states' important role in the creation and functioning of the Tribunals.

Overall, our study demonstrates that the Tribunals are managing the *amicus* practice in a conservative manner, and that there is limited evidence that *amici* have had direct impact on the outcome of the Tribunals' decisions. A largely cautious approach to the *amicus curiae* is generally appropriate given the primary role of judges and parties at the Tribunals. Claims of an overly permissive practice enabling the *amicus* mechanism to overwhelm the parties or to be used as an unregulated tool of lawfare by NGOs or states are not supported by our study. However, we do consider that the Tribunals' *amicus* practice can be improved, and propose reforms for how this might be done. These reforms could augment the positive impact of *amicus* participation both on the Tribunals' decisions, as well as on the markers of legitimacy we have identified. We suggest that the key values of participation, transparency, accountability and expertise, as well as broader notions of fairness, including independence, impartiality, equal treatment and fair processes should guide the ICC and other tribunals' management of their *amicus curiae* practice. International criminal tribunals should recognise the three functions that we have identified and recognise that the appropriate scope for each may differ. The criteria for *amicus* participation as well as the process followed may require modification depending on the actor and function sought to be fulfilled, which should be done openly in Chambers' decisions inviting or approving *amicus* applications. The express recognition of these functions, and their application by Chambers to admit *amici* only if they are likely to assist the Chambers by fulfilling an appropriate function (or perhaps a combination of such functions), is likely to lead to more consistent, fair, reasoned and predictable treatment of *amici*, benefiting the legitimacy of the proceedings. Further, Chambers should acknowledge where they have relied on *amicus* submissions more consistently, to confirm the value of *amicus* submissions and encourage actors to continue to participate as *amici* in the future. The Chambers have significant discretion to act within the parameters of the *amicus* mechanism. They can purposefully harness its potential to benefit normative and sociological legitimacy by actively seeking better and more diverse expertise, particularly on novel and complex matters, and seeking to ensure that the perspectives of all with interests directly affected by their determinations are effectively represented.

Annex A: Methodology for Data Collection and Analysis

I. INTRODUCTION

THIS ANNEX SETS out our approach to collating and analysing *amicus curiae* applications and briefs for a select group of international criminal tribunals between 2014 and 2019. As explained in chapter one, these are the ICC, ICTY, ICTR, ECCC, SCSL and STL. We acknowledge the limitations of our approach. While some are discussed below, they include selectivity, access, and bias issues, among others.

As documents, legal texts reflect the particular preferences and contexts of their authors.[1] They may not express the 'real' reasoning or intentions of their authors. Documents are also interpreted differently by each reader or researcher. The documents for this project were gathered by the authors, with the assistance at times of short-term research assistants, but all authors were involved with reviewing the method of collation and analysing the documents, no doubt each influenced by our training and work, expectations and perspectives. As lawyers, we endeavoured to analyse the stated positions in legal decisions using doctrinal legal interpretation methods as well as general thematic analysis (see below). However, we also drew on related documents such as media and NGO reports and a limited number of interviews to provide further context where available and known to us. For all the limitations of our methods, our approach produced a comprehensive sample of *amicus curiae* practice before the Tribunals.

II. COLLATION

Documents were collected from the official website of each institution and also from other public sources, for example, webpages of civil society actors. The Tribunals' websites have different formats and levels of functionality and completeness, and some changed during the project, but offered search functions to locate documents containing the words '*amicus curiae*' or the relevant internal

[1] A Orford, 'On International Legal Method' (2013) 1(1) *London Review of International Law* 166; D Smith, *Texts, Facts, and Femininity: Exploring the Relations of Ruling* (London, Routledge, 1993).

rule number. We gathered *amicus curiae* documents from the establishment of each Tribunal until the end March 2019. This approach did not locate all documents, since some applications or submissions do not include these words in the titles or, for in-text searches, retrieved too many documents. Thus, it was also necessary to review the listed court documents for each case online and attempt to identify titles that appeared likely to relate to an *amicus curiae* submission. We found a small number of decisions that appeared to rely solely upon the *amicus curiae* mechanism to admit submissions, but neither mentioned that term nor the applicable procedural rule. This suggests that there may have been other documents that also performed the 'function' of an *amicus curiae* that were not included in our data. On the other hand, since court documents often name related materials, including in the procedural history, once one decision was located it was often easier locate other relevant submissions or decisions (such as other applications, parties' responses or outcomes).

The data set is not complete; some applications and related decisions were not available, particularly for older documents (sometimes even after archive requests) and for those *amici curiae* that were unsuccessful, or sometimes where the *amicus* or Court decided not to make the application or submissions available publicly. Similarly, it has not been possible to source all *amicus* briefs. The search method may also not have retrieved every relevant document, although additional documents could become available subsequently, because there is sometimes a short lag between decisions being made and posted to tribunal websites and as older records are located, translated, and posted. Where we could not locate a particular document, sometimes we could identify its title and date, for instance from the procedural history of a related decision. In general, such identified documents were included within our table of documents. We also analysed only the English (or, very occasionally, French) versions of the documents, but did not identify relevant documents not in these languages (which are official languages of the Tribunals). Where identical or very similar *amicus curiae* submissions were submitted in more than one case (eg, in the *Ruto* and *Kenyatta* cases at the ICC or *Case 003* and *Case 004* at the ECCC), we counted these separately as while the content may be the same, the case is technically different. Most submissions by the same applicant in the same case were also counted separately, unless later documents were clearly clarifications or appeals related to an earlier brief on the same issue. Still, we did identify a large number of documents: 408 attempted *amicus curiae* submissions and 247 briefs accepted, including 78 (of 157) at the ICC.[2]

[2] In January 2016, Helen Brady of the OTP had located 63 *amicus curiae* applications at the ICC. We located 86 during a similar period, but believe the discrepancy comes from a difference in 'cut off' dates and our inclusion of 'duplicate' applications submitted in both the *Ruto* and *Kenyatta* cases. Neither number includes applications under Art 75(3) of the Rome Statute (though see ch 4 regarding the conflation of these procedures in some cases). We acknowledge there are multiple ways of counting these documents, but it does provide some comfort that at least we have more, rather than fewer, documents.

We use the term 'application' to include submissions in response to open calls and invitations as well as unsolicited applications and the total attempted submissions includes open calls or invitations that were not responded to.

We collected the details of applications and briefs made as *amici curiae* but excluded applications and briefs based on other mechanisms for participation. For example, we did not include submissions made by state actors in challenges to jurisdiction, referral or non-cooperation proceedings, unless the state was participating as an *amicus curiae* rather than on a specific statutory basis. We also did not capture *amicus curiae* submissions made by '*amicus curiae* prosecutors' or '*amicus curiae* defence' as we did not view these as serving the function of *amici curiae*. The exception to this is our approach to the reparations practice at the ICC, where we captured submissions labelled as *amicus curiae* as well as those labelled as pursuant to Article 75(3), as we wished to explore the interaction between these two provisions and this better reflected our functional approach.

III. ANALYSIS

To aid in analysis, wherever possible, for each actual or attempted submission as an *amicus curiae*, we extracted the following information, which was then recorded in a large spreadsheet, alongside the Tribunal and relevant case:[3]

(1) Name of applicant(s).
(2) The number of signatories. While some applications are signed once 'on behalf of' other groups,[4] the table includes a count of the number of listed authors or signatories to allow some consideration of the frequency of joint or multiple party submissions.
(3) Background: we attempted to categorise actors as 'national' (from the country where alleged crimes took place), 'international' (from any other country), or 'mixed', although this was an approximation since such classifications were difficult in many cases (as where apparently 'international' actors were long-term expatriates or worked with national NGOs or for institutions with 'national' chapters).
(4) Type of intervener: each applicant or invited *amicus* or other participant was classified (as a whole, regardless of the number of signatories)[5] according

[3] The spreadsheet became large and unwieldy as the number of documents we located escalated. We acknowledge that a different form of data collection application (such as thematic analysis software) may have been more effective.

[4] eg *Prosecutor v Katanga*, ICC TC II, 13 February 2015, ICC-01/04-01/07-3523 – counted as one applicant and one signatory, although it mentions being made on behalf of other agencies.

[5] eg, a co-submission by the NGO Redress and academic centre Queen's University Belfast Human Rights Centre was classified as an 'NGO' submission, although it could also have been considered 'academic': see *Prosecutor v Al Mahdi*, ICC TC VIII, 2 December 2016, ICC-01/12-01/15-188.

to whether they appeared to be predominantly an NGO, academic, government actor, 'legal' group (lawyers and bar and defence associations), or 'other', which included international organisations such as the United Nations and its organs, as well as individuals (including defendants in other cases).[6] Allocating these designations also required some subjective decision-making – for instance, for applications with large numbers of co-signatories of different 'types', or more activist research centres (typically 'academic').

(5) Apparent alignment of the application and brief with the defence, prosecution, victims, government, or 'legal' or 'other' (for examples, see chapter four) in substance. These were classified through making a general qualitative assessment of the main arguments in the application and any submissions.

(6) Stage of proceedings: pre-trial, trial, appeals, or post-appeals (reparations).

(7) The name and date of the submissions.

(8) The form of the *amicus curiae* – whether the *amicus curiae* submissions, if any, were made in a written brief, within oral proceedings, or both.[7]

(9) The process for the application or submission – was there an 'open call' for submissions on a particular topic, or was the *amicus curiae* invited or (as in the majority of cases) was there a voluntary application to participate.

(10) Where possible, the wording about the stated purpose for the invitation, call or request to provide *amicus curiae* submissions (and/or its proposed topic) was extracted from the relevant court document (call or invitation) or application, the names and dates of which were listed in the database.

(11) We allocated a broad category to the (proposed) issue to be addressed. Invitations, calls, or applications were classified in a subjective and general manner as seeking to offer: factual information, historical background, legal analysis, details about procedural or evidential matters (such as issues concerning witnesses), input concerning victims, defence representation issues, contempt proceedings, or 'other/mixed' matters (where a single allocation was inappropriate, usually because the submissions clearly addressed both factual and legal matters).[8]

(12) Outcome of request – was it accepted, rejected, or accepted with conditions placed upon the response (or withdrawn or not located).[9] Responses to invitations or open calls are typically not approved in an admissibility decision, but are counted as 'approved' since they are always admitted.

[6] Lawyers sometimes offered to provide advice in *amicus curiae* submissions and signed applications, but also represented individuals, including defendants in other cases. These were considered as being on behalf of other individuals and so characterised as 'other', rather than 'legal'.

[7] If both oral and written submissions were made by the same actor on the same issues and based on one application or invitation, this was typically still counted as a single application.

[8] For examples, see ch 4.

[9] Two applications were withdrawn and six application decisions could not be located, mostly at the ICTR.

(13) The name, date and Chambers for the admissibility decision or invitation.
(14) The extracted reasons provided for Chambers' decision (the 'test' applied, including whether there were references to other earlier *amicus curiae* decisions), as well as any specified time or length limits for the briefs themselves.
(15) Additional analysis of the admissibility decision was carried out, including: whether any party responded to the *application* to participate, the composition of the bench (the names of the judges and number of judges from civil, common, or mixed law countries, as listed on tribunal websites[10]), the length of the decision,[11] and the predominant reason[12] for acceptance or rejection (relevance/usefulness, duplication, timeliness/expeditiousness, providing additional information or arguments such as updates concerning other judicial proceedings, specified application procedures were not followed, the impartiality or otherwise of the applicant, or 'other' – including where there was an open call and thus no specific reason was provided).
(16) The specific issues addressed by the *amicus curiae* were listed, as well as which of each of the following types of arguments made or issues addressed (multiple topics could be selected): international criminal law issues (such as the elements of crimes or modes of liability), international humanitarian law, human rights law, general or public international law issues (such as concerning jurisdiction), procedural and evidence issues, victims participation and reparations, factual, political or historical background, and gender issues.
(17) The 'function' evident from the court's decision regarding accepting (or otherwise) the *amicus curiae* submissions, namely whether the brief was intended to fulfil the expertise, representative or communicative function. This focused on the predominant reason provided by the court, or if not evident, the likely intention or expectation of the applicant. Each was allocated to the three typologies or a mix, or any, all, or (in rare cases where the decision gave little detail) none of them.
(18) The names and dates of any written responses by the parties to the *amicus curiae* applications and arguments and other related documents and issues.

[10] While noting that there may be debates about which legal systems can be classified into each of these categories, if any, for the purposes of this research country systems were identified with reference to the CIA World Factbook, available at www.cia.gov/library/publications/the-world-factbook/fields/308.html, as at January 2018, or other public online sources.

[11] Some decisions deal with multiple applications, or cover a number of issues only one of which concerns an *amicus curiae*. Page lengths were therefore very approximate estimates of how much of each decision dealt with a particular application.

[12] Many decisions provide or suggest there were multiple reasons for accepting or rejecting an application to appear as an *amicus*. The categories were determined subjectively by reading the decision and deciding which reason was most emphasised – for instance, because it was the first reason provided.

Researchers then compared *amicus curiae* submissions to the documents reflecting the 'outcome' of the relevant proceedings, such as judgments and procedural rulings, in an attempt to determine whether and to what extent those submissions had influenced that outcome. This involved a textual analysis, comparing the structure, content and references of the *amicus* submissions to the most relevant court document.[13] This ability to analyse particular briefs in more depth was facilitated by the structure of the spreadsheet, which could be filtered across the range of measures (so as to extract, for example, only applications by NGOs in a specific court that were accepted).

IV. ICC ADDITIONAL ANALYSIS

Additional analysis was carried out for the ICC several years into our project in an effort to record some of our subjective and qualitative decisions and analysis in a more simplified manner, and to complement this with additional counting (more quantitative) techniques. First, after reading the *amicus curiae* briefs alongside the relevant judicial decision, submissions were scored '0' for no impact, '1' where the decision either referenced the brief or dealt with very similar arguments to the *amicus curiae*, or '2' where the decision (or a minority opinion) clearly engaged with or relied upon the brief to support a particular argument – for instance via citation to support or compare arguments.

The allocation of these scores remained qualitative and was complex and subjective, as illustrated by the following examples. A '0' was given where the *amicus* was not mentioned or appeared to have no impact. This included some instances where the Chambers noted the brief (for instance in the procedural history) but did not engage with the submissions, or the arguments were treated as being irrelevant. For instance, in the Kenyatta case concerning the Africa Centre for Open Justice,[14]

> The Appeals Chamber notes that the *Amicus Curiae* Observations advance arguments outside the scope of the issues certified on appeal and are therefore unhelpful for the proper determination of the present appeal. Under these circumstances, the Appeals Chamber will not address the submissions made in the *Amicus Curiae* Observations or in the responses thereto.

[13] For an example of the use of plagiarism software for this purpose, which proved too difficult to access and apply for this project but may warrant further exploration for future research, see PM Collins, PC Corley and J Hamner, 'The Influence of *Amicus Curiae* Briefs on U.S. Supreme Court Opinion Content' (2015) 49(4) *Law & Society Review* 917.

[14] *Prosecutor v Kenyatta*, ICC AC, 19 August 2015, ICC-01/09-02/11-1032.

A '1' was assigned where Chambers referred to *amicus* arguments, but did not explicitly engage with them to support their reasoning. Thus, in contrast to the previous example, a '1' was allocated where the Pre-Trial Chamber mentioned its interest in, but failure to draw upon, *amicus* submissions provided by the Uganda Victims Foundation and Redress Trust:[15]

> … the information submitted by the *Amicus curiae* regarding the difficulties encountered by victims of alleged LRA crimes … [etc.] *whilst interesting for the Chamber as a matter of information*, are equally unsuitable to build the background for a proper determination.

A score of '2' was given for a Pre-Trial decision in *Laurent Gbagbo* case, where the single judge was 'mindful of the potential difficulties in creating a collective narrative of events *as indicated by* the Defence, *REDRESS* and OPCV, particularly in cases where sensitive categories of victims are involved, such as victims of sexual crimes'.[16] Here, although the distinction is subtle, the judge relied upon *amicus curiae* submissions for at least one part of the analysis. More clearly, the *Al Mahdi* reparations decision frequently cited *amicus* submissions to support various findings, such as that '[c]ultural property also allows a group to distinguish and identify itself before the world community'.[17] This also supported a score of '2'.

Secondly, the database included a reflection on whether the outcome on the relevant issues was 'similar' to or 'different' from the position advanced by the *amicus curiae*. Determining similarity or difference was often complicated, however. For instance, Southern Africa Litigation Centre provided an *amicus curiae* brief that supported a finding that South Africa did not comply with its obligations under domestic law and the Rome Statute to arrest President Al-Bashir of Sudan.[18] This was 'similar' to the Chamber's finding, although the remedy (referral to the Assembly of States Parties) differed from SALC's proposal for referral to the Security Council.[19] Whereas the previous measure accounted for the extent to which decision-making engaged with *amicus* arguments (including disagreeing with them), this classification separately considered judicial outcomes – and therefore the possible correlation between the *amicus* and Chambers' conclusions. Despite their different focus, but similarly simplified approach, the previous scores of *amicus* influence (0–2) might be expected to correlate to findings of similarity versus difference. This was

[15] *Prosecutor v Kony et al*, ICC PTC II, 11 March 2009, ICC-02/04-01/15-156, para 50, emphasis added. See also para 49: 'The information summarized above, *albeit of enormous interest* to the Chamber, appears without any context which would allow the Chamber to properly address it in a full-fledged determination of the admissibility of the Case', emphasis added.

[16] *Prosecutor v L Gbagbo*, ICC TC I, 5 April 2012, ICC-02/11-01/11-86, para 29, emphasis added.

[17] *Prosecutor v Al Mahdi*, ICC TC VIII, 7 August 2017, ICC-01/12-01/15-236, para 16, fn 36, which cited submissions by the Queen's University of Belfast Human Rights Centre and the Redress Trust.

[18] *Prosecutor v Al-Bashir*, ICC PTC II, 10 March 2017, ICC-02/05-01/09-288.

[19] *Prosecutor v Al-Bashir*, ICC PTC II, 6 July 2017, ICC-02/05-01/09-302.

supported by the research, since for 70 per cent of decisions where the outcome was 'similar' to that proposed or implied by the *amicus*, the qualitative score of impact was either '1' or '2'. There were situations where the overall conclusion was 'different' but the brief scored '2'. These occurred where the Court discussed but disagreed with *amicus* arguments, or agreed with one or more of the *amici*'s points but ultimately reached a different conclusion.[20] Thus, these two methods provided complementary insights concerning the influence of *amicus curiae* briefs, though both really just recorded our qualitative assessment.

Thirdly, as noted above, drawing on a method adopted by Bürli to assess the success of activist and restraint arguments,[21] *amici* in all Tribunals were also classified by their alignment with the prosecution, defence, victims, government, or 'other' (alignment unclear). For the ICC, this alignment was then compared to whether the outcome in the case was broadly in favour of one or another of these actors. Again, this approach involved making subjective generalisations about the purpose and use of *amicus* briefs – and of the Chambers' findings. The results of this method were expected to coincide with those of the previous approach, since alignment was largely determined by the extent to which *amicus* arguments favoured one of the parties in substance. Thus, if the Chambers decided, for example, in favour of the prosecution, and the *amicus* appeared allied with the prosecution, the conclusion should also be 'similar' to that proposed by the *amicus*. Indeed, very few *amicus* briefs departed from this correlation. On closer examination, these were situations where the overall outcome favoured the party with which the *amicus* was arguably 'aligned', but the decision adopted different reasons or addressed different issues to the *amicus*.[22] The alignment comparison therefore offered an opportunity to cross-check the other results and further demonstrated the complexity of determining the influence of *amicus curiae* briefs.

Fourthly, to supplement this qualitative, but simplified analysis, the database also included the number of in-text[23] mentions or footnoted citations[24] and

[20] eg, a score of '2' was allocated to a brief by a number of countries concerning the presence of the accused at trial, even though the ultimate conclusion was different, because the Appeals Chamber noted that 'A measure of flexibility in the management of proceedings in such circumstances accords with the duty of the Trial Chamber ... and helps to ensure, *as mentioned by* the United Republic of Tanzania, the Republic of Rwanda, the Republic of Burundi, the State of Eritrea and the Republic of Uganda, "justice in each individual case"': *Prosecutor v Ruto and Sang*, ICC AC, 25 October 2013, ICC-01/09-01/11-1066, para 50, emphasis added.

[21] N Bürli, *Third-Party Interventions Before the European Court of Human Rights* (Cambridge, Intersentia, 2017) 45.

[22] eg see *Prosecutor v Kenyatta*, ICC AC, 19 August 2015, ICC-01/09-02/11-1032 regarding Africa Centre for Open Justice.

[23] 'In-text' in this context meant references within the main body of the document, rather than the footnotes, unless the footnoted material was clearly discursive.

[24] If an *amicus curiae* submitter was named within the decision, this was counted once, but if that mention was accompanied by a footnote, the additional citation was not counted to avoid double counting.

the approximate number of in-text lines mentioning the *amicus* submissions (including within the procedural history).[25] The database provides another, albeit rough, indicator for the extent to which the Chambers least reflected upon the *amici's* arguments, again, to cross-check the previous methods.

That said, counting lines and references provided merely an indicator of judicial consideration of *amicus curiae* arguments. For instance, some parts of the decisions may have incorporated points prompted by an *amicus* without citation. Other decisions summarised *amicus* arguments at length, alongside those of the parties, but then did not refer to them within the sections containing their analysis and reasoning. Moreover, the citations and lines did not demonstrate the level of *amicus* influence upon the actual *result*. In fact, the citation and length measures confirmed the importance of using a variety of methods for reviewing the use of *amicus curiae* briefs – and particularly their actual impact on judicial results. In decisions that showed a 'similar' outcome to that advanced by the *amicus*, the average number of lines addressing the submissions was 27 with 7 citations, whereas there were 50 lines and 10 citations when the outcome was 'different' (for this exercise, Article 75(3) submissions were also included). Although we did not apply any statistical analysis methods or controls, this suggested that a greater amount of decision 'space' devoted to discussing submissions did not correspond to a greater impact upon the result, perhaps indicating that Courts felt it necessary to engage with opposing arguments in more detail. As an example, some decisions in the *Ruto* case reached a different conclusion than was proposed by the Government of Kenya as an *amicus*, even though the Chambers summarised and engaged with Kenya's arguments to a significant degree.[26] In the *Lubanga* case, Trial Chamber I relied upon *amicus* submissions provided by counsel for several witnesses who were seeking asylum in The Netherlands, but reached a different conclusion.[27]

This combination of techniques was intended to combine 'the generalizability offered by quantitative studies with the depth provided by more traditional qualitative approaches that focus on the words used in judicial opinions'.[28] However, while this additional analysis for the ICC was interesting, rather than representing objective quantitative analysis, it mostly provided an opportunity

[25] Lines were manually counted, including headings and partial lines at the end of paragraphs and all related decisions (including of minority judgments). All figures should be considered approximate and rounded. This approach was inspired by that of Bürli, who analysed the practice of third party intervention before the ECHR. One aspect of her research involved examining references to interveners' submissions within judgments, as well as the number of pages dedicated to summarising the interveners' arguments: Bürli (n 21), 12–16.

[26] *Prosecutor v Ruto and Sang*, ICC TC V(A), 23 May 2014, ICC-01/09-01/11-1313 (approximately 200 lines, including in the minority decision by Judge Eboe-Osuji, which strongly disagreed with Kenya's submissions); *Prosecutor v Ruto and Sang*, ICC AC, 9 October 2014, ICC-01/09-01/11-1598 (approximately 165 lines).

[27] *Prosecutor v Lubanga*, ICC TC I, 15 December 2011, ICC-01/04-01/06-2835 (approximately 100 lines).

[28] Collins, Corley and Hamner (n 13), 919.

to record and compare qualitative textual assessments of the impact of *amicus curiae* briefs. As noted, the citations and length factors broadly supported the subjective analysis of the texts, but gathering this information was difficult to justify within the budget and time constraints of our project and would have been more helpful if further disaggregated, for instance by recording lines in different parts of the decisions. This more detailed data-gathering exercise was therefore not extended to the other tribunals, although if time and resources were unlimited it would have provided an extra opportunity to review the use of *amicus curiae* briefs.

V. INTERVIEWS

This book derives from a doctrinal analysis of legal documents concerning the *amicus curiae*, as well as from secondary literature including peer-reviewed academic literature and civil society reports. In order to check our understanding of certain events and to gain further insight into the reasons for (and against) appearing as an *amicus curiae*, we conducted a limited number of interviews (11) with legal practitioners, academics, and civil society representatives in Cape Town, London, the Hague and Sydney. Interviewees were purposively selected to capture direct experiences or knowledge of the *amicus curiae* procedure, meaning that accounts were biased toward those with an awareness, at least, of this process.

These recorded and transcribed interviews were conducted pursuant to UNSW ethics processes pursuant to Reference Number 14 122. Interviews followed a semi-structured interview guide designed to cover the interviewee's experience and responsibilities, especially concerning the *amicus curiae*, thoughts about the most effective ways to shape decisions about international criminal prosecutions, the role of different groups during trials, the challenges involved in influencing proceedings, changes in strategy, the main purposes of the *amicus curiae*, and accounts of their use.

This was clearly an inadequate number of interviews with individuals too selectively chosen to make any findings about these topics on the basis of the interviews alone. However, the interviews did help to provide further information about some uses of the *amicus curiae*, while also offering some examples of different perspectives of its role. Thus, some anonymised quotes are included in certain chapters for illustrative, though not generalisable, purposes.

VI. CONCLUSION

These multiple approaches toward analysing the *amicus curiae* across a number of tribunals (with additional analysis for the ICC), allowed us to derive broad observations about the use of *amicus curiae* briefs across international criminal tribunals. The table of documents also provided a source for identifying lesser-known examples of the *amicus*. In particular, it provided a useful source for identifying case studies for more detailed qualitative analysis, in order to remedy some of the simplification inherent in the above measures. This included a limited number of interviews, which served to clarify some points and presented examples of different perspectives of the purposes of the *amicus curiae*. A broad range of examples from the table is used throughout this book to demonstrate typical, illuminating, unusual or controversial examples of the *amicus curiae*.

Annex B: Table of Amicus Curiae *Rules and Directions*

ICC	ECCC	ICTY	ICTR	SCSL	STL
Rule 103 *Amicus curiae* and other forms of submission 1. At any stage of the proceedings, a Chamber may, if it considers it desirable for the proper determination of the case, invite or grant leave to a state, organisation or person to submit, in writing or orally, any observation on	**Rule 33. *Amicus curiae* Briefs** 1. At any stage of the proceedings, the Co-Investigating Judges or the Chambers may, if they consider it desirable for the proper adjudication of the case, invite or grant leave to an organisation or person to submit an *amicus curiae* brief in writing	**Rule 74. *Amicus Curiae*** A Chamber may, if it considers it desirable for the proper determination of the case, invite or grant leave to a state, organisation or person to appear before it and make submissions on any issue specified by the Chamber.	**Rule 74: *Amicus Curiae*** A Chamber may, if it considers it desirable for the proper determination of the case, invite or grant leave to any state, organisation or person to appear before it and make submissions on any issue specified by the Chamber.	**Rule 74: *Amicus Curiae*** A Chamber may, if it considers it desirable for the proper determination of the case, invite or grant leave to any state, organisation or person to make submissions on any issue specified by the Chamber.	**Rule 131: Third Parties and *Amicus Curiae*** (A) The Trial Chamber may decide, after hearing the Parties, that it would assist the proper determination of the case to invite or grant leave to a state, organisation or person to make written submissions on any issue, or to allow a state,

(*continued*)

(Continued)

ICC	ECCC	ICTY	ICTR	SCSL	STL
any issue that the Chamber deems appropriate. 2. The Prosecutor and the defence shall have the opportunity to respond to the observations submitted under sub-rule 1. 3. A written observation submitted under sub-rule 1 shall be filed with the Registrar, who shall provide copies to the Prosecutor and the defence. The Chamber shall determine	concerning any issue. The Co-Investigating Judges and the Chambers concerned shall determine what time limits, if any, shall apply to the filing of such briefs. 2. Briefs under this Rule shall be filed with the Greffier of the Co-Investigating Judges or Chamber concerned, who shall provide copies to the Co-Prosecutors and the lawyers	**Rule 77. Contempt of the Tribunal** (C) When a Chamber has reason to believe that a person may be in contempt of the Tribunal, it may: (i) direct the Prosecutor to investigate the matter with a view to the preparation and submission of an indictment for contempt; (ii) where the Prosecutor, in the view of the Chamber, has a	**Rule 77: Contempt of the Tribunal** (C) When a Chamber has reason to believe that a person may be in contempt of the Tribunal, it may: (i) direct the Prosecutor to investigate the matter with a view to the preparation and submission of an indictment for contempt; (ii) where the Prosecutor, in the view of the Chamber, has a	**Rule 46: Misconduct of Counsel** (F) This Rule is applicable to counsel for the Prosecution as well as counsel appearing for the Defence and to any counsel appearing as *amicus curiae*.	organisation or person to appear before it as *amicus curiae*. (B) The Parties shall have the opportunity to respond to any submissions made by *amicus curiae* or third parties under paragraph (A). **Rule 11** **Exercise of Jurisdiction over Attacks that May Fall Within the Jurisdiction of the Tribunal**

what time limits shall apply to the filing of such observations.	for the other parties, who shall be afforded the opportunity to respond. **Rule 67. Closing Orders by the Co-Investigating Judges** … 6. In the Closing Order, the Co-Investigating Judges shall make any necessary decisions concerning sealed items and, for this purpose, may grant leave or invite the submission of *amicus curiae* briefs.	conflict of interest with respect to the relevant conduct, direct the Registrar to appoint an *amicus curiae* to investigate the matter and report back to the Chamber as to whether there are sufficient grounds for instigating contempt proceedings; or (iii) initiate proceedings itself. (D) If the Chamber considers that there are sufficient grounds to proceed against a person for contempt, the Chamber may:	conflict of interest with respect to the relevant conduct, direct the Registrar to appoint an *amicus curiae* to investigate the matter and report back to the Chamber as to whether there are sufficient grounds for instigating contempt proceedings; or (iii) initiate proceedings itself. (D) If the Chamber considers that there are sufficient grounds to proceed against a person for contempt, the Chamber may:		(D) The Prosecutor may appeal the ruling by the Pre-Trial Judge within seven days, in which case the Appeals Chamber may request the Head of Defence Office to nominate independent counsel for appointment as *amicus curiae* to act in opposition to the Prosecutor's appeal. **Rule 60*bis*** **Contempt and Obstruction of Justice** …

(continued)

(Continued)

ICC	ECCC	ICTY	ICTR	SCSL	STL
	Rule 99. Effect of the Judgment … 3. When the judgment is pronounced, any bail order shall come to an end. The Chamber shall make any necessary decisions concerning sealed items and, for this purpose, may grant leave or invite the submission of *amicus curiae* briefs.	(i) in circumstances described in paragraph (C)(i), direct the Prosecutor to prosecute the matter; or (ii) in circumstances described in paragraph (C)(ii) or (iii), issue an order in lieu of an indictment and either direct *amicus curiae* to prosecute the matter or prosecute the matter itself.	(i) in circumstances described in paragraph (C) (i), direct the Prosecutor to prosecute the matter; or (ii) in circumstances described in paragraph (C)(ii) or (iii), issue an order in lieu of an indictment and either direct *amicus curiae* to prosecute the matter or prosecute the matter itself.		(E) When the Contempt Judge has reason to believe that a person may be in contempt of the Tribunal, he may: (i) invite the Prosecutor to consider investigating the matter with a view to the preparation and submission of an indictment for contempt; (ii) where the Prosecutor indicates a preference not to investigate the matter or submit an indictment himself, or

		Rule 91. False Testimony under Solemn Declaration (B) If a Chamber has strong grounds for believing that a witness has knowingly and wilfully given false testimony, it may: (i) direct the Prosecutor to investigate the matter with a view to the preparation and submission of an indictment for false testimony; or	**Rule 91: False Testimony under Solemn Declaration** (B) If a Chamber has strong grounds for believing that a witness has knowingly and wilfully given false testimony, it may: (i) direct the Prosecutor to investigate the matter with a view to the preparation and submission of an indictment for false testimony; or (ii) where the Prosecutor, in the view of the Chamber, has a conflict of interest with respect to the		where in the view of the Contempt Judge, the Prosecutor has a conflict of interest with respect to the relevant conduct, direct the Registrar to appoint an *amicus curiae* to investigate the matter and report back to the Contempt Judge as to whether there are sufficient grounds for instigating contempt proceedings; or (iii) initiate proceedings himself.

(continued)

(Continued)

ICC	ECCC	ICTY	ICTR	SCSL	STL
		(ii) where the Prosecutor, in the view of the Chamber, has a conflict of interest with respect to the relevant conduct, direct the Registrar to appoint an *amicus curiae* to investigate the matter and report back to the Chamber as to whether there are sufficient grounds for instigating proceedings for false testimony.	relevant conduct, direct the Registrar to appoint an *amicus curiae* to investigate the matter and report back to the Chamber as to whether there are sufficient grounds for instigating proceedings for false testimony. (C) If the Chamber considers that there are sufficient grounds to proceed against a person for giving false testimony, the Chamber may:		(F) If the Contempt Judge considers that there are sufficient grounds to proceed against a person for contempt, he may: (i) in circumstances described in paragraph (E)(i), direct the Prosecutor to prosecute the matter; or (ii) in circumstances described in paragraph (E)(ii) or (iii), issue an order in lieu of an indictment and either direct

		(C) If the Chamber considers that there are sufficient grounds to proceed against a person for giving false testimony, the Chamber may: (i) in circumstances described in paragraph (B)(i), direct the Prosecutor to prosecute the matter; or (ii) in circumstances described in paragraph (B)(ii), issue an order in lieu of an indictment and direct *amicus curiae* to prosecute the matter.	(i) in circumstances described in paragraph (B)(i), direct the Prosecutor to prosecute the matter; or (ii) in circumstances described in paragraph (B)(ii), issue an order in lieu of an indictment and direct *amicus curiae* to prosecute the matter.		*amicus curiae* to prosecute the matter or prosecute the matter himself. **Rule 152 False Testimony under Solemn Declaration** (B) The Contempt Judge may: (i) direct the Prosecutor to investigate the matter with a view to the preparation and submission of an indictment for false testimony; or

(continued)

(Continued)

ICC	ECCC	ICTY	ICTR	SCSL	STL
					(ii) where the Prosecutor, in the view of the Contempt Judge, has a conflict of interest with respect to the relevant conduct, direct the Registrar to appoint an *amicus curiae* to investigate the matter and report back to the Contempt Judge as to whether there are sufficient grounds for instigating proceedings for false testimony.

					(C) If the Contempt Judge considers that there are sufficient grounds to proceed against a person for giving false testimony, he may: (i) in circumstances described in paragraph (B)(i), direct the Prosecutor to prosecute the matter; or (ii) in circumstances described in paragraph (B)(ii), issue an order in lieu of an indictment and direct ***amicus curiae*** to prosecute the matter.

(continued)

(Continued)

ICC	ECCC	ICTY	ICTR	SCSL	STL
Code of Conduct	***Policies***	***Practice Directions***		***Practice Directions***	***Practice Directions***
Resolution ICC-ASP/4/Res.1 www.icc-cpi.int/NR/rdonlyres/BD397ECF-8CA8-44EF-92C6-AB4BEBD55BE2/140121/ICCASP432Res1_English.pdf Article 1 Scope This Code shall apply to defence counsel, counsel acting for states, *amici curiae* and counsel or legal representatives for victims	*Information on Submission of* Amicus Curiae *Briefs to Supreme Court Chamber* www.eccc.gov.kh/en/documents/legal/information-submission-amicus-curiae-briefs-supreme-court-chamber 1. Organisations or persons wishing to submit an *amicus* brief to the Supreme Court Chamber ('Chamber') must file an application with the Chamber	*Information Concerning the Submission of* Amicus Curiae *Briefs (IT/122/Rev.1) 16 February 2015* www.icty.org/x/file/Legal%20Library/Miscellaneous/it122_amicuscuriae_briefs_en.pdf SCOPE AND PURPOSE 1. This Information is intended to assist a state, organisation or person wishing to submit an		*Practice Direction on filing* Amicus Curiae *Briefs pursuant to Rule 74 of the Rules of Procedure and Evidence … 20 October 2004* www.rscsl.org/Documents/PRACTICE%20DIRECTION_RSCSL_on_Filing_Amicus_Curiae.pdf Article 1 1. Applications for leave to make written or oral submissions as *amicus curiae* may	*Practice Direction on* Amicus Curiae *Submissions before the Special Tribunal for Lebanon – 23 February 2012* www.stl-tsl.org/sites/default/files/documents/internal-regulatory-documents/practice-direction-on-amicus-curiae-submissions-before-the-stl/STL_PD_2011_05_Amicus_Curiae_WEB_EN.pdf

and witnesses practising at the International Criminal Court, hereinafter referred to as 'counsel'.	for leave to submit an *amicus* brief ('application for leave'). The application for leave must specify the following: (a) the applicant's name, address, and interest in the case and issue(s); (b) the issue(s) the applicant seeks to address, and the nature of the information or analysis the applicant proposes to submit; (c) the applicant's qualifications; (d) whether and why the applicant wishes to participate in oral	*amicus curiae* brief or to appear as an *amicus curiae* before the International Criminal Tribunal for the former Yugoslavia ('Tribunal') pursuant to Rule 74 of the Rules of Procedure and Evidence ('Rules'). 2. This Information does not apply to *amici curiae* appointed under Rule 77 or Rule 91 of the Rules.		be submitted at the applicant's own initiative or in response to a general invitation from the President, Designated Judge or Chamber. 2. At its discretion, the President, Designated Judge or Chamber may invite an *amicus curiae* submission from a particular State, organisation or person, in which case, no application for leave is required.	Article 1 *Amicus curiae* submissions upon specific invitation 1. Pursuant to Rule 131(A), a Judge or Chamber may invite a State, organisation or person to make written submissions or appear before it as *amicus curiae*. When such specific invitation is issued by the Judge or Chamber, no application for leave is required. The Judge or Chamber shall first allow the Parties to be heard on whether such invitation

(continued)

(Continued)

ICC	ECCC	ICTY	ICTR	SCSL	STL
	argument as *amicus curiae*; (e) the applicant's reasons for believing the *amicus* brief will aid in the proper adjudication of the case; and (f) a statement identifying and explaining any contact or relationship the applicant had, or has, with any party to the case. 2. Where possible, the application for leave should	APPLICATION FOR LEAVE 3. A state, organisation or person may submit an application for leave to file an *amicus curiae* brief or to appear as *amicus curiae*, unsolicited or in response to an invitation from a Chamber. An invitation by the Chamber may be specific (ie, directed at an individual state, organisation or person(s)) or general.		Article 2. 1. States, organisations or persons making an application under Article 1(1) of the present Practice Direction shall file an application specifying the following: (a) the applicant's name, address, telephone and fax numbers and email address; (b) whether the applicant is submitting the application:	would assist the proper determination of the case. The Judge or Chamber may also give other Participants an opportunity to be heard on the matter. 2. When *amici curiae* are invited to make written submissions, these submissions should fulfil the conditions of Articles 3, 4 and 5 of this Practice Direction, where applicable. The submissions will then be

	include the written *amicus* brief that the applicant seeks to have the Chamber accept. 3. Where the Chamber grants an application for leave that does not include the *amicus* brief, the Chamber shall determine the deadline for submitting the *amicus* brief. Upon receiving the *amicus* brief, the Chamber has the discretion to reject it. 4. Organisations and persons considering applying for leave	4. Unless responding to a specific invitation from a Chamber, a state, organisation or person(s) wishing to submit an *amicus curiae* brief or to appear as *amicus curiae* ('Applicant') must file an application, in writing, specifying the following: … etc. *Practice Direction on Procedure for the Investigation and Prosecution of Contempt Before the International Tribunal (IT/227)*		(i) at the applicant's own initiative; or (ii) in respect to a general invitation for application by the President, Designated Judge or a Chamber; (c) the issue or issues the applicant seeks to address, and the nature of the information or analysis the applicant proposes to submit; (d) the applicant' reasons for believing the submissions will aid in the proper determination of the case or issue;	automatically entered in the case file and sent to the Judge or Chamber. Article 2. Application for leave to make *amicus curiae* submissions Applications for leave to file *amicus curiae* briefs, or to appear as *amicus curiae*, from a particular State, organisation or person are submitted:

(continued)

(Continued)

ICC	ECCC	ICTY	ICTR	SCSL	STL
	and organisations and persons invited by the Chamber to submit an *amicus* brief should note the following: (a) *Amicus* briefs shall be made in writing. *Amici* may be invited to participate in oral argument at the Chamber's discretion; (b) *Amicus* briefs shall be limited to questions of law and may not include factual evidence relating to elements of a	www.icty.org/x/file/Legal%20 Library/Practice_ Directions/ it227_contempt_ procedure_en.pdf II. GENERAL 1. Part III of this practice direction applies to instances where the Prosecutor is directed or an *amicus curiae* is appointed to investigate an allegation of contempt pursuant to Rule 77(C)(i) or (ii) of the Rules, respectively … etc.		and e. a statement identifying and explaining any contact or relationship the applicant had, or has, with any party to the case, 2. The application shall be served on the Parties. Article 3. Any application under Article 1(1) of this Practice Direction may be accompanied by the proposed written *amicus curiae* submission. … etc.	(i) in response to a general invitation from the Judge or Chamber; or (ii) unsolicited by the Judge or Chamber. Article 3 Contents of application for leave to make *amicus curiae* submissions 1. An application for leave to make *amicus curiae* submissions, or to appear as *amicus curiae*, shall include in succinct form: … etc.

	crime charged or indicted; (c) The Chamber may set page limits on the length of an *amicus* brief; (d) *Amici* will not be subject to examination, nor will they be allowed to call witnesses or evidence; and (e) *Amici curiae* shall bear their own expenses. The Chamber may authorise the Office of Administration to reimburse the reasonable expenses incurred in connection				

(continued)

(Continued)

ICC	ECCC	ICTY	ICTR	SCSL	STL
	with participation in the ECCC's proceedings if the *amicus* has been specifically invited to submit an *amicus* brief to or appear …				

Annex C: Practical Guidance

PART A OF this Annex sets out some considerations for individuals and organisations considering applying as *amici curiae* before an international criminal tribunal. It draws from the practice directions and guides of international and domestic courts, as well as the practice of international criminal tribunals. The guidance is primarily directed at civil society actors, but is also relevant to states and international organisations that might seek to participate as *amici curiae*. Part B offers suggestions for Chambers in managing *amici curiae*.

PART A: GUIDANCE FOR POTENTIAL *AMICI*

A. When should you make a Submission?

- ***Purpose/function***: Applicants should identify the purpose of the proposed submission and the relevant function(s) of the *amicus curiae* identified in our study the submission will perform, namely: expertise, representative or communicative (see Table 1.1). The Chamber is likely to consider some or all of these functions in determining whether to accept the proposed briefs and which criteria to apply (see Table 4.1).
- ***Strategy***: How does the proposed topic relate to your core individual or organisational strategic priorities? What is the likely benefit to you and your priorities? (This might include legal, broader policy, or reputational outcomes and both short term and long term priorities). How likely is it that the proposed brief will be admitted? How likely that if it is accepted it will have the desired effect? How will it conflict with or supplement your other activities or other roles you perform, including trial monitoring or acting as a consultant to a court organ?
- ***Audience and stakeholders***: What other actors or groups comprise the intended audience for the brief? Who will the applicant 'speak for' in its submissions? What political sensitivities should be taken into account?
- ***Forum***: Is this the most appropriate Court, Chamber, case or proceedings for the proposed submissions and to achieve your strategic priorities? What is the background and expertise of the Bench? Are they from a common law or civil law background? How would the submissions assist the individuals who make up the Chambers to reach their decision? How have other similar applications been treated in the past?

- ***Rules and format***: What practice directions, rules and codes of conduct apply to submitting *amicus curiae* briefs? What criteria or additional rules has the Court adopted in the past toward *amici curiae*? What is the correct format for filing an *amicus curiae* application?
- ***Expertise***: Is the proposed topic within your expertise? Are you the best actor to provide legal arguments on the proposed topic? Or the best actor to provide particular information? If not, is appropriate expertise available to you, for example, pro bono lawyers to draft an application?
- ***Timing***: Have judicial proceedings commenced? At what stage of proceedings will the proposed submissions most aid in the determination of the case? Are the issues you wish to address raised in the present proceedings? When will the relevant Chamber hear the topic of the submissions? Is this the right time or stage of proceedings or will your intervention be too soon or too late? Has the Chamber already considered the issue you wish to address? Are you addressing your request to the right Chamber, for example, if an issue is now on appeal, your request should be directed to the Appeal Chamber?
- ***Alternatives***: Does an *amicus curiae* submission represent the most appropriate mechanism to achieve your strategic objectives? What other tools/avenues might bring similar benefits or outcomes? (Peer reviewed articles, NGO reports, other forms of advocacy, providing information or expertise to the parties or other participants directly). Which options appear transparent and ethical?
- ***Collaboration***: Who should draft the *amicus curiae* application and submission? Is legal advice required? Is there a benefit to partnering or co-signing with another actor, such as a local or international NGO or academic? Or inviting another actor to submit a separate brief? However, consider the benefits of quality over the quantity of *amici curiae*.

  You may also consider becoming a signatory to a joint brief, including one that may have many signatures. While such briefs are not as common in international criminal tribunals as in some national jurisdictions, they have been accepted. Signing such a brief offers some benefits, in particular not requiring resources to draft the brief and perhaps lending more weight to the brief (although there is no evidence for this in international criminal tribunals). However, such collaboration also results in a lack of control over the content and quality of a brief as well as which other actors are invited to support the brief, which may pose a reputational risk.
- ***Resources and planning***: What resources/tools/avenues might be needed to support the *amicus curiae* process to the desired (highest possible) level of quality? What time limits will be imposed and is it possible to produce a quality brief within the period allowed? Should the applicant plan ahead,

identifying issues that are likely to arise and organising possible arguments beforehand?

- ***Internal Controls and Ethics***: What internal review and risk or control procedures might be relevant or appropriate? Is there an internal *amicus curiae* policy? Who should authorise/approve the application and on what basis? Are there different considerations if a court has (specifically or generally) *invited* the applicant to provide *amicus curiae* submissions (as opposed to voluntarily applying for leave)? Are there any conflicts of interest, reputational risks, or ethical complexities? Has the applicant been in contact or have a relationship with any of the parties or participants or an affected state?

B. How Might the Proposed Submission Assist the *Chamber*?

The single criterion for admission of an *amicus curiae* submission is that it must assist the Chamber in its determination of an issue in dispute in the proceedings. In assessing whether a submission will be helpful, Chambers consider the following:

- **Does the proposed submission address a legal issue that is novel and/or important?** There are several topics where practice suggests a submission may assist a Chamber. These include:
    - Areas of novel or unsettled law or procedure, including issues of state cooperation, complementarity, reparations, immunity and statehood and others that may lie beyond the issues expected to fall within the core judicial competency of the Chamber.
    - Alerting the Chambers to an authoritative decision that may resolve a controversial issue or providing overviews of jurisprudence from other institutions, including other international criminal tribunals.
    - Unfamiliar national laws and legal practices, including how national legal proceedings operate in practice.
    - Comparative legal analysis, including international human rights and international humanitarian law, as well as information about different national laws or procedures.
    - Providing important information that the Court is unlikely to obtain otherwise or cannot obtain without considerable expense.
    - Analysis of actual situations in some circumstances, including where the information would otherwise be unavailable to the Court, including potentially in admissibility proceedings or in the implementation of reparations orders.
    - Sociological, cultural, or linguistic research, especially regarding the relevant country, or research concerning topics or perspectives that are less familiar to the Court.

- ○ In response to any call or standing invitation for submissions on a matter, such as in relation to reparations.

Less likely to be accepted are attempts to advise the Court of arguments about future possible events or broader policy consequences of a particular decision.

- To what extent will the proposed submission **overlap** with those of other actors already participating in the proceedings that are likely to address similar concerns? Submissions should not duplicate those of the parties or provide arguments or information that is already available to the Chamber through other means.
- Submissions must be **relevant** to the determination of the legal issue before the Chamber. Even if the topic of the submissions is novel or important, a submission is only useful if the Chamber is required to decide that issue as part of its determination in the proceedings.

C. How to make your Submission?

Amicus curiae participation is always at the discretion of the Chamber. Tribunals engage with potential *amici curiae* in three ways: issuing an invitation to specific *amici*; open calls to *amici*; and unsolicited or voluntary applications. For open calls and voluntary applications, there is usually a two-stage process: an applicant applies for leave to participate as an *amicus curiae* and, only if granted leave, would the *amicus curiae* be able to present their detailed submissions. Specifically invited *amici* generally do not need to seek leave to participate, but file submissions directly with the Chamber.

You may wish to wait to see if a Chamber issues an open call and then seek to participate. However, not all Chambers issue open calls in each stage of proceedings; the majority of *amici* participate by voluntary application. Therefore, if it is important to you to make submissions, you should make a voluntary application. There is no right to appeal a decision not to grant leave to an *amicus curiae* to participate; however, if denied permission, an *amicus* may apply again at a later stage of proceedings or before a different Chamber.

There is no requirement to notify the parties or other participants as to a potential *amicus curiae* submission.

Amici may participate by written submissions, oral submissions or a combination of the two. Most *amici* are only permitted to participate by filing written submissions and Chambers often decide issues without hearings. When requesting leave to participate in oral proceedings, you should consider the reason why the Chamber would benefit from hearing your submissions in person, as well as the likely cost of such participation, as *amici* are rarely reimbursed for their expenditure in attending hearings.

If you are specifically invited to participate as an *amicus curiae*, there is no obligation to do so. As with making any *amicus curiae* submission, you should evaluate the possible benefits and risks as well as whether it is appropriate for you to participate in the circumstances.

D. What to Include in an Application for Leave to Participate as an *Amicus Curiae*?

Amicus curiae applications should:

- Follow any practice directions, rules or practices that specify what applications should include. Applicants should also comply with any general requirements for filings, including format, language, page limits and referencing requirements as well as any specific instructions in a call for *amici* or invitation.
- Specify the legal basis on which the proposed submission is made. This is usually the rule addressing the *amicus curiae* (eg Rule 103 of the ICC RPE) but it may also be another provision, such as Article 75(3) of the Rome Statute in reparations proceedings. You should also specify if the application is relying on multiple, alternative legal bases for participation (for example, victim participation under Article 68(3) or as an *amicus curiae* in the alternative).
- Specify whether you are applying in response to a particular call for *amicus curiae* submissions, an invitation or on a voluntary basis.
- Provide adequate information: the addressee Judge or Chamber, contact information, references to any documents the application responds to in addition to the applicant's identity and contact details.
- Identify the reason for your interest in the case or the issues it raises and the function you seek to fulfil (see typology in Table 1.1). Where you are seeking to represent a particular interest (for example, you are directly affected or seek to represent those who are affected) set out this interest clearly, as well as the benefit of allowing your representation. Where you seek to represent the interest of others, you should indicate the basis on which you are authorised to represent others. Note that possessing an interest in the legal issue or the outcome should not mean you cannot be admitted as an *amicus curiae*; in fact, in some circumstances, having an interest may support your application. However, it is essential that the Chamber is made aware of the interest so it can weigh the application and any eventual submission accordingly.
- Spell out exactly why the proposed submission meets any criteria for admission and what the terms of the proposed participation would be

(including whether the applicant would seek to make written or oral submissions). You should refer to important decisions on the admission and role of *amici curiae* previously issued by that Court or Chamber.

- Set out briefly and clearly the issues to be addressed by the brief, and the nature of the proposed analysis. Explain why these issues are important for the specific case, are distinct from the arguments made or likely to be made by the parties and participants, and may affect its outcome – and how and why the submissions will aid in the determination of those issues. It is crucial to focus on how your submissions will be relevant and assist the Chamber to address issues that are currently before it. Define the parameters of the proposed submissions. Include only focused arguments that directly relate to the applicant's expertise and the contested issue before the Chambers.
- Particularly when seeking to perform an expertise function, outline why the applicant has the expertise and is best placed, *beyond* having a general concern about the issues, to provide the proposed submissions. What expertise and experience does the applicant have, including qualifications, time working in the relevant geographic location, access to information that is difficult to otherwise obtain, etc. This should include providing details of qualifications and relevant expertise, possibly by attaching a CV or summary of qualifications, experience and (as relevant) publications. Applicants should also demonstrate how that expertise is linked to the submissions and to the issues the Chamber needs to address. Applicants may wish to indicate any previous experience as an *amicus curiae*, whether at the same tribunal or in other institutions; while this is not determinative of admission, this knowledge may be useful to the tribunal.
- Provide details of any conflicts of interest, including any contact or relationships the applicant may have with the Court, the parties and other participants, and the state, as well as – if appropriate – the source of any request, payment or donor funding that supports the work for the *amicus curiae* brief.
- Maintain a professional, concise and clear style, but adjust for the intended audience(s). Follow any style and format directions in the rules. Unnecessarily emotive or advocacy-style language may reduce the likelihood of being accepted.
- Highlight that the proposed submissions will have no or minimal impact on defence rights or unduly delay proceedings.
- Subject to each Tribunal's practice (as this has been mixed), applications should avoid annexing the entire proposed submission unless this is accepted practice. However, applications should include a brief outline or summary of your proposed arguments so that the Chambers can see how they will be helpful.

E. Providing Oral or Written *Amicus Curiae* Submissions

The considerations relating to applications for leave to participate remain relevant for preparing submissions, as well as the following:

- Abide by any specifications included in the admission decision or call for submissions and any rules or conditions such as page limits or time deadlines. For those providing oral submissions, confirm the requirements for court room appearance, etiquette and procedure before your session and ensure that you do not exceed the time allocated to you for your presentation. Be prepared to respond to questions from the Chamber.
- Address the issues you have said in your application you would address or that the Chamber has asked you to address. Do not go beyond the issues approved, or it is likely your submissions will be ignored. Also, if fulfilling an expertise function, remain within the expertise you have established and that the Chamber considers relevant.
- Consider whether or how to react to any submissions that the parties may have made in response to the application or submissions.
- Depending on the stage of proceedings, do not make submissions that directly concern the individual criminal responsibility of the accused. Unless requested by the Chamber, *amici* should, in general, avoid factual or evidentiary submissions. Facts and evidence can be supplied to the parties or Chamber through other mechanisms. For legal arguments, rely upon facts advanced by the parties or determined by the Chambers, rather than advancing opposing factual scenarios.
- Avoid broader public interest arguments unless relevant to legal issues or requested or approved by the Chamber.
- Prepare objective submissions, with appropriate citations and references, including recognising opposing arguments and authorities where relevant.
- To the extent these submissions are available to you, do not provide evidence or materials already or likely to be provided by the parties or other participants or otherwise available to the Chamber.
- Clearly identify the 'gap' to be filled by these submissions and demonstrate that this focus is consistent with the leave that was granted. Avoid duplicating the parties' arguments or providing 'me too' briefs. If part of the brief supports points raised by a party or other *amici*, simply state this without rewriting those arguments. Duplicative submissions are not useful for the Chamber.
- Consider how to coordinate the submission with other *amici curiae* or (if appropriate) the parties.

- Consider your internal strategic plans concerning the submissions, which may involve, for example planning any complementary advocacy activities or publicity such as press releases, if appropriate.
- Comply with any requests from the Chamber for supplementary submissions.

F. Ethical and Fair Trial Issues

Amici curiae should assist the Chamber in a professional and ethical manner. This includes:

- Referring to the relevant Code of Conduct, eg the ICC Code of Conduct, which applies to *amicus curiae* applicants before the ICC.
- Not unduly delaying proceedings or creating additional, unnecessary workload for the parties, other participants or the Chambers or unduly affecting the fair trial rights of the accused.
- Deciding whether to request, accept or make payment for any services related to preparing the *amicus curiae* submissions – including indirect funding for the *amicus curiae* organisation – and how to disclose such decisions.
- Determining the nature and extent of the *amicus curiae*'s contact with any of the parties, whether any assistance or monetary contribution could be provided by the parties, and what disclosures may be necessary.
- Considering the *amicus curiae's* internal ethical procedures, including the protection of confidential relationships and sources.
- Advising the Court of any errors or inaccuracies in the application or brief in accordance with the Court's processes.

G. Evaluating the *Amicus Curiae* Experience

After applying and participating, *amici curiae* might consider reviewing each experience to:

- Compare the judicial, policy and reputational impact against initial expectations.
- Review internal procedures for deciding whether to act as an *amicus curiae*.
- Document and apply any lessons learned regarding the application or submissions-drafting procedures.
- Publicise and leverage any positive impact through other forms of advocacy.
- Identify any opportunities for providing training, experience-sharing or future collaboration with other actors.

B. CONSIDERATIONS FOR CHAMBERS

Rules allowing *amici curiae* give Chambers considerable discretion to determine when an *amicus curiae* submission may be helpful in judicial determinations. *Amicus curiae* participation offers several advantages for Chambers. *Amici* may provide additional information or expertise that is not otherwise available to the Chamber, or may allow the Chamber to be informed as to otherwise unrepresented interests. As outlined in chapter one, this may enhance the quality of judicial decision-making as well as contribute to building the legitimacy of the tribunal. However, participation also comes with certain risks, including:

- The additional work and cost to the parties, other participants and registry, as well as judicial costs related to reviewing and responding to *amicus curiae* applications and submissions.
- The potential to delay proceedings.
- The possibility that there may be a lack of clarity and consistency as to the admission of *amicus curiae* submissions, which may reduce the transparency of judicial proceedings.
- Whether the *amicus curiae* submissions might cause inconvenience, lack quality, relevance and usefulness, or duplicate parties' arguments.
- The possibility of conflicts of interest, lack of independence or impartiality and concerns about the representativeness of *amici curiae*.
- The potential for inaccurate information being provided, especially where *amici* make broad arguments in areas not central to their areas of expertise, commission research with certain parameters, or selectively provide factual information.
- Associated fair trial concerns related to the above and issues of equality of arms in criminal proceedings if *amici curiae* tend to support the prosecution.

Chambers must balance these benefits of *amicus curiae* participation against these risks. Moreover, Chambers must also strike an appropriate balance between the importance for judicial flexibility and retaining broad discretion in the admission of *amici curiae*, and having consistent, transparent and defined criteria for *amicus* admissions. This section offers suggestions for how Chambers may best manage *amicus curiae* practice to realise the benefits while minimising any risks.

Chambers may wish to consider whether practice directions or other forms of judicial guidance, including in specific orders, relating to the practice of *amicus curiae* briefs ought to be drafted that reflect these principles. Chambers might also consider and clarify the following matters.

A. Engaging with *Amici Curiae*: Open Calls, Voluntary Applications and Invitations

- Identifying when *amicus curiae* submissions may assist a Chamber or where voluntary applications are likely to help. It can be hard to predict, but actors are most likely to seek to participate as *amici curiae* where there are novel issues of substance or procedure, where the law is untested or unclear or there are conflicting views as to the relevant law or its interpretation. Applications are also likely where an issue is of significance beyond the immediate decision – an issue of 'constitutional' importance (such as interpreting for the first time a provision in the Statute, eg 'interests of justice' or an issue essential to effectiveness of the institution, eg head of state immunity and cooperation obligations of states) or will significantly develop jurisprudence (eg, the first interpretation of a 'new' crime, such as forced pregnancy).
- Before calling for or accepting *amici curiae*, Chambers should also consider whether more appropriate avenues of participation may be available, for example, victim participation, provision of material directly to the parties or calling expert witnesses.
- Where *amicus curiae* participation may be helpful or applications are likely, Chambers should consider issuing an open call to potential *amici*, or a class of potential *amici*. Open calls are generally preferable to specific invitations as they allow greater opportunity for a range of actors to seek to participate and are more transparent; however, where a specific actor is the only actor capable of providing certain expertise or information or has an interest that is directly engaged by the proceedings (eg a state), a specific invitation may be appropriate.
- Both open calls and specific invitations should list the particular topics or areas of expertise or information for which it might be useful to receive *amicus curiae* briefs. This will most likely take the form of a list of questions that will assist the Chamber in making a determination on the issues.
- Chambers should also consider whether an open call should be limited to a particular category of actor (eg NGOs, states or academics). Alternatively, an open call may encourage certain types of actors to apply (eg local actors with experience of implementing reparations projects on a particular type of harm or in a certain location), but not exclude others. Where appropriate, Chambers may consider the representativeness of *amici*, including whether perspectives from local actors and non-Western NGOs are represented.
- Where a Chamber is seeking submissions offering legal or other expertise, the open call should specify the nature and extent of expertise required, indicating if possible any minimum qualifications or level of experience required. The Chamber should direct potential *amici* to demonstrate their expertise in the application for leave. The Chamber should also consider the nature and

level of expertise when selecting *amici* it directly invites to participate, where *amici* are to provide expertise.

- Where possible, open calls should enable a two-stage process, requiring potential *amici* to first provide an application for leave to participate, accompanied by an overview of intended submissions (but not the full brief). This allows the Chamber to make an admission decision for each potential *amicus* based on quality, expertise and relevance and to eliminate or manage potential duplication between *amici* or with the parties. One method of managing multiple *amici* is to suggest *amici* collaborate on combined submissions.
- An open call or invitation should also indicate whether participation is to be by written submissions, oral submissions or a combination of the two.
- Open calls should also set a reasonable deadline, one that allows potential *amici* sufficient time to become aware of the call, to determine whether they should and can seek leave and to collaborate with other potential *amici* or to secure appropriate resources (eg legal support) to prepare a quality application. Timing will differ according to circumstances, but we suggest allowing a period of approximately one month. Late applicants should not be accepted unless there are exceptional grounds.
- The Chamber should request the Registry to publicise open calls on the Tribunal website and circulate open calls through appropriate mailing lists or partner websites. Open calls should be easily accessible (and locatable) on the website. The Registry may consider establishing a designated focal point for contact concerning *amicus curiae* participation and for managing the open call and application process, including guidance as to the relevant rules and filing requirements and procedures. The Registry may also wish to establish a part of the website in which rules and guidance on *amicus curiae* participation as well as previous decisions on admissibility and submissions may be collated and made available to potential *amici*.
- The Chamber may wish to appoint a single judge to consider *amicus curiae* applications and to manage the process.
- Where an *amicus curiae* has been involved at an earlier stage proceedings, the relevant Chamber may wish to consider inviting the *amicus* to participate in subsequent proceedings (an appeal), which may involve a further admissibility decision. This is not automatic, as the *amicus curiae* has no right to participate. A Chamber should always confirm that it is the appropriate Chamber to receive the *amicus curiae* submission, or whether the request should be directed to another Chamber.

B. Managing the Application Process

- Potential *amici* should be required to identify the case or proceedings to which the application relates and the relevant Judge or Chamber to whom the request is directed. *Amici* should also include sufficient and accurate contact information and specify whether the request is made in response to an open call or invitation (and provide details) or is a voluntary application.

- Require potential *amici curiae* (including specifically invited *amici*) to disclose any potential conflict of interest in their application for leave to participate (or brief for an invited *amicus curiae*). This should include any contact with or relationship to the Chamber, the Court (or its organs), parties or other participants (either formal or informal), as well as an affected state, and disclosure of funding or other support for the organisation generally or preparation of the *amicus* submission in particular. The existence of a relationship with the Court, the Chamber or a party or other participant need not exclude *amicus* participation; rather, it may affect the reliability of the submissions and the weight given to those submissions by the Chamber.
- The application should indicate the applicant's interest in the proceedings or the outcome, which may be a general interest or a specific interest. Chambers should elucidate and require transparency as to the nature or scope of permissible 'interests' in the case – in particular, where the requisite interests may be different for expertise as opposed to representative or communicative briefs. Again, the existence of a specific interest does not preclude participation as an *amicus curiae*; rather, it affects the weight the Chamber should give to the submissions.
- Potential *amici* should specify the issues on which they seek to make submissions and the nature of those submissions (eg factual or legal), identify how those submissions are relevant to the issues before the Chamber and outline why the applicant considers the proposed submission will assist the Chamber in reaching its decision.
- The applicant should be required to indicate whether they seek permission to participate by written submissions only or by oral submissions or a combination.
- The parties generally do not have a right to comment on potential *amici* and their applications; however, the Chamber may wish to consider inviting submissions from the parties and other participants as to the admission of specific *amici* before taking an admissibility decision.
- The Chamber should always make a decision as to admissibility of an *amicus curiae* and should not leave admissibility unaddressed or considered only in the final decision in the proceedings. This creates uncertainty both for the *amicus curiae* and the parties, and may raise fair trial issues if an *amicus curiae* is admitted without then allowing the parties an opportunity to respond to the submissions.
- In its admissibility decisions, the Chamber should provide clear reasoning rather than simply indicating that submissions may or may not be helpful. That is, providing transparent guidance that could prevent future rejections,

including by explaining why the proposed submissions would or would not be desirable or of assistance in the given case. This would ideally involve reference to the function of the particular *amicus curiae* applicant and applying the typology and criteria for admission we have highlighted in chapter four (see Table 4.1). We suggest that Chambers should be cautious in accepting briefs that seek to address non-legal issues, particularly exclusively 'communicative' briefs that seek to outline the public interests, wider impacts and views of an issue.

- Where the *amicus curiae* seeks to perform the expertise function, the Chamber should assess the information provided as to expertise and qualifications and should not accept submissions from *amici* that do not have appropriate relevant expertise. Similarly, where the *amicus curiae* seeks to perform a representative function, the Chamber should assess the interest that the *amicus curiae* claims to represent, whether that interest is directly implicated in the proceedings, the relationship between the interest and the proceedings, any alternative mechanisms of participation available and the benefits to be gained from allowing representation of that interest.
- Where the Chamber decides to admit *amici curiae*, the Chamber should set reasonable and feasible page or word limits and deadlines for filing the submission. Again, timing depends on the circumstances, but should allow reasonable time for the submissions to be prepared. We suggest this is generally at least two weeks and preferably one month from when the permission to participate (or invitation) is communicated. The decision should also specify the issues upon which *amici curiae* are permitted to make submissions (different *amici* may be required to address different issues, depending on their expertise and/or interest in the proceedings). As a general rule, *amicus curiae* briefs should be limited to legal submissions and should not make submissions of a factual nature or that directly concern the individual responsibility of the accused. However, we have identified some circumstances where factual material may be appropriate, for example the provision of information concerning national legal systems and proceedings by States or local NGOs.
- The admissibility decision should indicate whether the *amicus* may participate in writing only, or by oral submissions, or both. It should also indicate the legal basis upon which a submission is accepted, particularly where the applicant has relied on multiple provisions to support participation.
- *Amici* do not have a right to appeal the decision on admissibility.

C. Managing *Amicus Curiae* Submissions

- Chambers should enforce page and word limits and time deadlines. Submissions that do not comply should normally be rejected, unless there are exceptional grounds or permission has been sought from the Chamber. Similarly, a Chamber should reject submissions that do not address the issues specified in the admissibility decision or invitation. If submissions partly address the required issues but also address other issues, for which the Chamber had not given permission, the Chamber should disregard the submissions on those other issues and indicate this clearly in the decision or judgment.

- Where an *amicus curiae* is to participate in oral proceedings, the Chamber should set (and enforce) time limits for participation and indicate the likely timing, scheduling and format of proceedings. The Chamber should ensure that the *amicus curiae* does not address issues other than those indicated in the admissibility decision, other than at the request or by the leave of the Chamber.
- The parties must be given an opportunity to respond to *amicus curiae* submissions (both written and oral), and Chambers should set a reasonable time and page limit for this. To manage multiple *amici*, parties may be allowed to submit a consolidated response to all *amicus* submissions in one document. Chambers should also consider whether it is appropriate to permit other participants (including other *amici curiae*) to respond to *amicus* submissions. Generally, *amici* should not be given an opportunity to respond to the responses of parties and other participants.
- Generally, the role of the *amicus curiae* is limited to making submissions on legal issues, with access only to those filings on the public record. However, a Chamber should identify whether additional rights or conditions might reasonably be required for a particular *amicus curiae*, including whether *amici curiae* might tender factual material or evidence, inspect evidence or documents filed by the parties or respond to arguments raised by the parties in response to their submissions and the form (oral/written) and timing of such responses. Further, the Chamber should assess whether the circumstances justify the *amicus curiae* filing on a confidential basis. This should be the exception and justified only by a recognised ground, such as to protect the safety of the *amicus curiae* or their personnel or victims or confidential national security interests of states.
- *Amici curiae* do not as a general rule receive remuneration. However, a Chamber should consider whether it is appropriate for *amici* that have been specifically invited or who have participated in person to be reimbursed for their expenses.
- Chambers are not required to have any regard to *amicus curiae* submissions received nor refer to them in their decisions. However, Chambers should not call for and/or accept a brief where it will not read or consider the submission. Instead, Chambers should read all accepted submissions and determine what weight, if any, should be given to the submission in reaching

a determination. Best practice suggests that the *amicus curiae* submissions should be referred to in the procedural section of the decision and an overview of the key arguments provided. Where an *amicus curiae* submission has been taken into account during judicial deliberations and has influenced the substantive reasoning of a decision, Chambers should include a reference to the submission to acknowledge and make transparent the influence of the submission.

- Judges must also act in a transparent and ethical manner regarding any advice or information received or solicited regarding a matter before the Chamber, in particular through avenues other than the *amicus curiae* process – for instance, if a member of the Bench consults an expert informally for advice.
- As noted above, an *amicus curiae* has no right to participate in subsequent phases of proceedings, including an appeal from a decision.

Bibliography

Books

Aloisi, R and Meernik, J, *Judgment Day: Judicial Decision Making at the International Criminal Tribunals* (Cambridge, CUP, 2017).

Anheier, HK, Glasius, M and Kaldor, M, *Global Civil Society* (Oxford, OUP, 2001).

Arold, NL, *The Legal Culture of the European Court of Human Rights* (Leiden, Brill, 2007).

Baker, G, *Civil Society and Democratic Theory: Alternative Voices* (London, Routledge, 2003).

Brunee, J and Toope, S, *Legitimacy and Legality in International Law: An Interactional Account* (Cambridge, CUP, 2010).

Bürli, N, *Third-Party Interventions before the European Court of Human Rights* (Cambridge, Intersentia, 2017).

Chappell, L, *The Politics of Gender Justice at the International Criminal Court: Legacies and Legitimacy* (Oxford, OUP, 2016).

Collins, P, *Friends of the Supreme Court: Interest Groups and Judicial Decision Making* (New York, OUP, 2008).

Darcy, S and Powderley, J (eds), *Judicial Creativity at the International Criminal Tribunals* (Oxford, OUP 2010).

de Brouwer, AM, *Supranational Criminal Prosecution of Sexual Violence: The ICC and the Practice of the ICTY and the ICTR* (Oxford, Intersentia, 2005).

Duffy, H, *Strategic Human Rights Litigation: Understanding and Maximising Impact* (Oxford, Hart Publishing, 2018).

El-Hosseny, F, *Civil Society in Investment Treaty Arbitration: Shifts and Prospects* (Leiden, Brill, 2018).

Franck, TM, *The Power of Legitimacy Among Nations* (Oxford, OUP, 1990).

Glasius, M, *The International Criminal Court: A Global Civil Society Achievement* (Milton Park, Routledge, 2006).

Haddad, HN, *The Hidden Hands of Justice: NGOs, Human Rights and International Courts* (Cambridge, CUP, 2018).

Harlow, C and Rawlings, R, *Pressure Through Law* (London, Routledge, 1992).

Hurd, I, *After Anarchy: Legitimacy and Power in the United Nations Security Council* (Princeton, Princeton University Press, 2007).

Kaldor, M, *Global Civil Society: An Answer to War* (Cambridge, Polity Press, 2003).

Keane, J, *Global Civil Society?* (Cambridge, CUP, 2003).

Killean, RV, *Atrocity and International Criminal Justice: Lessons from Cambodia* (Milton Park, Routledge, 2018).

Leyh, BM, *Procedural Justice? Victim Participation in International Criminal Proceedings* (Cambridge, Intersentia, 2011).

Lindblom, AK, *Non-governmental Organisations in International Law* (Cambridge, CUP, 2005).

McCarthy, C, *Reparations and Victim Support in the International Criminal Court* (Cambridge, CUP, 2012).

Moffett, L, *Justice for Victims before the International Criminal Court* (Milton Park, Routledge, 2014).

Morris, V and Scharf, MP, *An Insider's Guide to the International Criminal Tribunal for the Former Yugoslavia* (New York, Transaction Publishers, vol 1, 1995).

Newton, M and Scharf, M, *Enemy of the State: The Trial and Execution of Saddam Hussein* (New York, St Martin's Press, 2008).

Pasqualucci, JM, *The Practice and Procedure of the Inter-American Court of Human Rights*, 2nd edn (Cambridge, CUP, 2016).
Schiff, BN, *Building the International Criminal Court* (New York, CUP, 2008).
Shaw, MN, *Rosenne's Law and Practice of the International Court of Justice, 1920–2015*, 5th edn (Leiden, Brill, vol III, 2016).
Smith, D, *Texts, Facts, and Femininity: Exploring the Relations of Ruling* (London, Routledge, 1993).
Tamanaha, B, *Law as a Means to an End: Threat to the Rule of Law* (Cambridge, CUP, 2009).
Webb, P, *International Judicial Integration and Fragmentation* (Oxford, OUP, 2013).
Wiik, A, *Amicus Curiae before International Courts and Tribunals* (Baden-Baden, Nomos, 2018).
Williams, S, *Hybrid & Internationalised Criminal Tribunals: Selected Jurisdictional Issues* (Oxford, Hart Publishing, 2012).
Williams, S and Woolaver, H (eds), *Civil Society and International Criminal Justice in Africa: Challenges and Opportunities* (Cape Town, Juta Law, 2016).
Woodward, B, *Global Civil Society in International Lawmaking and Global Governance: Theory and Practice* (Leiden, Martinus Nijhoff, 2010).

Book Chapters

Blackaby, N and Richard, C, '*Amicus Curiae*: A Panacea for Legitimacy in Investment Arbitration?' in M Waibel et al (eds), *The Backlash against Investment Arbitration* (Austin, Wolters Kluwer, 2010).
Bodansky, D, 'Legitimacy in International Law and International Relations' in JL Dunoff and MA Pollack (eds), *Interdisciplinary Perspectives on International Law and International Relations: The State of the Art* (New York, CUP, 2013).
Bodansky, D, 'The Concept of Legitimacy in International Law' in R Wolfrum and V Röben (eds), *Legitimacy in International Law* (Berlin, Springer, 2008).
Bohlander, M, 'The International Criminal Judiciary: Problems of Judicial Selection, Independence and Ethics' in M Bohlander (ed), *International Criminal Justice: A Critical Analysis of Institutions and Procedures* (London, Cameron May, 2007).
Buchanan, A, 'The Legitimacy of International Law' in S Besson and J Tasioulas (eds), *The Philosophy of International Law* (Oxford, OUP, 2010).
Budlender, G, '*Amicus Curiae*' in S Woolman et al (eds), *Constitutional Law of South Africa* (Cape Town, Juta Law, 2008).
Charnovitz, S, 'Judicial Independence in the World Trade Organization' in LB de Chazournes, CPR Romano and R Mackenzie (eds), *International Organizations and International Dispute Settlement* (Ardsley, New York, Transnational Publishers, 2002).
Cryer, R, 'The Ad Hoc Tribunals and the Law of Command Responsibility: A Quiet Earthquake' in S Darcy and J Powderly (eds), *Judicial Creativity at the International Criminal Tribunals* (Oxford, OUP, 2010).
di Rattalma, MF, 'NGOs Before the European Court of Human Rights: Beyond *Amicus Curiae* Participation?' in T Treves et al, *Civil Society, International Courts and Compliance Bodies, Project on International Courts and Tribunals* (The Hague, TMC Asser Press, 2005).
Duff, A, 'Authority and Responsibility in International Criminal Law' in S Besson and J Tasioulas (eds), *The Philosophy of International Law* (Oxford, OUP, 2010).
Ellis, MS, 'NGO Intervention in Court Proceedings Through *Amicus Curiae* Briefs' in LE Carter, MS Ellis and CC Jalloh (eds), *The International Criminal Court in an Effective Global Justice System* (Cheltenham, Edward Elgar, 2016).
Hansen, TO, 'The International Criminal Court and the Legitimacy of Exercise' in P Andersen, C Eriksen and B Viskum (eds), *Law and Legitimacy* (Denmark, DJØF Publishing, 2015).
Harlow, C and Rawlings, R, '"Striking Back" and "Clamping Down": An Alternative Perspective on Judicial Review' in J Bell et al (eds), *Public Law Adjudication in Common Law Systems: Process and Substance* (Oxford, Bloomsbury Publishing, 2016).

Hernández, GI, 'Non-state Actors From the Perspective of the International Court of Justice' in Jean d'Aspremont (ed), *Participants in the International Legal System: Multiple Perspectives on Non-state Actors in International Law* (Abingdon, Oxon, Routledge, 2011).

Jalloh, CC, 'Self-Representation and the Use of Assigned, Standby and *Amicus* Counsel' in L Carter and F Pocar (eds), *International Criminal Procedure: The Interface of Civil Law and Common Law* (Cheltenham, Edward Elgar, 2013).

Juaristi, F, 'The *Amicus Curiae* in the Inter-American Court of Human Rights (1982–2013)' in Y Haeck et al (eds), *The Inter-American Court of Human Rights: Theory and Practice, Present and Future* (Cambridge, Intersentia, 2015).

Kiyani, A, 'Legitimacy, Legality and the Possibility of a Pluralist International Criminal Law' in N Hayashi and CM Bailliet (eds), *The Legitimacy of International Criminal Tribunals* (Cambridge, CUP, 2017).

Langvatn, SA and Squatrito, T, 'Conceptualising and Measuring the Legitimacy of International Criminal Tribunals' in N Hayashi and CM Bailliet (eds), *The Legitimacy of International Criminal Tribunals* (Cambridge, CUP, 2017).

Linton, S, 'Joinder and Severance' in Göran Sluiter et al (eds) *International Criminal Procedure: Principles and Rules* (Oxford, OUP, 2013).

Linton, S, 'Testimony of Expert Witnesses, Journalists, ICRC, and UN staff' in Göran Sluiter et al (eds), *International Criminal Procedure: Principles and Rules* (Oxford, OUP, 2013).

Lohne, K, 'Global Civil Society, the ICC, and Legitimacy in International Criminal Justice' in N Hayashi and CM Bailliet (eds), *The Legitimacy of International Criminal Tribunals* (Cambridge, CUP, 2017).

Luban, D, 'Fairness to Rightness: Jurisdiction, Legality and the Legitimacy of International Criminal Law' in S Besson and J Tasioulas (eds), *The Philosophy of International Law* (Oxford, OUP, 2010).

May, L and Fyfe, S, 'The Legitimacy of International Criminal Tribunals' in N Hayashi and CM Bailliet (eds), *The Legitimacy of International Criminal Tribunals* (Cambridge, CUP, 2017).

Mégret, F, 'In Whose Name? The ICC and the Search for Constituency' in C De Vos, S Kendall and C Stahn (eds), *Contested Justice: The Politics and Practice of International Criminal Court Interventions* (Cambridge, CUP, 2015).

Morrison, H and Pountney, E, 'Victim Participation at the Special Tribunal for Lebanon' in A Alamuddin, NN Jurdi and D Tolbert (eds), *The Special Tribunal for Lebanon: Law and Practice* (Oxford, OUP, 2014).

Roht-Arriaza, N, 'Civil Society in Processes of Accountability' in MC Bassiouni (ed), *Post-Conflict Justice* (Ardsley, New York, Transnational Publishers, 2002).

Schabas, WA, 'Judicial Activism and the Crime of Genocide' in Shane Darcy and Joseph Powderly (eds), *Judicial Creativity at the International Criminal Tribunals* (Oxford, OUP, 2010).

Shahabuddeen, M, 'Judicial Creativity and Joint Criminal Enterprise' in S Darcy and J Powderly (eds), *Judicial Creativity at the International Criminal Tribunals* (Oxford, OUP, 2010).

Stahn, C, 'Justice Civilisatrice? The ICC, Post-colonial Theory, and Faces of "the Local"' in C De Vos, S Kendall and C Stahn (eds), *Contested Justice: The Politics and Practice of International Criminal Court Interventions* (Cambridge, CUP, 2015).

Struett, MJ, 'The Politics of Discursive Legitimacy: Understanding the Dynamics and Implications of Prosecutorial Discretion at the International Criminal Court' in SC Roach (ed), *Governance, Order, and the International Criminal Court* (Oxford, OUP, 2009).

Van Schaak, B, 'Engendering Genocide: The Akayesu Case before the ICTR' in DR Hurwitz, ML Satterthwaite and D Ford (eds), *Human Rights Advocacy Stories* (New York, Thomson Reuters/Foundation Press, 2009).

Vasiliev, S, 'Between International Criminal Justice and Injustice: Theorising Legitimacy' in N Hayashi and CM Bailliet (eds), *The Legitimacy of International Criminal Tribunals* (Cambridge, CUP, 2017).

Williams, S, 'Hybrid Courts and *Amicus Curiae* Briefing' in S Weill, KT Seelinger, and KB Carlson (eds), *Prosecuting the President: The Trial of Hissen Habré* (Oxford, OUP, forthcoming 2019).

Williams, S, 'Civil Society Participation in Preliminary Examinations' in M Bergsmo and C Stahn (eds), *Quality Control in Preliminary Examinations* (Torkel Opsahl Academic Epublisher, 2018).

Williams, S and Palmer, E, 'Civil Society and *Amicus Curiae* Interventions in the International Criminal Court' in S Williams and H Woolaver (eds), *Civil Society and International Criminal Justice in Africa: Challenges and Opportunities* (Cape Town, Juta Law, 2016).

Journal Articles

Acquaviva, G, 'New Paths in International Criminal Justice? The Internal Rules of the Cambodian Extraordinary Chambers' (2008) 6 *JICJ* 129.

Alarie, BRD and Green, AJ, 'Interventions at the Supreme Court of Canada: Accuracy, Affiliation, and Acceptance' (2010) 48 *Osgoode Hall Law Journal* 381.

Angell, E, 'The *Amicus Curiae*: American Development of English Institutions' (1967) 16 *ICLQ* 1017.

Appazov, A, 'International Criminal Court and the Decision-Making Heritage of the Ad Hoc Tribunals: A Study of Judicial Activism' (2016) 3 *Journal of Global Justice and Public Policy* 1.

Askin, KD, 'Prosecuting Wartime Rape and Other Gender-Related Crimes Under International Law: Extraordinary Advances, Enduring Obstacles' (2003) 21 *Berkeley Journal of international Law* 288.

Banner, S, 'The Myth of the Neutral *Amicus*: American Courts and Their Friends, 1790–1890' (2004) 20 *Constitutional Commentary* 111.

Bartholomeusz, L, 'The *Amicus Curiae* before International Courts and Tribunals' (2005) 5 *Non-State Actors and International Law* 209.

Bellhouse, J and Lavers, A, 'The Modern *Amicus Curiae*: A Role in Arbitration?' (2004) 23 *Civil Justice Quarterly* 187.

Berg, D, 'The Limits of Friendship: The *Amicus Curiae* in Criminal Trial Courts' (2012) 59 *Criminal Law Quarterly* 67.

Boas, G 'Self-Representation before the ICTY: A Case for Reform' (2011) 9 *JICJ* 53.

Bodansky, D 'The Legitimacy of International Governance: A Coming Challenge for International Environmental Law?' (1999) 93 *AJIL* 596.

Boesenecker, AP and Vinjamuri, L, 'Lost in Translation? Civil Society, Faith-Based Organizations and the Negotiation of International Norms' (2011) 5 *IJTJ* 345.

Boyle, D, 'The Rights of Victims: Participation, Representation, Protection, Reparation' (2006) 4 *JICJ* 307.

Brickhill, J, 'The Intervention of *Amici Curiae* in Criminal Matters: *S v Zuma* and *S v Basson* Considered' (2006) 123 *South African Law Journal* 391.

Buchanan, A and Keohane, RO, 'The Legitimacy of Global Governance Institutions' (2006) 20 *Ethics & International Affairs* 405.

Buckley, R and Blyschak, P, 'Guarding the Open Door: Non-Party Participation Before the International Centre for Settlement of Investment Disputes' (2007) 22 *Banking and Finance Law Review* 353.

Butler, N, 'Non-Disputing Party Participation in ICSID Disputes: Faux *Amici*?' (2019) 66 *Netherlands International Law Review* 143.

Cassese, A, 'The Legitimacy of International Criminal Tribunals and the Current Prospects of International Criminal Justice' (2012) 25 *LJIL* 491.

Chandra, MS, 'The *Amicus Curiae*: Friends no More?' (2010) *Singapore Journal of Legal Studies* 352.

Chayes, A, 'The Role of the Judge in Public Interest Litigation' (1976) 89 *Harvard Law Review* 1281.

Cimiotta, E, 'The Specialist Chambers and the Specialist Prosecutor's Office in Kosovo: The "Regionalization" of International Criminal Justice in Context' (2016) 14 *JICJ* 53.

Clark, JN, 'International Criminal Tribunals and Normative Legitimacy: An Achievable Goal?' (2015) 15 *ICLR* 763.

Clark, R, 'The International League for Human Rights and South West Africa 1947–1957: The Human Rights NGO as Catalyst in the International Legal Process' (1981) 3 *Human Rights Quarterly* 101.
Clements, R, 'From Bureaucracy to Management: The International Criminal Court's Internal Progress Narrative' (2019) 32 *LJIL* 149.
Copelon, R, 'Gender Crimes as War Crimes: Integrating Crimes Against Women into International Criminal Law' (2000) 46 *McGill Law Journal* 217.
Collins, P, Corley, P and Hamner, J, 'The Influence of *Amicus Curiae* Briefs on US Supreme Court Opinion Content' (2015) 49 *Law & Society Review* 917.
Collins, P and McCarthy, L, 'Friends and Interveners: Interest Group Litigation in a Comparative Context' (2017) 5 *Journal of Law and Courts* 55.
Copelon, R, 'Gender Crimes as War Crimes: Integrating Crimes Against Women into International Criminal Law' (2000) 46 *McGill Law Journal* 217.
Cupido, M, 'Facing Facts in International Criminal Law: A Casuistic Model of Judicial Reasoning' (2016) 14 *JICJ* 1.
Damaška, M, 'Reflections on Fairness in International Criminal Justice' (2012) 10 *JICJ* 611.
Damaška, M, 'Unacknowledged Presences in International Criminal Justice' (2012) 10 *JICJ* 1239.
Danner, AM, 'Enhancing the Legitimacy and Accountability of Prosecutorial Discretion at the International Criminal Court' (2003) 97 *AJIL* 510.
Davidson, C, 'Explaining Inhumanity: The Use of Crime-Definition Experts at International Criminal Courts' (2015) 48 *Vanderbilt Journal of Transnational Law* 359.
de Brabandere, E, 'NGOs and the "Public Interest": The Legality and Rationale of *Amicus Curiae* Interventions in International Economic and Investment Disputes' (2016) 12 *Chicago Journal of International Law* 85.
DeGuzman, MM, 'Gravity and the Legitimacy of the International Criminal Court' (2009) 32 *Fordham International Law Journal* 1400.
Dickens, BM, 'A Canadian Development: Non-Party Intervention' (1977) 40 *MLR* 666.
Dolidze, A, 'Bridging Comparative and International Law: *Amicus Curiae* Participation as Vertical Legal Transplant' (2015) 26 *EJIL* 851.
Dolidze, A, 'The Arctic Sunrise and NGO's in International Judicial Proceedings' (2014) 18 *ASIL Insights*.
Dolidze, A, 'Advisory Opinion on Responsibility and Liability for International Seabed Mining (ITLOS Case No 17) and the Future of NGO Participation in the International Legal Process' (2013) 19 *ILSA Journal of International and Comparative Law* 379.
Dosch, J, 'The Role of Civil Society in Cambodia's Peace-Building Process: Have Foreign Donors Made a Difference?' (2012) 52 *Asian Survey* 1067.
Fallon, R, 'Scholars' Briefs and the Vocation of Law Professors' (2012) 4 *Journal of Legal Analysis* 223.
Fitchelberg, A, 'Democratic Legitimacy and the International Criminal Court: A Liberal Defence' (2006) 4 *JICJ* 765.
Francioni, F, 'Access to Justice, Denial of Justice and International Investment Law' (2009) 20 *EJIL* 729.
Gillet, M and Schuster, M, 'The Special Tribunal for Lebanon Swiftly Adopts its Rules of Procedure and Evidence' (2009) 7 *JICJ* 885.
Glasius, M, 'Do International Criminal Courts Require Democratic Legitimacy?' (2012) 23 *EJIL* 43.
Gomez, KF, 'Rethinking the Role of *Amicus Curiae* in International Investment Arbitration: How to Draw the Line Favorably for the Public Interest' (2012) 35 *Fordham International Law Journal* 510.
Greenawalt, AKA, 'Justice Without Politics? Prosecutorial Discretion and the International Criminal Court' (2007) 39 *New York University Journal of international Law and Politics* 583.
Grossman, N, 'The Normative Legitimacy of International Courts' (2013) 86 *Temple Law Review* 61.
Haddad, HN, 'Judicial Institution Builders: NGOs and International Human Rights Courts' (2012) 11 *Journal of Human Rights* 126.

Hannett, S, 'Third Party Interventions: In the Public Interest?' [2003] *Public Law* 128.
Harlow, C, 'Public Law and Popular Justice' (2002) *MLR* 1.
Haslam, E, 'Subjects and Objects: International Criminal Law and the Institutionalization of Civil Society' (2011) 5 *IJTJ* 221.
Heinze, A, 'The Kosovo Specialist Chambers' Rules of Procedure and Evidence A Diamond Made Under Pressure?' (2017) 15 *JICJ* 985.
Helfer, LR and Slaughter, AM, 'Toward a Theory of Effective Supranational Adjudication' [1997] *Yale LJ* 273.
Hovil, L and Okello, MC 'Editorial Note' (2011) 5(3) *IJTJ* 333.
Howse, R, 'The World Trade Organization 20 Years On: Global Governance by Judiciary' (2016) 27 *EJIL* 9.
Howse, R, 'Membership and Its Privileges: The WTO, Civil Society, and the *Amicus* Brief Controversy' (2003) 9 *European Law Journal* 496.
Hunt, D, 'The International Criminal Court: High Hopes, 'Creative Ambiguity' and an Unfortunate Mistrust in International Judges' (2004) 2 *JICJ* 56.
Kearney, JD and Merrill, TW, 'The Influence of *Amicus Curiae* Briefs on the Supreme Court' (2000) 148 *University of Pennsylvania Law Review* 743.
Kendall, S and Nouwen, S, 'Representational Practices at the International Criminal Court: The Gap Between Juridified and Abstract Victimhood' (2013) 76 *Law and Contemporary Problems* 235.
Kent, A and Trinidad, J, 'The Management of Third-party *Amicus* Participation before International Criminal Tribunals: Juggling Efficiency and Legitimacy' (2017) 17 *ICLR* 728.
Kent, A and Trinidad, J, 'International Law Scholars as *Amici Curiae*: An Emerging Dialogue (of the Deaf)?' (2016) 29 *LJIL* 1081.
Kiyani, A, 'The Antinomies of Legitimacy: On the (Im)possibility of a Legitimate International Criminal Court' (2015) 8 *African Journal of Legal Studies* 1.
Knahr, C, 'Transparency, Third Party Participation and Access to Documents in International Investment Arbitration' (2007) 23 *Arbitration International* 327.
Knoops, GJA, 'The Dichotomy between Judicial Economy and Equality of Arms within International and Internationalized Criminal Trials: A Defense Perspective' (2004) 28 *Fordham International Law Journal* 1566.
Koch, J, 'Making Room: New Directions in Third Party Intervention' (1990) 48 *University of Toronto Faculty of Law Review* 151.
Kochevar, S, '*Amici Curiae* in Civil Law Jurisdictions' [2013] 122 *Yale LJ* 1653.
Krislov, S, 'The *Amicus Curiae* Brief: From Friendship to Advocacy' [1963] 72 *Yale LJ* 694.
Larsen, AO, 'The Trouble With *Amicus* Facts' (2014) 100 *Virginia Law Review* 1757.
Lasser, M de S-O-l'E, *Judicial Transformations: The Rights Revolution in the Courts of Europe* (Oxford, OUP, 2009).
Levine, E, '*Amicus Curiae* in International Investment Arbitration: The Implications of an increase in Third-Party Participation' (2011) 29 *Berkeley Journal of International Law* 200.
Lowman, MK, 'The Litigating *Amicus Curiae*: When Does the Party begin After the Friends Leave?' (1992) 41 *American University Law Review* 1243.
Loux, AC, 'Hearing a "Different Voice": Third Party Interventions in Criminal Appeals' (2000) 53 *Current Legal Problems* 449.
Mayer, LH, 'NGO Standing and Influence in Regional Human Rights Courts and Commissions' (2011) 36(3) *Brooklyn Journal of International Law* 911.
McDermott, Y, 'The International Criminal Court's Chambers Practice Manual: Towards a Return to Judicial Law Making in International Criminal Procedure?' (2017) 15 *JICJ* 873.
Meernik, J, King, KL and Dancy, G, 'Judicial Decision Making and International Tribunals: Assessing the Impact of Individual, National and International Factors' (2005) 86 *Social Science Quarterly* 683.
Mégret, F, 'The Anxieties of International Criminal Justice' (2016) 29 *LJIL* 197.
Mégret, F, 'Beyond Fairness: Understanding the Determinants of International Criminal Procedure' (2009) 14 *UCLA Journal of International Law and Foreign Affairs* 37.

Mercer, C, 'NGOs, Civil Society and Democratization: A Critical Review of the Literature' (2002) 2(1) *Progress in Development Studies* 5.

Mistry, H, 'The Significance of Institutional Culture in Enhancing the Validity of International Criminal Tribunals' (2017) 17 *ICLR* 703.

Mohamed, AA, 'Individual and NGO Participation in Human Rights Litigation before the African Court of Human and Peoples' Rights: Lessons from the European and Inter-American Courts of Human Rights' (1999) 43 *Journal of African Law* 201.

Mohan, SC, 'The *Amicus Curiae*: Friends No More' (2010) 2 *Singapore Journal of Legal Studies* 352.

Moriarty, M and Sibley, E, 'Counting the True Costs of Section 87 of the Criminal Justice and Courts Act 2015' (2015) 20(3) *Judicial Review* 147.

Morris, M, 'The Democratic Dilemma of the International Criminal Court' (2002) 5 *Buffalo Criminal Law Review* 591.

Muldoon, P and Scriven, D, 'Intervention as Added Party: Rule 13 of the Ontario Rules of Civil Procedure' (1985) 6(2) *The Advocate's Quarterly* 129.

Murray, C, 'Litigating in the Public Interest: Intervention and the *Amicus Curiae*' (1994) 10 *South African Journal on Human Rights* 240.

Neudorf, L, 'Intervention in the UK Supreme Court' (2013) 2 *Cambridge Journal of International and Comparative Law* 16.

Nouwen, SMH and Werner, WG, 'Doing Justice to the Political: The International Criminal Court in Uganda and Sudan' (2010) 21 *EJIL* 941.

Olasolo, H and Mendoza, JMFR, 'The Colombian Integrated System of Truth, Justice, Reparation and Non-Repetition' (2017) 15 *JICJ* 1011.

Oloka-Onyango, J and Mbazira, C, 'Befriending the Judiciary: Behind and Beyond the 2016 Supreme Court *Amicus Curiae* Rulings in Uganda' (2016) 1 *African Journal of Comparative Constitutional Law* 1.

Oosterveld, V, 'Gender-sensitive Justice and the International Criminal Tribunal for Rwanda: Lessons Learned for the International Criminal Court' (2005) 12 *New England Journal of International and Comparative Law* 119.

Orford, A, 'On International Legal Method' (2013) 1 *London Review of International Law* 166.

Overton, A and Rothe, D, 'The International Criminal Court and the External Non-Witness Expert(s), Problematic Concerns: An Exploratory Endeavour' (2010) 10(3) *ICLR* 345.

Palchetti, P, 'Opening the International Court of Justice to Third States: Intervention and Beyond' (2002) 6 *Max Planck Yearbook of United Nations Law* 139.

Palmer, N, 'Transfer or Transformation?: A Review of the Rule 11 *Bis* Decisions of the International Criminal Tribunal for Rwanda' (2012) 20(1) *The African Journal of International and Comparative Law* 1.

Pomson, O, 'Does the *Monetary Gold* Principle Apply to International Courts and Tribunals Generally?' (2019) 10 *Journal of International Dispute Settlement* 88.

Roach, SC, 'Legitimising Negotiated Justice: The International Criminal Court and Flexible Governance' (2013) 17 *International Journal of Human Rights* 619.

Ronen, Y, 'Participation of Non-State Actors in ICJ Proceedings' (2012) 11 *The Law and Practice of International Courts and Tribunals* 77.

Rustad, M and Koenig, T, 'The Supreme Court and Junk Social Science: Selective Distortion in *Amicus* Briefs' (1994) 72 *North Carolina Law Review* 91.

Santivasa, S, 'The NGO's Participation in the Proceedings of the International Court of Justice' (2012) 5 *Journal of East Asia and International Law* 377.

Saul, B, '*Amicus Curiae* Brief on the Notion of Terrorist Acts Submitted to the Appeals Chamber of the Special Tribunal for Lebanon Pursuant to Rule 131 of the Rules of Procedure and Evidence' (2011) 22 *Criminal Law Forum* 365.

Saul, B, 'Legislating from a Radical Hague: The United Nations Special Tribunal for Lebanon Invents an International Crime of Transnational Terrorism' (2011) 24 *LJIL* 677.

Scharf, MP, 'The Iraqi High Tribunal A Viable Experiment in International Justice?' (2007) 5 *JICJ* 258.

Scharf, MP, 'Self-Representation Versus Assignment of Defence Counsel Before International Criminal Tribunals' (2006) 4 *JICJ* 31.
Schomburg, W, 'The Role of International Criminal Tribunals in Promoting Respect for Fair Trial Rights' (2009) 8 *Northwestern University Journal of International Human Rights* 1.
Seelinger, KT, 'Uganda's Case of *Thomas Kwoyelo*: Customary International Law on Trial' (2017) 8 *Californian Law Review* 19.
Shah, S, Poole, T and Blackwell, M, 'Rights, Interveners and the Law Lords' (2014) 34 *Oxford Journal of Legal Studies* 295.
Sheffield, K, 'Speak Softly and Carry a Sealed Warrant: Building the International Criminal Court's Legitimacy in the Wake of Sudan' (2013) 18 *Appeal* 163.
Shelton, D, 'The International Court of Justice and Nongovernmental Organisations' (2007) 9 *International Community Law Review* 139.
Shelton, D, 'The Jurisprudence of the Inter-American Court of Human Rights' (1994) 10 *American University International Law Review* 333.
Shelton, D, 'The Participation of Nongovernmental Organizations in International Judicial Proceedings' (1994) 88 *AJIL* 611.
Sluiter, G, 'Due Process and Criminal Procedure in the Cambodian Extraordinary Chambers' (2006) 4 *JICJ* 314.
Sperfeldt, C, 'The Trial Against Hissène Habré: Networked Justice and Reparations at the Extraordinary African Chambers' (2017) 9 *International Journal of Human Rights* 1.
Sperfeldt, C, 'Cambodian Civil Society and the Khmer Rouge Tribunal' (2012) 6 *IJTJ* 149.
Stahn, C, 'Between "Faith" and "Facts": By What Standards Should We Assess International Criminal Justice?' (2012) 25 *LJIL* 251.
Starygin, S, 'Internal Rules of the Extraordinary Chambers in the Courts of Cambodia (ECCC): Setting an Example of the Rule of Law by Breaking the Law?' (2011) 3 *Journal of Law and Conflict Resolution* 20.
Struett, MJ, 'Why the International Criminal Court Must Pretend to Ignore Politics' (2012) 26 *Ethics & International Affairs* 83.
Subotić, J, 'Legitimacy, Scope, and Conflicting Claims on the ICTY: In the Aftermath of *Gotovina, Haradinaj* and *Perišić*' (2014) 13 *Journal of Human Rights* 170.
Sunga, LS, 'How Can UN Human Rights Special Procedures Sharpen ICC Fact-Finding?' (2011) 15 *International Journal of Human Rights* 187.
Tuinstra, JT, 'Assisting an Accused to Represent Himself' (2006) 4 *JICJ* 47.
Umbricht, GC, 'An "*Amicus Curiae* Brief" on *Amicus Curiae* Briefs at the WTO' (2000) 4 *Journal of International Economic Law* 773.
Van Den Eynde, L, 'An Empirical Look at the *Amicus Curiae* Practice of Human Rights NGOs before the European Court of Human Rights' (2013) 31(3) *Netherlands Quarterly Human Rights* 271.
Varaki, M, 'Introducing a Fairness-Based Theory of Prosecutorial Legitimacy before the International Criminal Court' (2016) 27 *EJIL* 769.
Viljoen, F and Abebe, AK, '*Amicus* Participation before Regional Human Rights Bodies in Africa' (2014) 58(1) *Journal of African Law* 22.
Warbrick, C, 'International Criminal Courts and Fair Trial' (1998) 3 *Journal of Armed Conflict Law* 45.
Willheim, E, '*Amici Curiae* and Access to Constitutional Justice in the High Court of Australia' (2010) 22 *Bond Law Review* 126.
Williams, G, 'The *Amicus Curiae* and Intervener in the High Court of Australia: A Comparative Analysis' (2000) 28 *Federal Law Review* 365.
Williams, J, 'Slobodan Milosevic and the Guarantee of Self-Representation' (2006) 3(2) *Brooklyn Journal of International Law* 553.
Williams, S, 'The Specialist Chambers of Kosovo: The Limits of Internationalization?' (2016) 14 *JICJ* 25.
Williams, S, 'Aggression, Affected States, and a Right to Participate: A Response to Koh and Buchwald' (2015) 109 *AJIL Unbound* 246.

Williams, S and Woolaver, H, 'The Role of the *Amicus Curiae* before International Criminal Tribunals' (2006) 6(2) *ICLR* 151.

Woolaver, H and Palmer, E, 'Challenges to the Independence of the International Criminal Court from the Assembly of States Parties' (2017) 15 *JICJ* 641.

Woolaver, H and Williams, S, 'The Role of the *Amicus Curiae* Before International Criminal Tribunals' (2006) 6 *ICLR* 15.

Zachariasiewicz, M, '*Amicus Curiae* in International Investment Arbitration: Can it Enhance the Transparency of Investment Dispute Resolution? (2012) 29 *Journal of International Arbitration* 205.

Further Material

Al Hussein, ZR et al, 'The International Criminal Court Needs Fixing', *Atlantic Council* (24 April 2019), available at www.atlanticcouncil.org/blogs/new-atlanticist/the-international-criminal-court-needs-fixing.

Ambos, K and Adoueldahab, S, 'Foreign Jurists in the Colombian Special Jurisdiction for Peace: A New Concept of *Amicus Curiae*?' (*EJIL: Talk!*, 19 December 2017), available at www.ejiltalk.org/foreign-jurists-in-the-colombian-special-jurisdiction-for-peace-a-new-concept-of-amicus-curiae/.

Aminah, S, 'Menjadi Sahabat Keadilan: Panduan Menyusun *Amicus* Brief' ('Becoming a Friend of the Court: Guidelines for Preparing an *Amicus* Brief'), Indonesian Legal Resource Center (ILRC) and HiVOS (November 2014), 'Untuk berpartisipasi dalam mewujudkan negara hukum yang demokratis', available at www.mitrahukum.org/wp-content/uploads/2015/02/Amicus-Brief.pdf.

Brimelow, K, Ellis, M, Williams, S, and Woolaver, H, 'Shaping the Law: Civil Society Influence at the International Courts' (*Chatham House*, 25 January 2016), available at www.chathamhouse.org/sites/default/files/events/160125-meeting-summary-shaping-law-civil-society-influence-international-criminal-courts.pdf.

'Civil Society and International Criminal Justice in Africa' (4–5 February 2015), available at http://archive.ahrcentre.org/sites/ahrcentre.org/files/Civil%20Society%20and%20ICJ%20in%20Africa%20Exec%20Summary.pdf.

Defensoría del Pueblo, 'El *amicus curiae*: ¿qué es y para qué sirve? Jurisprudencia y labor de la Defensoria del Pueblo, Serie Documentos Defensoriales – Documento N° 8' ('The *amicus curiae*: what is it and what is it for? Jurisprudence and the work of the Ombudsman's Office, Ombudsman's Document Series – Document No. 8' (October 2009), available at www.corteidh.or.cr/tablas/26654.pdf.

Fujimori, A, Sala Penal Especial de la Corte Suprema, 'Resolución del 1 de agosto del 2008, recaida en el proceso penal contra Alberto Fujimori por los crimenes de Barrios Altos y La Cantuta' (1 August 2008), available at http://historico.pj.gob.pe/CorteSuprema/spe/Documentos/SPE_RESOLUCION_CSJP_070808.pdf.

Horwitz, P 'Is Fallon's Article a No-Brainer?' (*PrawfsBlawg*, 31 October 2011), available at https://prawfsblawg.blogs.com/prawfsblawg/2011/10/is-fallons-article-a-no-brainer.html.

International Centre for Transitional Justice, 'ICTJ Written Submission: Legality of Truth and Reconciliation Commission' (July 2006), available at www.ictj.org/publication/ictj-written-submission-legality-truth-and-reconciliation-commission.

International Justice Resource Center, 'Advocacy before the African Human Rights System: A Manual for Attorneys and Advocates Preventing and Remedying Human Rights Violations through the International Framework' (November 2016), available at https://ijrcenter.org/wp-content/uploads/2016/11/Advocacy-before-the-African-Human-Rights-System.pdf.

Justice, To Assist the Court: Third Party Interventions in the Public Interest (2016), available at https://2bquk8cdew6192tsu41lay8t-wpengine.netdna-ssl.com/wp-content/uploads/2016/06/To-Assist-the-Court-Web.pdf.

Karnavas, M 'The *Amicus Curiae* in International Criminal Justice' (18 January 2016), available at http://michaelgkarnavas.net/files/ExecutiveSummaryAmicusCuriaeICJ.pdf.

Kersten, M 'The ICC was Wrong to Deny Prosecution Request for Afghan Probe', *Al Jazeera* (12 April 2019), available at www.aljazeera.com/indepth/opinion/icc-wrong-deny-prosecution-request-afghan-probe-190412101757533.html.

Leon-Manco, H, 'Human Rights In Practice: The Work of the Peruvian Ombudsman – and how it Contributes to Legal Empowerment of the Poor', (ANLEP Working Paper No 3, December 2011), available at http://lnweb90.worldbank.org/exteu/SharePapers.nsf/(ID)/FB647574177F9B17852579FE00075A5A/$File/human+rights+i+practice.pdf.

Moyer, C, 'The Role of the *Amicus Curiae* in the Inter-American Court of Human Rights', available at www.corteidh.or.cr/tablas/a11770.pdf.

Open Society Justice Initiative, Strategic Litigation Impacts: Insights from Global Experience (2018), available at www.opensocietyfoundations.org/sites/default/files/strategic-litigation-impacts-insights-20181023.pdf.

Schiff, BN, 'Evolution of ICC Legitimacy' (International Studies Association Annual Meeting, New Orleans, February 2010) 6.

Schlesinger, N, 'Making International Criminal Law: Factors Influencing Judicial Behaviour at the ICTY and ICTR' (PhD thesis, the University of Melbourne).

Wintour, P, Bowcott O and Borger, J, 'US Revokes ICC Prosecutor's Visa Over Afghanistan Inquiry', *The Guardian* (5 April 2019), available at www.theguardian.com/law/2019/apr/05/us-revokes-visa-of-international-criminal-courts-top-prosecutor.

Yau, Sean Shun Ming 'Academic *Amici* and the Legitimacy of International Criminal Court: Some Reflections on the Al Bashir Appeal' (*Cambridge International Law Journal Blog*, 2018), available at http://cilj.co.uk/2018/11/19/academic-amici-and-the-legitimacy-of-international-criminal-court-some-reflections-on-the-al-bashir-appeal/.

Index

Introductory Note

References such as '178–79' indicate (not necessarily continuous) discussion of a topic across a range of pages. Wherever possible in the case of topics with many references, these have either been divided into sub-topics or only the most significant discussions of the topic are listed. Because the entire work is about '*amici curiae*', the use of this term (and certain others which occur constantly throughout the book) as an entry point has been minimised. Information will be found under the corresponding detailed topics.

www.ingramcontent.com/pod-product-compliance
Ingram Content Group UK Ltd.
Pitfield, Milton Keynes, MK11 3LW, UK
UKHW021911150926
475560UK00003B/313

9 781509 913329